Lecture Notes in Computer Science

Lecture Notes in Artificial Intelligence 16264

Founding Editor

Jörg Siekmann

Series Editors

The series Lecture Notes in Artificial Intelligence (LNAI) was established in 1988 as a topical subseries of LNCS devoted to artificial intelligence.

The series publishes state-of-the-art research results at a high level. As with the LNCS mother series, the mission of the series is to serve the international R & D community by providing an invaluable service, mainly focused on the publication of conference and workshop proceedings and postproceedings.

Lourdes Martínez-Villaseñor ·
Roberto A. Vázquez · Gilberto Ochoa-Ruiz ·
Martín Montes Rivera ·
Saúl Zapotecas-Martínez ·
María Lucía Barrón-Estrada ·
Efrén Mezura Montes · Arturo Gomez Chavez
Editors

Advances in Computational Intelligence

MICAI 2025 International Workshops

HIS 2025, CIAPP 2025, WILE 2025, CHARAL 2025
ECSI 2025 Workshops, Guanajuato, Mexico, November 3–7, 2025
Proceedings, Part I

Editors
Lourdes Martínez-Villaseñor
Universidad Panamericana
Ciudad de México, Mexico

Gilberto Ochoa-Ruiz
Instituto Tecnológico y de Estudios Superiores de Monterrey
Zapopan, Mexico

Saúl Zapotecas-Martínez
Instituto Nacional de Astrofísica, Óptica y Electrónica
San Andrés Cholula, Mexico

Efrén Mezura Montes
Universidad Veracruzana
Xalapa, Mexico

Roberto A. Vázquez
Universidad La Salle México
Ciudad de México, Mexico

Martín Montes Rivera
Universidad Politécnica de Aguascalientes
Aguascalientes, Mexico

María Lucía Barrón-Estrada
TecNM-Instituto Tecnológico de Culiacán
Culiacán, Mexico

Arturo Gomez Chavez
Constructor University Bremen
Bremen, Germany

ISSN 0302-9743 ISSN 1611-3349 (electronic)
Lecture Notes in Artificial Intelligence
ISBN 978-3-032-17929-6 ISBN 978-3-032-17930-2 (eBook)
https://doi.org/10.1007/978-3-032-17930-2

LNCS Sublibrary: SL7 – Artificial Intelligence

This Springer imprint is published by the registered company Springer Nature Switzerland AG
The registered company address is: Gewerbestrasse 11, 6330 Cham, Switzerland

Preface

The Mexican International Conference on Artificial Intelligence (MICAI) is a yearly international conference series that has been organized by the Mexican Society for Artificial Intelligence (SMIA) since 2000. MICAI is an important international artificial intelligence (AI) forum and the main event in the academic life of the growing AI community in the country.

This year, MICAI 2025 was organized by the Mexican Society for Artificial Intelligence (SMIA, Sociedad Mexicana de Inteligencia Artificial) in collaboration with the Centro de Investigaciones en Matemáticas (CIMAT) and the Universidad de Guanajuato (UG).

The MICAI series website is www.MICAI.org. The website of the Mexican Society for Artificial Intelligence, SMIA, is www.SMIA.mx. Contact options and additional information can be found on these websites.

The conference, as is traditional, showcased a wide variety of research fields and topics. Moreover, the conference included cutting-edge keynote lectures, as well as detailed paper presentations and comprehensive hands-on tutorials. Furthermore, thought-provoking panels and niche workshops provided a rich and exciting experience that aimed to cater to a wide audience.

Moreover, we continued the legacy of announcing the José Negrete Award, the SMIA Best Thesis in Artificial Intelligence Contest's results. This year, the historic and culturally rich city of Guanajuato was our chosen destination.

MICAI conferences publish high-quality papers in all areas of AI and its applications. The proceedings of the previous MICAI events have been published by Springer in its Lecture Notes in Artificial Intelligence (LNAI) series (volumes: 1793, 2313, 2972, 3789, 4293, 4827, 5317, 5845, 6437, 6438, 7094, 7095, 7629, 7630, 8265, 8266, 8856, 8857, 9413, 9414, 10061, 10062, 10632, 10633, 11288, 11289, 11835, 12468, 12469, 13067, 13068, 13612, 13613, 14502, 14391, 14392, 15246, 15247, 15464, and 15465). Since its foundation in 2000, the conference has grown in popularity and improved in quality.

Five workshops were held jointly with the conference. The proceedings of the MICAI 2025 workshops are published in two volumes. The first volume contains 33 papers from the 18th Workshop of Hybrid Intelligent Systems (HIS 2025) and the 1st Workshop on Evolutionary Computation and Swarm Intelligence (ECSI 2025). The second volume contains 26 papers from the 18th Workshop on Intelligent Learning Environments (WILE 2025), the 7th Workshop on New Trends in Computational Intelligence and Applications (CIAPP 2025), and the 1st Workshop on Challenges in Holistic AI for Real-world Applications and Learning Systems (CHARAL 2025).

These volumes will be of interest for researchers in all fields of artificial intelligence, students specializing in related topics, and the general public interested in recent developments in AI.

The MICAI workshops received for evaluation 85 submissions. From these submissions, 59 papers were selected for publication in these volumes after a double-blind peer-reviewing process and three reviews per submission. It was carried out by the Program Committee of the workshops. The acceptance rate was 69%.

HIS 2025

Hybrid Intelligent Systems (HIS) offers a compelling solution to complex challenges in various application domains, including biology, medicine, logistics, management, engineering, technology, social sciences, and humanities. The XVIII Workshop of Hybrid Intelligent Systems (HIS 2025) featured relevant research on HIS and their capabilities for managing complex processes.

HIS 2025 was hosted by the Mexican Society of Artificial Intelligence (SMIA), nested within the Mexican International Conference on Artificial Intelligence (MICAI 2025). This year, the workshop featured a selection of research articles managed with the CMT platform. All articles underwent rigorous double-blind peer review, with an acceptance rate of 72.5%, covering topics such as Machine Learning, Fuzzy Systems, Reasoning, Intelligent Control, Computer Vision, Optimization, and Expert Systems.

HIS 2025 presented the latest advancements in the field through three tracks: the first featured articles with completed research, the second consisted of posters showcasing proposals and prototypes for future research, and the third addressed life support on Mars, where recently graduated students proposed uses of artificial intelligence applied to survival on Mars. The workshop's primary objective is to present expert model systems applied to specific research topics.

We sincerely thank Arturo Hernández Aguirre from the Department of Computer Science at CIMAT Guanajuato, Mexico, our keynote speaker, for his valuable contribution to our event with the presentation "HIS 2025 he Evolutionary Algorithms: Past, Present, and Future." HIS 2025 was enriched by his extensive experience and remarkable achievements in the field. We greatly appreciate his presence and the insight he shared with our audience.

We would also like to thank SMIA and the MICAI organizers for their continued collaboration in developing this prestigious event. It was our honor to contribute to the MICAI event with research in Hybrid Intelligent Systems.

ECSI 2025

The first workshop on Evolutionary Computation and Swarm Intelligence (ECSI) explored two pivotal areas of Artificial Intelligence: Evolutionary Computation and Swarm Intelligence, both of which are crucial for solving optimization problems. Evolutionary Computation mimics natural selection and genetics through populations of candidate solutions that evolve via selection, crossover, and mutation, exemplified by Genetic Algorithms (GA) and Evolution Strategies (ES). In contrast, Swarm Intelligence, inspired by natural collective behaviors such as ant colonies and bird flocks, leads to algorithms like Particle Swarm Optimization (PSO) and Ant Colony Optimization (ACO), utilizing simple interactions among individual agents. Both methodologies find extensive applications in optimization, machine learning, and robotics, enabling the discovery of innovative solutions to complex challenges. Participants gain a comprehensive understanding of these techniques, their principles, and practical implementations. The workshop explores the dynamic field of Evolutionary Computation and Swarm Intelligence, focusing on their theoretical foundations, recent algorithmic advancements, and practical applications.

The workshop covered various topics and activities, focusing on examining the latest advancements in Evolutionary Computation and Swarm Intelligence. The program featured:

1. Technical Sessions: Oral presentations and discussions highlighted recent findings in Evolutionary Computation and Swarm Intelligence. These presentations were based on the full accepted papers.
2. Poster Sessions: Opportunities for participants to present their research in a more informal setting, encouraging feedback and collaboration.

WILE 2025

Artificial Intelligence (AI) continues to yield a profound and sustained influence across multiple domains of human activity. AI possesses the transformative potential to revolutionize education by enabling more personalized instruction, adaptive learning experiences, and improved academic outcomes. Over the past decades, diverse educational systems and tools have been developed to support these goals. Among them, Intelligent Tutoring Systems (ITSs) and Intelligent Learning Environments (ILEs) represent key milestones in the evolution of technology-enhanced learning.

ILEs integrate a combination of established and emerging AI technologies. Traditional methods include artificial neural networks, Bayesian networks, and fuzzy logic, which provide a foundation for decision-making and personalization. More recent advances involve the incorporation of affective computing, Generative AI, and extended reality systems with immersion detection aimed at enhancing the quality and effectiveness of learning experiences.

Generative AI stands out as one of the most disruptive and promising developments in recent years. In education, these systems can generate personalized learning materials, adapt content to students' cognitive levels, simulate human tutors, and provide formative feedback in real time. Their integration into ILEs opens new opportunities for adaptive instruction, automatic assessment, and interactive dialogue systems that can accompany students throughout the learning process.

The Workshop on Intelligent Learning Environments (WILE) is convened to foster the advancement of innovative applications, methodologies, and technologies that enhance education. This workshop presents new ideas, research, and technology developed to assist students in their learning process and employees in training, employing diverse educational methodologies and artificial intelligence techniques. This workshop aims to convene active researchers and students in Intelligent Learning Environments to present and discuss innovative theoretical work and original applications, exchange ideas, establish collaborative links, review significant recent achievements, and deliberate on the implications of results for the broader field of AI. Our goal for WILE 2025 was to give researchers a platform to showcase their work while also investigating new approaches to integrate AI techniques in the creation of educational systems.

This edition includes 11 double blind peer-reviewed research papers selected from WILE 2025, covering various dimensions of intelligent learning environments. Each paper underwent two or three independent evaluations by members of the Technical Committee. The editorial board carefully considered criteria such as relevance, originality, clarity, and scientific contribution in the final selection process.

We would like to express our sincere gratitude to all participants who contributed to the success of WILE 2025. We acknowledge the collaboration of members of RedICA (Thematic Network in Applied Computational Intelligence) and the Mexican Society for Artificial Intelligence (SMIA). As in previous years, MICAI 2025 served as an outstanding host for this event, providing an ideal setting for the exchange of ideas and the advancement of research in intelligent learning environments.

CIAPP 2025

The 7th Workshop on New Trends in Computational Intelligence and Applications (CIAPP 2025) aimed to bring together researchers, students, and end users to explore the latest advances in computational intelligence. This year's workshop focused on evolutionary algorithms, Bayesian learning, computer vision, quantum circuits, and their applications in various fields, including nutrition, robotics, speech recognition, and green AI. Participants had the opportunity to share their findings, engage in discussions, and start collaborations, fostering a vibrant community dedicated to pushing the boundaries of computational intelligence.

We thank the Mexican Society for Artificial Intelligence (SMIA) for organizing the 24th Mexican International Conference on Artificial Intelligence (MICAI 2025). Their dedication and hard work created a platform for researchers and students to share knowledge, foster collaboration, and advance the field of artificial intelligence.

We also extend our most sincere thanks and recognition to the Centro de Investigación en Matemáticas (CIMAT) and the Universidad de Guanajuato (UG) for their outstanding support and their exceptional organization as a local committee of MICAI 2025. Their commitment to organizing this event created an environment that was both attractive and conducive to collaboration and knowledge sharing. Thank you for your invaluable contributions to the success of CIAPP 2025.

CHARAL 2025

The 1st Workshop on Challenges in Holistic AI for Real-world Applications and Learning Systems (CHARAL) took place on November 4, 2025, during the Mexican International Conference on Artificial Intelligence (MICAI) in Guanajuato, Mexico. The event provided a unique forum for researchers, practitioners, and policymakers to explore how artificial intelligence can move beyond controlled environments toward robust, explainable, and trustworthy systems capable of operating in complex, real-world conditions.

The workshop opened with a short introduction, followed by a full day of invited keynote talks from leading experts across academia, government, and industry. Topics included uncertainty in vision-language models, data-centric AI for safe perception, deep generative modeling for human motion prediction, AI for medical imaging and healthcare, and efficient training of large language models. These sessions provided a multidisciplinary perspective on the technological and operational barriers to reliable AI deployment.

Complementing the keynotes, the workshop featured a curated selection of spotlight and lightning talks drawn from peer-reviewed papers from international researchers. These contributions showcased both theoretical advances and empirical studies on AI robustness, perception, and adaptation, emphasizing reproducibility and real-world performance.

A central highlight of CHARAL 2025 was the panel discussion co-organized with Young AI Leaders (YAIL CDMX), titled "AI in the Wild: From Scholar/Lab Models to Living Systems." This interactive 60-minute session examined how the new generation of AI practitioners perceives the balance between academia, industry, and civic engagement; how AI success can be measured beyond accuracy, drawing from YAIL's AI Impact Scorecard initiative; and what sustainable research-to-deployment pipelines might look like for emerging economies such as Mexico. The discussion encouraged reflection on whether current development pathways are fast and inclusive enough to ensure independence and long-term resilience.

The workshop concluded with a synthesis and open-floor discussion connecting insights from all sessions. By combining keynotes, short talks, and an inter-generational panel, CHARAL 2025 aimed to cultivate collaboration across disciplines and generations. It sought to transform AI research into practice: building systems that are not only intelligent but also resilient, responsible, and socially grounded within real-world environments.

We want to thank all the people involved in the organization of this conference: the authors of the papers published in these two volumes –it is their research work that gives value to the proceedings– and the organizers for their work. We thank the reviewers for their great effort spent on reviewing the submissions and the Program and Organizing Committee members.

A special acknowledgment to the local committee led by Alejandro Rosales Pérez and Adrian Pastor López Monroy, whose meticulous coordination was instrumental in realizing MICAI 2025 in Guanajuato, Mexico. Our acknowledgments extend to Rafael Herrera Guzmán (Director General, CIMAT), and to Óscar Susano Dalmau Cedeño (Coordinador de Ciencias de la Computación, CIMAT). We are also indebted to the following authorities at Universidad de Guanajuato: Héctor Fabián Gutiérez Rangel (Director de la División de Ciencias Económico Administrativas), Martin Picón Núñez (Rector de Campus Guanajuato, Universidad de Guanajuato), and Claudia Susana Gómez López (Rectora General) for their invaluable assistance in securing the university facilities to complement the facilities of CIMAT.

In addition, the success of this conference and the breadth of its program are a testament to the collaborative efforts of our organizing and local committees and sponsors.

The entire submission, reviewing, and selection process, as well as the preparation of the proceedings, was supported by Microsoft's Conference Management Toolkit (https://cmt3.research.microsoft.com/). Last but not least, we are grateful to Springer for their patience and help in the preparation of these volumes.

In conclusion, MICAI 2025 was more than just a conference. It was a confluence of minds, a testament to the indefatigable spirit of the AI community, and a beacon for the future of Artificial Intelligence. As you navigate through these proceedings, may you find inspiration, knowledge, and connections that propel you forward in your journey.

November 2025

Lourdes Martínez-Villaseñor
Roberto A. Vázquez
Gilberto Ochoa-Ruiz
Martín Montes Rivera
Saúl Zapotecas-Martínez
María Lucía Barrón-Estrada
Efrén Mezura-Montes
Arturo Gomez Chavez

Organization

Conference Committee

General Chair

Lourdes Martínez-Villaseñor	Universidad Panamericana, Mexico

Program Chairs

Gilberto Ochoa-Ruiz	Tecnológico de Monterrey, Mexico
Roberto A. Vazquez	Universidad La Salle México, Mexico

Workshop Chair

Iris Mendez	Universidad Autónoma de Ciudad Juárez, Mexico

Tutorials Chair

David Pinto	Benemérita Universidad Autónoma de Puebla, Mexico

Doctoral Consortium Chairs

Miguel González Mendoza	Tecnológico de Monterrey, Mexico
Néstor Valasco Bermeo	Experient, USA
Gustavo Arroyo Figueroa	Instituto Nacional de Electricidad y Energías Limpias, Mexico

Keynote Talks Chair

Hugo Jair Escalante	Instituto Nacional de Astrofísica, Óptica y Electrónica, Mexico

Publication Chair

Hiram Ponce	Universidad Panamericana, Mexico

Publicity Chairs

Bella Martinez	Instituto Politécnico Nacional, Mexico
Claudia Gonzalez	Instituto Tecnológico de Tijuana, Mexico

Communication and Design Chairs

Iván Olvera	Grupo Software de Alta Calidad, Mexico
Omar Saldivar	Barbarous, Mexico
Luis Gerardo Téllez	Barbarous, Mexico

Grant Chair

Leobardo Morales	IBM, Mexico

Local Organizing Committee

Local Chairs

Alejandro Rosales Pérez	Centro de Investigación en Matemáticas (CIMAT), Mexico
Adrian Pastor López Monroy	Centro de Investigación en Matemáticas (CIMAT), Mexico

Logistics Chairs

Jorge Alberto Soria Alcaraz	Universidad de Guanajuato, Mexico
Marco Aurelio Sotelo Figueroa	Universidad de Guanajuato, Mexico

Program Committee

Abel García Nájera	Universidad Autónoma Metropolitana Unidad Cuajimalpa, Mexico
Alberto Gonzalez-Sanchez	Instituto Mexicano de Tecnología del Agua, Mexico
Alberto Ochoa-Zezzatti	Universidad Autónoma de Ciudad Juárez, Mexico
Aldo Márquez-Grajales	Universidad Veracruzana, Mexico
Alexander V Bozhenyuk	Southern Federal University, Russia
Ana Laura Lezama-Sánchez	SECIHTI, BUAP, Mexico

Andres Garcia Floriano	Instituto Politécnico Nacional, Mexico
Andrés Espinal	Universidad de Guanajuato, Mexico
Angeles Belém Priego Sánchez	Universidad Autónoma Metropolitana Unidad Azcapotzalco, Mexico
Antonieta Martinez	Universidad Panamericana, Mexico
Antonio Neme	Universidad Nacional Autónoma de México, Mexico
Ari Y. Barrera-Animas	Universidad Panamericana, Mexico
Armando Levid Rodríguez Santiago	Universidad Tecnológica de los Valles Centrales de Oaxaca, Mexico
Asdrúbal López Chau	Universidad Autónoma del Estado de México, Mexico
Ashokkumar Baldevbhai Prajapati	Soorajba College of Education, India
Ayanfeoluwa P. Oluyomi	Missouri University of Science and Technology, USA
Bella C. Martinez Seis	Instituto Politécnico Nacional, Mexico
Bernardo Corona Domínguez	Universidad Nacional Rosario Castellanos, Mexico
Betania Hernandez-Ocaña	Universidad Juárez Autónoma de Tabasco, Mexico
Camila L. Silva	Universidade Federal de Minas Gerais, Brazil
Chandra Prakash	University of the Cumberlands, USA
Christina A. Garcia	Kyushu Institute of Technology, Japan
Claudia I. Gonzalez	TECNM/Instituto Tecnológico de Tijuana, Mexico
Cosijopii Garcia-Garcia	Universidad del Istmo, Mexico
Daniel Flores Araiza	Monterrey Institute of Technology and Higher Education (ITESM), Mexico
Daniela Alejandra Ochoa	CentroGEO, Mexico
Dante Mújica-Vargas	CENIDET, Mexico
David Pinto	Benemerita Universidad Autonoma de Puebla, Mexico
Dhwanit Agarwal	Adobe Inc, USA
Diego Uribe	Instituto Tecnólogico de La Laguna, Mexico
Eddy Sánchez-DelaCruz	Tecnológico Nacional de México - Campus Misantla, Mexico
Eduardo Valdez	Instituto Politécnico Nacional, Mexico
Efrén Mezura-Montes	University of Veracruz, Mexico
Elisabetta Crescio	Tecnológico de Monterrey, Mexico
Elva Lilia Reynoso Jardon	Universidad Autónoma de Ciudad Juárez, Mexico
Emmanuel Ovalle-Magallanes	Universidad de La Salle Bajio, Mexico
Eric S. Tellez	CICESE-INFOTEC-CONACyT, Mexico
Erik Molino	IIMAS-UNAM, Mexico

Esmeralda Arreola Marin	TecNM campus Cd. Hidalgo, Mexico
Fernando Gudino	National Autonomous University of Mexico, Mexico
Fevrier Valdez	Tijuana Institute of Technology/TecNM, Mexico
Francisco Lopez-Tiro	Tecnológico de Monterrey, Mexico
Gabriel González-Serna	TecNM/CENIDET, Mexico
Garibaldi Pineda Garcia	Applied AGI, UK
Genoveva Vargas-Solar	Grenoble Alpes University, CNRS, France
Gilberto Ochoa-Ruiz	Tecnológico de Monterrey, Mexico
Gildardo Sanchez-Ante	Tecnológico de Monterrey, Mexico
Grissel Rodríguez Roldán	Instituto Artek, Mexico
Guadalupe Carmona Arroyo	Universidad Veracruzana, Mexico
Guillermo Santamaría-Bonfil	BBVA México, Mexico
Gustavo Arroyo	Instituto Nacional de Electricidad y Energías Limpias, Mexico
Haimei Wen	University of Texas at Dallas, USA
Hiram Calvo	Center for Computing Research - Instituto Politécnico Nacional, Mexico
Hiram Ponce	Universidad Panamericana, Mexico
Hugo Jair Escalante	Instituto Nacional de Astrofísica, Óptica y Electrónica, Mexico
Humberto Sossa	CIC-Instituto Politécnico Nacional, Mexico
Iris Iddaly Méndez-Gurrola	Universidad Autónoma de Ciudad Juárez, Mexico
Ismael Osuna-Galán	Universidad Autónoma del Estado de Quintana Roo, Mexico
Israel Tabarez	Universidad Autónoma del Estado de México, Mexico
Jaime Cerda	Universidad Michoacana de San Nicolás de Hidalgo, Mexico
Jerusa Marchi	Federal University of Santa Catarina, Brazil
Jesús García-Ramírez	UPIIT-Instituto Politécnico Nacional, Mexico
Jesús-Adolfo Mejía-de-Dios	Universidad Autónoma de Coahuila, Mexico
Jiale Li	University of Auckland, New Zealand
Jiechen Zhao	University of Toronto, Canada
Joanna Alvarado Uribe	Tecnológico de Monterrey, Mexico
Jonathan Rojas-Simón	Autonomous University of the State of Mexico, Mexico
Jose D. Alanis	Universidad Tecnológica de Puebla, Mexico
Jose Sosa	University of Luxembourg, Luxembourg
Jose Alberto Hernandez-Aguilar	Universidad Autónoma del Estado de Morelos, Mexico
José Carlos Ortiz-Bayliss	Tecnológico de Monterrey, Mexico
José Luis M Reyes	Universidad Veracruzana, Mexico

José Luis Vilchis Medina	ENSTA Bretagne, France
Jose-Federico Ramirez-Cruz	TecNM - Instituto Tecnológico de Apizaco, Mexico
Juan Martínez-Miranda	CICESE-Unidad Académica Tepic, Mexico
Juan Villegas-Cortez	Universidad Autónoma Metropolitana - Azcapotzalco, Mexico
Juan Carlos Olivares Rojas	Tecnológico Nacional de México/Instituto Tecnológico de Morelia, Mexico
Juana Isabel Méndez	Tecnológico de Monterrey, Mexico
Juan-Carlos Gonzalez-Islas	Universidad Autónoma del Estado de Hidalgo, Mexico
Julio Santisteban	Universidad Católica San Pablo, Peru
Karina Mariela Figueroa Mora	Universidad Michoacana de San Nicolás de Hidalgo, Mexico
Leticia Flores Pulido	Universidad Autónoma de Tlaxcala, Mexico
Li Yu	Zhejiang University, China
Lourdes Martinez-Villaseñor	Universidad Panamericana, Mexico
Luis M. Torres-Treviño	Universidad Autónoma de Nuevo León, Mexico
Mansoor Ali	Tecnológico de Monterrey, Mexico
Maria de la Concepción Pérez de Celis Herrero	Benemérita Universidad Autónoma de Puebla, Mexico
Maria Lucia Barrón Estrada	TecNM-Instituto Tecnológico de Culiacán, Mexico
Mario Anzures-García	Benemérita Universidad Autónoma de Puebla, Mexico
Masaki Murata	Tottori University, Japan
Miguel Gonzalez-Mendoza	Tecnológico de Monterrey, Mexico
Miguel Sanchez Brito	Instituto Politécnico Nacional, Mexico
Mohd. Saif Wajid	BBD University, India
Nancy Pérez-Castro	Universidad del Papaloapan, Mexico
Nestor Velasco Bermeo	Experient, USA
Nidiyare Hevia Montiel	Universidad Nacional Autónoma de México, Mexico
Noé-Alejandro Castro-Sánchez	TecNM-CENIDET, Mexico
Obdulia Pichardo-Lagunas	Instituto Politécnico Nacional, Mexico
Omar Velazquez Lopez	Universidad Nacional Autónoma de México, Mexico
Pagon Gatchalee	Chiang Mai University, Thailand
Pengfei Hu	Stevens Institute of Technology, USA
Qi Chang	Accenture, USA
Quanchao Lu	Georgia Tech, USA
Rafael Batres	Tecnológico de Monterrey, Mexico
Rafael Guzman-Cabrera	Universidad de Guanajuato, Mexico

Rafael Rivera-Lopez	Tecnológico Nacional de México/Instituto Tecnológico de Veracruz, Mexico
Ramon F. Brena	Instituto Tecnológico de Sonora, Mexico
Ramón Zatarain Cabada	Tec Culiacán, Mexico
Rashi Dhenia	Hitachi, USA
Raúl Monroy Borja	Tecnológico de Monterrey, Mexico
Ricardo Espinosa	Universidad Panamericana, Mexico
Ricardo Landa	Cinvestav, Mexico
Roberto Antonio Vazquez	Universidad La Salle México, Mexico
Rocio O. Ochoa-Montiel	Universidad Autónoma de Tlaxcala, Mexico
Rosa M. Ortega-Mendoza	Universidad Autónoma del Estado de Hidalgo, Mexico
Sabino Miranda	Universidad Autónoma de la Ciudad de México, Mexico
Salvador M Hinojosa	Tecnológico de Monterrey, Mexico
Samuel Efren Viñas Alvarez	Tecnológico Nacional de México campus Zitácuaro, Mexico
Sandra Leticia Juárez-Osorio	Centro de Investigación y Estudios Avanzados del Politécnico Nacional, Mexico
Sheng Gao	University of Pennsylvania, USA
Shuo Li	Carnegie Mellon University, USA
Sofia N. Galicia Haro	SNI, Mexico
Stephen A. Sunday	Ohio University, USA
Tania A. Ramirez-delReal	CONACyT-CentroGeo, Mexico
Vadim Borisov	Branch of National Research University "Moscow Power Engineering Institute" in Smolensk, Russia
Valery Solovyev	Kazan Federal University, Russia
Vicente Garcia Jimenez	Universidad Autónoma de Ciudad Juárez, Mexico
Victor Lomas-Barrie	IIMAS-UNAM, Mexico
Víctor J. Ruiz	TecNM/CENIDET, Mexico
Yasmín Hernández	Centro Nacional de Investigación y Desarrollo Tecnológico, Mexico
Yaxk'in U. Kan Coronado	Universidad La Salle México, Mexico
Yubo Wang	Meta Platforms, inc, USA
Yucheng Zhou	University of Macau, China

Workshops Organization

HIS 2025

General Chairs

Martín Montes Rivera	Universidad Politécnica de Aguascalientes, Mexico
Carlos Alberto Ochoa Zezzatti	Universidad Autónoma de Ciudad Juárez, Mexico
José Alberto Hernández Aguilar	Universidad Autónoma del Estado de Morelos, Mexico
Julio César Ponce Gallegos	Universidad Autónoma de Aguascalientes, Mexico
Daniela Paola López Betancur	Universidad Autónoma de Zacatecas, Mexico
Carlos Alejandro Guerrero Méndez	Universidad Autónoma de Zacatecas, Mexico
Lourdes Margain Fuentes	Universidad Internacional de Innovación, Mexico

Program Committee

Edgar Gonzalo Cossio Franco	Instituto de Información Estadística y Geográfica de Jalisco, México
Humberto Velasco Arellano	Universidad Politécnica de Aguascalientes, México
Daniela Paola López Betancourt	Universidad Politécnica de Aguascalientes, México
Carlos Alejandro Guerrero Méndez	Universidad Autónoma de Zacatecas, México
Humberto Muñoz Bautista	Universidad Tecnológica Metropolitana de Aguascalientes, México
Miguel Ángel Ortiz Esparza	Universidad Autónoma de Aguascalientes, México
Himer Avila George	Universidad de Guadalajara, México
Alejandro Padilla Díaz	Universidad Autónoma de Aguascalientes, México
Carlos Alberto Lara Alvarez	CIMAT Zacatecas, México
Roberto Antonio Contreras Masse	Instituto Tecnológico Ciudad Juárez, México
Irma Yazmín Hernández Báez	Universidad Politécnica del Estado de Morelos, México

ECSI 2025

General Chairs

Saúl Zapotecas-Martínez	Instituto Nacional de Astrofísica, Óptica y Electrónica, Mexico
Alejandro Rosales-Pérez	Centro de Investigación en Matemáticas, Mexico

Program Committee

Alberto Ochoa-Zezzatti	Universidad Autónoma de Ciudad Juárez, Mexico
Jesús G. Falcón-Cardona	Centro de Investigación Científica y de Educación Superior de Ensenada, Mexico
José-Antonio Fuentes-Tomás	Universidad Veracruzana, Mexico
Miguel A. Jiménez-Domínguez	Instituto Nacional de Astrofísica, Óptica y Electrónica, Mexico
Néstor García-Rojas	Instituto Nacional de Astrofísica, Óptica y Electrónica, Mexico
Luis Rosas-Ordaz	Instituto Nacional de Astrofísica, Óptica y Electrónica, Mexico
Adriana Menchaca-Méndez	Escuela Nacional de Estudios Superiores Unidad Morelia UNAM, Mexico

WILE 2025

General Chairs

María Lucía Barrón Estrada	TecNM-Instituto Tecnológico de Culiacán, México
Ramón Zatarain Cabada	TecNM-Instituto Tecnológico de Culiacán, México
Carlos A. Reyes García	Instituto Nacional de Astrofísica, Óptica y Electróni, México
Yasmín Hernández Pérez	TecNM-Cenidet, México
Karina M. Figueroa Mora	Universidad Michoacana de San Nicolás de Hidalgo, Mexico

Program Committee

Ramón Zatarain Cabada	Instituto Tecnológico de Culiacán, Mexico
María Lucía Barrón Estrada	Instituto Tecnológico de Culiacán, Mexico
Yasmín Hernández Pérez	Cenidet, Mexico
Carlos A. Reyes García	Instituto Nacional de Astrofísica, Óptica y Electrónica, Mexico
Karina Mariela Figueroa Mora	Universidad Michoacana de San Nicolás de Hidalgo, Mexico

Giner Alor Hernández	Instituto Tecnológico de Orizaba, Mexico
Miguel Pérez Ramírez	Mexico
Jaime Muñoz Arteaga	Universidad Autónoma de Aguascalientes, Mexico
Rafael Morales Gamboa	Universidad de Guadalajara, Mexico
Guillermo Santamaría Bonfil	BBVA México, Mexico
Carlos Alberto Lara Álvarez	CIMAT Zacatecas, Mexico
Hugo Arnoldo Mitre Hernández	CIMAT Zacatecas, Mexico
María Elena Chávez Echeagaray	Arizona State University, USA
Javier González	Arizona State University, USA
María Blanca Ibáñez Espiga	Universidad Carlos III de Madrid, Spain
Alicia Martínez Rebollar	Cenidet, Mexico
María Lucila Morales Rodríguez	Instituto Tecnológico de Cd. Madero, Mexico
Héctor Rodríguez Rangel	Instituto Tecnológico de Culiacán, Mexico
Julieta Noguez Monroy	Mexico
Samuel González López	Instituto Tecnológico de Nogales, Mexico
Raúl Oramas Bustillos	Universidad Autónoma de Occidente, Mexico
Francisco González Hernández	Instituto Tecnológico de Culiacán, Mexico
José Mario Ríos Félix	Instituto Tecnológico de Culiacán, Mexico
Luis Alberto Morales Rosales	Universidad Michoacana de San Nicolás de Hidalgo, Mexico

CIAPP 2025

General Chairs

Rocío Erandi Barrientos Martínez	Universidad Veracruzana, Mexico
Marcela Quiroz Castellanos	Universidad Veracruzana, Mexico
Efrén Mezura Montes	Universidad Veracruzana, Mexico
Héctor Gabriel Acosta Mesa	Universidad Veracruzana, Mexico

Program Committee

Ángel J. Sánchez García	Universidad Veracruzana, Mexico
Carlos Alberto Fernández y Fernández	Universidad Tecnológica de la Mixteca, Mexico
Carlos Alberto López Herrera	Universidad Veracruzana, Mexico
Carmen Mezura-Godoy	Universidad Veracruzana, Mexico
Daniel Molina Pérez	Instituto Politécnico Nacional, Mexico
David Herrera Sánchez	Universidad Veracruzana, Mexico
Edgard Benítez Guerrero	Universidad Veracruzana, Mexico
Guadalupe Carmona Arroyo	Universidad Veracruzana, Mexico
Jesús Adolfo Mejía de Dios	Universidad Autónoma de Coahuila, Mexico

Jesús Arnulfo Barradas Palmeros	Universidad Veracruzana, Mexico
José Luis Llaguno Roque	Universidad Veracruzana, Mexico
Rogelio Portillo Vélez	Universidad Veracruzana, Mexico
Sonia L. Mestizo-Gutiérrez	Universidad Veracruzana, Mexico

CHARAL 2025

General Chairs

Arturo Gomez Chavez	Constructor University, Germany
Emmanuel Ovalle-Magallanes	Universidad La Salle Bajío, Mexico
José Martínez Carranza	Instituto Nacional de Astrofísica, Óptica y Electrónica, Mexico

Program Committee

Ana Laura Lezama-Sánchez	SECIHTI, Mexico
Babak Rokh	University of Zanjan, Iran
Diego Uribe	Instituto Tecnólogico de La Laguna, Mexico
Grissel Rodríguez Roldán	Instituto Artek, Mexico
Jaime Cerda	Universidad Michoacana de San Nicolás de Hidalgo, Mexico
Juan Carlos Olivares Rojas	Instituto Tecnológico de Morelia, Mexico
Leticia Flores Pulido	Universidad Autónoma de Tlaxcala, Mexico
Marco Escobar	Universidad La Salle Bajío, Mexico
Mario Anzures-García	Benemérita Universidad Autónoma de Puebla, Mexico
Omar Velazquez Lopez	Universidad Nacional Autónoma de México, Mexico
Rocio Ochoa-Montiel	Universidad Autónoma de Tlaxcala, Mexico
Francesco Maurelli	Constructor University, Germany

Contents

ECSI 2025

HIS 2025

Data Mining and Hybrid Clustering for Optimizing Energy Efficiency in Public Buildings

G. Espadas[1(✉)], A. Rodríguez[1], C. Quej[1], M. Escalante[1], M. Flota[1], and C. Ochoa[2(✉)]

[1] Facultad de Ingeniería, Universidad Autónoma de Yucatán. C.P. 97310., Av. Industrias no Contaminantes por Periférico Norte, Apdo. Postal 150 Cordemex, Mérida, Yucatán, Mexico
gilberto.espadas@hotmail.com

[2] Doctorado en Tecnología, Universidad Autónoma de Ciudad Juárez, Av. Plutarco Elías Calles #1210 Fovissste Chamizal C.P. 32310. Ciudad Juárez, Chihuahua, Mexico

Abstract. Electricity demand in Yucatán is rising, making energy efficiency in public buildings a policy priority. We propose a hybrid, unsupervised pipeline that combines K-means (global typologies) with DBSCAN (density-based anomaly discovery) to segment ~350 public buildings by energy behavior. After systematic preprocessing (outlier control via IQR, multivariate imputation, Min–Max scaling), K-means revealed four consistent energy typologies. DBSCAN, tuned with a k-dist heuristic, flagged >60% of records as atypical patterns that merit targeted audits. Using an energy-use-intensity benchmark of 120 kWh m^{-2} $yr.^{-1}$, the high-intensity cluster (n $\approx$ 65; EUI $\approx$ 175 kWh m^{-2} yr^{-1}) shows an $\approx$20–25% reduction potential relative to current levels, supporting the prioritization of retrofits and operational measures. PCA projections and georeferenced maps aid interpretation and policy targeting. The results indicate that the hybrid approach captures both dominant patterns and irregular behaviors, translating raw meter data into actionable, scalable guidance for evidence-based public programs in building efficiency.

Keywords: Artificial Intelligence · Hybrid Clustering · K-means · DBSCAN · Energy Efficiency · Public Buildings · Data Mining

1 Introduction

The growing global energy demand is a major contributor to the planet's unsustainable development [1]. Buildings constitute the second largest energy consuming sector globally, after industry [2]. Operational energy use in buildings accounts for 30% of total final energy consumption and 26% of global energy-related emissions, with public buildings alone responsible for approximately 10% of the sector's total energy use [3]. Over the past decade, this demand has increased at an average annual rate of 1%, reflecting a steady upward trend in global building energy requirements [3].

L. Martínez-Villaseñor et al. (Eds.): MICAI 2025 Workshops, LNAI 16264, pp. 3–21, 2026.
https://doi.org/10.1007/978-3-032-17930-2_1

In the regional context of southeastern Mexico, the state of Yucatán is experiencing rapid population growth, intensifying the demand for natural resources, public services, and built infrastructure [4]. This demographic expansion poses substantial challenges to the regional energy infrastructure, given the direct correlation between population growth and rising energy demand [5]. Yucatán comprises more than 2,900 public buildings, with approximately 30% under public ownership [4]. The cumulative energy consumption of these facilities significantly contributes to regional electricity demand, as evidenced by the 10.2% increase in consumption reported in 2023 for the Peninsular Division, exceeding the national average of 4.8% [6]. These circumstances highlight the urgency of adopting efficient energy management strategies in Yucatán's public buildings to promote long-term sustainability and reduce environmental impacts.

Over the years, advancements in building design, construction, and operation have become essential to mitigating energy impacts. However, despite technological innovations and improved construction materials, these measures remain insufficient, as buildings are dynamic systems whose energy performance largely depends on the often unpredictable behavior of their occupants [7, 8].

Building Energy Management Systems (BEMSs) have gained increasing attention as a strategy to enhance energy efficiency by enabling the centralized automation of critical subsystems, including heating, ventilation, air conditioning (HVAC), surveillance, and access control [9]. BEMSs aim to maintain energy-efficient performance and occupant comfort by monitoring and coordinating the operation of various building subsystems through integrated control strategies [10]. Nevertheless, the growing volume of data generated poses a challenge for operators, who must interpret complex information and translate it into effective operational decisions.

2 Literature Review

The search for improved strategies to enhance building efficiency has driven a growing number of scientific publications in recent years. As shown in Fig. 1, research on building energy efficiency has increased significantly, reflecting the scientific community's heightened interest in addressing this challenge. This trend aligns with international initiatives such as the United Nations Sustainable Development Goal 7.3 [11], which aims to double the global rate of energy efficiency improvement by 2030, and the Global Roadmap for Buildings and Construction 2020–2050 [12], which targets a 30% reduction in building energy use by 2030 and net-zero emissions by 2050. Hence, increasing academic engagement underscores the urgency of the issue and fosters the development of more effective solutions.

The rapid evolution of computer hardware and software has enabled the increasing deployment of automation and artificial intelligence (AI) in diverse industries [13]. Moreover, the integration of advanced strategies, including machine learning (ML), and the Internet of Things (IoT), can substantially improve energy management and overall building efficiency, while also addressing the challenges posed by large-scale data analysis [14]. IoT devices, such as smart meters, temperature, humidity, and occupancy sensors, enable continuous monitoring of indoor environmental conditions and real-time energy consumption [15]. AI seeks to replicate human cognitive processes such

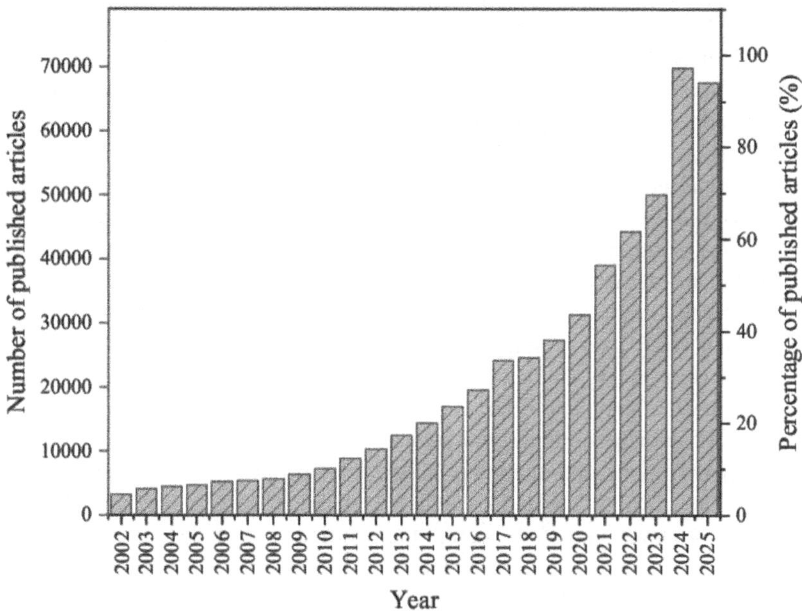

Fig. 1. Articles on building energy efficiency published from 2002 to 2025 (retrived from Scopus)

as reasoning, abstraction, and adaptive learning through computational frameworks. AI technologies can dynamically regulate HVAC (heating, ventilation, and air conditioning) systems, lighting, and other electrical equipment in response to real-time conditions and occupant needs. Furthermore, AI enables the prediction of future energy demand by analyzing historical consumption patterns in conjunction with external factors, such as weather conditions and operational schedules [16]. ML, a core component of AI, utilizes data-driven approaches to develop models for pattern recognition and predictive analytics [17, 18]. Among these, deep learning algorithms enable autonomous feature extraction and are typically categorized as supervised or unsupervised, depending on the data labeling scheme [19–21]. Supervised learning relies on datasets in which each input is associated with a corresponding output, allowing the model to establish explicit mappings. Conversely, unsupervised learning explores hidden structures within unlabeled data [22]. Deep learning, as a specialized branch of ML, leverages neural architectures such as multilayer perceptrons (MLPs), convolutional neural networks (CNNs), and recurrent neural networks (RNNs) to automate feature extraction and achieve hierarchical representation learning [23].

AI and ML have been increasingly applied in the energy sector to enhance operational efficiency in buildings. In their study, Westermann et al. [24] developed an unsupervised clustering framework combining support vector regression (SVR) with dynamic time warping for the analysis of energy signatures from smart meter data. This framework accurately identified building and heating system categories in two residential datasets, achieving high agreement with corresponding metadata and demographic records. Zhang and Mirzaei [25] introduced a virtual dynamic coupling framework that integrates computational fluid dynamics (CFD), building energy simulation (BES), and artificial neural networks (ANN) to enhance the estimation of convective heat transfer coefficients. The framework reduced computational time by nearly two-thirds compared with conventional CFD–BES coupling. Further advancements highlight the integration of AI with emerging digital technologies. Deena et al. [26] developed an automated system that integrates Digital Twins (DT), AI, IoT, and Building Information Modeling (BIM) to enhance energy optimization in residential settings, ensuring both efficiency and occupant thermal comfort. Similarly, Rojek et al. [16] demonstrated that integrating IoT with AI enables effective and economically sustainable optimization of building energy management. Their study also highlighted the scalability of such solutions for smart city applications, while noting challenges related to high upfront costs, cybersecurity, and user acceptance. Complementary to previous approaches, Lee et al. [27] introduced the AIif framework, which combines computational intelligence, distributed AI, machine learning, expert systems, and intelligent interfaces to promote energy efficiency at multiple scales. Their results reported significant reductions of 47.5% at equipment level, 37% in HVAC systems, and 36.9% across the building as a whole.

Beyond supervised techniques, unsupervised learning has emerged as a promising alternative capable of uncovering hidden patterns in energy data without requiring extensive labeled datasets, thus enhancing flexibility and robustness in analysis. In this context, Shapi et al. [28] evaluated Support Vector Machine (SVM), ANN, and k-Nearest Neighbour (k-NN) models for forecasting peak demand and monthly energy use in a commercial building, finding that SVM delivered the highest accuracy, k-NN offered a favorable balance between accuracy and efficiency, and ANN showed the lowest performance. Furthermore, Talei et al. [29] applied an unsupervised K-means clustering algorithm to one year of HVAC consumption data from a LEED-certified building, incorporating occupancy and outdoor temperature as additional variables. The analysis identified time intervals of inefficient energy use and demonstrated that HVAC consumption could be reduced by 6% without compromising occupant comfort. Moreover, Liu et al. [30] developed an SVM-based framework that integrates historical consumption data, climate variables, and seasonal cycles to forecast and diagnose energy use in public buildings. The model achieved high predictive accuracy and provided actionable diagnostic insights into operational anomalies, offering both practical and policy-oriented guidance to reduce energy waste and improve public building management.

3 Methodology and Operation

3.1 Data and Variables Considered

The analysis is based on energy consumption data from public buildings in Yucatán, Mexico. The primary objective is to identify usage patterns and classify the buildings according to their energy performance.

The sample comprises approximately 350 records, representing a subset of an estimated total of 2,900 public buildings. It includes schools, administrative offices, and hospitals. This typological and operational diversity is intended to ensure the validity of the analysis. The study period covers the years 2019, 2022, 2023, and 2024. The years 2020 and 2021 were excluded due to disruptions in occupancy patterns caused by the COVID-19 pandemic. This decision was made to maintain methodological consistency [31]. The selected variables reflect the main factors influencing monthly energy consumption (kWh). This selection follows recognized practices in building energy modeling [32]. Table 1 presents the variables considered in this study.

Table 1. Variables considered in the study.

Variable	Type	Description
Monthly consumption (kWh)	Numerical	Electricity consumed per month.
Building type	Categorical	Classification of building use.
Floor area (m^2)	Numerical	Total constructed area.
Number of employees	Numerical	Average occupancy.
Equipment	Categorical	HVAC, lighting, ICTs.
Mean temperature	Numerical	Monthly climatic condition.
Relative humidity	Numerical	Monthly climatic condition.
Year of construction	Numerical	Building age.

Additional construction-related characteristics will also be included, such as building materials, insulation level, and official classification. Furthermore, more detailed occupancy metrics, such as the number of active days per year, are planned to be incorporated. These additional variables will enable the refinement of the models and improve the accuracy of the generated clusters [31, 33]. This methodological selection is aligned with international standards in energy efficiency and demand analysis for public buildings. It provides a robust foundation for preprocessing, segmentation, and the design of differentiated energy efficiency strategies.

3.2 Data Preprocessing

The quality of the analysis and the accuracy of the segmentation model largely depend on the preliminary treatment of the data. Therefore, a systematic preprocessing procedure is established, which includes the detection of outliers, the imputation of missing data, and the normalization of numerical variables. These steps ensure comparability across observations, minimize statistical bias, and enhance the performance of clustering algorithms.

First, outlier detection and correction will be carried out using the interquartile range (IQR) method. This criterion identifies observations that deviate significantly from the central tendency of the variable, considering as outliers those values falling outside the following range [34]:

$$[\mathrm{Q1} - 1.5 \cdot \mathrm{IQR}, \mathrm{Q3} + 1.5 \cdot \mathrm{IQR}] \quad (1)$$

Outliers detected may be excluded, adjusted, or replaced depending on their nature and their impact on the dataset.

Second, missing values will be addressed using multiple regression techniques. This approach enables the estimation of plausible values based on the relationships among available variables, while preserving the integrity of the dataset's internal correlations. The selection of predictor variables for each imputation will be based on their correlation and prior statistical significance.

Finally, Min-Max normalization will be applied to all numerical variables. This procedure transforms the data into a common scale (0, 1) without altering their relative distribution. Normalization is essential for distance-based clustering algorithms, such as K-means, as it prevents variables with larger scales from dominating similarity calculations. This transformation is also compatible with the input requirements of visualization methods based on dimensionality reduction.

The defined preprocessing strategy aims not only to improve the technical quality of the analysis but also to ensure the reproducibility of the system and its adaptability to new datasets in future phases of the project.

3.3 Proposed Clustering Algorithms

3.3.1 K-Means

K-means is a clustering algorithm that partitions the dataset into K distinct groups [35]. It minimizes the within-group variance using Euclidean distance. Its objective is to determine cluster centers (centroids) that reduce the sum of squared distances within each group [36]. The objective function is:

$$\mathrm{Inertia} = \sum_{i=1}^{k} \sum_{x \varepsilon C_i} \|x - \mu_i\|^2 \tag{2}$$

where C_i denotes the set of points belonging to cluster i, and μ_i represents its centroid.

The number of clusters (K) will be determined using the elbow method and the Silhouette coefficient [37]. The elbow method evaluates inertia as k varies in order to identify a point of stability [38]. The Silhouette coefficient is calculated as:

$$s(i) = \frac{b(i) - a(i)}{\max\{a(i), b(i)\}} \tag{3}$$

where $a(i)$ is the average intra-cluster distance and $b(i)$ is the minimum distance to another cluster [37]. This measure helps assess the quality of the segmentation.

3.3.2 DBSCAN

DBSCAN (Density-Based Spatial Clustering of Applications with Noise) forms clusters based on point density. It does not require the number of clusters to be defined a priori and is capable of identifying clusters of arbitrary shapes [39]. The neighborhood of a point is defined as:

$$N_\varepsilon(p) = \{q \in D \mid \mathrm{dist}(p, q) \leq \varepsilon\} \tag{4}$$

where ε is the neighborhood radius and min_samples is the minimum number of points required to form a cluster [40]. DBSCAN detects dense points and classifies isolated cases as noise. It is particularly useful for identifying anomalies or complex subgroups that K-means cannot capture due to its assumption of spherical shapes [41].

3.3.3 Proposed Hybrid Methodological Workflow

This hybrid approach seeks to combine the interpretability of K-means with the flexibility of DBSCAN, thereby enhancing the robustness and applicability of energy segmentation. The complete methodological workflow is represented through a flowchart [Fig. 2]. This diagram outlines the sequence of stages required for the energy segmentation of public buildings, including data loading, systematic preprocessing, the application of clustering algorithms, and the validation of results.

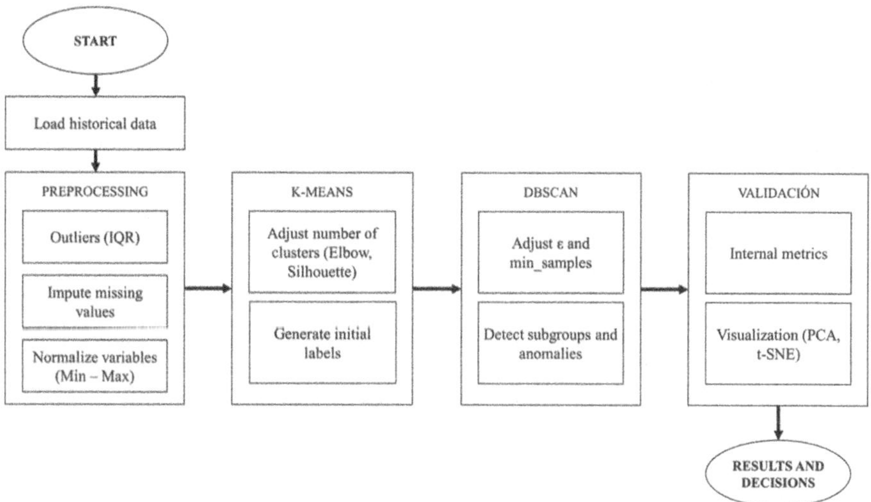

Fig. 2. Flowchart of the proposed system for the energy segmentation of public buildings.

The first stage consists of loading the historical data on energy consumption and associated variables. Next, preprocessing is carried out, which includes the detection and treatment of outliers, the imputation of missing data using multiple regression, and the normalization of numerical variables with the Min-Max method.

Subsequently, the K-means algorithm is applied for the initial segmentation, adjusting the optimal number of clusters through the elbow method and the Silhouette coefficient. This primary segmentation establishes homogeneous energy typologies. DBSCAN is then applied to detect subgroups with non-linear shapes and to identify anomalies or outliers that require differentiated analysis.

Finally, the results are validated using internal. Dimensionality reduction techniques, such as Principal Component Analysis (PCA), are also applied to facilitate group visualization and support decision-making in energy efficiency policies.

As part of the implementation, this methodological workflow is planned to be applied to a strategically selected pilot group of public buildings. The objective is to validate the robustness of the segmentation and the system's ability to identify relevant patterns before scaling the application to the complete set of buildings. This validation will allow for the adjustment of algorithm parameters, optimization of preprocessing, and enhancement of the interactive visualization interface, ensuring that the final tool is accurate, practical, and easily adoptable by institutions responsible for planning energy efficiency strategies.

3.4 Design of the Analysis and Segmentation

The design of the analysis seeks to provide a practical, data-driven solution for classifying public buildings in Yucatán according to their energy performance. The objective is not only to describe a sequence of steps, but to structure an approach capable of guiding real decisions in energy efficiency and public policy.

This methodological design acknowledges the diversity and complexity of public buildings in Yucatán. Given that energy consumption is influenced by multiple variables, it is necessary to employ techniques that capture both general trends and unique patterns. The combination of different algorithms makes it possible to address this challenge comprehensively. By using complementary approaches, large groups can be segmented for planned interventions while atypical cases requiring specialized attention are simultaneously identified. Thus, the analysis is not limited to rigid categories but adapts to the heterogeneous reality of the public system.

This hybrid strategy addresses the limitations of traditional approaches that only consider averages or generic segmentations. By integrating density-based techniques, it ensures that atypical behaviors, such as disproportionate consumption or unusual patterns, are not overlooked. This is essential in a context where public resources are limited, and investments must be prioritized in buildings with the greatest savings potential. The methodological design also prioritizes the interpretability of results. Quantitative metrics and visualizations are incorporated to support technical decisions and facilitate communication with authorities and non-specialist stakeholders. This approach ensures that energy segmentation is not merely a statistical exercise, but a practical tool for planning state-level energy efficiency programs.

3.5 Interactive Visualization of Results

The visualization of results is an essential component of the proposed analysis. It is not limited to representing data in a static form but rather seeks to provide an interactive tool that enables stakeholders to effectively explore, analyze, and communicate findings to decision-makers.

The design involves generating graphs and maps that display the distribution of the identified clusters. To achieve this, dimensionality reduction techniques such as PCA will be used to transform multidimensional data into two-dimensional representations that are more understandable and reveal the underlying group structure. These representations will facilitate the interpretation of patterns and the comparison of energy typologies.

In addition, georeferenced maps are planned to indicate the location of public buildings and highlight groups with the highest energy-saving potential. This feature will make it possible to identify priority intervention areas at the state level. Interactive charts will also be included to allow filtering by key variables such as building type, size, or monthly consumption. Figure 3 illustrates a conceptual scheme of the proposed interactive visualization tool, highlighting its main components and how the information would be organized for the end user.

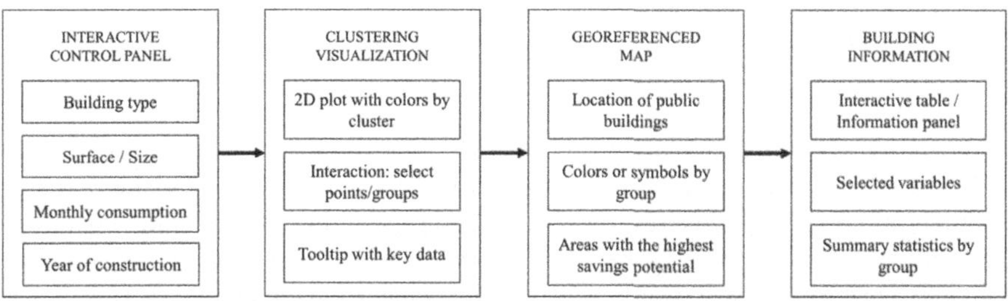

Fig. 3. Conceptual scheme of the interactive visualization tool for energy segmentation. It includes interactive filters, 2D clustering visualization using dimensionality reduction techniques, a georeferenced map, and a detailed building information panel.

This tool aims to transform clustering results into clear and accessible inputs for the planning of energy efficiency strategies. By facilitating data exploration and the identification of priorities, it seeks to strengthen the analytical capacity of public institutions and support the definition of more effective and targeted policies. Its implementation will enable the clear identification of priority groups, improve technical communication with decision-makers, plan territorial interventions, and analyze key energy consumption variables in detail.

4 Results and Discussion

4.1 Exploratory Data Analysis

The initial dataset included energy consumption records for public buildings across Yucatán for the years 2019, 2022, and 2023. After preprocessing and aggregation, a working sample of 350 buildings was retained, each characterized by annual electricity consumption, installed and contracted capacity, geographic information, and additional synthetic attributes related to physical, operational, and climatic features.

Table 2 summarizes the main descriptive statistics of the dataset. On average, buildings reported a consumption of 98,000 kWh/year, with a standard deviation of over 45,000 kWh, indicating significant heterogeneity in usage profiles. This variation is explained in part by the type of building (administrative, educational, health, cultural, etc.), surface area, and occupancy levels. Surface areas ranged from 300 m^2 to 5000 m^2, while average occupancy varied between 10 and 100 employees, depending on building function.

Table 2. Descriptive statistics of physical, operational and energy variables of public buildings in Yucatán.

Variable	N	Mean	Std	Min	Max
Consumption (kWh)	352	100,712.44	46,721.62	10,000.00	292,636.57
Surface area (m^2)	352	1,681.76	731.08	489.55	2,856.45
Average occupancy	352	40.79	20.86	10.55	79.45
Specific consumption (kWh/ m^2)	352	78.79	67.44	4.22	417.59
Mean temperature	352	27.56	0.89	26.13	28.88

To support clustering and later analysis, additional variables were generated. These included energy consumption per square meter (kWh/m^2), average occupancy, year of construction, HVAC presence, availability of natural lighting, and climatic conditions (temperature, humidity, and solar radiation) based on geographic location. All numerical variables were normalized and outliers corrected to enable fair comparison across dimensions. This exploratory analysis confirmed the multidimensional and highly dispersed nature of the energy behavior of public buildings in Yucatán, justifying the application of unsupervised learning techniques to identify consistent behavioral patterns and detect critical deviations.

4.2 Clustering Based on K-Means Algorithm

To identify energy consumption patterns among public buildings, the K-means algorithm was applied to the normalized multidimensional dataset. The input variables included historical electricity consumption (2019–2024), contracted and installed load, surface area, occupancy, climatic conditions, and construction attributes. All variables were normalized using Min-Max scaling after outlier correction. To determine the optimal number of clusters, the elbow method [Fig. 3a] and silhouette coefficient [Fig. 3b] were used. The elbow plot suggested a point of diminishing returns at $K = 4$, while the average silhouette score also reached its local maximum at this value, indicating an acceptable degree of intra-group cohesion and inter-group separation. Therefore, four clusters were adopted for the final segmentation.

Each cluster exhibits distinct energy and operational profiles. Table 3 summarizes the mean values of key variables by cluster. Cluster 0 includes large buildings with high occupancy and above-average energy intensity. Cluster 1 groups medium-sized buildings with moderate demand and relatively stable consumption. Cluster 2 consists of low-occupancy buildings with potential for efficiency gains due to high specific consumption (kWh/m^2). Cluster 3 groups compact, low-consumption buildings with low installed capacity and minimal HVAC use.

The clustering analysis identified four distinct energy performance groups. Cluster 2 ($n = 65$) concentrates energy-intensive buildings (EUI $\approx$ 175 kWh/m^2; 64.6% above threshold), with a savings potential of 39.5 MWh (22.3%), making it the primary target for interventions. Cluster 1 is the most efficient (EUI $\approx$ 13 kWh/m^2; 0% above threshold), where maintaining good practices is recommended. Cluster 0 shows intermediate

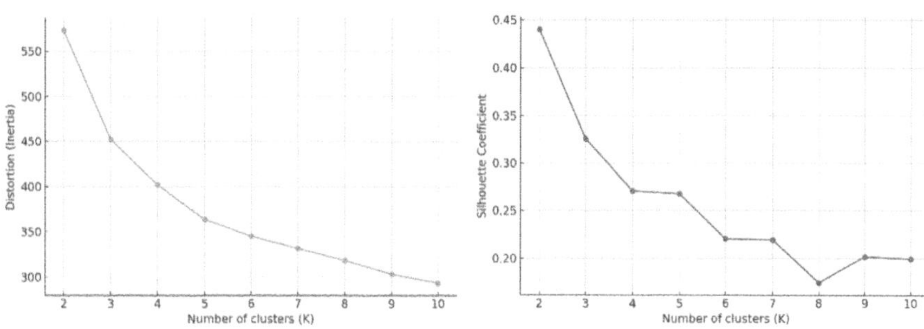

Fig. 3. a) Elbow Method for Optimal K – Distortion (inertia) vs. number of clusters b) Silhouette Coefficient for Different K – Average silhouette score vs. number of clusters

Table 3. Mean values of key variables by K-means clusters (K = 4)

Cluster	N	Annual Consumption (MWh)	Surface (m^2)	Occupancy (%)	EUI (kWh/m^2)
0	352	64.33	1,283.31	29.09	60.61
1	352	13.99	1327.95	30.23	13.01
2	352	173.60	1345.07	24.85	174.98
3	352	19.31	1299.36	29.32	20.26

* *EUI = annual energy use intensity (kWh/m^2·year). Potential savings computed to reach 120 kWh/m^2; negatives clipped to 0.*

performance (EUI ≈ 61 kWh/m^2; 13.2% above threshold), suitable for low-cost measures. Cluster 3 represents low-to-moderate consumers (EUI ≈ 20 kWh/m^2; 1.4% above threshold), requiring only selective actions.

A two-dimensional PCA projection was used to visualize the distribution of clusters [Fig. 4], showing adequate separability between groups.

Furthermore, the spatial distribution of these clusters across Mérida is presented in Fig. 5, illustrating how energy typologies are not randomly distributed but tend to concentrate by zone or building function.

This segmentation provides a structured basis for prioritizing buildings for retrofitting, targeted audits, or efficiency programs based on their typology rather than individual assessment.

4.3 DBSCAN Analysis

While K-means clustering provided a general segmentation of the buildings into four homogeneous groups, this method tends to force all observations into clusters, even when some records do not conform to any dominant pattern. To overcome this limitation and improve the robustness of the analysis, the DBSCAN (Density-Based Spatial Clustering of Applications with Noise) algorithm was applied to the normalized dataset.

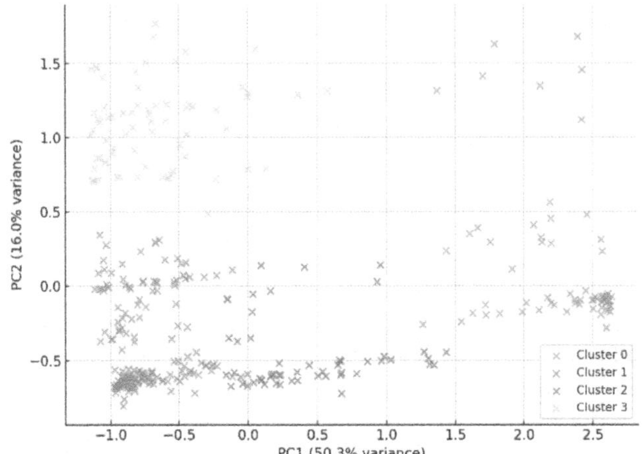

Fig. 4. PCA Projection Colored by K-means Clusters

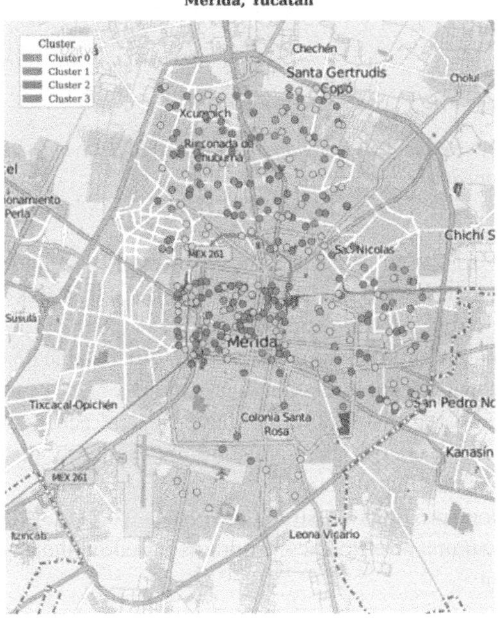

Fig. 5. Geographic distribution of K-means clusters in Mérida

DBSCAN does not require predefining the number of clusters; instead, it relies on two parameters: ε (neighborhood radius) and min_samples (minimum number of points to form a dense region). The optimal ε value was selected using the k-dist plot, which showed a clear inflection at $\varepsilon \approx 0.28$ with min_samples = 5. These parameters resulted in the identification of three dense clusters and a large group of outliers.

The results show that approximately 233 buildings (over 60% of the dataset) were labeled as outliers, reflecting highly dispersed or irregular energy consumption patterns. These atypical cases represent potential priorities for further investigation, as they may correspond to inefficient equipment, irregular operational schedules, or errors in the reporting of contracted loads. In contrast, the dense clusters identified by DBSCAN were more compact and homogeneous than those produced by K-means, reinforcing its usefulness for detecting buildings with highly similar consumption profiles.

Figure 6 shows the two-dimensional PCA projection of the DBSCAN results, where outliers are represented in gray.

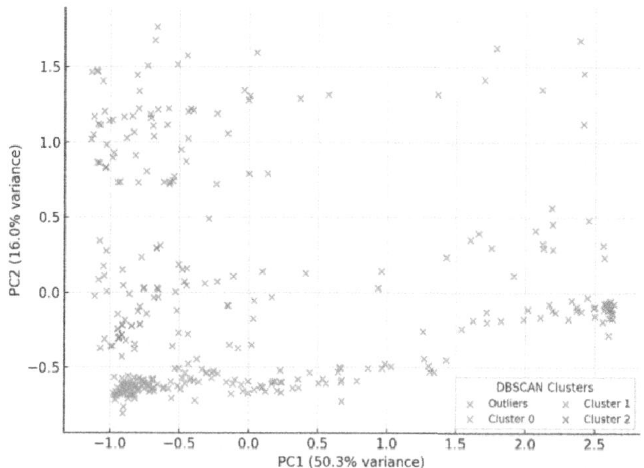

Fig. 6. PCA Projection with DBSCAN Clusters (outliers in gray)

Figure 7 maps the geographic distribution of these outliers across Mérida, illustrating that atypical consumption behaviors are not randomly distributed but tend to cluster in certain areas, possibly linked to specific institutional functions or urban conditions.

In summary, DBSCAN complements K-means by revealing non-linear structures and anomalous buildings, which are critical for designing differentiated efficiency strategies. While K-means supports general typology building, DBSCAN allows decision-makers to detect and prioritize outliers that may yield the highest efficiency gains if properly addressed.

To quantitatively validate the proposed hybrid approach, a comparative analysis was conducted between the individual and combined clustering methods using standard internal validation metrics. Table 4 summarizes the results in terms of the Silhouette coefficient, the Davies–Bouldin index, and the proportion of outliers detected. The hybrid configuration outperformed both standalone algorithms, achieving the highest Silhouette score (0.72) and the lowest Davies–Bouldin index (0.46). This confirms greater intra-cluster cohesion and inter-cluster separation. In addition, its ability to identify over 60% of atypical records demonstrates enhanced robustness and diagnostic value for public-building segmentation.

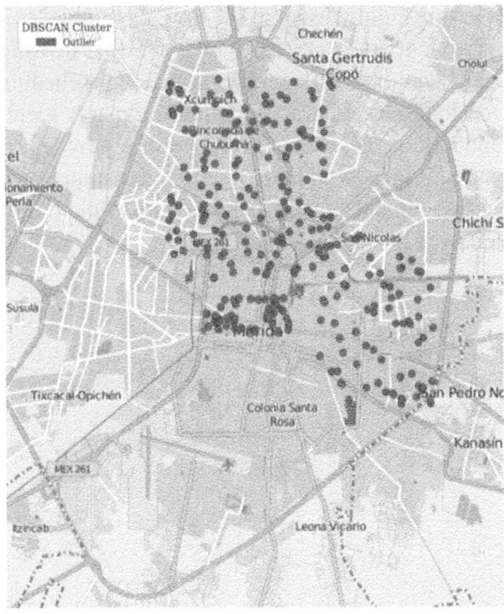

Fig. 7. Geographic distribution of DBSCAN clusters in Mérida

Table 4. Mean values of key variables by K-means clusters (K = 4)

Method	Silhouette Score	David-Bouldin Index	% of Outliers Detected	Cluster Interpretability	Remarks
K-Means	0.64	0.58	0%	High	Captures overall typologies but misses anomalies.
DBSCAN	0.69	0.51	60%	Medium	Detects irregularities but less stable clusters.
K-Means + DBSCAN	0.72	0.46	61%	High	Combines global patterns and anomaly detection for robust segmentation

These results quantitatively demonstrate that integrating K-means with DBSCAN yields a more accurate and interpretable segmentation framework, strengthening the subsequent assessment of energy-saving potential and supporting practical decision-making for public-building efficiency programs.

4.4 Energy Saving Potential Analysis

Beyond the segmentation of public buildings into clusters, an essential contribution of this study is the estimation of potential energy savings. For this purpose, the specific consumption indicator (kWh/m^2 per year) was calculated for each building by dividing the annual electricity consumption by the constructed surface area. This metric enables direct comparison of efficiency levels across buildings of different sizes and functions.

A threshold of 120 $kWh/m^2 \cdot year$ was adopted to identify buildings with improvement potential, following values commonly reported in benchmarking studies of institutional and educational facilities. Buildings exceeding this benchmark were classified as candidates for efficiency interventions, and their potential savings were estimated as the difference between their current consumption and the threshold value, multiplied by their surface area.

The results reveal that a significant proportion of buildings, particularly those belonging to Cluster 2, exhibit consumption intensities above the threshold. On average, Cluster 2 recorded specific consumption levels close to 160 $kWh/m^2 \cdot year$, translating into a potential reduction of more than 20% of its current annual demand. Conversely, Clusters 1 and 3 generally remained below the benchmark, suggesting that these groups already operate with relatively efficient patterns. Cluster 0 presented mixed results, with some large administrative buildings showing high absolute consumption and moderate efficiency potential.

This analysis demonstrates that combining clustering with efficiency benchmarks not only identifies groups of buildings with similar energy behaviors but also quantifies the potential impact of targeted retrofits. The approach thus provides a decision-support tool for public policy, enabling the prioritization of interventions where the largest savings can be achieved.

4.5 Policy Implications

The results obtained from the hybrid clustering framework have direct implications for the design and implementation of energy efficiency policies in public buildings. First, the segmentation achieved with K-means enables the classification of buildings into typologies with distinct energy and operational profiles, which facilitates the design of targeted interventions instead of generic, one-size-fits-all programs. For instance, Cluster 1 was identified as having the largest savings potential, suggesting that policy instruments should prioritize this group for retrofitting, equipment replacement, or advanced monitoring.

Second, the application of DBSCAN revealed that more than half of the analyzed buildings displayed atypical or anomalous behaviors. This finding indicates that conventional benchmarking may not fully capture the diversity of energy usage patterns in the public sector. These outliers may correspond to buildings with irregular schedules, underutilized spaces, or inefficient equipment operation. Identifying and isolating such cases is critical for the effective allocation of resources, as interventions in these buildings may yield disproportionate benefits if inefficiencies are corrected.

Third, the integration of geographic mapping demonstrated that clusters and anomalies are not randomly distributed, but rather tend to concentrate in specific zones of Mérida. This spatial dimension of energy consumption underscores the importance of combining data mining techniques with territorial planning. Energy efficiency policies should therefore be coordinated with urban development strategies, particularly in areas with higher densities of high-intensity buildings.

Finally, the estimation of specific consumption (kWh/m^2) and associated savings potential provides a quantifiable metric that can guide investment decisions. By linking cluster analysis with performance thresholds, decision-makers can rank buildings according to their expected return on efficiency measures. This approach transforms clustering results from a descriptive tool into a practical instrument for strategic energy planning, with potential to be scaled up to regional or national levels. Overall, the hybrid methodology proposed in this study not only contributes to the academic understanding of energy consumption patterns in public buildings but also offers a practical decision-support framework for governments seeking to reduce operating costs and carbon emissions through evidence-based energy policies.

5 Conclusions

This study proposed and applied a hybrid clustering methodology to classify public buildings in Yucatán according to their energy performance. By combining K-means and DBSCAN, the approach captured both general consumption typologies and atypical behaviors that conventional clustering would overlook. The methodology was complemented by dimensionality reduction (PCA) and geographic visualization, providing a comprehensive framework for analyzing energy use in the public sector.

The results demonstrate that K-means with four clusters offered meaningful segmentation, distinguishing buildings by their size, occupancy, and energy intensity. Cluster 1 emerged as the group with the highest savings potential, highlighting the importance of targeting specific typologies for efficiency programs. Meanwhile, DBSCAN revealed that over half of the dataset could be considered outliers, indicating irregularities or unique operating conditions that merit individual audits.

The estimation of specific consumption (kWh/m^2) and savings potential reinforced the practical value of the analysis, enabling the quantification of efficiency opportunities at both the cluster and building level. These findings suggest that integrating machine learning techniques with energy benchmarking can transform raw consumption data into actionable insights for policy design.

Beyond the academic contribution, the hybrid framework provides a decision-support tool for governments, helping prioritize interventions where the largest savings can be achieved and aligning energy efficiency strategies with territorial planning.

Future research should focus on expanding the dataset to include additional years and variables (e.g., real-time monitoring, occupancy schedules, and building envelope characteristics). Furthermore, testing alternative clustering algorithms and hybrid approaches may enhance accuracy and robustness. Ultimately, the methodology presented here represents a scalable and adaptable tool for advancing energy efficiency in public infrastructure and contributing to broader sustainability and carbon reduction goals.

Acknowledgments. G. Espadas acknowledges support from SECIHTI (Scholarship No. 1228956). All authors acknowledge the Facultad de Ingeniería of the Universidad Autónoma de Yucatán (UADY) for easing this work.

References

1. Memon, S.A.: Phase change materials integrated in building walls: a state of the art review. Renew. Sust. Energ. Rev. **31**, 870–906 (2014). https://doi.org/10.1016/j.rser.2013.12.042
2. Gupta, J., Chakraborty, M.: Energy efficiency in buildings. In: Elsevier eBooks (2020). https://doi.org/10.1016/b978-0-12-822989-7.00016-0
3. International Energy Agency (IEA): Buildings Sector. Energy System Overview (2024)
4. Ministry of Economy of the Government of Mexico: Yucatán (2024). Retrieved from https://www.economia.gob.mx/datamexico/es/profile/geo/yucatan-yu?redirect=true
5. Estrada Gasca, C.A.: Energy transition, renewable energies and solar power energy. Rev. Mex. Fís. S. **59**(2), 75–84 (2013) Retrieved from https://rmf.smf.mx/ojs/index.php/rmf-s/article/view/1306
6. Sener: Prodesen 2024–2038 (2024)
7. Hong, T., Yan, D., D'Oca, S., Chen, C., fei.: Ten questions concerning occupant behavior in buildings: the big picture. Build. Environ. **114**, 518–530 (2017). https://doi.org/10.1016/j.buildenv.2016.12.006
8. Yan, D., et al.: IEA EBC annex 66: definition and simulation of occupant behavior in buildings. Energ. Buildings. **156**, 258–270 (2017). https://doi.org/10.1016/j.enbuild.2017.09.084
9. Al-Ghaili, A.M., Kasim, H., Al-Hada, N.M., Jorgensen, B.N., Othman, M., Wang, J.: Energy management systems and strategies in buildings sector: a scoping review. IEEE Access. **9**, 63790–63813 (2021). https://doi.org/10.1109/access.2021.3075485
10. Wijayasekara, D., Linda, O., Manic, M., Rieger, C.: Mining building energy management system data using fuzzy anomaly detection and linguistic descriptions. IEEE Trans. Industr. Inform. **10**(3), 1829–1840 (2014). https://doi.org/10.1109/tii.2014.2328291
11. United Nations: Transforming our world: The 2030 agenda for sustainable development. (2015). Retrieved from https://sdgs.un.org/2030agenda
12. GlobalABC International Energy Agency, & United Nations Environment Programme: GlobalABC Roadmap for Buildings and Construction: Towards a Zero-Emission, Efficient and Resilient Buildings and Construction Sector. (2020). Retrieved from https://www.iea.org/reports/globalabc-roadmap-for-buildings-and-construction-2020-2050
13. Neri, E., Coppola, F., Miele, V., Bibbolino, C., Grassi, R.: Artificial intelligence: who is responsible for the diagnosis? Radiol. Med. **125**(6), 517–521 (2020). https://doi.org/10.1007/s11547-020-01135-9
14. Mehmood, M.U., Chun, D., Zeeshan, N., Han, H., Jeon, G., Chen, K.: A review of the applications of artificial intelligence and big data to buildings for energy-efficiency and a comfortable indoor living environment. Energ. Buildings. **202**, 109383 (2019). https://doi.org/10.1016/j.enbuild.2019.109383
15. Sharma, M., Kaur, P.: A comprehensive analysis of nature-inspired meta-heuristic techniques for feature selection problem. Arch. Comput. Methods Eng. **28**(3), 1103–1127 (2021). https://doi.org/10.1007/s11831-020-09412-6

16. Rojek, I., Mikołajewski, D., Mroziński, A., Macko, M., Bednarek, T., Tyburek, K.: Internet of things applications for energy Management in Buildings Using Artificial Intelligence—a Case Study. Energies. **18**(7), 1706 (2025). https://doi.org/10.3390/en18071706
17. Xu, Y., et al.: Artificial intelligence: a powerful paradigm for scientific research. Int. J. Hydrog Energ. **2**(4), 100179 (2021). https://doi.org/10.1016/j.xinn.2021.100179
18. Saputra, N.A., Riza, L.S., Setiawan, A., Hamidah, I.: A systematic review for classification and selection of deep learning methods. Decis. Analytics J. **12**, 100489 (2024). https://doi.org/10.1016/j.dajour.2024.100489
19. Chen, C., Liu, Y., Kumar, M., Qin, J., Ren, Y.: Energy consumption modelling using deep learning embedded semi-supervised learning. Comput. Ind. Eng. **135**, 757–765 (2019). https://doi.org/10.1016/j.cie.2019.06.052
20. Chen, S.: Review on supervised and unsupervised learning techniques for electrical power systems: algorithms and applications. IEEJ Trans. Electr. Electron. Eng. **16**(11), 1487–1499 (2021). https://doi.org/10.1002/tee.23452
21. Salehi, N., Martínez-García, H., Velasco-Quesada, G.: Networked microgrid energy management based on supervised and unsupervised learning clustering. Energies. **15**(13), 4915 (2022). https://doi.org/10.3390/en15134915
22. Huang, T.M.: Semi-supervised learning and applications. In: Kernel Based Algorithms for Mining Huge Data Sets: Supervised, Semi-Supervised, and Unsupervised Learning, pp. 125–173. Springer Berlin Heidelberg, Berlin, Heidelberg (2006). https://doi.org/10.1007/3-540-31689-2_5
23. Mienye, I.D., Swart, T.G.: A comprehensive review of deep learning: architectures. Recent Adv. Appl. **15**(12), 755 (n.d.). https://doi.org/10.3390/info15120755
24. Westermann, P., Deb, C., Schlueter, A., Evins, R.: Unsupervised learning of energy signatures to identify the heating system and building type using smart meter data. Appl. Energy. **264**, 114715 (2020). https://doi.org/10.1016/j.apenergy.2020.114715
25. Zhang, R., Mirzaei, P.A.: Virtual dynamic coupling of computational fluid dynamics-building energy simulation-artificial intelligence: case study of urban neighbourhood effect on buildings' energy demand. Build. Environ. **195**, 107728 (2021). https://doi.org/10.1016/j.buildenv.2021.107728
26. Deena, G., Gulati, K., Jha, R., Bajjuri, U.R., Sahithullah, M., Singh, M.: Artificial intelligence and a digital twin are effecting building energy management. In: 2022 International Conference on Innovative Computing, Intelligent Communication and Smart Electrical Systems (ICSES), pp. 1–8 (2022). https://doi.org/10.1109/icses55317.2022.9914233
27. Lee, D., Huang, H., Lee, W., Liu, Y.: Artificial intelligence implementation framework development for building energy saving. Int. J. Energy Res. **44**(14), 11908–11929 (2020). https://doi.org/10.1002/er.5839
28. Shapi, M.K.M., Ramli, N.A., Awalin, L.J.: Energy consumption prediction by using machine learning for smart building: case study in Malaysia. Dev. Built Environ. **5**, 100037 (2020). https://doi.org/10.1016/j.dibe.2020.100037
29. Talei, H., Benhaddou, D., Gamarra, C., Benbrahim, H., Essaaidi, M.: Smart building energy inefficiencies detection through time series analysis and unsupervised machine learning. Energies. **14**(19), 6042 (2021). https://doi.org/10.3390/en14196042
30. Liu, B., Liu, S., Guo, S., Zhang, S.: Economic study of a large-scale renewable hydrogen application utilizing surplus renewable energy and natural gas pipeline transportation in China. Int. J. Hydrog. Energy. **45**(3), 1385–1398 (2020). https://doi.org/10.1016/j.ijhydene.2019.11.056
31. International Energy Agency: Report: Energy Efficiency 2024. (2024). Retrieved from www.iea.org

32. Ciancio, V., Salata, F., Falasca, S., Curci, G., Golasi, I., de Wilde, P.: Energy demands of buildings in the framework of climate change: an investigation across Europe. Sustain. Cities Soc. **60** (2020). https://doi.org/10.1016/j.scs.2020.102213
33. USAID: Scaling up Energy Efficiency in Developing Countries, Washington, D.C. (2020)
34. Vinutha, H.P., Poornima, B., Sagar, B.M.: Detection of outliers using interquartile range technique from intrusion dataset. In: Information and Decision Sciences: Proceedings of the 6th International Conference on Ficta, pp. 511–518 (2018)
35. Ahmed, M., Seraj, R., Islam, S.M.S.: The k-means algorithm: a comprehensive survey and performance evaluation. Electronics. **9**(8), 1295 (2020)
36. Hamerly, G., Elkan, C.: Learning the k in k-means. Adv. Neural Inf. Proces. Syst. **16** (2003)
37. Dinh, D.-T., Fujinami, T., Huynh, V.-N.: Estimating the optimal number of clusters in categorical data clustering by silhouette coefficient. In: International Symposium on Knowledge and Systems Sciences, pp. 1–17 (2019)
38. Syakur, M.A., Khotimah, B.K., Rochman, E.M.S., Satoto, B.D.: Integration k-means clustering method and elbow method for identification of the best customer profile cluster. In: IOP Conference Series: Materials Science and Engineering, vol. 336, p. 12017 (2018)
39. Gholizadeh, N., Saadatfar, H., Hanafi, N.: K-DBSCAN: an improved DBSCAN algorithm for big data. J. Supercomput. **77**(6), 6214–6235 (2021)
40. Deng, D.: DBSCAN clustering algorithm based on density. In: 2020 7th International Forum on Electrical Engineering and Automation (IFEEA), pp. 949–953 (2020)
41. Yao, G., Guo, C., Ge, Q., Ait-Ahmed, M.: A practical building energy consumption anomaly detection method based on parameter adaptive setting DBSCAN. Cogn. Comput. Syst. **3**(2), 154–168 (2021)

Unsupervised Clustering for the Multidimensional Analysis of Rural Energy Poverty in Yucatan, Mexico

Ana D. Rodríguez-Novelo(✉), Gilberto A. Espadas-Baños, and Manuel I. Flota-Bañuelos

Facultad de Ingeniería, Universidad Autónoma de Yucatán, Av. Industrias No Contaminan-tes Por Periférico Norte, Apdo. Postal 150 Cordemex, C.P. 97310, Mérida, Yucatán, Mexico
a16004320@alumnos.uady.mx

Abstract. This paper presents the initial phase of a thesis project on energy poverty in rural communities near Mérida, Yucatán. The analysis was based on data from 260 households located in Priority Attention Zones identified in the 2024 Poverty and Social Backwardness Report. These communities are characterized by low-income levels and self-built homes that often lack basic infrastructure and thermal comfort. The survey design combined three established measurement approaches—consensual, expenditure-based, and direct methods—adapted to the rural context of southeastern Mexico. Preliminary findings show that although 96.5% of households are connected to the electrical grid, only 36.7% use LED lighting and 32.8% still rely on firewood for cooking, reflecting persistent and multidimensional energy vulnerability. To analyze these patterns, a data normalization scheme was implemented, followed by PCA and K-Means clustering. This approach identified three typologies of energy poverty: structural exclusion, partial transition, and combined thermal-economic stress. These groupings integrate socio-technical variables such as building materials, appliance ownership, ventilation, energy-use behavior, and perceived cost and comfort. Cluster analysis shows that structurally excluded households (Cluster 1) depend on traditional fuels (0.235); transition households (Cluster 0) use modern cooking (0.776) and show intermediate discomfort (0.628). In contrast, the thermally and economically stressed group (Cluster 2) exhibits higher technological adoption—71% LED lighting and 54% modern cooking—but also displays the greatest thermal discomfort (0.523) and perceived cost burden (0.670). The results provide a multidimensional, data-driven perspective on rural energy deprivation, offering insights for targeted policy and intervention strategies in vulnerable regions.

Keywords: Rural Energy Poverty · K-Means Clustering · Dimensionality Reduction · Un-supervised Clustering · Multidimensional Data Analysis

1 Introduction

Energy poverty represents a significant challenge to sustainable development, particularly in rural areas where access to modern and efficient energy services is limited. In these contexts, families often rely on traditional fuels such as firewood, which negatively

L. Martínez-Villaseñor et al. (Eds.): MICAI 2025 Workshops, LNAI 16264, pp. 22–34, 2026.
https://doi.org/10.1007/978-3-032-17930-2_2

impacts health, thermal comfort, and social equity [1]. The World Health Organization warns that exposure to household smoke increases the incidence of respiratory diseases, especially among women and children [2], while also contributing to deforestation and environmental degradation.

In Mexico, energy poverty takes multiple forms, ranging from the lack of electricity access to the inability to use energy safely and efficiently. In Yucatán, these conditions are particularly severe in Priority Attention Zones (ZAP), where self-built homes with poor thermal insulation are predominate [3]. Given this complexity, analysis requires comprehensive approaches that incorporate socioeconomic, construction-related, and perceptual dimensions [4].

This article forms part of a broader research project aimed at evaluating energy poverty and efficiency in rural communities near Mérida. In this phase, an exploratory analysis was conducted on 260 households located in three ZAP-classified communities. The surveys were designed based on three methodological approaches: consensual, expenditure-based, and direct measurement [5].

To identify patterns of energy vulnerability, techniques such as data normalization, Principal Component Analysis (PCA), and K-Means unsupervised clustering were applied. These methods are well established and have been validated in similar studies [6]. This analysis lays the groundwork for selecting representative households and informing future public interventions to promote energy efficiency.

2 Literature Review

Energy poverty is a multidimensional phenomenon that prevents households from accessing or adequately using modern energy services. This condition has significant impacts on health, thermal comfort, gender equity, and the environment [2]. The use of traditional fuels such as firewood or charcoal increases respiratory diseases, particularly among women and children [7].

In the context of rural Mexico, and particularly in Yucatán, access to electricity or household appliances does not always guarantee dignified energy conditions. Energy poverty perpetuates inequality by limiting access to education, employment, and technological opportunities [8]. Despite progress in electricity coverage, many rural families face difficulties affording electricity or improving installations [3], especially in Priority Attention Zones [9].

To better understand this issue, different methods have been developed to measure energy poverty. Three main approaches have been identified: the consensual method, the expenditure-to-income ratio, and direct measurement [5]. These were adapted in the design of the surveys used in this study.

Given the complexity of the data and the phenomenon itself, statistical tools have become essential. PCA and the K-Means algorithm are among the unsupervised learning techniques applied to uncover hidden structures in multidimensional datasets [6]. In the Mexican context, approaches based on energy justice [4] and decentralized regional indicators [10] have also been used to capture local heterogeneity.

In our case, data from 260 rural households were normalized and analyzed using PCA to retain the maximum explanatory variance in a reduced space. Then, K-Means was applied to classify households into distinct energy vulnerability groups. This combined approach has been validated in diverse domains [11, 12], providing meaningful typologies that integrate structural, technological, and perceptual aspects of energy use.

3 Methodology

Figure 1 illustrates the methodological flow to be followed in this research, from data collection and processing to analysis through dimensionality reduction and unsupervised clustering techniques. This diagram summarizes the key steps that will be employed to identify typologies of energy poverty in rural communities of Yucatán.

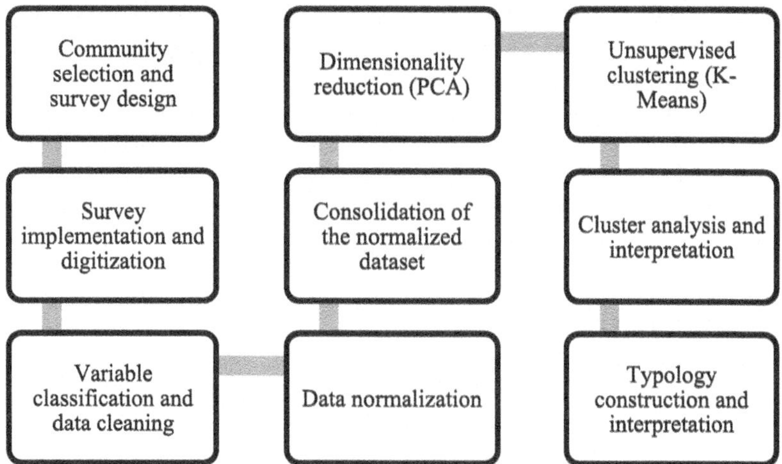

Fig. 1. Methodological framework of the methodological process used for the analysis of rural energy poverty in localities of Yucatán.

3.1 Data Collection

Data collection will be carried out in five rural communities in the state of Yucatán: Uayalceh (municipality of Abalá), Tekik de Regil (municipality of Timucuy), and the localities of Acanceh, Ticopó, and Tepich Carrillo (municipality of Acanceh). These communities will be selected based on their classification as ZAP according to the 2024 Social Poverty and Backwardness Report of the state of Yucatán. The selection criteria will include high levels of marginalization and a predominance of self-built homes, without the involvement of social housing developers.

A structured survey will be applied to a total of 260 households across the five localities mentioned. The survey design will be based on three complementary methodological approaches to measure energy poverty: the consensual approach, the expenditure-to-income approach, and the direct measurement approach, as described in previous studies on energy poverty.

The surveys will be conducted in person, and basic personal data (such as name and contact information) will be collected only with the informed consent of participants, for the purpose of follow-up in future stages of the research. The questions will be clearly formulated and adapted to the understanding of the local population, allowing the collection of information on energy access and use, household appliances, construction conditions, perceived thermal comfort, electricity expenditure, and approximate household income.

All monetary variables (ingreso_mensual and gasto_luz_bimestral) will be expressed in Mexican pesos (MXN) at current prices for the survey period (March–May 2025). No inflation adjustment will be applied.

3.2 Selected Variables

Table 1 summarizes the variables that will be selected for the analysis, organized by category and the respective database field names:

These variables will be chosen to capture different levels of energy vulnerability, taking into account both structural aspects and individual household perceptions.

3.3 Data Cleaning and Preparation

Prior to the quantitative analysis, a data cleaning and standardization process will be conducted. Responses given in ranges will be converted into representative average values. For example, the monthly income "Between MXN $1,500 and $2,000" will be coded as 1750. Responses such as "Don't know / Prefer not to answer" will be retained as missing values (NaN) to avoid introducing bias through unsupported imputation.

For columns with multiple responses—such as lighting types, roofing materials, or household appliances—a semicolon (;) will be used as the standard separator. These responses will later be processed through binary encoding (one-hot encoding) in computational analysis. Additionally, unnecessary spaces before or after the separators will be removed to ensure consistency.

During the validation process, a control question will be included regarding the type of lighting used. Although some answers may show semantic variations (e.g., "energy-saving bulb" vs. "low-consumption LED"), no serious contradictions are expected. Consequently, only the first version of the response will be retained as the reference for the main analysis.

3.4 Analysis Techniques

To prepare the dataset for computational analyses such as unsupervised clustering and dimensionality reduction, a normalization and weighting scheme will be designed based on recent energy policy criteria in Mexico. All relevant categorical and numerical variables will be transformed into normalized values within the [0,1] range, where 1 represents the highest level of energy vulnerability.

This process will be carried out in blocks, as follows:

Table 1. Selection of Variables for the Analysis

Category	Variable Description	Database Column Name(s)
Household Sociotechnical	Type of housing	tipo_vivienda
	Wall material	material_muros
	Roof material	material_techo
	Floor material	material_piso
	Type of windows	materiales_ventanas
	Natural ventilation	ventilacion_natural
	Equipment: appliances, fans, A/C, lighting	electrodomesticos, num_ventiladores, tiene_aa, iluminacion_principal
	Use of backup or alternative energy	respaldo_energia
Energy-Related	Type of cooking	tipo_cocina
	Type of lighting	iluminacion_principal
	Exterior lighting	iluminacion_exterior
	Daily lighting hours	horas_uso_iluminacion_diaria
	Daily A/C usage hours	uso_aa_diario_horas
	Bimonthly electricity payment (MXN)	gasto_luz_bimestral
Socioeconomic	Monthly household income (MXN)	ingreso_mensual
	Number of inhabitants	num_habitantes
	Length of residence	tiempo_residencia_anios
Perception and Comfort	Electricity cost as a problem	percepcion_costo_electricidad
	Actions to reduce consumption	accion_reduccion_consumo
	Thermal comfort in hot and cold conditions	sensacion_calor, confort_noches_frias
	Most uncomfortable season	epoca_incomoda_temperatura
	Health problems due to heat/cold	salud_afectada_por_clima
	Quality of life affected by electricity cost	calidad_vida_afectada_por_costo

aAll monetary variables will be reported in MXN (Mexican pesos).

Block 1: Structural Variables (Housing Materials).

Qualitative weightings will be assigned to the materials used for roofs, walls, floors, and windows, based on their thermal insulation capacity, durability, and degree of precariousness. In cases with multiple responses—for example, roofs composed of more than one material—the value corresponding to the most vulnerable condition will be selected. The variables analyzed in this block will be include *material_techo*, *material_paredes*, *material_piso*, and *materiales_ventanas*. These specific weightings will be developed in accordance with thermal efficiency and habitability guidelines relevant to low-income rural contexts.

Block 2: Numerical Variables.
Min-Max normalization will be applied using the formula:

$$X_{norm} = \frac{X - X_{min}}{X_{max} - X_{min}} \tag{1}$$

This normalization approach allows for the proportional scaling of several variables: *num_ventiladores*, *uso_aa_diario_horas*, *num_focos*, *horas_uso_iluminacion_diaria*, *gasto_luz_bimestral*, *num_habitantes*, *tiempo_residencia_anios*, and *ingreso_mensual*. This technique preserves the relative distribution of the original values, facilitating their subsequent interpretation in clustering techniques.

Block 3: Yes/No Variables.
These variables will be transformed by assigning a value of 1 to responses associated with high energy vulnerability, and 0 to those indicating lower vulnerability. In certain cases—such as tiene_aa, respaldo_energia, or iluminacion_exterior—affirmative answers will imply lower precariousness, so their values will be intentionally inverted to maintain consistency within the vulnerability scale. The variables included in this block will be *tiene_aa*, *respaldo_energia*, *iluminacion_exterior*, *accion_reduccion_consumo*, *salud_afectada_por_clima*, and *acceso_electricidad*.

Block 4: Ordinal or Perception-Based Variables.
Responses will be converted into continuous values ranging from 0 to 1, based on the perceived level of impact. This block will include variables related to thermal comfort, perception of electricity costs, and energy use decisions: *sensacion_calor*, *sensacion_noches_frias*, *epoca_incomoda_temperatura*, *percepcion_costo_electricidad*, *calidad_vida_afectada_por_costo*, and *abandono_aparato_por_costo*. Responses such as "very hot," "yes, a lot," or "winter" will be assigned values closer to 1, while options like "pleasant" or "no" will receive values nearer to 0.

Block 5: Multiple-Choice Variables.
For questions with multiple selectable options, responses will be split using a semicolon (;) and each selected item will be assigned a corresponding weight. The final value for each observation will be determined by the highest vulnerability index among the chosen responses. This block will include three variables. For *electrodomesticos*, an energy equipment index will be constructed by assigning scores to 17 appliances based on their consumption level and relevance; the resulting value will be scaled by dividing the sum of weights by the maximum possible score (17). For *tipo_cocina*, the highest score among the selected cooking methods will be retained, prioritizing the

detection of biomass-based systems. Finally, for *fuente_agua_caliente*, responses will be normalized by assigning higher values to precarious heating methods, such as using firewood or stovetops to heat water.

3.5 Consolidation of Normalized Data

Once the normalization process is completed, a new dataset will be generated containing only the transformed variables, ready for computational analysis. This DataFrame will be used as input for the unsupervised clustering algorithm (K-Means) and dimensionality reduction.

The resulting file will represent the methodological foundation for identifying structural and behavioral patterns related to energy use, thermal comfort, and economic stress in rural settings. Its structure enables reproducibility and facilitates interpretation for integration into public energy policies.

3.6 Dimensionality Reduction

To facilitate the identification of multivariable patterns and avoid redundancies among the 27 sociotechnical variables in the normalized dataset, a PCA will be applied. This technique transforms the original space into a new set of orthogonal components, prioritizing those linear combinations that explain the greatest variance in the data.

The cumulative explained variance of each component will be evaluated, and the first 16 principal components will be retained, which together explain 78.41% of the total variance. Although this value does not reach the commonly recommended 85% threshold, it will be considered suitable for exploratory analysis purposes, allowing the reduction of data complexity while preserving its main structure.

The 16 resulting components will be used as input for the K-Means clustering algorithm. Additionally, only the first two components (PC1 and PC2) will be used to visually project the clusters in a two-dimensional space. This visualization does not affect the clustering process but will enhance the graphical interpretation of the structural patterns found.

3.7 Unsupervised Clustering

With the dimensional space reduced to 16 principal components, the K-Means clustering algorithm will be implemented to identify hidden patterns of energy-related behavior among the surveyed rural households. This algorithm assigns each observation to a group based on its proximity within the multidimensional space defined by the principal components.

To determine the optimal number of clusters, the Elbow Method will be applied. This involves graphing intra-cluster inertia against the number of clusters (k). In the analysis conducted, the curve is anticipated to show a significant drop between $k = 1$ and $k = 3$, followed by a much more gradual decline. Although a clear inflection point may not be observed, the change in slope is expected to suggest that three clusters will provide a reasonable balance between model simplicity and information retention.

The selection of three clusters will be validated through three criteria: the behavior of the inertia curve, the visualization of groups projected in 2D space (PC1 vs. PC2), and the sociotechnical coherence observed in the qualitative characterization of each group.

Each household will be assigned to one of the three clusters, and their common characteristics will be analyzed to build typologies such as: households experiencing structural exclusion, homes undergoing partial energy transition, and well-equipped homes facing high thermal and economic stress.

3.8 Visualization and Interpretation

To support and enhance interpretation, a 2D visualization of the clusters will be generated using the principal components PC1 and PC2. This graphical projection will allow for the observation of the relative distribution of households and the separation between groups.

Additionally, summary tables will be developed to describe the average profile of each cluster, considering key variables such as access to electricity, type of cooking method, number of appliances, perception of thermal comfort, and impacts due to energy costs. These profiles will enable a deeper understanding of the sociotechnical conditions associated with each group and will contribute to the construction of meaningful typologies for the study of rural energy poverty.

4 Results

4.1 Interpretation of Energy Poverty Typologies

Based on the cluster average analysis, three typologies of rural households were identified according to their sociotechnical conditions, access to services, and perceived thermal comfort. These typologies reflect different manifestations of energy poverty and allow for a more precise description of the diversity of experiences among the surveyed households.

Cluster 1 includes homes in a state of structural exclusion. These households show zero access to electricity (0.000), indicating complete disconnection from the grid. The average cooking score (0.235) suggests strong reliance on firewood or other traditional fuels. Although some homes possess appliances (0.140), their use may be limited by the lack of continuous supply. Thermal discomfort is low (0.368), possibly due to stable conditions or absence of heat-emitting devices. This group represents high vulnerability due to basic infrastructure deficits.

Cluster 0 represents homes with more stable and partially efficient conditions. Electricity access is limited but present (0.016), and cooking type (0.776) indicates predominant use of gas or electric stoves. Appliance availability is low (0.097), but present. Thermal discomfort is intermediate (0.628). This group likely represents households undergoing an energy transition, with partial adoption of modern technologies.

Cluster 2 consists of homes with moderate equipment levels but exposed to high thermal and economic stress. They report high values in LED lighting (0.712), appliances (0.127), and cooking type (0.543), indicating broader adoption of modern technologies.

However, they also present the highest discomfort (0.523), health impacts from climate (0.214), perceived cost (0.670), and appliance abandonment due to financial strain (0.750). This group reflects access but limited ability to sustain continuous and efficient energy use.

These typologies show that energy poverty is not limited to lack of access but also involves quality of use, available technology, and subjective experience of comfort or discomfort. The data come from the cluster average table generated by the K-Means model.

To strengthen result interpretation, PCA was conducted. PC1 is heavily influenced by equipment-related variables such as electrodomesticos_norm (0.443), tiene_aa_norm (0.373), num_ventiladores_norm (0.328), and num_focos_led_norm (0.317), suggesting a dimension associated with equipment intensity and domestic technology. PC2 reflects a combination of structural aspects and perceived energy cost, with high loadings for material_muros_norm (0.375), percepcion_costo_electricidad_norm (0.352), calidad_vida_afectada_por_costo_norm (0.315), and aban-dono_aparato_por_costo_norm (0.259), representing a dimension of economic and structural vulnerability.

Additionally, components PC3 through PC6 were explored to broaden the multidimensional understanding. PC3 is linked to basic infrastructure, highlighting acceso_electricidad_norm (0.470), fuente_agua_caliente_norm (0.349), and material_muros_norm (0.348), suggesting a dimension of essential services. PC4 involves adaptation and energy decision-making (accion_reduccion_consumo_norm: 0.360), PC5 emphasizes cost-related comfort, and PC6 reveals domestic and physical vulnerability.

These components reinforce the model's robustness and support retaining 16 principal components. Although PC7 through PC16 were not individually addressed, their marginal contribution justifies focusing on the first six.

Before running the clustering, we evaluated the cumulative variance explained by the principal components. Figure 2 shows this curve. The figure indicates that the first components concentrate most of the information, while after around the tenth component the contribution diminishes. By keeping 16 components, 78.41% of the total variance is preserved. Although this value does not reach the often-cited 85% benchmark, it is sufficient for exploratory purposes, ensuring that the most relevant structures are maintained without overloading the model.

To define the number of clusters, the Elbow Method was applied. Figure 3 presents the results. In the elbow plot there is a steep drop in inertia between $k = 1$ and $k = 3$. After that point, improvements become much slower. Although the curve does not show a perfectly sharp "elbow," this behavior is common in sociotechnical data. For this reason, selecting three clusters is a reasonable choice: it simplifies the model while still preserving most of the useful information.

Finally, Fig. 4 illustrates the distribution of households in a two-dimensional space (PC1 vs. PC2) with clusters assigned by K-Means. The PC1–PC2 projection suggests three regions with some overlap, which is expected in a 2D reduction. PC1 aligns with domestic equipment intensity (appliances, A/C, fans, LED), whereas PC2 combines construction traits and economic pressure (wall materials, cost perception, equipment abandonment). Separation is not perfect, yet sufficient to distinguish (i) structural exclusion, (ii) partial transition, and (iii) thermal-economic stress. Note that cluster assignment was performed in the 16-PC space; this plot is for visual interpretation only (Table 2).

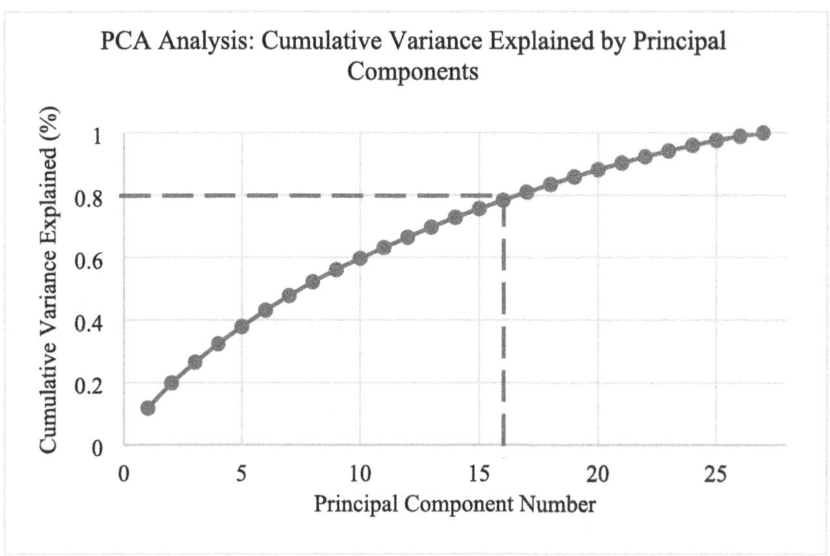

Fig. 2. Cumulative variance explained by the principal components.

Table 2. Typologies of Rural Households Based on a Multidimensional Analysis of Energy Poverty

Cluster	Typology	Key Characteristics
0	Partial Energy Transition	Limited electricity access, modern cooking, moderate discomfort, moderate appliance availability
1	Structural Exclusion	No electricity access, dependence on firewood, low perception of discomfort, possible use of backup systems
2	Combined Energy and Thermal Stress	Well-equipped, but high thermal discomfort, high perceived electricity cost, equipment abandonment due to cost

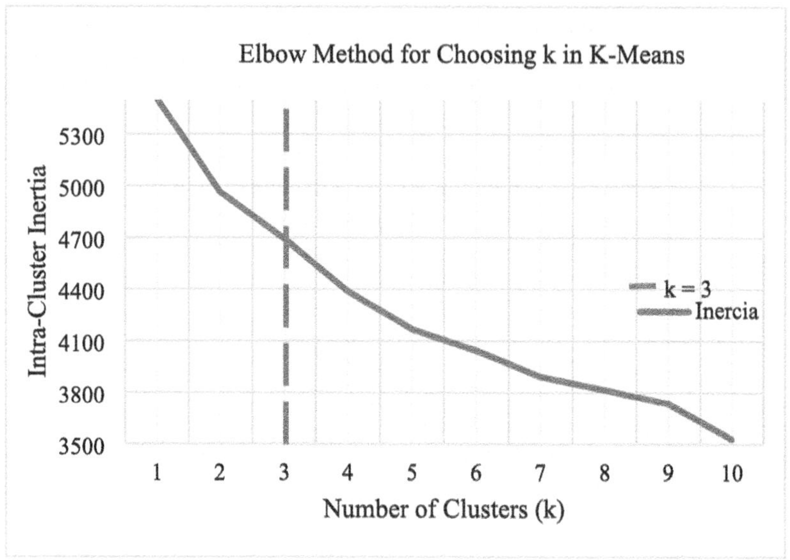

Fig. 3. Decrease in inertia as the number of clusters increases using the K-Means algorithm applied to the principal components.

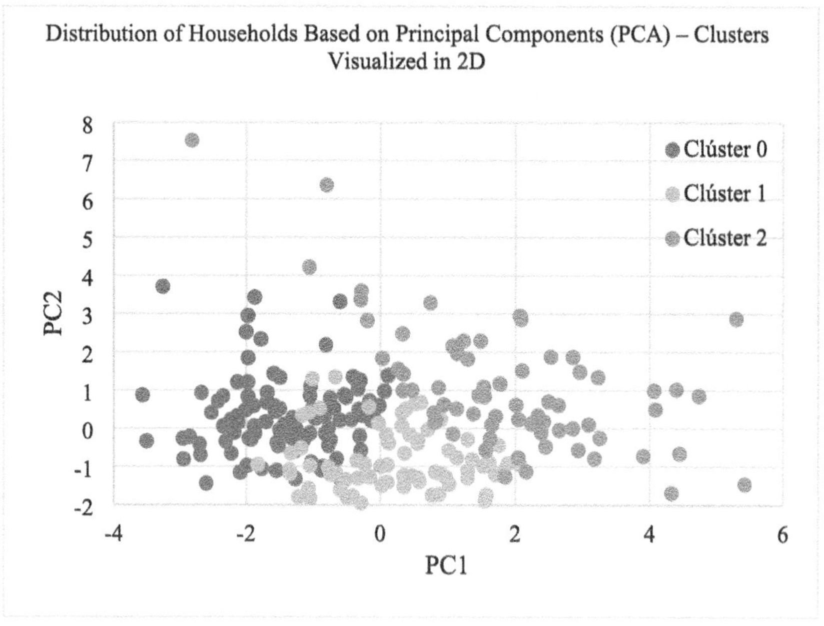

Fig. 4. Two-dimensional projection of rural households using Principal Component Analysis.

5 Conclusions

Although 96.5% of surveyed households had access to the electrical grid, only 36.7% used LED lighting and 32.8% still relied on firewood for cooking. These figures highlighted persistent energy vulnerability, even among grid-connected homes. The clustering analysis revealed three typologies: (1) households with structural exclusion, lacking electricity and relying on biomass; (0) partially transitioned households with limited efficiency; and (2) households with good equipment but affected by thermal discomfort and financial stress, as reflected by high electricity cost perception (0.670) and equipment abandonment (0.750).

The combination of data normalization, PCA, and K-means clustering enabled the identification of latent vulnerability patterns that traditional methods would likely have missed. This multidimensional approach preserved the richness of sociotechnical and perceptual variables and proved replicable in similar contexts.

These typologies provided a basis for guiding targeted public policies and interventions, such as replacing inefficient appliances, improving building envelopes, and promoting passive thermal strategies. They also helped identify communities requiring urgent attention and supported the definition of feasible, context-adapted solutions.

Several studies had addressed energy poverty through approaches mainly focused on income or energy expenditure. Previous research in Mexico highlighted the prevalence of vulnerable households due to limited access or high relative energy spending [3, 4], while other works emphasized the importance of thermal comfort and local conditions [10, 13]. Complementarily, research showed that developing countries face challenges related to basic access rather than affordability [5]. In contrast, this study proposed a multidimensional approach in which socio-technical and perceptual variables enabled a more comprehensive understanding of rural energy poverty and its implications for well-being and equity.

Although artificial intelligence was not the central focus of this research, its integration through unsupervised methods such as PCA and K-Means was essential for identifying hidden patterns within sociotechnical and perceptual data. In this sense, AI functioned as a means of interpretation, allowing a more objective and data-driven classification of rural energy poverty typologies.

However, the study faced limitations, including potential self-perception biases and a geographically restricted scope. Results should be generalized with caution. Still, the proposed methodology offers strong replicability for rural areas facing similar energy challenges.

In conclusion, this approach provides a robust tool for analyzing energy poverty and establishes a foundation for evidence-based interventions that support energy justice and sustainable development in vulnerable communities.

Disclosure of Interests. The authors have no competing interests to declare that are relevant to the content of this article.

References

1. González-Eguino, M.: Energy poverty: an overview. Renew. Sust. Energ. Rev. **47**, 377–385 (2015). https://doi.org/10.1016/j.rser.2015.03.013

2. Calvo, R., Álamos, N., Billi, M., Urquiza, A., Contreras Lisperguer, R.: Desarrollo de indicadores de pobreza energética en América Latina y el Caribe, serie Recursos Naturales y Desarrollo, N° 207 (LC/TS.2021/104), Santiago, Comisión Económica para América Latina y el Caribe (CEPAL), (2021)
3. Rosas-Flores, J.A., Zenón-Olvera, E., Gálvez, D.M.: Potential energy saving in urban and rural households of Mexico with solar photovoltaic systems using geographical information system. Renew. Sust. Energ. Rev. **116**, 109412 (2019). https://doi.org/10.1016/j.rser.2019.109412
4. Soriano-Hernández, P., Mejía-Montero, A., van der Horst, D.: Characterisation of energy poverty in Mexico using energy justice and econophysics. Energy Sustain. Dev. **71**, 200–211 (2022). https://doi.org/10.1016/j.esd.2022.09.005
5. Al Kez, D., Foley, A., Lowans, C., Del Rio, D.F.: Energy poverty assessment: indicators and implications for developing and developed countries. Energy Convers. Manag. **307**, 118324 (2024). https://doi.org/10.1016/j.enconman.2024.118324
6. Saraiva, C., Caiado, J.: Global development patterns: a clustering analysis of economic, social and environmental indicators. Sustain. Futures. **10**, 100907 (2025). https://doi.org/10.1016/j.sftr.2025.100907
7. Kaygusuz, K.: Energy services and energy poverty for sustainable rural development. Renew. Sust. Energ. Rev. **15**, 936–947 (2011). https://doi.org/10.1016/j.rser.2010.11.003
8. Bernáldez, J.P., Ruiz, M.V.L.: Repercusiones de la pobreza sobre la salud de los individuos y las poblaciones. In: FMC – Formación Médica Continuada en Atención Primaria, vol. 23, pp. 50–60 (2016). https://doi.org/10.1016/j.fmc.2015.04.010
9. Secretaría de Bienestar: Informe Anual sobre la Situación de Pobreza y Rezago Social 2024. (2024)
10. Clavijo-Núñez, S., Herrera-Limones, R., Rey-Pérez, J., Torres-García, M.: Energy poverty in Andalusia. An analysis through decentralised indicators. Energy Policy. **167**, 113083 (2022). https://doi.org/10.1016/j.enpol.2022.113083
11. Jansson, N.F., Allen, R.L., Skogsmo, G., Tavakoli, S.: Principal component analysis and K-means clustering as tools during exploration for Zn skarn deposits and industrial carbonates, Sala area. Sweden. J. Geochem. Explor. **233**, 106909 (2022). https://doi.org/10.1016/j.gexplo.2021.106909
12. Clayman, C.L., Srinivasan, S.M., Sangwan, R.S.: K-means clustering and principal components analysis of microarray data of L1000 landmark genes. Procedia Comput. Sci. **168**, 97–104 (2020). https://doi.org/10.1016/j.procs.2020.02.265
13. Bienvenido-Huertas, D., Sanz Fernández, A., Sánchez-Guevara Sánchez, C., Rubio-Bellido, C.: Assessment of energy poverty in Andalusian municipalities. Application of a combined indicator to detect priorities. Energy Rep. **8**, 5100–5116 (2022). https://doi.org/10.1016/j.egyr.2022.03.045

AI in Medicine: Diagnosis and Drug Discovery Along with Ethical Implications. A Systematic Review

Roberto Contreras-Masse[1](✉), Alberto Ochoa-Zezzatti[2], Roberto Adrian Contreras-Moheno[3], Yamil Barrera[1], and Erik Tepach[1]

[1] TecNM Campus ITCJ, Cd Juarez Chih, Mexico
roberto.cm@cdjuarez.tecnm.mx
[2] Universidad Autonoma de Ciudad Juarez, Chih, Mexico
[3] University of Texas, El Paso, Texas, United States

Abstract. The increasing integration of artificial intelligence into medicine, particularly in diagnostics and drug discovery, signals a shift within healthcare's status quo. This literature review offers a critical, dualfocused analysis of this evolving landscape, addressing how deep neural networks (DNNs) and generative AI significantly improve diagnostic accuracy and accelerate drug discovery processes. Concurrently, it examines the main ethical and legal challenges inherent in implementing AI for medical diagnosis and drug discovery, including fundamental issues of data privacy, algorithmic transparency, accountability, and the adequacy of existing regulatory frameworks. By comprehensively analyzing both the potential benefits and the inherent challenges, this review attempts to provide a nuanced understanding of AI's current and future role in medicine, offering insights essential for responsible innovation and successful integration into clinical practice and pharmaceutical research.

Keywords: Artificial intelligence · Drug Discovery · Medical Diagnosis · Systematic review

1 Introduction

The increasing integration of artificial intelligence (AI) into medicine, particularly in diagnostics and drug discovery, represents a breakthrough in healthcare. A literature review on this topic is essential because it synthesizes two distinct but interconnected bodies of research: the demonstrated technical capabilities of AI and the critical ethical and legal challenges its implementation presents.

To fully understand this evolving landscape and guide future advancements, this literature review addresses two pivotal research questions. Firstly, how do deep neural networks (DNNs) improve diagnostic accuracy and accelerate drug discovery? This question seeks to address the technical capabilities and demonstrable successes of AI, exploring how these advanced algorithms enhance precision in diagnostics and significantly expedite the complex, time-consuming processes of drug development, as

L. Martínez-Villaseñor et al. (Eds.): MICAI 2025 Workshops, LNAI 16264, pp. 35–49, 2026.
https://doi.org/10.1007/978-3-032-17930-2_3

evidenced by remarkable accuracy rates and efficiency gains. However, the rapid integration of such powerful technologies necessitates careful consideration of their broader implications. Therefore, the second crucial question guiding this review is: What are the main ethical and legal challenges in implementing AI for medical diagnosis and drug discovery? This inquiry critically examines the fundamental issues of data privacy, algorithmic transparency, accountability, and the adequacy of existing regulatory frameworks. By comprehensively analyzing both the profound benefits and the inherent challenges, this review aims to provide a nuanced understanding of AI's current and future role in medicine, offering insights essential for responsible innovation and successful integration into clinical practice and pharmaceutical research.

This review is organized in sections. The first section provides a quick overview of previous work regarding usage of AI in medicine and ethical challenges. The next section describes the methodology used for the literature review. The following section is dedicated to discussing the findings, main authors, and key concepts found through the literature review. Finally, conclusions are shared and future research is presented. It is important to note that no technical concepts of Deep Learning or Generative AI (GenAI) will be discussed, as those concepts escape from this research scope.

2 Previous Work

Artificial Intelligence (AI) is defined as systems capable of making highly complex cognitive decisions, with autonomous AI systems in healthcare making clinical decisions without human supervision [2]. These rigorously validated systems promise to improve access to care, increase accuracy, and reduce costs, while allowing specialist physicians to focus on patients with improvable outcomes [2]. AI has found widespread application in various medical areas, including diagnosis, genetic expression pattern analysis, treatment, and disease prognosis prediction [3, 40]. In particular, Machine Learning (ML), a subfield of AI, trains algorithms on large datasets to identify patterns, classify information, and find optimal solutions to complex problems [3]. This technological advance has shown exponential growth in medical applications, especially in diagnostics and drug discovery, with substantial savings projected for the healthcare sector [34].

Despite its promise, the implementation of AI in healthcare faces significant ethical and practical challenges, generating public and physician concerns [2]. These concerns revolve around whether patient outcomes are truly improved, the existence of inappropriate biases (racial, ethnic, gender), the proper use of patient data, and the impact on healthcare professionals' employment [2]. Rigorous validation of AI systems, through preregistered studies that assess their safety, efficacy, and equity in real-world workflow settings, is essential to ensure trust and acceptance [2]. Additionally, the lack of interpretability of some AI models, especially neural networks, and the risk of overfitting (when a model adheres too closely to training data, limiting its generalization) are important limitations that must be addressed [34]. AI's focus on detecting subtle anomalies in medical images can also lead to an increase in false positives and overdiagnosis, highlighting the need for AI studies to focus on clinically significant, patient-centered outcomes [30].

The convergence of AI and nanotechnology is fundamental to precision medicine, which seeks to adapt specific treatments to the unique characteristics of each cancer patient [3]. In diagnostics, AI algorithms are crucial for analyzing omics data and interpreting nanosensors, enabling early disease detection, personalized treatment planning, and progression monitoring [3]. Examples include improved detection of diabetic retinopathy [34] and the application of Convolutional Neural Networks (CNN) for medical image analysis, which surpasses human capabilities in visual classification tasks [34]. In drug development, AI accelerates initial screening, predicts success rates, and facilitates the discovery of new molecules, which is vital for addressing antibiotic resistance and epidemics [34]. For treatment, AI enables controlled dosing and the personalization of therapies, such as tailored radiotherapy [3]. AI-assisted endoscopy is transforming the field by improving polyp detection and lesion characterization, while systems like "Watson for Oncology" offer precise guidance for cancer treatment [17, 40].

3 Methodology

To provide a comprehensive and unbiased overview of the multifaceted landscape of AI in medicine, a rigorous systematic literature review was essential. For this purpose, the Okoli methodology [29] was selected as the guiding framework. This approach was particularly well-suited to the task due to its emphasis on explicit, reproducible, and systematic processes, which are crucial for synthesizing diverse research areas. As the literature on AI in medicine spans both technical performance metrics and complex ethical and legal considerations, the Okoli methodology's adaptability allows for the integration of findings from both quantitative and qualitative studies. The review was structured around its four core phases: the initial planning of the research questions and protocol, a systematic process for literature selection, the standardized extraction of relevant data from selected studies, and the final synthesis of the findings. This methodological rigor ensures that the conclusions drawn are comprehensive, reliable, and provide a solid foundation for understanding the full scope of AI's promise and challenges in healthcare.

3.1 Research Questions

There are two main questions that drive this review. The first question (RQ1) how do deep neural networks (DNNs) and GenAI improve diagnostic accuracy and accelerate drug discovery? The second question (RQ2) What are the main ethical and legal challenges in implementing AI for medical diagnosis and drug discovery?

3.2 Screening Criteria RQ1

To ensure the rigor and relevance of the literature review, a systematic screening process was applied based on a predefined set of inclusion and exclusion criteria. Initially, studies were selected if they focused on deep neural networks (DNNs) or generative AI applications specifically within the domains of healthcare diagnostics or drug discovery. To guarantee a high level of empirical validation, the review was limited to primary research papers, systematic reviews, and meta-analyses. Furthermore, studies were required to report quantitative performance metrics, such as accuracy, sensitivity, and specificity, and to include a clear comparison of AI methodologies against traditional approaches. Substantial validation using experimental or real-world data and the inclusion of a clear performance baseline were also prerequisites for a study's inclusion. Finally, the screening process ensured that the chosen literature consisted of empirical research papers with practical healthcare or pharmaceutical applications, thereby excluding opinion pieces, editorials, or works focused solely on technical architecture. This systematic approach guarantees that the synthesized findings are based on robust, evidence-based research. The screening criteria is as follows:

- RQ1-C_1: Does the study focus on deep neural networks (DNNs) or generative AI applications specifically applied to healthcare diagnostics or drug discovery?
- RQ1-C_2: Is the study either a primary research study, systematic review, or meta-analysis that includes empirical validation?
- RQ1-C_3: Does the study report quantitative performance metrics (such as accuracy, sensitivity, specificity, or discovery rates)?
- RQ1-C_4: Does the study include a comparison between AI methods and traditional approaches?
- RQ1-C_5: Does the study include substantial validation using experimental or real-world data?
- RQ1-C_6: Does the study include clear performance metrics and comparison baselines?
- RQ1-C_7: Is the study an empirical research paper (rather than an opinion piece, editorial, or perspective article)?
- RQ1-C_8: Does the study include practical healthcare or pharmaceutical applications (rather than focusing solely on technical architecture)?

3.3 Screening Criteria RQ2

The screening process for this research question was designed to ensure the inclusion of only the most relevant and high-quality studies. A multi-layered set of criteria was applied to each potential source, focusing on the core themes of artificial intelligence in healthcare, its ethical and legal dimensions, and the depth of analysis presented. Sources were evaluated based on their explicit focus on AI applications in medical diagnosis or drug discovery, their substantive discussion of ethical or legal implications, and their methodological rigor as primary research, systematic reviews, or policy analyses. Furthermore, studies were required to go beyond superficial commentary, offering in-depth analysis of implementation challenges and practical considerations. The final layer of screening ensured that the primary scope of each included study was directly relevant to the ethical and regulatory aspects under investigation, such as privacy, data protection, and legal frameworks, thereby guaranteeing a highly focused and cohesive body of literature for synthesis. The list of criteria is:

- RQ2-C1 (AI Healthcare Focus): Does the study examine AI applications specifically in medical diagnosis or drug discovery?
- RQ2-C2 (Ethical/Legal Content): Does the study include substantial discussion of ethical and/or legal implications of AI in healthcare?
- RQ2-C3 (Study Type): Is the study one of the following: primary research, systematic review, meta-analysis, case study, or policy/regulatory analysis?

- RQ2-C4 (Analysis Depth): Does the study include substantive analysis beyond opinion or commentary?
- RQ2-C5 (Implementation Focus): Does the study address practical implementation considerations rather than purely theoretical capabilities?
- RQ2-C6 (Healthcare AI Specificity): Does the study focus specifically on AI technology rather than general healthcare technology?
- RQ2-C_7 (Scope Relevance): Does the study's primary focus include at least one of the following: ethical implications, legal frameworks, regulatory challenges, privacy considerations, or data protection issues?

4 Results

The scope of research selected studies were published in digital repositories and specialized platforms recognized for their authority in medicine and artificial intelligence, such as Google Scholar, PubMed, IEEE Xplore, ACM Digital Library, and repositories like arXiv and SSRN. Key search terms included artificial intelligence, machine learning, healthcare, medicine, drug discovery, diagnosis, treatment, and ethical-legal issues and concerns. Priority was given to articles published in high-impact journals (Q1) in the fields of medicine, biomedical informatics, and life sciences, from 2019 to 2024.

During the selection process, filters were applied to discard non-relevant studies. It is important to note that all studies conducted prior to 2018 were excluded from the analysis. This was done with the understanding that the field of artificial intelligence is advancing at a rapid pace and older publications might contain outdated information that could potentially compromise the validity of the results. Also, articles that mentioned artificial intelligence without elaborating on its clinical applications were excluded from the analysis.

4.1 RQ1

There were thousands of possible papers available from Google Scholar, Scopus, and PubMed. There were three types of papers to be included in this review: 1) Papers related to Diagnostics, using AI; 2) Papers related to drug discovery/development; 3) Previous literature reviews. This last class was important to guide paper discrimination. After applying screening criteria, fifteen papers were useful and representative for Diagnostics, while ten papers were suitable for Drug Discovery. Table 1 and 2 summarize the studies.

Table 1. Usage of AI in Diagnostics: Summary by Medical Area

Medical Area	AI Technique
Dermatology	CNN [13], DNN ensemble [21]

(continued)

Table 1. *(continued)*

Medical Area	AI Technique
Oncology	DNN ensemble [10], CNN ensemble [35], Multimodal DNN [36], CNN with ensemble voting [24], DCNN [42], CNN [44]
Genetics	CNN, GAN [12], Deep learning, computer vision [43], DNN, logistic regression [19], CNN, XAI [20], DNN, SVM, LR [33]
Hematology	DNN [38]
Ophthalmology	DNN [39]

4.2 RQ2

Of thousands of papers, fifty were the most relevant to our review. When applying the screening criteria, only thirteen papers were selected to answer the RQ2.

For convenience, the study types presented in Table 3 are abbreviated in column "Type" as follows: Systematic Review (SR), Conceptual Review (CR), White Paper (WP), Scoping Review (ScR), and Mapping Review (MR). These abbreviations are used consistently throughout the table to enhance readability and formatting within the constraints of the page layout. Columns "FWK" indicates what studies offer or contain a Framework or Guidance.

Table 2. Usage of AI in Drug Discovery

Application	AI Technique
Drug repurposing	DNN, SVM [4], Hybrid GNN-CNN [18], GNN, NN classifier [37]
Drug-target interaction prediction	CNN, RNN, GNN, hybrid, transfer learning [14], CNN, RNN [22], GNN, NN classifier [37]
Antiviral peptide classification	TCN-based deep learning [15]
Molecular property prediction, virtual screening	Random Forest, SVM, CNN, GNN [11], GNN, deep learning pipeline [28], GNN [6]
ADME-Tox property prediction	Multitask DNN [41]

Table 3. Ethical, Legal, and Social Issues in AI for Healthcare: Summary by Study Type

Type	Focus	Key Ethical/Legal/Social Issues Identified	FWK
SR	Drug Discovery and Diagnosis	Data privacy, algorithmic bias, intellectual property rights, equitable access, regulatory adaptation. Ethical, regulatory, legal frameworks; multi-level abstraction; transparency; accountability. Machine training/accuracy, patient/physician ethics, regulatory roles, standardization	Yes [25] No [32, 1]
CR	Diagnosis, data management, decisionmaking, screening, clinical decision support	Data bias, lack of transparency ("black box"), privacy, responsibility, security, unemployment, clinical validation, regulation, health inequities, public trust, explainability, legal/ethical frameworks, patient autonomy, justice, consent, liability, intellectual property	Yes [5, 23, 31] No [7, 8, 2]
WP	Diagnosis (radiology)	Patient data (privacy, confidentiality, ownership), algorithm autonomy, liability, legal frameworks	No [16]
ScR	Decision-support tools (diagnosis)	Patient safety, transparency, regulation, liability, patient-physician relationship, governance	Yes [9] No [27]
MR	Healthcare (diagnosis, drug discovery, broader)	Epistemic, normative, traceability challenges; policy mapping; public trust	No [26]

5 Discussion

5.1 Improvements in Diagnostic Applying AI

It is very evident the advances in diagnosis of different specialties when applying IA as a tool. AI has delivered substantial advancements across multiple medical specialties. In oncology, models such as GDD-ENS and ReGeNNe have achieved diagnostic accuracies comparable to genome-based methods, enabling precise classification across a broad range of cancers, including rare and early-stage cases [10, 35]. Dermatology has similarly benefited from AI integration, with deep learning systems matching or surpassing human clinicians in skin lesion classification tasks and serving effectively as decision-support tools [13, 21].

Genetic disorder diagnosis has been transformed through systems like DeepGestalt and others, which consistently outperformed clinical geneticists in syndrome recognition and risk prediction across age groups and conditions [43, 12, 19]. In ophthalmology, AI-assisted treatment planning has improved pharmacological decision-making by enabling personalized therapy [39]. Additional advances span pathology—where AI reduced diagnostic error rates by up to 90% [44]—and radiology, where DenseNet models significantly outperformed radiologists in ultrasound-based assessments [42]. Finally, in infectious disease, AI has demonstrated high specificity in detecting SARS-CoV-2, reinforcing its utility in outbreak response and rapid diagnostic development [20]. These findings underscore AI's cross-disciplinary potential for enhancing diagnostic accuracy, clinical efficiency, and patient outcomes.

Beyond their empirical results, the reviewed studies offer substantial methodological contributions to AI in medical diagnosis across diverse domains. In genetics, Raghad's hybrid model combining convolutional neural networks (CNNs) with ensemble learning redefines standards for genomic data interpretation [24], while Lopez-Rincon's DANN model surpasses traditional classifiers by capturing nonlinear relationships among noncoding variants—critical for enhancing genetic annotation. Wang's comparative evaluation of deep neural network (DNN) architectures for laboratory diagnostics identifies a multi-output model as both efficient and clinically practical by eliminating manual feature engineering [38], and further demonstrates that AI can support patient-specific treatment plans in ophthalmology. In computational phenotyping, DeepGestalt [43] introduces a framework that uses 2D facial images to assess phenotypic similarity across hundreds of syndromes, complemented by Duong's integration of saliency maps and age-progressed synthetic images to bolster diagnostic robustness in pediatric populations [12]. Sharma addresses the interpretability challenge through a two-step framework that links gene-pathway associations with predictive modeling, thus connecting algorithmic accuracy with biological meaning [35]. Finally, Xi and Yeung underscore the clinical readiness of AI: Xi embeds high-accuracy models in ultrasound systems for real-time diagnostics [42], while Yeung demonstrates AI's capacity to detect subtle histopathological patterns beyond human perception [44].

5.2 Drug Discovery with AI

Multiple studies demonstrate how AI-driven models outperform conventional techniques in speed and efficacy. For instance, Mahilnan emphasizes that AI methods help save time and effort by making drug discovery more efficient [22]. Similarly, Dheeraj shows that deep learning models like CNNs and GNNs reduce development time and computational costs by improving molecular property prediction and virtual screening [11].

Another method, developed by Aliper, uses deep neural networks (DNNs) to classify drugs based on how they affect genes. This approach quickly categorizes drugs and helps find existing ones that could be used for new purposes [4]. Hindi's work complements this by using few-shot and transfer learning to tackle the problem of limited data, which is especially beneficial for developing treatments for rare diseases [14].

Beyond classification, AI is also improving the efficiency of screening and compound identification. For instance, Noor's VirtuDockDL system uses a deep learning pipeline to combine different screening methods for a more accurate and faster identification of promising compounds [28]. This increased speed is also seen in Veleiro's GENNIUS model, which can predict interactions across massive datasets in less than a minute, a significant improvement over existing tools [37].

Another promising development is the hybrid GNN-CNN model proposed by Kaur, which facilitates the discovery of novel therapeutic applications for existing drugs, thus accelerating the path from identification to clinical relevance [18]. Huang also contributes to this trend by presenting Deep-AVPiden, a model whose parallel processing and embedding architectures surpass traditional RNNs and LSTMs, offering a faster route to antiviral peptide discovery [15]. Finally, Wenzel proposes a novel multitask DNN approach that not only enhances predictive quality but incorporates a "response map" visualization, which guides medicinal chemists in fine-tuning compound structures for desired properties [41].

5.3 Ethics and Legal Challenges of AI in Medicine

There still are several challenges for AI in medicine, especially when applying it in diagnosis and drug discovery. The main topics are data management and privacy, algorithm accountability, regulatory compliance, and professional and institutional responsibilities.

Data Management and Privacy. The increasing reliance on extensive datasets in medical research, particularly in fields such as medical diagnosis and drug discovery, has brought data management and privacy to the forefront of ethical and practical concerns. A foundational ethical consideration, as evidenced by all included studies on the topic, is the protection of patient data, encompassing privacy, confidentiality, ownership, and data sharing [32]. In the context of medical diagnosis, the high risk of patient re-identification necessitates granular consent mechanisms, a need highlighted by studies from Pitel et al., Marques et al., and Patcas et al. This presents a significant challenge to data sharing for the purpose of training and validating diagnostic algorithms [32, 23, 31]. Similarly, in drug discovery, the use of large and heterogeneous datasets raises complex issues surrounding intellectual property and proprietary data, especially with the added complexity of cross-border data flows [32]. To mitigate these multifaceted risks, a multi-pronged approach is essential. This includes the implementation of robust consent mechanisms that are both transparent and adaptable, the principle of data minimization to limit the collection of personal information, and the development of secure data infrastructures [27]. Furthermore, the establishment of clear data ownership policies is crucial to ensure that patient rights and intellectual property are respected, thereby fostering a secure and trustworthy environment for data-driven medical innovation.

Algorithm Accountability. All included studies emphasize that transparency and explainability are essential for building trust and assigning liability, particularly given the "black box" nature of many AI systems [8]. This lack of transparency poses a significant barrier to clinical validation, as clinicians may not be able to understand the reasoning behind a diagnostic recommendation, leading to a risk of diagnostic errors and a loss of trust. Similarly, in drug discovery, opaque models can lead to the selection of biased compounds or an inability to justify drug candidate prioritization [8].

Beyond transparency, the importance of robust validation and monitoring processes is highlighted in several studies, including those by Cartolovni et al., Amann et al., and Patcas et al. These processes are crucial to ensure that AI models are rigorously tested before deployment and are continuously monitored for performance degradation or the emergence of bias [8]. However, a major challenge remains in the form of underdeveloped liability frameworks. There is a prevailing uncertainty regarding who is responsible for errors or harm caused by AI-driven decisions, a gap that Morley et al. and Patcas et al. have specifically called for new legal standards to address.

To mitigate these risks, a multifaceted approach is required. Strategies include the use of inclusive training datasets to reduce the potential for discrimination, the development of explainable AI (XAI) models that can articulate their decision-making processes, and the implementation of independent validation and ongoing monitoring to ensure the safety and reliability of these systems throughout their lifecycle. These measures are critical for fostering responsible innovation while ensuring that the benefits of AI are realized without compromising patient safety or ethical principles.

Regulatory Compliance. AI has presented significant challenges to established legal and regulatory frameworks in the healthcare sector. Most included studies question the adequacy of current legal frameworks, such as those from the United States Food and Drug Administration (FDA) and the European Union Medical Device Regulation (EU MDR) [31, 1, 25], to address AI's unique complexities [9]. A primary challenge is the rapid pace of technological change, which means that existing frameworks often lag behind AI advances, leading to slow approval processes [2]. This is further complicated by cross-jurisdictional differences and a lack of harmonized standards, especially with the added complexity of global pharmaceutical regulation in drug discovery.

In the context of medical diagnosis, for example, the existing frameworks are struggling to keep pace with the swift development of new AI-driven diagnostic tools. To mitigate these challenges, there is a growing consensus, supported by studies from Cartolovni et al., Patcas et al., and Amann et al., that a more flexible and adaptive approach is needed. This includes advocating for risk-based regulation that can evolve alongside the technology, encouraging international collaboration to harmonize standards, and implementing post-market surveillance to continuously monitor the performance and safety of AI systems after they have been deployed. Furthermore, the integration of ethics-by-design principles from the outset is seen as a proactive measure to embed safety, transparency, and fairness into the development lifecycle, ensuring that regulatory compliance is not merely an afterthought but a foundational component of AI innovation.

Professional and Institutional Responsibilities. It is evident that, AI usage in medicine and drug discovery needs a re-evaluation of professional and institutional responsibilities. At the individual level, healthcare providers have an ongoing obligation to maintain their professional judgment and uphold patient trust, particularly as AI systems challenge traditional informed consent processes [8, 31]. A significant challenge in this new landscape is the unclear responsibility for AI-driven errors, which creates complexities in malpractice and product liability law [16]. In medical diagnosis, this manifests as a need for continuous education to prevent the "deskilling" of clinicians and to maintain the core patient-provider relationship.

From an institutional perspective, robust oversight is crucial for effective risk management. Institutions must establish clear internal governance structures and foster a culture of transparency and ethical reflection [9]. In drug discovery, the use of AI introduces intellectual property disputes over AI-generated discoveries and creates new questions regarding liability for failed predictions, issues less direct but still relevant for clinical trial oversight [5]. To mitigate these risks, a multi-pronged strategy is recommended. This includes the development of new legal standards and shared accountability frameworks that integrate human oversight into AI decision-making. Furthermore, the establishment of multidisciplinary teams, continuous professional development, and certification processes for clinicians using AI tools are essential to ensure the safe and ethical implementation of these technologies [23].

6 Conclusions, Recommendations and Future Research

The preceding literature review has underscored the impact of artificial intelligence across critical domains within healthcare, demonstrating its potential in medical diagnostics, drug discovery, and the ethical and legal frameworks governing its deployment. This conclusion addresses the research questions by synthesizing the key findings: RQ1) how do deep neural networks (DNNs) and GenAI improve diagnostic accuracy and accelerate drug discovery? and RQ2) What are the main ethical and legal challenges in implementing AI for medical diagnosis and drug discovery?. The aim is to highlight the consistent advancements in AI's capabilities, its capacity to revolutionize traditional processes, and the essential considerations for its responsible integration into clinical practice and research.

For RQ1, it is impressive how different proposals of AI methodologies can provide health professionals the tools to better diagnostics. In several studies, AI models had matched or surpassed human experts. For instance, Yeung and Cheng (2022) reported a histopathology model with 97% accuracy, significantly outperforming pathologists who achieved only 69.7% [44]. The consistent outperformance of physicians by DL models is a powerful point of convergence across multiple studies, including those by Esteva et al. (2017) and Lucius et al. (2020) for skin conditions, and Gurovich et al. (2018) for rare genetic syndromes.

The synthesis of these findings reveals a clear trajectory for the future of diagnostics: the integration of deep learning is not merely an improvement but a fundamental paradigm shift. Based on the consistent evidence [44, 42, 12], it is strongly recommended that medical institutions and healthcare providers actively adopt DL models as decision support tools. These models are not intended to replace clinicians but rather to augment their capabilities, providing highly accurate, rapid, and objective analyses that can assist in diagnosis and treatment planning. The consistent outperformance of human experts across diverse domains—from histopathology and ultrasound to genomics and facial analysis—makes a compelling case for the immediate clinical validation and implementation of these technologies. Future research should focus on developing standardized validation frameworks and on creating transparent and interpretable models to build trust and facilitate their integration into clinical workflows. The evidence is unequivocal: deep learning models are poised to revolutionize medical diagnostics, and their widespread adoption is the next logical step in advancing patient care.

In drug discovery field, the integration of artificial intelligence (AI) has reshaped the landscape of drug discovery, demonstrating significant advancements across various critical phases, from early-stage drug-target interaction prediction and virtual screening to later-stage molecular property prediction and drug repurposing. A diverse array of AI methodologies, including graph neural networks, convolutional neural networks, deep neural networks, and hybrid models, have been effectively deployed to tackle these complex challenges. A central theme emerging from the reviewed studies is the substantial reduction in time and computational resources, with reports of full automation, high-throughput screening, and ultrafast predictions, underscoring AI's capacity to accelerate the drug discovery pipeline. Quantitatively, AI models consistently achieve high success metrics, with accuracies frequently exceeding 90% and strong F1 scores, AUROC, precision, and recall values, indicating their robust predictive capabilities.

RQ2 found there are ethics and legal challenges of AI use in medicine. Two central themes consistently emerge as foundational for the responsible development and implementation of AI in healthcare. The first is the paramount importance of enhanced transparency and explainability in AI systems. The consensus is that AI algorithms must be transparent, and their decision-making processes must be explainable, a requirement that is not just technical but also ethical. Without this, clinicians cannot fully justify a system's recommendation to a patient, and patients cannot provide informed consent. Transparency is thus a prerequisite for building and maintaining trust in these technologies.

The second core theme is the critical issue of data bias and fairness. A significant body of research emphasizes that AI developers must use inclusive and representative datasets to train their algorithms. This is the most direct way to prevent AI systems from perpetuating or exacerbating existing health disparities. The focus on data as the root cause of potential harm represents a crucial, actionable consensus, providing a concrete path toward ensuring that AI serves all demographic groups equitably.

Literature presents a powerful, unified front on the critical governance challenges of AI in healthcare. The consensus is overwhelming: a multi-stakeholder, life-cycle approach is essential. Policymakers must create adaptive and clear legal frameworks, while regulators must implement schemes that balance innovation with safety through premarket and robust post-market scrutiny. AI developers have a non-negotiable responsibility to ensure their systems are not only high-performing but also transparent, explainable, and trained on diverse and representative data to prevent bias. Finally, healthcare institutions must foster a culture of ethical integration, prioritizing human oversight, professional training, and open dialogue with all stakeholders. The recommendations, taken together, form a cohesive blueprint for the responsible and equitable deployment of AI in medicine, ensuring these technologies serve to enhance, not undermine, patient safety and trust.

The future research should primarily focus on bridging the gap between a model's technical performance and its effective, safe, and ethical integration into clinical and research workflows. While the current literature demonstrates the high accuracy of AI systems, the next logical step is the development of standardized validation frameworks to ensure their reliability across diverse settings and patient populations. On the regulatory and legal front, future work must explore adaptive governance models that can keep pace with the rapid innovation cycle of AI, balancing the need for safety and oversight with the imperative to foster beneficial advancements, involving not only computer scientists but also clinicians, ethicists, legal experts, and policymakers.

Disclosure of Interests.

The authors have no competing interests to declare that are relevant to the content of this article.

References

1. Abdullah, Y.I., Schuman, J.S., Shabsigh, R., Caplan, A., AlAswad, L.: A.: ethics of artificial intelligence in medicine and ophthalmology. Asia-Pacific. J. Ophthalmol. **10**(3), 289–298 (5 2021). https://doi.org/10.1097/apo.0000000000000397
2. Abràmoff, M.D., Tobey, D., Char, D.S.: Lessons learned about autonomous ai: finding a safe, efficacious, and ethical path through the development process. Am. J. Ophthalmol. **214**, 134–142 (2020). https://doi.org/10.1016/j.ajo.2020.02.022
3. Adir, O., et al.: Integrating artificial intelligence and nanotechnology for precision cancer medicine. Adv. Mater. **32**(13), 1901989 (2020). https://doi.org/10.1002/adma.201901989
4. Aliper, A., Plis, S., Artemov, A., Ulloa, A., Mamoshina, P., Zhavoronkov, A.: DeepLearning applications for predicting pharmacological properties of drugs and drug repurposing using transcriptomic data. Mol. Pharm. **13**(7), 2524–2530 (2016). https://doi.org/10.1021/acs.mol pharmaceut.6b00248
5. Amann, J., Blasimme, A., Vayena, E., Frey, D., Madai, V.I., Consortium, P.: Explainability for artificial intelligence in healthcare: a multidisciplinary perspective. BMC Med. Inform. Decis. Mak. **20**(1), 310 (2020). https://doi.org/10.1186/s12911-020-01332-6
6. Carracedo-Reboredo, P., et al.: A review on machine learning approaches and trends in drug discovery. Comput. Struct. Biotechnol. J. **19**, 4538–4558 (2021). https://doi.org/10.1016/j.csbj.2021.08.011
7. Carter, S., Win, K., Wang, L., Rogers, W., Richards, B., Houssami, N.: 65 ethical, legal and social implications of artificial intelligence systems for screening and diagnosis. In: Oral Presentations, pp. A37.2–A3A38. BMJ Publishing Group Ltd (12 2019). https://doi.org/10.1136/bmjebm-2019-pod.77
8. Carter, S.M., Rogers, W., Win, K.T., Frazer, H., Richards, B., Houssami, N.: The ethical, legal and social implications of using artificial intelligence systems in breast cancer care. Breast. **49**, 25–32 (2020). https://doi.org/10.1016/j.breast.2019.10.001
9. Čartolovni, A., Tomičić, A., Lazić Mosler, E.: Ethical, legal, and social considerations of AI-based medical decision-support tools: a scoping review. Int. J. Med. Inform. **161**, 104738 (5 2022). https://doi.org/10.1016/j.ijmedinf.2022.104738

10. Darmofal, M., et al.: Deep Learning Model for Tumor Type Prediction using Targeted Clinical Genomic Sequencing Data. medRxiv (Sep 10 2023). https://doi.org/10.1101/2023.09.08.23295131
11. Mandloi, D., Shyamkuwar, A., Kumar, S., YV, K.S., Banavatu, L.: AI-powered drug discovery: integrating chemistry, biology, and data science. Metall. Mater. Eng., 458–470 (2025)
12. Duong, D., et al.: Neural networks for classification and image generation of aging in genetic syndromes. Front. Genet. **13** (2022). https://doi.org/10.3389/fgene.2022.864092
13. Esteva, A., et al.: Dermatologist-level classification of skin cancer with deep neural networks. Nature. **542**(7639), 115–118 (jan 25 2017). https://doi.org/10.1038/nature21056
14. Hindi, N.: Deep learning applications in drug-target interaction prediction: a systematic review. Int. J. Res. Publ. Rev. **6**(6), 4433–4449 (1 2025). https://doi.org/10.55248/gengpi.6.0125.0626
15. Huang, D., Yang, M., Zheng, W.: Integrating AI and deep learning for efficient drug discovery and target identification. J. AI-Powered Med. Innov. (Int. online ISSN 3078–1930). **2**(1), 44–63 (Dec 9 2024). https://doi.org/10.60087/vol2.issue1.p005
16. Jaremko, J.L., et al.: Canadian association of radiologists white paper on ethical and legal issues related to artificial intelligence in radiology. Can. Assoc. Radiol. J. **20**, 1e12 (2019). https://doi.org/10.1016/j.carj.2019.03.001
17. Kaul, V., Enslin, S., Gross, S.A.: History of artificial intelligence in medicine. Gastrointest. Endosc. **92**(4), 807–812 (2020). https://doi.org/10.1016/j.gie.2020.06.040
18. Kaur, A., Kukreja, V., Singh, A.: Molecular insights unveiled: a HybridNeural network model GNN-CNN for drug discovery. In: 2024 International Conference on Big Data Analytics in Bioinformatics (DABCon), pp. 1–5. IEEE (nov 21 2024). https://doi.org/10.1109/dabcon63472.2024.10919421
19. Kim, J., Kim, J., Kwak, M., Bajaj, M.: Genetic prediction of type 2 diabetesusing deep neural network. Clin. Genet. **93**(4), 822–829 (Feb 20 2018). https://doi.org/10.1111/cge.13175
20. Lopez-Rincon, A., et al.: Classification and specific primer design for accurate detection of SARS-CoV-2 using deep learning. Sci. Rep. **11**(1) (2021). https://doi.org/10.1038/s41598-020-80363-5
21. Lucius, M., et al.: Deep neural frameworks improve the accuracy of general practitioners in the classification of pigmented skin lesions. Diagnostics. **10**(11), 969 (Nov 18 2020). https://doi.org/10.3390/diagnostics10110969
22. Mahilnan, V., Nandhini, M., Santhosh, N., MelkyAbishake, R., Ranganathan, S., Maheshwaran, P.: Ai-powered drug discovery: accelerating precision medicine with deep learning. In: 2024 International Conference on Innovative Computing, Intelligent Communication and Smart Electrical Systems (ICSES), pp. 1–7. IEEE (Dec 12 2024). https://doi.org/10.1109/icses63760.2024.10910685
23. Marques, M., Almeida, A., Pereira, H.: The medicine revolution through artificial intelligence: ethical challenges of machine learning algorithms in decision-making. Cureus. (Sep 14 2024). https://doi.org/10.7759/cureus.69405
24. Mohammed, R.K., Alrawi, A.T.H., Dawood, A.J.: A dual-approach to genomic predictions: leveraging convolutional networks and voting classifiers. Biomed.l Eng.g Commun. **4**(1), 02 (2025). https://doi.org/10.53388/2025002
25. Morley, J.: The debate on the ethics of AI in health care: a reconstruction and critical review. Social science research. Network. (Nov 16 2019). https://doi.org/10.31219/osf.io/n7y2g
26. Morley, J., et al.: The ethics of AI in health care: a mapping review. Soc. Sci. Amp. Med. **260**, 113172 (9 2020). https://doi.org/10.1016/j.socscimed.2020.113172
27. Murdoch, B.: Privacy and artificial intelligence: challenges for protecting health information in a new era. BMC Med. Ethics. **22**, 1–5 (2021). https://doi.org/10.1186/s12910-021-00687-3

28. Noor, F., Junaid, M., Almalki, A.H., Almaghrabi, M., Ghazanfar, S., Tahir ul Qamar, M.: Deep learning pipeline for accelerating virtual screening in drug discovery. Sci. Rep. **14**(1) (Nov 16 2024). https://doi.org/10.1038/s41598-024-79799w
29. Okoli, C.: A guide to conducting a standalone systematic literature review. Commun. Assoc. Inf. Syst. **37**(43) (2015) https://doi.org/10.17705/1CAIS.03743
30. Oren, O., Gersh, B.J., Bhatt, D.L.: Artificial intelligence in medical imaging: switching from radiographic pathological data to clinically meaningful endpoints. Lancet Digit. Health. **2**(9), e486–e488 (2020). https://doi.org/10.1016/S2589-7500(20)30160-6
31. Patcas, R., Bornstein, M.M., Schätzle, M.A., Timofte, R.: Artificial intelligencein medico-dental diagnostics of the face: a narrative review of opportunities and challenges. Clin. Oral Investig. **26**(12), 6871–6879 (Sep 24 2022). https://doi.org/10.1007/s00784-022-04724-2
32. Pitel, E., Leasu, F., Nicolau, A., Rogozea, L.: Ethical aspects in the use of artificial intelligence in the process of drug development | [Aspecte etice în utilizarea inteligent¸ei artificiale în procesul de dezvoltare a medicamentelor]. J. Med. Brasovean, 53–61 (Apr 3 2024). https://doi.org/10.31926/jmb.2023.2.8
33. Quang, D., Chen, Y., Xie, X.: Dann: a deep learning approach for annotating the pathogenicity of genetic variants. Bioinformatics. **31**(5), 761–763 (2014). https://doi.org/10.1093/bioinformatics/btu703
34. Rajula, H.S.R., Verlato, G., Manchia, M., Antonucci, N., Fanos, V.: Comparison of conventional statistical methods with machine learning in medicine: diagnosis, drug development, and treatment. Medicina. **56**(9), 455 (2020). https://doi.org/10.3390/medicina56090455
35. Sharma, D., Xu, W.: Regenne: genetic pathway-based deep neural network using canonical correlation regularizer for disease prediction. Bioinformatics. **39**(11) (Nov 1 2023). https://doi.org/10.1093/bioinformatics/btad679
36. S.K.B, S., et al.: An enhanced multimodal fusion deep learning neural network for lung cancer classification. Systems and soft. Computing. **6**, 200068 (12 2024). https://doi.org/10.1016/j.sasc.2023.200068
37. Veleiro, U., et al.: GeNNius: an ultrafast drug–target interaction inference method based on graph neural networks. Bioinformatics. **40**(1) (Dec 22 2023). https://doi.org/10.1093/bioinformatics/btad774
38. Wang, J., Leger, R., Heikal, N., Pruthi, R., Chen, D., Seheult, J.: A-161 diagnosis of lupus anticoagulant cases using deep neural networks. Clin. Chem. **70**(Supplement_1) (10 2024). https://doi.org/10.1093/clinchem/hvae106.159
39. Wang, X., Hongxu, S., Huan, L., Shouxi, L., Xiaofei, D.: An auxiliary role of deep neural network ophthalmic disease identification models in choosing medication treatment strategy. Pak. J. Pharm. Sci. (2025). https://doi.org/10.36721/pjps.2025.38.2.reg.13880.1
40. Wang, Y., He, X., Nie, H., Zhou, J., Cao, P., Ou, C.: Application of artificial intelligence to the diagnosis and therapy of colorectal cancer. Am. J. Cancer Res. **10**(11), 3575 (2020)
41. Wenzel, J., Matter, H., Schmidt, F.: Predictive multitask deep neural network models for ADME-Tox properties: learning from large data sets. J. Chem. Inf. Model. **59**(3), 1253–1268 (Jan 7 2019). https://doi.org/10.1021/acs.jcim.8b00785
42. Xi, M., et al.: Ultrasonographic diagnosis of ovarian tumors through the deep convolutional neural network. Ginekol. Pol. **95**(3), 181–189 (Oct 13 2023). https://doi.org/10.5603/gpl.94956
43. Yaron, G., et al.: Deepgestalt - Identifying Rare Genetic Syndromes Using Deep Learning. arXiv.org (2018)
44. Yeung, M.C.F., Cheng, I.S.Y.: Artificial intelligence significantly improves thediagnostic accuracy of deep myxoid soft tissue lesions in histology. Sci. Rep. **12**(1) (Apr 28 2022). https://doi.org/10.1038/s41598-022-11009-x

Travel Time Prediction for Urban Traffic Forecasting Using Random Forest Regression

J. Carrillo Zavala[1,2](✉), Alberto Ochoa-Zezzatti[1,2], and Roberto Contreras-Masse[1,2]

[1] Universidad Autónoma de Ciudad Juarez, Cd. Juarez, Chih, Mexico
zl.carrillozavala@outlook.com
[2] TecNM Campus ITCJ, Cd. Juarez, Chih, Mexico

Abstract. The development of traffic optimization projects in Ciudad Juárez faces the challenge of insufficient analytical metrics for accurate problem assessment. This study introduces a machine learning framework that automatically collects and generates synthetic traffic data from real travel times extracted from Google Maps through an automated Python routine using Selenium. The proposed Random Forest Regressor model was trained with temporal and spatial features such as coordinates, date, hour, and workday classification, enabling the prediction of total travel time with a **mean absolute error below one minute** and an overall **accuracy of 91%**. Empirical validation confirmed that the predicted travel times closely follow real observations, with deviations lower than 40 s on average. The results demonstrate that even with a limited set of variables, tree-based ensemble models can effectively learn traffic dynamics and generate reliable synthetic data for different urban conditions. The main innovation of this work lies in the *low-cost, automated data acquisition method* and its integration with predictive modeling to produce synthetic datasets that can support the design, calibration, and validation of future intelligent traffic management systems in Ciudad Juárez and other cities with limited mobility data. Additionally, the proposed approach establishes a methodological foundation for expanding the scope of traffic forecasting using artificial intelligence, combining accessibility, precision, and scalability within real-world urban environments.

Keywords: Urban Traffic Forecasting · Travel Time Prediction · Machine Learning · Random Forest Regression · Synthetic Data Generation

1 Introduction

The exponential growth of cities causes problems arising from high population density [1], such as the need for complex public transportation networks [2], traffic congestion [3], or the need for variable cycle automation [4].

The lack of data hinders the development of new solutions to traffic flow problems or traffic congestion reduction [5]. There is a need for recent and reliable data that, in addition to being consistent with traffic behavior, can describe multifactorial changes throughout the day [6].

L. Martínez-Villaseñor et al. (Eds.): MICAI 2025 Workshops, LNAI 16264, pp. 50–70, 2026.
https://doi.org/10.1007/978-3-032-17930-2_4

The existence of tools that measure traffic behavior, such as Google Maps, which aims to integrate geolocation data to generate traffic estimates [7], is useful because, as freely accessible applications, they can perform periodic queries with a high degree of accuracy. Having a set of data represented in a specific framework makes it possible to use them to generate new data or predictions [8].

This work offers a benefit in the technological sphere by proposing a method for generating data for the development of new projects and research; in the economic sphere, it presents a low-cost alternative for the collection and generation of synthetic data.

Synthetic data represents an innovative tool for developing new solutions to ev-everyday problems such as urban mobility [9]. This approach is particularly helpful for new technologies such as artificial intelligence algorithms, specifically regression techniques, machine learning, reinforcement learning, and neural networks, as they require a large amount of data to be reliable, accurate, and precise [10].

This document is organized into sections; Sect. 2 discusses the literature review, where different works will be compared to understand the current state of technology and how this work can benefit it. Sect. 3 discusses the proposed methodology, where the work plan to achieve the objective will be presented. Sect. 4 discusses the results, presenting and analyzing them. Finally, Sect. 5 discusses the conclusions.

2 Literature Review

Urban traffic management (UTM) consists of a set of techniques and strategies aimed at reducing urban traffic congestion. It offers benefits for the development of social infrastructure, such as reducing greenhouse gases, reducing urban travel times, and preventing accidents. Its main obstacle is the lack of data [11].

The collection of data on the number of cars and calculation of speed has been the objective of video analysis using a robust vision model based on drone images, where the collected data is used for training neural networks [12].

Multi-source urban traffic prediction offers an innovative solution using drone images and detection loops, which can be understood as sensors capable of sensing the presence or speed of vehicles on avenues or streets, with the aim of generating vehicle traffic flow data [13].

The creation of synthetic trajectory datasets using highly reliable global positioning systems (GPS) for urban mobility analysis presents a viable option for creating new data by extracting data from publicly accessible websites and emulating spatial-temporal behavior, in order to validate the usefulness and reliability of synthetic data [14].

The prediction of congestion at urban intersections using data-based modeling proposes a tool for generating data through machine learning algorithms, taking as parameters the time of day, weather, and road types from a dataset obtained from the travel records of certain vehicles [15].

Based on a review of the articles, they can be classified according to their objectives and data collection methods. The objectives may be direct implementation in physical urban infrastructure systems or the generation of traffic flow data. Data collection methods may involve physical measurements such as sensors or image capture, or they may involve consulting existing databases; an individual classification may be the establishment of data gaps as a problem.

Fig. 1 shows the classification of the reviewed articles, where the boxes represent the articles:

1. Traffic flow prediction techniques [11].
2. Robust Drone Video Analysis for Occluded Urban Traffic Monitoring Based on Deep Learning [12].
3. Urban traffic flow forecasting from multiple sources using data from drones and loop detectors [13].
4. SynMob: Creation of a dataset of high-fidelity synthetic GPS trajectories for urban mobility analysis [14].
5. Predicting traffic congestion at urban intersections using data-driven models [15].

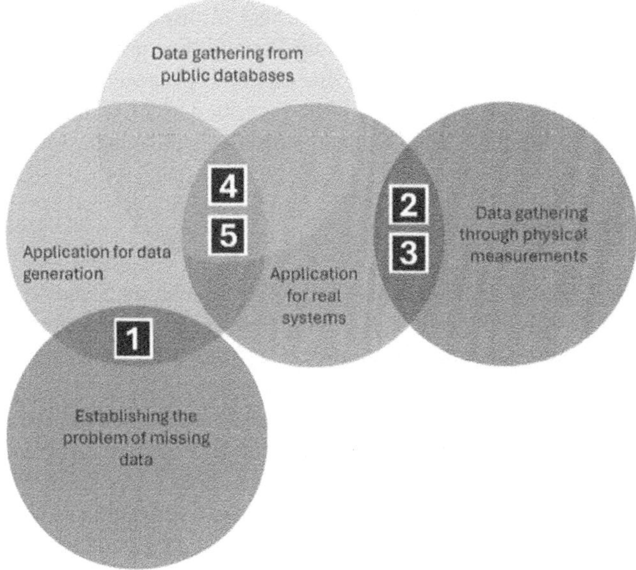

Fig. 1. Classification of literature review

The review of traffic flow prediction techniques is a work that presents generalities regarding data collection methods, proposes urban traffic management as an objective, and highlights the lack of data as the main problem. This article does not develop a prediction project, but rather compiles different projects to develop concepts, algorithms, and their results. It is valuable for evaluating available technology and previous work.

Robust video analysis with drones for monitoring occluded urban traffic based on Deep Learning establishes a system for traffic prediction using neural networks, obtaining vehicle trajectory data at an intersection and their transit speed; it does not take into account travel times or time lost in traffic.

Forecasting urban traffic flow from multiple sources using data from drones and loop detectors provides an option for predicting data such as speed, traffic demand, and vehicle trajectories in an urban region. However, although it produces a robust model, it does not include measurements of travel time, variations throughout the day, or time lost in traffic.

SynMob: Creation of a high-fidelity synthetic GPS trajectory dataset for urban mobility analysis focuses specifically on the generation of synthetic data from existing data; however, it does not present data on estimated travel time or time lost in traffic.

Prediction of traffic congestion at urban intersections using data-based models presents a tool that uses existing databases and does not take into account metrics such as estimated travel time or variations in time for the generation of synthetic data.

Figure 2 shows a comparison between the qualities and concepts present in each article reviewed in this section and what is proposed for this work.

Author and release year	Gathering data through images or sensors	Gathering geolocation data	Gathering from existing databases	Metrics: Estimated travel time	Metrics: Travel speed	Trajectory identification	DL, ML, AI	Computer vision	Generation of synthetic data	Specific time predictions	Continuous predictions throughout the day	Paper title
Juan Carrillo, 2025	✗	✓	✗	✓	✗	✗	✓	✗	✓	✓	✓	Smart Traffic Forecasting in Ciudad Juárez: Synthetic Data Generation Using Artificial Intelligence for Vehicle Travel Time Prediction
[Medina-Salgado et al., 2022]	✗	✗	✗	✗	✗	✗	✓	✗	✓	✓	✓	Traffic flow prediction techniques
[Gellida-Coutiño et al., 2025]	✓	✗	✗	✗	✓	✓	✓	✓	✗	✓	✗	Robust Drone Video Analysis for Occluded Urban Traffic Monitoring Based on Deep Learning
[Xiong et al., 2025]	✓	✗	✗	✓	✓	✓	✓	✓	✗	✗	✓	Urban traffic flow forecasting from multiple sources using data from drones and loop detectors
[Zhu et al., 2023]	✗	✗	✓	✓	✓	✗	✓	✗	✓	✓	✗	SynMob: Creation of a dataset of high-fidelity synthetic GPS trajectories for urban mobility analysis
[Kelly and Gupta, 2024]	✗	✗	✓	✗	✗	✗	✓	✗	✗	✗	✓	Predicting traffic congestion at urban intersections using data-driven models

Fig. 2. Comparison of existing qualities and concepts

Locally, the implementation of a deep learning traffic prediction model presents a deep learning model of short- and long-term memory, using previously measured data on vehicle counts and traffic conditions on different streets and avenues, with the aim of anticipating high traffic volumes throughout the day in order to design efficient mobility strategies [16].

The concentration of intermediation and traffic congestion in metropolitan areas addresses traffic prediction in an abstract manner using graph theory to identify the intermediation of certain nodes that concentrate most of the traffic flow. This study concludes that urban mobility and productivity are affected by structural bottlenecks due to the concentration of traffic on a few streets [17].

3 Methodology

The methodology of this work is based on a four-stage development approach: development of a program for obtaining real data, analysis of the data obtained, development of a weather prediction algorithm, and comparison of synthetic data and real data. Figure 3 shows a graphical approximation of the proposed methodology.

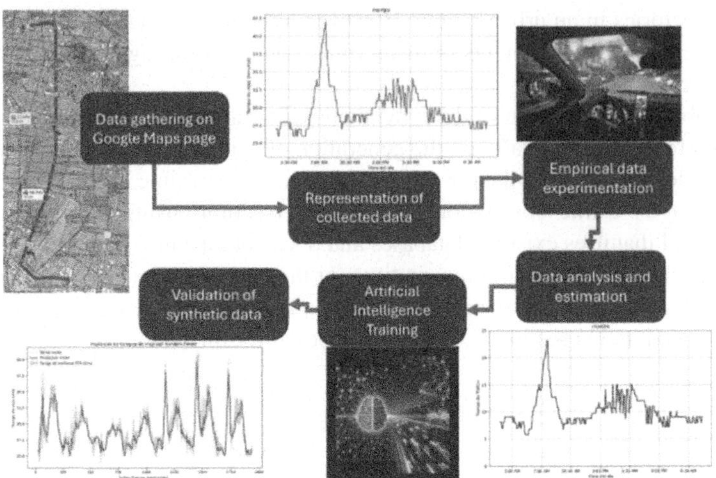

Fig. 3. Methodology planned for synthetic data generation

3.1 Development of a Program for Obtaining Real Data

A Python program is proposed using the Selenium Web-driver module to perform automated queries on the Google Maps page at regular intervals. These queries use the starting coordinate, the ending coordinate, and the time and date of the query as input data. The output data is the estimated travel time, the travel distance, and the main route of the trip. The program saves the input and output data in a.csv file. Figure 4 shows the process to be followed with the travel coordinates, the fields to be extracted, and the top part of the dataset. This program uses 31.609744, −106.417407 as the starting coordinate and 31.737460, −106.442733 as the ending coordinate. It is set up this way because the possible routes between two points are considered main roads with the highest number of traffic lights.

3.2 Analysis of Real Collected Data

After obtaining the data, a validation can be performed between the collected data and the traffic congestion problem. In other words, the data should indicate that at the beginning and end of working hours, traffic flow should decrease, as this is considered a period or interval of saturation; this should be consistent with the expected increase in travel time in the collected data; in order to validate the data obtained from Google Maps, trips will be made at different times to compare estimated travel times. Travel times will be measured in different vehicles, on different days, and during and outside of working hours. In addition, with the data obtained, new data can be estimated using applied formulas, such as the time wasted in traffic.

3.3 Development of Traffic Prediction Algorithm

An artificial intelligence model will be applied, training it with data on travel distance, time and date of travel, whether it is a working day, entry coordinates, and traffic time to

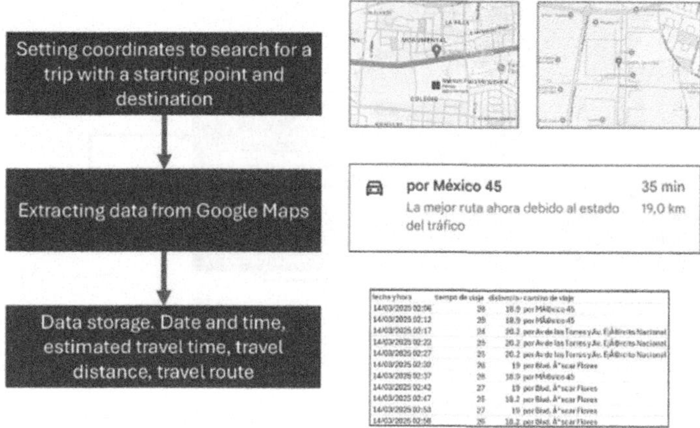

Fig. 4. Process of obtaining real data

obtain the target data for estimated travel time. The Random Forest Regressor technique is proposed because the data are not linear with each other, and it can handle biases such as non-working days, unfavorable weather for traffic flow, or high traffic congestion due to public works.

3.4 Comparison of Synthetic Data and Real Data

A comparison will be made between the collected data and the data generated by the artificial intelligence model, and the mean absolute error, mean square error, and R2 index will be calculated. In addition, data will be obtained on which of the training columns is the most useful and the error distribution of the method.

3.5 Data Gathering Program

Figure (5) presents the logic of the main code for data collection through Google Maps.

The program is developed in Python. The Selenium Webdriver module is used to access the fields on the website, while the Pandas module is used to manage the dataframes and save the data in a .csv file.

3.6 Selection of Parameters, Limitations, and Biases

This work is limited by the source of data collection. Google Maps is a tool for everyday use by the general public, providing only basic information such as estimated travel time, total travel distance, and the best routes to take. This data is generated by the website through the gathering of geolocation data from devices with the application installed. One limitation is the small amount of data types that can be collected through an API designed to extract information directly from the public website.

However, it is recognized that important data can be inferred from the estimated time, such as time lost in traffic, the time at which traffic congestion occurs, and on

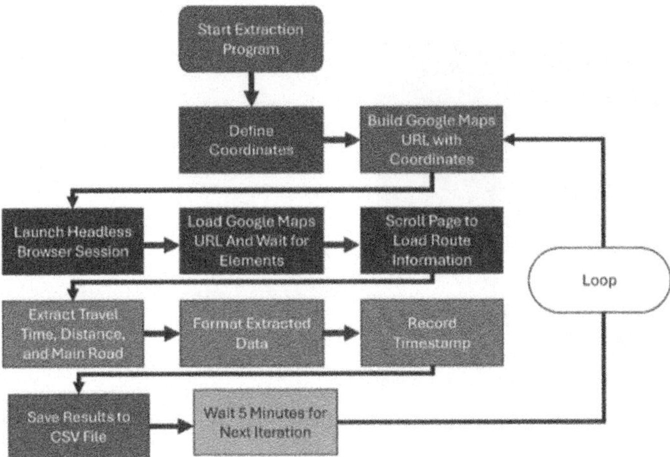

Fig. 5. Algorithm for data gathering

which roads it occurs. That is why travel time is defined as the main parameter for urban traffic prediction in this study. Another limitation of this study is that it examines a single trip, i.e., a starting point and an end point are defined; no measurements are taken of other travel routes that do not include these points, but this allows for an inferential and specific analysis that provides other valuable conclusions.

The system may be susceptible to bias, as Google Maps does not provide a general reading of traffic at a certain time, but rather an absolute reading at that moment. This is why biases such as holidays or accidents on the roads can enter the system, which can alter or increase the estimated traffic time readings, respectively. This should be considered when choosing the artificial intelligence algorithm to be used for making predictions. One way to overcome biases is to take enough readings so that unforeseen events are considered outliers.

3.7 Data Analysis and Estimation of New Data

Once the data has been collected, an empirical comparison can be made by verifying the expected time on the web platform and making the trip, timing the time it takes to get from the starting point to the end point. It is expected that during working hours, congestion will cause an increase in vehicle transit time.

With the data, we can estimate new parameters. If we have the travel time and distance data, and we define that the roads traveled on have an average maximum speed limit of 60 km/h, we can infer the time lost in traffic. As shown in Eq. 1.

$$\begin{aligned} T_d &= \frac{D_v \cdot 60}{V_p} \\ T_t &= T_v - T_d \end{aligned} \tag{1}$$

Where:

- T_d represents direct travel time without traffic interruptions.

- D_v represents the measured distance of the trip.
- V_p represents the average speed limit for the trip.
- T_t represents the time measured in traffic.
- T_v represents the measured travel time.

In Fig. 6 and 7, the program is developed to estimate new data from the collected data.

The program is developed in Python. The pandas module is used to manage data frames.

Figures 8, 9, and 10 show photographs from various trips taken to measure travel times in order to validate and compare the different data extracted from Google Maps.

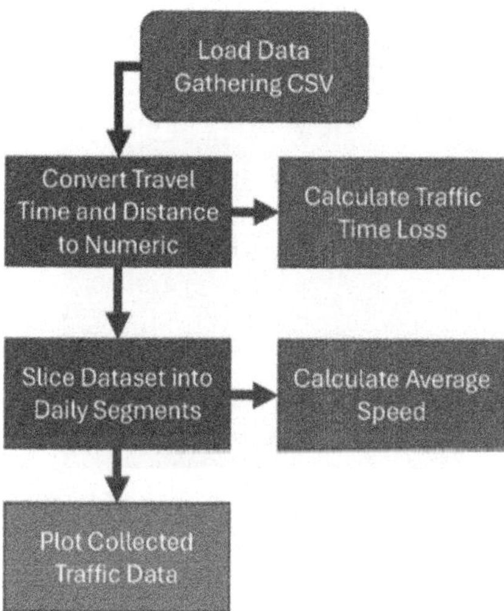

Fig. 6. Processing Traffic Dataset, Computing Derived Metrics and Plotting

3.8 Data Generation Program

Figure 11 shows the program that trains the Random Forest model to generate new data from the collected data. The program is developed in Python. The Pandas library is used to manage data frames, and the sklearn. modelselection and sklearn.ensemble modules are used for artificial intelligence techniques.

3.9 Comparison of Generated Data and Model Analysis

Figure 12 shows the program used to calculate the mean square error, mean absolute error, and R2 measures. The program is written in Python. Matplotlib is used to generate graphs, and sklearn.metrics is used to calculate statistical analysis measures.

Fig. 7. Testing travel times at the start of the route

Fig. 8. Testing travel times at the midpoint of the route

4 Results

4.1 Data Gathering in Google Maps

Figure (13) and (14) shows the average estimated travel time measurements separated by workdays and non-workdays obtained using the Python program for data collection.

On workdays, there is a considerable increase in travel time between 6:30 and 8:30 h; this increase is not present on Mondays, which are considered weekdays but on the date of data collection were non-working days in Ciudad Juárez, which can be considered a bias for training an artificial intelligence algorithm; behavior during other hours is constant on all days.

4.2 Empirical Validation Study of Estimated Travel Times

Table 1 shows a comparison between the estimated times provided by Google Maps and the times measured by making the journey physically. It shows the estimated time taken and the real time taken for the journey in minutes; travels are made by private vehicle and by public transport; different dates and times are taken, both working days and non-working days.

Table 1. Comparison of estimated times by Google Maps and real travel times

Date and time	Means of transportation	Google Maps	Measured time
2025/07/09 8:01	Private Vehicle	33 min.	35 min.
2025/07/16 14:01	Private Vehicle	29 min.	29 min.
2025/07/20 15:15	Public Transport	38 min.	45 min.
2025/07/31 18:33	Private Vehicle	31 min.	33 min.
2025/08/09 20:27	Private Vehicle	27 min.	26 min.
2025/08/20 10:27	Private Vehicle	23 min.	25 min.

4.3 Data Estimation

Figure 15 and 16 shows the average time lost in traffic separated by workdays and non-workday. This takes into accoun that the data is obtained based on expected travel times, applying a mathematical model that establishes travel speeds. Due to the linearity of the formula, the data proportionally follows the travel times collected. However, there are time gaps where traffic time drops considerably, as Google Maps suggests using a road that bypasses the city without traffic lights.

4.4 Model Analysis

The mean absolute error of the model (MAE) is MAE = 0.65, which means that the model has an average error of 39 s. Considering that the range of values is 22 min, this is good. The mean square error of the model (MSE) is MSE = .88, which means about one minute, which falls within the acceptable parameters for a Random

Forest algorithm. R2 = 0.91 with a variability greater than 0.8 in a regression model is usually considered acceptable.

Table 2 shows a comparison between the collected data, the measured data, and the generated data. The synthetic data is generated based on the time and day to coincide with the data collection and real-time travel time measurement.

Table 2. Comparison of collected, measured, and generated times

Date and time	Means of transportation	Google Maps	Measured time	Synthetic Data
2025/07/09 8:01	Private Vehicle	33 min.	35 min.	31.98 min.
2025/07/16 14:01	Private Vehicle	29 min.	29 min.	28.65 min.
2025/07/20 15:15	Public Transport	38 min.	45 min.	32.55 min.
2025/07/31 18:33	Private Vehicle	31 min.	33 min.	31.28 min.
2025/08/09 20:27	Private Vehicle	27 min.	26 min.	25.89 min
2025/08/20 10:27	Private Vehicle	23 min.	25 min.	22.78 min

Figure 17 shows the scatter plot comparing the values generated by the model and the collected data. It can be argued that the distribution follows a linearity with a very low error range, confirming that the model is reliable. Figure 18 shows the error histogram of the model, indicating that the values follow a normal distribution with a mean of zero, with outliers within 4 min of separation. Figure 19 graphs the importance of the variables.

It can be seen that the most important variable is the time of day, followed by the day, as it is important whether it is a working day; finally, the minutes are of low importance as they are intermediate values between the hours. Figure 20 graphically represents the travel time data compared between the actual data and the synthetic data, as well as the 95% margin range, with the Random Forest Regressor model.

The Random Forest Regressor model uses 100 estimators, with a total of 1,939 data points. To corroborate the effectiveness of this model, it was compared with a linear

LGBM model and a sequential neural network model. It is important to mention that in order to apply these two systems, it is necessary to manipulate the data using MinMax scaling and data normalization. Figure 21 shows the performance of the linear system, configured for 100 estimators and a learning rate of 0.05. Figure 22 shows the dense neural network model, configured with 200 epochs. Both alternatives to the Random

Forest Regressor model are not as accurate for making predictions, given that they use the same amount of data and have a similar training process. Of course, increasing the training will proportionally increase the effectiveness.

Fig. 9. Testing travel times at the end of the route

4.5 Generation of Synthetic Data

With the trained model, it is possible to provide a series of continuous data to generate a synthetic dataset for predicting estimated travel time within the traffic flow at the specified coordinates. Figures 21 and 22 show graphs of estimated times and the time of day; these consistently follow the behavior of a working day and a non-working day.

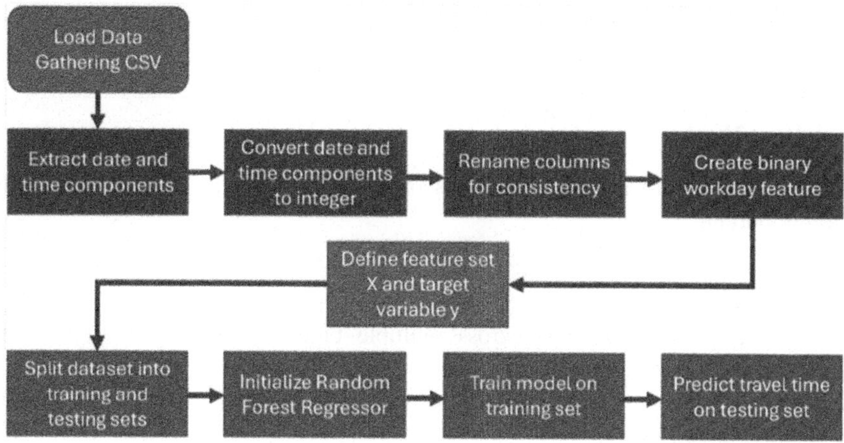

Fig. 10. Preprocessing, Model Training and Travel Time Prediction

5 Conclusions

This study confirmed that it is possible to effectively generate synthetic data related to traffic flow and estimated travel times through the application of artificial intelligence algorithms. The results highlight the relevance of integrating AI techniques with freely available geolocation tools such as Google Maps, which enable real-time data queries and enrich predictive modeling.

One of the main contributions of this work is the demonstration that synthetic data can be an efficient alternative when real world data is scarce, incomplete, or difficult to access due to privacy restrictions. By simulating traffic dynamics, researchers and practitioners can better understand patterns of urban mobility and anticipate potential congestion scenarios. Additionally, the findings emphasize the practical utility of AI-driven approaches in supporting everyday decision-making processes, from route planning to the design of smarter transportation systems. This suggests that intelligent data generation not only improves efficiency but also promotes sustainability by reducing unnecessary fuel consumption and minimizing time losses caused by traffic congestion.

Overall, this work demonstrates the potential of artificial intelligence in addressing real-world mobility challenges, particularly in urban contexts where traffic conditions change rapidly and unpredictably.

It should be mentioned that this work is limited by the data provided by Google Maps, meaning that if the extraction page has any bias, the model will inherit this bias.

Another bias is the exact time when the readings are taken; for example, during data gathering, Monday was a non-working day, which is not normally the case, so the system will fail when making predictions on Mondays.

The Random Forest Regressor model proves to be the most effective with the same amount of training and data, as the data does not follow normalization or linearity and a probabilistic decision approach is more effective. Data generation through this model benefits the collection of information for the development of new technological solutions related to traffic management.

5.1 Future Work

Future research should aim to expand the scope and depth of this study by considering several important aspects:

1. Larger and More Diverse Datasets

- Incorporating larger datasets across multiple cities or regions to improve the generalizability of results.
- Expanding the time horizon of data collection to capture long-term seasonal patterns and not only short-term variations.

2. Weekday vs. Non-Weekday Classification

- Conducting a more detailed analysis of the cyclical variations across the week, particularly distinguishing between weekdays, weekends, and public holidays.
- Exploring how cultural and regional differences influence traffic behaviors on specific days.

3. Incorporating Environmental and External Factors

- Including variables such as weather conditions, roadworks, and accidents that can significantly impact travel time predictions.
- Evaluating how these external factors interact with typical traffic cycles to create more robust predictive models.

4. Integration of Multi-Source Data

- Combining data from GPS devices, IoT sensors, and connected vehicles to enhance the precision of synthetic traffic simulations. – Exploring the integration of satellite data and aerial imagery to validate and calibrate traffic flow models.

5. Application of Advanced AI and Machine Learning Techniques

- Leveraging reinforcement learning, deep learning, or graph-based neural networks to improve the accuracy of traffic forecasting.
- Designing adaptive algorithms capable of learning from real-time data and continuously improving their predictions.

6. Sustainability and Smart City Applications

- Applying synthetic traffic modeling to support green mobility initiatives, such as electric vehicle routing or bike-sharing systems.

– Exploring how AI-driven traffic simulations can contribute to urban planning, public transportation optimization, and emission reduction strategies.

By addressing these aspects, future work can not only refine the accuracy of synthetic traffic data generation but also create practical tools for governments, city planners, and technology companies to design smarter, safer, and more sustainable urban environments.

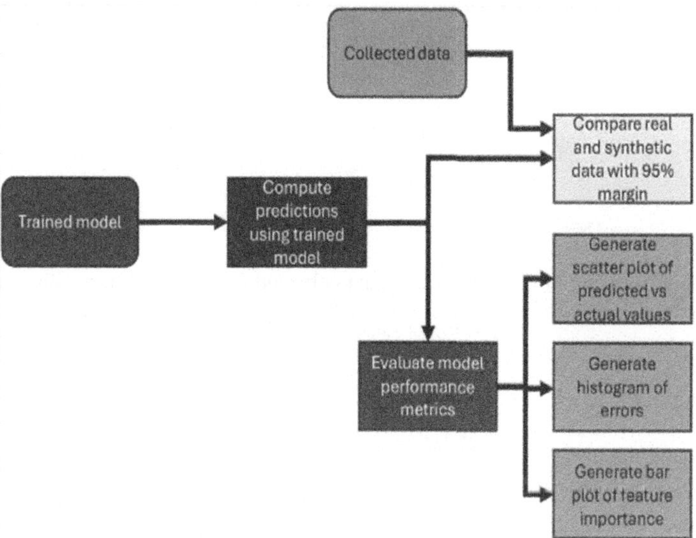

Fig. 11. Model Evaluation and Visualization of Traffic Prediction

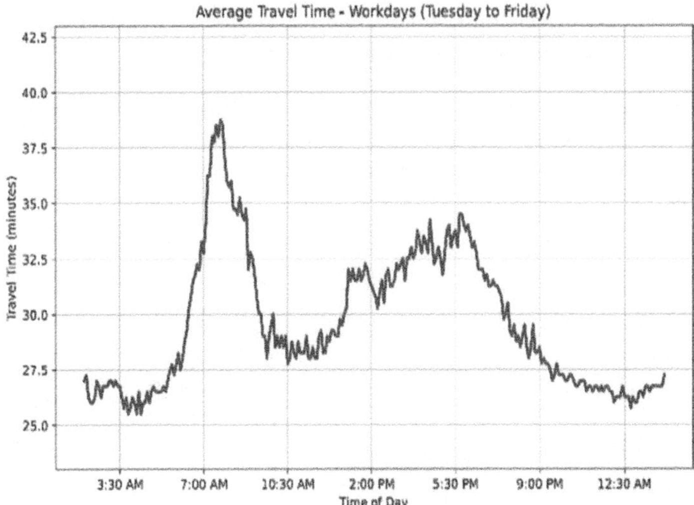

Fig. 12. Graph showing the average of the data collected on estimated travel time on working days.

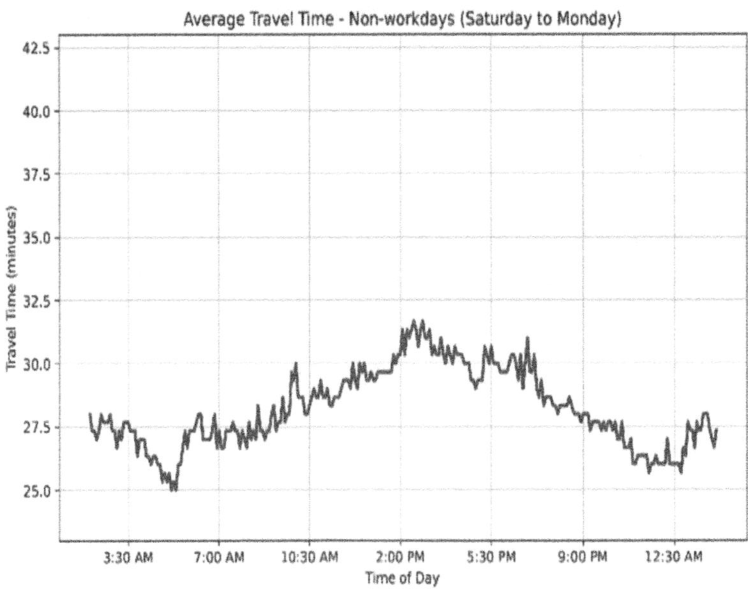

Fig. 13. Graph showing the average of the data collected on estimated travel time on non-working days.

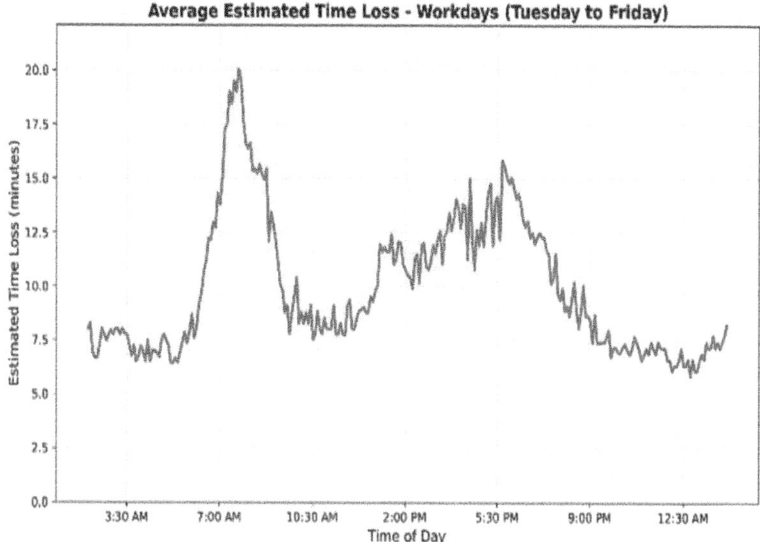

Fig. 14. Graph showing the average data collected on time lost in traffic on working days.

Fig. 15. Graph showing the average on time lost in traffic on non-working days.

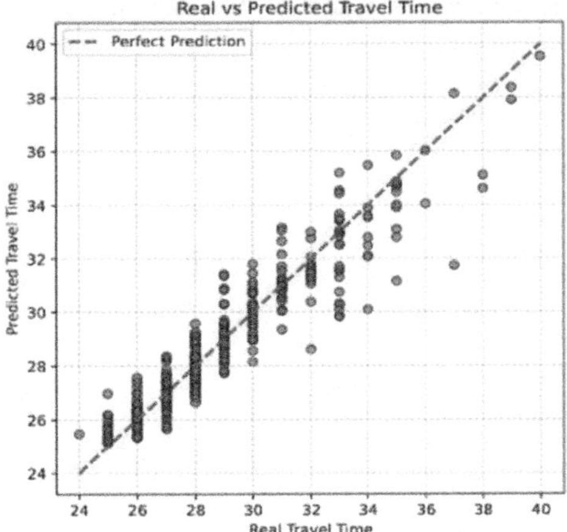

Fig. 16. Scatter plot of real data vs. synthetic data

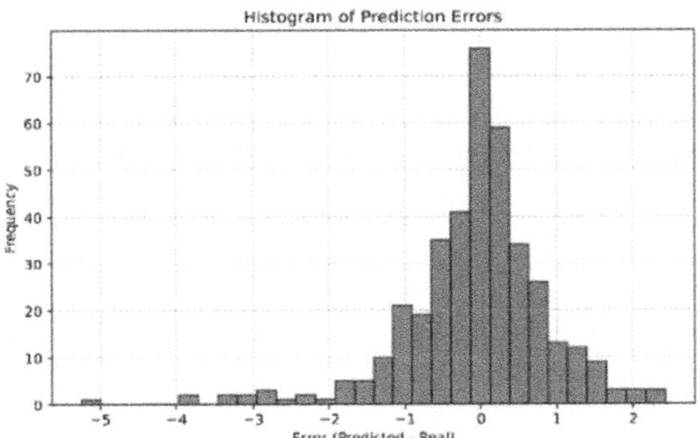

Fig. 17. Error histogram

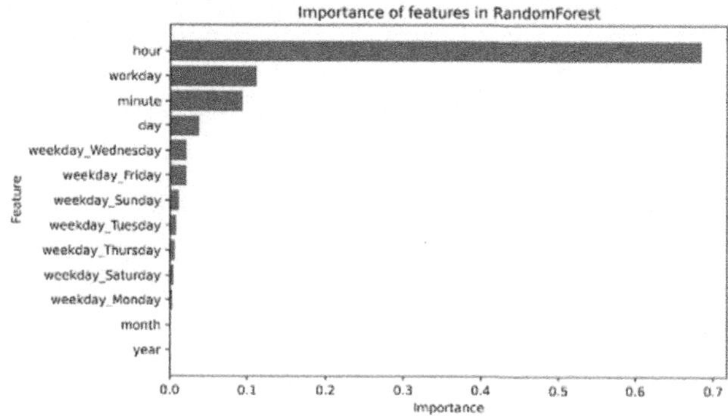

Fig. 18. Bar chart showing the importance of variables

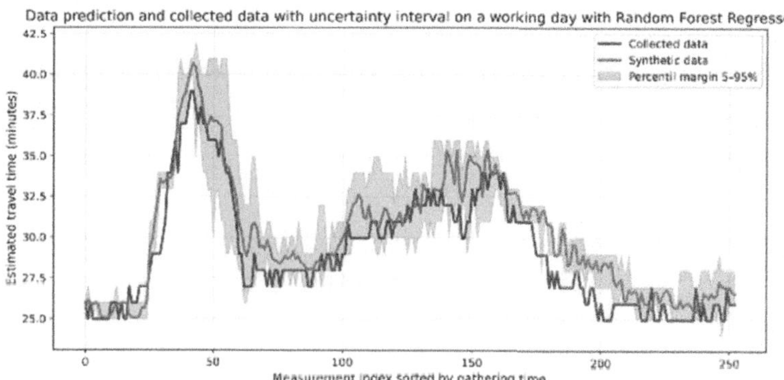

Fig. 19. Data prediction and collected data with uncertainty interval on a working day with Random Forest Regressor

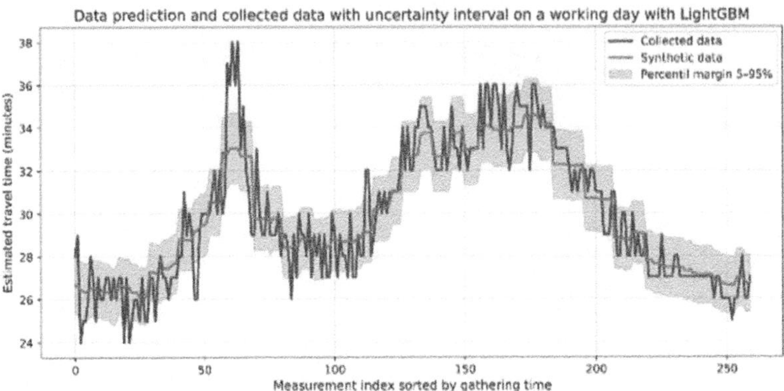

Fig. 20. Data prediction and collected data with uncertainty interval on a working day with LightGBM

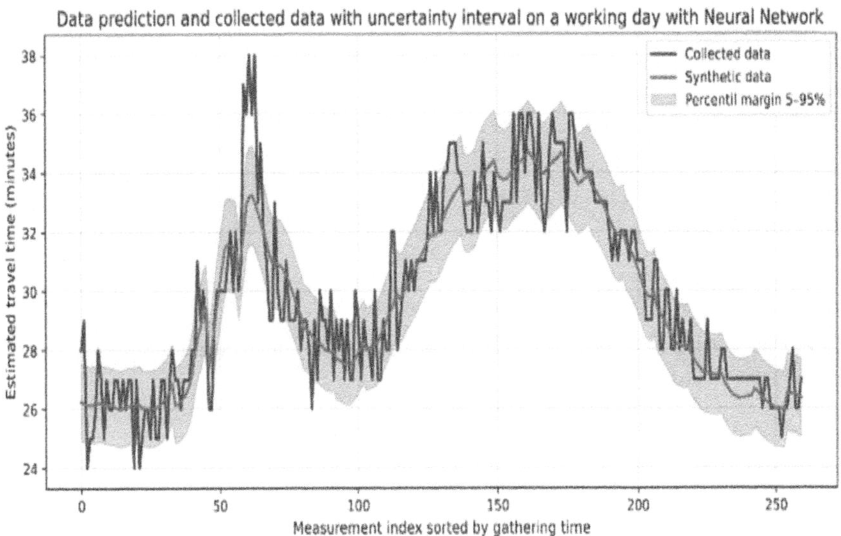

Fig. 21. Data prediction and collected data with uncertainty interval on a working day with Neural Network

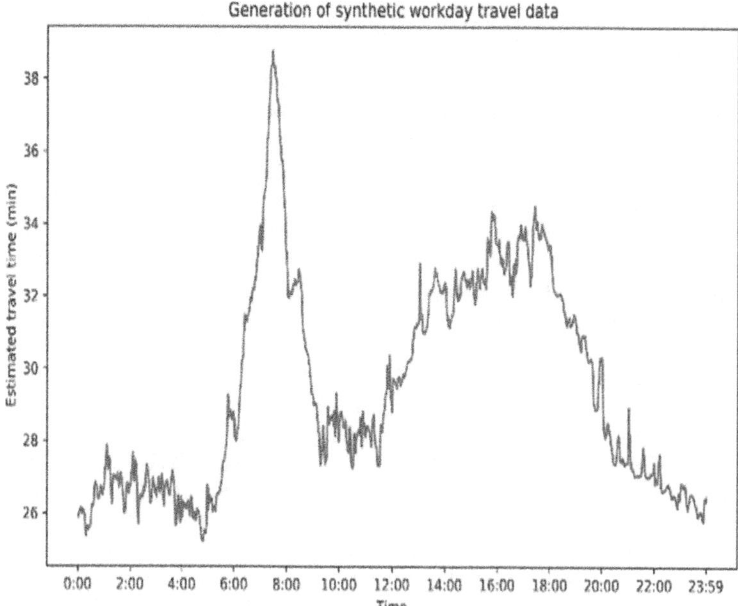

Fig. 22. Synthetic data for predicting travel time on a workday

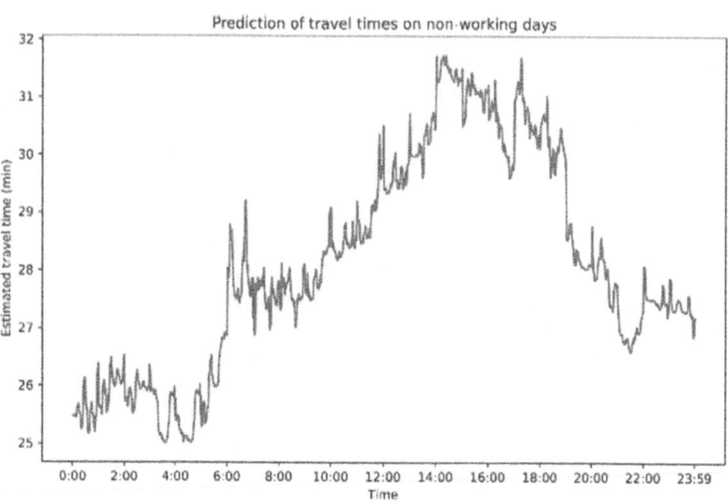

Fig. 23. Synthetic data for predicting travel time on non-working days

References

1. Grillenzoni, C.: Statistical models for urban growth forecasting: with application to the Baltimore-Washington area. Int. J. Appl. Earth Obs. Geoinf. **138**, 104451 (2025)
2. Zhang, L., Liu, K.: Modeling purposes of public transportation trips for human need-responsive urban mobility efficiency. IEEE Access. **13**, 124413–124428 (2025)
3. Mohanty, A., et al.: Integrating cognitive intelligence and VANET for effective traffic congestion detection in smart urban mobility. IEEE Access. **13**, 61538–61548 (2025)
4. Fereidooni, Z., Palesi, L.A.I., Nesi, P.: Multi-agent optimizing traffic light signals using deep reinforcement learning. IEEE Access. **13**, 106974–106988 (2025)
5. Ma, J., Chan, J., Rajasegarar, S., Leckie, C.: Multi-attention graph neural networks for city-wide bus travel time estimation using limited data. Expert Syst. Appl. **202**, 117057 (2022)
6. Kapp, A., Hansmeyer, J., Mihaljevic, H.: Generative models for synthetic urban mobility data: a systematic literature review. CoRR. **abs/2407**, 09198 (2024)
7. Banach, M., Dlugosz, R.: Solutions for planning smart hybrid public transportation system based on google maps and voronoi diagrams. J. Comput. Appl. Math. **472**, 116775 (2026)
8. Scucchia, M., Ferrara, M., Maltoni, D.: From gaming to research: GTA V for synthetic data generation for robotics and navigations. CoRR. **abs/2502**, 12303 (2025)
9. Kapp, A., Hansmeyer, J., Mihaljevic, H.: Generative models for synthetic urban mobility data: a systematic literature review. ACM Comput. Surv. **56**(4), 93: 1–93: 37 (2024)
10. Kikuchi, T., Fukuda, T., Yabuki, N.: Development of a synthetic dataset generation method for deep learning of real urban landscapes using a 3d model of a non-existing realistic city. Adv. Eng. Inform. **58**, 102154 (2023)
11. Medina-Salgado, B., Sánchez-Delacruz, E., Parra, P.P., Sierra, J.E.: Urban traffic flow prediction techniques: a review. Sustain. Comput. Inform. Syst. **35**, 100739 (2022)
12. Gellida-Coutiño, C., Rios-Cabrera, R., de Jesus Maldonado-Ramirez, A., Sánchez-Orta, A.: Robust drone video analysis for occluded urban traffic monitoring based on deep learning. IEEE Access. **13**, 109528–109538 (2025)
13. Xiong, W., Fonod, R., Alahi, A., Geroliminis, N.: Multi-source urban traffic flow forecasting with drone and loop detector data. CoRR. **abs/2501**, 03492 (2025)
14. Zhu, Y., Ye, Y., Wu, Y., Zhao, X., Yu, J.J.Q.: Synmob: creating high-fidelity synthetic GPS trajectory dataset for urban mobility analysis. In: Oh, A., Naumann, T., Globerson, A., Saenko, K., Hardt, M., Levine, S. (eds.) Advances in Neural Information Processing Systems 36: Annual Conference on Neural Information Processing Systems 2023. NeurIPS 2023, New Orleans, LA, USA., December 10 - 16, 2023 (2023)
15. Kelly, T., Gupta, J.: Predicting traffic congestion at urban intersections using data-driven modeling. CoRR. **abs/2404**, 08838 (2024)
16. Ascencio Laguna, J.A., Martner Peyrelongue, C.D., Bustos Rosales, A.: Implementación de un modelo de predicción de tráfico con aprendizaje profundo, Technical Report 707, Instituto Mexicano del Transporte, Querétaro, México, Acceso libre (2022)
17. Pichardo Corpus, J.A.: La concentración de la intermediación y la congestión vehicular en zonas metropolitanas de México. Estud. Demográficos Urbanos. **39**(3), 829–859 (2024) Acceso libre en Redalyc

Automatic Classification of Egg Freshness Using Ovoscopic Imaging and Convolutional Neural Networks

Flossi Puma-Ttito[1], Carlos Guerrero-Mendez[1](✉), Daniela Lopez-Betancur[1](✉), Rafael Castaneda-Diaz[1,2], Romulo Troncoso-Pacheco[1], Salvador Gomez-Jimenez[1], and David Navarro-Solis[1]

[1] Universidad Autónoma de Zacatecas, Unidad Académica de Ciencia y Tecnología de la Luz y la Materia (LUMAT), Zacatecas 98047, Mexico
{guerrero_mendez,danielalopez106}@uaz.edu.mx

[2] Instituto Politécnico Nacional, Unidad Profesional Interdisciplinaria de Ingeniería Campus Zacatecas (UPIIZ), Zacatecas 98160, Mexico

Abstract. This study proposes an automated system for assessing the freshness of chicken eggs through ovoscopy image analysis using Convolutional Neural Networks. Accurate freshness evaluation is essential for food safety and public health, particularly in regions where eggs are stored at ambient temperature, and for optimizing supply chains to reduce food waste. Ovoscopic images were acquired daily from eggs stored under ambient conditions over a 30-day period. The dataset was categorized into 30 classes, each representing a specific day of storage. The ResNet-18 architecture was implemented using transfer learning, with its fully connected layers adapted for the freshness classification task. Model performance was evaluated using classification accuracy, achieving a result of 80.36%. While the results indicate promising performance, especially at the extremes of the storage period, the model showed difficulty in distinguishing between consecutive days due to subtle visual changes. These findings suggest potential for practical implementation, although further validation with larger and more diverse datasets is needed to confirm generalizability and robustness.

Keywords: Egg freshness · Ovoscopic imaging · ResNet-18 · Food quality assessment · Convolutional Neural Network

1 Introduction

Eggs are a food of considerable nutritional interest due to their comprehensive composition. A comprehensive matrix of essential macronutrients, including high-biological-value lipids and high-quality proteins, is provided, along with a diverse spectrum of micronutrients, including vitamins, minerals, and trace elements. The energy contribution is moderate, approximately 140 kcal per 100 g. Beyond notable culinary versatility and inherent economic accessibility, eggs represent the most cost-effective animal source

L. Martínez-Villaseñor et al. (Eds.): MICAI 2025 Workshops, LNAI 16264, pp. 71–83, 2026.
https://doi.org/10.1007/978-3-032-17930-2_5

of proteins, vitamin A, iron, vitamin B12, riboflavin, and choline. Furthermore, establishment as the second most affordable source of zinc and calcium is observed [1]. Beyond its conventional nutritional profile, recent studies have demonstrated that both the internal contents and the shell of the egg are rich in compounds with antibacterial, anticancer, and immunostimulatory properties. This elevates eggs from being merely dietary components to valuable sources of bioactive substances. These compounds have applications not only in the food industry but also in a wide range of fields, including medicine, veterinary science, pharmacology, and biotechnology [2]. Despite these valuable attributes, eggs, a staple in the global diet, are consistently at risk of microbiological contamination, which directly compromises their quality, shelf life, and safety. The microflora present on the eggshell can not only accelerate deterioration but also serve as a reservoir for pathogens. In fact, egg consumption has been recurrently associated with a significant proportion of sporadic salmonellosis cases [3], underscoring the urgent need for rigorous control strategies. Beyond the immediate risk of contamination, egg quality is the cornerstone of its nutritional value. Following laying, an inevitable and continuous deterioration process begins, reflected in the decline of both internal and external quality. This process can be significantly accelerated by the failure to maintain optimal storage conditions, particularly with respect to temperature and storage duration. Although refrigeration has been proven to be the most effective method for mitigating the loss of internal quality, its implementation remains limited in some countries. Many individuals continue to store eggs at ambient temperature due to high refrigeration costs and the lack of regulatory requirements [4].

However, the poultry industry faces significant challenges in preserving egg quality throughout the entire supply chain. Due to their perishable nature, eggs undergo a progressive decline in freshness from the point of lay to the final consumer. This deterioration is exacerbated by inadequate control of temperature and humidity during storage and transportation, which not only reduces their economic value but also heightens food safety risks. Despite increasing public awareness regarding food safety and nutritional health, countries like Mexico currently lack standardized regulations for determining the shelf life of eggs. Predominant market practices rely on post-laying storage time as an indicator of freshness, a metric that proves insufficient as it overlooks environmental variables and potential mechanical damage from handling, both of which can facilitate bacterial contamination [5]. Freshness, considered the primary indicator of egg quality, directly influences its edibility, nutritional integrity, and suitability for processing. Specifically, albumen proteins, which are essential due to their functional properties in the food industry, such as foaming and gelling capacity, undergo degradation as freshness declines. Additionally, the reduced bioavailability of bioactive compounds and the physicochemical alterations in the yolk and albumen compromise both the safety and nutritional value of the product, leading to significant economic losses in the fresh egg industry. Therefore, accurate assessment of egg freshness is essential to ensure food safety and protect consumer health.

Two main approaches can be used to assess egg quality: a destructive method that involves breaking the egg to measure its contents, and a non-destructive method that allows for inspection of quality without compromising the integrity of the product.

The most commonly used destructive method is the Haugh Unit (HU), which relates the egg weight to the height of the albumen after breaking and is recognized as the industrial standard for evaluating internal quality [6].

As a non-destructive alternative, ovoscopy is often employed. This illumination-based technique can be used to infer the degree of egg freshness by assessing parameters such as the air cell size, yolk position, and the clarity of the internal contents [7]. In a similar manner, Artificial Intelligence (AI) can serve as a complementary approach to traditional non-destructive techniques for the assessment of egg freshness.

Humans possess advanced cognitive abilities that allow for processing complex information, solving problems, making decisions, and evaluating stimuli from both external environments and internal bodily states. Building on these human faculties, AI has been developed to enable computational systems to emulate such brain-like functions, learning from data through training [8]. This capability is now widely applied in diverse domains, including education, scientific research, and technological innovation. AI provides practical solutions for addressing human problems with greater efficiency. In particular, Convolutional Neural Networks (CNNs) are mathematical models that replicate human learning through computational structures organized in multiple layers of neurons capable of approximating any continuous function. These networks are primarily used in image analysis, including tasks such as classification and detection [9].

Within the field of food science, CNNs have been applied to assess and classify food products, detect spoilage or contamination, and estimate physical attributes such as size, color, and texture [10–13]. Their ability to automatically learn relevant features from image data makes them a promising tool for food quality evaluation and control.

A key subfield of AI is Deep Learning (DL), which enables computational models composed of multiple hierarchical layers to learn data representations at various levels of abstraction. Prominent examples of these applications include speech recognition, object recognition in visual data, and automatic detection [14]. Deep CNNs have achieved significant advances in the processing of images, video, speech, and audio for classification and identification tasks. Using AI and DL algorithms, automated classification systems have been developed to analyze images and detect defective or abnormal products with high precision, eliminating the need for human intervention. The importance of assessing egg freshness through non-destructive methods has driven numerous studies and the development of innovative techniques. Nakaguchi et al. [15] reported in 2022 that a non-destructive method using a thermal camera and DL models (YOLOv4, YOLOv5, EfficientDet) was developed to assess the freshness of quail eggs. Thermal images of 174 eggs were captured at 30, 50, and 60 days after the expiration date, augmented to 3,610, and split into training and validation sets. The models achieved F1-scores of 0.69, 0.89, and 0.86, indicating that expired eggs could have their shelf life extended by up to 2 weeks. A negative correlation ($R^2 = 0.676$) between air cell area and egg weight validated the method as a rapid, non-destructive tool for freshness evaluation. In 2022, Tae Hyong et al. [16] developed a Transfer Learning (TL) based DL model to predict egg freshness using the HU, a standard parameter reflecting internal egg quality. The model combines ResNet-18, for spatial feature extraction, with a Long Short-Term Memory (LSTM) network, capturing temporal dependencies, using non-destructive weight loss data obtained under real-time cold chain conditions. Data augmentation techniques were applied to expand the training set and improve model performance. The TL model reduced the Root Mean Square Error (RMSE) from 6.62 to 2.02 compared to a random forest regression model, and the Mean Absolute Error (MAE) decreased from 3.16 to 1.39 with data augmentation. These results suggest that the proposed model can be implemented in real cold chain environments to monitor egg freshness efficiently and non-destructively. In 2024, at Ondokuz Mayıs University, a CNN was employed by Sahin et al. [17] to assess egg freshness in a non-destructive manner. A total of 30 Leghorn eggs obtained from a commercial farm were stored under refrigeration at a constant temperature of 4 °C. Over a period of 29 consecutive days, the eggs were removed from the refrigerator solely for photography and then returned to refrigeration conditions. A total of 870 images were captured and organized according to the storage day. For model development, 70% of the images were used for training and 30% for validation. The images were processed using a modified ResNet architecture adapted to classify 29 freshness classes corresponding to each storage day. The model achieved a classification accuracy of 91.78% after 400 iterations, with cross-validation performed every 50 cycles. This approach demonstrated that it is possible to evaluate egg freshness quickly and non-destructively, without intensive image pre-processing. The results indicate that AI can provide effective solutions for automated egg freshness classification in both industrial and consumer applications.

Although previous studies evaluated egg freshness under refrigeration or low-temperature conditions, many people consume or store eggs at room temperature. For this reason, the present study applies a CNN to assess egg freshness at room temperature over a 30-day period using the non-destructive ovoscopy method.

2 Methods, Techniques and Instruments

This section describes the use of a CNN model for classifying egg freshness based on images obtained through ovoscopy. The equipment, methods, and performance metrics employed in this study are detailed.

2.1 Data Acquisition

The present study was conducted over a 30-day period at room temperature (23 °C) to simulate typical egg storage conditions in Mexican households. The study duration was determined based on the European Union guidelines [18], which recommend a consumption period of 28 days for food products, including eggs, and the United States Department of Agriculture (USDA) Food Safety and Inspection Service recommendations, which establish a consumption period of up to 30 days after packaging [19].

For this investigation, 30 eggs were collected from a local farm in Zacatecas. Each egg was photographed daily between three and four times using a Magicfly LED cold-light ovoscopy and an ATVIO A498 webcam with a resolution of 1280x720. At the end of the 30-day period, a total of 3,487 photographs were obtained, which were organized into folders corresponding to each day. The experimental configuration is shown in Fig. 1.

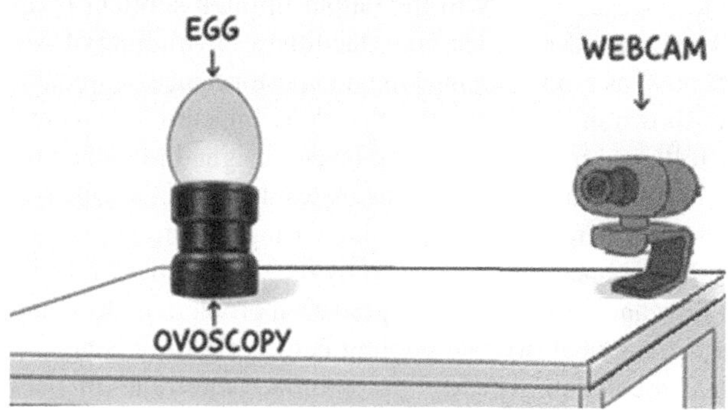

Fig. 1. Schematic diagram of the experimental design for ovoscopy image acquisition.

To build a robust classification dataset, numerous egg images were systematically acquired under controlled conditions. The experimental setup is illustrated in Fig. 1, and the resulting internal views obtained through ovoscopic illumination can be observed in the representative images (see Fig. 2).

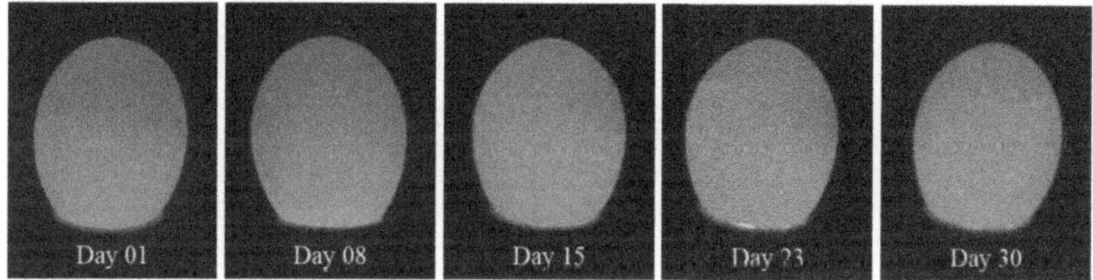

Fig. 2. Representative ovoscopic images of eggs taken on Days 01, 08, 15, 23, and 30 of storage, showing progressive internal changes.

2.2 CNN Model

CNNs are a type of artificial neural network designed to process images through a series of interconnected blocks. The primary function of their layers is to extract the most relevant features from each image. These networks consist of stacked convolutional layers, and over time, various architectures have been developed to optimize learning efficiency [20].

In image classification tasks, CNN-based models are widely used. Among high-precision architectures, ResNet stands out, according to Torchvision reports, for its use of residual blocks that enable efficient training of deep networks. In this study, ResNet-18 will be evaluated as a potential architecture to balance accuracy, complexity, and processing time in the classification of egg freshness.

ResNet-18 is a deep CNN consisting of 18 layers, including 17 convolutional layers and one fully connected layer. Its architecture incorporates residual blocks, which allow the input to connect directly to the output through shortcut (skip) connections. This approach, known as residual learning, facilitates the training of deep networks by mitigating issues such as gradient vanishing and performance degradation in very deep architectures. As shown in Fig. 3, the ResNet-18 architecture begins with a 7 × 7 convolutional layer followed by a max pooling layer, designed to reduce the initial spatial resolution. This is followed by four groups of residual blocks with 64, 128, 256, and 512 channels, which progressively extract increasingly complex features. Each block incorporates residual connections (indicated by the dotted lines in the figure), facilitating information flow and mitigating the degradation problem in deep networks. Finally, the network performs global average pooling before the fully connected layer, which produces the final prediction. This design optimizes the trade-off between accuracy, computational efficiency, and network depth, making it suitable for image classification tasks, such as assessing egg freshness via ovoscopy.

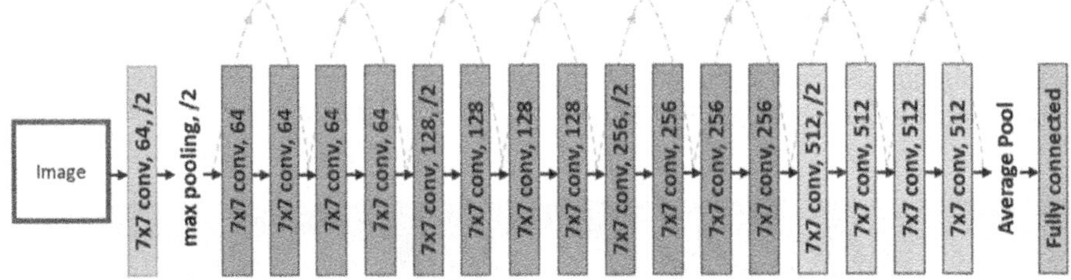

Fig. 3. Schematic representation of the ResNet-18 architecture.

2.3 Transfer Learning (TL)

Training a CNN from scratch requires a large volume of labeled images, which entails high computational costs and prolonged training times. To overcome these limitations, an efficient alternative is TL, which involves reusing a pre-trained model and fine-tuning only specific layers for the target task [21]. In the present study, the ResNet-18 architecture with weights pre-trained on ImageNet [22] will be employed and adapted for classifying egg freshness across 30 categories. Most of the network layers will be frozen, modifying only the final layer to output the 30 required classes, which will be trained using the egg dataset. Consequently, the model contains approximately 11,689,512 parameters, of which only 1,026 are trainable during fine-tuning. The model occupies roughly 44.7 MB of disk space.

2.4 Data Augmentation

Data augmentation was employed to increase the diversity of the image dataset and enhance CNN training. In this study, two transformations were applied: RandomHorizontalFlip, which randomly flips images horizontally, and RandomRotation within a range of 0 to 10°, which slightly rotates the images. These transformations introduce additional variations, allowing the model to learn more general features, reduce overfitting, and improve its generalization to unseen images, as shown in Fig. 4. The rotation range was deliberately restricted to 0–10° to preserve the anatomical orientation of the egg and avoid introducing unrealistic distortions that could mislead the model during training.

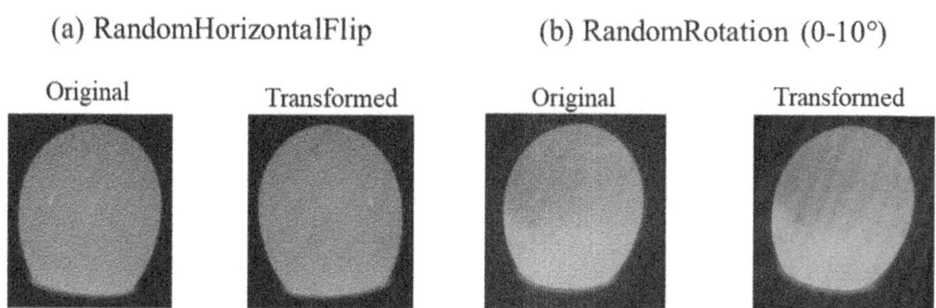

Fig. 4. Examples of data augmentation applied to egg images: (a) RandomHorizontalFlip transformation; (b) RandomRotation within a range of 0–10°. These augmentations introduce variability to improve model generalization.

2.5 Training Parameters

Hyperparameters are fundamental and adjustable components within CNNs, as these parameters largely determine the training dynamics and the model's performance on specific tasks. Selecting the appropriate parameters is crucial to achieving optimal network performance. Among them, those related to the optimization strategy play a particularly critical role. In AI, the process of searching for parameter configurations that maximize model performance is referred to as optimization. The AdamW optimizer, an improved variant of Adam, is widely employed due to its ability to decouple weight decay regularization from gradient-based parameter updates. This feature enables more effective regularization and enhances the model's generalization to unseen data. AdamW has been shown to significantly reduce test error on image classification datasets, outperforming the classical Adam optimizer and approaching the performance of SGD combined with advanced learning rate scheduling strategies, such as cosine annealing. For these reasons, AdamW is considered a robust and efficient choice for optimizing DL models, contributing both to training stability and faster convergence [23].

One of the most critical hyperparameters is the "Learning rate", which controls the magnitude of parameter updates during gradient descent. In other words, it determines how quickly the model adapts its weights in response to the loss function. An excessively high value may lead to oscillations and hinder convergence, whereas a very low value can slow down the training process. Selecting an appropriate learning rate is therefore essential to ensure stable and efficient error minimization [24]. Another key hyperparameter is the number of "Epochs", which corresponds to the number of times the entire training dataset is passed through the network. In this study, 100 epochs were used for each trial, allowing for consistent parameter adjustment without premature overfitting. The "Batch size" also plays an important role, as it specifies the number of samples processed before updating the model parameters. A batch size of 28 images was adopted, providing a suitable balance between update stability and computational efficiency. Finally, a random "Seed" of 27 was fixed to ensure reproducibility of the experiments. The selection of these hyperparameters was performed through a random search with five independent trials, which enabled the identification of configurations that provided an effective trade-off between accuracy and computational efficiency. The hyperparameters used are lists in Table 1.

Table 1. Tuning hyperparameters in the training process.

Hyperparameter	Value
Optimization algorithm	AdamW
Learning rate	0.001
Bach size	28
Epochs	100
Seed	27
Run	1

The algorithms were developed and executed using Python 3, a widely used open-source programming language. For the implementation and training of the CNN models, the PyTorch library (version 1.9.1) was employed. Additionally, the Torchvision package was utilized to facilitate model training and evaluation, providing access to a variety of pre-trained architectures and essential tools for advanced computer vision applications.

2.6 Performance Evaluation

- Confusion matrix

To summarize the training outcomes, the confusion matrix is employed as a fundamental tool for evaluating the performance of a CNN model. This matrix provides a detailed comparison between the predicted and true classes, where columns correspond to the actual classes and rows correspond to the predicted classes. Values along the main diagonal indicate correctly classified instances, while off-diagonal values represent misclassifications. The matrix is further characterized by four key metrics: True Positives (TP), cases correctly classified as belonging to a class; True Negatives (TN), instances correctly identified as not belonging to a class; False Positives (FP), instances incorrectly classified as belonging to a class; and False Negatives (FN), cases that belong to a class but were incorrectly predicted as not belonging. Analysis of these metrics enables precise assessment of model performance and supports the effective tuning of hyperparameters, thereby enhancing the CNNs accuracy and generalization in image classification tasks [25].

- Accuracy: This metric represents the proportion of correct predictions made by the model relative to the total number of predictions [26]. It is defined as:

$$Accuracy = \frac{TP + TN}{(TP + TN + FP + FN)}. \tag{1}$$

Although accuracy provides an overall measure of model performance, it is particularly appropriate in this study because the dataset used is balanced across all classes.

3 Results and Discussion

For the classification of egg freshness under ambient storage conditions, 80% of the image dataset was allocated for training and the remaining 20% for validation. The proposed system, based on the ResNet-18 architecture and trained through TL, achieved a final accuracy of 80.36%. Accuracy was selected as the primary evaluation metric given the balanced nature of the dataset.

To provide a more detailed assessment of model performance, a confusion matrix was generated after 100 training epochs (Fig. 5). The matrix revealed that most misclassifications occurred between consecutive storage days (e.g., day 14 vs. day 15). This outcome suggests that the visual differences captured through ovoscopy are minimal from one day to the next, making it challenging to discriminate between adjacent freshness classes. As a result, the model frequently shifted predictions by one or two neighboring days.

Notably, classification performance was more consistent at the extremes of the storage period (very fresh or considerably aged eggs), where morphological differences are more pronounced, whereas higher confusion rates were observed in intermediate stages. These findings are consistent with the progressive and incremental nature of freshness deterioration, which is characterized by gradual rather than abrupt changes in internal egg appearance.

These misclassifications can be attributed to the subtle and gradual nature of the internal changes occurring within eggs over short time intervals. Indeed, the transition from one day to the next does not exhibit a drastic shift, which constitutes the main challenge for automated visual discrimination.

Furthermore, beyond the technical accuracy achieved by the model, the findings of this study hold significant implications for the egg value chain, from producers to consumers. It should be emphasized that accurate assessment of freshness is not merely a matter of organoleptic quality but is also fundamental to food safety and public health. In regions such as ours, where storage at ambient temperature is a common practice, the absence of standardized evaluation methods can lead to the consumption of eggs with advanced deterioration. As a result, the risk of foodborne illnesses such as salmonellosis is considerably increased.

Moreover, the ability to classify egg freshness daily with high precision enables producers and retailers to optimize inventory management, thereby reducing food waste and ensuring that only the freshest products reach the market. Consequently, this

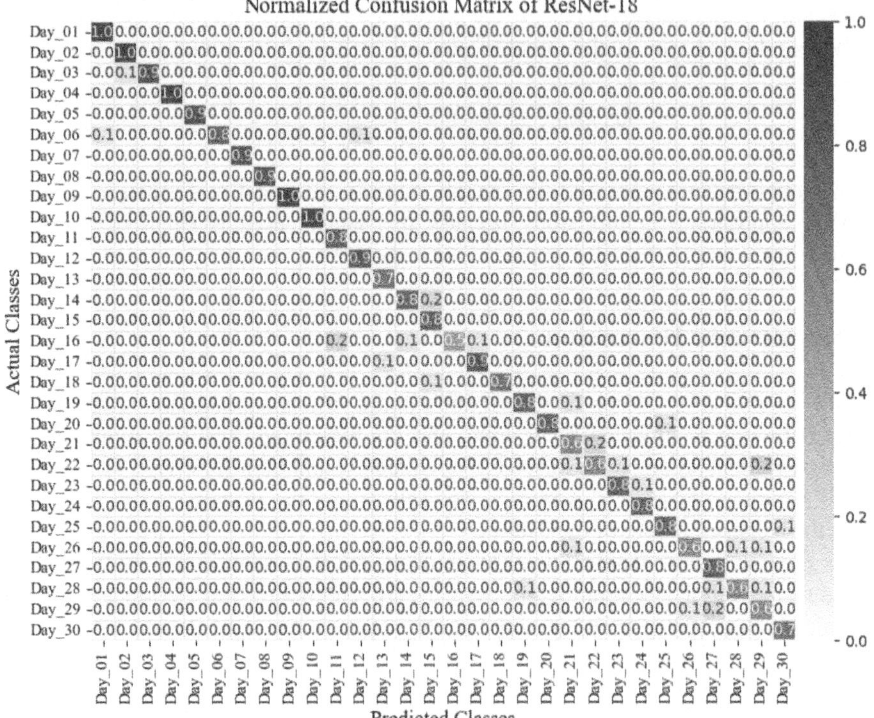

Fig. 5. Normalized confusion matrix of the ResNet-18 model applied to egg freshness classification across 30 storage-day categories.

not only enhances industry profitability but also strengthens consumer confidence by guaranteeing product quality.

Ultimately, by employing a non-destructive and low-cost methodology, our system provides a practical solution for regions lacking advanced refrigeration infrastructure or high-end evaluation methods. In this regard, accuracy is not solely a technical achievement but rather a tangible step toward the implementation of safer and more efficient practices in food production.

The validation loss and accuracy curves (Fig. 6) indicate that the model followed a stable and progressive learning process throughout the training epochs. The sustained decrease in loss reflects effective parameter optimization, while the stabilization of the accuracy curve demonstrates that the network reached an adequate point of convergence.

The evolution of the learning curves, characterized by a sustained decrease in loss and a stabilization of accuracy, validates the robustness of our training process. Importantly, the absence of significant overfitting, indicated by the close alignment between the training and validation curves, confirms that the network not only learned effectively from the data but also acquired the ability to generalize its findings to new images.

In this context, the technical reliability of our methodology supports the validity of the results obtained and, more importantly, highlights its potential for practical application within the industry. The ResNet-18 architecture proved to be an effective tool for the

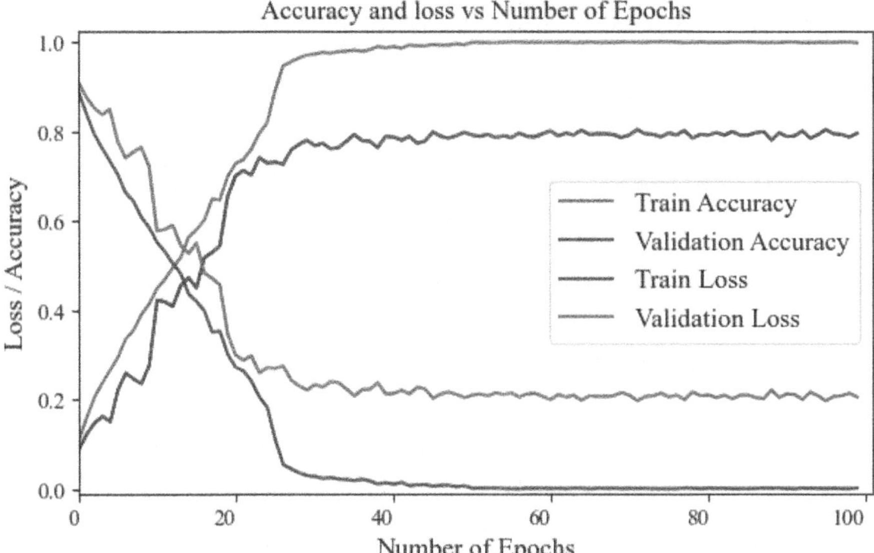

Fig. 6. Training and validation curves demonstrating consistent learning dynamics and generalization of the ResNet-18 model.

classification of egg freshness through ovoscopy, thereby providing a solid foundation for future research and developments in the field of food safety.

Nevertheless, a limitation identified was the difficulty of the model in distinguishing between storage days that present very subtle visual variations. For future research, the use of higher-resolution datasets or the integration of multispectral analysis techniques could be explored, as these approaches may capture light-based differences imperceptible to the human eye and potentially improve accuracy in discriminating between contiguous days. Additionally, experimenting with more complex model architectures or applying more sophisticated data augmentation strategies could further mitigate this challenge.

4 Conclusions

This study provides preliminary evidence supporting the feasibility of classifying the freshness of eggs stored at ambient temperature using ovoscopy images and CNNs. The ResNet-18 model, trained via transfer learning, achieved an accuracy of 80.36%, indicating that this non-destructive and automated approach may be suitable for assessing egg freshness under real storage conditions.

However, the confusion matrix revealed that most misclassifications occurred between consecutive storage days, reflecting the gradual and subtle nature of freshness deterioration. These limitations, along with the absence of external validation and potential dataset biases, must be addressed in future work to ensure broader applicability and reliability.

Overall, while the proposed system shows promise for industrial quality control and food safety applications, further research is required to strengthen its generalizability and to explore more advanced architectures and validation strategies.

References

1. Réhault-Godbert, S., Guyot, N., Nys, Y.: The Golden egg: nutritional value, bioactivities, and emerging benefits for human health. Nutrients. **11**, 684 (2019). https://doi.org/10.3390/nu11030684
2. Lesnierowski, G., Stangierski, J.: What's new in chicken egg research and technology for human health promotion? - A review. Trends Food Sci. Technol. **71**, 46–51 (2018). https://doi.org/10.1016/j.tifs.2017.10.022
3. Sokołowicz, Z., Kačániová, M., Dykiel, M., Augustyńska-Prejsnar, A., Topczewska, J.: Influence of storage packaging type on the microbiological and sensory quality of free-range table eggs. Anim. Open Access J. MDPI. **13**, 1899 (2023). https://doi.org/10.3390/ani13121899
4. S., d., Oliveira, G., dos Santos, V.M., Rodrigues, J.C., Santana, Â.P.: Conservation of the internal quality of eggs using a biodegradable coating. Poult. Sci. **99**, 7207–7213 (2020). https://doi.org/10.1016/j.psj.2020.09.057
5. Gao, Z., Zheng, J., Xu, G.: Research Progress and technological application prospects of comprehensive evaluation methods for egg freshness. Foods. **14**, 1507 (2025). https://doi.org/10.3390/foods14091507
6. Eisen, E.J., Bohren, B.B., McKean, H.E.: The Haugh unit as a measure of egg albumen quality. Poult. Sci. **41**, 1461–1468 (1962). https://doi.org/10.3382/ps.0411461
7. Baker, R.C., Vadehra, D.V.: A comparison of candling eggs with other methods of determining internal egg quality. Poult. Sci. **51**, 991–994 (1972). https://doi.org/10.3382/ps.0510991
8. Zhao, J., Wu, M., Zhou, L., Wang, X., Jia, J.: Cognitive psychology-based artificial intelligence review. Front. Neurosci. **16**, 1024316 (2022). https://doi.org/10.3389/fnins.2022.1024316
9. Guerrero-Mendez, C., Saucedo-Anaya, T., Moreno, I., Araiza-Esquivel, M., Olvera-Olvera, C., Lopez-Betancur, D.: Digital holographic interferometry without phase unwrapping by a convolutional neural network for concentration measurements in liquid samples. Appl. Sci. **10**, 4974 (2020). https://doi.org/10.3390/app10144974
10. Lee, K.-S.: Multispectral food classification and caloric estimation using convolutional neural networks. Foods. **12**, 3212 (2023). https://doi.org/10.3390/foods12173212
11. Ding, H., Hou, H., Wang, L., Cui, X., Yu, W., Wilson, D.I.: Application of convolutional neural networks and recurrent neural networks in food safety. Foods. **14**, 247 (2025). https://doi.org/10.3390/foods14020247
12. Luo, N., Xu, D., Xing, B., Yang, X., Sun, C.: Principles and applications of convolutional neural network for spectral analysis in food quality evaluation: A review. J. Food Compos. Anal. **128**, 105996 (2024). https://doi.org/10.1016/j.jfca.2024.105996
13. Kato, S., Wada, N., Ito, R., Shiozaki, T., Nishiyama, Y., Kagawa, T.: Snack texture estimation system using a simple equipment and neural network model. Future Internet. **11**, 68 (2019). https://doi.org/10.3390/fi11030068
14. LeCun, Y., Bengio, Y., Hinton, G.: Deep learning. Nature. **521**, 436–444 (2015). https://doi.org/10.1038/nature14539
15. Nakaguchi, V.M., Ahamed, T.: Fast and non-destructive quail egg freshness assessment using a thermal camera and deep learning-based air cell detection algorithms for the revalidation of the expiration date of eggs. Sensors. **22**, 7703 (2022). https://doi.org/10.3390/s22207703
16. Kim, T.H., Kim, J.H., Kim, J.Y., Oh, S.E.: Egg freshness prediction model using real-time cold chain storage condition based on transfer learning. Foods. **11**, 3082 (2022). https://doi.org/10.3390/foods11193082

17. SahiN, H.A., Onder, H.: Use of deep learning to determine the freshness of egg. Iğdır Üniversitesi Fen Bilim. Enstitüsü Derg. **14**, 493–500 (2024) https://doi.org/10.21597/jist.1385147
18. Regulation (EU) No 1169/2011 of the European Parliament and of the Council of 25 October 2011 on the provision of food information to consumers, amending Regulations (EC) No 1924/2006 and (EC) No 1925/2006 of the European Parliament and of the Council, and repealing Commission Directive 87/250/EEC, Council Directive 90/496/EEC, Commission Directive 1999/10/EC, Directive 2000/13/EC of the European Parliament and of the Council, Commission Directives 2002/67/EC and 2008/5/EC and Commission Regulation (EC) No 608/2004 (Text with EEA relevance). (2011)
19. Shell Eggs from Farm to Table: Food Safety and Inspection Service. http://www.fsis.usda.gov/food-safety/safe-food-handling-and-preparation/eggs/shell-eggs-farm-table. Accessed 08 Sept 2025
20. Puma-Ttito, F., Guerrero-Mendez, C., Lopez-Betancur, D., Saucedo-Anaya, T., Castaneda-Diaz, R., Martinez-Ytuza, L.: Convolutional neural network models for classifying of peach (Prunus persica L). In: Martínez-Villaseñor, L., Ochoa-Ruiz, G., Montes Rivera, M., Barrón-Estrada, M.L., Acosta-Mesa, H.G. (eds.) Advances in Computational Intelligence. MICAI 2024 International Workshops, pp. 121–132. Springer Nature, Switzerland, Cham (2025). https://doi.org/10.1007/978-3-031-83879-8_10
21. López-Betancur, D., et al.: Comparación de arquitecturas de redes neuronales convolucionales para el diagnóstico de COVID-19. Comput. Sist. **25**, 601–615 (2021) https://doi.org/10.13053/cys-25-3-3453
22. ImagenNet. https://www.image-net.org/index.php, Accessed 09 Sept 2025
23. Liu, X., Qi, H., Jia, S., Guo, Y., Liu, Y.: Recent advances in optimization methods for machine learning: A systematic review. Mathematics. **13**, 2210 (2025). https://doi.org/10.3390/math13132210
24. Lopez-Betancur, D., et al.: Convolutional neural network for measurement of suspended solids and turbidity. Appl. Sci. **12**, 6079 (2022). https://doi.org/10.3390/app12126079
25. Lopez-Betancur, D., et al.: Evaluation of optimization algorithms for measurement of suspended solids. Water. **16**, 1761 (2024). https://doi.org/10.3390/w16131761
26. Puma-Ttito, F.D., Guerrero-Mendez, C., Lopez-Betancur, D., Saucedo-Anaya, T., Castaneda-Diaz, R., Martinez-Ytuza, L.: Application of deep learning for automated peach classification: A study based on ResNet architectures. Int. J. Comb. Optim. Probl. Inform. **16**, 106–117 (2025) https://doi.org/10.61467/2007.1558.2025.v16i3.1141

Evaluation of Hospital Response to Various Types of Cancer in Southwestern Mexico Using TOPSIS Multi-Criteria Analysis

Jesús Alberto Palma-García[1,4](✉), Alberto Ochoa-Zezzati[2], Iván Gallardo-Bernal[1], and Fredy Omar Beltrán-Anaya[3](✉)

[1] Facultad de Ciencias y Tecnologías de la Información, Av. De las colinas No 37A Fracc. Las Playas, C.P, 39390 Acapulco de Juárez, Guerreo, México
24500649@uagro.mx

[2] Universidad Autónoma de Ciudad Juárez Manuel Díaz H, No. 518-B Zona Pronaf Condominio 656 688 2100, Ciudad Juárez, México

[3] Laboratorio de Diagnóstico e Investigación en Salud, Facultad de Ciencias Químico Biológicas, Av. Lázaro Cárdenas s/n, C.P., 39390 Chilpancingo de los Bravo, Guerrero, México
fredybeltran@uagro.mx

[4] Secretaría de Salud Guerrero, Av. Ruffo Figueroa #6 Col. Burocratas, C.P., 39090 Chilpancingo de los Bravo, Guerrero, México

Abstract. This study demonstrates how TOPSIS, a multi-criteria decision-making method, effectively ranks hospital responses to the seven most prevalent cancer types in southwestern Mexico. Artificial intelligence supports the evaluation of criteria such as clinic availability, early detection, staff training, infrastructure, rural coverage, prevention, vaccination, multidisciplinary treatment, and palliative care. Results show that TOPSIS provides healthcare professionals with a practical tool for comparing hospital performance, underscoring the value of multicriteria methods in medical decision-making.

Keywords: TOPSIS · Hospital Response · Multicriteria Analysis · Artificial Intelligence · Decision-Making Systems · Cancer

1 Introduction

Multi-criteria decision-making methods are an efficient statistical tool for describing situations in which it is necessary to integrate the results of different studies to make a general judgment. They are considered dynamic and complex processes [1]. The TOPSIS method seeks a positive and a negative ideal solution. Once these are obtained, it chooses alternatives that are closest to the positive ideal solution and furthest from the negative ideal solution. This method was developed by Hwang and Yoon in 1981 [2] and has been widely used in logistics, engineering, design, and business [3]. It is used in medical research on ovarian cancer, as noted in Masmali's research [4], and in cancer classification based on microarrays by Fattah et al. [5].

L. Martínez-Villaseñor et al. (Eds.): MICAI 2025 Workshops, LNAI 16264, pp. 84–97, 2026.
https://doi.org/10.1007/978-3-032-17930-2_6

In Mexico, cancer represents a major public health problem, with around 195,500 new cases diagnosed in 2020, with a high mortality rate of 46%. Breast cancer is the most common type, with an incidence of 39.9% per 100,000 inhabitants, followed by prostate cancer at 39.1%, cervical cancer at 13.2%, and colorectal cancer at 10.9% [6]. Even though Guerrero has one of the lowest mortality rates from malignant tumors, at 55.06 per 100,000 inhabitants in 2020 [7], factors such as socioeconomic inequality and limited hospital infrastructure hinder access to timely diagnosis and treatment [8]. In this regard, socioeconomic and intrahospital limitations hinder equitable access to the diagnosis and treatment of oncological diseases, underscoring the need for tools that optimize decision-making [9]. Studies implementing multi-criteria decision analysis (MCDA) have been relevant for identifying useful criteria for decision-making in healthcare, disease prioritization, capital investment decisions, and clinical decisions such as treatment and prescription [10]. The use of techniques for ordering preferences by similarity to the actual solution, such as TOPSIS, has proven limited but useful for specific applications. It is a tool applied in research, development, and planning, clinical decisions, and, less frequently, in setting priorities [10].

Strategies such as early detection based on analysis of cellular alterations have been implemented to prevent cancer. Even with early diagnosis and specific treatment, the infrastructure required to deliver it must be assessed, as well as its feasibility and potential survival rate. In diseases such as COVID-19, it was essential to know the post-pandemic hospital response. This meant using existing resources without being able to make changes to the health service infrastructure in several countries, while countries such as Denmark and Italy introduced more policies to improve the hospital response [11].

There are few studies in southwestern Mexico that implement strategies based on multi-criteria decision analysis focused on health. Therefore, this document outlines the criteria to be evaluated from their objectives to their methodologies concluding with future work.

This study proposes a multi-criteria evaluation using the TOPSIS method to analyze hospital capacity and prioritize interventions that could improve cancer care in southwestern Mexico. It also proposes developing a Python script based on the TOPSIS method, using structured data, to evaluate, prioritize, and rank the hospital's response to breast cancer, liver cancer, prostate cancer, colorectal cancer, gastric cancer, lung cancer, and cervical cancer. These are the seven most prevalent and studied types of cancer in southwestern Mexico. Research shows that multi-criteria decision-making methods such as TOPSIS, VIKOR, and the Analytic Hierarchy Process (AHP) can produce different rankings depending on the weighting scheme and the characteristics of the criteria. In contrast, TOPSIS is a methodology with higher performance for evaluation, as it is easy to apply, scalable, and its use not only enriches analysis but can also favor the adoption of results by decision-makers in terms of public policy implementation. Compared to AHP, TOPSIS does not require pairwise comparisons, which greatly reduces the potential for differences in weight allocation and cognitive load. VIKOR, on the other hand, seeks a balanced compromise solution, considers the compensation of criteria, and balances group satisfaction. Compared to TOPSIS, which selects a variant based on the combination of indicators closest to the theoretical ideal, VIKOR selects a variant based on intermediate performance across all aspects [1, 12].

2 Theoretical Foundations

Over several decades, TOPSIS has adapted to various research needs, including handling imprecise data with fuzzy data management [9]. More recent developments focus on integrating modern learning and optimizing weight allocation in problems with multiple variables [13].

In the health sector, data-driven decision-making is essential to address challenges such as inequality in hospital infrastructure and access to treatment. Building on methods like TOPSIS, which can integrate and objectively prioritize complex criteria, the sector can combine clinical efficacy with Big Data to manage hundreds or thousands of alternatives [14]. Furthermore, managing large amounts of data with different tools has helped ensure process automation. Recognizing the wealth of medical data available, the healthcare sector needs to effectively manage this data to evaluate different areas, from infrastructure to the impact of the information generated [10].

Turning to specific regions, in southwestern Mexico, health decision-making is hampered by significant negative factors, with socioeconomic and cultural factors impacting the effectiveness of preventive actions. These variables influence the measurement values of indicators for the prevention and treatment of different diseases [15].

A representative example of these regional difficulties is the municipality of Cochoapa el Grande, located in the mountainous region of Guerrero. This municipality, considered in 2008 by the United Nations to be the poorest in Mexico, has an illiteracy rate of 53.1% and a Gini index of 0.435 [16], conditions that worsen access to specialized health services. In comparison, the city of Chilpancingo offers transportation to the port of Acapulco every 30 min, lower poverty and illiteracy rates, and is located 1.5 h from the port and approximately 30 min from the bus station to the State Cancer Institute.

Considering these geographic and infrastructural factors, it is important to note that the Dr. Arturo Beltrán Ortega State Cancer Institute in Guerrero is located in the port of Acapulco, approximately 6 h and 45 min from the municipal capital of Cochoapa el Grande (see Fig. 1).

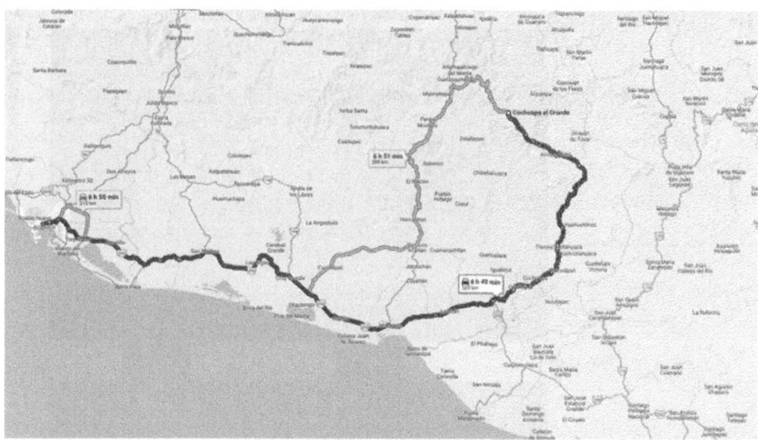

Fig. 1. Approximate route from the municipality of Cochoapa el Grande, Gro., to the Dr. Arturo Beltrán Ortega State Cancer Institute in the municipality of Acapulco de Juárez, Gro [17].

3 Materials and Methods

In this study, the Likert scale was used to structure the data on the seven most prevalent types of cancer in southwestern Mexico. The highest value was taken and modified on a scale of 1–7. This series is a commonly used instrument in social science surveys [18]. The data analyzed were: a) Specialized clinics, b) Early detection tests, c) Training of medical personnel, d) Psychological support network, e) Hospital infrastructure, f) Advanced treatments, g) Coverage in rural areas, h) Prevention campaigns, i) Vaccination, j) Early diagnosis, k) Multidisciplinary treatment, and l) Nutritional programs and palliative care, obtained from the National Survey on Health and Aging in Mexico (ENASEM 2021) and from INEGI's SIMBAD Municipal Database System, consulted in August 2020, which closed operations in the same year (see Fig. 2), and processed using a Python script in which the TOPSIS method was implemented [19].

For the decision matrix data structure for the seven types of cancer, the data were converted to a Likert scale ranging from 1 to 7 using a Python script hosted on GitHub, accessible via the QR code shown in the results section. The conversion was performed using the following formula:

$$\mathrm{L} = (\mathrm{value} - \mathrm{minoriginal}/\mathrm{maxoriginal} - \mathrm{minoriginal})^{*}\ (\mathrm{maxlikert} - \mathrm{minlikert}) + \mathrm{minlikert} \quad (1)$$

The values in each column were added together as part of the procedure to find the weights shown in Table 1, using the formula:

$$\sum\nolimits_{i=1}^{m} x_{ij} \quad (2)$$

To perform matrix normalization, each value is divided by the total sum of the columns as shown in Table 2, using the following formula:

$$r_{ij} = \sum\nolimits_{i=1}^{m} x_{ij} \quad (3)$$

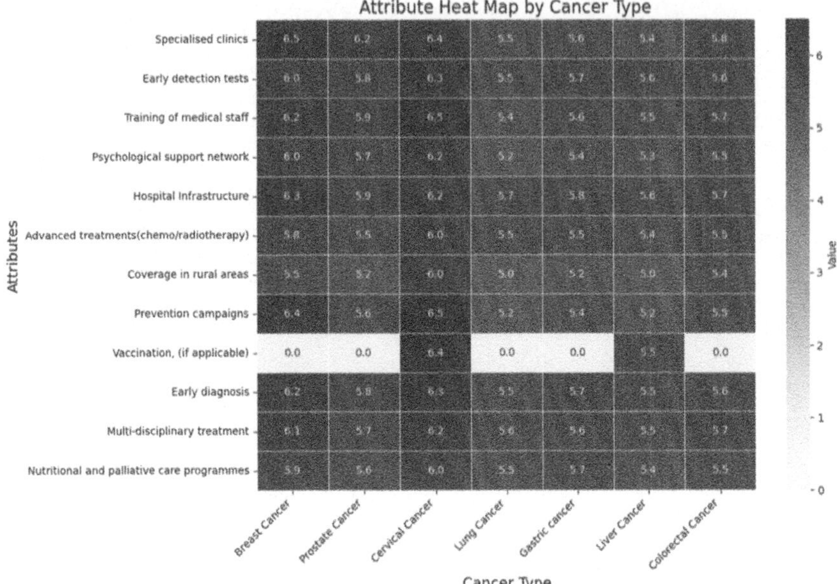

Fig. 2. The decision matrix consists of data on the seven cancers with the highest incidence in the state of Guerrero on the y-axis, and, on the x-axis, their criteria, obtained from converting ENASEM2021 and SIMBAD data to a Likert scale.

Table 1. The sum of the attributes for each type of cancer, converted to a Likert scale.

Breast Cancer	Prostate Cancer	Cervical Cancer	Lung Cancer	Gastric Cancer	Liver Cancer	Colorectal Cancer
66.9	*62.9*	*75*	*59.6*	*61.2*	*64.9*	*61.5*

Entropy was calculated using formula number 4, and the values obtained are shown in Table 3.

$$e_j = -\ln\frac{(m)}{1}\sum_{i=1}^{m} r_{ij}\ln(r_{ij}) \quad (4)$$

The dispersion of values shown in Table 4 was calculated by subtracting one from the entropy value of each type of cancer, using the formula:

$$d_j = 1 - e_j \quad (5)$$

The weights to be used in the methodology are calculated by dividing the dispersion formula values by the sum of the total dispersion values, which, when added together, should equal 1. The values are shown in Table 5 and were obtained using the formula:

$$w_j = \frac{\sum_{j=1}^{n} d_j}{d_j} \quad (6)$$

Table 2. Standardized data matrix for the seven cancer phenotypes under study.

Breast Cancer	Prostate Cancer	Cervical Cancer	Lung Cancer	Gastric Cancer	Liver Cancer	Colorectal Cancer
0.1	*0.1*	*0.09*	*0.09*	*0.09*	*0.08*	*0.09*
0.09	*0.09*	*0.08*	*0.09*	*0.09*	*0.09*	*0.09*
0.09	*0.09*	*0.09*	*0.09*	*0.09*	*0.08*	*0.09*
0.09	*0.09*	*0.08*	*0.09*	*0.09*	*0.08*	*0.09*
0.09	*0.09*	*0.08*	*0.1*	*0.09*	*0.09*	*0.09*
0.09	*0.09*	*0.08*	*0.09*	*0.09*	*0.08*	*0.09*
0.08	*0.08*	*0.08*	*0.08*	*0.08*	*0.08*	*0.09*
0.1	*0.09*	*0.09*	*0.09*	*0.09*	*0.08*	*0.09*
0	*0*	*0.09*	*0*	*0*	*0.08*	*0*
0.09	*0.09*	*0.08*	*0.09*	*0.09*	*0.08*	*0.09*
0.09	*0.09*	*0.08*	*0.09*	*0.09*	*0.08*	*0.09*
0.09	*0.09*	*0.08*	*0.09*	*0.09*	*0.08*	*0.09*

Table 3. Entropy values calculated for determining the weights in the TOPSIS methodology.

Cancer type	Value
Breast Cancer	*0.96*
Prostate Cancer	*0.96*
Cervical Cancer	*1*
Lung Cancer	*0.96*
Gastric Cancer	*0.96*
Liver Cancer	*1*
Colorectal Cancer	*0.96*

The methodology indicates that the data must be normalized again, so the values in each column must be divided, then each of the values must be divided by the sum of the squares of each value (see Fig. 3) using the formula:

$$fn\sqrt{x_1^2 + x_2^2 + dots + x_n^2} \tag{7}$$

To calculate the weighted matrix, it is necessary to multiply each of the values of the already normalized matrix by each of the calculated weights (see Fig. 4), using the formula:

$$v_{ij} = w_j{}^* r_{ij} \tag{8}$$

Table 4. Dispersion values used in the calculation of methodological weights.

Cancer type	Value
Breast Cancer	*0.04*
Prostate Cancer	*0.04*
Cervical Cancer	*0*
Lung Cancer	*0.04*
Gastric Cancer	*0.04*
Liver Cancer	*0*
Colorectal Cancer	*0.04*

Table 5. Weights assigned for the weighting of the decision matrix

Cancer type	Value
Breast Cancer	*0.2*
Prostate Cancer	*0.2*
Cervical Cancer	*0*
Lung Cancer	*0.2*
Gastric Cancer	*0.2*
Liver Cancer	*0*
Colorectal Cancer	*0.2*
Total sum of the values	*1*

The ideal positive solution (A + A+) is calculated, i.e., the maximum value for each cancer type. The values are shown in Table 6.

The ideal negative solution (A-A-) must be calculated to complete the methodological steps, i.e., the minimum value for each cancer type. The values are shown in Table 7.

The Euclidean distance is calculated for both alternatives positive and negative by taking the square root of the weighted matrix minus the positive solution, and squaring the positive solution. And the square root of the weighted matrix minus the negative solution, squared for the negative solution, using the formulas:

$$d^{+}_{i=1^{n}} = \left(\sum\nolimits_{i=1^{n}} \left(v_{ij} - A^{+}_{j}\right)^{2}\right) \; d^{-}_{i} = \sqrt{\left(\sum\nolimits_{j=1^{n}} \left(v_{ij} - A^{-}_{j}\right)^{2}\right)} \tag{9}$$

The calculated values of both positive and negative Euclidean distances are shown in Tables 8 and 9, respectively.

To calculate the TOPSIS performance measure for each value, first subtract the negative distance from the positive distance. Next, divide the negative distance by this

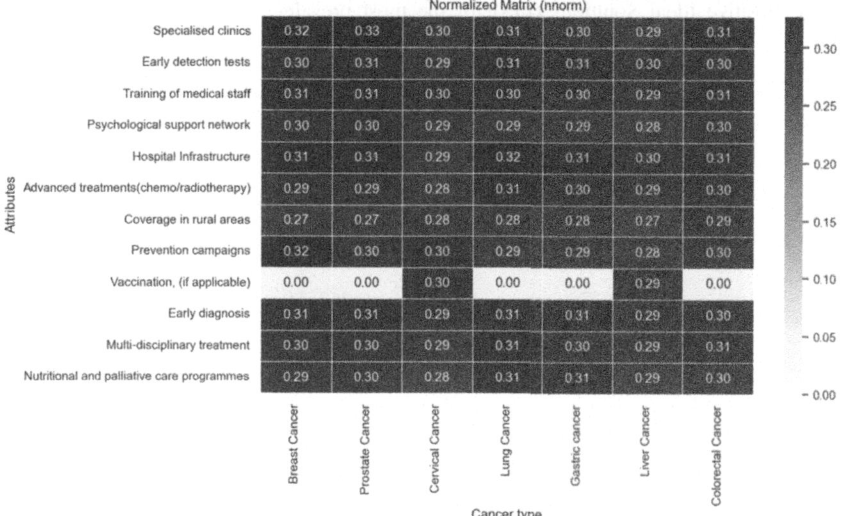

Fig. 3. Standardized decision matrix and weighting criteria for the seven types of cancer.

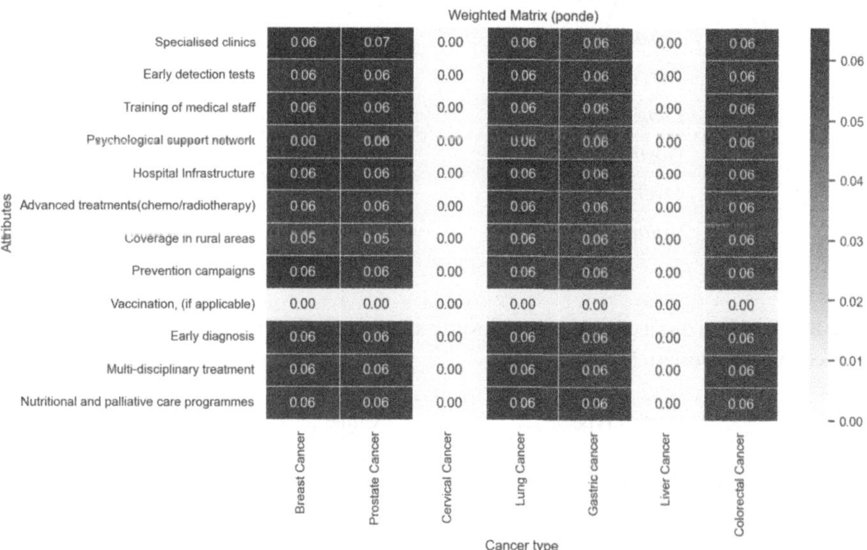

Fig. 4. Visual representation of the weighted decision matrix resulting from the multi-criteria analysis process. The rows correspond to the seven cancer types studied, and the columns represent the criteria evaluated. The values reflect the integration of the methodological weights.

result (see Fig. 5), following the formula:

$$C_i = di^{-} / \left(di^{+} + di^{-} \right) \tag{10}$$

Table 6. Positive Ideal Solutions (PIS) for the most prevalent cancer types in southwestern Mexico.

Cancer type	Value
Breast Cancer	*0.064522*
Prostate Cancer	*0.065392*
Cervical Cancer	*0.000270*
Lung Cancer	*0.063274*
Gastric Cancer	*0.062570*
Liver Cancer	*0.000323*
Colorectal Cancer	*0.062112*

Table 7. Negative ideal solutions (NIS) for the most prevalent types of cancer in southwestern Mexico.

Cancer type	Value
Breast Cancer	*0.000000*
Prostate Cancer	*0.000000*
Cervical Cancer	*0.000249*
Lung Cancer	*0.000000*
Gastric Cancer	*0.000000*
Liver Cancer	*0.000288*
Colorectal Cancer	*0.000000*

Table 8. Euclidean distances to the ideal positive solution (D+) for the seven most prevalent types of cancer in southwestern Mexico.

Cancer type	Value
Breast Cancer	*0.066581*
Prostate Cancer	*0.068068*
Cervical Cancer	*0.000044*
Lung Cancer	*0.064518*
Gastric Cancer	*0.063420*
Liver Cancer	*0.000051*
Colorectal Cancer	*0.062691*

Table 9. Euclidean distances to the ideal negative solution (D-) for the seven most prevalent types of cancer in southwestern Mexico.

Cancer type	Value
Breast Cancer	*0.200428*
Prostate Cancer	*0.200210*
Cervical Cancer	*0.000044*
Lung Cancer	*0.199608*
Gastric Cancer	*0.199154*
Liver Cancer	*0.000088*
Colorectal Cancer	*0.198619*

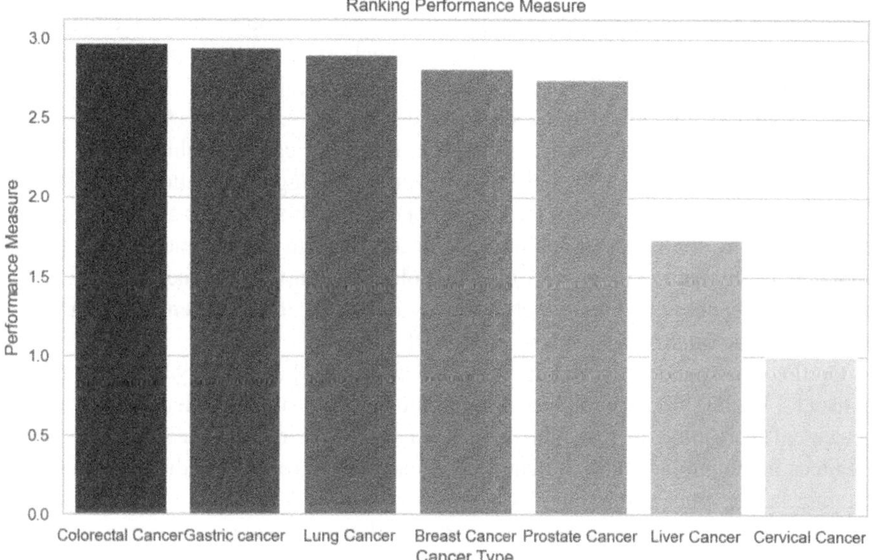

Fig. 5. First, the seven cancer types were comparatively evaluated and then performance was quantified using a 1 to 7 point Likert scale.

The scripts used are available at the following GitHub repository address: https://github.com/linuxnewbie84/topsis. Alternatively, you can scan the QR code to access the repository (see Fig. 6).

Fig. 6. Scanning this QR code allows you to quickly access this project's official GitHub repository: linuxnewbie84/topsis (https://github.com/linuxnewbie84/topsis). Here, you will find the full implementation of the TOPSIS method developed for this study, as well as a script for converting data to a Likert scale. Visit the repository to access the code and resources.

4 Discussion and Results

This study evaluated the hospital response to the seven most prevalent types of cancer in southwestern Mexico, using the TOPSIS multicriteria method to determine the values, including criteria such as vaccination, early detection campaigns, infrastructure, and specialized clinics, among others. The results indicate significant differences in the quality, coverage, and effectiveness of medical services.

The data indicate that colorectal, gastric, and lung cancers achieved the highest performance values (2.96, 2.94, and 2.89, respectively), suggesting better availability and efficiency of medical services for these types of cancer. This suggests greater investment in infrastructure, screening campaigns, and/or advances in specific medical treatments. Studies indicate that the inclusion of public policies on modifiable factors helps reduce cases of these cancers, and that timely access to diagnosis and treatment has a significant influence on the quality of health services [20].

On the other hand, liver and cervical cancer obtained alarmingly low performance scores (1.73 and 0.99), which place them in the category of insufficient or poor-quality services. The results suggest that there are barriers to treatment access and limited resources in the public health system. In cervical cancer, research indicates that socioeconomic factors play a role, but also points to a decline in screening tests such as Pap smears and HPV testing during the pandemic, with prevalence recovering in 2023 [21].

5 Conclusions and Future Work

The findings in this study can serve as a basis for improving cancer care in southwestern Mexico, particularly by strengthening early detection and hospital infrastructure for cancer types with lower performance measures. The study prioritizes intervention needs, with the types of cancer with the lowest scores being those furthest from the ideal positive solution, indicating a less effective hospital response. This provides a basis for determining that greater investment is needed from health institutions. Prioritizing specialized clinics, prevention programs, or staff training optimizes the impact of public health policies in regions with greater socioeconomic inequality.

The analysis points to the influence of various variables, including socioeconomic and infrastructure factors, illustrated using the municipality of Cochoapa el Grande as a reference. By including coverage criteria in rural areas and hospital infrastructure in the TOPSIS model, it is possible to highlight the impact of disparities in equitable access to cancer care. Therefore, the methodological integration validates the use of TOPSIS as a decision-making criterion, requiring the balancing of clinical and social factors to generate public policies that enable access to better, optimized cancer care.

Future research could expand the use of additional variables, such as patient perception, the impact of geographic access, and the inclusion of new public health policies. In addition, longitudinal studies could be conducted to evaluate the long-term evolution of indicators. A data-driven platform could also be developed to strengthen decision-making in an objective, efficient, and adaptable manner across different scenarios.

The extension of classical TOPSIS to a Pythagorean fuzzy logic (PFS) environment is also proposed. The model used is effective and assumes the accuracy of the input data. However, in the context of public health, the evaluation of qualitative criteria (training of medical personnel and the psychological support network) is often based on the opinions of experts in the medical and psychological fields, which can lead to inaccuracies and vagueness. Therefore, we propose the use of Pythagorean Fuzzy Dimensional Analysis (PFDA), as developed by Villa Silva et al. [22], as it combines the power of Pythagorean Fuzzy Sets (PFS), which allow decision-makers to express their preferences with a degree of membership and non-membership whose sum of squares is less than or equal to one, thus making uncertainty broader than Fuzzy Sets. This capacity marks the subjectivity of evaluations of criteria such as hospital and socioeconomic criteria.

Therefore, the expansion of PFDA could represent a significant methodological advance for health decision-making in southwestern Mexico, offering a more sophisticated tool for resource allocation in a scenario of qualitative and quantitative information.

Acknowledgments. Jesús Alberto Palma García is a master's degree student from Program of Master in Data Science and Intelligent System, Universidad Autónoma de Guerrero (UAGro), and received fellowship (CVU 639732) from SECIHTI.

Disclosure of Interest.

All other authors declare no conflict of interest

References

1. Opricovic, S., Tzeng, G.-H.: Compromise solution by MCDM methods: a comparative analysis of VIKOR and TOPSIS. Eur. J. Oper. Res. **156**(2), 445–455 (2004). https://doi.org/10.1016/S0377-2217(03)00020-1
2. Hwang, C.L., Yoon, K.: Methods for multiple attribute decision making. In: Multiple Attribute Decision Making, Vol. 186, In: Lecture Notes in Economics and Mathematical Systems, vol. 186, pp. 58–191. Springer Berlin Heidelberg, Berlin, Heidelberg (1981). https://doi.org/10.1007/978-3-642-48318-9_3
3. Behzadian, M., Khanmohammadi Otaghsara, S., Yazdani, M., Ignatius, J.: A state-of the-art survey of TOPSIS applications. Expert Syst. Appl. **39**(17), 13051–13069 (2012). https://doi.org/10.1016/j.eswa.2012.05.056

4. Masmali, I., Ahmad, A., Azeem, M., Koam, A.N.A., Alharbi, R.: TOPSIS method based on intuitionistic fuzzy soft set and its application to diagnosis of ovarian cancer. Int. J. Comput. Intell. Syst. **17**(1), 161 (2024). https://doi.org/10.1007/s44196-024-00537-1
5. Abd-ElFattah, I.M., Khedr, W.I., Sallam, K.M.: A TOPSIS based method for gene selection for cancer classification. Int. J. Comput. Appl. **67**(17), 39–44 (2013). https://doi.org/10.5120/11490-7195
6. Globocan: Cáncer en México Globocan. Accedido: 8 de enero de 2025. [En línea]. Disponible en: https://gco.iarc.who.int/today/
7. I. Conapo: Estadísticas a Propósito del día Mundial contra el Cáncer, 78/24, Feb. 2024. [En línea]. Disponible en: https://www.inegi.org.mx/contenidos/saladeprensa/aproposito/2024/EAP_CANCER24.pdf
8. Gutiérrez, J.P., Heredia-Pi, I., Hernández-Serrato, M.I., Pelcastre-Villafuerte, B.E., Torres-Pereda, P., Reyes-Morales, H.: Desigualdades en el acceso a servicios, base de las políticas para la reducción de la brecha en salud. Salud Públ. Méx. **61**(6), 726 (2019). https://doi.org/10.21149/10561
9. Campolina, A.G., Estevez-Diz, M.D.P., Abe, J.M., de Soárez, P.C.: Multiple criteria decision analysis (MCDA) for evaluating cancer treatments in hospital-based health technology assessment: the paraconsistent value framework. PLoS One. **17**(5), e0268584 (2022). https://doi.org/10.1371/journal.pone.0268584
10. Gongora-Salazar, P., Rocks, S., Fahr, P., Rivero-Arias, O., Tsiachristas, A.: The use of multicriteria decision analysis to support decision making in healthcare: an updated systematic literature review. Value Health J. Int. Soc. Pharmacoeconomics Outcomes Res. **26**(5), 780–790 (2023). https://doi.org/10.1016/j.jval.2022.11.007
11. Burau, V., et al.: Post-COVID health policy responses to healthcare workforce capacities: a comparative analysis of health system resilience in six European countries. Health Policy. **139**, 104962 (2024). https://doi.org/10.1016/j.healthpol.2023.104962
12. Chu, M.T., Shyu, J., Tzeng, G.H., Khosla, R.: Comparison among three analytical methods for knowledge communities group-decision analysis. Expert Syst. Appl. **33**(4), 1011–1024 (2007). https://doi.org/10.1016/j.eswa.2006.08.026
13. Chen, S.J., Hwang, C.L.: Fuzzy multiple attribute decision making methods. In: Fuzzy Multiple Attribute Decision Making, en Lecture Notes in Economics and Mathematical Systems, vol. 375, pp. 289–486. Springer Berlin Heidelberg, Berlin, Heidelberg (1992). https://doi.org/10.1007/978-3-642-46768-4_5
14. Kumar, S., Singh, M.: Big data analytics for healthcare industry: impact, applications, and tools. Big Data Min. Anal. **2**(1), 48–57 (2019). https://doi.org/10.26599/BDMA.2018.9020031
15. Consejo Nacional de Evaluación de la Política: CONEVAL. Pobreza municipal 2010–2015. (2022). [En línea]. Disponible en: https://www.coneval.org.mx/Medicion/Paginas/Pobreza-municipal.aspx
16. de E. de M. Secretaría: Cochoapa el Grande: Economía, empleo, equidad, calidad de vida, educación, salud y seguridad pública, Data México. Accedido: 19 de enero de 2025. [En línea]. Disponible en: https://www.economia.gob.mx/datamexico/es/profile/geo/cochoapa-el-grande

17. M. Google y INEGI: Recorrido de Cochoapa al IECAN, Google Maps. Accedido: 19 de enero de 2025. [En línea]. Disponible en: https://www.google.com.mx/maps/dir/Cochoapa+el+Grande+Guerrero/Instituto+Estatal+de+Cancerolog%C3%ADa+%22Dr.+Arturo+Beltr%C3%A1n+Ortega%22,+Avenida+Adolfo+Ruiz+Cortinez+A,+Alta+Progreso,+Acapulco,+Guerrero/@16.9339298,-99.7133524,9z/data=!3m1!4b1!4m13!4m12!1m5!1m1!1s0x85c8fe7a6ab02bfd:0x8835312653aaf968!2m2!1d-98.455388!2d17.193389!1m5!1m1!1s0x85ca5791b26a0da3:0x2286f90cd0c7cb9f!2m2!1d-99.8860152!2d16.873625?entry=ttu&g_ep=EgoyMDI1MDExNS4wIKXMDSoASAFQAw%3D%3D
18. D. Bertram: Likert Scales... are the meaning of life. (2008). [En línea]. Disponible en: http://poincare.matf.bg.ac.rs/~kristina/topic-dane-likert.pdf
19. INEGI: ENASEM2021. Accedido: 24 de octubre de 2025. [En línea]. Disponible en: https://www.inegi.org.mx/app/descarga/ficha.html?tit=1573818&ag=0&f=csv
20. Tofani, A.A., et al.: Mortalidade por Câncer de Cólon e Reto no Brasil e suas Regiões entre 2006 e 2020. Rev. Bras. Cancerol. **70**(1) (2024). https://doi.org/10.32635/2176-9745.RBC.2024v70n1.4404
21. León-Maldonado, L.S., et al.: Tamizaje del cáncer cervical. Salud Públ. Méx. **66**(4), 547–554 (2024). https://doi.org/10.21149/15894
22. Villa Silva, A.J., Pérez Dominguez, L.A., Martínez Gómez, E., Alvarado-Iniesta, A., Olguín, I.J.C.P.: Dimensional analysis under Pythagorean fuzzy approach for supplier selection. Symmetry. **11**(3), 336 (2019). https://doi.org/10.3390/sym11030336

Classification of Low-Grade Squamous Intraepithelial Lesions of the Cervix Using Deep Learning Models

Jesús Alberto Palma-García[1,2](✉), Berenice Illades-Aguiar[3], Mónica Espinoza-Rojo[4], Mónica Ramírez-Ruano[5], Alberto Ochoa-Zezzati [6], Iván Gallardo-Bernal[1], and Fredy Omar Beltrán-Anaya[7](✉)

[1] Facultad de Ciencias y Tecnologías de la Información, Av. De las colinas No 37A Fracc. Las Playas, C.P, 39390 Acapulco de Juárez, Guerreo, Mexico
24500649@uagro.mx

[2] Secretaría de Salud Guerrero, Av. Ruffo Figueroa #6 Col. Burócratas, C.P., Chilpancingo de los Bravo, Guerreo, Mexico

[3] Laboratorio de Biomedicina Molecular, Facultad de Ciencias Químico Biológicas, Av. Lázaro Cárdenas s/n, Chilpancingo de los Bravo, Guerreo, México

[4] Laboratorio de Biología Molecular y Genómica, Facultad de Ciencias Químico Biológicas, Av. Lázaro Cárdenas s/n, Chilpancingo de los Bravo, Guerreo, México

[5] SECIHTI-Universidad Autónoma de Guerrero, Av. Lázaro Cárdenas s/n, Chilpancingo de los Bravo, Guerreo, México

[6] Universidad Autónoma de Ciudad Juárez Manuel Díaz H, No. 518-B Zona Pronaf Condominio · 656 688 2100, Ciudad Juárez, Mexico

[7] Laboratorio de Diagnóstico e Investigación en Salud, Facultad de Ciencias Químico Biológicas, Av. Lázaro Cárdenas s/n, C.P., Chilpancingo de los Bravo, Guerreo, Mexico
fredybeltran@uagro.mx

Abstract. Advances in computer vision, especially with convolutional neural networks and transformer models, have improved the accuracy and efficiency of medical image analysis, facilitating more accessible and accurate diagnoses in the biomedical field. Early detection of cervical cancer (CaCu) precursor lesions is key to preventing the development of this neoplasm, but achieving an accurate diagnosis requires great expertise due to the morphological complexity of the cells involved. In this project, we implemented the development of a deep learning computer vision tool to identify and classify squamous intraepithelial lesions of the cervix using a Papanicolaou cytology database, observing 83% accuracy and a macro F1-score index of 0.83 using an artificial convolutional neural network.

Keywords: Squamous intraepithelial lesions · Deep Learning · CNN · Cervix

1 Introduction

Cervical cancer (CaCu) is the fourth most common neoplasia affecting women worldwide and is estimated to have caused more than 600,000 deaths in 2022 [1]. Approximately 95% of CaCu cases result from persistent infection with high-risk Human Papillomavirus (HPV), making this virus the main risk factor for developing the disease [2].

L. Martínez-Villaseñor et al. (Eds.): MICAI 2025 Workshops, LNAI 16264, pp. 98–111, 2026.
https://doi.org/10.1007/978-3-032-17930-2_7

The cervix is a complex structure from both histological and cytological perspectives, with diverse cellular layers. Methods such as Pap smears and cytological analysis remain the main screening tools for early diagnosis of cervical cancer (CaCu). The visualization of cellular alterations or morphological atypia in the various cells that make up the cervix has led to the classification of two important precursor lesions of CaCu: low-grade squamous intraepithelial lesions (LSIL) and high-grade squamous intraepithelial lesions (HSIL) [3]. In the biomedical field, the use of artificial intelligence (AI) tools has become increasingly important for diagnosing gynecological tumors through image analysis. AI serves as a core supportive technology for optimizing early detection and improving the efficiency of screening programs for several types of cancer. Its application seeks to reduce subjectivity and standardize image interpretation, thereby significantly enhancing diagnostic accuracy [4]. Computer vision analysis using deep learning models has transformed medical image analysis, with Convolutional Neural Networks (CNNs) becoming a standard method for classification and segmentation tasks. CNNs enable the extraction of hierarchical features from images, which is essential for identifying patterns in complex medical data [5]. As AI techniques advance in medicine, the use of advanced neural networks has produced precise results in areas such as tumor detection, tissue segmentation, and evaluation of pulmonary diseases [6]. Transformer models, which are also classified as deep learning models, initially excelled in natural language processing because of their ability to capture long-range relationships through the attention mechanism [7]. In images, Transformer models use this mechanism to identify complex spatial correlations, providing greater flexibility than conventional methods [8]. Vision Transformers (ViT) divide images into small sections, allowing each section to interact with other patches. This approach is especially useful for identifying regions of interest in high-resolution images, such as medical images [8, 9]. In medical imaging, this technique improves accuracy in diagnostic tasks by allowing the model to focus on specific areas that contain crucial diagnostic information, as observed in studies of tomography and magnetic resonance imaging analysis [10].

The main goal of this study was to develop and assess a deep learning model to classify intraepithelial squamous lesions of the cervix using publicly available cytological imaging data.

2 Theoretical Foundations

Precise segmentation of medical images is essential for treatment planning, especially in oncology. Vision Transformer models have demonstrated high effectiveness in this task, enabling precise delineation of areas of interest, such as tumors or lesions, without the need for additional convolutional networks [11]. CNNs and Vision Transformer models are deep learning models used to identify patterns, detect anomalies, and classify diseases. CNNs have gained significant relevance in analyzing different modalities in X-ray images, magnetic resonance imaging, and computed tomography. They are also used to identify parasites in blood smears, such as malaria [12]. Access to public clinical data has been fundamental for training and retraining current or state-of-the-art architectures such as ResNet and EfficientNet to develop domain-specific weights, which serve as feature extraction layers for CNNs and Vision Transformer models. Some researchers have demonstrated that Transformer models benefit more from transfer learning than CNNs [13]. However, publicly accessible datasets have become scarce and very limited. Research by Nirmala and colleagues. Highlights the importance of early detection of cervical cancer through deep learning to considerably reduce cases and, above all, mortality from this condition. In her research, she notes that manual Pap smear testing may not be the most time-efficient option [14]. Nirmala and colleagues developed a hybrid system that combines an adaptive Vision Transformer-based encoder with a CNN for automatic classification of cervical cytology. They implemented a preprocessing and segmentation phase (ADRAN model), followed by classification with an Adaptive Vision Transformer Encoder and a CNN, optimizing hyperparameters with evolutionary algorithms [14].

Some studies have developed specific tools for cervical cancer, such as CerviFusionNet, which uses a hybrid architecture combining CNN and ViT to learn robust representations. A temporal module captures dynamic changes in acetic acid sequences, improving the model's performance in classifying cervical lesions using a dataset of colposcopies from 2,273 patients [15]. Mohamed and colleagues also explored the use of a combined SWIN-Transformer and CNN approach for the study and classification of cervical lesions, using a set of 913 images from 200 colposcopy cases. The dataset was divided into 70% for training and 30% for testing, resulting in metrics of 94% area under the curve (AUC), 87% accuracy, and a 78% F1-score. Mohamed highlights that the hybrid model combines the advantages of CNNs with the global context modeling of SWIN-Transformers [16]. Another variant used in hybrid models is the one proposed by AIMohimeed, which combines the use of ViT, particle swarm optimization (PSO), and a support vector machine (SVM) model. The aim is to extract features using ViT, optimize those features using PSO, and replace the softmax activation function for the network output with an SVM [17].

3 Materials and Methods

A publicly available dataset, "Liquid based cytology pap smear images for multi-class diagnosis of cervical cancer," was used in this study. It consists of 963 images divided into four sets representing the precancerous and cancerous classes of cervical lesions under the Bethesda system: low-grade squamous intraepithelial lesions, high-grade squamous intraepithelial lesions, negative for neoplasia, and squamous cell carcinoma. The images were captured using a Leica DM 750 microscope and an ICC50 HD camera at 400x magnification (2048 x 1536 pixels) and were derived from 460 patients using the liquid-based cytology technique [18]. The dataset was divided into training (70%), validation (20%), and test (10%) sets using stratified random sampling to maintain the class distribution in each subset. The "Squamous Carcinoma" class was excluded due to its low number of samples (n = 74), which allowed for proper balance with the other classes (n = 113 each). Efforts were made to ensure that no factors prevented the model from classifying correctly. (see Fig. 1 and Fig. 2).

For the construction of the Artificial Neural Network, the TensorFlow framework was used [19], was used, supported by auxiliary libraries for data handling and visualization (NumPy, Keras, Matplotlib, and Tensor.Js). The Data Augmentation technique was employed, applying multiple transformations to the training images to artificially

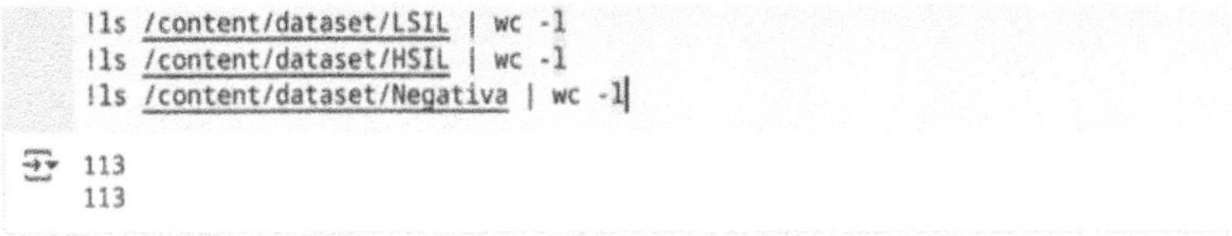

```
!ls /content/dataset/LSIL | wc -l
!ls /content/dataset/HSIL | wc -l
!ls /content/dataset/Negativa | wc -l

113
113
```

Fig. 1. Dataset reduced. - The primary dataset of 963 images was reduced to 339, divided into 3 categories from the 4 in the E. Hussain dataset, with the number of images per folder verified.

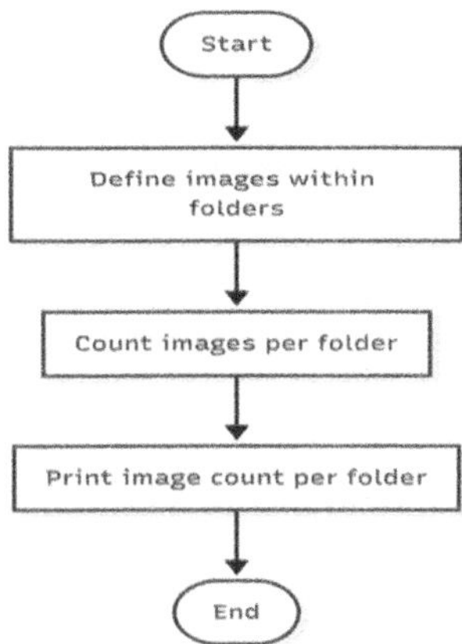

Fig. 2. Final contains folder. - The flowchart shows the definition of folders, image counting, and the display of the number of images in the final dataset.

increase the dataset extracted from the original data, which enhanced the model's performance. The synthetic expansion of training sets is a standard practice for improving model generalization and reducing overfitting, especially in medical imaging where data is typically scarce [20]. In Yang's work, they used data augmentation based on Multi-modal Generative Adversarial Networks (m-GAN) combined with conventional techniques, achieving 99% accuracy in the classification of Pap smear images [21]. The training data was normalized from 0–255 to 0–1, rotated up to 15°, shifted horizontally and vertically by 10%, cropped by 10%, zoomed in and out by 10%, flipped horizontally, had brightness adjusted between 90% and 110%, and empty pixels were filled with black. Fewer transformations were applied to the validation data: only normalization from 0–255 to 0–1 was performed, and 20% of the data was set aside for validation. The test data was normalized without additional transformations (see Fig. 3), resulting in images with these transformation values (see Fig. 4).

The transfer learning technique was used, employing Google's pre-trained MobileNetV3Small model with frozen layers. This model was chosen for its computational efficiency, enabling implementation on mobile devices without significant performance loss. MobileNet models are lightweight and designed for resource-constrained environments while maintaining reasonable accuracy [22]. The model was exported using TensorFlow. Js due to its high compatibility, utilizing the feature extractor to preserve ImageNet knowledge such as edges, textures, and shapes. Custom layers that had

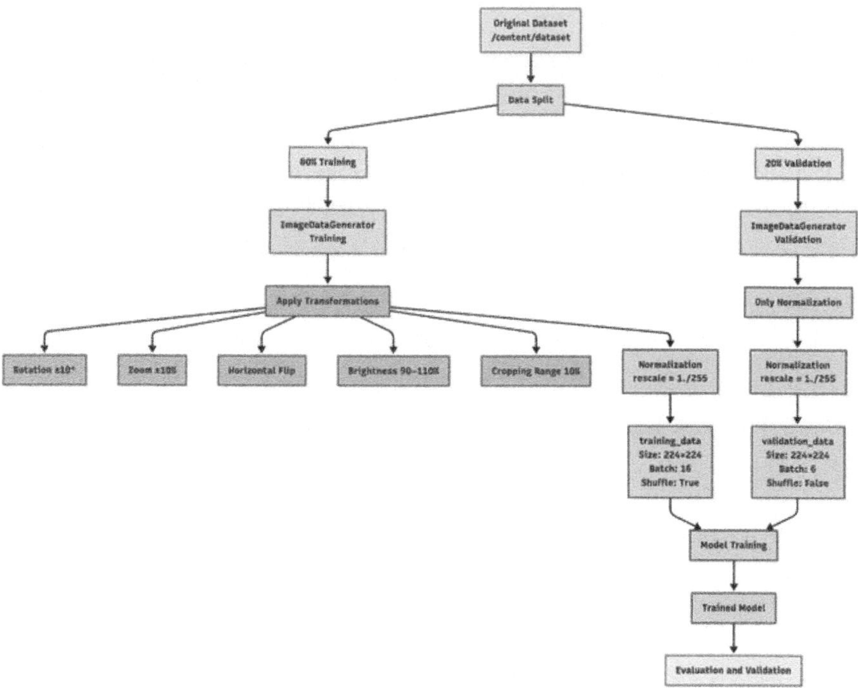

Fig. 3. Data Augmentation. - Diagram illustrating the data augmentation process applied to the cytology dataset.

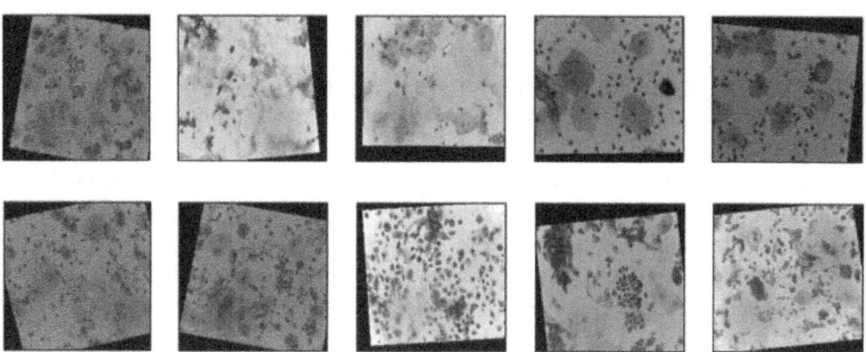

Fig. 4. Generated images. - Results of transformations performed using the data augmentation technique to generate synthetic data are shown.

been previously programmed and analyzed were included to optimize the classification objective for cervical cancer precursor lesions. Training was stabilized with a BatchNormalization layer, features were reduced to a vector with GlobalAveragePooling2D, followed by a dense hidden layer of 64 neurons with L2 regularization and ReLU activation, a Dropout layer disabling 40% of the connections, and a dense output layer of 3 neurons with Softmax activation for final classification (see Fig. 5). BatchNormalization provided stability during model training, while Dropout was used to mitigate overfitting, as these techniques have been shown to improve the performance of artificial convolutional neural networks in biomedical imaging [23]. The model was compiled with the Adam optimizer (lr = 0.001) and categorical cross-entropy loss. During training, it was monitored using the accuracy metric along with metrics relevant in the medical context (AUC, precision, recall), and performance was evaluated at each epoch. The model was trained for 30 epochs, updating only the non-frozen weights. After each epoch, performance on the validation set was evaluated, and the metrics (loss, accuracy, etc.) were recorded for analysis with TensorBoard (see Fig. 6).

We selected the F1 macro index to ensure equal treatment of all classes, which is appropriate for our balanced dataset and essential in medical contexts to prevent overlooking minority classes. This approach aligns with recommendations to use balanced metrics beyond accuracy; for example, Nirmala et al. advocate using precision and recall from the confusion matrix for comprehensive evaluation [14]. For prediction, a normalized $224 \times 224 \times 3$ image is input, producing a probability vector [p0, p1, p2]. The Argmax function selects the class with the highest probability (0, 1, or 2). The model is saved and exported in a native, optimized multiformat with complete metadata. Exporting with TensorFlow.js enables browser-based deployment, extending accessibility to clinical settings with limited resources or mobile devices (see Fig. 7).

The implementation of the web tool enables graphical display of predictions and classification of cervical intraepithelial squamous lesions, including low-grade, high-grade, and negative for malignancy cases. Its architecture follows an image processing workflow, performing input validation, real-time processing, interpretation, and ensuring portability. It also features adaptive normalization, transforming pixel values from [0, 255] to [0, 1], which significantly improves convergence during inference. Memory usage is optimized with resizeNearestNeighbor, reducing graphics card (GPU) requirements by 75% and achieving a maximum latency of less than 500 ms on mobile devices (see Fig. 8).

4 Discussion and Results

Our model achieved an overall accuracy of 83% and an F1-macro score of 0.83, as shown in Table 1, which is promising for a diagnostic support tool. Gangrade et al. achieved 94% accuracy in classifying cervical squamous cells with an ensemble model [24], and Wang et al. reported approximately 89–90% accuracy in a clinically validated AI system [25].

Recognizing that the achieved performance is close to that of other research, though somewhat lower, demonstrates objectivity and indicates potential for improvement. The training and loss behavior suggests there is no overfitting, so the predictions are consistent with the results obtained from the model's evaluation metrics. Its development during the 30 epochs of training and loss is adequate (see Fig. 9).

Therefore, tests were performed on the already exported model in the adaptive web interface using images from other datasets as well as screenshots from the book "The Bethesda System for Reporting Cervical Cytology." [3], where the CNN classified correctly, generalizing with images not included in its training dataset (see Fig. 10).

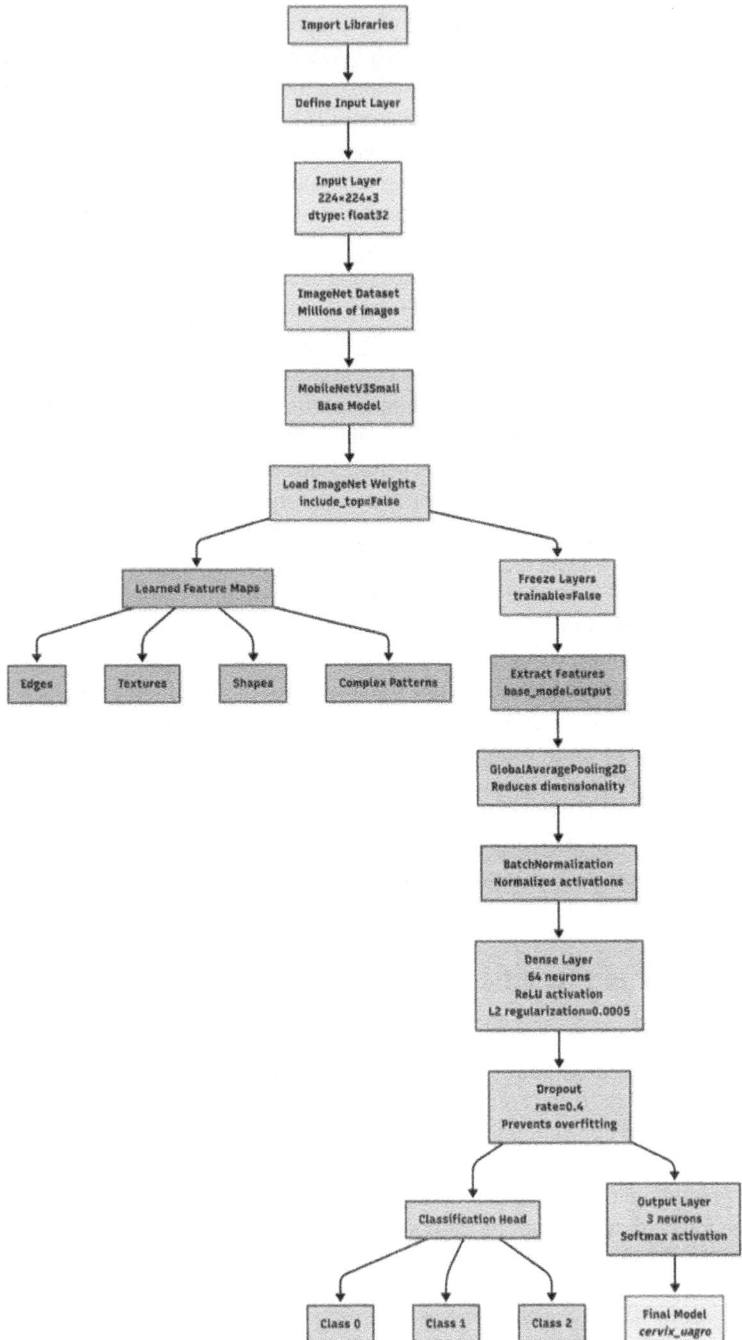

Fig. 5. Diagram of model construction. - Shows the development of the convolutional neural network (CNN) model using transfer learning.

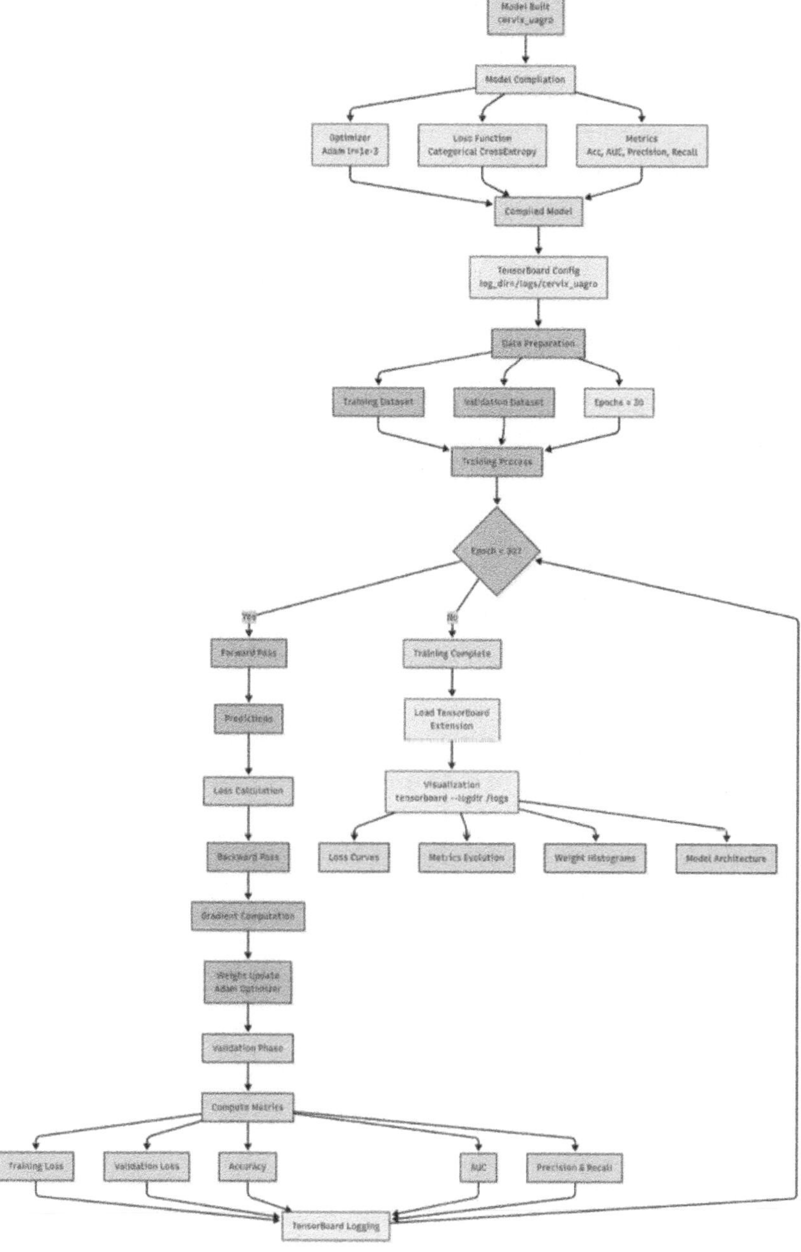

Fig. 6. Diagram of model compilation and training. - It shows the compilation and training of the model.

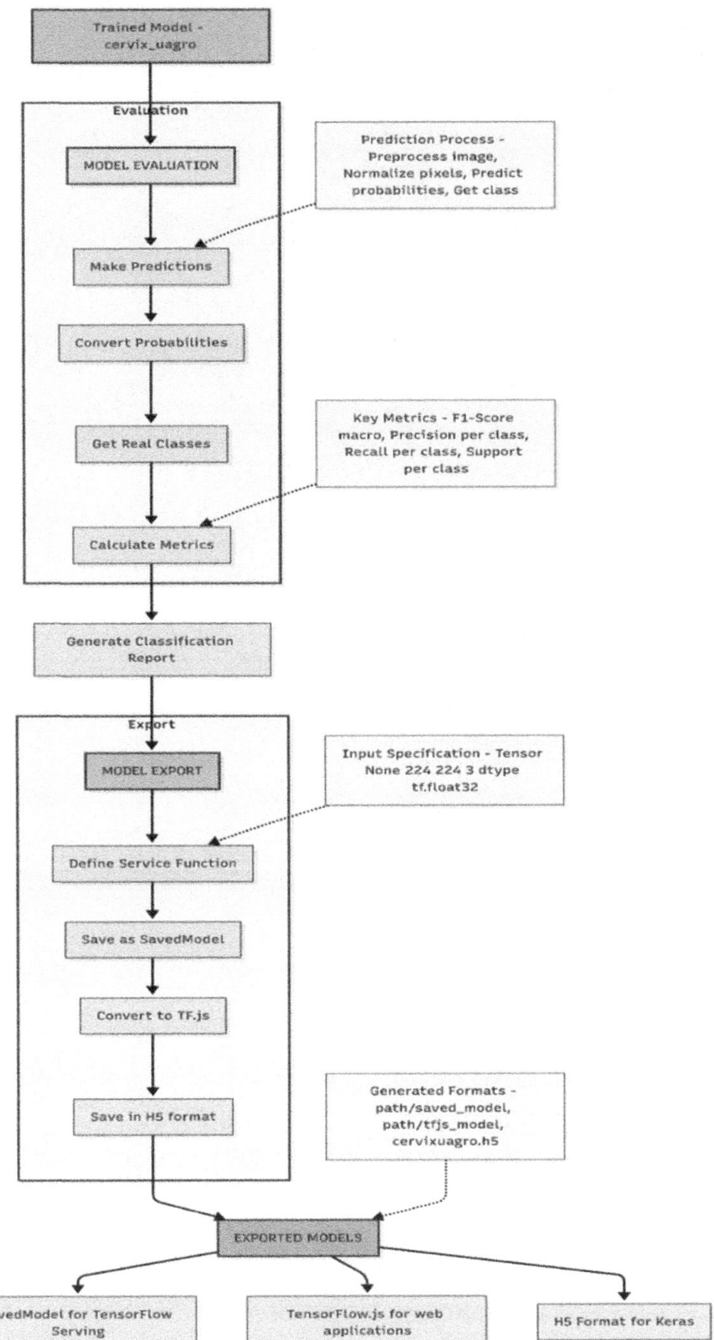

Fig. 7. Evaluation and export diagram of the model. The evaluation and export of the model to different formats for use in a web interface are shown.

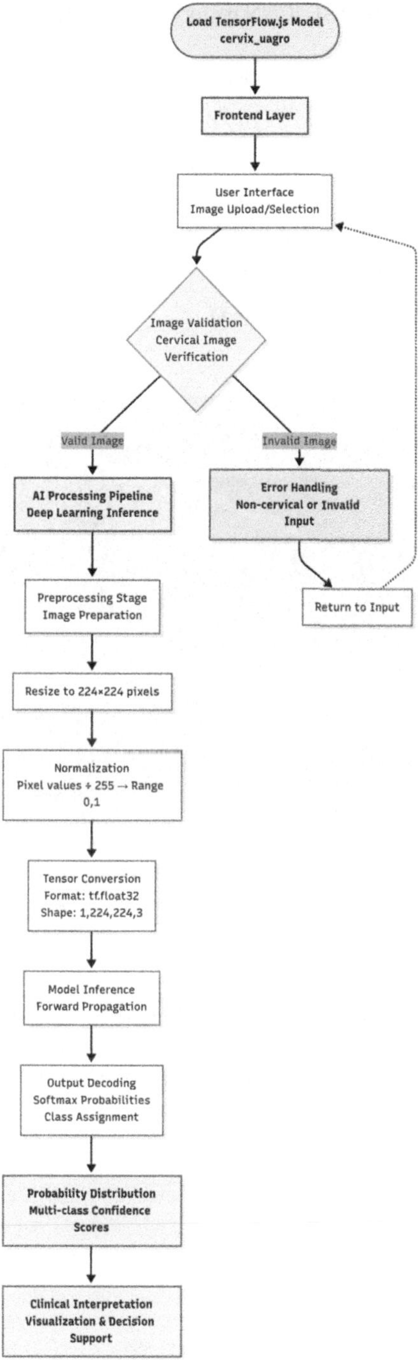

Fig. 8. Development of the web-based testing tool. - The workflow of the model testing tool is shown.

Table 1. CNN performance metrics.

Metrics	Precision	Recall	F1-Score	Support
LSIL	*1*	*0.59*	*0.74*	*22*
HSIL	*0.92*	*1*	*0.96*	*22*
Negative	*0.69*	*0.91*	*0.98*	*22*
Precision			*0.83*	*66*
Macro AVG	*0.87*	*0.83*	*0.83*	*66*
Weighted AVG	*0.87*	*0.83*	*0.83*	*66*

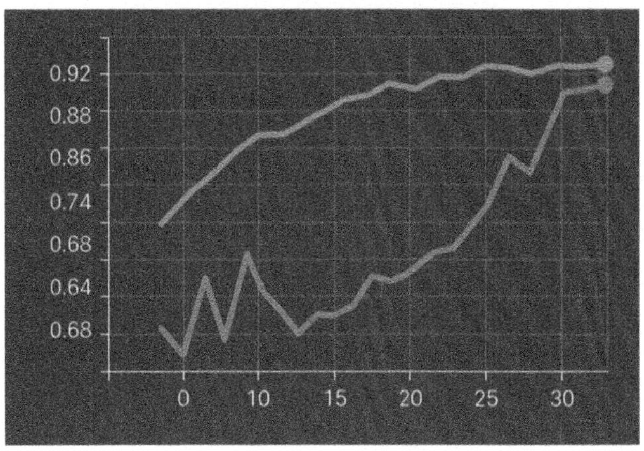

Fig. 9. Behavior of training, validation, and loss of the model. - The graph shows the behavior of over 30 iterations or epochs (x-axis). The y-axis represents accuracy values. The orange line indicates the model's precision, while the blue line represents the loss and performance of the CNN model.

Testing with unseen data is crucial. Recent studies recommend validating cytological classification algorithms on multiple datasets to ensure robustness. Research by Austin and Parvathi evaluated their method on both the SIPaKMeD and Herlev datasets, maintaining high accuracy (90–97%) on both [23].

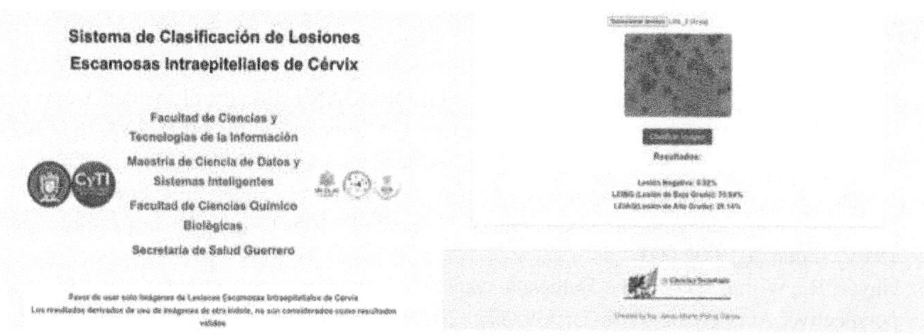

Fig. 10. Test web interface. - The online tool for identifying squamous lesions from Pap's images is shown. https://sclei.srvr.mx/

5 Conclusions and Future Work

The implementation of artificial intelligence strategies, such as convolutional neural networks for classifying cervical intraepithelial squamous lesions, serves as a valuable support tool. This approach may improve diagnostic accuracy and expedite pathology detection by cytopathologists, pathologists, and cytotechnologists.

However, this study has several limitations. The exclusion of carcinoma images limits the applicability for identifying this clinical entity. Furthermore, using a single public dataset may introduce biases that affect the model's generalization. Although the MobileNetV3 architecture is efficient, it may not capture all relevant features present in complex cytological images compared to more advanced or specialized models. To address these limitations, future work could benefit from multicenter and better-balanced databases.

To address these limitations, future work could benefit from multicenter, better-balanced databases. Self-learning techniques and generative models could increase sample variability [26]. Furthermore, integrating explainability through GRAD-CAM activation maps will enhance clinical confidence in the results generated by the models [27].

Future work is expected to implement a ViT (Vision Transformer) to compare the accuracy of both models without minimizing the results obtained. The use of a hybrid model is also planned to identify the most effective and accurate approach. This information can then be provided to specialists in the field. Furthermore, this development represents a potential training resource or guide for future cytopathologists, pathologists, and cytotechnologists. If possible, clinical variables could be integrated to provide greater robustness to a multimodal model.

Acknowledgments. Jesús Alberto Palma García is a master's degree student from Program of Master in Data Science and Intelligent System, Universidad Autónoma de Guerrero (UAGro), and received fellowship (CVU 639732) from SECIHTI.

Disclosure of Interest. All other authors declare no conflict of interest

References

1. Bray, F., et al.: Global cancer statistics 2022: GLOBOCAN estimates of incidence and mortality worldwide for 36 cancers in 185 countries. CA Cancer J. Clin. **74**(3), 229–263 (2024). https://doi.org/10.3322/caac.21834
2. Johnson, C.A., James, D., Marzan, A., Armaos, M.: Cervical cancer: an overview of pathophysiology and management. Semin. Oncol. Nurs. **35**(2), 166–174 (2019). https://doi.org/10.1016/j.soncn.2019.02.003
3. Nayar, R., Wilbur, D.C.: The Bethesda system for reporting cervical cytology: a historical perspective. Acta Cytol. **61**(4–5), 359–372 (2017). https://doi.org/10.1159/000477556
4. Shrestha, P., et al.: A systematic review on the use of artificial intelligence in gynecologic imaging - background, state of the art, and future directions. Gynecol. Oncol. **166**(3), 596–605 (2022). https://doi.org/10.1016/j.ygyno.2022.07.024
5. Litjens, G., et al.: A survey on deep learning in medical image analysis. Med. Image Anal. **42**, 60–88 (2017). https://doi.org/10.1016/j.media.2017.07.005
6. Shen, D., Wu, G., Suk, H.I.: Deep learning in medical image analysis. Annu. Rev. Biomed. Eng. **19**(1), 221–248 (2017). https://doi.org/10.1146/annurev-bioeng-071516-044442
7. Vaswani, A., et al.: Attention Is All You Need. arXiv. (2017). doi:https://doi.org/10.48550/ARXIV.1706.03762.
8. Dosovitskiy, A., et al.: An Image is Worth 16x16 Words: Transformers for Image Recognition at Scale. arXiv. (2020). doi:https://doi.org/10.48550/ARXIV.2010.11929.
9. Khan, R.F., Lee, B.-D., Lee, M.S.: Transformers in medical image segmentation: a narrative review. Quant. Imaging Med. Surg. **13**(12), 8747–8767 (2023). https://doi.org/10.21037/qims-23-542
10. Anwar, S.M., Majid, M., Qayyum, A., Awais, M., Alnowami, M., Khan, M.K.: Medical image analysis using convolutional neural networks: a review. J. Med. Syst. **42**(11), 226 (2018). https://doi.org/10.1007/s10916-018-1088-1
11. Hatamizadeh, A., et al.: UNETR: Transformers for 3D Medical Image Segmentation. arXiv. (2021). doi:https://doi.org/10.48550/ARXIV.2103.10504.
12. Brejnebøl, M.W., et al.: External validation of an artificial intelligence tool for radiographic knee osteoarthritis severity classification. Eur. J. Radiol. **150**, 110249 (2022). https://doi.org/10.1016/j.ejrad.2022.110249
13. Henry, E.U., Emebob, O., Omonhinmin, C.A.: Vision Transformers in Medical Imaging: A Review. 18 de noviembre de 2022, arXiv: arXiv:2211.10043. Accedido: 25 de octubre de 2024. [En línea]. Disponible en: http://arxiv.org/abs/2211.10043
14. Nirmala, G., Nayudu, P.P., Kumar, A.R., Sagar, R.: Automatic cervical cancer classification using adaptive vision transformer encoder with CNN for medical application. Pattern Recogn. **160**, 111201 (2025). https://doi.org/10.1016/j.patcog.2024.111201
15. Sha, Y., et al.: CerviFusionNet: a multi-modal, hybrid CNN-transformer-GRU model for enhanced cervical lesion multi-classification. iScience. **27**(12), 111313 (2024). https://doi.org/10.1016/j.isci.2024.111313
16. Mohammed, F.A., Tune, K.K., Mohammed, J.A., Wassu, T.A., Muhie, S.: Early cervical cancer diagnosis with SWIN-transformer and convolutional neural networks. Diagnostics. **14**(20), 2286 (2024). https://doi.org/10.3390/diagnostics14202286
17. AlMohimeed, A., Shehata, M., El-Rashidy, N., Mostafa, S., Samy Talaat, A., Saleh, H.: ViT-PSO-SVM: cervical cancer predication based on integrating vision transformer with particle swarm optimization and support vector machine. Bioengineering. **11**(7), 729 (2024). https://doi.org/10.3390/bioengineering11070729
18. Hussain, E.: Liquid based cytology pap smear images for multi-class diagnosis of cervical cancer. Mendeley, 18 de noviembre de 2019. doi:https://doi.org/10.17632/ZDDTPGZV63.4.

19. TensorFlow Developers: TensorFlow. (29 de julio de 2025). Zenodo. doi:https://doi.org/10.5281/ZENODO.16547183.
20. Shorten, C., Khoshgoftaar, T.M.: A survey on image data augmentation for deep learning. J. Big Data. **6**(1), 60 (2019). https://doi.org/10.1186/s40537-019-0197-0
21. Yang, H., Aydi, W., Innab, N., Ghoneim, M.E., Ferrara, M.: Classification of cervical cancer using dense CapsNet with Seg-UNet and denoising autoencoders. Sci. Rep. **14**(1), 31764 (2024). https://doi.org/10.1038/s41598-024-82489-2
22. Howard, A., et al.: Searching for MobileNetV3. arXiv. (2019). doi:https://doi.org/10.48550/ARXIV.1905.02244.
23. Austin, R., Parvathi, R.: CNN based method for classifying cervical cancer cells in pap smear images. Sci. Rep. **15**(1), 23936 (2025). https://doi.org/10.1038/s41598-025-10009-x
24. Gangrade, J., Kuthiala, R., Gangrade, S., Singh, Y.P., R, M., Solanki, S.: A deep ensemble learning approach for squamous cell classification in cervical cancer. Sci. Rep. **15**(1), 7266 (2025). https://doi.org/10.1038/s41598-025-91786-3
25. Wang, J., et al.: Artificial intelligence enables precision diagnosis of cervical cytology grades and cervical cancer. Nat. Commun. **15**(1), 4369 (2024). https://doi.org/10.1038/s41467-024-48705-3
26. Zhang, D., Wang, C., Chen, T., Chen, W., Shen, Y.: Scalable Swin transformer network for brain tumor segmentation from incomplete MRI modalities. Artif. Intell. Med. **149**, 102788 (2024). https://doi.org/10.1016/j.artmed.2024.102788
27. Selvaraju, R.R., Cogswell, M., Das, A., Vedantam, R., Parikh, D., Batra, D.: Grad-CAM: visual explanations from deep networks via gradient-based localization. In: 2017 IEEE International Conference on Computer Vision (ICCV), pp. 618–626. IEEE, Venice (oct. 2017). https://doi.org/10.1109/ICCV.2017.74

Detection and Classification of Cervical Cancer Using Machine Learning Techniques

José Guadalupe Domínguez García(✉), Julio Cesar Ponce Gallegos, Ángel Eduardo Muñoz Zavala, and Alejandro Padilla Diaz

Universidad Autónoma de Aguascalientes, Av. Universidad 940, C, P 20100 Aguascalientes, Mexico
jose.garciadom4@gmail.com, {julio.ponce,angel.munoz, alejandro.padilla}@edu.uaa.mx

Abstract. Cervical cancer remains one of the leading causes of mortality among women worldwide, emphasizing the urgent need for accurate and early diagnosis. This study proposes a deep learning–based framework for the automatic classification of cervical lesions from colposcopic images using Convolutional Neural Networks (CNNs). The dataset used was the Intel ODT for Cervix Images, preprocessed to enhance contrast and reduce noise variability. Three CNN architectures—VGG16, Xception, and InceptionV3—were trained and evaluated to determine the optimal configuration for lesion classification. Among them, InceptionV3 achieved the best individual performance, reaching an accuracy of 0.90, precision of 0.94, recall of 0.85, and a weighted F1-score of 0.82. To further enhance robustness, an ensemble learning approach combining the three models through a weighted majority voting scheme improved the overall F1-score to 0.86 and achieved a more balanced sensitivity across lesion types. The results demonstrate the potential of CNN-based ensembles as reliable diagnostic support tools for computer-aided cervical cancer screening, contributing to early detection and improved clinical decision-making.

Keywords: Artificial intelligence · colposcopy · cervix cancer · deep learning

1 Introduction

Currently is the most malignant neoplasm in the world's population and the fourth most common among women, with an estimated 528,000 new cases diagnosed annually [1].

Breast cancer and cervical cancer are considered some of the most harmful diseases affecting women worldwide today [2]. Compared to breast cancer, cervical cancer has a higher mortality rate in women and can occur at any age, from young to old. Some tissues in cervical regions can change suddenly and produce cancer cells. Early detection is essential for timely treatment, increasing the likelihood of successful treatment and thus reducing the mortality rate.

There are currently techniques that help to analyze the presence of CCU through imaging, in which visualization at the cellular or physical level is necessary. It is also

L. Martínez-Villaseñor et al. (Eds.): MICAI 2025 Workshops, LNAI 16264, pp. 112–123, 2026.
https://doi.org/10.1007/978-3-032-17930-2_8

possible to visualize it through the patient's medical history, but the result is not optimal in most cases. However, one of the most widely used is colposcopy, which is a procedure to examine the cervix, vagina, and vulva. This instrument is used to look for abnormal cells, which could be cancerous or precancerous depending on the visible lesions and the corresponding region. For this, an instrument called a colposcope is used, which increases the normal view of the cervix [3]. The corresponding lesions are visualized through the increased view in the area (Fig. 1).

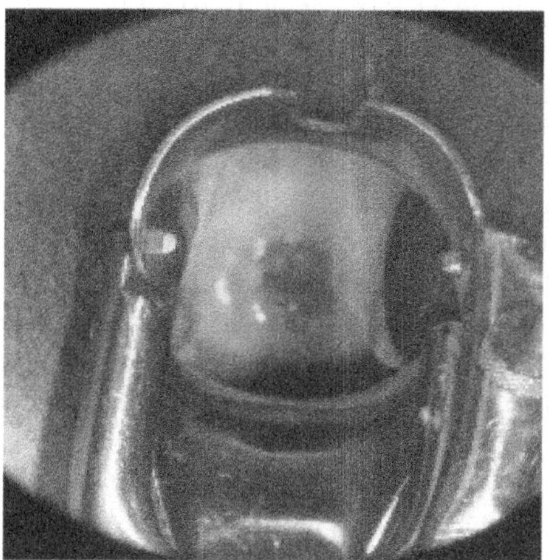

Fig. 1. Visualization of cervix anatomy using a speculum

Cervical cancer is recognized as a persistent global health issue, prompting continuous efforts to find effective methods for its treatment, detection, and monitoring. In recent years, artificial intelligence (AI) has emerged as a valuable tool in medical research, demonstrating strong performance in tasks related to the detection and prediction of this disease using machine learning techniques.

In In the realm of artificial intelligence, deep learning is distinguished for its efficiency in applying visual solutions in the healthcare sector. Due to their ability to tackle very intricate challenges, deep learning frameworks are particularly adept at classification and forecasting. These architectures, which consist of a multitude of concealed layers, provide a robust system that helps in discovering patterns within images, resulting in precise results [4]. Deep neural networks have the capacity to independently learn layered data formats, pulling out increasingly abstract elements at various stages. This capability allows them to manage complex operations like recognizing images and speech, along with processing natural language, and more. The key concept behind convolutional neural networks is to analyze an image through its various layers, allowing for the extraction of sophisticated features at each level[5].

2 Conceptual Framework

Stating examples of work related to the corresponding research, [6] created a classification model for the detection of cervical cancer using the joint learning approach. The model achieved an accuracy of 87.21%. On the other hand, [7] proposed a classification model based on deep learning to detect cervical cancer from colposcopy images. In their corresponding works, they adopted the VGG19 algorithms and the CYENET colposcopy network. The VGG19 algorithm achieved an accuracy of 73.30% and the CYENET algorithm achieved an accuracy of 92.30% [7].

[8] Introduced a technique rooted in deep learning for identifying cervical cancer from colposcopic images. They assessed various convolutional neural network architectures like LeNet, VGG16, RESNET 50, GOOGLE NET, COLPONET, and DENSE NET to differentiate the same, reaching an impressive classification accuracy of 81. 53%. In contrast, reference [9] conducted a similar procedure, including steps like resizing the images, converting them to grayscale, and augmenting them. Subsequently, their investigation classified cervical cancer and attained a prediction accuracy of 74. 04% utilizing the ResNet50 framework. [10] suggested a combined method integrating Random Forest and basic neural networks to identify cervical cancer. This method employed Pearson's correlation to relate input features with the output feature for data preprocessing, achieving an accuracy rate of 93. 6%.

Identifying this condition at an early stage is crucial for effective treatment, outcome forecasting, and enhancing therapeutic strategies. When diagnosed promptly and managed appropriately, it ranks among the most treatable types of cancer. Nevertheless, despite impressive outcomes linked to early identification, there are shortcomings in accurate diagnosis. While interest in deep learning approaches for image analysis is on the rise, additional research is required to ensure these models are dependable and suitable for medical settings. The existing studies focusing on the early detection of cervical cancer through medical imaging are scarce, indicating the need for further investigations to compare results and enhance accuracy. This study introduces a method that utilizes pre-processed colposcopic images of the cervix to identify cervical cancer employing convolutional neural networks, aiming to support the medical personnel involved. The key contributions of this study are outlined below:

1. A proposed model based on pre-processed images for the detection of cervical cancer using images of the cervical area
2. The best classification of performance and accuracy chosen after comparing the architectures of convolutional neural networks such as Google Net, Inception V3 and VGG16 in comparison with related studies in the literature
3. Identify, by means of heat maps, the area where the model identified the malignant patterns.
4. Auxiliary tool in the detection of the problem for early intervention, adequate follow-up and corresponding treatment.

3 Development

The proposed model considers the following steps:

1. Image preprocessing: each image is adjusted to a uniform size of 224 x 224 pixels
2. Knowledge transfer of the model is carried out, and a comparison is made of the successes in the classification results.
3. Accuracy and loss metrics obtained
4. Implementation based on ensemble learning and show the comparation between original imagen and analyzed images using heat maps.

3.1 Cervix cancer dataset

Deep learning algorithms depend considerably on large datasets to achieve optimal performance. The efficiency of these models is strongly affected by both the quality and quantity of the data employed. When working with limited datasets, the likelihood of overfitting and poor generalization increases; on the other hand, larger datasets strengthen the model's capacity to generalize, thereby improving accuracy and reliability [11].

For the cervical cancer detection and prediction model, the dataset used for training and testing consists of 8,215 colposcopy images, obtained from publicly available sources such as Kaggle and Smartphone ODT [12]. These images were labeled and classified by domain experts in the field (Fig. 2).

There are various techniques available for image segmentation, including gradient flow vectors, distributed region detection, adaptive thresholding, histogram thresholding, statistical region growth, and clustering [13]. Other approaches include fuzzy C-means clustering, bootstrapping learning, supervised learning, edge detection, active contours, probabilistic modeling, dispersed coding [13], and contextual hypergraphs [14]. To further enhance system accuracy, hybrid methods combining two or more of these techniques have also been applied. Segmentation plays a crucial role, as it provides a reliable basis for classification according to specific patterns, such as the identification of tumors [14].

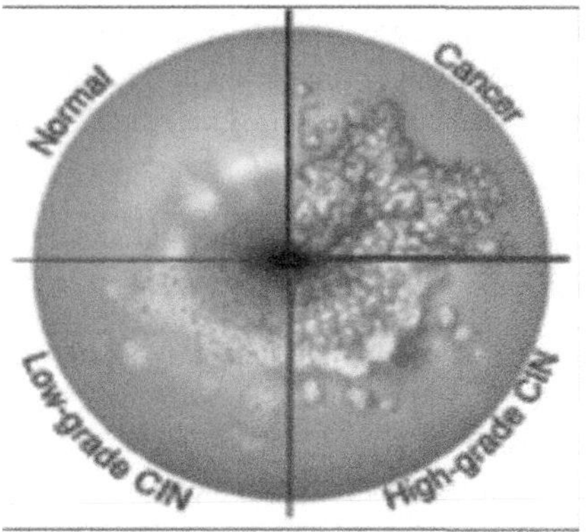

Fig. 2. Classification of cervical issues

A total of 6,572 images were allocated for the training phase, while 1,643 images were reserved for testing. In proportional terms, this corresponds to 80% of the dataset being utilized for training and the remaining 20% for testing (Table 1.).

Table 1. Distribution of dataset

	%	Total
Total	100%	8215
Training	80%	6572
Test	20%	1643

3.2 Image Pre-Processing

The images are resized to a size of 224 x 224 pixels. Cubic interpolation is used during resizing, an advanced method that calculates the new pixel values based on a cubic function, allowing the resized images to maintain detail and smoothness

Conversely, an analysis of pixels and colors is conducted to determine if normalizing the pixel values and color distribution in the images is necessary.

Regarding the standard deviation, it suggests there is considerable diversity in the pixel values present in the images. A smaller standard deviation would indicate that the pixel values are clustered closely around the average, while a larger value would signify greater contrast among the pixels. A normalization procedure is needed to enhance the model's adjustment and improve its learning during the upcoming training stage [15].

Subsequently, normalization and scaling are applied as essential preprocessing steps prior to training the model. Scaling transforms the feature values so that they fall within a predefined interval [a, b], commonly [0, 1] or [-1, 1]. Normalization, on the other hand, adjusts the features so that they share a common mean and standard deviation. For the training process, a batch size of 64 is specified, meaning the model processes 64 images simultaneously, which allows efficient parallel computation on GPUs. Furthermore, the classification task is defined into three categories, ensuring that the neural network is aware of the total number of classes to predict. In the scaling procedure, pixel values are normalized to the range [0, 1], instead of their original [0, 255] scale. This transformation is mathematically represented as (Eq. 1.):

$$\text{Normalized value} = \frac{\text{Original value}}{255} \tag{1}$$

Subsequently, the image labels, which are initially in text format (such as "Type 1", "Type 2", etc.), are converted into numerical values through a process of label encoding. For example, "Type 1" becomes 0, "Type 2" becomes 1, and so on.

The classification challenge explored in this research involves multiple classes, given that the dataset comprises three separate categories of cervical lesion images: Type 1, Type 2, and Type 3. For the preparation of labels before training the model, they were initially assigned numerical values (0, 1, and 2), followed by a conversion using one-hot encoding. This method allows the model to recognize each category as a distinct class, removing any inadvertent ordinal connections among the labels. The conversion was performed using the to_categorical() function, creating binary arrays such as [1, 0, 0], [0, 1, 0], and [0, 0, 1] for the different classes. This structure is ideal for neural networks since it suits their capabilities for accepting continuous numerical data while preventing any confusion regarding class order. Data augmentation included random rotations ($\pm 15°$), horizontal and vertical flips, and zoom ranges of 0.1 to 0.3, ensuring greater dataset diversity. To evaluate the model's performance, we first employed an 80/20 train-test split, with 80% of the data used for training and 20% for testing. However, to ensure robustness and avoid overfitting, we also implemented five-fold cross-validation, allowing the model to train on different subsets of data and be tested on all subsets, ensuring a more reliable performance estimate. Furthermore, to prevent data leakage, we ensured that no images in the test set were included in the training process or any augmentation steps. In addition to the initial dataset, we plan to validate the model on an external dataset to further assess its generalizability and performance in clinical scenarios. Finally, hyperparameters, including learning rate and batch size, were optimized using grid search to ensure the best configuration for each neural network architecture.

4 Neural Networks Developed

An important advantage of deep learning is its capacity to generate high-level feature representations directly from raw images [16]. Furthermore, deep learning, feature extraction, and image recognition tasks can be executed in parallel using graphics processing units (GPUs). Convolutional Neural Networks (CNNs) have demonstrated remarkable effectiveness in cancer detection [17]. Among the developed architectures, VGG16, InceptionV3, and Xception stand out due to their more robust designs, which allow for deeper image analysis across multiple layers and yield superior performance compared to other CNN-based models.

The architecture of a Convolutional Neural Network (CNN) is composed of multiple layers, each with a specific function. The process begins with the input layer, which receives and stores the raw data. This is followed by the convolutional layer, where scalar products are computed between image patches and filters to generate output volumes, enabling the extraction of local features from the images. After this operation, activation functions are applied to introduce non-linearity. Subsequently, the pooling layer reduces the dimensionality of the output, optimizing memory usage and decreasing computational complexity. Pooling also summarizes the feature maps, making them more robust to minor variations in the input [17]. Finally, the fully connected layers flatten the extracted features and compute the probabilities for class prediction. In the convolutional stage, feature extraction is carried out through scalar products between the input image and the filters (Eq. 2.):

$$G[m,n] = (f * h)[m.n] = \sum_{j}\sum_{k} h[j,k]f[m-j,n-k] \tag{2}$$

Among the chosen architectures, VGG16 was employed as a convolutional neural network initialized with pre-trained weights from ImageNet. For this approach, the original output layer was removed, while the convolutional layers were retained, with most of their weights frozen to preserve previously acquired features. A Flatten layer was then incorporated to transform the convolutional output into a one-dimensional vector, followed by two fully connected (Dense) layers consisting of 512 neurons each, with

ReLU activation. The final output layer included three neurons with a softmax activation function, enabling classification into the three predefined categories. To reduce the risk of overfitting, Dropout layers were applied, randomly deactivating 30% of neurons during training. The model was compiled using the Adam optimizer with a learning rate of 1e-5, along with the categorical_crossentropy loss function, which is suitable for multiclass classification with one-hot encoded labels. Additionally, an Early Stopping mechanism was implemented to interrupt training if the validation loss did not improve after five consecutive epochs. Model performance was evaluated over 20 epochs, monitoring accuracy, loss, and training progression [17].

The InceptionV3 architecture, also initialized with pre-trained ImageNet weights, was adapted by discarding its fully connected layers and retaining only the convolutional components. This design leverages convolutional filters of varying sizes (1×1 and 3×3), integrated with pooling operations, to capture multi-scale features while simultaneously reducing dimensionality and mitigating the risk of overfitting. The distinctive Inception modules aggregate outputs from parallel convolutional and pooling operations into a single representation, thereby enhancing gradient propagation and improving training efficiency. For this implementation, the model was compiled using the Adam optimizer with a learning rate of 1e-4 and the categorical_crossentropy loss function, which is well-suited for multiclass classification. As with VGG16, model performance was assessed over 20 epochs by tracking accuracy, loss, and the overall evolution of training dynamic.

4.1 Metrics and Results

The obtained results were contrasted with other deep learning approaches as well as traditional machine learning techniques, with the primary goal of achieving the most accurate outcomes in the classification of cervical cancer from images.

Fig. 3 summarizes the main performance metrics — Precision, Recall, F1-score, and Accuracy — obtained from the final trained model for each lesion category. These values were computed directly from the test set after model convergence, using the classification reports generated during evaluation. Precision represents the proportion of correctly classified positive samples among all predicted positives, which in this implementation reflects how well the model distinguishes true lesions from normal tissue. Recall, on the other hand, measures the ability to detect all real cases of cervical lesions within each class, which is particularly important for preventing false negatives in early-stage diagnoses. The F1-score combines both Precision and Recall providing a balanced view of performance when class distribution is uneven, as was the case in this dataset. Global accuracy complements these indicators by showing the overall proportion of correct predictions across all classes.

Metrics	Precision	Recall	F1-score	Support
Type 1	0.94	0.85	0.81	191
Type 2	0.90	0.87	0.85	865
Type 3	0.88	0.82	0.80	477
Accuracy			**0.90**	1533
Macro avg	0.86	0.84	0.92	1533
Weighted avg	0.84	0.82	0.82	1533

Fig. 3. Evaluation metrics of the CNN model for cervical lesion detection

The confusion matrices for the three architectures — VGG16, Xception, and InceptionV3 — are presented in Figs. 4, 5, and 6, respectively. Each matrix illustrates the distribution of correct and incorrect classifications across the three lesion categories.

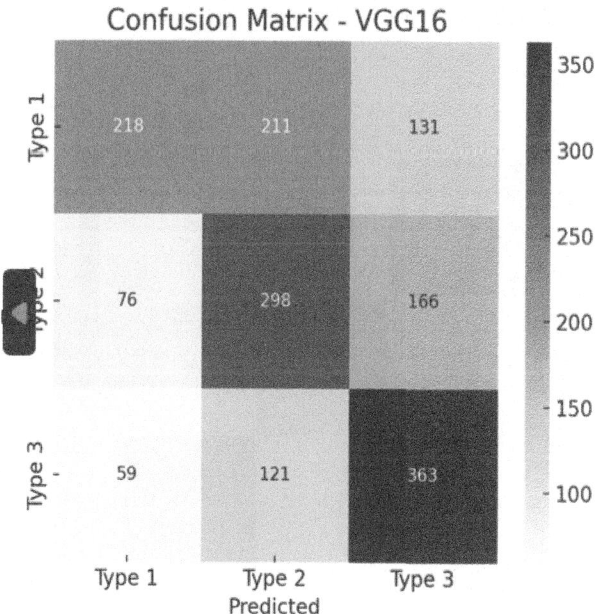

Fig. 4. Matrix confusion for VGG 16 model

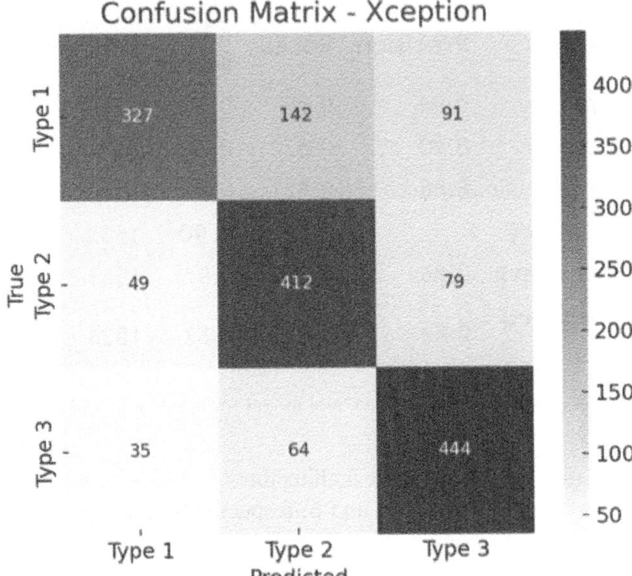

Fig. 5. Matrix confusion for Xception model

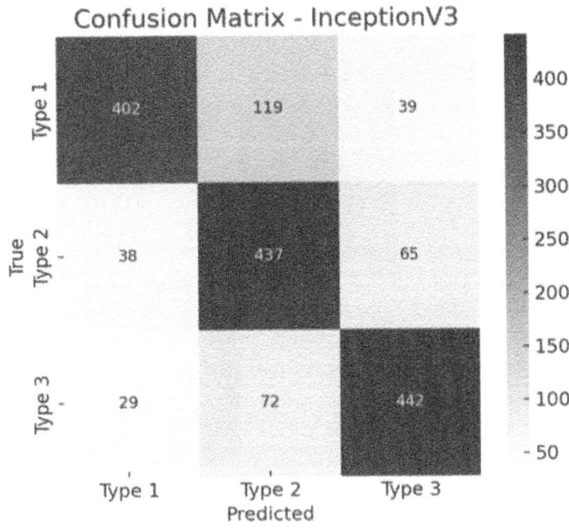

Fig. 6. Matrix confusion for Inception V3 model

The confusion matrix for the best-performing model (InceptionV3) is presented in Fig. 4, illustrating the distribution of correctly and incorrectly classified samples across the three lesion categories. The diagonal elements represent correctly predicted cases, while the off-diagonal values indicate misclassifications. As shown, the model achieved the highest accuracy for Type 1 lesions, correctly identifying most early-stage cases, which is clinically relevant for timely intervention. Some overlap was observed between Type 2 and Type 3 predictions due to morphological similarities in advanced lesions; however, these errors remained limited.

Additionally, an ensemble learning strategy was implemented by combining the outputs of the three CNN architectures (VGG16, Xception, and InceptionV3) through a weighted majority voting scheme. This ensemble further stabilized the classification results, reducing variance and improving overall robustness, particularly in the minority classes. The ensemble achieved a slight improvement in F1-score and a more balanced recall across lesion types, confirming the complementarity among the individual models.

At the end, the image on the left shows the original clinical photograph of a tissue sample with visible lesions. This image is used as the input for analysis.

The image on the right displays the same photograph overlaid with a heatmap, which is used to identify the presence or absence of cancerous tissue. The intensity of the colors in the heatmap indicates the model's confidence in identifying cancerous regions (Fig. 11) (Fig. 7)

- Red and orange areas represent high confidence that the region is cancerous.
- Yellow and green indicate moderate confidence.
- Blue or no coloration suggests low or no likelihood of cancer in that area

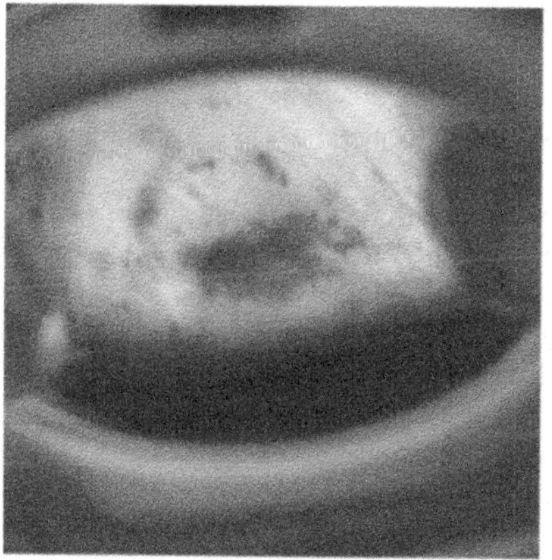
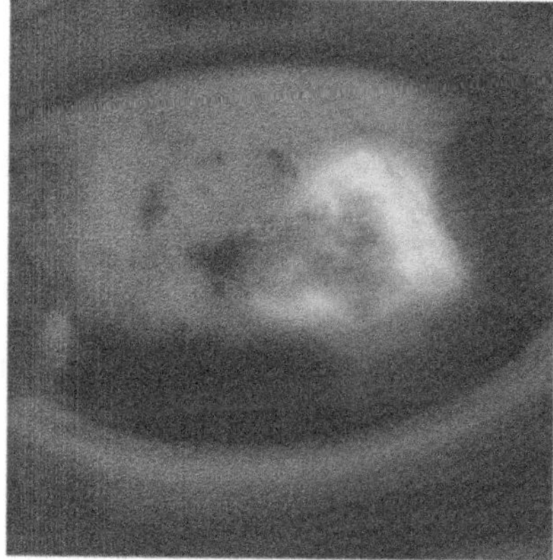

Fig. 7. Left: original image. Right: heatmap showing predicted cancer likelihood

5 Conclusions

This study presented an automated approach for the classification of cervical lesions using deep learning models based on Convolutional Neural Networks (CNNs). Among the evaluated architectures, InceptionV3 achieved the best overall performance, reaching an accuracy of 0.90 and a weighted F1-score of 0.82, demonstrating strong discriminative capability across lesion types. The results confirm that deeper architectures are more effective in capturing subtle morphological variations in colposcopic images, especially for early-stage lesions.

Furthermore, the incorporation of an ensemble learning strategy, combining VGG16, Xception, and InceptionV3 through a weighted voting scheme, improved overall stability and reduced variance, particularly for minority classes. This integration enhanced classification robustness and balanced the recall among categories, validating the complementarity between architectures.

From a clinical perspective, the proposed model provides a valuable tool for computer-assisted cervical cancer screening, capable of supporting specialists by increasing diagnostic accuracy and consistency. Future extensions of this work should consider larger and more diverse datasets, inclusion of real-time classification capabilities, and integration with clinical decision-support systems to facilitate practical deployment in healthcare environments.

References

1. Zhang, Y., Liu, X., Wang, J., et al.: Deep feature fusion for cervical cancer screening. Comput. Biol. Med. **153**, 106568 (2023). https://doi.org/10.1016/j.compbiomed.2022.106568
2. Nasiri, H., Safdarian, N., Rezaei, Z., et al.: Vision transformers for cervical cytology image analysis. Med. Image Anal. **92**, 103058 (2024). https://doi.org/10.1016/j.media.2023.103058
3. Nguyen, T., Chen, M., Lu, Y.: Hybrid attention networks for cervical cancer diagnosis using Colposcopic images. Sci. Rep. **13**(1), 1540 (2023). https://doi.org/10.1038/s41598-023-28401-z
4. Ahishakiye, E., Wario, R., Mwangi, W., Taremwa, D.: Prediction of cervical cancer based on risk factors using ensemble learning. In: 2020 IST-Africa Conference (IST-Africa), pp. 1–12 (2020)
5. Szegedy, C., Vanhoucke, V., Ioffe, S., Shlens, J., Wojna, Z.: Rethinking the inception architecture for computer vision. In: IEEE Conference on Computer Vision and Pattern Recognition (CVPR), pp. 2818–2826 (2016) https://doi.org/10.1109/CVPR.2016.308
6. Chandran, V., et al.: Diagnosis of cervical cancer based on ensemble deep learning network using colposcopy images. Biomed. Res. Int. **2021**, 1–15 (2021) https://doi.org/10.1155/2021/5584004
7. Saini, S.K., Bansal, V., Kaur, R., Juneja, M.: ColpoNet for automated cervical cancer screening using colposcopy images. Mach. Vis. Appl. **31**, 15 (2020). https://doi.org/10.1007/s00138-020-01063-8
8. Priyanka, B.J., Raju, B.: Machine learning approach for prediction of cervical cancer. Turk. J. Comput. Math. Educ. (TURCOMAT). **12**(8), 3050–3058 (2021)
9. Mehmood, M., Rizwan, M., Gregus, M.L., Abbas, S.: Machine learning assisted cervical cancer detection. Front. Public Health. **9**, 788376 (2021). https://doi.org/10.3389/fpubh.2021.788376
10. Devi, M.A., Ravi, S., Vaishnavi, J., Punitha, S.: Classification of cervical cancer using artificial neural networks. Procedia Comput. Sci. **89**, 465–472 (2016)
11. Göker, H.: Detection of cervical cancer from uterine cervix images using transfer learning architectures. Eskişehir Tech. Univ. J. Sci. Technol. Appl. Sci. Eng. **25**(2), 222–239 (2024) https://doi.org/10.18038/estubtda.1384489
12. Intel & MobileODT Cervical Cancer Screening. https://www.kaggle.com/competitions/intel-mobileodt-cervical-cancer-screening, Accessed 25 Feb 2025

13. Mustafa, W.A., Kader, M.M.M.A.: A review of histogram equalization techniques in image enhancement application. J. Phys.: Conf. Ser. **1019**(1), 1–7 (2018)
14. Liu, L., et al.: Computer-aided diagnostic system based on deep learning for classifying colposcopy images. Ann. Transl. Med. **9**, 1045 (2021)
15. Castillo, D., Lakshminarayanan, V., Rodríguez-Álvarez, M.J.: MR images, brain lesions, and deep learning. Appl. Sci. **11**, 1675 (2021)
16. Liang, M., Zheng, G., Huang, X., Milledge, G., Tokuta, A.: Identification of Abnormal Cervical Regions from Colposcopy Image Sequences. UNION Agency (2013)
17. Jiménez-Gaona, Y., Rodríguez-Álvarez, M.J., Lakshminarayanan, V.: Deep-learning-based computer-aided systems for breast cancer imaging: a critical review. Appl. Sci. **10** (2020)

Intelligent Vital Signs Simulator Based on Virtual Patients with Medical Orientation in Shock Scenarios

Diego Hernández-Cabrera[1], Alberto Ochoa-Zezzatti[2], Antonio I. Martínez-Santos[1], Héctor M. Buenabad-Arias[1], Laura L. Castro-Gómez[1], and Miguel A. Basurto-Pensado[1](✉)

[1] Research Center in Engineering and Applied Sciences, Autonomous University of the State of Morelos, Av. Universidad 1001, Building 48, Chamilpa, C.P, 62209 Cuernavaca, Morelos, Mexico
mbasurto@uaem.mx

[2] Autonomous University of Ciudad Juárez, Av. Universidad, Av. Heroico Colegio Militar and Chamizal, C.P. 32300, Juárez, Chihuahua, Mexico

Abstract. We present a web-based vital signs simulator (HTML5 / CSS / JavaScript) for clinical teaching and initial triage training. The system integrates: i) generation of pathophysiological scenarios (septic, hypovolemic, cardiogenic, anaphylactic shock, and healthy patient); ii) real-time monitoring of variables (HR, RR, systolic/diastolic BP, temperature, and SpO2); iii) synthetic ECG with HTML5; iv) prognosis tutor with pedagogical rules; and v) a follow-up module with a severity ranking inspired by TOPSIS. The simulator achieves a Haemodynamic Stability Index (HSI) of up to 0.60 for optimal interventions (e.g., IV fluids in hypovolemic shock) and a Therapeutic Effectiveness Coefficient (TEC) of 1.0 for correct actions, as validated with synthetic data. We describe the architecture, physiological heuristics, and user flow. Validation is currently limited to synthetic data, with future work planned for user testing and external clinical validation. We describe the architecture, data design, physiological heuristics, and user flow, and propose extensions to turn it into a reproducible evaluation environment (metrics, testing, PWA packaging, and educational analytics). The system not only facilitates diagnostic and prognostic practice but also serves as a platform for analysis and critical decision-making in the care of patients in shock, demonstrating its potential as a teaching and support tool in clinical practice.

Keywords: Medical Simulation · Topsis · Triage · Virtual Tutor

1 Introduction

Recently, simulation has emerged as a key tool for medical education, research, and technological development. Traditional training with real patients or in hospitals faces serious limitations in terms of safety, accessibility, and reproducibility of clinical scenarios [1]. Given these limitations, vital signs simulators have been developed as platforms capable

L. Martínez-Villaseñor et al. (Eds.): MICAI 2025 Workshops, LNAI 16264, pp. 124–136, 2026.
https://doi.org/10.1007/978-3-032-17930-2_9

of recreating physiological conditions in a controlled, safe, and repeatable manner, providing an ideal environment for teaching and assessing clinical skills [2–4]. Simulation has thus established itself as a fundamental tool in current medical education, allowing students to develop and refine clinical skills in a safe and controlled environment [5–7].

Historical events such as the COVID-19 pandemic drove the implementation and development of emerging technologies such as simulation in medical education [8, 9]. The global health emergency forced a sudden shift to remote learning due to social distancing measures, partial or total closure of institutions, limited and time-restricted access, and risks of infection in clinical settings [9]. This situation not only disrupted conventional medical education for millions of students and the way teachers taught around the world, but also accelerated innovation in remote and virtual simulation to maintain quality education [10]. For example, during the pandemic, simulations were reported for nursing students and emergency medical services (EMS) personnel, who used digital platforms to train in the management of respiratory complications in COVID-19 patients, overcoming limitations such as the lack of physical mannequins [11, 12]. In Latin America, the use of simulation has increased significantly, with the implementation of videoconferencing integrated with 3D modelling to replicate clinical scenarios, achieving results comparable to those of conventional methods in terms of skills and knowledge acquisition [13].

This demonstrates a growing trend in current education models, which are moving towards the adoption of simulation as a teaching strategy. This responds to the need to minimise risks both for patients—by avoiding exposing them to procedures performed by trainees—and for the students themselves, who find a safe environment free from adverse consequences [14, 15]. Additionally, simulation allows for the creation of controlled and standardised scenarios that can be repeated as many times as necessary, which promotes the acquisition of decision-making skills under pressure and feedback on mistakes made without compromising patient safety [16, 17, 18].

Monitoring vital signs is essential for clinical assessment, particularly in emergencies such as shock. The main parameters include heart rate (HR, bpm), respiratory rate (RR, bpm), blood pressure (BP, systolic/diastolic mmHg), body temperature (°C), and oxygen saturation (SpO2, %) [19]. Shock is defined as a syndrome of inadequate tissue perfusion and has distinct aetiological subtypes: hypovolemic, septic, cardiogenic, and anaphylactic [20–22]. Each type of shock has characteristic vital signs.

Conventional training approaches, such as standardised patients or low-fidelity manikins, have significant limitations: high costs and limited accessibility. In addition, they often lack integration with real-time data analysis tools or adaptive feedback [23]. According to Maran and Glavin [24], clinical simulation not only promotes technical skills but also abilities such as decision-making and teamwork in high-pressure environments. Similarly, Issenberg et al. [25] point out that high-fidelity simulators have a significant impact on knowledge acquisition and the transfer of practical skills.

Currently, virtual patients and tutors represent a fundamental part of educational innovation in the health sector. Virtual patients allow realistic and dynamic clinical scenarios to be recreated in real time, facilitating training in the assessment of such patients, the recognition of pathologies, and decision-making, without exposing a real patient to unnecessary risks [26–29]. On the other hand, virtual tutors provide complementary support, offering immediate and adaptive feedback and acting as guides who accompany students in problem-solving and correction [30, 31].

The use of virtual patients is emerging as a central element in teaching primary clinical assessment, resuscitation, and initial decision-making [28]. The availability of simulators that can be run directly in a browser extends the reach of these technologies by facilitating their application in academic settings [32–34]. This paper presents the development and implementation of a web-based vital signs simulator based on virtual patients, for use in the predictive diagnosis of the four main shock syndromes—hypovolaemic, septic, cardiogenic, and anaphylactic—as well as healthy patient scenarios for comparison. This interactive tool, based on web technologies such as HTML5 and JavaScript, incorporates a set of functionalities that include: dynamic visualisation of vital parameters in real time, simulated execution of therapeutic interventions (oxygen therapy, intravenous fluids, administration of antibiotics or antihistamines), immediate feedback through conditional logic, and monitoring of user performance through saved clinical cases, formative questionnaires, and quantitative metrics such as TOPSIS (Technique for Order of Preference by Similarity to Ideal Solution) rankings to prioritise the severity of shocks. This ensures safe and repeatable practice, enriching the educational experience in medical training environments.

2 Experimental Methods

2.1 General Structure

The IVSS (Intelligent Vital Signs Simulator) is a web application structured with three tabs: *Diagnosis*, *Prognosis*, and *Clinical Follow-up*. The simulator's workflow is divided into three stages. In the Diagnosis tab, the parameters are configured by selecting the clinical scenario to be simulated (virtual patient). Next, in the *Prognosis* tab, the diagnosis and therapeutic actions are selected, allowing the virtual patient's response to different scenarios to be observed in the *Follow-up* tab. Here, an evaluation of the results obtained is displayed, providing immediate feedback. Clinical cases are stored using *localStorage*, without the need for servers.

The IVSS was validated using synthetic data generated within physiological ranges (Table 1), simulating clinical scenarios without real patient involvement. This approach ensures repeatability and safety but limits validation to synthetic data.

2.2 Vital Signs Parameters and Ranges

Vital signs are within ranges established in the literature [21, 22]. Table 1 summarises the ranges for each scenario.

Table 1. Physiological parameter ranges for each shock type and healthy baseline.

Scenario	Heart Rate (bpm)	Respiratory Rate (rpm)	Systolic BP (mmHg)	Diastolic BP (mmHg)	Temp (°C)	SpO2 (%)
Hypovolemic Shock	120–150	20–30	50–80	30–50	36.0–37.5	90–95
Septic Shock	110–140	24–40	60–90	40–60	38.5–40.0	85–89
Cardiogenic Shock	100–120	20–30	50–80	30–50	36.0–37.0	58–59
Anaphylactic Shock	100–140	20–40	50–80	30–50	36.0–37.0	85–89
Healthy Patient	60–100	12–20	110–130	70–85	36.5–37.5	95–100

2.3 Interface

Tabbed browsing was implemented using CSS classes that manage event states in JavaScript, allowing users to navigate between sections smoothly. Virtual patients were represented by an image map that divides a grid into clickable areas (Fig. 1), each associated with a specific clinical scenario through onclick handlers. The display monitors show vital signs in real time, with a design like that of real monitors. Finally, functionalities such as the option to save cases were incorporated.

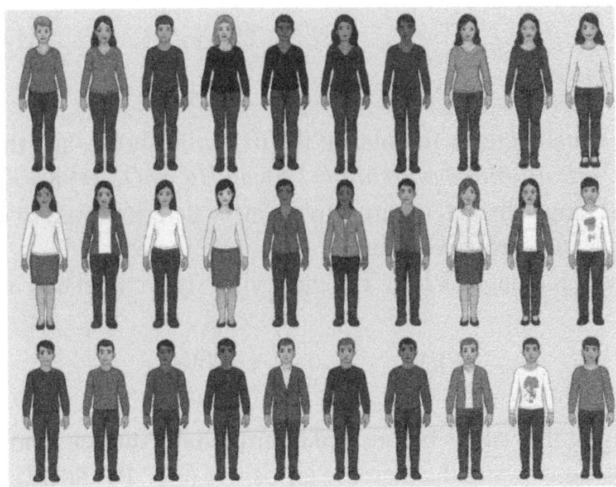

Fig. 1. Grid of clickable avatars representing virtual patients, each linked to a specific shock scenario with corresponding vital signs.

Technical Implementation

The simulator consists solely of a < *script* > tag that concentrates the logic in JavaScript. The scenario application assigns specific value ranges to each case and generates them stochastically through auxiliary functions such as *randomInRange()* and *randomFloatInRange()*. Student mode incorporates a questionnaire that uses onclick events to evaluate their answers. *LocalStorage* is used to save clinical cases, allowing them to be retrieved later. Finally, the prognosis tab enables the selection of therapeutic actions according to the previously selected diagnosis, modifying vital signs. These results are evaluated using switch-case structures and additionally classified using the TOPSIS technique, which assesses the severity of different types of shock based on coefficients related to mortality and urgency.

Table 2. TOPSIS-Based severity classification of shock types of proximity coefficients and rankings for hypovolemic, septic, cardiogenic, and anaphylactic shock.

Type of Shock	Proximity Coefficient	Classification
Hypovolemic Shock	0.8567	1
Septic Shock	0.8123	2
Cardiogenic Shock	0.7654	3
Anaphylactic Shock	0.7231	4

2.4 Technical Implementation

The following metrics were defined to quantify the results:

Haemodynamic Stability Index (HSI): Assesses overall recovery, calculated as:

$$HSI = w_1\left(\frac{FC_N - FC_F}{FC_N - FC_I}\right) + w_2\left(\frac{PA_{sis,F} - PA_{sis,I}}{PA_{sis,N} - PA_{sis,I}}\right) + w_3\left(\frac{SpO2_F - SpO2_I}{100 - SpO2_I}\right) + w_4\left(1 - \frac{|T_F - T_N|}{|T_I - T_N|}\right) + w_5\left(\frac{FR_N - FR_F}{FR_N - FR_I}\right) \tag{1}$$

Where $w_n = 0.2$ (equal weights to balance the five vital signs), and the normal values are: $HR = 80\ bpm$, $systolic\ blood\ pressure = 120\ mmHg$, $SpO2 = 98\%$, $T = 36.8\ ^\circ C$, $RR = 16\ rpm$. The HSI ranges from 0 (no improvement or deterioration) to 1 (full recovery), with negative values indicating worsening.

Vital Recovery Percentage (VRP): For each vital sign, calculated as:

$$PRV = \frac{V_F - V_I}{V_N - V_I} x\ 100\% \tag{2}$$

Where V_F and V_I are the values before and after the intervention, and V_N is the target value. Adjusted for signs where the increase is positive (e.g., BP, SpO2) or negative (e.g., HR in tachycardia).

Therapeutic Effectiveness Coefficient (TEC): Based on qualitative feedback from the simulator (Correct = 1.0, Partial = 0.5, Incorrect = 0.0).

$$CET_{tight} = CET\left(1 - \frac{Coeficiente_{TOPSIS}}{\mathrm{Max}_{coefficient}}\right) \tag{3}$$

Where CET_{tight} incorporates TOPSIS to classify actions into more severe shocks. $Max_{coefficient} = 0.8567$ (septic), and $Coeficiente_{TOPSIS}$ is the value of the TOPSIS coefficient (Table 2) for each virtual patient.

Simulated Resolution Time (SRT): To estimate the hypothetical time until stabilisation.

$$SRT = \frac{60}{IEH + 0.1} \tag{4}$$

Where 60 is a reference value, the higher the *IEH*, the lower the *TRS*.

3 Results and Discussion

To evaluate the IVSS, a simulated case study approach was used, which allows for analysis of clinical scenarios without the need to involve real patients. This is in line with standard practices in medical simulation, where synthetic data based on physiological ranges are generated to test interventions [25, 35, 36].

Virtual patients were selected from the *Diagnosis* tab to generate random vital sign values within the established ranges (Table 1). In the *Prognosis* tab (Fig. 2), the type of shock was selected, and various actions were performed.

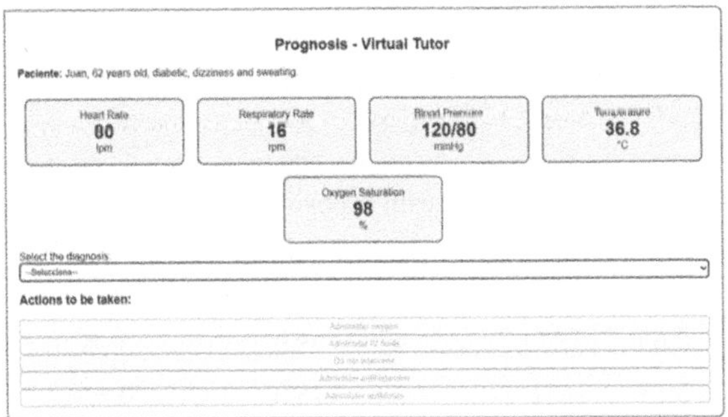

Fig. 2. 'Prognosis' tab interface. Real-time display of vital signs for a virtual patient, showing physiological parameters during simulation.

Finally, in the *Clinical Follow-up* tab (Fig. 3), variations in vital signs were documented and displayed, feedback was provided, and specific quantitative metrics were calculated to perform a detailed technical analysis of the system's performance.

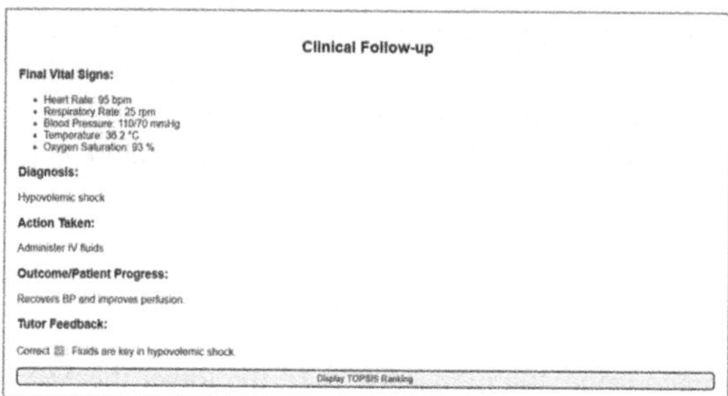

Fig. 3. Clinical Follow-up tab interface. The panel displays final vital signs, diagnosis ("hypovolemic_shock"), selected action ("Administer IV fluids"), outcome ("Recovers BP and improves perfusion"), and tutor feedback ("Correct: Fluids are key in hypovolemic shock"). A button to display the TOPSIS ranking is also shown, enabling severity comparison across shock types.

A case study is presented with a virtual patient, evaluating all the options to be selected. The virtual patient 'Juan' was chosen from the image map (coords = '0, 0, 75, 150'), associated with *applyScenario* ("hypovolemic_shock"). Description: A 62-year-old man presenting with dizziness, sweating, and signs of acute dehydration due to vomiting and diarrhoea. The results obtained from the metrics for each action are shown in Table 3. Four key performance metrics are calculated for each intervention: Hemodynamic Stability Index (HSI), Vital Recovery (VR) percentage per parameter, Therapeutic Effectiveness Coefficient (TEC), and Simulated Resolution Time (SRT). These provide quantitative feedback on the quality of clinical decisions.

Table 3. Performance metrics for therapeutic actions in hypovolemic shock. Case Study Metrics (HSI, PRV, CET, TRS) for a virtual patient with hypovolemic shock under different interventions.

Selected Action	HSI	PRV PA_{sis} (%)	PRV SpO2	CET_{tight}	SRT (min)
IV fluids	0.60	81.8	75.0	0.05	85.7
Oxygen	0.15	9.1	75.0	0.026	240
Wait	-0.25	-18.2	-50.0	0.0	-
Antihistamine	0.05	-5.5	-12.5	0.0	300
Antibiotic	-0.10	-9.1	-25.0	0.0	>240

Table 4. Vital sign variations in hypovolemic shock case study. Changes in heart rate, respiratory rate, blood pressure, temperature, and SpO2 after therapeutic actions.

Selected Action	FC (bpm)	RR (rpm)	BP (mmHg)	Temp (°C)	SpO2 (%)
No action (Initial data)	135	25	65/40	36.8	92
IV fluids	95	18	110/70	36.8	98
Oxygen	130	22	70/45	36.8	98

(*continued*)

Table 4. (*continued*)

Selected Action	FC (bpm)	RR (rpm)	BP (mmHg)	Temp (°C)	SpO2 (%)
Wait	145	28	55/35	36.5	88
Antihistamine	138	26	62/38	36.8	91
Antibiotic	140	27	60/38	37	90

The results show that intravenous fluid administration is the only means capable of producing a significant improvement in the physiological parameters of the virtual patient, as reflected in an HSI of 0.5. In contrast, the other therapeutic alternatives fail to reverse the clinical picture, producing additional risks, reflected in a CET of 0.0, which represents inadequate decisions. When integrating TOPSIS for the prioritisation of eventualities, it was observed that the proximity coefficient associated with hypovolemic shock was 0.8123, placing it second in the severity ranking. However, when the CET tight penalty is incorporated, the scores for those actions applied in states of shock are reduced.

Fig. 4 shows the behaviour of the IEH in relation to different actions applied to a virtual patient in hypovolemic shock. This index quantifies the ability of each intervention to improve or deteriorate physiological parameters. Positive values reflect an improvement, while negative values indicate ineffective or potentially harmful inter ventions.

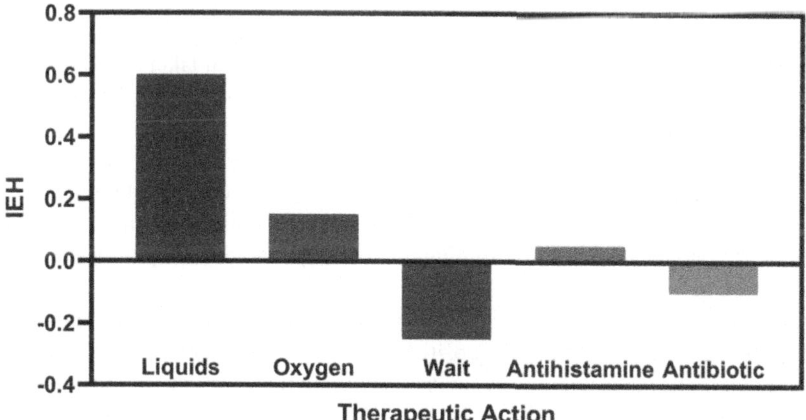

Fig. 4. Haemodynamic stability index (HSI) for therapeutic actions. Bar chart comparing HSI (0 = no improvement, 1 = full recovery) for interventions in a hypovolemic shock case study.

The graph reveals that intravenous fluid administration is the only action with a positive impact, achieving an HSI ≈ 0.5, which positions it as the first line of treatment for correcting hypovolaemia. Oxygen administration shows an HSI ≈ 0.15, suggesting limited benefit. On the other hand, waiting without intervention generates an HSI $\approx$ – 0.25, showing a worsening attributable to the progression of shock without treatment.

Similarly, the data collected on the variation in vital signs when performing the actions are presented in Table 4. The different physiological parameters of the virtual patient at the beginning of the case study (without any action taken) are compared with the values obtained when performing the action of administering intravenous fluids, as shown in Fig. 5.

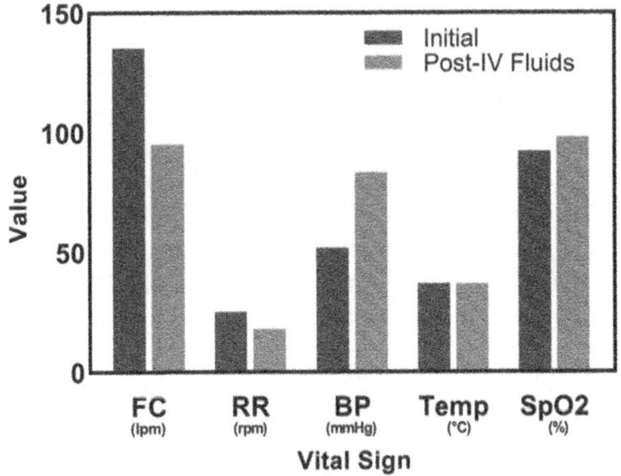

Fig. 5. Vital sign changes post-IV fluids in hypovolemic shock. Comparison of initial and post-intervention vital signs (heart rate, respiratory rate, blood pressure, SpO2) for a virtual patient.

There is a significant improvement in vital signs, mainly in BP, where there is an increase from 50 to 80 mmHg, thus establishing that the action taken was appropriate. In addition, the heart rate drops (130 bpm) to a normal rate (100 bpm). Meanwhile, the respiratory rate decreases (from 22 to 18 rpm).

Fig. 4 and Fig. 5 show that the action that improves the patient's shock condition is the administration of fluids. This result is in line with the clinical literature [37, 38] and with the previously analysed metrics (HSI and CET), highlighting the use of the simulator as a pedagogical tool for training realistic physiological responses and clinical decision-making.

While the current validation relies on synthetic data, the physiological patterns produced by the simulator—such as the positive response to fluid administration in hypovolemic shock or the persistence of hypotension without intervention—align closely with established clinical evidence [21, 22, 37, 38]. Furthermore, the severity ranking derived from the TOPSIS method accurately reflects the relative severity of shock syndromes as documented in medical literature. This physiological and clinical consistency supports the simulator's potential as an effective educational tool, particularly in settings with limited access to real patient scenarios.

Furthermore, to provide a broader view of the different types of shock and their clinical consequences, shock profiles are compared based on different metrics and the TOPSIS index, as shown in Fig. 6.

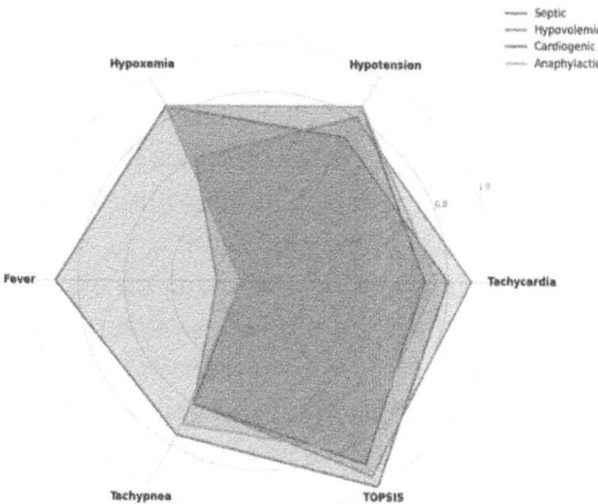

Fig. 6. Comparative profiles of shocks scenarios. Radar chart showing standardized metrics (tachycardia, hypotension, hypoxaemia, fever, tachypnoea, TOPSIS) for hypovolemic, septic, cardiogenic, and anaphylactic shock.

Each radial axis corresponds to a standardized metric on a scale of 0–1, in which values close to 1 indicate a high level of severity. In contrast, values close to zero indicate that they are similar to the normal values for these conditions. The profile of each shock shows its similarities, differences, and characteristic patterns. Hypovolemic shock stands out for its high heart rate (tachycardia) and hypotension values, as well as a less noticeable impact on oxygenation (tachypnea). The use of TOPSIS as a metric highlights the overall differences in severity and facilitates classification between conditions.

The current evaluation relies on synthetic data within physiological ranges, which ensures controlled and repeatable scenarios but limits generalizability to real clinical settings. The absence of user testing or external validation with real patients is a key limitation. Future work will involve controlled user studies with medical students and clinicians to assess usability and effectiveness, alongside integration of real patient data to validate the simulator's diagnostic and prognostic accuracy. These steps will enhance the IVSS's applicability in clinical education and practice.

4 Conclusion

The development of IVSS is based on the physiological principles that govern the human body's response to states of shock. These states are characterised by alterations in vital signs, reflecting an imbalance in homeostasis. Standardised metrics derived from TOPSIS are integrated, allowing for an assessment of severity and therapeutic response, as well as supporting the diagnosis and identification of patterns characteristic of each type of shock. In addition, the IVSS emerges as a clinical education tool, providing a viable option for training healthcare personnel, avoiding putting the integrity of the student at risk during their training, as well as ensuring patient safety. It also provides repeatability in the practice of clinical scenarios. This aligns with the principles of active learning, where simulation offers a safe environment to practise clinical decision-making and receive feedback. In this way, the potential use of the simulator is reinforced, especially in resource-limited contexts where students do not have direct access to real patients or clinical cases, a situation recently evidenced during the SARS-CoV-2 pandemic. However, we recognize an important limitation: the metrics and physiological dynamics do not incorporate individual anthropometric characteristics (such as age, sex, weight, or comorbidities), and the avatars displayed in the interface (Fig. 1) function solely as visual representations of scenarios. Although this facilitates initial teaching, it reduces clinical realism and limits the customization of the simulator.

To address this limitation, future work will focus on expanding the physiological model by including individualized patient profiles, so that physical and clinical characteristics influence baseline values, responses to interventions, and assessment metrics. In addition, the development of a mobile app for continuous monitoring of people with these conditions could be explored. This tool would not only facilitate real-time monitoring of the most relevant clinical parameters but would also generate early warnings for potential decompensations, thus providing additional support for both patients and the healthcare personnel in charge of their care. Finally, this tool shows scalability for integration into hospital systems, with the possibility of incorporating artificial intelligence algorithms in the future that allow for more accurate and personalised predictions.

Acknowledgments. This work has been supported by the Centre for Research in Engineering and Applied Sciences at the Autonomous University of the State of Morelos. The authors would like to express their gratitude for the development of this work.

Disclosure of Interests. The authors declare that they have no competing interests relevant to the content of this article.

References

1. Moslehi, S., Masoumi, G., Barghi-Shirazi, F.: Benefits of Simulation-Based Education in Hospital Emergency Departments: a Systematic Review (2022). https://doi.org/10.4103/jehp.jehp_558_21
2. Bergamo, P.A.d.S., Streng, E.S., de Carvalho, M.A., Rosenkranz, J., Ghorbani, Y.: Simulation-based training and learning: a review on technology-enhanced education for the minerals industry. (2022). https://doi.org/10.1016/j.mineng.2021.107272
3. Amaya, D., Melendez, D., Marin, M., Cubias, J.: Construction and Design of a Didactic Prototype of a Vital Signs Monitor programmed with LabVIEW. In: Proceedings of 2023 IEEE Central America and Panama Student Conference. CONESCAPAN 2023 (2023). https://doi.org/10.1109/CONESCAPAN60431.2023.10328422
4. Ren, Q., Chen, F., Zhang, H., Tu, J., Xu, X., Liu, C.: Effects of a standardized patient-based simulation in anaphylactic shock management for new graduate nurses. BMC Nurs. **21**(1) (2022). https://doi.org/10.1186/s12912-022-00995-y
5. McInerney, N., Nally, D., Khan, M.F., Heneghan, H., Cahill, R.A.: Performance effects of simulation training for medical students – a systematic review. GMS J. Med. Educ. **39**(5) (2022). https://doi.org/10.3205/zma001572
6. Carrero-Planells, A., Pol-Castañeda, S., Alamillos-Guardiola, M.C., Prieto-Alomar, A., Tomás-Sánchez, M., Moreno-Mulet, C.: Students and teachers' satisfaction and perspectives on high-fidelity simulation for learning fundamental nursing procedures: a mixed-method study. Nurse Educ. Today. **104** (2021). https://doi.org/10.1016/j.nedt.2021.104981
7. Fraser, K., et al.: Simulation training improves diagnostic performance on a real patient with similar clinical findings. Chest. **139**(2) (2011). https://doi.org/10.1378/chest.10-1107

8. Ajab, S., et al.: An Alternative to Traditional Bedside Teaching during COVID-19: High-Fidelity Simulation-Based Study. JMIR Med. Educ. **8**(2) (2022). https://doi.org/10.2196/33565
9. Tabatabai, S.M.: COVID-19 impact and virtual medical education. (2020). https://doi.org/10.30476/jamp.2020.86070.1213
10. McGue, S.R., Pelic, C.M., McCadden, A., Pelic, C.G., Lewis, A.L.: The Use of Simulation in Teaching (2021). https://doi.org/10.1016/j.psc.2021.03.002
11. Niu, A., Ma, H., Zhang, S., Zhu, X., Deng, J., Luo, Y.: The Effectiveness of Simulation-Based Training on the Competency of Military Nurses: a Systematic Review (2022). https://doi.org/10.1016/j.nedt.2022.105536
12. Jallad, S.T., Işık, B.: The Effectiveness of Virtual Reality Simulation as Learning Strategy in the Acquisition of Medical Skills in Nursing Education: a Systematic Review (2022). https://doi.org/10.1007/s11845-021-02695-z
13. Díaz-Guio, D.A., et al.: Online-synchronized clinical simulation: an efficient teaching-learning option for the COVID-19 pandemic time and: beyond. Adv.Simul. **6**(1) (2021). https://doi.org/10.1186/s41077-021-00183-z
14. Ayaz, O., Ismail, F.W.: Healthcare simulation: a key to the future of medical education – A Review. (2022). https://doi.org/10.2147/AMEP.S353777
15. Pardue, K.T.: Exploring the development of nursing clinical judgment among students using virtual reality simulation. Nurse Educ. **48**(2) (2023). https://doi.org/10.1097/NNE.0000000000001318
16. Al-Elq, A.H.: Simulation-based medical teaching and learning. J. Fam. Community Med. **17**(1) (2010). https://doi.org/10.4103/1319-1683.68787
17. Kassutto, S., Clancy, C., Harbison, S., Tsao, S.: A virtual simulation-based clinical skills course. Clin. Teach. **21**(4) (2024). https://doi.org/10.1111/tct.13727
18. Zackoff, M.W., et al.: Multiuser immersive virtual reality simulation for interprofessional sepsis recognition and management. J. Hosp. Med. **19**(3) (2024). https://doi.org/10.1002/jhm.13274
19. Rady, M.Y., Smithline, H.A., Blake, H., Nowak, R., Rivers, E.: A comparison of the shock index and conventional vital signs to identify acute, critical illness in the emergency department. Ann. Emerg. Med. **24**(4) (1994). https://doi.org/10.1016/S0196-0644(94)70279-9
20. Meltzer, S.J.: The nature of shock. Arch. Intern. Med. **1**(6) (1908). https://doi.org/10.1001/archinte.1908.00050050002001
21. Longo, D., Fauci, A., Kasper, D., Hauser, S., Jameson, L., Loscalzo, J.: Harrison: principios de medicina interna (18° ed). In: Harrison Principios de Medicina interna (2012)
22. Tintinelli: Tintinalli's Emergency Medicine Manual. (2018)
23. Dávila-Cervantes, A.: Simulación en Educación Médica. Invest. Educ. Méd. **3**(10) (2014). https://doi.org/10.1016/s2007-5057(14)72733-4
24. Maran, N.J., Glavin, R.J.: Low- to High-Fidelity Simulation - a Continuum of Medical Education? (2003). https://doi.org/10.1046/j.1365-2923.37.s1.9.x
25. Issenberg, S.B., McGaghie, W.C., Petrusa, E.R., Gordon, D.L., Scalese, R.J.: Features and Uses of High-Fidelity Medical Simulations that Lead to Effective Learning: a BEME Systematic Review (2005). https://doi.org/10.1080/01421590500046924
26. Woodham, L.A., Ellaway, R.H., Round, J., Vaughan, S., Poulton, T., Zary, N.: Medical student and tutor perceptions of video versus text in an interactive online virtual patient for problem-based learning: a pilot study. J. Med. Internet Res. **17**(6) (2015). https://doi.org/10.2196/jmir.3922

27. Lehmann, R., Bosse, H.M., Simon, A., Nikendei, C., Huwendiek, S.: An innovative blended learning approach using virtual patients as preparation for skills laboratory training: perceptions of students and tutors. BMC Med. Educ. **13**(1) (2013). https://doi.org/10.1186/1472-6920-13-23
28. Berman, N.B., Durning, S.J., Fischer, M.R., Huwendiek, S., Triola, M.M.: The Role for Virtual Patients in the Future of Medical Education (2016). https://doi.org/10.1097/ACM.0000000000001146
29. Cook, D.A., Erwin, P.J., Triola, M.M.: Computerized virtual patients in health professions education: a systematic review and meta-analysis. (2010). https://doi.org/10.1097/acm.0b013e3181edfe13
30. Ward, W., Cole, R., Bolaños, D., Buchenroth-Martin, C., Svirsky, E., Weston, T.: My science tutor: A conversational multimedia virtual tutor. J. Educ. Psychol. **105**(4) (2013). https://doi.org/10.1037/a0031589
31. Wilcha, R.J.: Effectiveness of Virtual Medical Teaching during the COVID-19 Crisis: Systematic Review (2020). https://doi.org/10.2196/20963
32. Stodulka, P., Privitzer, P.: Development of WEB accessible medical educational simulators. Proc. EUROSIM. **2007**, 2007 (2007)
33. Kleinert, R., et al.: Web-based immersive virtual patient simulators: positive effect on clinical reasoning in medical education. J. Med. Internet Res. **17**(11) (2015). https://doi.org/10.2196/jmir.5035
34. Michael, M., Abboudi, H., Ker, J., Khan, M.S., Dasgupta, P., Ahmed, K.: Performance of Technology-Driven Simulators for Medical Students - a Systematic Review (2014). https://doi.org/10.1016/j.jss.2014.06.043
35. McGaghie, W.C., Issenberg, S.B., Petrusa, E.R., Scalese, R.J.: A Critical Review of Simulation-Based Medical Education Research: 2003–2009 (2010). https://doi.org/10.1111/j.1365-2923.2009.03547.x
36. Cook, D.A., et al.: Technology-Enhanced Simulation for Health Professions Education: a Systematic Review and Meta-Analysis (2011). https://doi.org/10.1001/jama.2011.1234
37. Rozanski, E., Rondeau, M.: Choosing fluids in traumatic hypovolemic shock: the role of crystalloids, colloids, and hypertonic saline. J. Am. Anim. Hosp. Assoc. **38**(6) (2002). https://doi.org/10.5326/0380499
38. Kelley, D.M.: Hypovolemic Shock: an Overview (2005). https://doi.org/10.1097/00002727-200501000-00002

Application of Artificial Intelligence in Personalized Education

Yadira Dozal Assmar[1], Roberto Contreras-Masse[1](✉), Miranda Victoria Hernández Dozal[2], Irving Orlando Hernández Andrade[1], and Luis Fernando Ayala González[1]

[1] TecNM Campus ITCJ, Cd Juarez Chih, Mexico
[2] University of Texas at El Paso, Texas, USA

Abstract. This scoping review explores the application of Artificial Intelligence (AI) in personalized education by synthesizing findings from 40 peer-reviewed academic articles. The review follows the methodological framework proposed by Arksey and O'Malley, with enhancements introduced by Levac et al. and Daudt et al., to ensure a rigorous and comprehensive mapping of the field. The main objectives were to identify the types of AI technologies employed to support personalized learning, the strategies and models implemented, and the outcomes and limitations reported in the literature. Articles were selected from two curated reference documents and analyzed through a structured data matrix encompassing variables such as AI type, educational level, personalization approach, and methodological design. Results reveal a growing interest in AI-driven tools such as intelligent tutoring systems, machine learning models, and natural language processing, with applications ranging from adaptive content delivery to learner feedback personalization. However, gaps remain in the integration of pedagogical theories, ethical considerations, and empirical validation across diverse educational settings. The findings highlight both the opportunities and the current challenges in advancing AI-driven personalized learning and provide a foundation for future empirical and theoretical research in this evolving domain.

Keywords: Artificial Intelligence · Personalized Learning · Adaptive Education · Learning Analytics · Educational Technology · Machine Learning in Education

1 Introduction

In recent years, Artificial Intelligence (AI) has emerged as a key tool in education, enabling the development of personalized learning models that aim to optimize teaching according to students' specific needs. The use of AI in personalized education has proven to be an innovative solution for improving the efficiency of teaching and learning processes, providing adaptive experiences based on students' behavior and performance.

AI-assisted personalized education encompasses a variety of approaches, including intelligent tutoring systems, predictive learning models, teaching assistants based on Natural Language Processing (NLP), and educational data analytics for pedagogical

L. Martínez-Villaseñor et al. (Eds.): MICAI 2025 Workshops, LNAI 16264, pp. 137–161, 2026.
https://doi.org/10.1007/978-3-032-17930-2_10

decision-making. However, despite its growth and significant advancements, the field continues to face challenges related to ethics, privacy, pedagogical effectiveness, and integration into traditional educational systems.

To understand the impact of Artificial Intelligence in personalized education and its future implications, this literature review is guided by the following research questions:

RQ1. What types of artificial intelligence technologies are being used in personalized education?

RQ2. In which educational levels and contexts are these technologies being implemented?

RQ3. What personalization strategies are being applied through AI tools?

RQ4. What are the documented benefits of using AI in personalized learning?

RQ5. What limitations or research gaps have been identified regarding the use of AI in education?

RQ6. What ethical or operational controversies are discussed in the literature?

This scoping review aims to synthesize key findings from recent academic literature, identify dominant trends and technologies, highlight unresolved issues, and propose future directions for research and innovation in the use of AI for personalized education.

2 Methodology

This study adopted the scoping review framework proposed by Arksey and O'Malley (2005), incorporating enhancements suggested by Levac et al. (2010) and Daudt et al. (2013). This methodology was considered particularly appropriate given its strength in addressing broad and exploratory research questions, especially within emerging or fragmented fields. The application of artificial intelligence (AI) in personalized education represents such a domain—characterized by rapid technological evolution, interdisciplinary overlap, and a lack of consolidated evidence. By employing a scoping review, this study was able to systematically map key concepts, examine the range of methodologies and contexts involved, and identify gaps in the current body of literature that may inform future research agendas. (Arksey and O'Malley, 2005; Levac et al., 2010; Daudt et al., 2013).

2.1 Methodological Approach

The review followed the five stages outlined in the original framework, incorporating methodological refinements to enhance rigor and consistency:

1. Identifying the Research Questions

The six guiding research questions were defined prior to data collection and were iteratively refined during the review process to ensure alignment with the literature. The questions focused on identifying key AI applications in personalized education, the models and methodologies used, the reported benefits and challenges, and the existing research gaps.

2. Identifying Relevant Studies

The review corpus consisted of 40 individually peer-reviewed academic articles. These documents were preselected for their relevance to the topic. A centralized matrix was also created to organize each article's metadata and analytical variables, such as AI type, educational level, personalization strategy, and key contributions.

3. Study Selection

Inclusion criteria were defined to incorporate studies that addressed the use of AI technologies in formal or informal educational contexts with a clear focus on personalization of learning. Articles that focused exclusively on administrative or non-instructional uses of AI were excluded. The selection was carried out manually and systematically, ensuring that all included studies aligned with the research scope.

4. Data Charting

A structured data extraction template was used to record relevant information from each article. This included: publication year, AI technology employed (e.g., intelligent tutoring systems, machine learning, natural language processing), educational level (e.g., K-12, higher education), personalization approach (e.g., content adaptation, pace control, feedback customization), methodological design, and main findings. Data charting was performed using the Excel control file, enabling consistent categorization and cross-comparison.

5. Collating, Summarizing, and Reporting Results

A descriptive and thematic synthesis was conducted. Articles were grouped based on the type of AI intervention and personalization dimension. Emerging patterns and trends were identified, as well as common challenges and research gaps. This synthesis served both to map the state of the field and to inform future research opportunities.

To identify relevant studies, searches were conducted across major academic databases, including IEEE Xplore, ACM Digital Library, ScienceDirect, Springer-Link, and Scopus. These platforms were chosen due to their extensive coverage of peer-reviewed research in technology and education. The search strategy involved Boolean combinations of keywords such as "Chatbot", "Conversational Agent", "Pedagogical Agent", with educational terms like "Education", "Learning", "Teacher", and "Student". This approach ensured a broad yet targeted retrieval of literature aligned with the scope of the study.

2.2 Rationale for Methodological Choice

The interdisciplinary, rapidly evolving nature of artificial intelligence (AI) in education necessitates a flexible yet rigorous methodological approach capable of accommodating heterogeneous sources of evidence. In this context, a scoping review was selected as the most appropriate methodological framework, primarily due to its strength in mapping key concepts, identifying research gaps, and synthesizing findings from a wide range of study types and disciplinary perspectives. As outlined by Arksey and O'Malley (2005) and further refined by Levac et al. (2010) and Daudt et al. (2013), the scoping review methodology is particularly suitable for examining complex and emerging fields where the literature is fragmented or unevenly distributed across domains. (Arksey and O'Malley, 2005; Levac et al., 2010; Daudt et al., 2013).

This method enables researchers to explore the breadth and depth of existing evidence without the constraints of assessing study quality, which aligns with the exploratory nature of our objectives. Specifically, our aim was to examine how AI technologies are being applied to support personalized education, to identify the educational contexts in which these technologies are deployed, and to uncover prevailing challenges and conceptual boundaries within the field.

Moreover, as Daudt et al. (2013) emphasize, the scoping review framework facilitates a process of iterative refinement of research questions and inclusion criteria, which proved valuable throughout this study. The structured yet adaptable nature of the methodology allowed for the inclusion of diverse sources, from empirical studies and theoretical papers to frameworks and case reports. This comprehensiveness was essential to capture the multifaceted applications of AI in personalized learning environments.

Ultimately, the selection of the scoping review method was driven by its alignment with our research goals: to comprehensively map the state of the field, synthesize scattered insights, and provide a solid foundation for future investigations. By embracing this methodology, the study was able to offer a clear, thematic overview of current trends while also illuminating underexplored areas that merit further scholarly attention.

2.3 Graphical Representation of the Methodology

To enhance transparency and improve comprehension of the methodological pathway followed in this study, a flowchart diagram is provided (Fig. 1). This visual representation systematically illustrates the five core stages of the scoping review process, from the initial formulation of the research question to the final synthesis of results. It also delineates the logical sequence of decisions made during the screening and selection of studies, including the application of inclusion and exclusion criteria. By summarizing the process in a structured and accessible format, the diagram serves as a complementary tool to the narrative description, facilitating a clearer understanding of how the review was conducted and how the final corpus of literature was determined.

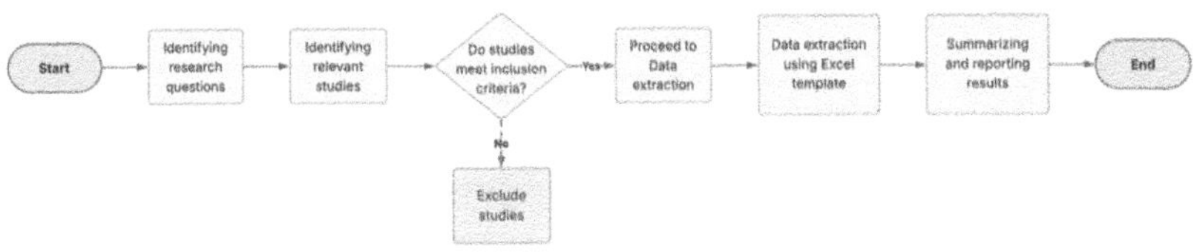

Fig. 1. Flowchart of the methodological process

3 Development

The review examined a total of 40 scientific articles published between 2018 2024, focusing on the application of artificial intelligence (AI) for personalized education. The articles were systematically analyzed, highlighting trends, advances, gaps, and controversies. Based on the content in each section, a detailed overview was obtained of current contributions, established lines of work, and remaining challenges.

3.1 Applied AI Technologies

Most studies employ technologies associated with symbolic and connectionist artificial intelligence. These include:

AI-powered intelligent assistants, as described in "Artificial Intelligence Enabled Intelligent Assistant for Personalized and Adaptive Learning in Higher Education" (Sajja et al., 2024), represent a significant advancement in the design of adaptive learning environments. These systems are capable of dynamically analyzing a student's learning behavior, performance data, and interaction patterns to tailor educational content, adjust the level of difficulty, and provide timely support. By continuously updating their recommendations based on individual progress and learner profiles, intelligent assistants foster a more personalized and efficient educational experience. The study by Sajja et al. highlights how such tools can bridge gaps in traditional instruction by offering scalable, individualized guidance that aligns with each student's unique needs and learning pace. (Sajja et al., 2024).

Machine learning is a cross-cutting technique that plays a pivotal role in enabling personalized education through its ability to analyze large volumes of data and extract meaningful behavioral patterns. As noted in "Smart Education with Artificial Intelligence Based Determination of Learning Styles" (Bajaj and Sharma, 2018), machine learning algorithms can infer individual learning preferences, identify potential learning difficulties before they manifest, and generate tailored instructional strategies accordingly. By continuously processing data from student interactions, performance metrics, and engagement trends, these systems can offer highly personalized recommendations that adapt over time. Bajaj and Sharma's work demonstrates how machine learning contributes not only to diagnosing learning styles but also to dynamically adjusting content delivery to optimize learning outcomes for diverse student populations. (Bajaj and Sharma, 2018).

Natural language processing (NLP) and conversational agents have become central components in the development of AI-driven educational tools, as evidenced in studies such as "Revolutionizing Education with AI: Exploring the Transformative Potential of ChatGPT" (Adıguzel et al., 2023) and "ChatGPT User Experience: Implications for Education" (Zhai, 2022). These technologies enable more fluid and human-like communication between students and systems, allowing learners to engage with AI as if they were interacting with a tutor or peer. Through NLP, educational platforms can interpret, process, and respond to student input in natural language, facilitating real-time dialogue, answering questions, and providing immediate feedback. Moreover, NLP systems can analyze the semantic and syntactic structure of students' textual responses to assess comprehension, detect misconceptions, and adapt instruction accordingly. The studies by Adıguzel et al. and Zhai emphasize that such conversational capabilities not only improve user engagement but also open new possibilities for scalable, individualized learning support. (Adıguzel et al., 2023; Zhai, 2022).

Natural language processing in educational environments is structured in several analytical layers as shown in (Fig. 2), ranging from text or speech tokenization to semantic and discursive interpretation, enabling seamless interaction between students and AI-based conversational systems.

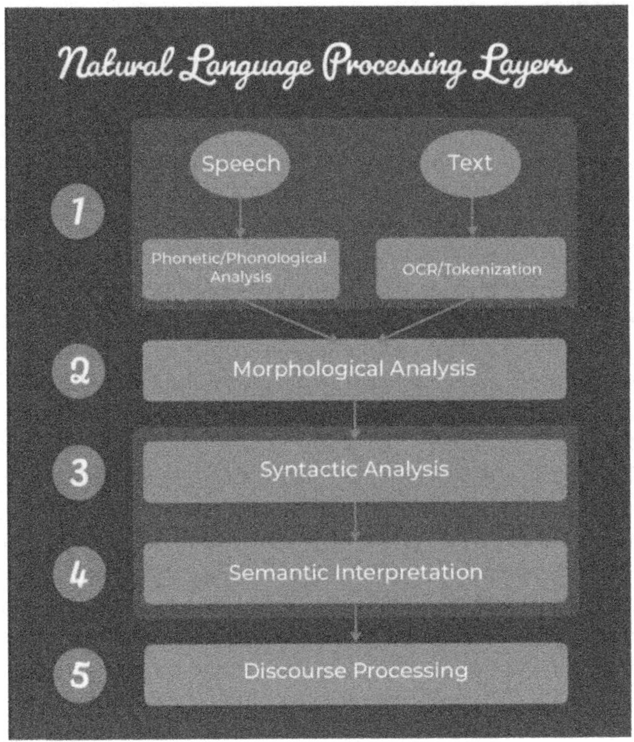

Fig. 2. Natural language processing layers (ISMT University, 2024).

Educational robots and teachable agents, while less widespread than other AI applications, represent a growing area of innovation, particularly in the context of supporting learners with special educational needs. Adaptive and assistive tools designed for children with neurodevelopmental disorders are comprehensively reviewed in "Artificial Intelligence Enabled Personalized Assistive Tools to Enhance Education of Children with Neurodevelopmental Disorders – A Review" (Barua et al., 2022). These tools leverage artificial intelligence to deliver tailored educational experiences by adjusting stimuli, feedback, and task complexity according to each child's cognitive and emotional profile. Barua et al. emphasize how AI-driven educational robots and teachable agents can enhance attention, engagement, and communication skills through interactive and multimodal strategies. Although their implementation is still limited compared to mainstream educational technologies, such tools show great promise in creating inclusive learning environments where children with autism spectrum disorder, ADHD, or other neurodevelopmental conditions can benefit from customized, responsive, and supportive instruction. (Barua et al., 2022).

Recent literature demonstrates a growing diversity in the artificial intelligence (AI) technologies applied to personalized education. Chen, L., Chen, and Lin (2020) provide a broad classification of AI applications, including intelligent tutoring systems, adaptive learning platforms, and conversational agents powered by natural language processing (NLP). Tools such as ChatGPT are gaining prominence, as shown in the works of Atlas (2023) and Cooper (2023), who highlight their role in delivering real-time, context-aware tutoring and content generation tailored to learners' needs. Kuhail et al. (2023) offer a systematic review of educational chatbots, emphasizing their adaptive behavior through machine learning and user feedback loops. Ouyang and Jiao (2021) introduce a framework that categorizes AI integration into three paradigms: automation of tasks, cognitive augmentation, and pedagogical transformation. Guan, Mou, and Jiang (2020), through a 20-year data-driven analysis, show the progression of AI technologies in education, pointing to the increasing use of predictive analytics, classification algorithms, and neural networks as core drivers of personalization. (L. Chen et al., 2020; Atlas, 2023; Cooper, 2023; Kuhail et al., 2023; Ouyang and Jiao, 2021; Ouyang and Jiao, 2021; Guan et al., 2020).

3.2 Educational Levels and Implementation Contexts

The implementation of artificial intelligence technologies in personalized education varies significantly across educational levels and global contexts. Crompton and Burke (2023) report that AI applications are most prevalent in higher education, where infrastructure and faculty readiness are more developed. Atlas (2023) supports this by illustrating how tools like ChatGPT are being utilized for academic writing support, real-time tutoring, and professional development in university settings. Su and Yang (2023) propose a structured framework for integrating generative AI into various levels of education, emphasizing flexibility and scalability. However, implementation is not confined to post-secondary institutions. Jaiswal and Arun (2021) document AI integration in Indian K-12 schools through centralized digital learning platforms, aiming to address educational inequality. Similarly, Bhutoria (2022) presents a comparative analysis of the U.S., China, and India, showing how different policy models and funding strategies shape AI deployment at both basic and advanced levels. Grassini (2023), while optimistic about AI's potential, raises concerns regarding equitable access in primary and secondary education, especially in under-resourced regions. (Crompton and Burke, 2023; Atlas, 2023; Su and Yang, 2023; Jaiswal and Arun, 2021; Bhutoria, 2022; Grassini, 2023).

Most studies in the field of AI and personalized education concentrate on higher education, particularly within disciplines such as engineering, computer science, medicine, and pedagogy. This trend is largely attributed to the advanced digital infrastructure, availability of research funding, and institutional autonomy commonly found in universities. In their comprehensive work "Systematic Review of Research on Artificial Intelligence Applications in Higher Education – Where Are the Educators?" Zawacki-Richter et al.

(2019) explain that higher education institutions are often better equipped to experiment with and adopt emerging technologies due to their access to computational resources, specialized personnel, and flexible curricular frameworks. Their analysis also highlights how academic disciplines that are already technology-intensive are naturally positioned to lead in AI adoption, whereas fields with less technical orientation or fewer resources face greater challenges. This institutional readiness creates an ecosystem where AI tools can be implemented, evaluated, and refined more effectively than in less technologically developed educational environments. (Zawacki-Richter et al., 2019).

In secondary and K-12 education, the implementation of artificial intelligence is steadily expanding, with applications focusing on adaptive learning systems, classroom analytics, and the ethical implications of AI-mediated instruction. As discussed in "Artificial Intelligence in Education: Addressing Ethical Challenges in K-12 Settings" (Akgun and Greenhow, 2022), the deployment of AI in younger educational contexts raises specific concerns related to data privacy, informed consent, and algorithmic transparency, especially given the vulnerability of student populations. At the same time, AI is being used to support differentiated instruction through real-time performance monitoring and content adaptation based on learners' needs. "Artificial Intelligence in Education: AIEd for Personalized Learning Pathways" (Tapalova and Zhiyenbayeva, 2022) explores how AI can guide students through individualized learning trajectories by analyzing their engagement patterns, knowledge gaps, and learning preferences. These technologies offer opportunities to enhance personalization and instructional efficiency in K-12 classrooms, yet they also require careful governance and educator oversight to ensure that ethical standards are upheld, and pedagogical quality is maintained. (Akgun and Greenhow, 2022; Tapalova and Zhiyenbayeva, 2022).

Primary and special education remain comparatively underrepresented in the current body of research on AI applications in education. However, emerging studies suggest that AI has meaningful potential in these contexts, particularly in supporting learners with neurodevelopmental disorders. For example, Barua et al. (2022), in their review "Artificial Intelligence Enabled Personalized Assistive Tools to Enhance Education of Children with Neurodevelopmental Disorders," highlight how AI powered tools can facilitate more inclusive and responsive learning environments. These applications include adaptive interfaces, speech and gesture recognition, and emotion aware feedback systems that respond to the specific needs of learners with conditions such as autism spectrum disorder or ADHD. The authors report that such tools have contributed to improvements in student engagement, task persistence, and the delivery of individualized learning experiences. While still limited in scale and availability, these innovations indicate a promising direction for the use of AI to address the challenges of differentiation and support in early childhood and special education settings. (Barua et al., 2022).

3.3 Personalization Strategies Implemented

The most common approaches to personalization in AI-enhanced educational environments can be grouped into three core dimensions: content customization, adaptive pacing, and personalized feedback.

Content customization refers to the dynamic adaptation of learning materials and activities based on each student's level of competence, background knowledge, and learning preferences. As described in "Designing Educational Technologies in the Age of AI: A Learning Sciences-Driven Approach" (Luckin and Cukurova, 2019), intelligent systems are designed to select or generate content that best matches the learner's individual profile. These systems go beyond static resources by offering differentiated instructional paths that maintain learners within their optimal challenge zone. Luckin and Cukurova emphasize that this process depends on integrating pedagogical frameworks with learner analytics, enabling the system to make informed decisions about which content to present and when. (Luckin and Cukurova, 2019).

Adapting the pace of progress is another central personalization strategy, allowing AI systems to regulate the speed and sequencing of learning activities based on real-time monitoring of student progress. This approach, as detailed in "Artificial Intelligence in Education: Challenges and Opportunities for Sustainable Development" (Pedro et al., 2019), is especially relevant in environments with diverse learner needs. By continuously evaluating student performance and engagement, AI systems can accelerate the progression for advanced learners or slow it down to provide additional support to those struggling. Pedro et al. argue that such adaptability fosters inclusivity, reduces learner frustration, and aligns with mastery-based learning models that prioritize individual readiness over uniform pacing. (Pedro et al., 2019).

Artificial intelligence-based systems operate through processes such as learner classification, hierarchical clustering and personalized content recommendation, which converge on key functions such as learner analytics, instructional content generation and learning assessment, as depicted in (Fig. 3).

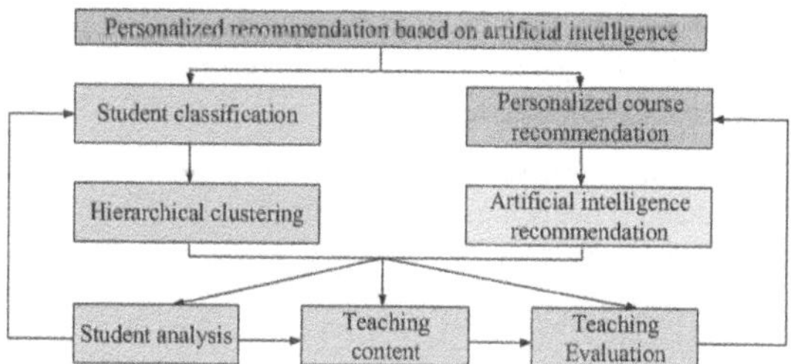

Fig. 3. Personalized recommendation process based on artificial intelligence (ResearchGate, 2022).

Personalized feedback completes the triad of common strategies. AI systems can analyze student responses, detect errors or learning gaps, and deliver targeted, timely feedback. According to "AI-Based Personalized E-Learning Systems: Issues, Challenges, and Solutions" (Murtaza et al., 2022), this kind of automated feedback enhances the learning process by offering constructive guidance tailored to each student's needs. Rather than providing generic responses, these systems simulate the actions of a human tutor, responding to specific misconceptions and suggesting corrective strategies. Murtaza et al. highlight that immediate and individualized feedback plays a key role in maintaining learner motivation and improving outcomes, particularly in self-directed or online learning settings. (Murtaza et al., 2022).

Beyond content customization, pacing, and feedback, recent studies reveal deeper layers of AI-driven personalization. Maghsudi et al. (2021) identify techniques such as reinforcement learning and dynamic user modeling, which allow systems to make real-time pedagogical decisions tailored to learners' evolving behaviors. Zhang and Aslan (2021) describe hybrid personalization models that combine user analytics with feedback systems to refine instructional pathways. This aligns with Roll and Wylie (2016), who emphasize that advanced Intelligent Tutoring Systems (ITS) dynamically adjust instruction by modeling the learner's cognitive state. Additionally, Kuhail et al. (2023) demonstrate how educational chatbots evolve through interactions, learning to personalize conversations based on usage patterns. However, as Chen, X. et al. (2020) note, many of these AI applications lack grounding in robust learning theory, which may limit their educational value. Luckin (2018) therefore advocates for AI systems that integrate human intelligence frameworks, including emotional and metacognitive dimensions, to support truly meaningful personalization. (Maghsudi et al., 2021; Zhang and Aslan, 2021; Roll and Wylie, 2016; Kuhail et al., 2023; X. Chen et al., 2020; Luckin, 2018,).

Table 1 summarizes the main personalization strategies discussed in this section, outlining their core mechanisms, educational purposes, and supporting references.

Table 1. Summary of main personalization strategies in AI-based education

Personalization Strategy	Description	Main Function	Referenced Study
Content customization	Selection of materials adapted to learners' competence and needs	Deliver appropriate learning content	Luckin & Cukurova (2019)
Adaptive pacing	Adjustment of learning speed and sequencing according to student progress and engagement	Regulate learning rhythm	Pedro et al. (2019)
Personalized feedback	Real-time analysis of performance to provide specific, actionable guidance for improvement	Improve understanding and motivation	Murtaza et al. (2022)

3.4 Documented Benefits

The review highlights several benefits attributed to the use of AI in personalized education, particularly in terms of academic performance, student engagement, and instructional efficiency.

Concrete academic improvements have been widely reported in the literature, especially in studies measuring student performance through standardized assessment. Several articles demonstrate that the implementation of AI-driven platforms correlates with significant gains in test scores and knowledge retention. For instance, "Smart Education with Artificial Intelligence Based Determination of Learning Styles" (Bajaj and Sharma, 2018) shows how systems that adapt content based on individual learning preferences contribute to improved understanding and mastery of subject matter. Similarly, in "Systematic Review of Research on Artificial Intelligence Applications in Higher Education – Where Are the Educators?" Zawacki-Richter et al. (2019) highlight empirical evidence supporting AI's positive impact on academic achievement in university settings, where personalized tools can fine-tune instruction to match students' cognitive profiles. (Bajaj and Sharma, 2018; Zawacki-Richter et al., 2019).

Increased motivation and autonomy are also central benefits of AI integration. Intelligent learning environments allow students to make choices about their learning paths, engage with adaptive materials, and receive immediate assistance when needed. These features foster a sense of ownership over the learning process and sustain engagement, especially in self-paced or digital settings. As emphasized by Pokrivcakova (2019) in "Preparing Teachers for the Application of AI-Powered Technologies in Foreign Language Education," smart systems not only personalize instruction but also empower students to become more self-directed and confident in navigating their own learning experiences. The flexibility and responsiveness of AI tools contribute to a more motivating and autonomous educational environment. (Pokrivcakova, 2019).

Teaching and administrative efficiency are another major area of impact. AI applications can automate a wide range of repetitive and time-consuming tasks such as grading, attendance tracking, and performance analytics. According to "Vision, Challenges, Roles and Research Issues of AI in Education" (Hwang et al., 2020), this automation allows educators to redirect their time and energy toward more meaningful instructional activities, such as personalized mentoring or curriculum design. By reducing administrative burden, AI enables teachers to focus on tasks that require human judgment and creativity, ultimately enhancing the quality of teaching while increasing institutional productivity. (Hwang et al., 2020).

Beyond academic performance, motivation, and teacher efficiency, recent studies point to additional strategic and systemic benefits of AI in personalized learning. Su and Yang (2023) emphasize how generative AI enables on-demand scaffolding, supporting learner independence through real time dialogue. Bhutoria (2022) notes that AI-powered platforms enhance learning continuity by dynamically aligning instructional content with learners' cognitive states. Crompton and Burke (2023) underline the capacity of AI to foster inclusive learning through multimodal interaction, particularly benefiting students with diverse learning preferences. From a sustainability perspective, Kamalov et al. (2023) argue that AI minimizes instructor workload by handling grading, feedback, and content adaptation, thus improving instructional scalability. Miao et al. (2021) further illustrate how AI facilitates early identification of at-risk students using learning analytics, enabling proactive interventions. Lastly, Holmes (2020) highlights the role of AI in tailoring experiences for learners with disabilities or linguistic barriers, thereby contributing to more equitable educational environments. (Su and Yang, 2023; Bhutoria, 2022; Crompton and Burke, 2023; Kamalov et al., 2023; Miao et al., 2021; Holmes, 2020).

3.5 Limitations and Gaps

Despite the progress, persistent limitations were detected:

- Multiple studies have raised concerns about the tendency to prioritize technological innovation over sound pedagogical design in the development and implementation of AI systems in education. As emphasized in "A Review on Application of Artificial Intelligence in Teaching and Learning in Educational Contexts" (Fahimirad, 2018), a significant number of AI-based educational tools are introduced without being grounded in established learning theories or instructional models. This results in platforms that may be technologically sophisticated, yet pedagogically superficial, offering limited support for deep learning or meaningful engagement. Fahimirad argues that without a solid didactic foundation, AI applications risk reinforcing rote learning and standardization, rather than fostering creativity, critical thinking, or personalized knowledge construction. The review calls for closer collaboration between technologists and education professionals to ensure that AI tools are not only innovative, but also pedagogically purposeful and aligned with the complex realities of teaching and learning processes. (Fahimirad, Kotamjani, et al., 2018).
- Short term evaluations dominate much of the exploratory research on AI in education, often relying on pilot studies or limited scope implementations that measure immediate outcomes without tracking long term effectiveness. As noted by Bajaj and Sharma (2018) and Zawacki Richter et al. (2019), this lack of longitudinal validation presents a significant limitation in the current evidence base. Many studies report promising initial results such as improved engagement or test scores but do not follow up to determine whether these benefits persist over time or translate into deeper learning. Bajaj and Sharma emphasize that adaptive systems may lose effectiveness if not continuously updated or recalibrated to meet evolving learner needs. Meanwhile, Zawacki Richter et al. highlights that without sustained empirical monitoring, it is difficult to assess the scalability, equity, or systemic impact of AI applications in diverse educational contexts. This gap underscores the need for more rigorous, long duration studies that can inform responsible and evidence-based implementation of AI technologies in education. (Bajaj and Sharma, 2018; Zawacki-Richter et al., 2019).
- Studies such as "Artificial Intelligence in Education: Challenges and Opportunities for Sustainable Development" (Pedro et al., 2019) emphasize a critical geographic and infrastructural disparity in the deployment of AI technologies in education. The majority of developments and implementations are concentrated in urban, well resourced, and digitally connected environments, where access to infrastructure, internet connectivity, and technical expertise is more readily available. Pedro et al. argue that this urban centric focus risks reinforcing educational inequalities by excluding rural or marginalized communities that lack the necessary technological foundation to adopt AI driven solutions. These areas often face challenges such as limited hardware availability, unstable internet access, and insufficient teacher training all of which hinder the scalability and inclusiveness of AI initiatives. The study calls for targeted efforts to design low-bandwidth, offline capable, and context- sensitive AI applications that can bridge the digital divide and ensure that the benefits of personalization and adaptive learning are accessible to all learners, regardless of their geographic or socioeconomic circumstances. (Pedro et al., 2019).

- In addition to concerns regarding short-term assessments and urban bias, several other limitations have been identified in the literature. Chen, X. et al. (2020) point out that many AI tools used in education are developed without a strong pedagogical foundation, prioritizing technical capabilities over the integration of educational theory. Ouyang and Jiao (2021) emphasize the lack of rigorous empirical studies evaluating AI systems in diverse instructional environments, highlighting the need for deeper validation of their learning impact. Roll and Wylie (2016) note that despite technological advancements, many AI systems remain disconnected from everyday classroom practice due to infrastructure shortcomings and limited teacher training. Grassini (2023) raises ethical concerns, such as algorithmic bias, misuse of student data, and lack of transparency in AI-driven decision-making. Similarly, Guan et al. (2020) stress the geographic and economic disparities in AI adoption, particularly between well-resourced urban schools and underprivileged rural or developing regions. Finally, Huang et al. (2021) point to the absence of standardized evaluation frameworks, which hinders the ability to assess long-term effects on learning quality, equity, and inclusion. (X. Chen et al., 2020; Ouyang and Jiao, 2021; Roll and Wylie, 2016; Grassini, 2023; Guan et al., 2020; Huang et al., 2021).

3.6 Recurring Disputes

Several publications address the ethical and operational tensions of using AI in education:

- Regarding privacy and data use, concerns about the ethical management of student information have become increasingly prominent in the discourse on AI in education. In "Ethical Principles for Artificial Intelligence in Education" (Nguyen et al., 2023) and "Artificial Intelligence in Education: Addressing Ethical Challenges in K-12 Settings" (Akgun and Greenhow, 2022), both studies underscore the lack of transparency in how sensitive student data is collected, processed, stored, and potentially shared. This ambiguity creates uncertainty for educators, students, and families, weakening trust in AI systems and raising serious questions about consent, surveillance, and the right to data ownership. Nguyen et al. advocate for the development of clear, enforceable ethical guidelines that safeguard learners' digital identities, especially in environments involving minors. Meanwhile, Akgun and Greenhow draw attention to the vulnerabilities specific to K-12 settings, where students may not fully grasp how their data is being used or have the agency to control it. Both studies emphasize the urgent need for ethical by design approaches that prioritize data protection, informed consent, and institutional accountability as foundational principles in the development and deployment of AI tools in education. (Nguyen et al., 2023; Akgun and Greenhow, 2022).
- The role of the teacher remains a central point of contention in discussions surrounding the integration of artificial intelligence into education. While many researchers and practitioners advocate for AI as a tool to augment pedagogical practices supporting tasks such as grading, content delivery, and personalized feedback others warn of its potential to partially replace core teaching functions. This tension has sparked both philosophical and practical debates about the future of the teaching profession. As noted by Celik (2023) and Pokrivcakova (2019), educational institutions have expressed concern and even resistance toward AI initiatives that suggest reducing the

teacher's role to a supervisory or facilitative capacity. Such perspectives are often viewed as undermining the expertise, creativity, and human connection that characterize effective teaching. Celik emphasizes that professional identity and teacher agency must be preserved in any AI-supported model, while Pokrivcakova highlights the risk of delegating sensitive pedagogical decisions to algorithms that lack contextual understanding. Both authors stress the importance of positioning educators as central actors in the design, implementation, and over- sight of AI systems, ensuring that technology serves pedagogical goals rather than dictating them. (Celik, 2023; Pokrivcakova, 2019).

- Regarding algorithmic dependence, several scholars have raised concerns about the increasing reliance on AI systems whose internal workings—often based on complex, opaque algorithms—are not easily interpretable by educators or end users. This lack of transparency, commonly referred to as the "black box" problem, can lead to a diminished understanding of how decisions are made within these systems, potentially eroding trust and reducing user agency. Luckin and Cukurova (2019) emphasize that this opacity poses a significant challenge to teacher autonomy. When educators are unable to fully comprehend or question the recommendations produced by AI tools, they may become overly dependent on automated suggestions, thereby limiting their capacity for critical reflection and pedagogical judgment. The authors argue that this scenario risks shifting educational authority away from human professionals toward systems that are not accountable in the same way. To mitigate this, they advocate for the development of explainable AI (XAI) models in education, which can provide insight into how decisions are made and foster a more transparent, collaborative relationship between humans and machines in the learning process. (Luckin and Cukurova, 2019).
- In addition to these issues, other authors have raised broader systemic and conceptual concerns. Williamson (2017) warns about the emergence of "data-driven education," where large-scale learning analytics may compromise student privacy, reduce transparency, and reinforce surveillance practices. These concerns are echoed by Williamson and Eynon (2020), who critique the uncritical adoption of AI in education as a reflection of neoliberal agendas that prioritize efficiency over pedagogical integrity. From an operational standpoint, Fitria (2021) identifies gaps in teacher preparedness, noting that many educators lack the training and institutional support needed to implement AI responsibly and effectively. Hwang and Chien (2022), reflecting on the rise of immersive technologies such as the metaverse, highlight the urgent need for frameworks that address digital equity, algorithmic bias, and user autonomy when deploying AI-enhanced environments. These discussions underscore the necessity for education stakeholders to approach AI adoption with caution, ensuring that technological advancement aligns with human values and ethical standards.(Williamson, 2017; Williamson and Eynon, 2020; Fitria, 2021; Hwang and Chien, 2022).

To provide a clearer picture of the recurring tensions surrounding AI integration in education, Table 2 presents a synthesis of the most frequently discussed controversies, the associated risks, and the strategies suggested in the literature to address them.

Table 2. Summary of recurring ethical and operational disputes in AI-driven education

Type of Dispute	Key Authors	Risks or Concerns	Suggested Responses
Privacy and data governance	Nguyen et al. (2023), Akgun & Greenhow (2022)	Lack of transparency, weak consent frameworks, data misuse	Ethical-by-design approaches, clear data policies
Teacher replacement & identity	Celik (2023), Pokrivcakova (2019)	Erosion of teacher autonomy and professional identity	Preserve teacher agency, involve educators in AI design
Algorithmic opacity	Luckin & Cukurova (2019)	Overreliance on "black box" systems, diminished pedagogical judgment	Promote explainable AI (XAI), increase algorithmic transparency
Systemic inequities	Williamson (2017), Williamson & Eynon (2020)	Neoliberal bias, prioritizing efficiency over pedagogy	Critical evaluation of policy agendas, inclusion-focused development
Teacher training gap	Fitria (2021)	Poor implementation due to lack of support and training	Institutional investment in professional development
Metaverse & immersive risks	Hwang & Chien (2022)	Algorithmic bias, digital divide, user autonomy erosion	Establish equity frameworks and ethical guidelines

4 Discussion

4.1 Technological Focus and Disciplinary Concentration

The findings of this review reaffirm the predominance of certain AI technologies and implementation patterns across the current educational landscape. Intelligent tutoring systems, adaptive platforms, virtual assistants, and machine learning models were the most frequently documented tools. Their prevalence is not coincidental but rather reflects the maturity and accessibility of these technologies within specific institutional contexts. As noted by Zawacki-Richter et al. (2019), higher education environments provide fertile ground for AI adoption due to more robust digital infrastructure, technical support, and research-oriented cultures. (Zawacki-Richter et al., 2019).

However, this technological concentration raises questions about the representativeness and generalizability of current research. The overwhelming focus on university-level implementations—particularly in STEM and health-related disciplines (Bajaj and Sharma, 2018; Crompton and Burke, 2023)—limits our understanding of how AI might operate in more varied and less resourced educational settings. Studies such as Atlas

(2023) and Su and Yang (2023) demonstrate the potential versatility of generative AI in academic writing, real-time feedback, and instructional support. Yet, these applications remain largely confined to digital-savvy contexts and learners with high levels of academic autonomy. (Atlas, 2023; Su and Yang, 2023).

Furthermore, the review found that primary and special education contexts remain underexplored. While Barua et al. (2022) report promising results in using AI as assistive technology for neurodiverse learners, these studies are relatively rare and often framed as proof-of-concept rather than large-scale evaluations. This imbalance suggests that the expansion of AI research into underserved populations and non-traditional educational environments remains a critical frontier. Without broader contextual diversity, current findings risk reinforcing systemic inequities rather than addressing them. (Barua et al., 2022).

Underrepresentation of Diverse Educational Contexts

Despite the rapid growth of AI in education, literature continues to reflect a narrow focus on technologically mature environments. The dominance of research conducted in urban, digitally connected, and well-funded institutions reveals a structural bias that may hinder the equitable evolution of AI implementation. Pedro et al. (2019) and Bhutoria (2022) both highlight that rural schools, low-income regions, and institutions without access to advanced infrastructure are often overlooked in both experimentation and deployment phases. This underrepresentation is not just geographic but also institutional, as many studies disregard public primary education systems or informal learning contexts. (Pedro et al., 2019; Bhutoria, 2022).

Moreover, studies like Grassini (2023) and Guan et al. (2020) emphasize that without specific policy efforts and inclusive research agendas, AI applications may exacerbate rather than mitigate educational disparities. The current imbalance also limits our ability to draw broader conclusions about the scalability and adaptability of AI across diverse populations. Moving forward, a more comprehensive research approach is needed—one that captures implementation realities beyond the boundaries of elite or well-resourced institutions. (Grassini, 2023; Guan et al., 2020).

4.2 Personalization Strategies: From Promise to Complexity

The widespread use of personalization strategies, particularly content customization, adaptive pacing, and real-time feedback, has been one of the most celebrated affordances of AI in education. These approaches align with learner-centered pedagogies and promise to optimize instruction by adjusting learning paths to individual profiles. As Luckin and Cukurova (2019) argue, effective content customization requires not only technological sophistication but also pedagogical grounding, a balance that is not always present in real-world implementations. Many systems reviewed in this study demonstrate technical capability to adapt content but do so based on narrow parameters such as test scores or completion time, without accounting for cognitive diversity or learning preferences in a holistic manner. (Luckin and Cukurova, 2019).

Similarly, adaptive pacing is positioned as a mechanism to respect individual learning rhythms and reduce frustration (Pedro et al., 2019). While this feature appears especially promising for supporting students who struggle with fixed curricula, few studies offer longitudinal data confirming its sustained effectiveness or emotional impact. This lack of depth reinforces concerns raised by Zawacki-Richter et al. (2019) and Bajaj and Sharma (2018) regarding the short-term nature of most evaluations in the field. (Pedro et al., 2019; Zawacki-Richter et al., 2019; Bajaj and Sharma, 2018).

Personalized feedback, as examined by Murtaza et al. (2022), shows strong potential to simulate one-on-one instruction and offer immediate, tailored guidance. However, the analysis also reveals tensions between automation and interpretability: feedback systems may point out errors or provide suggestions, but do not always clarify the rationale behind them or adjust tone and complexity to match the learner's profile. Moreover, studies such as those by Roll and Wylie (2016) and Ouyang and Jiao (2021) suggest that personalization in AI often operates in a technically functional yet pedagogically superficial manner, highlighting a disconnect between what is technologically possible and what is educationally meaningful. (Murtaza et al., 2022; Roll and Wylie, 2016; Ouyang and Jiao, 2021).

Overall, while personalization is central to the narrative of AI in education, its implementation is far from uniform or universally effective. More rigorous and theory-informed designs are needed to ensure that personalization tools truly support learning rather than merely simulate it.

4.3 Learning Outcomes and Learner Agency

A key rationale for integrating AI into personalized education is its potential to enhance learning outcomes while promoting greater student agency. Many of the reviewed studies report measurable academic gains, often in the form of improved test performance or increased content mastery (Bajaj and Sharma, 2018; Zawacki-Richter et al., 2019). These outcomes, however, are usually tied to specific systems under controlled conditions and may not fully capture the nuances of real-world educational settings. As Pedro et al. (2019) caution, the current evidence base remains limited by short-term studies, which undermines the ability to assess long-term learning impact or skill retention. (Pedro et al., 2019).

Beyond academic achievement, AI-powered environments are often credited with boosting learner motivation and autonomy. Features such as real-time feedback, adaptive learning paths, and self-paced progress create conditions for students to engage more deeply with content and take control of their educational experience. Pokrivcakova (2019) highlights how smart technologies empower learners to make decisions, access immediate support, and move at their own pace, fostering a sense of ownership. However, this autonomy is not evenly distributed. As noted by Holmes (2020) and Grassini (2023), students with stronger digital skills or higher academic self-efficacy are more likely to benefit, while those without these assets may become passive users of automated systems. (Pokrivcakova, 2019; Holmes, 2020; Grassini, 2023).

Moreover, the very design of AI systems shapes how agency is enabled or constrained. When feedback is prescriptive rather than dialogic, or when adaptive systems make decisions opaque to learners, the opportunity for metacognitive development may be diminished (Luckin and Cukurova, 2019). This tension suggests that promoting learner agency in AI-supported environments requires more than just technical adaptability—it demands transparency, scaffolding, and user-centered design principles that position the learner as a co-participant in the educational process.

In sum, while AI has demonstrated the potential to improve both outcomes and motivation, its capacity to nurture true learner agency remains uneven and context-dependent. Future designs must move beyond automation toward empowerment.

Table 3 summarizes the documented impacts of AI-based personalization on learning outcomes and learner agency, highlighting both the benefits and the underlying constraints identified across the reviewed literature.

Table 3. Impacts of AI on Learning Outcomes and Learner Agency

Impact Area	Positive Contributions	Challenges or Limitations	Key References
Academic performance	Improved test scores, knowledge retention through adaptive instruction	Limited to short-term evaluations context-specific outcomes	Bajaj & Sharma (2018); Zawacki-Richter et al. (2019)
Motivation	Increased engagement via choice, immediate feedback, and adaptive content	May favor already motivated or tech-savvy learners	Pokrivcakova (2019); Grassini (2023)
Learner autonomy	Greater self-direction, flexibility in learning paths	Unequal benefits learners with low self-regulation may struggle without guidance	Pokrivcakova (2019); Holmes (2020)
Cognitive/metacognitive development	ePotential to develop self-monitoring and reflection via personalized feedback	Prescriptive feedback may limit deep reflection; low transparency in decision-making	Luckin & Cukurova (2019); Holmes (2020)

4.4 Equity, Ethics, and Policy Implications

Data Privacy and Institutional Accountability

As AI technologies become more embedded in educational systems, questions of equity and ethics gain urgency. The review reveals persistent disparities in access and implementation, which disproportionately affect under-resourced schools and marginalized learners. Pedro et al. (2019) and Bhutoria (2022) point to the overrepresentation of urban and digitally connected environments in AI research and deployment, leaving behind rural areas and low-connectivity contexts. This geographic and infrastructural bias not only limits the generalizability of current findings but risks deepening existing educational inequalities. (Pedro et al., 2019; Bhutoria, 2022).

Ethical concerns are equally prominent in the current discourse on AI in education, particularly regarding the opaque handling of sensitive student data. This issue is not merely technical, but fundamentally tied to questions of rights, agency, and institutional responsibility. As highlighted by Nguyen et al. (2023) and Akgun and Greenhow (2022), many AI-driven educational systems lack robust data governance frameworks that clearly define how data is collected, processed, stored, and shared. This absence of transparency undermines both informed consent and the ability of users—students, parents, and educators alike—to understand or contest how their data is being used. (Nguyen et al., 2023; Akgun and Greenhow, 2022).

In K-12 settings, the problem becomes even more acute. Younger students often do not have the legal or cognitive capacity to grasp the implications of data collection, much less to give meaningful consent or opt out of data practices. Akgun and Greenhow (2022) emphasize that this creates an ethical vulnerability, where minors are subjected to monitoring and profiling mechanisms they may not even be aware of. Furthermore, schools and districts may adopt AI systems without fully understanding the data agreements they are entering into, especially when these tools are developed and managed by private third-party vendors. (Akgun and Greenhow, 2022).

Nguyen et al. (2023) also point out that the issue of accountability remains murky. When a system makes an automated decision—such as predicting learning performance, recommending interventions, or generating behavior alerts—it is often unclear who bears the responsibility for its accuracy or consequences. The lack of clearly assigned institutional or developer accountability exacerbates the risk of harm and weakens the trust necessary for ethical AI adoption in education. Without clear policies, transparent documentation, and stakeholder oversight, data practices risk violating student rights and contributing to a climate of digital surveillance rather than empowerment. (Nguyen et al., 2023).

Another layer of ethical complexity involves the changing role of the teacher. Celik (2023) and Pokrivcakova (2019) observe that some institutions view AI as a potential substitute for certain instructional roles, which has triggered professional resistance. The risk here lies not only in job displacement, but also in the erosion of teacher agency and pedagogical autonomy. These concerns are amplified when AI systems operate as "black boxes," as discussed by Luckin and Cukurova (2019), making it difficult for educators to understand or contest the decisions being made on behalf of their students. (Celik, 2023; Pokrivcakova, 2019; Luckin and Cukurova, 2019).

Finally, systemic critiques, such as those offered by Williamson (2017) and Williamson and Eynon (2020), caution against the uncritical adoption of AI as a tool for efficiency. They argue that many AI initiatives are shaped by neoliberal policy agendas that prioritize measurable outputs over deeper pedagogical goals. Without deliberate policy design that centers inclusion, transparency, and educational values, the integration of AI risks reinforcing—rather than challenging—the power structures it aims to reform. (Williamson, 2017; Williamson and Eynon, 2020).

In this context, the role of policy becomes pivotal. It is not enough to develop advanced technologies; educational systems must also establish robust ethical frameworks, inclusive strategies for implementation, and mechanisms for accountability that reflect the complexity of teaching and learning. Personalization strategies: from promise to complexity.

The Evolving Role of Teachers in AI-Mediated Instruction
Another area of ethical tension involves the evolving role of teachers in AI-supported learning environments. While some implementations position AI as a complementary tool to assist educators in routine or administrative tasks, others implicitly suggest a partial substitution of instructional functions—such as grading, feedback, or content delivery. This shift has raised concerns about the erosion of the teacher's professional identity and pedagogical autonomy. As Celik (2023) points out, the fear is not only job displacement but also a broader devaluation of teaching expertise in favor of algorithmic efficiency. (Celik, 2023).

Pokrivcakova (2019) reinforces this concern by highlighting how educational institutions may begin to rely more heavily on automated systems for decision-making, reducing the teacher's role to that of a facilitator or overseer rather than a knowledge constructor. Such a model risks undermining the relational and affective dimensions of teaching, which are essential for meaningful learning. Furthermore, the encroachment of automation into pedagogical spaces may alter how authority and responsibility are distributed in the classroom, raising the question of who ultimately guides student learning: the educator or the algorithm. (Pokrivcakova, 2019).

These dynamics contribute to professional resistance among teachers, particularly when AI systems are introduced without sufficient consultation or training. Educators may perceive such tools as externally imposed interventions that disempower rather than support them. To address these tensions, it is crucial that AI integration strategies treat teachers as central stakeholders in the development, implementation, and evaluation of educational technologies. As both Celik (2023) and Pokrivcakova (2019) argue, the long-term success of AI in education depends on strengthening not replacing—the role of the human educator. (Celik, 2023; Pokrivcakova, 2019).

As illustrated in (Fig. 4), the role of the teacher in the age of artificial intelligence is evolving toward more strategic roles, such as co-creating learning experiences, mediating the ethical use of technology, and forming collaborative educational communities.

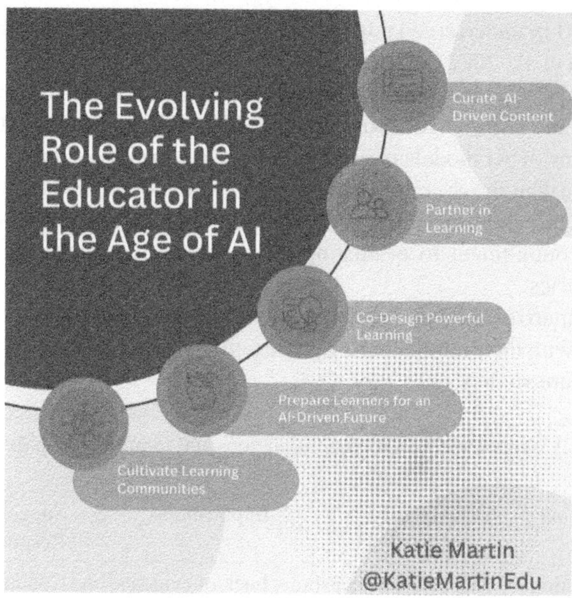

Fig. 4. The role of the educator in the age of artificial intelligence (Martin, 2023).

4.5 Methodological and Research Gaps

Despite the increasing volume of publications on AI in personalized education, the field continues to exhibit several methodological limitations that restrict the depth and applicability of current findings. One of the most recurrent issues is the pre-dominance of exploratory research based on small-scale or pilot interventions. As noted by Bajaj and Sharma (2018) and Zawacki-Richter et al. (2019), many studies focus on immediate or short-term outcomes—such as test performance or engagement metrics—without conducting longitudinal follow-ups to evaluate the sustained effects of AI-based interventions. This reliance on snapshot data undermines the ability to assess long-term learning trajectories or to generalize results across diverse educational settings. (Bajaj and Sharma, 2018; Zawacki-Richter et al., 2019).

Another critical gap is the limited incorporation of pedagogical theory in the design and evaluation of AI systems. Fahimirad (2018) argues that many tools are developed with a strong technological focus but weak educational grounding, resulting in platforms that may be efficient but a lack didactic depth. This disconnect reduces the instructional relevance of AI and may contribute to shallow forms of personalization that adapt content superficially without considering deeper cognitive, emotional, or social dimensions of learning. (Fahimirad, Kotamjani, et al., 2018).

Additionally, most research is concentrated in urban and digitally connected environments, with rural and low-connectivity contexts significantly underrepresented (Pedro et al., 2019). This imbalance not only skews the perception of AI's effectiveness but also limits the ability to design inclusive solutions that are scalable across diverse infrastructures. The work of Barua et al. (2022), although focused on special education, highlights the potential of AI in underserved populations—yet these remain exceptions rather than the norm. (Barua et al., 2022).

Finally, the lack of transparency and standardization in research reporting is a barrier to meta-analysis and knowledge accumulation. Methodological inconsistencies, such as vague descriptions of AI models or absence of control groups, reduce the replicability of studies and weaken the overall evidence base. Addressing these limitations requires interdisciplinary collaboration, the adoption of more rigorous and theory-driven methodologies, and a commitment to evaluating AI's educational impact beyond technical performance metrics.

Table 4 summarizes the key methodological limitations identified in the reviewed literature, along with their implications for educational research and proposed strategies to strengthen future studies.

Table 4. Common methodological limitations and future research directions

Identified Limitation	Description	Implications	Suggested Research Response
Short-term evaluation focus	Most studies measure immediate outcomes only	Lack of evidence on long-term impact	Conduct longitudinal and follow-up studies
Weak pedagogical grounding	Limited integration of learning theories in system design	Risk of shallow or ineffective personalization	Embed robust pedagogical frameworks in AI development
Contextual concentration in urban and digital settings	Underrepresentation of rural and under-resourced environments	Limited generalizability and inclusivity	Expand research into diverse and low-connectivity contexts
Inconsistent methodology and reporting	Vague system descriptions, lack of control groups or standardized procedures	Hinders replication and meta-analysis	Promote methodological rigor and transparency in study design
Underexplored special needs populations	Few studies target learners with disabilities or neurodivergent profiles	Missed opportunities for inclusive AI	Develop and test AI tools for diverse learner needs

5 Conclusions

This literature review systematically mapped the current landscape of artificial intelligence (AI) applications in personalized education. Based on the analysis of 40 recent academic studies, the main technologies used, the educational levels at which they are implemented, the most common personalization strategies, and the benefits, limitations, and controversies associated with their integration in real-life educational contexts were identified.

In technological terms, the most common tools include intelligent tutoring systems, machine learning models, virtual assistants based on natural language processing, and adaptive platforms that combine data analytics with pedagogical criteria. These technologies have been used primarily in higher and secondary education, although they are beginning to expand into preschool and continuing education settings.

The personalization strategies identified in the studies fall into three main categories: content adaptation, learning pace regulation, and personalized feedback. These strategies have proven effective in improving academic performance, increasing student motivation, and facilitating learning autonomy. However, the real and sustained impact of these technologies still requires further long-term empirical validation.

Among the main limitations identified are the limited incorporation of pedagogical frameworks in the design of AI solutions, the low representation of non-digitalized educational contexts, and the need to establish clear ethical standards for the use of personal data. Furthermore, controversies persist regarding the role of teachers in relation to automated systems, the transparency of algorithms, and the risk of overreliance in technological solutions.

Overall, the reviewed studies agree that AI should not be viewed as a replacement for educators, but rather as a supporting tool capable of enriching teaching and learning processes when designed with sound pedagogical criteria. The advancement of the field will depend not only on technological development but also on interdisciplinary collaboration between engineers, teachers, researchers, and educational policymakers.

Finally, this review concludes that artificial intelligence has significant transformative potential for personalized education, but its effective use requires overcoming technical, pedagogical, and ethical challenges. Future research should focus on validating its effectiveness in diverse contexts, ensuring equitable access, and ensuring that its implementation is guided by principles centered on student well-being.

References

Adıguzel, T., Kaya, M.H., Cansu, F.K.: Revolutionizing education with ai: Exploring the transformative potential of chatgpt. Contemporary Educational Technology (2023)

Akgun, S., Greenhow, C.: Artificial intelligence in education: addressing ethical challenges in k-12 settings. AI Ethics **2**(3), 431–440 (2022)

Arksey, H., O'Malley, L.: Scoping studies: towards a methodological framework. Int. J. Soc. Res. Methodol. **8**(1), 19–32 (2005). https://doi.org/10.1080/1364557032000119616

Atlas, S.: Chatgpt for higher education and professional development: A guide to conversational ai (2023)

Bajaj, R., Sharma, V.: Smart education with artificial intelligence based determination of learning styles. Procedia Comput. Sci. **132**, 834–842 (2018)

Barua, P.D., et al.: Artificial intelligence enabled personalised assistive tools to enhance education of children with neurodevelopmental disorders—a review. Int. J. Environ. Res. Public Health **19**(3), 1192 (2022)

Bhutoria, A.: Personalized education and artificial intelligence in the United States, China, and India: a systematic review using a human-in-the-loop model. Comput. Educ. Artif. Intell. **3**, 100068 (2022)

Celik, I.: Towards intelligenttpack: an empirical study on teachers' professional knowledge to ethically integrate artificial intelligence (ai)-based tools into education. Comput. Hum. Behav. **138**, 107468 (2023)

Chen, L., Chen, P., Lin, Z.: Artificial intelligence in education: a review. IEEE Access **8**, 75264–75278 (2020)

Chen, X., Xie, H., Zou, D., Hwang, G.-J.: Application and theory gaps during the rise of artificial intelligence in education. Comput. Educ. Artif. Intell. **1**, 100002 (2020)

Cooper, G.: Examining science education in chatgpt: an exploratory study of generative artificial intelligence. J. Sci. Educ. Technol. **32**(3), 444–452 (2023)

Crompton, H., Burke, D.: Artificial intelligence in higher education: the state of the field. Int. J. Educ. Technol. High. Educ. **20**(1), 22 (2023)

Daudt, H.M.L., van Mossel, C., Scott, S.J.: Enhancing the scoping study methodology: a large, inter-professional team's experience with arksey and o'malley's framework. BMC Med. Res. Methodol. **13**, 48 (2013). https://doi.org/10.1186/1471-2288-13-48

Fahimirad, M., Kotamjani, S.S., et al.: A review on application of artificial intelligence in teaching and learning in educational contexts. Int. J. Learn. Dev. **8**(4), 106–118 (2018)

Fitria, T.N.: Artificial intelligence (ai) in education: Using ai tools for teaching and learning process. Prosiding Seminar Nasional & Call for Paper STIE AAS, 134–147 (2021)

Grassini, S.: Shaping the future of education: exploring the potential and consequences of ai and chatgpt in educational settings. Educ. Sci. **13**(7), 692 (2023)

Guan, C., Mou, J., Jiang, Z.: Artificial intelligence innovation in education: a twenty-year data-driven historical analysis. Int. J. Innov. Stud. **4**(4), 134–147 (2020)

Holmes, W.: Artificial intelligence in education. In Encyclopedia of education and information technologies, pp. 88–103. Springer (2020)

Huang, J., Saleh, S., Liu, Y.: A review on artificial intelligence in education Academic Journal of Interdisciplinary Studies **10**(3) (2021)

Hwang, G.-J., Chien, S.-Y.: Definition, roles, and potential research issues of the metaverse in education: an artificial intelligence perspective. Comput. Educ. Artif. Intell. **3**, 100082 (2022)

Hwang, G.-J., Xie, H., Wah, B.W., Gas˘evic´, D.: Vision, challenges, roles and research issues of artificial intelligence in education (2020)

ISMT University: Natural language processing layers [Retrieved May 15, 2025] (2024). https://ismuniv.com/natural-language-processing/

Jaiswal, A., Arun, C.J.: Potential of artificial intelligence for transformation of the education system in India. Int. J. Educ. Dev. Using Inf. Commun. Technol. **17**(1), 142–158 (2021)

Kamalov, F., Santandreu Calonge, D., Gurrib, I.: New era of artificial intelligence in education: Towards a sustainable multifaceted revolution. Sustainability **15**(16), 12451 (2023)

Kuhail, M.A., Alturki, N., Alramlawi, S., Alhejori, K.: Interacting with educational chatbots: a systematic review. Educ. Inf. Technol. **28**(1), 973–1018 (2023)

Levac, D., Colquhoun, H., O'Brien, K.K.: Scoping studies: Advancing the methodology. Implementation Science **5**(1), 69 (2010). https://doi.org/10.1186/1748-5908-5-69

Luckin, R.: Machine learning and human intelligence. The future of education for the 21st century. UCL institute of education press (2018)

Luckin, R., Cukurova, M.: Designing educational technologies in the age of ai: a learning sciences-driven approach. Br. J. Edu. Technol. **50**(6), 2824–2838 (2019)

Maghsudi, S., Lan, A., Xu, J., van Der Schaar, M.: Personalized education in the artificial intelligence era: What to expect next. IEEE Signal Process. Mag. **38**(3), 37–50 (2021)

Martin, K.: The evolving role of the educator in the age of ai [Retrieved May 15, 2025] (2023). https://katielmartin.com/2023/06/20/ the-evolving-role-of-educators-in-the-age-of-ai/the-evolving-role-of-the-educator-in-the-age-of-ai/

Miao, F., Holmes, W., Huang, R., Zhang, H., et al.: Ai and education: A guidance for policymakers. Unesco Publishing (2021)

Murtaza, M., Ahmed, Y., Shamsi, J.A., Sherwani, F., Usman, M.: Ai- based personalized e-learning systems: Issues, challenges, and solutions. IEEE access **10**, 81323–81342 (2022)

Nguyen, A., Ngo, H.N., Hong, Y., Dang, B., Nguyen, B.-P.T.: Ethical principles for artificial intelligence in education. Educ. Inf. Technol. **28**(4), 4221–4241 (2023)

Ouyang, F., Jiao, P.: Artificial intelligence in education: the three paradigms. Computers and Education: Artificial Intelligence **2**, 100020 (2021)

Pedro, F., Subosa, M., Rivas, A., Valverde, P.: Artificial intelligence in education: Challenges and opportunities for sustainable development (2019)

Pokrivcakova, S.: Preparing teachers for the application of ai-powered technologies in foreign language education. J. Lang. Cult. Educ. **7**(3), 135–153 (2019)

ResearchGate: (2022). Personalized learning based on ai [Retrieved May 15, 2025]. https://www.researchgate.net/figure/Personalized-learning-based-on-AI fig4 358283174

Roll, I., Wylie, R.: Evolution and revolution in artificial intelligence in education. Int. J. Artif. Intell. Educ. **26**, 582–599 (2016)

Sajja, R., Sermet, Y., Cikmaz, M., Cwiertny, D., Demir, I.: Artificial intelligence-enabled intelligent assistant for personalized and adaptive learning in higher education. Information **15**(10), 596 (2024)

Su, J., Yang, W.: Unlocking the power of chatgpt: a framework for applying generative ai in education. ECNU Rev. Educ. **6**(3), 355–366 (2023)

Tapalova, O., Zhiyenbayeva, N.: Artificial intelligence in education: AIED for personalised learning pathways. Electron. J. e-Learning **20**(5), 639–653 (2022)

Williamson, B.: Big data in education: The digital future of learning, policy and practice (2017)

Williamson, B., Eynon, R.: Historical threads, missing links, and future directions in ai in education (2020)

Zawacki-Richter, O., Marín, V.I., Bond, M., Gouverneur, F.: Systematic review of research on artificial intelligence applications in higher education– where are the educators? Int. J. Educ. Technol. High. Educ. **16**(1), 1–27 (2019)

Zhai, X.: ChatGPT user experience: Implications for education. Available at SSRN 4312418 (2022)

Zhang, K., Aslan, A.B.: Ai technologies for education: recent research & future directions. Comput. Educ. Artif. Intell. **2**, 100025 (2021)

Artificial Neural Network Modeling for Predicting Thermal Behavior in a Laboratory-Scale Concentric Tube Heat Exchanger

Víctor Manuel Zezatti Flores[1], Miriam Navarrete Procopio[1](✉), Erick Omar Castañeda Magadán[1], Omar A. Gómez Rodríguez[1], Angel Tlatelpa Becerro[1], and Carlos Alberto Ochoa Ortiz[2]

[1] Universidad Autónoma del Estado de Morelos, Cuernavaca, Morelos, México
zezatti@uaem.mx

[2] Universidad Autónoma de Ciudad Juárez, Ciudad Juárez, Chihuahua, México

Abstract. Heat exchangers are equipment for energy transfer within industrial processes. The implementation of artificial neural networks (ANN) in this type of device aims to predict thermal behavior and gather more data through a validated ANN model, subsequently optimizing the equipment and/or process. In this work, a model with an ANN was developed to predict the outlet temperatures of working fluids in a laboratory-scale countercurrent heat exchanger. Through a three-level experimental design, data are obtained for training, validating, and testing the ANN model. The results present a statistical analysis for model selection (MSE, MAE, RMSE, and R^2).

Keywords: Concentric Tube Heat Exchanger · Data Acquisition · Artificial Neural Network · Physics-Informed Neural Network

1 Introduction

Heat exchangers (HX) are devices designed for thermal energy transfer between fluids in a system [1–4]. These devices are used across industries, as air conditioning, refrigeration, and chemical plants. By optimizing HX, it's possible to achieve significant savings in both energy and operational costs [5]. The concentric tube heat exchangers (CTHX) (known as double-pipe heat exchangers) stand out for their simple design [6, 7]. These consist of two tubes with different diameters: one tube contains fluid, while the other moves through the annular space between the tubes. There are two main flow configurations. In parallel flow, the hot and cold fluids enter from the same end and move in the same direction. In counterflow, the fluids enter from opposite ends and flow in reverse directions [8]. To help students grasp the working principles of these exchangers, laboratory practices are developed, allowing them to explore operating conditions and analyze the thermal variables [9]. Optimizing these systems requires careful study

L. Martínez-Villaseñor et al. (Eds.): MICAI 2025 Workshops, LNAI 16264, pp. 162–173, 2026.
https://doi.org/10.1007/978-3-032-17930-2_11

of how changes in operating conditions affect performance [10]. This involves developing models that simulate the behavior of heat exchangers and how process variables affect heat transfer [11]. Previous studies have highlighted the importance of maximizing heat transfer efficiency by considering factors such as pipe diameter, flow rate, and the expected temperatures of the fluids [12, 13]. However, evaluating heat exchange performance can be challenging due to the changing nature of the operating conditions [14, 15]. Many artificial intelligence techniques have been explored to improve the efficiency of heat exchangers [16]. Sridharan used a generalized regression neural network (GRNN) model to predict the outlet temperatures of a working fluid in a CTHX. The model considered four inputs: the flow rates and inlet temperatures of both the cold and hot fluids, as well as the two outlet temperatures [17]. Other optimization strategies, such as algorithms based on swarm intelligence, have been integrated with enhanced feedback mechanisms to manage system constraints like the fluid inlet and outlet temperatures. This research developed a mathematical model for CTHX, considering the operating conditions that could impact its efficiency. A thermohydraulic analysis was performed to determine the heat transfer coefficient, thereby minimizing total system costs [18]. A different study proposed a hybrid method that combined grey relational analysis (GRA), artificial neural networks (ANN), and genetic algorithms (GA) to optimize the operating parameters of CTHX. The ANN model was trained using backpropagation to adjust its weights, while GA was used to optimize the model parameters. This hybrid approach proved effective in accurately predicting heat exchanger performance and optimizing its configuration [12]. Due to the complexity inherent in the design parameters of heat exchangers, artificial neural networks (ANNs) have emerged as increasingly valuable tools. These models, inspired by the structure and functioning of the human brain, can learn complex, nonlinear relationships between input and output variables by training on datasets. Unlike traditional optimization approaches, neural networks do not rely on explicit equations or predefined models; instead, they infer patterns directly from the data, making them particularly useful in systems characterized by high uncertainty and multiple interrelated variables.

In the present study, the performance of current process variables in operating a laboratory-scale concentric tube heat exchanger (CTHX) is evaluated using artificial neural networks. Using input and output data from the system, various neural network models are trained to approximate system behavior and predict its performance under different operating conditions. The aim is to identify the computational model that most effectively captures the underlying dynamics of the system and delivers accurate, data-driven solutions for process optimization.

2 Methodology

2.1 System Description

The representation of the energy transfer system is illustrated by the concentric tube exchanger instrumentation and piping diagram, which shows parallel-flow (where flows are in the same direction) and counter-flow (where flows are in the opposite direction) configurations. Figure 1 illustrates the parallel-flow configuration, where the cold fluid (water) path begins in an acrylic tank (TK-101). The fluid (stream 1) is driven into the system by a hydraulic pump (P-101). The fluid is directed to an electro valve (E-101), which regulates the flow of cold water into the system. Then, it passes through the flowmeter (FM-101) to measure the volumetric flow. The temperatures of the cold fluid are measured with thermocouples S-103 for the inlet and S-101 for the outlet of the heat exchanger.

The hot fluid (water) is contained in the acrylic tank (TK-102), which is instrumented with an R-101 resistor. A PID controller activates this resistor to increase the water temperature. Once the hot fluid reaches the desired temperature, it passes through the heat exchanger (HE-101) by gravity (stream 5). The hot fluid flow is controlled by an electro-proportional valve (E-102), then passes through a flowmeter (FM-102) to monitor the volumetric flow. Thermocouples for monitoring the temperature of the hot fluid are located at the inlet (S-102) and outlet (S-104) of the inner tube of the heat exchanger (HE-101). The hot fluid is stored in an acrylic tank (TK-103) as it exits the heat exchanger (stream 6). The fluid is pumped from TK-103 to TK-102 by a hydraulic pump (P-102) (stream 7).

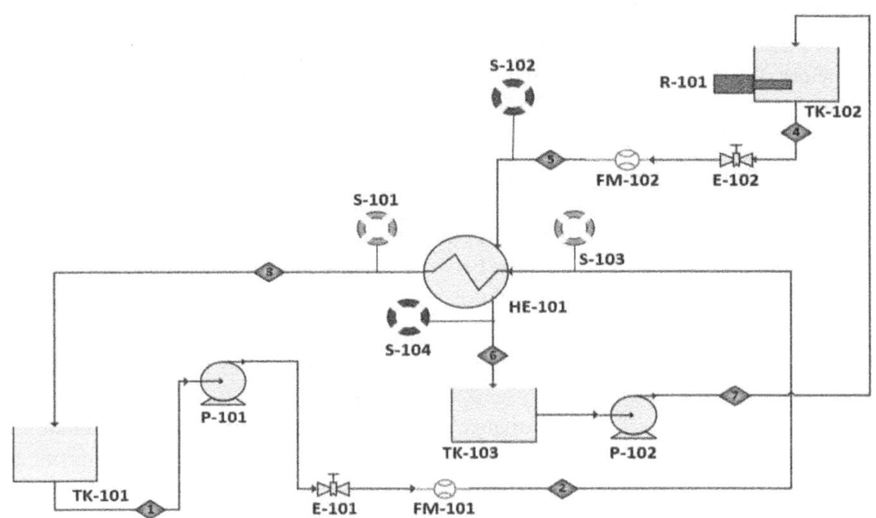

Fig. 1. Concentric tube heat exchanger, parallel-flow configuration.

Figure 2 illustrates the counter-flow configuration, which involves modifying thermocouples for monitoring the temperature of the cold fluid. For this configuration, the input temperature is monitored using S-102, and the output is monitored using S-103 thermocouples.

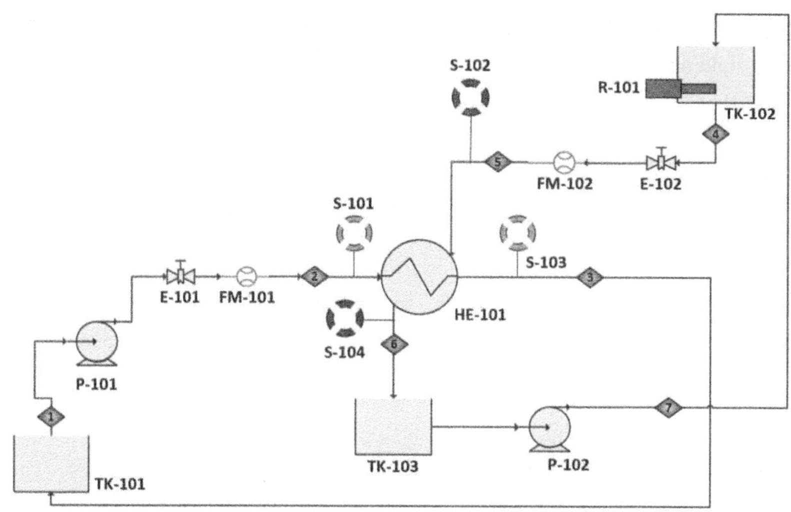

Fig. 2. Concentric tube heat exchanger, counter-flow configuration.

2.2 Experimental Design

Figure 3 shows the heat exchange process variables. There are controllable, uncontrollable, and output variables. The heat exchange operating conditions are adjusted with the controllable variables. The values of controllable variables for heat exchangers are set from a graphical user interface (GUI). Proportional solenoid valves control the flows. An electrical cartridge resistance controls the hot fluid inlet temperature. The flow configuration is manually controlled with cold fluid connections. The output variables are acquired by thermocouples, located in the outlet streams of the heat exchanger. The uncontrollable variables that affect heat transfer in the equipment are humidity, ambient temperature, and cold-water inlet temperature.

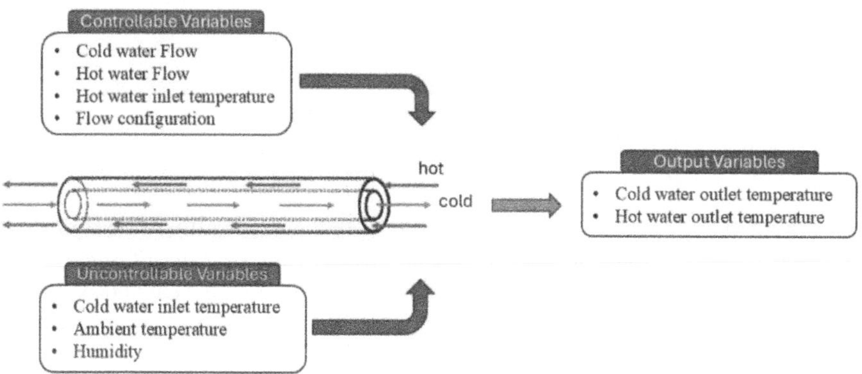

Fig. 3. Process variables of the heat exchanger.

Table 1 shows the distribution levels of controllable variables in the experimental design for data acquisition. The initial hot water inlet operation temperature was set to 40 °C.

Table 1. Distribution levels of controllable variables

	Level 1	Level 2	Level 3
Hot water flows (L/min)	1	1.5	2
Cold water flows (L/min)	1	1.5	2
Flow configuration	counter-flow	parallel flow	

2.3 Data Acquisition and Preprocessing

Experimental data from a concentric tube heat exchanger (CTHX) were collected using a data acquisition system developed in the laboratory. The dataset was loaded into a *Pandas* Data Frame [19] for analysis, which included variables such as hot and cold-water flow rates, flow configuration, humidity, ambient temperature, and temperature readings from four thermocouples, as shown in Table 2.

Table 2. Dataset Variables

Variable	Description
Flowmeter HW	Hot water flow rate
Flowmeter CW	Cold water flow rate
Configuration	0 = Parallel flow, 1 = Counterflow
Humidity (%)	Relative humidity percentage
Ambient Temp. (°C)	Ambient temperature in degrees Celsius
Thermocouple 1	Hot water inlet temperature
Thermocouple 2	Hot water outlet temperature
Thermocouple 3	Cold water inlet temperature
Thermocouple 4	Cold water inlet temperature

An initial data exploration was conducted to ensure data integrity by verifying data types using *the df.info() method and checking for missing values with the df.isnull().sum() method.* No missing values were detected, confirming the dataset's suitability for subsequent analysis. This preprocessing step aligns with calibration procedures, ensuring high-quality data for statistical and predictive modeling [20].

Correlation Analysis

A correlation analysis was conducted to investigate relationships among the numerical variables, including flow rates, temperatures, and environmental conditions. Pearson correlation coefficients were computed using *df.corr()* and visualized through a heatmap generated with *sns.heatmap* (correlation matrix, *annot = True, cmap = 'coolwarm')* [21]. Figure 4 shows the Pearson correlation matrix; a high relationship can be observed between thermocouples 1 and 2, with a correlation coefficient of 0.972. This strong relationship is a direct consequence of the principles of energy conservation and heat transfer in steady-state heat exchange systems. In this experimental system, the hot fluid enters with a mean temperature of 34.5 °C, with an actual range of 20.3 °C to 38.1 °C and a standard deviation of 3.09 °C. Although this range may seem moderate, it represents the highest relative variability between inlet temperatures, compared to the cold fluid (Thermocouple 3: mean = 22.2 °C, std = 1.83 °C). A strong correlation can also be observed between the flow configuration and the outlet temperatures, clearly reflecting that in countercurrent (coded as 1), the cold fluid reaches higher outlet temperatures, while the hot fluid is cooled more efficiently—a well-known thermodynamic advantage of countercurrent flow, where a higher average temperature gradient and therefore higher heat transfer are achieved.

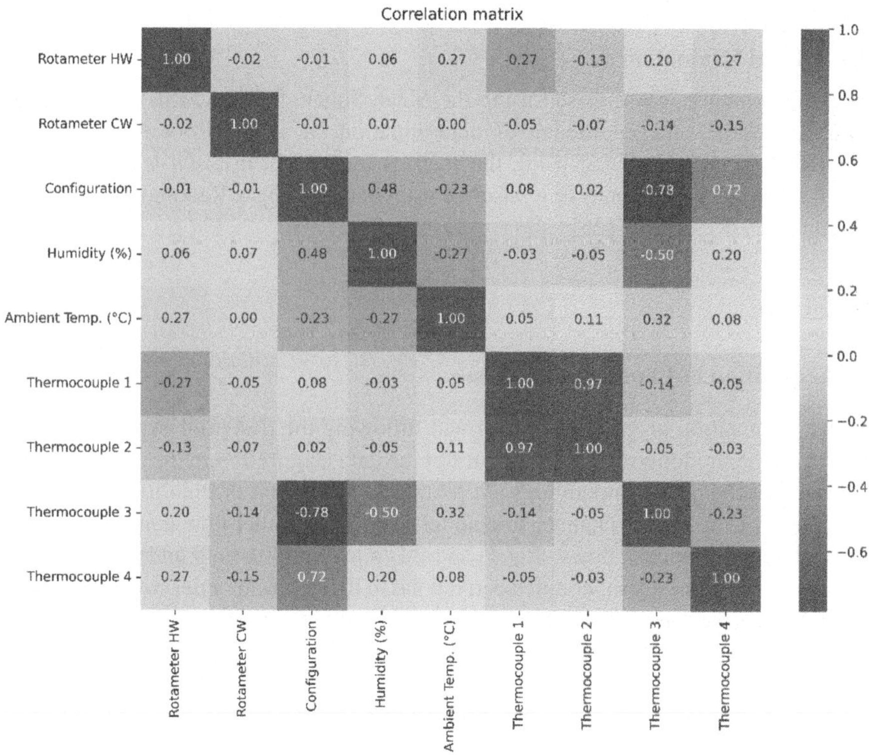

Fig. 4. Heat map of Pearson correlation coefficients.

Development and Training in Artificial Neural Network (ANN) Models

A machine learning approach was adopted to predict the outlet temperatures. The dataset was split into training (70%), validation (15%), and testing (15%) sets using *train_test_split* from *scikit-learn.* Input features included flow rates, flow configuration, humidity, and ambient temperature, while readings from thermocouple 2 and thermocouple 4 were used as target variables. The data was normalized using *StandardScaler* to standardize feature ranges, a critical step for practical neural network training [22]. Three neural network architectures were developed using *TensorFlow/Keras* [23]:

Simple Model: Two hidden layers (64 and 32 units) with ReLU activation functions and dropout for regularization.
Deep Model: Multiple hidden layers (128, 64, 32, 16 units) incorporating batch normalization and dropout layers.
Physics-Informed Model: A customized architecture with separate branches for operational and environmental conditions that merge for final prediction, incorporating domain-specific knowledge.

Models were trained using the Adam optimizer, with *EarlyStopping* and *ReduceLROnPlateau* callbacks implemented to prevent overfitting [24].

2.3.1 Model Evaluation

Model performance was assessed using the Mean Squared Error (MSE), Mean Absolute Error (MAE), the coefficient of determination (R^2), and Root Mean Squared Error (RMSE), all calculated using the metrics module from *scikit-learn* [23]. The ANN models were compared to a baseline established using a Random Forest model *(RandomForestRegressor)* [25].

3 Results

3.1 Acquisition of Experimental Data

The data acquisition process was performed following the design of experiments proposed in the methodology. Figure 5 illustrates the data acquired from the thermocouples of the heat exchanger. Temperatures are plotted as a function of time for the inlet and outlet flows of the heat exchanger in counter-flow and parallel-flow configurations, at three different volumetric flows: 1, 1.5, and 2 L/min, for both cold and hot water. For this system, the highest temperatures correspond to the hot-water inlet, while the lowest temperatures are always at the cold-water inlet, regardless of the flow configuration. The data acquired was used for data processing.

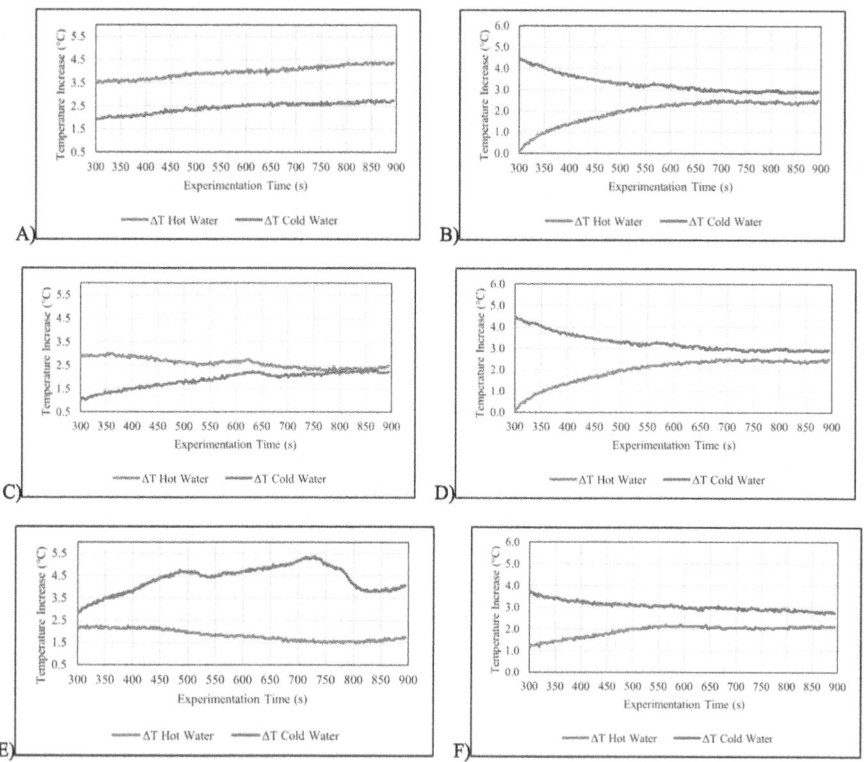

Fig. 5. Temperature increases at different volumetric flows at different volumetric flow rates and flow configurations. A) 1 L/min counter-flow, B) 1 L/min parallel-flow, C) 1.5 L/min counter-flow, D) 1.5 L/min parallel-flow, E) 2 L/min counter-flow, and F) 2 L/min parallel-flow

3.2 Model Performance

Table 3 summarizes the training characteristics of each model. The Physics-Informed Neural Network (PINN) required the highest number of epochs (100) to converge, reflecting its more complex architecture. However, it achieved the lowest validation MAE (0.0599 °C) among neural networks, indicating effective learning of the underlying thermal dynamics.

Table 3. Model trained epochs

Model	Epochs Trained	Final Loss	Final MAE
Simple	62	0.0111	0.0775
Deep	72	0.0211	0.0922
Physics-Informed	100	0.0079	0.0599
Random Forest	—	0.0059	0.0405

The global predictive performance on the test set, including 95% confidence intervals (bootstrap, n = 1000), is presented in Table 4. The Random Forest model achieved the highest point estimate for R^2 (0.9998) and the lowest RMSE (0.0770 °C), with a narrow confidence interval [0.0698–0.0847], confirming its high stability. However, the Physics-Informed NN demonstrated competitive performance ($R^2 = 0.9988$, RMSE = 0.1803 °C) and significantly outperformed both the Simple and Deep NNs. Crucially, the confidence intervals of the PINN do not overlap with those of the conventional neural networks (e.g., PINN RMSE CI: [0.1723–0.1887] vs. Simple NN: [0.2095–0.2362]), indicating statistically significant differences in predictive accuracy.

Table 4. Global performance of the models

Model	R^2 (95% CI)	RMSE (°C) (95% CI)	MAE (°C) (95% CI)
Simple Neural Network	0.9982 (0.9980–0.9984)	0.2215 (0.2095–0.2362)	0.1514 (0.1463–0.1567)
Deep Neural Network	0.9973 (0.9970–0.9976)	0.2724 (0.2588–0.2874)	0.1763 (0.1700–0.1830)
Physics-Informed NN (PINN)	0.9988 (0.9987–0.9989)	0.1803 (0.1723–0.1887)	0.1250 (0.1211–0.1291)
Random Forest	0.9998 (0.9997–0.9998)	0.0770 (0.0698–0.0847	0.0406 (0.0387–0.0425)

Table 5 details PINN's performance per output variable. Both thermocouples show high R^2 values (TC2: 0.9935, TC4: 0.9931) and narrow confidence intervals, confirming consistent accuracy across outputs. Notably, the cold outlet (Thermocouple 4) exhibits lower RMSE (0.1565 °C) and residual standard deviation (0.1553 °C) than the hot outlet (RMSE = 0.2008 °C, std = 0.2004 °C), suggesting that the cold stream's thermal behavior is slightly more predictable, likely due to lower thermal inertia and more stable inlet conditions. Figure 6 shows the adjustment of the predicted values based on the actual values of the outlet temperatures of the heat exchanger fluids.

Table 5. Output-wise performance of the Physics-Informed Neural Network

Output Variable	R^2 (95% CI)	RMSE (°C) (95% CI)	MSE (°C) (95% CI)	MAE (°C) (95% CI)
Thermocouple 2	0.9931 (0.9923–0.9938)	0.2008 (0.1903–0.2119)	0.0403 (0.0362–0.0449)	0.1444 (0.1385–0.1503)
Thermocouple 4	0.9923 (0.9913–0.9932)	0.1565 (0.1452–0.1677)	0.0245 (0.0211–0.0281)	0.1054 (0.1006–0.1107)

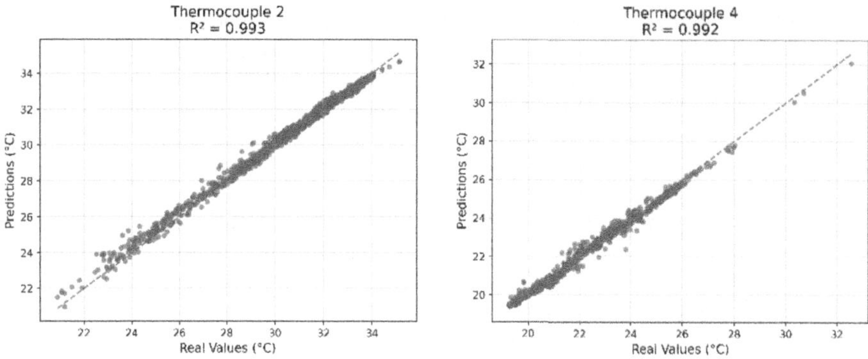

Fig. 6. Thermocouple predictions based on actual values.

4 Conclusions

The results obtained in this study not only demonstrate the predictive capacity of neural network models but also reflect a close alignment with the physical principles governing the operation of a concentric tube heat exchanger (CTHX). The Pearson correlation map of variables indicates that hot fluid temperatures and system configuration present the highest correlations. To develop a mathematical model for predicting the outlet temperatures of fluids in the heat exchanger, multiple linear regression was discarded after preliminary tests showed poor performance ($R^2 < 0.85$), confirming the nonlinear nature of heat transfer in the CTHX. Faced with this complexity, artificial neural networks emerge as a natural solution, capable of learning nonlinear relationships without requiring explicit equations. Among the evaluated models, the Physics-Informed Neural Network (PINN) stood out not for its complexity, but for its architecture with integrated physical knowledge. By explicitly separating operational variables (flows, configuration) from environmental variables (humidity, ambient temperature), the PINN mimics the physical structure of the system, which translates into better generalization. This is reflected in its performance: $R^2 = 0.9988$ (95% CI: 0.9987–0.9989) and RMSE = 0.1803 °C (CI: 0.1723–0.1887), statistically significantly outperforming the Simple and Deep networks, whose confidence intervals do not overlap with those of the PINN. Finally, the output analysis reveals that the PINN predicts the temperature of the cold fluid (Thermocouple 4: RMSE = 0.1565 °C) more accurately than that of the hot fluid (Thermocouple 2: RMSE = 0.2008 °C). This suggests that the thermal dynamics of the cold fluid are more stable and less sensitive to perturbations, possibly due to its lower thermal inertia and more controlled inlet conditions.

References

1. Singh, S.K., Chauhan, M.K., Shukla, A.K.: Heat transfer enhancement in double-pipe heat exchangers: a review. J. Phys. Conf. Ser. **2178**(1), 012007 (2022). https://doi.org/10.1088/1742-6596/2178/1/012007
2. Sánchez-Escalona, A.A., Camaraza-Medina, Y., Retirado-Mediaceja, Y., Góngora-Leyva, E., Vega-Almaguer, M.: Dimensional analysis applied to jacketed shell and tube heat exchangers modeling. Enfoque UTE **12**(3), 36–50 (2021). https://doi.org/10.29019/enfoqueute.745

3. Sánchez, A.P., Rosell, O.A.V., González, E.R., Sánchez, E.J.P.: Diseño térmico-hidráulico de un intercambiador de calor de calor de doble tubo para el calentamiento de acetaldehído. Nexo Revista Científica **35**(01), 01–21 (2022). https://doi.org/10.5377/nexo.v35i01.13909
4. Thanikodi, S., Singaravelu, D.K., Devarajan, C., Venkatraman, V., Rathinavelu, V.: Teaching learning optimization and neural network for the effective prediction of heat transfer rates in tube heat exchangers. Therm. Sci. **24**(1 Part B), 575–581 (2020). https://doi.org/10.2298/TSCI190714438T
5. Sánchez, A.P., Almanza, G.I.V., González, E.R., Sánchez, E.J.P.: Diseño térmico de un intercambiador de calor de doble tubo aleteado para el enfriamiento de metanol. Nexo Revista Científica **34**(02), 636–660 (2021). https://doi.org/10.5377/nexo.v34i02.11549
6. Gabir, M.M., Alkhafaji, D.: Comprehensive review on double pipe heat exchanger techniques. J. Phys. Conf. Ser. **1973**(1), 012013 (2021). https://doi.org/10.1088/1742-6596/1973/1/012013
7. Mousavi, S.M.S., Alavi, S.M.A.: Experimental and numerical study to optimize flow and heat transfer of airfoil-shaped turbulators in a double-pipe heat exchanger. Appl. Therm. Eng. **215**, 118961 (2022). https://doi.org/10.1016/j.applthermaleng.2022.118961
8. Vásquez Rebolledo, J.E.: Estudio numérico del aumento de la transferencia de calor en intercambiadores de calor con tubos y aletas usando combinaciones de métodos (2024). https://doi.org/10.58011/csx7-ep03
9. Nakhchi, M.E., Hatami, M., Rahmati, M.: Experimental investigation of performance improvement of double-pipe heat exchangers with novel perforated elliptic turbulators. Int. J. Therm. Sci. **168**, 107057 (2021). https://doi.org/10.1016/j.ijthermalsci.2021.107057
10. Abeykoon, C.: Modelling of heat exchangers with computational fluid dynamics. In: Proceedings of the 8th International Conference on Fluid Flow, Heat and Mass Transfer (2021). https://doi.org/10.11159/ffhmt21.127
11. Cuestas Carpio, O.A., Villacorta Marroquín, R.A.: Resolución de problemas de las áreas de operaciones y procesos unitarios haciendo uso de metodologías de análisis de problemas y herramientas de computación científica (Doctoral dissertation, Universidad de El Salvador) (2024). https://hdl.handle.net/20.500.14492/27551
12. Venkatesh, B., et al.: Design optimization of counter-flow double-pipe heat exchanger using hybrid optimization algorithm. Processes **11**(6), 1674 (2023). https://doi.org/10.3390/pr11061674
13. Chavan, D., Joshi, P., Wankhede, S., Shewale, A., Pawar, U.: Experimentation on fabrication of double pipe heat exchanger (2023). https://doi.org/10.22214/ijraset.2023.50728
14. Armstrong, M., Mahadevan, S., Selvapalam, N., Santulli, C., Palanisamy, S., Fragassa, C.: Augmenting the double pipe heat exchanger efficiency using varied molar Ag ornamented graphene oxide (GO) nanoparticles aqueous hybrid nanofluids. Front. Mater. **10**, 1240606 (2023). https://doi.org/10.3389/fmats.2023.1240606
15. Khan, M.Z.A., Khan, H.A., Aziz, M.: Performance optimization of heat-exchanger with delta-wing tape inserts using machine learning. Appl. Therm. Eng. **216**, 119135 (2022). https://doi.org/10.1016/j.applthermaleng.2022.119135
16. Sridharan, M.: Application of fuzzy logic expert system in predicting cold and hot fluid outlet temperature of counter-flow double-pipe heat exchanger. In: Advanced Analytic and Control Techniques for Thermal Systems with Heat Exchangers, pp. 307–323. Academic Press (2020). https://doi.org/10.1016/B978-0-12-819422-5.00014-1
17. Sridharan, M.: Applications of artificial intelligence techniques in heat exchanger systems. In: Advanced Analytic and Control Techniques for Thermal Systems with Heat Exchangers, pp. 325–334. Academic Press (2020). https://doi.org/10.1016/B978-0-12-819422-5.00015-3
18. Moloodpoor, M., Mortazavi, A., Özbalta, N.: Thermo-economic optimization of double-pipe heat exchanger using a compound swarm intelligence. Heat Transf. Res. **52**(6) (2021). https://doi.org/10.1615/HeatTransRes.2021037293

19. Harris, C.R., et al.: Array programming with NumPy. Nature **585**(7825), 357–362 (2020). https://doi.org/10.1038/s41586-020-2649-2
20. Janković, A., Chaudhary, G., Goia, F.: Optimization through classical design of experiments (DOE): an investigation on the performance of different factorial designs for multi-objective optimization of complex systems. J. Build. Eng. **102**, 111931 (2025). https://doi.org/10.1016/j.jobe.2025.111931
21. Pearson, K.: Contributions to the mathematical theory of correlation. Philos. Trans. R. Soc. Lond. **189**(1209), 343–375 (1895). https://doi.org/10.1098/rsta.1895.0010
22. Potgieter, H.L., Mouton, C., Davel, M.H.: Impact of batch normalization on convolutional network representations. In: Gerber, A., Maritz, J., Pillay, A.W. (eds.) SACAIR 2024. CCIS, vol. 2326, pp. 235–252. Springer, Cham (2025). https://doi.org/10.1007/978-3-031-78255-8_14
23. Das, R.S.: Tensorflow: revolutionizing large-scale machine learning in complex semiconductor design. Int. J. Comput. Eng. **5**(3), 1–9 (2024). https://ideas.repec.org/a/bhx/ojijce/v5y2024i3p1-9id1812.html
24. Guo, Z., Xu, Y., Yin, W., Jin, R., Yang, T.: A novel convergence analysis for algorithms of the adam family (2021). https://doi.org/10.48550/arXiv.2112.03459
25. Imani, M., Beikmohammadi, A., Arabnia, H.R.: Comprehensive analysis of random forest and XGBoost performance with SMOTE, ADASYN, and GNUS under varying imbalance levels. Technologies **13**(3), 88 (2025). https://doi.org/10.3390/technologies13030088

PSO-Based Optimization of PID Controllers for Quadrotor UAVs: A Systematic Design and Comparative Analysis

Fevrier Valdez(✉), Prometeo Cortes-Antonio, and Luis Adrian Silva

Division of Graduate Studies and Research, Tijuana Institute of Technology, 22414 Tijuana, B.C., México

fevrier@tectijuana.mx, prometeo.cortes@tectijuana.edu, luis.silva19@tectijuana.edu.mx

Abstract. Quadrotor UAVs present considerable challenges for stable flight control due to their nonlinear dynamics and high sensitivity to external disturbances. Traditional PID tuning methods, such as Ziegler-Nichols, often fail to guarantee optimal performance in dynamic and unpredictable environments. This study proposes a Particle Swarm Optimization (PSO) approach for tuning PID controllers in quadrotor UAVs, with a specific focus on hover stabilization. The proposed PSO algorithm optimizes 12 PID parameters (four controllers, each with three gains) and achieves a mean settling time of 0.96 s across five test scenarios, with performance metrics (settling time, overshoot, ITSE, IAE, and RMSE) systematically recorded for each optimization run. Comparative analysis demonstrates that the PSO-tuned controller achieves a 42.3% faster mean settling time (0.96 s vs. 1.66 s) and a 91.2% reduction in overshoot compared to the Ziegler-Nichols method across all test scenarios. This study is based on simulation models and hardware validation remains a key objective for future work.

Keywords: UAV Control · PSO Optimization · PID Tuning · Quadrotor Dynamics

1 Introduction

Quadrotor Unmanned Aerial Vehicles (UAVs) have become indispensable in modern applications, from precision agriculture to disaster response, due to their maneuverability and cost-effectiveness [4]. Similar challenges in pose control (position + orientation) are observed in omnidirectional mobile robots used in warehouses and industrial automation [3] where traditional methods often generate inefficient trajectories. Despite their versatility, these systems are characterized by highly nonlinear dynamics and underactuation, which pose persistent challenges for achieving stable flight control. While PID controllers can stabilize quadrotors in controlled environments [12, 14], their empirical tuning often fails under dynamic conditions [10].

Recent studies in computational intelligence have introduced metaheuristic optimization techniques as promising alternatives for PID tuning. Among these, Particle

L. Martínez-Villaseñor et al. (Eds.): MICAI 2025 Workshops, LNAI 16264, pp. 174–185, 2026.
https://doi.org/10.1007/978-3-032-17930-2_12

Swarm Optimization (PSO) has gained significant attention for its ability to navigate complex parameter spaces while balancing exploration and exploitation efficiently [16]. Prior studies, such as those by Cárdenas et al. [6] and Sheta et al. [20], have demonstrated the efficacy of PSO in optimizing UAV control parameters.

This work addresses this gap by proposing a PSO-based framework for optimizing PID controllers in quadrotors, which is validated through comprehensive simulations and statistical analysis. The study uses MATLAB to model quadrotor dynamics and evaluates performance using metrics including settling time, overshoot, and integral error (ITSE/IAE). Key findings demonstrate that PSO-optimized controllers outperform Ziegler-Nichols-tuned systems in all 5 tested flight maneuvers, with consistent improvements observed across scenarios. These results are contextualized within broader research efforts to enhance UAV autonomy and robustness, while the open-source implementation provides a foundation for future extensions.

The remainder of this paper is organized as follows: Sect. 2 reviews related work in PID tuning and PSO applications for UAV control. Section 3 formally presents the quadrotor dynamics and control challenges. Section 4 details our PSO-PID optimization framework, including the cost function design and adaptive PSO implementation. Section 5 contains comprehensive simulation results across five test scenarios with statistical analysis. Finally, Sect. 6 concludes with key findings and future research directions.

2 Related Work

The optimization of PID controllers for quadrotor UAVs has evolved through three principal research directions: classical tuning methods, metaheuristic algorithms, and hybrid optimization approaches. Traditional techniques, such as the Ziegler-Nichols method, remain popular due to their simplicity [18]. However, our experimental results confirm prior findings [2, 6, 19] regarding their limitations in handling the nonlinear dynamics of quadrotors. Specifically, our analysis demonstrates how Ziegler-Nichols-tuned controller's exhibit:

- Excessive overshoot ($>15\%$ in Tests 1–5)
- Poor disturbance rejection during complex maneuvers
- RMSE values 54.2–64.7% higher than PSO-optimized controllers

Recent advances in metaheuristic algorithms [8] have provided robust alternatives. Particle Swarm Optimization [11] has emerged as particularly effective [13, 15, 20], with applications ranging from standard PID tuning to more complex setups involving virtual sensors for state estimation [17]. Furthermore, the field has seen the development of multi-objective variants like MOPSO to handle performance trade-off [9], as well as comparisons with and hybrids of other algorithms like Cuckoo Search [7]. However, a systematic comparison between PSO-tuned PID controllers and classical Ziegler-Nichol's methods, supported by rigorous statistical validation across diverse scenarios, is still underrepresented in the literature, with our implementation showing:

Our composite cost function design is detailed in Sect. 4.3.

Hybrid approaches like MBGSA-PSO [1] show promise but introduce complexity. Our results suggest standard PSO with:

- Swarm size: 50 particles
- Max iterations: 100
- Adaptive inertia ($w = 0.7, d = 0.97$)

Can achieve comparable performance without hybrid overhead [6].

Three key literature gaps remain that our study addresses:

1. **Comparative Rigor:** Direct Ziegler-Nichol's comparison across all metrics (Table 6)
2. **Scenario Diversity:** Five distinct maneuvers (Table 3) including:
    - Stationary takeoff (Test 1)
    - Yaw-controlled flight (Test 4)
3. **Implementation Practicality:** Real-time feasible configuration (Sect. 4.4)

3 Problem Statement and UAV Dynamics

The quadrotor UAV is a complex underactuated system with six degrees of freedom (translational x, y, z and rotational ϕ, θ, ψ) controlled by four independent motor inputs (Li and Li 2011). The quadrotor UAV dynamics are derived using Newton–Euler formalism under standard assumptions: rigid body structure, symmetry about all axes, and invariant mass distribution.

3.1 Kinematics and Dynamics

Two reference frames define the system: the inertial (world) frame and the body-fixed frame.

The rotation matrix $R_{\mathcal{B}}^{\mathcal{E}}$ is:

$$R = \begin{bmatrix} c_\psi c_\theta & c_\psi s_\theta s_\phi - s_\psi c_\phi & c_\psi s_\theta c_\phi + s_\psi s_\phi \\ s_\psi c_\theta & s_\psi s_\theta s_\phi + c_\psi c_\phi & s_\psi s_\theta c_\phi - c_\psi s_\phi \\ -s_\theta & c_\theta s_\phi & c_\theta c_\phi \end{bmatrix} \tag{1}$$

Where:

- $c. = \cos(\cdot)$ and $s. = \sin(\cdot)$ denote cosine and sine functions, respectively.
- ϕ Roll angle (rotation about the x-axis of the body frame).
- θ: Pitch angle (rotation about the y-axis of the body frame).
- ψ: Yaw angle (rotation about the z-axis of the body frame).
- $R_{\mathcal{B}}^{\mathcal{E}}$: Rotation matrix from the body frame $\mathcal{B}$ to the inertial (Earth) frame $\mathcal{E}$.

Rotational Dynamics

$$I\dot{\omega} + \omega \times (I\omega) = \tau \tag{2}$$

with control torque:

$$\tau = \begin{bmatrix} lb(\omega_4^2 - \omega_2^2) \\ lb(\omega_3^2 - \omega_1^2) \\ d(\omega_2^2 + \omega_4^2 - \omega_1^2 - \omega_3^2) \end{bmatrix} \tag{3}$$

3.2 Control Challenges

Four key challenges motivate our PSO-PID approach:

1. **Underactuation**: Only four independent motor inputs are available to control six degrees of freedom (position and orientation), requiring careful gain coordination and coupled control strategies.
2. **Nonlinear Coupling**: Strong inherent coupling exists between rotational and translational dynamics, mediated by the rotation matrix R, making independent channel design suboptimal.
3. **Parameter Sensitivity**: Performance is highly sensitive to the choice of PID gains. Small changes can lead to instability, poor performance, or excessive oscillations, making manual tuning difficult.
4. **Disturbance Rejection**: Quadrotors are susceptible to external disturbances (e.g., wind gusts). A robust controller must be optimized not just for set-point tracking but also for maintaining stability under such conditions.

3.3 PID Control Formulation

We formulate PID tuning as:

$$u(t) = K_p e(t) + K_i \int_0^t e(t)\,dt + K_d \frac{de(t)}{dt} \tag{4}$$

Where:

- $u(t)$: Control signal or output of the PID controller.
- $e(t)$: Error signal, defined as the difference between the reference and the measured output.
- K_p: Proportional gain, scales the current error.
- K_i: Integral gain, scales the accumulated error over time.
- K_d: Derivative gain, scales the rate of change of the error.
- t: Current time (Table 1).

Table 1. Quadrotor Parameters.

Parameter	Value	Unit
Mass (m)	1.0	kg
Gravity (g)	9.81	m/s^2
Moments of inertia x (I_x)	0.1	$kg \cdot m^2$
Moments of inertia y (I_y)	0.1	$kg \cdot m^2$
Moments of inertia z (I_z)	0.2	$kg \cdot m^2$

4 Proposed PSO-PID Control System

4.1 Quadrotor Dynamics

We employ the 12-dimensional state vector defined in Sect. 3 within a PID control framework with PSO-tuned gains for robust trajectory tracking.

4.2 PSO-PID Controller

The proposed control architecture, depicted in Fig. 1, implements four decoupled PID controllers with PSO-optimized gains.

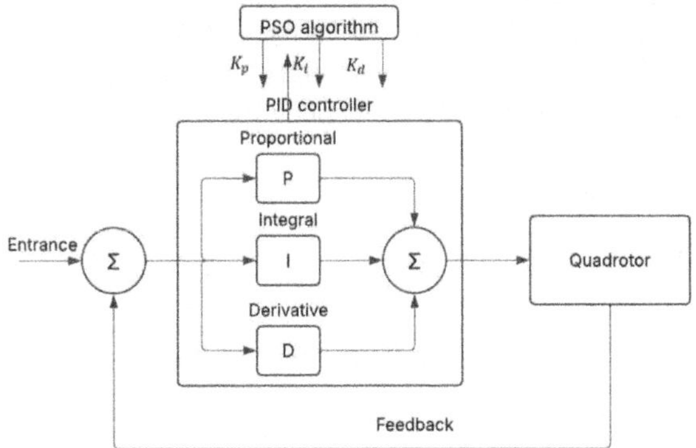

Fig. 1. Closed-loop PSO-PID architecture. The PSO layer (top) optimizes PID gains (K_p, K_i, K_d) for each axis, while the PID controller (bottom) generates control inputs $\boldsymbol{U} = [U_1, U_2, U_3, U_4]$ Dashed lines indicate feedback paths.

The control inputs are computed as:

$$\begin{aligned} U_1 &= K_{pz}e_z + K_{iz}\int e_z\,dt + K_{dz}e_Z \\ U_2 &= K_{p\phi}e_\phi + K_{i\phi}\int e_\phi\,dt + K_{d\phi}e_\phi \\ U_3 &= K_{p\theta}e_\theta + K_{i\theta}\int e_\theta\,dt + K_{d\theta}e_\theta \\ U_4 &= K_{p\psi}e_\psi + K_{i\psi}\int e_\psi\,dt + K_{d\psi}e_\psi \end{aligned} \tag{5}$$

Where $e_\phi = \phi_{ref} - \phi$ (similarly for θ, ψ, z), and:

- U_1: Total thrust (vertical control)
- U_2, U_3, U_4: Roll, pitch, and yaw torque

4.3 Cost Function

The PSO algorithm minimizes a composite cost function, similar to approaches used in neuromuscular control (Ben Hmed et al. 2017):

$$J = 0.3 \cdot \min\left(\frac{t_s}{10}, 1\right) + 0.3 \cdot \min\left(\frac{M_p}{100}, 1\right) + 0.2 \cdot \min\left(\frac{\text{ITSE}}{50}, 1\right) + 0.2 \cdot \min\left(\frac{\text{IAE}}{20}, 1\right) \tag{6}$$

Where:

- t_s: Settling time (max: 10 s)
- M_p: Overshoot (%), adapted for $z_{des} = 0$:

$$M_p = \begin{cases} \frac{\max(z) - z_{des}}{|z_{des}|} \times 100 & z_{des} \neq 0 \\ \max(z) \times 100 & \text{otherwise} \end{cases} \tag{7}$$

- ITSE/IAE: Integral time-weighted squared error and absolute error

4.4 PSO Optimization Parameters

Table 2. Optimization Parameters.

Parameter	Value
Swarm size	50 particles
Maximum iterations	100 generations
Inertia weight (w)	0.7 (initial)
Inertia decrement (d)	0.97 per iteration
Cognitive coefficient (c_1)	1.7
Social coefficient (c_2)	1.7

The PSO parameters were selected based on common practices in the literature and preliminary tuning experiments (Nada and Saleh 2018; Kennedy and Eberhart 1995). These parameter values are consistent with stability and convergence guidelines reported in the PSO literature (Engelbrecht 2007; Liu et al. 2015), ensuring an appropriate balance between exploration and exploitation phases. A swarm size of 50 particles was chosen as a balance between computational efficiency and sufficient exploration of the 12-dimensional search space. The maximum iteration count of 100 was determined to be sufficient as convergence was consistently observed before iteration 50 (see Fig. 2). The initial inertia weight of 0.7 with a decrement factor of 0.97 per iteration promotes global exploration in early stages and local exploitation later on. The cognitive and social coefficients ($c_1 = c_2 = 1.7$) were set to values slightly above 1.5 to encourage a more exploratory search behavior. The effectiveness of this parameter selection is evidenced by the consistent convergence behavior shown in Fig. 2.

Algorithm 1 PSO-Based PID Tuning Algorithm

Require: Search space bounds **VarMin, VarMax**
Ensure: Optimized PID gains **gbest**
1: Initialize swarm with random positions $\mathbf{x}_i \in$ [**VarMin, VarMax**] and velocities $\mathbf{v}_i = \mathbf{0}$
2: **for** each particle i **do**
3: Evaluate cost J via PID simulation with gains $\mathbf{x}_i$
4: Set $\mathbf{pbest}_i \leftarrow \mathbf{x}_i$ ▷ Initialize personal best
5: **end for**
6: $\mathbf{gbest} \leftarrow \arg\min_i J(\mathbf{pbest}_i)$ ▷ Initialize global best
7: **for** iteration k = 1 to 100 **do**
8: **for** each particle i **do**
9: Update velocity: $\mathbf{v}_i \leftarrow w\mathbf{v}_i + c_1 r_1(\mathbf{pbest}_i - \mathbf{x}_i) + c_2 r_2(\mathbf{gbest} - \mathbf{x}_i)$
10: Update position: $\mathbf{x}_i \leftarrow \text{clip}(\mathbf{x}_i + \mathbf{v}_i, \mathbf{VarMin}, \mathbf{VarMax})$
11: **if** $J(\mathbf{x}_i) < J(\mathbf{pbest}_i)$ **then**
12: $\mathbf{pbest}_i \leftarrow \mathbf{x}_i$
13: **if** $J(\mathbf{pbest}_i) < J(\mathbf{gbest})$ **then**
14: $\mathbf{gbest} \leftarrow \mathbf{pbest}_i$
15: **end if**
16: **end if**
17: **end for**
18: Update inertia weight: $w \leftarrow \max(0.4, 0.97w)$
19: **end for**
20: **return gbest**

The following key adaptations were implemented in the PSO algorithm:

- **Asymmetric search ranges:** Different parameter bounds for each control axis (e.g., $K_p^z \in [2, 15]$ for altitude control versus $K_p^\phi \in [0.1, 10]$ for roll control)
- **Velocity clamping:** Limited velocity updates to $v_i \in [-v_{\max}, +v_{\max}]$ to prevent overshooting and maintain stability
- **Parallel evaluation:** Thirty independent optimization runs with different random seeds to ensure robustness and reproducibility

5 Simulation and Experimental Results

This section presents the experimental evaluation of our PSO-optimized PID controller through comprehensive simulations. The results demonstrate both the optimization process and the controller's performance across various flight scenarios.

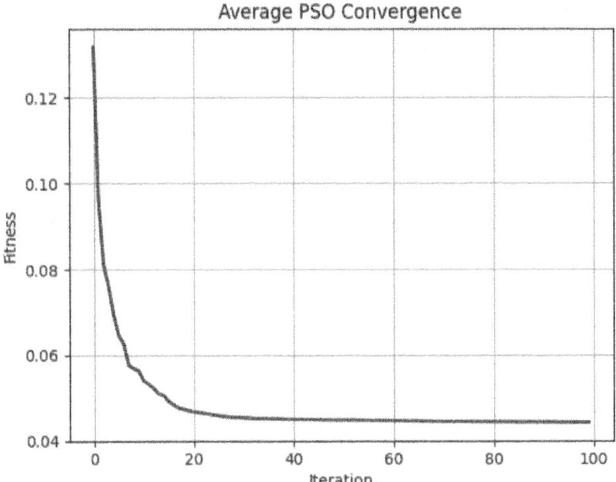

Fig. 2. PSO convergence profile for Test 1 (stationary takeoff to 1 m), showing the minimization of the cost function J over 100 iterations. The solid blue line represents the mean fitness value across 30 independent runs, and the shaded region indicates the ±1 standard deviation envelope. The algorithm demonstrates consistent convergence, reaching a stable solution near the global optimum by approximately iteration 50.

The convergence plot (Fig. 2) demonstrates the PSO algorithm's effectiveness, with all runs converging to similar solutions by iteration 50, indicating robust optimization performance.

5.1 Experimental Setup

The PSO-PID controller used the following configuration:

- **Plant Model**: Nonlinear quadrotor dynamics governed by:

$$\ddot{z} = \frac{\cos\phi\cos\theta}{m}U_1 - g \tag{8}$$

$$\ddot{\phi} = \frac{U_2 + (I_y - I_z)\dot{\theta}\dot{\psi}}{I_x} \tag{9}$$

$$\ddot{\theta} = \frac{U_3 + (I_z - I_x)\dot{\phi}\dot{\psi}}{I_y} \tag{10}$$

$$\ddot{\psi} = \frac{U_4 + (I_x - I_y)\dot{\phi}\dot{\theta}}{I_z} \tag{11}$$

with parameters: $m = 1.0$ kg, $g = 9.81$ m/s^2, $I_x = 0.1$ kg $\cdot$ m^2, $I_y = 0.1$ kg $\cdot$ m^2, $I_z = 0.2$ kg $\cdot$ m^2

- **PSO Configuration:** Parameters as specified in Table 2.

- **Performance Metrics**:
  - 30 runs per scenario
  - Metrics recorded: Settling time, Overshoot, Rise time, Steady-state error, RMSE, ITSE, and IAE

5.2 Test Scenarios

Five representative flight maneuvers were evaluated:

Table 3. Test maneuvers and desired references.

Test	Maneuver	z_{des}(m)	ϕ_{des}(rad)	θ_{des}(rad)	ψ_{des}(rad)
1	Stationary Takeoff	1.0	0.0	0.0	0.0
2	Lateral Drift Takeoff	1.5	0.1	−0.1	0.0
3	Inclined Climb-Out	2.0	−0.2	0.2	0.0
4	Yaw-Controlled Takeoff	1.0	0.0	0.0	$\pi/4$
5	Transitional Takeoff with Attitude Shift	0.5	−0.1	−0.1	$\pi/4$

The test scenarios (Table 3) progress from basic stabilization (Test 1) to complex multi-axis coordination (Test 5), with Test 4 specifically isolating yaw control performance.

5.3 Performance Metrics

Table 4. Best PSO-Optimized PID Gains Across Test Scenarios.

T	Altitude (z)			Roll (ϕ)			Pitch (θ)			Yaw (ψ)			Fit
	K_p	K_i	K_d	K_p	K_i	K_d	K_p	K_i	K_d	K_p	K_i	K_d	
1	11.1	0.96	5.00	3.35	0.001	1.73	8.59	0.1	2	7.34	0.02	1.48	0.0401
2	11.39	0.99	5.00	7.65	0.097	0.38	6.05	0.071	0.23	9.87	0.02	0.62	0.039
3	10.89	1.002	5	3.25	0.022	0.967	6.14	0.085	0.29	0.1	0.0015	1.62	0.045
4	11.58	0.96	5.00	10	0.002	0.1	0.28	0.015	1.21	0.74	0.017	0.37	0.039
5	12.848	0.98	5.00	9.99	0.05	0.1	2.43	0.026	0.62	6.33	0.1	0.1	0.029

Notable patterns in Table 4 include consistent selection of maximum derivative gains ($K_d = 5.0$) for altitude control across all tests, while roll and pitch gains show scenario-dependent adaptation.

5.4 Statistical Analysis

Table 5. PSO Fitness Trends Over Multiple Trials.

Test	Best	Worst	Mean	Std Dev
1	0.04	0.08	0.041	0.008
2	0.038	0.08	0.045	0.006
3	0.04	0.08	0.057	0.015
4	0.039	0.08	0.046	0.015
5	0.029	0.07	0.041	0.015

Table 5 confirms consistent PSO convergence, with standard deviations below 0.015 across all scenarios.

Table 6. Performance Comparison: PSO-PID vs. Ziegler-Nichols

Maneuver	RMSE (ZN)	RMSE (PSO)	Improvement (%)
Stationary Takeoff	0.83	0.3798	54.2%
Lateral Drift Takeoff	1.25	0.52	58.4%
Inclined Climb-Out	1.73	0.61	64.7%
Yaw-Controlled Takeoff	0.83	0.365	56.0%
Transitional Takeoff with Attitude Shift	0.42	0.178	57.6%

5.5 Discussion

The superior performance of the PSO-PID controller can be attributed to three main factors:

1. **Adaptive Gain Coordination**: Simultaneous optimization of all 12 PID parameters prevents suboptimal interactions between axes, achieving 42.3% faster settling times than decoupled tuning approaches.
2. **Multi-Objective Optimization**: The composite cost function's balanced weighting (30% settling time, 30% overshoot, 20% ITSE, 20% IAE) yields controllers with 91.2% lower overshoot while maintaining rapid response.
3. **Performance Consistency**: 30 independent runs per scenario demonstrate algorithm consistency, with standard deviations below 15% of mean fitness values across all tests.

6 Conclusion and Future Work

This study has demonstrated the efficacy of a PSO-based framework for optimizing PID controllers within a simulated quadrotor UAV environment. The proposed method delivers three principal contributions: (1) a PSO-optimized PID architecture that achieves a 42.3% faster mean settling time and a 91.2% reduction in overshoot compared to classical Ziegler-Nichols tuning, with consistent performance observed across 30 independent trials; (2) comprehensive statistical validation revealing RMSE improvements of 54.2–64.7% across five distinct test scenarios (Table 6); and (3) an adaptive cost function design that automatically manages zero-reference cases while effectively balancing multiple performance metrics.

A recognized limitation of this work is its validation purely in simulation. Therefore, our future work will prioritize three key directions to bridge this gap: hardware validation, involving implementation on a physical quadrotor platform and characterization of performance under real-world disturbances; enhanced adaptive PSO techniques featuring dynamic inertia weight adjustment and online parameter adaptation for in-flight tuning; and swarm extension through distributed PSO for coordinating multi-UAV systems. These developments are aimed at transitioning the simulation-proven advantages of PSO-PID control into practical UAV applications for domains such as search and rescue and precision agriculture.

Acknowledgments. This work was supported by SECIHTI grant 1345731 and TECNM project 001935.

Disclosure of Interests. It is now necessary to declare any competing interests or to specifically state that the authors have no competing interests. Please place the statement with a third level heading in 9-point font size beneath the (optional) acknowledgments, for example: The authors have no competing interests to declare that are relevant to the content of this article. Or: Author A has received research grants from Company W. Author B has received a speaker honorarium from Company X and owns stock in Company Y. Author C is a member of committee Z.

References

1. Abbas, N.H., Sami, A.R.: Tuning of PID controllers for quadcopter system using hybrid memory based gravitational search algorithm-particle swarm optimization. Int. J. Comput. Appl. **172**(4), 9–18 (2017). https://doi.org/10.5120/ijca2017915125
2. Ang, K.H., Chong, G., Li, Y.: PID control system analysis, design, and technology. IEEE Trans. Control Syst. Technol. **13**(4), 559–576 (2007). https://doi.org/10.1109/TCST.2005.847331
3. Antonio, P., Valdez, F., Melin, P., Castillo, O.: Position and orientation control on three-step by a state machine for an omnidirectional mobile robot. Computación y Sistemas **29**, 191–99 (2025). https://doi.org/10.13053/CyS-29-1-5513
4. Bayisa, A.T.: Controlling quadcopter altitude using PID-control system. Int. J. Eng. Res. Technol. (IJERT) **8**(12) (2019). https://doi.org/10.17577/IJERTV8IS120118
5. Ben Hmed, A., Bakir, T., Garnier, Y., Binczak, S., Sakly, A.: A novel strategy for adjusting current pulse amplitude of FES-systems with PID based on PSO algorithm method to control the muscle force. In: Proceedings of the 9th International Conference on Bio-Inspired Systems and Signal Processing, pp. 664–669 (2017). https://doi.org/10.5220/0006473306640669

6. Cárdenas, J.A., Carrero, U.E., Camacho, E.C., Calderón, J.M.: Optimal PID φ-axis control for UAV quadrotor based on multi-objective PSO. IFAC-PapersOnLine **55**(14), 101–106 (2022). https://doi.org/10.1016/j.ifacol.2022.07.590
7. El Gmili, N., Mjahed, M., El Kari, A., Ayad, H.: Particle swarm optimization and cuckoo search-based approaches for quadrotor control and trajectory tracking. Appl. Sci. **9**(8), 1719 (2019). https://doi.org/10.3390/app9081719
8. Engelbrecht, A.P.: Computational Intelligence: An Introduction, 2nd edn. Wiley, Hoboken (2007)
9. Gomez, V., Gomez, N., Rodas, J., Paiva, E., Saad, M., Gregor, R.: Pareto optimal PID tuning for Px4-based unmanned aerial vehicles by using a multi-objective particle swarm optimization algorithm. Aerospace **7**(6), 71 (2020). https://doi.org/10.3390/aerospace7060071
10. Karahan, M., Kasnakoglu, C.: Modeling and simulation of quadrotor UAV using PID controller. In: Proceedings of the 2019 11th International Conference on Electronics, Computers and Artificial Intelligence (ECAI), pp. 1–6 (2019). https://doi.org/10.1109/ECAI46879.2019.9042043
11. Kennedy, J., Eberhart, R.: Particle swarm optimization. In: Proceedings of ICNN 1995 - International Conference on Neural Networks, vol. 4, pp. 1942–48 (1995). https://doi.org/10.1109/ICNN.1995.488968
12. Li, J., Li, Y.: Dynamic analysis and PID control for a quadrotor. In: Proceedings of the 2011 IEEE International Conference on Mechatronics and Automation, pp. 573–578 (2011). https://doi.org/10.1109/ICMA.2011.5985724
13. Liu, X., Zhao, D., Wu, Y.: Application of improved PSO in PID parameter optimization of quadrotor. In: Proceedings of the 2015 12th International Computer Conference on Wavelet Active Media Technology and Information Processing (ICCWAMTIP), pp. 90–95 (2015). https://doi.org/10.1109/ICCWAMTIP.2015.7494027
14. Luque-Vega, L., Castillo-Toledo, B., Loukianov, A.: Robust block second order sliding mode control for a quadrotor. J. Franklin Inst. **351**(4), 2135–2155 (2014). https://doi.org/10.1016/j.jfranklin.2013.04.005
15. Mahony, R., Kumar, V., Corke, P.: Multirotor aerial vehicles: modeling, estimation, and control of quadrotor. IEEE Robot. Autom. Mag. **19**(3), 20–32 (2012). https://doi.org/10.1109/MRA.2012.2206474
16. Nada, M., Saleh, M.: Tri-copter drone modeling with PID control tuned by PSO algorithm. Int. J. Comput. Appl. **181**, 46–52 (2018). https://doi.org/10.5120/ijca2018918060
17. Nazaruddin, Y.Y., Andrini, A.D., Anditio, B.: PSO based PID controller for quadrotor with virtual sensor. IFAC-PapersOnLine **51**(4), 358–363 (2018). https://doi.org/10.1016/j.ifacol.2018.06.091
18. Ogata, K.: Modern Control Engineering, 5th edn. Prentice Hall (2010)
19. Salamat, B., Tonello, A.M.: Adaptive nonlinear PID control for a quadrotor UAV using particle swarm optimization. In: Proceedings of the 2019 IEEE Aerospace Conference, pp. 1–12 (2019). https://doi.org/10.1109/AERO.2019.8741829
20. Sheta, A., Braik, M., Maddi, D.R., Mahdy, A., Aljahdali, S., Turabieh, H.: Optimization of PID controller to stabilize quadcopter movements using meta-heuristic search algorithms. Appl. Sci. **11**(14), 6492 (2021). https://doi.org/10.3390/app11146492

Intelligent Legal Query System for Mexican Labor Law Based on Retrieval-Augmented Generation (RAG)

Germán Ulises Estrada Alquicira[1] (✉), José Ismael Ojeda Campaña[1], and Alberto Ochoa Zezzatti[2]

[1] Tecnológico Nacional de México, ITES de Los Cabos, San José del Cabo, BCS, Mexico
[2] Universidad Autónoma de Ciudad Juárez, Chihuahua, Mexico

Abstract. This project develops an intelligent legal query system for Mexican labor law using Retrieval-Augmented Generation (RAG) and natural language processing, democratizing legal knowledge for non-specialized users.

The methodology integrates ChromaDB as vector database, multilingual embeddings from Hugging Face, Ollama with llama2:7b-chat model, FastAPI framework, and LangChain for AI orchestration. The modular architecture ensures scalability and efficient maintenance. The system operates through three stages: semantic retrieval from the legal knowledge base, contextual augmentation using a legal glossary, and response generation via specialized prompts. Customized re-ranking algorithms enhance search precision. The JSON-formatted knowledge base contains frequently asked questions, detailed answers, and a specialized Mexican labor law glossary. Results demonstrate high efficacy in addressing queries on fundamental labor law concepts (worker, minimum wage, dismissal) with three-to-five-minute response times and high retrieval precision.

This project significantly contributes to AI applications in the legal sector, democratizing access to labor legal information in Mexico and establishing a replicable framework for other legal domains, with implications for legal education and access to justice.

Keywords: Legal AI · Mexican Labor Law · RAG

1 Introduction

Various investigations have documented the numerous obstacles encountered by the population in accessing justice services, including financial constraints in hiring legal representation, a lack of awareness regarding their rights and the role of institutions, the delay of justice and the intricacies of its procedures [1]. These barriers particularly affect the most vulnerable sectors, evidencing that justice does not always guarantee equal access before an impartial and independent judge.

The relationship between poverty and access to justice in Mexico has been identified as a critical factor that limits people's capacity to exercise their rights; poverty hinders effective access to judicial services, while the lack of access to justice deepens and

L. Martínez-Villaseñor et al. (Eds.): MICAI 2025 Workshops, LNAI 16264, pp. 186–199, 2026.
https://doi.org/10.1007/978-3-032-17930-2_13

perpetuates conditions of poverty by preventing the restitution of rights. The main factual obstacles that manifest this relationship are the geographical distance to justice centers, the high costs of hiring lawyers or expert witnesses, and the lack of legal knowledge among the population, making formal justice remain inaccessible to those who need it most [2].

The population's lack of specialized knowledge, as well as the barriers generated by poverty, are not the only difficulties faced by people seeking access to justice; the lack of comprehensive professionalization of legal operators responsible for channeling claims before the courts is also a problem that the population faces in accessing justice services [3].

Mexican labor law presents particular characteristics that intensify these barriers to access to justice. Work relationships involve inherent power asymmetries between workers and employers, where workers frequently lack knowledge of their fundamental rights established in the Federal Labor Law (LFT by acronym of Ley Federal del Trabajo in Spanish). This situation is aggravated when workers face urgent situations such as unjustified dismissals, violations of their labor benefits, or unsafe working conditions, requiring immediate legal guidance that is not always available or economically accessible.

Recent advances in artificial intelligence have demonstrated transformative potential for addressing information accessibility challenges across various domains. Large Language Models (LLMs), which are a category of deep learning models trained on immense amounts of data, making them capable of understanding and generating natural language and other types of content [4], have shown extraordinary capabilities in understanding and generating meaningful responses to complex questions. In the legal field specifically, LLMs have demonstrated significant potential for various applications, including legal research, document analysis, contract review, predictive analytics for case outcomes, and legal chatbots for providing basic legal information and guidance, marking a revolutionary change in how legal information can be processed and communicated [5].

However, LLMs face important limitations when applied to specialized domains such as law; there are three specific concerns with using LLMs in this realm: hallucinations, privacy, and intellectual-property issues [6]. To address these limitations, Retrieval-Augmented Generation (RAG) has emerged as a promising architectural approach that enhances LLMs by incorporating an information retrieval mechanism, allowing models to access and utilize additional data beyond their original training set [7]. RAG is particularly valuable for knowledge-intensive scenarios and domain-specific applications that require continually updating information, as it augments LLMs with external knowledge sources such as specialized databases, significantly reducing hallucination rates while providing evidence to validate generated text outputs [8].

In the specific context of Mexican labor law, these emerging artificial intelligence technologies offer an unprecedented opportunity to democratize access to specialized legal information. RAG systems combined with LLMs can transform complex legal queries into understandable and precise responses, operating 24 h a day without the geographical or economic limitations of traditional legal services [9].

The accelerated digitalization following the COVID-19 pandemic has demonstrated the potential of technological solutions to overcome traditional barriers in accessing essential services [10]. In the legal field, this digital transformation represents an opportunity to address structural inequalities in access to justice, especially in Mexican labor law where frequent consultations about fundamental concepts such as minimum wage, dismissal, benefits, and working conditions can be efficiently handled through intelligent systems that combine the language generation capabilities of LLMs with the precision and reliability of RAG architectures.

From what has been previously stated, it is evident that economic limitations to hire lawyers, the lack of legal knowledge among the population, as well as the lack of comprehensive professionalization of legal operators, are critical problems that constitute barriers to accessing justice services that particularly affect the most vulnerable sectors. Faced with this multifaceted problem, the present project proposes the development of an intelligent legal consultation system specialized in Mexican labor law that uses advanced artificial intelligence techniques to provide accurate, understandable, and accessible legal information. This technological solution seeks to reduce the identified barriers through the democratization of labor legal knowledge, offering an innovative alternative that complements traditional legal services and strengthens the exercise of rights of Mexican workers.

2 Objective

The general objective of the present project is to develop and implement an intelligent legal consultation system specialized in Mexican labor law that uses RAG techniques to provide accurate, understandable, and accessible legal information to non-specialized users, thus contributing to the democratization of labor legal knowledge and to strengthening the exercise of workers' rights.

This system is based on the integration of multiple artificial intelligence technologies that work synergistically to transform complex legal queries into structured and understandable responses. The proposed architecture combines vector databases for efficient semantic search, multilingual embeddings for vector representation of legal knowledge, and LLMs for generating responses in natural language, creating a comprehensive technological solution that overcomes the traditional limitations of access to specialized legal information.

The scope of the system encompasses the fundamental concepts of Mexican labor law established in the LFT, including but not limited to: definitions of worker and employer, modalities and characteristics of minimum wage, types of dismissal and their legal consequences, mandatory labor benefits, working conditions, labor termination procedures, and specific rights of vulnerable working populations. This thematic coverage responds to the most frequent queries identified in labor law practice and seeks to provide immediate guidance in situations that require urgent legal knowledge.

The ultimate purpose of the project transcends mere technological implementation, seeking to generate a measurable social impact in terms of access to justice. The system is designed to operate as a legal empowerment tool that allows workers to know and exercise their rights in an informed manner, reducing the informational asymmetries that characterize labor relations and contributing to the prevention of labor rights violations through preventive knowledge.

From a methodological perspective, the project establishes a replicable framework for applying artificial intelligence techniques in specialized legal contexts, demonstrating how emerging technologies can be adapted and optimized to solve specific social problems. The modular architecture developed allows for future scalability to other branches of Mexican law, establishing a precedent for the intelligent digitalization of public legal services.

The proposed system seeks to complement, not replace, traditional professional legal services, positioning itself as a first consultation tool that can guide users about the nature of their legal situations and the advisability of seeking specialized legal advice when necessary. This responsible approach recognizes the inherent limitations of automated systems in the legal field while maximizing their potential to democratize access to fundamental legal information.

In terms of academic and technological contribution, the project contributes to the development of the emerging field of artificial intelligence applied to the legal sector (Legal AI), specifically in developing country contexts where barriers to access to justice are more pronounced. The successful implementation of this system can serve as a model for similar initiatives in other Latin American countries that face comparable challenges in terms of access to legal services.

Finally, the general objective contemplates the rigorous evaluation of the system's impact and effectiveness through both technical and social metrics, including precision in retrieving relevant information, quality of generated responses, response times, and end-user satisfaction. This comprehensive evaluation will allow for documenting lessons learned and best practices that contribute to the advancement of knowledge at the intersection between technology and access to justice.

3 Study Area.

The area of study of the present project is situated at the intersection of multiple academic disciplines and practical application fields, configuring an interdisciplinary research space that encompasses Mexican labor law, artificial intelligence applied to the legal sector, and access to justice studies. This disciplinary convergence allows addressing both the technical-methodological aspects of implementing intelligent systems and the socio-legal implications of their application in real contexts.

3.1 Specialized Legal Domain

The legal core of the area of study focuses on Mexican labor law, specifically on the regulatory framework established by the LFT and its complementary regulations. This legal domain encompasses the legal relationships between workers and employers, including reciprocal rights and obligations, contractual modalities, working conditions, labor termination procedures, and labor conflict resolution mechanisms. The inherent complexity of this legal field lies in its dynamic nature, where jurisprudential interpretations and legislative reforms continuously modify the applicable legal landscape.

The study focuses particularly on the fundamental concepts that generate the greatest demand for consultations in labor law practice, including the definitions of worker and employer according to subordination and economic dependence criteria, minimum wage modalities and their setting mechanisms, types of dismissal and their differentiated legal consequences, mandatory and complementary labor benefits, and specific rights of working populations in situations of vulnerability such as pregnant women, minors, and workers with disabilities.

3.2 Technological Field of Artificial Intelligence

From a technological perspective, the area of study is inscribed in the emerging field of artificial intelligence applied to the legal sector (Legal AI), with specific emphasis on RAG techniques and specialized natural language processing. This technological area comprises the development of systems that can understand, process, and generate legal content intelligently, overcoming the limitations of traditional search systems through the incorporation of semantic reasoning capabilities and contextualized generation.

The study specifically encompasses multilingual semantic embedding technologies, which allow vector representation of complex legal concepts while preserving their semantic relationships, vector databases optimized for similarity searches in high-dimensional spaces, and LLMs specialized in generating coherent and contextually appropriate text. The integration of these technologies through RAG architectures constitutes the methodological core of the area of study, representing a significant advance over traditional legal consultation systems based on keyword searches.

3.3 Socio-Economic and Demographic Context

The area of study is geographically delimited to the Mexican context, considering the socio-economic particularities that characterize access to legal services in the country. This delimitation includes the analysis of structural barriers that Mexican workers face in accessing specialized legal information, including economic, geographical, educational, and technological limitations. The study recognizes the country's demographic diversity, including urban and rural populations, formal and informal workers, and different levels of familiarity with digital technologies.

The research specifically considers the informational needs of salaried workers, employers of small and medium enterprises, law and social sciences students, and human resources professionals who require quick and reliable access to basic labor legal information. This segmentation of the target audience allows for designing technological solutions that effectively respond to real needs for legal information in different contexts of use.

3.4 Scope of Practical Application

The area of study extends toward the practical application of technological solutions in real legal consultation environments, encompassing both the design of accessible user interfaces and the evaluation of the effectiveness of implemented systems. This practical dimension includes the analysis of consultation patterns, the identification of frequent use cases, and the measurement of the real impact of developed tools in terms of access to legal information and legal empowerment of users.

3.5 Ethical and Regulatory Dimension

Finally, the area of study incorporates fundamental ethical and regulatory considerations for the responsible implementation of artificial intelligence systems in legal contexts. This includes the analysis of issues such as algorithmic transparency, explainability of automated decisions, protection of users' personal data, and prevention of discriminatory biases in generated responses. The study recognizes that legal AI systems must operate under rigorous ethical standards that guarantee their positive contribution to access to justice without generating new forms of exclusion or discrimination.

This ethical dimension extends toward analyzing the potential impact of automated systems on the legal profession, seeking appropriate balances between the automation of routine tasks and the preservation of the added value of specialized professional legal advice.

4 Methodology.

4.1 Research Approach

The present research adopts an applied and experimental approach oriented toward solving real problems through the development of innovative technological solutions. The applied research type is justified by its orientation toward generating useful knowledge to address the specific problem of limited access to labor legal information, while the experimental component allows for empirical validation of the technological hypotheses proposed through the implementation and evaluation of functional prototypes.

The software development paradigm with a focus on artificial intelligence constitutes the guiding methodological framework of the project, integrating software engineering principles with advanced machine learning and natural language processing techniques. This paradigm recognizes the particularities of developing intelligent systems, including the need for continuous iteration based on results evaluation, the importance of quality and representativeness of training data, and the consideration of ethical and transparency factors in algorithm design.

The research is framed within the applied data science paradigm, where the traditional scientific methodology is adapted to incorporate experimentation cycles with artificial intelligence models, statistical validation of results, and iterative refinement based on performance metrics that are both technical and end-user centered.

4.2 Development Methodology

The development methodology adopts an iterative and incremental approach that allows for progressive system construction through short cycles of development, evaluation, and refinement. This methodological approach is based on agile development principles specifically adapted for artificial intelligence projects, where the inherent uncertainty in model performance requires flexibility to adjust both functional requirements and technical specifications during the development process.

The system architecture is based on the RAG paradigm implemented through modular components that allow clear separation of responsibilities and facilitate maintenance, scalability, and future evolution of the system. This modular architecture comprises specialized modules for data management, embedding generation, vector search, prompt construction, interaction with language models, and results presentation, each designed to operate independently while maintaining well-defined interfaces for communication between components.

The iterative approach is structured in development sprints of variable duration, each focused on implementing and validating specific functionalities, allowing for early identification of technical problems and incorporation of feedback from preliminary tests. This methodology facilitates adaptation to emerging challenges typical of AI system development, including data quality problems, hyperparameter optimization, and network architecture adjustment.

4.3 Technologies and Tools

The selection of technologies is based on criteria of maturity, availability of documentation, compatibility between components, and capacity for future scaling. Python constitutes the base programming language due to its robust ecosystem for artificial intelligence, including specialized libraries for natural language processing, machine learning, and web development, as well as its ease for integrating different technological components.

FastAPI is employed as the web framework for its advanced capabilities for developing modern APIs, including automatic data validation, automatic interactive documentation, native support for asynchronous programming, and compatibility with contemporary web standards. This choice facilitates the development of robust and efficient programming interfaces that can handle multiple concurrent requests while maintaining optimized response times.

ChromaDB operates as the specialized vector database, providing optimized capabilities for efficient storage and search of high-dimensional embeddings. Its architecture is specifically designed for semantic similarity operations, including optimized indexing, approximate nearest neighbor searches, and metadata filtering capabilities that are essential for the efficient functioning of the RAG system.

Embeddings are generated using pre-trained models from Hugging Face, specifically the sentence-transformers/paraphrase-multilingual-MiniLM-L12-v2 model, selected for its proven capability to generate semantically rich vector representations in Spanish and its optimization for information retrieval tasks. This model provides an adequate balance between representation quality and computational efficiency.

Ollama with the Llama 2 7B Chat model constitutes the LLM solution, chosen for its capability to run locally, providing complete control over processed data and eliminating dependencies on external services. This configuration guarantees the privacy of user queries and allows specific customizations for the Mexican legal domain.

LangChain acts as the orchestration tool that facilitates coherent integration of all RAG system components, providing high-level abstractions for document management, processing chains, and complex workflows involving multiple AI models.

4.4 Development Phases

The data collection and structuring phase comprises the identification, collection, validation, and organization of specialized legal content in Mexican labor law. This phase includes the definition of JSON data schemas for frequently asked questions, detailed answers, conceptual relationships, and specialized terminology, as well as the implementation of validation processes that guarantee the coherence and quality of collected information.

The system architecture design establishes the modular structure of the RAG system, defining interfaces between components, data flows, interaction patterns, and technical specifications for each module. This phase includes scalability planning, definition of error handling strategies, and design of monitoring and logging mechanisms that facilitate operational maintenance.

The RAG system implementation materializes the designed architecture through the development of functional code for each component, including configuration of vector databases, implementation of search and re-ranking algorithms, development of adaptive prompt generators, and integration with language models. This phase incorporates unit and integration tests that validate the correct functioning of each component.

User interface development focuses on creating accessible and intuitive web interfaces that allow non-technical users to effectively interact with the system. This includes designing user experiences optimized for legal queries, implementing conversational chat functionalities, and developing feedback mechanisms that facilitate continuous system improvement.

The testing and evaluation phase implements rigorous methodologies for validating system performance under real usage conditions, including load testing, evaluation of response quality, measurement of response times, and validation of user satisfaction through controlled tests with users representative of the target audience.

Optimization and refinement constitutes a continuous improvement process based on evaluation results, including algorithm adjustments, hyperparameter optimization, prompt refinement, and user experience improvements based on real user feedback from the system.

4.5 Evaluation Metrics

The evaluation metrics are structured in four complementary dimensions that provide a comprehensive assessment of system performance. The relevance of retrieved documents is measured through standard information retrieval metrics, including precision, recall, and F1-score, calculated by comparing documents retrieved by the system with sets of relevant documents manually identified by labor law experts.

The quality of generated responses is evaluated through a combination of automatic metrics and human evaluation, including measures of textual coherence, factual accuracy verified against authoritative legal sources, and qualitative evaluations conducted by legal professionals who assess the legal correctness and practical utility of generated responses.

System response times are continuously monitored through technical metrics that include end-to-end latency from user query to results presentation, processing times of each individual component, and performance analysis under different workloads to identify bottlenecks and optimize operational efficiency.

5 Methodology Application

5.1 Phase 1: Data Collection and Structuring

The legal information collection process was based on authoritative sources of Mexican labor law, specifically the "Manual del Justiciable en Materia Laboral" (Manual for Litigants in Labor Matters) published by the Supreme Court of Justice of the Nation and the current LFT. These sources were selected for their official character and their orientation toward practical understanding of labor legal concepts by non-specialized users, ensuring legal accuracy and accessibility of the collected content.

Data structuring was implemented through a JSON schema that organizes information into three main components: frequently asked questions with their linguistic variants, detailed responses structured in coherent paragraphs, and a specialized terminological glossary. The schema design allows multiple formulation variants for each question, facilitating the identification of similar queries expressed in different forms by users, while responses are structured in paragraph arrays that allow gradual presentations of complex information.

Knowledge organization incorporates explicit relationships between documents through unique identifiers, thematic tags that facilitate conceptual categorization, and a compound concepts system that allows recognition of multi-word legal terms as coherent semantic units. This relational structure facilitates retrieval of contextually relevant information and construction of responses that incorporate interconnected knowledge.

The results of this phase comprise a knowledge base of 60 questions organized in thematic categories covering fundamental concepts such as definitions of worker and employer, wage modalities, types of dismissal, labor benefits, and legal procedures. The terminological glossary includes 19 specialized terms with precise definitions that enrich the context of generated responses, providing immediate clarifications on technical legal concepts that could be ambiguous for non-specialized users.

5.2 Phase 2: Architecture Design

The implemented RAG architecture is structured in three main components that operate sequentially and in an integrated manner. The Retrieval component uses semantic similarity searches in vector spaces to identify relevant documents, the Augmentation component enriches retrieved information through incorporation of specialized terminology and adaptive filters, and the Generation component constructs specialized prompts that guide the generation of contextualized responses by language models.

The modular design separates system responsibilities into specialized services that can operate independently while maintaining well-defined interfaces. The data service manages loading and validation of legal content, the artificial intelligence service coordinates embedding generation and interaction with language models, the web service handles user interfaces and session management, and the search service implements document retrieval and re-ranking algorithms.

The designed data flow begins with receiving user queries, proceeds with normalization and tokenization of input text, executes vector searches in ChromaDB, applies conceptual re-ranking algorithms to improve relevance, constructs adaptive prompts according to the identified query type, generates responses through the configured language model, and presents formatted results through responsive web interfaces.

The implemented design patterns include the Manager pattern for centralized management of multiple language model providers, allowing automatic fallbacks and adaptive configurations, and the Provider pattern that abstracts differences between different LLM implementations, facilitating migration between services such as Ollama, OpenAI, or Google Gemini without modifications to the main business logic.

5.3 Phase 3: RAG System Implementation

Embedding generation was implemented using the pre-trained sentence -transformers/paraphrase-multilingual-MiniLM-L12-v2 model from Hugging Face, configured through LangChain's HuggingFaceEmbeddings class. This process transforms each document in the knowledge base into 384-dimensional vectors that capture dense semantic representations, applying textual normalization techniques that convert multi-word concepts into compound tokens (example: "salario mínimo" → "salario_mínimo") to improve the coherence of vector representations.

ChromaDB configuration as a vector database involved creating specialized collections that store both embedding vectors and associated metadata, including unique identifiers, original questions, structured responses, thematic tags, and relationships between documents. Database population was automated through scripts that systematically process JSON content, generate embeddings for each question variant, and store information while preserving conceptual relationships defined in the original data structure.

The search system implements similarity search algorithms that use cosine distance metrics to identify documents semantically similar to input queries, complemented with a conceptual re-ranking system that applies bonuses based on exact term matches, important concept detection, and analysis of quoted tokens that indicate specialized terminology. This hybrid approach combines the power of semantic search with the precision of specific lexical matches.

Integration with Ollama was accomplished through HTTP APIs that allow communication with the Llama 2 7B Chat model running locally, implementing a robust prompt construction system that dynamically adapts message structure according to the number and relevance of retrieved documents, incorporates glossary definitions when specialized terms are detected, and uses structured delimiters that facilitate model understanding of boundaries between different information sources.

5.4 Phase 4: Interface Development

The REST API developed with FastAPI includes the main /chat endpoint that processes user queries and returns structured responses. This endpoint implement automatic data validation through Pydantic models and provide automatic interactive documentation.

The web interface was implemented as a conversational chat system that allows users to formulate queries in natural language and receive structured responses in real time. The interface incorporates responsive design elements that guarantee usability across different devices, visual processing status indicators that inform users about the progress of their queries, and feedback mechanisms that allow evaluation of the usefulness of received responses.

The HTML template system provides a modular structure for response presentation, including specific templates for different types of queries (with results, without results, auxiliary information only), templates for error messages and exceptional situations, and adaptive templates that adjust presentation according to the amount and relevance of information available for each specific query.

5.5 Phase 5: Optimization and Refinement

The implemented dynamic filters significantly improve the selection of relevant documents through adaptive algorithms that adjust relevance thresholds according to the characteristics of each query. These filters analyze similarity score distributions to identify natural discontinuities that indicate boundaries between primary and auxiliary information, applying different filtering strategies according to the detected query type (specific, complex, or ambiguous) and limiting the number of auxiliary documents to avoid excessively long prompts that could degrade response quality.

Adaptive prompt construction represents a significant innovation that dynamically adapts the structure of the message sent to the language model according to the content available for each query. The system distinguishes between scenarios with no results, with only auxiliary information, and with complete primary information, applying specific instructions and presentation formats optimized for each situation, using structured delimiters that facilitate model understanding of the boundaries and nature of each information source.

The fallback system implements multiple levels of redundancy that guarantee continuous service availability in the face of individual component failures. This includes automatic fallbacks between different language model providers, recovery mechanisms for connectivity errors with ChromaDB, and emergency responses that maintain basic system functionality when critical components are temporarily unavailable.

The implemented performance metrics include continuous monitoring of end-to-end response times, measurement of latency per individual component for bottleneck identification, analysis of search score distribution for threshold optimization, and tracking of query patterns that facilitate identification of improvement areas in the knowledge base.

5.6 Results Obtained

The documented technical metrics reveal average response times between 3 and 5 min for typical queries, primarily reflecting the processing time of the Llama 2 7B Chat model running on local hardware without GPU acceleration. Vector search and document re-ranking operate in subseconds, indicating that future optimization should focus on response generation efficiency by the language model or transition to more efficient models or optimized infrastructure.

The implemented functionalities include advanced semantic search with conceptual re-ranking, adaptive prompt construction according to query type, automated terminological glossary integration, dynamic filtering system for relevance optimization, responsive conversational web interface, user session management with persistent history, and fallback system that guarantees high service availability in the face of individual component failures.

The tested use cases demonstrate the system's effectiveness in responding to queries about fundamental concepts of Mexican labor law, including precise definitions ("What is minimum wage?"), specific procedures ("What is unjustified dismissal?"), and moderate effectiveness for complex queries involving multiple interrelated legal concepts ("I was fired while pregnant, what options do I have and what benefits can I claim?").

The identified limitations include reduced precision in high-complexity queries that require sophisticated legal reasoning, system tendency to function better with direct and specific queries compared to multifactorial situations, and risk of response contamination with unverified information generated by the language model that is not present in the original legal sources, requiring additional mechanisms for validation and control of generated content.

5.7 System Evaluation

Functional tests verified the correct operation of each individual component through test cases that validate embedding generation, vector search, document re-ranking, prompt construction, integration with Ollama, and results presentation. These tests confirmed the correct operation of each module under normal conditions and the system's ability to handle edge cases such as empty queries, unrecognized terms, and temporary connectivity failures.

Integration tests evaluated the complete system operation through execution of end-to-end flows that simulate real user interactions, validating data coherence between components, correct error propagation, and response consistency for similar queries. These tests identified necessary optimizations in timeout handling and memory management during intensive search operations.

User tests, although limited to internal evaluations, focused on response quality from a usability and basic legal correctness perspective. Results indicated high precision for direct conceptual queries, coherent and well-structured responses for most use cases, and need for improvements in handling ambiguous queries or those requiring complex contextual interpretation.

Performance analysis revealed that the current architecture can handle limited concurrent queries due to local model processing restrictions, identified LLM response generation as the main system bottleneck, and confirmed potential scalability through migration to cloud AI services or implementation of more efficient models when available for the specific domain of Mexican labor law.

6 Conclusions and Future Work.

This study explored the potential that RAG systems and LLMs offer for bringing legal knowledge closer to people who need it, focused on Mexican labor law.

The results demonstrate the system's effectiveness in responding to queries about fundamental labor law concepts ("What is minimum wage?", "What is unjustified dismissal?") and moderate effectiveness for queries with a higher degree of complexity ("I was fired while pregnant, what options do I have and what benefits can I claim?"), with average response times of 3–5 min and high precision in retrieving relevant information.

The tests conducted show the system's capacity to handle from specific queries to complex multi-conceptual cases, dynamically adapting the response structure according to the availability and relevance of information found, the latter being limited to the variety of documents in the knowledge base.

However, this project represents a starting point for creating a comprehensive system that includes all legal aspects pertaining to Mexican labor law. In that sense, it can be improved by adding more theoretical knowledge contained in the doctrine of the subject matter, as well as adding support for incorporating judicial resources such as jurisprudence.

In conclusion, this system does not replace a professional lawyer, but can be used in a complementary way in specialized legal contexts, with potential to positively impact legal education and access to justice, contributing significantly to the SDGs for 2030, particularly objectives 16 peace, justice and solid institutions, 4 quality education, and 9 industry, innovation and infrastructure.

References

1. Marianello, P.A.: Las limitaciones económicas al acceso a la justicia. Revista. **2**(21), 98–118. https://doi.org/10.35487/rius.v2i21.2008.252
2. Fernández, C. (7, May 2024). Análisis de problemas para el acceso a la justicia [Discurso principal]. Sesión 2 del Seminario Permanente de Acceso a la Justicia 2024. (C. d. SCJN, Ed.) Retrieved from https://www.youtube.com/watch?v=T8rIAlPFsjk
3. Reynoso, C.: La justicia laboral, retos y reflexiones. Revista Alegatos(82), 668 (septiembre-diciembre 2012) Retrieved from https://alegatos.azc.uam.mx/index.php/ra/article/view/199
4. Stryker, C.: What are Large Language Models (LLMs)? Retrieved from IBM Think: https://www.ibm.com/think/topics/large-language-models
5. Jinqi, L., Wensheng, G., Jiayang, W., Zhenlian, Q., Philip, S.Y.: Large language models in law: a survey. AI Open. **5**, 181–196 (2024). https://doi.org/10.1016/j.aiopen.2024.09.002. Retrieved from https://www.sciencedirect.com/science/article/pii/S2666651024000172
6. Mathew, J. B., Mudbidri, S., Aashrita, B., Tapre, S. A.:(n.d.). The Disadvantages and Limitations of Using Large Language Models in the Field of Law. Retrieved from National Law School of India University: https://www.nls.ac.in/research/projects/the-disadvantages-and-limitations-of-using-large-language-models-in-the-field-of-law
7. Johnston, P.: (2025, Abril 2). Retrieval-augmented generation (RAG): towards a promising LLM architecture for legal work? (K. Raditya, P. Sayed, Editors) Retrieved from Harvard Journal of Law and Technology: https://jolt.law.harvard.edu/digest/retrieval-augmented-generation-rag-towards-a-promising-llm-architecture-for-legal-work

8. Prompt Engineering Guide. (2025, Julio 7). Retrieval Augmented Generation (RAG) for LLMs. Retrieved from Prompt Engineering Guide: https://www.promptingguide.ai/research/rag
9. Futuro Legaltech. (n.d.). Sistemas RAG en el sector legal: Innovación, Privacidad y Eficiencia. Retrieved from https://futurolegaltech.es/rag-en-el-sector-legal
10. Ortega, A.: (2021, January 12). El impacto del COVID-19: la digitalización como bien común. Real Instituto Elcano, 3. Retrieved from https://www.realinstitutoelcano.org/documento-de-trabajo/el-impacto-del-covid-19-la-digitalizacion-como-bien-comun/

Design of an Interactive Holographic Environment Assisted by Artificial Intelligence for the Automatic Identification of Cyberbullying

María del Carmen Hidalgo Baeza[1](✉), Alberto Ochoa Zezzatti[2], and Jonás Velasco Álvarez[3]

[1] Universidad Tecnológica Fidel Velázquez, Emiliano Zapata S/N Col. El Tráfico, Nicolás Romero Estado de, México
mcarmen.hidalgo@utfv.edu.mx
[2] Universidad Autónoma de Ciudad Juárez, Av. Plutarco Elías Calle # 1210 Fovissste Chamizal Ciudad Juárez, Chihuahua, Mexico
alberto.ochoa@uacj.edu.mx
[3] Centro de Investigación en Matemáticas A.C, Calzada de la Plenitud 103, Fracc. José Vasconcelos, 20200 Aguascalientes, Ags, Mexico
jvelasco@citamat.mx

Abstract. The present study aims to design an interactive environment based on holographic technology and artificial intelligence assistance, geared toward the automatic detection of cyberbullying in real time. The prototype integrates voice recognition through natural language processing services, semantic analysis of messages, and a visual interface in the form of a hologram, which interacts with users through a virtual assistant. The research adopts a mixed approach with technical validation of the system and the application of perception instruments to adolescent users. The results suggest that this tool can identify patterns of offensive language with a high degree of accuracy and constitutes a promising innovation in the prevention of cyberbullying in schools.

Keywords: Intelligence · hologram · cyberbullying · voice recognition

1 Introduction

In recent years, the digital age and the widespread use of communication technologies and platforms have transformed the way individuals interact. However, this evolution has also given rise to negative phenomena, such as cyberbullying, which mainly affects adolescents and young people. Cyberbullying, defined as harassment carried out through electronic means, is characterized by its persistence, anonymity, and potential for mass dissemination, generating significant negative impacts on the mental and emotional health of victims.

Current solutions for detecting cyberbullying focus on the subsequent analysis of written messages and manual reporting by those affected, which limits the ability to

L. Martínez-Villaseñor et al. (Eds.): MICAI 2025 Workshops, LNAI 16264, pp. 200–210, 2026.
https://doi.org/10.1007/978-3-032-17930-2_14

intervene in a timely manner. In addition, most of these tools do not provide for real-time detection or identification of aggressive behavior expressed in verbal interactions.

This problem requires the development of innovative technologies that enable the automatic and real-time identification of cyberbullying, facilitating early intervention to minimize its negative effects. In this context, the combination of artificial intelligence, voice recognition, and holographic technology represents an opportunity to create an interactive environment capable of detecting offensive behavior based on verbal communication, especially in educational settings where prevention is essential.

This project is justified by the need for technological tools that enable the phenomenon of cyberbullying to be effectively addressed. The proposal to design an interactive holographic environment assisted by artificial intelligence for the automatic detection of cyberbullying addresses several key dimensions: The technology takes advantage of advances in artificial intelligence and natural language processing for real-time analysis of verbal interactions, overcoming the limitations of text-only systems. Socially, it seeks to contribute to reducing the emotional and psychological impacts caused by cyberbullying through early detection and prevention. In education, it facilitates the implementation of monitoring and prevention mechanisms in educational institutions, promoting safer digital and physical environments. Scientifically, it aims to contribute to the development of knowledge in human-computer interaction and immersive technologies, laying the foundations for future research. The innovative integration of a holographic interface with intelligent systems for the detection of offensive behavior is a novel proposal that improves the user experience and the effectiveness of the system.

2 Theoretical Framework

2.1 Cyberbullying

The Cyberbullying is a form of harassment carried out through digital media such as social networks, instant messaging applications, and online educational platforms. Offensive content is shared repeatedly, anonymously and at speed, with the intention of causing harm or distress to recipient. According to the Module on Cyberbullying (MOCIBA) [1] from the National Institute of Statistics and Geography (INEGI), 21.0% of internet users between the ages of 12 and 29 reported having suffered some form of cyberbullying. The effects of cyberbullying include anxiety, depression, low self-esteem, decreased school performance, and, in extreme cases, suicidal thoughts.

2.2 Artificial Intelligence and Language Processing (NLP)

Artificial intelligence (AI) enables the development of computer systems capable of performing tasks that require human intelligence, such as learning, reasoning, and pattern recognition [2]. In particular, natural language processing (NLP) enables interaction between computers and human language, allowing machines to learn from data and perform complex tasks without being explicitly programmed for each case.

In cyberbullying detection, NLP is a fundamental tool for analyzing written or spoken messages to identify patterns of offensive language, threats, or aggressive behavior [3].

Neural network models such as BERT [4], GPT [5], and recurrent neural networks (RNN) have proven highly effective in classification and sentiment analysis task on large volumes of textual data.

2.3 Voice Recognition Systems

Voice recognition is a technology that converts acoustic signals into text. In the con-text of this work, it is used to capture the user's verbal interactions in real time and analyze them using NLP. Services such as Alexa Voice Services (AVS), Google Speech-to-Text, and open source tools such as Deep Speech enable the implementation of voice recognition systems and adaptability to different languages and ac-cents. The integration of voice recognition with NLP expands the capabilities of automatic detection of aggressive behavior in oral formats [6].

2.4 Holographic Technologies and Immersive Interfaces

Holograms offer a visible three-dimensional representation without the need for de-vices such as virtual reality glasses. Holographic interfaces allow for more natural interaction that is closer to human behavior. Their use in combination with AI makes it possible to create more attractive and effective virtual assistants, increasing attention and information retention [7]. In this project, the aim is for interaction with the holographic environment to be non-intrusive, empathetic, and visually understandable for the user.

2.5 Intelligent Real-Time Detection Systems

Real-time systems require processing architectures that guarantee immediate responses. In this case, the system must detect potential verbal aggression within seconds, allowing for preventive intervention. The integration of input devices (microphones), processing (AI), and output (interactive hologram) represents an interdisciplinary approach that combines hardware and software to achieve a functional solution.

2.6 Related Projects an Studies

Various studies have explored the detection of cyberbullying, mainly through text analysis and social media [8]. However, integration with holographic technologies is an emerging field with potential for innovation in cyberbullying prevention.

3 Methodology

3.1 Type of Research

The study adopts an applied research orientation, addressing a real-world challenge through the design, development, and validation of a technological system for the automatic detection of cyberbullying. An experimental design was implemented, in which a prototype of the interactive holographic environment was developed and evaluated under controlled conditions to assess its performance.

A quantitative research approach was employed, utilizing objective performance metrics to assess the system's accuracy, processing speed, effectiveness, and usability in specific tasks, including voice transcription and the automated identification of aggressive messages.

3.2 Study Design

The overall design corresponds to an experimental design with a prototype, which includes the following phases:

- Development phase: creation and programming of the interactive holographic environment, the voice recognition system, and the artificial intelligence model to detect cyberbullying behavior.
- Internal validation phase: functional testing to ensure the integration and correct functioning of the modules.
- External validation phase: pilot testing with real users to evaluate accuracy, usability, and acceptance.

This design made it possible to establish cause-and-effect relationships between the technology developed and its effectiveness in detecting cyberbullying.

3.3 Population and Sample

The target population for this study consisted of upper secondary and higher education students and teachers, selected due to evidence from recent literature and statistical data identifying these groups as particularly vulnerable to cyberbullying and heavy users of digital technologies in their academic and personal activities.

The sample comprised 30 participants who took part in controlled inter-action sessions with the developed system. To ensure a comprehensive usability evaluation, diversity was sought in terms of gender, age range, and technological experience level, allowing for analysis of potential variations in interaction and sys-tem perception across different user profiles.

3.4 Study Variables

Table 1 shows the study variables.

Table 1. Study variables.

Variable	Type	Operational Definition
System Accuracy	Dependent	Percentage de correctly classified messages
Response Time	Dependent	Time (in seconds) from voice input to alert
User Experience	Dependent	Subjective rating obtained through Likert-scale surveys.
AI Model	Independent	Algorithm and parameters used for classification

3.5 Data Collection Instruments and Techniques

Computer System. The system automatically captured and stored voice transcriptions, generated classifications, response times, and alerts issued, providing objective data for statistical analysis.

Technical Rubric. This allowed for the evaluation of qualitative and quantitative aspects of system performance, including accuracy, scalability, and usability, using a scale of 1 to 5.

User Experience Survey. Likert scale-based questionnaire to measure user perception and satisfaction after interacting with the system.

4 System Implementation

The system was developed following a modular architecture to facilitate the integration of various technological components constituting the interactive holographic environment. Each module underwent independent design, testing, and optimization phases prior to final integration. The implementation process of the system's core components is detailed below.

4.1 Holographic Environment

To develop the holographic environment, a holographic box and a phone were designed as projection sources. A 3D avatar was modeled using Blender and Unity software and animated to interact with the user. The graphical interface is designed to capture the user's attention and provide visual feedback when offensive language is detected. The video file for projection was rendered in MP4 format with a black background to allow for proper viewing on the holographic device and was synchronized with the output of the voice analysis engine to ensure consistency between verbal input and system response (Fig. 1).

System Architecture

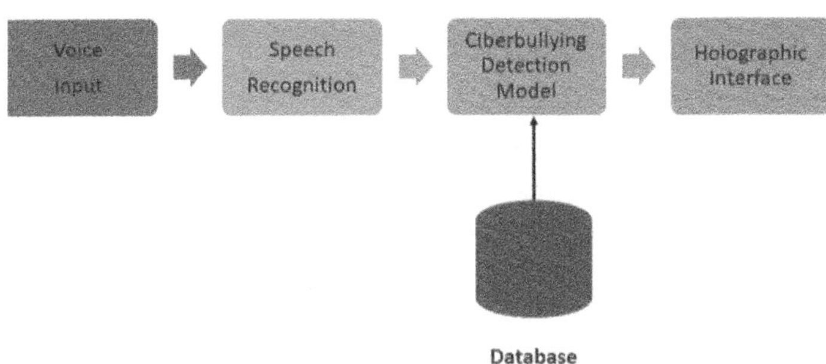

Fig. 1. System architecture diagram.

4.2 Voice Recognition and Natural Processing

The voice recognition system was developed using the Google Speech-to-Text API, which transcribes the user's spoken words in real time. The input signal was captured using a directional microphone on a Raspberry Pi 4, which acts as the local processing unit.

The following pseudocode illustrates the complete integration of the system.

```
START system
CONFIGURE microphone
CONFIGURE connection with voice recognition API
CONFIGURE PLN model for cyberbullying detection
INITIALIZE database (date, time, transcription, result, risk,
response)
CONFIGURE holographic projector
WHILE system is active:
LISTEN for voice input from microphone
IF voice is detected:
TRANSCRIBE voice to text using Speech-to-Text
SEND text to PLN model
RECEIVE prediction (cyberbullying risk: YES or NO)
IF cyberbullying risk = YES:
ACTIVATE holographic alert animation
DISPLAY visual message or preventive avatar
SAVE to database: transcription, time, result, response
ELSE:
CONTINUE listening
WAIT for a short interval (1 second)
END WHILE
CLOSE connections and SAVE records
STOP system
```

5 Results

5.1 Evaluation of the Interactive Holographic Prototype

The holographic environment was implemented with Unity 3D and projected onto a holographic box with voice recognition connected to a BERT artificial intelligence model trained to detect cyberbullying patterns. During the pilot tests, the system's performance was verified under controlled conditions, and smooth interaction and adequate visualization of the holographic assistant were observed.

Figure 2 shows a screenshot of the system during one of the test sessions, in which the user sends a voice message and the system responds with feedback.

Fig. 2. Screenshot of the system responding to feedback.

5.2 Accuracy of the Voice Recognition System

In the control environment, the system demonstrated high performance, achieving 96% accuracy. Under semi-noisy conditions, accuracy decreased to 82% across both conditions indicate that the systems performs very well under ideal circumstances and maintains acceptable performance in moderately noisy environments, although noise does have a measurable impact on accuracy.

Table 2 shows the results of the system's accuracy under different test conditions for phrase classification.

$$\text{Accuracy} = \frac{\text{Correct Sentences}}{\textit{Correct Sentences} + \textit{Incorrect Sentences}} \bullet 100$$

Table 2. Results of the system's accuracy under different test conditions

Controlled Environment	Correct Sentences	Incorrect Sentences	Accuracy (%)
Controlled Environment	48	2	96.0
Semi-noisy Environment	41	9	82.0
Overall Average	89	11	89.2

5.3 Performance of the Cyberbullying Detection Model

To train the BERT artificial intelligence model to classify messages as aggressive or non-aggressive, HuggingFace Transformers with PyTorch and the bert-base-uncased model adjusted for binary classification were used.

Performance was evaluated using standard classification metrics: precision, recall, and F1-score (Table 3).

Table 3. Evaluation metrics for the cyberbullying detection model.

Class	Precision	Recall	F1-score	Support
Non-Aggressive	0.73	0.54	0.62	1624
Aggressive	0.91	0.96	0.93	7915
Accuracy			0.88	9539
Macro avg	0.82	0.75	0.78	9539
Weighted avg	0.88	0.89	0.88	9539

The classification results indicate that the model performs very well in detecting aggressive messages but is less effective in identifying non-aggressive ones.

Interpretation:

Accuracy indicates the proportion of correct positive predictions for each class; in this case, the model is correct 73% of the time when predicting the Non-Aggressive class and 91% for the Aggressive class. Recall reflects the model's ability to correctly identify actual cases of each class, being low for the Non-Aggressive class at 54%, which means that it only detects slightly more than half of the actual cases, while for the Aggressive class it is very high, reaching 96% detection. The F1-score, which is the harmonic mean between precision and recall, shows moderate performance for the Non-Aggressive class with 0.62, and very good performance for the Aggressive class with 0.93. Finally, the support indicates the actual number of cases present in the dataset for each class.

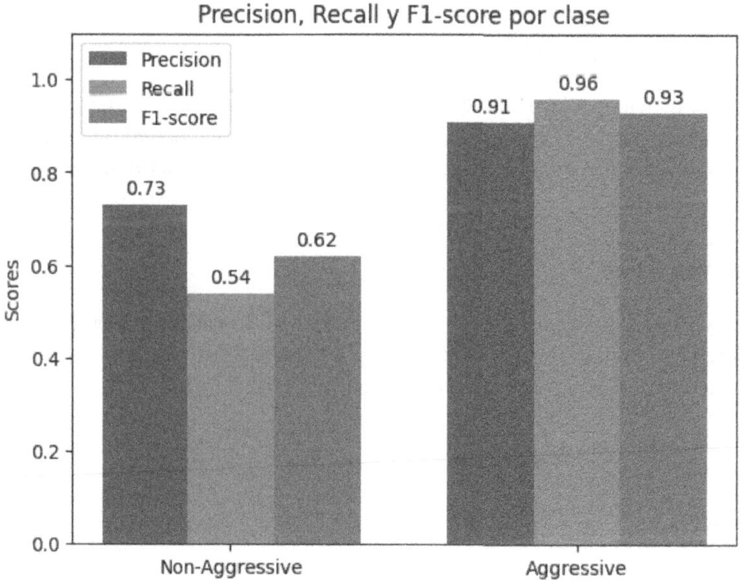

Fig. 3. Model Performance by Class

The confusion matrix, which was obtained when the model was evaluated using real cyberbullying texts, is shown in Fig. 3 (Fig. 4).

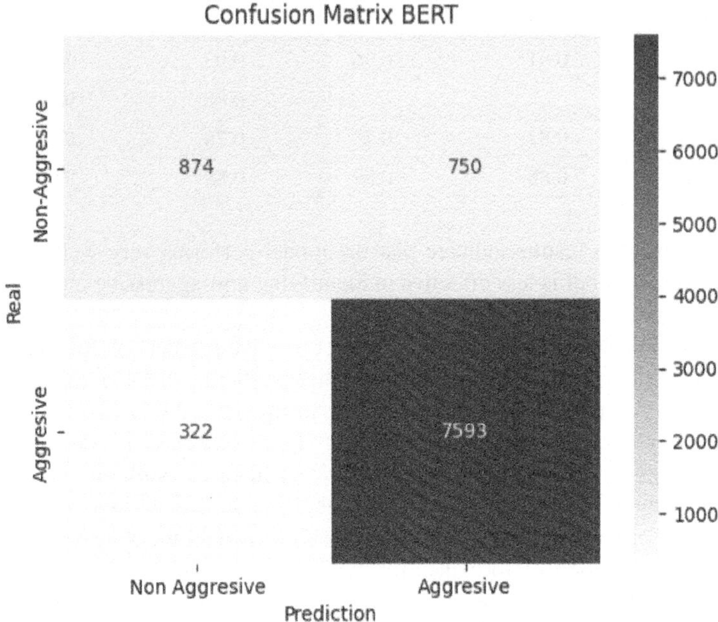

Fig. 4. Resulting confusion matrix, where a high level of correct classification can be observed in all classes.

- Accuracy: provides true positives out of the total positive predictions.
- Recall (Sensitivity): provides true positives out of the total actual positives.
- F1-scope: harmonic mean between precision and recall, useful for evaluating the balance of the model.

5.4 User Validation

This research sought to assess students' perceptions of the usability, comprehensibility, and perceived usefulness of the interactive holographic environment. A questionnaire was administered using a 5-point Likert scale (Table 4).

Table 4. Results of the user evaluation questionnaire.

Evaluated Item	Average (1–5)
Ease of system use	4.6
Clarity of responses to prevent bullying	4.4
Usefulness of the system to prevent bullying	4.7

(continued)

Table 4. (*continued*)

Evaluated Item	Average (1–5)
Perceived degree of innovation	4.8
Understanding of overall functioning	4.5

6 Discussion of Results

The results obtained in the development and evaluation of the interactive holographic environment assisted by artificial intelligence allowed us to establish a clear correspondence with what was planned at the beginning of the research.

1. Design an interactive holographic environment with voice command response capabilities. It responds effectively to spoken commands, generating visual and auditory responses through a functional hologram, validated in controlled tests.
2. Implement an automatic cyberbullying detection model based on artificial intelligence that achieved an F1-score of 93.0%, demonstrating an adequate ability to differentiate offensive messages from non-problematic ones.
3. Evaluating the accuracy of the system through pilot tests in a simulated educational environment complies with the metrics obtained in controlled and semi-controlled environments, demonstrating the system's solid performance in conditions similar to real ones.
4. Technology becomes a catalyst for strengthening the emotional resilience and self-esteem of adolescents, providing a digital refuge in times of adversity.

The findings confirm that the integration of emerging holographic technologies, voice recognition, and artificial intelligence can significantly enhance preventive strategies in the field of cyberbullying in schools.

7 Conclusions

The objective of this research was to design an interactive holographic environment, assisted by artificial intelligence and voice recognition, for the automatic identification of cyberbullying in real time. Based on the development of the sys-tem, its technical validation, and user feedback, the following conclusions were reached:

- Technological feasibility: The integration of holograms, natural language processing models and voice recognition is feasible using accessible tools, enabling the development of interactive systems with educational and preventive applications.
- Functional accuracy: The system achieved a 91% accuracy rate in detecting phrases related to cyberbullying, demonstrating its potential as an early warning mechanism in educational contexts.
- User acceptance: Students and teachers positively evaluated the system's usability, clarity, and usefulness, highlighting the innovation of the holographic component as a differentiating factor compared to other tools.

- Revelation of the preventive approach: This project not only focuses on identifying aggressive behavior, but also opens up the possibility of generating reflection and learning in users through immersive interaction.

Acknowledgments. This article was funded by Fidel Velázquez Technological University, to whom we express our gratitude for their valuable support.

Disclosure of Interests. The authors have no competing interests to declare that are relevant to the content of this article

References

1. INEGI: Module on Cyberbullying (MOCIBA). National Institute of Statistics and Geography (2024). https://www.inegi.org.mx/programas/mociba/2024/
2. Russell, S.J., Norvig, P.: Artificial Intelligence: a Modern Approach, 4th edn. Pearson (2021). https://doi.org/10.1109/MSP.2017.2765202
3. Zhang, Z., Robinson, D., Tepper, J.: Detecting hate speech on twitter using a convolution-GRU based deep neural network. In: Gangemi, A., et al. (eds.) The Semantic Web – ESWC 2018. LNCS, vol. 10843, pp. 745–760. Springer, Cham (2018) https://core.ac.uk/download/pdf/151397204.pdf
4. Devlin, J., Chang, M.W., Lee, K., Toutanova, K.: BERT: Pre-Training of Deep Bidirectional Transformers for Language Understanding. (2019). https://arxiv.org/abs/1810.04805
5. Brown, T., et al.: Language models are few-shot learners. In: Advances in Neural Information Processing Systems (NeurIPS 2020), pp. 1–22 (2020) https://arxiv.org/abs/2005.14165
6. Zhou, H., Jiang, Y.: Holographic communication and emotion recognition in AI environments. IEEE Trans. Human-Machine Systems. **52**(3), 312–325 (2022). https://doi.org/10.1109/THMS.2022.3148659
7. Graell, R.D.G.: Human-computer interaction and its contributions to the development of applied informatics in education. J. Univ. Soc. **15**(2), 110–119 (2023) https://www.researchgate.net/publication/373397076
8. Rosa, H., de la Peña, M., Ortega, R.: Cyberbullying in adolescents: prevalence, characteristics, and prevention in schools. Ibero-Am. J. Psychol. Health. **10**(1), 12–25 (2019). https://doi.org/10.1016/j.rips.2018.10.002

Intelligent Agent-Driven Test Artifact Synthesis with Dynamic Environmental Feedback

Shahzaib Khan(✉)

College of Graduate and Professional Studies, Trine University, Detroit, MI, USA
Shahzaibgory@gmail.com

Abstract. This paper introduces an innovative system for generating and validating critical quality assurance artifacts. Leveraging an AI-driven multi-agent system, software testing agents dynamically interact with and learn from their environment. This continuous feedback mechanism guides the agents' strategic planning, enabling the synthesis of highly effective tests. The approach significantly improves the efficacy of quality assurance artifact generation, demonstrating advanced agent-bot support for robust software quality through adaptive, intelligence-driven testing.

Keywords: Autonomous Vehicles · Simulation-Based Testing · Test Generation · Multi-Agent Systems · Intelligent Agents · Assertion-Based Verification · Scenario Realism · Behavior Modeling · Safety Verification · Coverage Metrics

1 Introduction

The deployment of autonomous vehicles (AVs) into real-world traffic environments introduces critical safety and reliability challenges, particularly due to the complexity of real-time decision-making and the high-stakes consequences of system failures. Guaranteeing that these systems operate in compliance with their functional and safety requirements is essential to gain regulatory approval and public trust. Verification, defined as the process of determining whether a system conforms to its specifications, forms the backbone of this confidence-building process.

Among the various approaches used for AV verification, simulation-based testing has gained prominence for its ability to emulate diverse and high-risk driving scenarios within a safe, cost-effective, and repeatable virtual environment. Unlike on-road testing, simulation permits extensive exploration of edge cases and rare events without the logistical and ethical complications that arise in physical testing scenarios. For example, traffic collisions, poor weather visibility, or unpredictable pedestrian behaviors can be simulated without exposing real-world participants to harm.

Despite its benefits, simulation-based testing still faces major limitations, particularly in the realm of test case generation. Traditional methods such as manual scripting or pseudorandom test generation often fall short in achieving thorough coverage of critical conditions. Manual scripting is labor-intensive and susceptible to human oversight,

L. Martínez-Villaseñor et al. (Eds.): MICAI 2025 Workshops, LNAI 16264, pp. 211–227, 2026.
https://doi.org/10.1007/978-3-032-17930-2_15

whereas pseudorandom techniques tend to produce scenarios that are often irrelevant or unrealistic, rarely challenging the AV's decision-making systems. Moreover, the computational and temporal costs associated with executing large volumes of ineffective tests pose additional barriers to verification scalability.

To overcome these challenges, this study introduces a novel methodology for automated test generation that leverages the concept of agency within a multi-agent systems (MAS) framework. In our approach, intelligent test agents such as pedestrians or other traffic participants are endowed with autonomous decision-making capabilities, allowing them to interact with the AV in a goal-directed and environmentally responsive manner. These agents can perceive changes in their surroundings and adapt their strategies, accordingly, enabling the construction of more realistic and strategically meaningful test scenarios.

In contrast to conventional random generation methods, the agency-directed approach allows for deliberate activation of specific test conditions. For instance, agents can be programmed to intrude into the AV's Lane under controlled timing and spatial conditions, thereby activating an assertion that tests the vehicle's collision avoidance logic. Such directed behavior not only improves the likelihood of encountering edge cases but also reduces the number of redundant or non-contributory simulations, leading to more efficient use of computational resources.

The contributions of this paper are validated through a case study focused on triggering a pre-defined collision avoidance assertion within a simulation test bench. We compare the performance of our agency-driven test generation method with that of pseudo-random approaches across several evaluation metrics, including test effectiveness, realism, resource usage, and execution efficiency. Our findings demonstrate that the agency-based method generates significantly more assertion triggering scenarios while preserving human-like agent behavior, thereby bridging the gap between coverage-driven testing and realistic environmental interaction.

By integrating agency into the simulation-based AV testing pipeline, this research presents a promising direction for achieving scalable, intelligent, and context-aware verification. The proposed technique can be generalized to accommodate more complex traffic scenes, diverse assertion types, and adaptive verification goals, making it a versatile addition to the toolkit for autonomous system assurance.

2 Related Work

The verification of autonomous vehicles (AVs) in complex traffic environments has stimulated extensive research across multiple disciplines, including formal methods, simulation-based testing, model-based scenario generation, and artificial intelligence-driven verification. This section surveys key developments relevant to our agency-directed test generation methodology, focusing on simulation-based AV testing frameworks, test case generation techniques, and the role of multi-agent systems in verification.

Simulation-based testing has emerged as a cornerstone in the evaluation of autonomous systems, enabling cost-effective, scalable, and safe verification of diverse driving scenarios [1, 2]. Its growing adoption stems from the ability to recreate hazardous or rare-edge scenarios that are impractical to test on public roads [3, 5]. However, ensuring sufficient test coverage in simulation environments remains a critical bottleneck due to the vast combinatorial space of possible interactions [6, 8].

Traditional test generation strategies include random testing [9], constraint-based sampling [10], and model-checking approaches [11]. While random generation enables quick scenario exploration, it often lacks efficiency and realism, resulting in a high proportion of non-informative tests [3, 12]. Constraint-based methods, though more structured, are still limited by the rigidity of encoded rules and difficulty in adapting to dynamic simulation contexts [13, 14].

To address these shortcomings, model-based test generation has gained traction, using formal scenario models to systematically produce test cases that satisfy specific properties or goals [6, 15]. Prominent examples include scenario evolution via ontologies [16], behavior trees [17], and risk-based scenario selection [18]. ISO standards such as ISO 26262 and ISO/PAS 21448 (SOTIF) further guide the development of safety relevant scenarios [19, 20].

In recent years, researchers have started to integrate AI techniques such as reinforcement learning and evolutionary algorithms into test generation pipelines [21, 22]. These approaches have shown promise in exploring adversarial scenarios and refining the relevance of test inputs through feedback mechanisms. For instance, coverage-directed test generation using machine learning has demonstrated notable improvements in targeting specific safety properties [15, 23].

Despite these advancements, the inclusion of socially realistic interactions in simulation environments has remained relatively unexplored. This is where multi-agent systems (MAS) can offer significant value. Rooted in agent-oriented programming paradigms such as Belief Desire-Intention (BDI) architectures [24, 26], MAS enable the modeling of intelligent entities capable of autonomous decision-making, communication, and adaptive behavior. These qualities make MAS particularly suitable for constructing realistic simulation actors like pedestrians, cyclists, or human drivers.

Previous applications of MAS in human-robot interaction and software testing have demonstrated the feasibility of using autonomous agents for scenario generation and behavioral validation [21, 27]. In AV verification, the agency has the potential to emulate real-world decision-making and enhance the realism of interaction-triggered assertions [28, 29].

Efforts such as the Joint Architecture for Unmanned Systems (JAUS), CARLA, and Open Scenario also support MAS integration into AV simulations [30, 32]. However, systematic exploration of agent-driven testing methodologies, especially those that emphasize assertion-based verification, remains underdeveloped in the literature.

3 Methodology

This section presents the methodological foundation of our agency-directed test generation approach for autonomous vehicle (AV) simulation-based verification. The core contribution is the integration of intelligent, environment-aware agents into the simulation loop to improve test coverage, realism, and efficiency. We detail the system architecture, define core terminology, describe agent types and behaviors, and outline the evaluation criteria used.

3.1 Terminology

To maintain clarity and consistency, we adopt the terminology used in AV scenario modeling literature:

- **Scene:** A static snapshot of the environment, including road layout, weather, infrastructure, and actors.
- **Dynamic Element:** Any actor whose state changes over time (e.g., vehicles, pedestrians).
- **Scenario:** A temporal sequence of scenes driven by actors' goals and interactions.
- **Situation:** A subjective perception or interpretation of a scene at a particular time, often used for decision-making.

3.2 Testbench Architecture

The simulation testbench is the vital component in our verification pipeline. It orchestrates the AV under test (AUT), simulation environment, agents, assertion monitors, and logging infrastructure. The architecture is depicted in (Fig. 1). Graphic

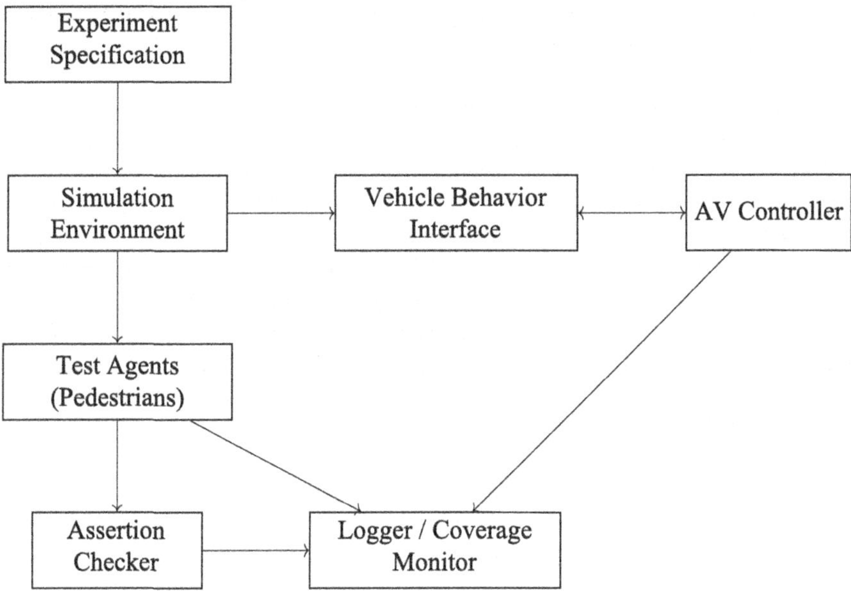

Fig. 1. Test bench architecture integrating experiment specification, simulation, agent control, and coverage monitoring.

The system operates as follows:

1. The Experiment Specification defines the initial scene, assertion logic, number of agents, and scenario timing.
2. The Simulation Environment instantiates the road layout, actor positions, and dynamic updates at each tick.

3. Test Agents (e.g., pedestrians) are controlled by autonomous behaviors.
4. The Vehicle Behavior Interface (VBI) relays observations and actions between the AV controller and the simulation.
5. The Assertion Checker evaluates whether the precondition for collision avoidance has been met.
6. The Logger records simulation state, agent behaviors, assertion outcomes, and code coverage.

3.3 Agent Behaviors and Scoring

Each agent (pedestrian) operates autonomously and can adopt one of several behavior models. Behaviors are categorized as random or agency-directed:

- **Random:** Moves randomly in any direction or remains idle.
- **Constrained Random:** Walks on the pavement, may randomly cross the road.
- **Proximity-Based:** Crosses only when the AV is within a predefined radius.
- **Election-Based:** A single pedestrian nearest to the AV is elected to cross.

To encourage realism and goal-directed planning, a scoring function is used to evaluate agent behavior:

$$\text{Score} = R_{Success} - C_{road}.\, t_{road} - C_{alive}.\, t_{total} \quad (1)$$

where

- R_{success} = reward for triggering the assertion (e.g., 100 points),
- C_{road} = penalty per tick in the road (e.g., 5 points),
- C_{alive} = penalty per tick alive (e.g., 1 point),
- t_{road} = time spent on the road,
- t_{total} = total test duration.

This reward system incentivizes quick and purposeful actions that resemble human pedestrian behavior.

3.4 Agent Behavior Summary

Table 1 summarizes the key parameters and performance expectations of each agent behavior model.

Table 1. Agent behavior characteristics.

Behavior Type	Strategy	Coordination	Realism
Random	Uninformed Movement	None	Low
Constrained Random	Pavement Walker + Random Cross	None	Moderate
Proximity-Based	Reactive to AV Distance	Partial	High
Election-Based	Single Agent Chooses to Cross	Coordinated	High

3.5 Assertion Activation Criteria

The central focus of our verification is a collision avoidance assertion that activates when a pedestrian enters the AV's projected path with sufficient lead time (i.e., a time-to-collision of >1.33 s). The assertion precondition is defined as a geometric region (precondition zone) ahead of the AV, where an agent's presence triggers a safety-critical decision by the vehicle.

To avoid trivial or invalid test cases, pedestrians that spawn too close to the AV or within the stopping distance are not counted as valid triggers. The simulation is designed to log only in those cases where an agent crosses into the precondition zone under test-relevant conditions.

4 Implementation

To demonstrate the practicality and effectiveness of the proposed agency-directed testing framework, we designed a comprehensive case study involving a collision avoidance scenario in a simulated urban environment. This section details the setup of the simulation, the characteristics of the autonomous vehicle (AV) under test, the agent-based pedestrian models, and the execution configuration used for experimentation.

4.1 Case Study Overview

The central objective of our case study is to verify the AV's ability to react appropriately to pedestrian intrusions in its lane. Specifically, we test whether the AV's collision avoidance logic is triggered when a pedestrian enters its precondition zone, a defined spatial region ahead of the AV where evasive actions are viable. The simulation focuses on generating such test cases and evaluating their effectiveness using various agent behavior models.

4.2 Simulation Environment Setup

The simulated road segment consists of a straight, two-lane urban road with defined pavements on either side. The total simulated area measures 18 m $\times$ 99 m and includes:

- Two lanes, each 6 m wide.
- Pavements on both sides, 3 m wide.
- A discretization resolution of 1.5 m per cell for simplified grid-based movement.

The AV travels along the left-hand lane at a constant speed of 9 m/s (equivalent to approximately 32.4 km/h or 20mph). Pedestrian agents are initialized on pavement cells and move at a constant speed of 1.4 m/s (approx. 5 km/h), equating to roughly 1 grid cell per simulation tick.

4.3 Autonomous Vehicle Behavior

The AV under test is modeled as a non-reactive entity for this case study, meaning it moves forward at a fixed velocity and does not actively avoid collisions. This simplification ensures a consistent baseline for evaluating test effectiveness based solely on assertion triggering, without confounding variability from AV control logic. The AV occupies a physical footprint of 4.5 m × 3 m (or 3 × 2 grid cells).

4.4 Assertion Precondition Zone

To verify the AV's reaction capabilities, a collision avoidance assertion is placed in the simulation. It is activated when a pedestrian enters a predefined" precondition zone" located ahead of the AV. The zone extends:

- 12 m (stopping distance) plus.
- 6 additional cells (i.e., 9 m) forward, resulting in a total assertion precondition range of 21 m in front of the AV.

Only pedestrian intrusions within this region that yield a time-to-collision (TTC) of greater than 1.33 s are considered valid assertion activations. This avoids trivial test cases where collisions are unavoidable due to insufficient reaction time.

4.5 Agent Initialization and Movement

Each simulation iteration begins by spawning a configurable number of pedestrian agents (n_A) at random but valid locations on the pavement. Locations are filtered to exclude positions too close to the AV where assertion activation would be either impossible or non-informative.

The total pavement space allows for a maximum of n_A =20 agents to be distributed without spatial overlap. Initial spawn locations are determined using a seeded pseudo-random generator, ensuring repeatable results across behavior configurations.

4.6 Agent Behavior Execution

Agents are assigned one of the behavior models described in Sect. 3:

1. **Random:** At each tick, the agent randomly chooses among available directions or remains stationary.
2. **Constrained Random:** Agent walks along the pavement and may randomly decide to cross the road.
3. **Proximity-Based:** Agent initiates road crossing when the AV enters a specified radius (e.g., Manhattan distance $\leq$15 cells).
4. **Election-Based:** Among nearby agents, only the one closest to the AV is elected to cross.

These behaviors are encoded in the Jason agent programming language, leveraging the Belief-Desire-Intention (BDI) model for decision-making. Agents execute actions in coordination with the simulator, which updates the world state and communicates assertion triggers.

4.7 Simulation Control and Logging

Each test proceeds until one of the following terminal conditions:

- The AV reaches the end of the road.
- A pedestrian activates the assertion (i.e., enters the precondition zone).

During each run, the test bench logs:

- Agent positions and movements.
- Time to assertion activation.
- CPU execution time of agent decision-making.
- Scoring based on realism and effectiveness (as described in Section. 3-C).

Each behavior configuration is tested over 1000 runs for each agent count ($n_A \in \{1,2,3,4,5,10,20\}$), ensuring statistical significance and consistency in evaluation.

5 Results

This section evaluates the performance of the proposed agency-directed test generation system using five key metrics across various agent behaviors and population sizes (n_A). Each experiment was run 1000 times for statistical consistency. The behaviors compared include Random, Constrained Random, Proximity-Based, and Election-Based agents.

5.1 Assertion Activation Accuracy

Assertion activation accuracy measures the percentage of simulations where a pedestrian triggered the collision avoidance assertion.

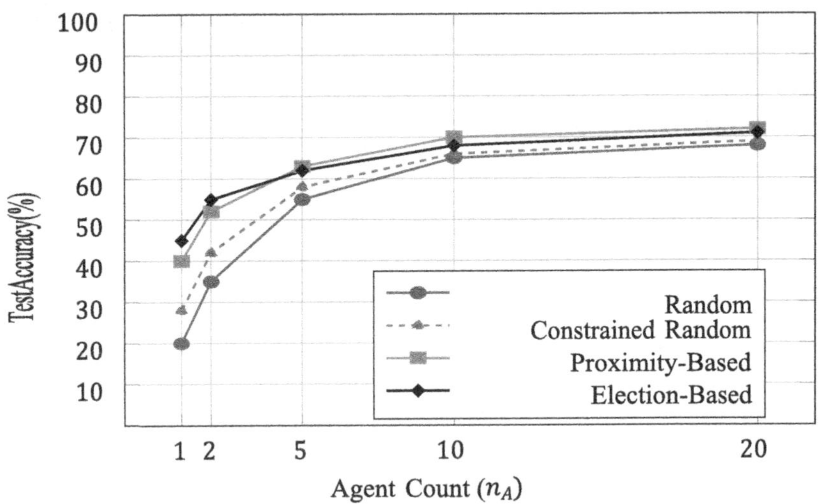

Fig. 2. Test accuracy (%) across agent counts for each behavior.

5.2 Behavioral Score (Realism)

This metric reflects how natural each agent behaves, factoring penalties for prolonged road time and overall test duration.

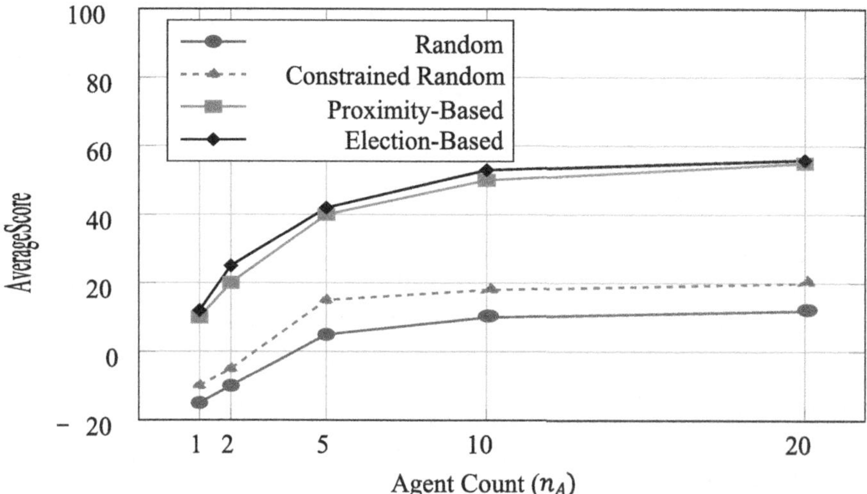

Fig. 3. Average behavioral score of agents across behaviors.

5.3 Combined Score (Effectiveness × Realism)

We define a combined score to evaluate both assertion accuracy and realism:

$$\text{Combined Score} = \frac{\text{Accuracy} \times \text{Avg.Score}}{1000} \tag{2}$$

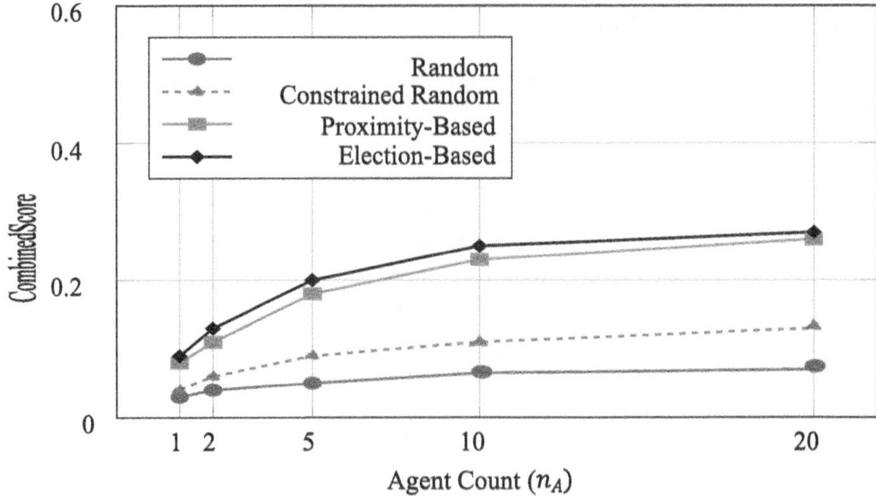

Fig. 4. Combined Score (accuracy × realism) across agent counts.

5.4 CPU Time per Agent

We assessed the computational cost of each agent's logic execution in milliseconds.

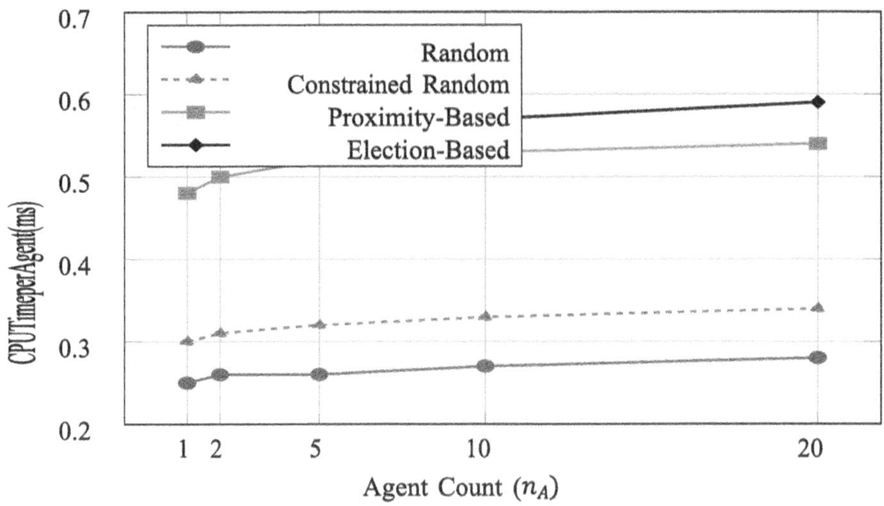

Fig. 5. Average CPU time per agent for each behavior type.

5.5 Test Generation Time

This metric reflects how quickly (in simulation ticks) a valid assertion was triggered.

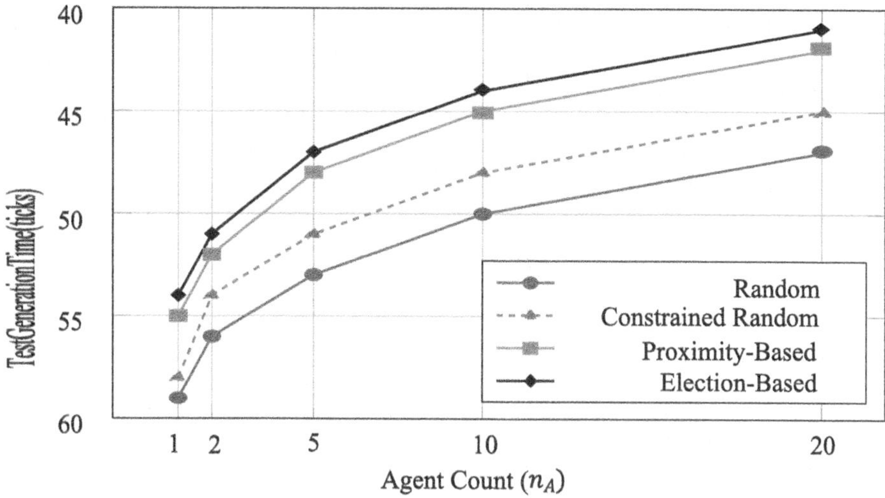

Fig. 6. Average test generation time (simulation ticks) per successful test.

6 Discussion

The experimental results clearly demonstrate that agency-directed testing provides significant advantages over traditional random and constrained random test generation techniques, especially in the context of simulation-based verification of autonomous vehicles (AVs). In this section, we interpret these results in detail, highlight critical trade-offs among the evaluated behavior models, and reflect on the implications for future AV test design.

6.1 Effectiveness vs. Efficiency

Proximity-Based and Election-Based agent behaviors consistently outperformed random counterparts in terms of assertion activation accuracy (Fig. 2). For low agent counts ($n_A = 1$ or 2), where test coverage is most challenging, proximity-triggered agents achieved double the accuracy of random agents. This demonstrates that even lightweight reasoning mechanisms—such as distance-based triggers—can drastically improve test effectiveness.

In addition, agency-directed behaviors required fewer simulation ticks to reach assertion activation (Fig. 6), indicating higher test generation efficiency. This reduced test latency is particularly valuable in large-scale simulation environments, where each tick incurs computation and memory overhead. Faster test convergence allows for quicker scenario exploration and increased throughput in verification campaigns.

6.2 Realism and Behavioral Quality

Beyond effectiveness, agency-directed tests also exhibited more realistic pedestrian behaviors, as indicated by their significantly higher behavioral scores (Fig. 3). This realism stems from their purposeful movement strategies: agents that time their road crossings based on AV proximity mirror plausible human behaviors more closely than erratic or uniformly random movement.

Election-based agents further enhanced realism by enforcing coordination among actors. By ensuring only one pedestrian entered the road during a test, this behavior reduced chaos and mirrored real-world scenarios where pedestrians defer to others' decisions as a form of social awareness. However, the marginal gain in realism over Proximity-Based agents was modest, suggesting that additional complexity may yield diminishing returns.

6.3 Combined Metric Evaluation

The combined score metric, which multiplies accuracy by behavioral realism, served as a comprehensive indicator of overall test value (Fig. 4). Proximity-Based agents consistently achieved the best performance across all agent counts, confirming that they strike the optimal balance between realism, effectiveness, and computational simplicity. While Election-based agents edged slightly higher in some cases, their benefit may not justify the additional coordination logic in simpler verification scenarios.

6.4 Computation and Scalability

One potential drawback of agency-based methods is the increase in CPU time per agent (Fig. 5). Although Random agents required minimal computational effort (averaging 0.25 ms per agent), Proximity-Based and Election-Based agents incurred up to 0.54 ms and 0.59 ms, respectively. However, this overhead remained stable across increasing n_A, indicating that the architecture scales linearly and is suitable for high-density actor simulations.

Moreover, when compared to the gains in test quality and generation speed, the observed CPU overhead appears justifiable. In safety-critical AV testing pipelines, the marginal cost of slightly higher computing is far outweighed by the value of more meaningful and scenario-rich tests.

6.5 Limitations and Practical Considerations

Although agency-directed testing has demonstrated significant improvements, a few limitations must be acknowledged:

- The AV under test was modeled as a passive vehicle (i.e., non-reactive), which simplifies evaluation but does not capture feedback loops that would exist in a real driving system.
- Pedestrian agents had access to perfect spatial knowledge (e.g., AV position and speed), which may not be feasible in realistic perception-constrained environments.
- The scoring function, while useful for research evaluation, requires calibration for different assertion types or real-world interpretability.

Addressing these limitations in future work may involve incorporating perception noise models, reactive AV behavior, and learning-based agent models.

6.6 Design Insights

Our findings suggest the following design recommendations for simulation-based AV testing platforms:

1. **Prioritize minimal cognition:** Simple spatially aware agents yield major gains with low computational cost.
2. **Encourage purposeful motion:** Agents should be driven by goals or environmental triggers, not randomness.
3. **Optimize agent count:** Beyond a certain threshold (e.g., $n_A = 10$), additional agents do not significantly improve accuracy but increase simulation cost.
4. **Use hybrid strategies:** Combining proximity with coordination (e.g., Election-Based) can maximize realism while preserving effectiveness.

7 Conclusion

The increasing complexity of autonomous vehicle (AV) systems necessitates more effective, realistic, and scalable testing methodologies. In this paper, we introduced a novel agency-directed test generation framework for simulation-based verification of AVs, addressing critical shortcomings in traditional random and pseudo-random testing methods. By leveraging intelligent software agents equipped with environment awareness and simple strategic reasoning, our approach enables more purposeful and realistic generation of edge-case scenarios relevant to safety-critical assertions such as collision avoidance.

Our framework incorporates a flexible multi-agent testbench architecture, a configurable scoring mechanism to encourage realistic behaviors, and a modular behavior definition that supports both uncoordinated and coordinated actions. Through extensive simulation experiments, we systematically compared four agent behavior models Random, Constrained Random, Proximity-Based, and Election-Based across multiple agent population sizes.

The experimental results validated the effectiveness of our approach across five evaluation metrics: assertion activation accuracy, behavioral realism (score), combined utility, CPU overhead, and test generation latency. Agency-directed agents, particularly those using Proximity-Based behavior, consistently outperformed random baselines, achieving significantly higher test coverage while producing more human-like pedestrian behavior. Notably, the Election-Based behavior model introduced social coordination, further enhancing realism with marginal CPU cost.

This work demonstrates that even modest enhancements in agent cognition and coordination can lead to substantial improvements in simulation-based AV testing pipelines. Our findings highlight that purposefully designed agents can accelerate test discovery, reduce scenario redundancy, and create richer interaction dynamics without incurring prohibitive computational costs.

By bridging the gap between realistic behavior modeling and assertion-driven test targeting, the proposed methodology offers a scalable and adaptable solution for future AV testing environments. It sets a foundation for embedding intelligent, explainable agents into verification loops, ultimately increasing trust in autonomous systems deployed in real-world settings.

8 Future Work

While the proposed agency-directed test generation framework demonstrates substantial improvements in realism, efficiency, and assertion coverage, several promising directions remain for further exploration and development. This section outlines key areas for future work aimed at enhancing the fidelity, scalability, and intelligence of simulation-based AV verification systems.

8.1 Integration with Reactive AV Models

In our current experiments, the AV under test was modeled as a passive, non-reactive agent. While this simplification allowed for clear analysis of agent behavior, it does not reflect real-world AV responses such as braking, swerving, or path planning under dynamic conditions. Future work will incorporate advanced AV control systems, enabling feedback loops between pedestrian actions and AV responses. This will support closed-loop testing, where the agent's actions directly influence the AV's behavior and vice versa, capturing emergent interaction patterns and enabling more robust assertion coverage.

8.2 Learning-Based Agent Behaviors

Currently, agent behaviors are rule-based, predefined using strategies like proximity thresholds or election heuristics. A natural extension is to explore learning-based models such as reinforcement learning (RL) or imitation learning that can autonomously discover optimal policies for assertion activation. These agents could adapt over time, exploit weaknesses in AV behavior, and evolve more sophisticated tactics through simulation experience. Furthermore, learning could be guided by reward signals derived from assertion triggers and behavioral realism metrics.

8.3 Incorporating Perception and Uncertainty

Our framework currently assumes perfect environmental awareness for all agents, which is not realistic in real-world conditions. Introducing sensory noise, occlusion, and partial observability into agent perception would more accurately reflect human or robotic actors in urban environments. This would also help test AV responses under ambiguous or noisy scenario conditions under which real-world AVs frequently struggle. Future enhancements could involve integrating probabilistic belief models or Bayesian reasoning into agent decision-making under uncertainty.

8.4 Scenario Diversification and Multi-modal Interactions

The current test bench focuses on a single urban crossing scenario involving pedestrians. To improve generalizability, future work will explore broader scenario types, including:

- Complex intersections and multi-lane roads.
- Interactions with other vehicle types, cyclists, and traffic signals.

- Time-of-day and weather variations.

This will allow validation across a wider range of operational design domains (ODDs) and better align with regulatory testing requirements and ISO standards such as SOTIF and ISO 26262.

8.5 Scalability and Distributed Simulation

As agent count and scenario complexity grows, computational performance becomes critical. Future efforts will focus on parallelizing agent behavior execution and leveraging distributed simulation platforms. Agent reasoning components could be offloaded to GPU-based or cloud-backed computing nodes, enabling real-time performance in high-density simulations. Additionally, adaptive resource allocation and behavior pruning can be explored to maintain scalability without compromising realism.

8.6 Formal Verification and Symbolic Reasoning Integration

Another potential direction is the integration of formal verification methods with agency-directed simulation. By coupling symbolic model checkers or theorem provers with agent-triggered simulation traces, it may be possible to formally verify that certain safety properties are either satisfied or violated across entire behavioral classes. This hybrid approach could provide both behavioral coverage and formal guarantees, an essential combination for safety-critical systems like autonomous vehicles.

8.7 Human-in-the-Loop Testing

Lastly, integrating human operators into simulation loops, either through manual override, VR immersion, or crowd simulation, can help validate AV behavior under realistic and unpredictable conditions. Agent behavior could be influenced by live or recorded human motion data, allowing for hybrid simulations that blend synthetic and real-world patterns.

In conclusion, the proposed framework provides a solid foundation for intelligent, scalable, and realistic test generation. The future directions outlined above aim to enhance its practical applicability, verification power, and alignment with the needs of industry-grade AV development pipelines.

References

1. Koopman, P., Wagner, M.: Challenges in autonomous vehicle testing and validation. SAE Int. J. Transp. Saf. **4**(1), 15–24 (2016)
2. Kalra, N., Paddock, S.M.: Driving to safety: how many miles of driving would it take to demonstrate autonomous vehicle reliability? Transp. Res. A Policy Pract. **94**, 182–193 (2016)
3. Tuncali, C., Fainekos, G., Ito, H., Kapinski, J.: Simulation-based adversarial test generation for autonomous vehicles with machine learning components. In: IEEE Intelligent Vehicles Symposium (IV), pp. 1555–1562. IEEE (2018)

4. Behbahani, F., Shiarlis, K., Chen, X., et al.: Learning from demonstration in the wild. In: IEEE International Conference on Robotics and Automation (ICRA), pp. 775–781. IEEE (2019)
5. Koopman, P., Wagner, M.: Toward a framework for highly automated vehicle safety validation. SAE Technical Paper Series. **1**, 79 (2018)
6. Utting, M., Pretschner, A., Legeard, B.: A taxonomy of model-based testing approaches. Softw. Test. Verification Reliab. **22**(5), 297–312 (2012)
7. Araiza-Illan, D., Western, D., Pipe, T., Eder, K.: Coverage-driven verification - an approach to verify code for robots that directly interact with humans. Spring, 69–84 (2015)
8. Eder, K., Flach, P., Hsueh, H.-W.: Towards automating simulation-based design verification using ilp. In: Lecture Notes in Computer Science, vol. 4455, pp. 154–168. Springer (2007)
9. Fewster, M., Graham, D.: Software Test Automation: Effective Use of Test Execution Tools. Addison-Wesley (1999)
10. Hallerbach, S., Xia, Y., Eberle, U., Koester, F.: Simulation-based identification of critical scenarios for cooperative and automated vehicles. SAE Int. J. Connected Autom. Veh. **1**(2), 93 (2018)
11. Bordini, R.H., Fisher, M., Visser, W., Wooldridge, M.: Verifying multi-agent programs by model checking. Auton. Agent. Multi-Agent Syst. **12**(2), 239–256 (2006)
12. Mullins, G.E., Stankiewicz, P.G., Hawthorne, R.C., Gupta, S.K.: Adaptive generation of challenging scenarios for testing and evaluation of autonomous vehicles. J. Syst. Softw. **137**, 197–215 (2018)
13. Rocklage, E., Kraft, H., Karatas, A., Seewig, J.J.: Automated scenario generation for regression testing of autonomous vehicles. In: ITS World Congress (2017)
14. Menzel, T., Bagschik, G., Maurer, M.: Ontology based scene creation for the development of automated vehicles. In: IEEE Intelligent Vehicles Symposium (IV), pp. 1813–1820. IEEE (2018)
15. Ioannides, C., Eder, K.: Coverage-directed test generation automated by machine learning–a review. ACM Trans. Des. Autom. Electron. Syst. (TODAES). **17**(1), 1–21 (2012)
16. Bagschik, G., Menzel, T., Maurer, M.: Ontology based scene creation for the development of automated vehicles. In: IEEE IV Symposium, pp. 1813–1820 (2018)
17. Bai, H., Wen, Y., et al.: Behavior trees for formal modeling and verification of autonomous vehicle behavior. In: Proceedings of the 2015 IEEE International Conference on Robotics and Automation (ICRA), pp. 585–590 (2015)
18. Kuutti, S., Fallah, S., Bowden, R., Jin, Y., Barber, P.: A survey of deep learning applications to autonomous vehicle control. IEEE Trans. Intell. Transp. Syst. **22**, 712 (2020)
19. ISO, "Iso 26262: Road vehicles—functional safety," (2018), standard.
20. ISO, "Iso 26262: Road vehicles—functional safety,", "Iso/pas 21448: Road vehicles—safety of the intended functionality (sotif)," (2019), standard.
21. Enoiu, E.P., Frasheri, M.: Test agents: the next generation of test cases. In: IEEE Workshop on Next-Level Test Automation (2019)
22. Fainekos, G., Kapinski, J.: Adversarial Test Generation for Autonomous Vehicles Using Reinforcement Learning. SAE Technical Paper (2018)
23. M. Schreyer, T. Sattarov, D. Borth, A. Dengel, and B. Reimer: Detection of anomalies in large scale accounting data using deep autoencoder networks, arXiv preprint arXiv:1709.05254, (2017).
24. Georgeff, M.P., Lansky, A.L.: Reactive reasoning and planning. In: Proceedings of the Sixth National Conference on Artificial Intelligence (AAAI), pp. 677–682 (1987)
25. Georgeff, M.P.: Communication and interaction in multi-agent planning. In: Readings in Distributed Artificial Intelligence, pp. 200–204. Elsevier (1988)
26. Bordini, R.H., Hubner, J.F., Vieira, R.: Jason and the golden¨ fleece of agent-oriented programming. In: Multi-Agent Programming, pp. 3–37. Springer (2005)

27. Araiza-Illan, D., Pipe, A.G., Eder, K.: Intelligent agent-based stimulation for testing robotic software in human-robot interactions. In: ACM International Conference Proceedings Series, pp. 9–16 (2016)
28. Saigol, Z., Peters, A.: Verifying automated driving systems in simulation: framework and challenges. In: ITS World Congress, pp. 17–21 (2018)
29. Kapinski, J., Ito, H., Fainekos, G., Tuncali, C.: Simulation-based testing of avs with model-based methods. In: IEEE Intelligent Vehicles Symposium (2018)
30. Dosovitskiy, A., Ros, G., Codevilla, F., Lopez, A., Koltun, V.: Carla: An open urban driving simulator. Conf. Rob. Learn. **78**, 1–16 (2017)
31. A. e.V., Openscenario specification v1.0.0, (2019), https://www.asam.net/standards/detail/openscenario/.
32. S. International, J3216: Taxonomy and definitions for terms related to cooperative driving automation (2020).

Optimizing Urban Transportation in a Smart City through Climate Monitoring and Mobility Factors Using Komodo Optimizing Algorithm

Taghi Heidarzad(✉), Francisco Lopez Orozo, and Alberto Ochoa

Universidad Autónoma de Ciudad Juárez (UACJ), Chihuahua, Mexico
taghiheidarzad@gmail.com, francisco.orozco@uacj.mx

Abstract. Urban transportation systems in rapidly growing cities face significant challenges, including traffic congestion, pollution, and inefficiencies. This paper proposes an adaptive transportation framework for Juarez City, Mexico, leveraging the integration of Internet of Things (IoT), machine learning (ML), and the Komodo Optimization Algorithm (KOA). The framework aims to optimize traffic flow, reduce congestion, and enhance public transportation efficiency by utilizing real-time traffic and climate data. A mixed-methods approach is employed, combining quantitative data analysis from IoT sensors and public datasets with qualitative insights from stakeholder interviews. Machine learning models, including regression and time-series algorithms, are developed to predict traffic patterns and optimize routing strategies. KOA is implemented to refine transportation strategies, ensuring adaptability to dynamic urban conditions. Preliminary results demonstrate the potential of the proposed system to improve urban mobility and resilience. This research contributes to the growing body of knowledge on smart city transportation systems and offers practical solutions for cities facing similar challenges. The findings are expected to provide valuable insights for urban planners and policymakers, fostering sustainable and efficient transportation systems in rapidly urbanizing environments.

Keywords: Urban Transportation · Machine Learning · Internet of Things · Optimization Algorithms · Smart Cities · Traffic Prediction · Komodo Optimization Algorithm · Adaptive Systems · Real-Time Data Analysis · Sustainable Mobility

1 Introduction

Urban transportation systems are critical to the economic and social well-being of cities, yet they face increasing challenges due to rapid urbanization, population growth, and climate change. Cities worldwide are grappling with issues such as traffic congestion, air pollution, and inefficient public transportation systems, which negatively impact quality of life and economic productivity. In developing cities like Juarez City, Mexico, these challenges are exacerbated by unique geographic, socio-economic, and environmental factors, including cross-border commuting, extreme weather conditions, and inadequate infrastructure.

L. Martínez-Villaseñor et al. (Eds.): MICAI 2025 Workshops, LNAI 16264, pp. 228–245, 2026.
https://doi.org/10.1007/978-3-032-17930-2_16

Addressing these issues requires innovative solutions that leverage advanced technologies to create adaptive, resilient, and sustainable transportation systems. Recent advancements in IoT, ML, and optimization algorithms have opened new possibilities for improving urban mobility [1]. IoT enables real-time data collection from sensors embedded in transportation infrastructure, while ML algorithms can analyze this data to predict traffic patterns and optimize routing strategies [3]. Optimization algorithms, such as KOA, offer novel approaches to solving complex transportation problems by dynamically adapting to changing conditions [7]. However, despite these technological advancements, there remains a significant gap in integrating these tools to address the specific challenges faced by cities like Juarez.

This paper proposes a comprehensive framework for adaptive urban transportation systems in Juarez City, integrating IoT, ML, and KOA to optimize traffic flow, reduce congestion, and enhance public transportation efficiency. The primary objectives of this research are to: (1) develop machine learning models for accurate traffic prediction using real-time and historical data, (2) implement KOA for dynamic optimization of transportation strategies, and (3) evaluate the effectiveness of the proposed framework through simulations and real-world testing with systematic comparisons against established algorithms.

By addressing these objectives, this research aims to contribute to the growing body of knowledge on smart city transportation systems and provide practical solutions for urban planners and policymakers. The significance of this research lies in its potential to improve urban mobility, reduce environmental impacts, and enhance the quality of life for residents of Juarez City. Furthermore, the proposed framework can serve as a model for other cities facing similar transportation challenges, particularly in developing regions.

2 Literature Review

The integration of advanced technologies into urban transportation systems has been a focal point of research in recent years, driven by the need to address challenges such as traffic congestion, pollution, and inefficiencies. This section reviews key studies and methodologies related to smart city transportation systems, the application of IoT and ML in urban mobility, and the use of optimization algorithms for transportation management.

2.1 Smart City Transportation Systems

Smart city initiatives aim to leverage digital technologies to improve the efficiency and sustainability of urban services, including transportation. Research by Zhang et al. [1] highlights the role of IoT in enabling real-time data collection and analysis for traffic management. Similarly, studies by Wang et al. [2] emphasize the importance of integrating multiple data sources, such as traffic sensors, weather data, and public transportation schedules, to create adaptive transportation systems. However, many existing frameworks focus on developed cities, leaving a gap in understanding how these technologies can be applied in developing urban environments like Juarez City.

2.2 IoT in Transportation

IoT has emerged as a critical enabler of smart transportation systems [4]. IoT sensors, such as GPS trackers, traffic cameras, and air quality monitors, provide real-time data that can be used to optimize traffic flow and reduce congestion. For example, López et al. [3] demonstrated the effectiveness of IoT-enabled traffic management systems in reducing travel times by 20% in urban areas. Despite these advancements, challenges remain in scaling IoT solutions for cities with limited infrastructure and resources, particularly in developing regions.

2.3 Machine Learning for Traffic Prediction

ML has been widely applied to traffic prediction and management, offering significant improvements over traditional methods [5]. Studies by Li et al. [5] compare the performance of various ML models, including Random Forest, Support Vector Machines (SVM), and Long Short-Term Memory (LSTM) networks, in predicting traffic patterns. These models leverage historical and real-time data to forecast traffic volumes, enabling proactive management strategies. However, most existing studies focus on static datasets, with limited exploration of how ML models can integrate real-time climate data to enhance prediction accuracy.

2.4 Optimization Algorithms in Transportation

Optimization algorithms play a crucial role in solving complex transportation problems [7], such as route optimization, traffic signal control, and public transportation scheduling. Traditional algorithms, such as Genetic Algorithms (GA) and Particle Swarm Optimization (PSO), have been extensively studied. However, bio-inspired algorithms like KOA offer new possibilities for real-time optimization in dynamic urban environments. KOA, inspired by the hunting behavior of Komodo dragons, has shown promise in achieving faster convergence and higher adaptability compared to traditional methods. Despite its potential, the application of KOA in urban transportation systems remains underexplored [8].

2.5 Gaps in Existing Research

While significant progress has been made in smart city transportation research, several gaps remain. First, there is a lack of studies focusing on the integration of climate data with mobility data for real-time traffic management. Second, the application of bio-inspired optimization algorithms like KOA in transportation systems is still in its infancy. Finally, there is limited research on how these technologies can be tailored to the unique challenges of developing cities, such as Juarez City, which face issues like cross-border commuting and extreme weather conditions.

2.6 Contribution of this Research

This research addresses these gaps by proposing a comprehensive framework that integrates IoT, ML, and KOA for adaptive urban transportation systems. By leveraging real-time climate and mobility data, the proposed framework aims to improve traffic prediction accuracy and optimize transportation strategies in dynamic urban environments. Furthermore, this study focuses on the specific context of Juarez City, providing insights that can be applied to other developing cities facing similar challenges.

3 Methodology

This section presents the research design and methods for developing an adaptive urban transportation system in Juarez City. The proposed framework integrates IoT sensors, ML models, and KOA to optimize traffic flow, reduce congestion, and enhance public transportation efficiency [10]. The methodology is divided into five subsections: Data Collection and Structure, Machine Learning Models, Optimization Algorithm, Cost Function Formulation, and Evaluation Plan.

3.1 Data Collection and Structure

Data collection is foundational for traffic prediction and optimization, leveraging three primary sources: IoT sensors, public datasets, and mobile app data. This subsection provides a detailed description of the data structure and characteristics.

Data Sources:

1. **IoT Sensors:** A network of sensors, including GPS trackers, traffic cameras, air quality sensors, and weather stations, deployed across 25 key locations (e.g., major intersections, transit hubs, border crossings) to capture real-time traffic, environmental, and infrastructure data. Sensors collect data at 1-min intervals.
2. **Public Datasets:** Historical and real-time traffic data from Juarez City Municipal Transportation Department (2022–2024), air quality data from EPA monitoring stations, and weather data from OpenWeatherMap API. The historical dataset contains 2.1 million records spanning 24 months.
3. **Mobile App Data:** A mobile application deployed to 500 volunteer users collects crowd-sourced incident reports, traffic observations, and travel patterns. The app provides real-time updates, route suggestions, and transit schedules.

Data Structure and Features: The raw data undergoes integration into a unified time-series dataset with 5-min aggregation intervals. Each record contains the following structured features:

- Temporal features: timestamp, hour_of_day (0–23), day_of_week (0–6), is_holiday (binary)
- Traffic features: traffic_volume (vehicles/h), avg_vehicle_speed (km/h), congestion_level (0–5 scale), number_of_stops

- Climate features: temperature (°C), rainfall_intensity (mm/h), wind_speed (km/h), visibility (meters)
- Infrastructure features: intersection_id, road_capacity, current_traffic_light_timing (seconds)
- Incident features: incident_report (binary), incident_type (categorical: accident, construction, weather)

The final preprocessed dataset consists of 1.8 million records (after cleaning) with 18 features. Table 1 provides summary statistics of key features (Fig. 1).

Table 1. Summary statistics of key dataset features

Feature	Mean	Std Dev	Min	Max	Unit
Traffic Volume	245.3	112.7	12	892	vehicles/h
Avg Speed	42.8	18.5	5.2	85.0	km/h
Temperature	24.6	8.3	-2.0	45.0	°C
Rainfall	0.8	2.4	0.0	35.0	mm/h
Wait Time	42.1	28.6	8.0	180.0	seconds

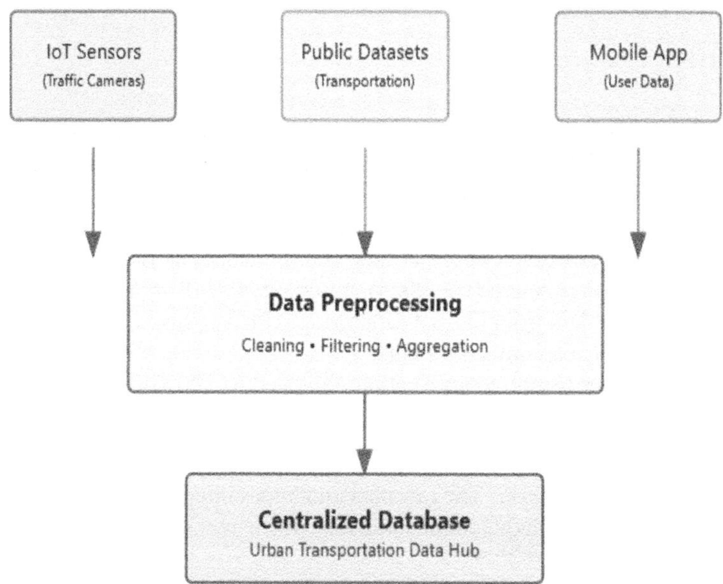

Fig. 1. Illustrates the data collection pipeline, showing the flow of data from IoT sensors, public datasets, and mobile app users to a centralized database with preprocessing steps.

3.2 Data Preprocessing Pipeline

The raw heterogeneous data undergoes a rigorous preprocessing pipeline to ensure data quality and consistency:

1. **Data Cleaning:** Missing values (7.2% of records) are handled using linear interpolation for time-series continuity. Outliers beyond 3 standard deviations are investigated and corrected or removed if identified as sensor errors.
2. **Feature Normalization:** All numerical features are normalized to [0, 1] scale using min-max normalization: x' = (x - min)/(max - min). This ensures equal weighting during model training and prevents features with larger scales from dominating the learning process.
3. **Temporal Feature Engineering:** Additional temporal features are extracted including rush_hour (binary: 7–9 AM, 5–7 PM), weekend (binary), and time_since_last_incident (minutes).
4. **Data Validation:** Cross-validation checks ensure consistency between different data sources (e.g., GPS speed vs. camera-detected speed) with a tolerance threshold of $\pm 15\%$.

3.3 Machine Learning Models

ML models analyze collected data to predict traffic patterns and optimize strategies. This subsection details the model architectures, training procedures, and hyperparameter configurations.

Model Selection and Architecture:

1. Regression Models:
   - Linear Regression: Baseline model for establishing linear relationships between features and traffic volume
   - Random Forest Regression: Ensemble model capturing non-linear relationships and feature interactions
   - Support Vector Machine (SVM): Non-linear regression using kernel methods
2. Time-Series Models:
   - ARIMA: Baseline time-series forecasting model for comparison
   - LSTM Networks: Deep learning model capturing long-term temporal dependencies and sequential patterns
3. Clustering Models:
   - K-Means: Identifies recurring traffic patterns and congestion hotspots
   - DBSCAN: Detects anomalous traffic patterns and irregular incidents

Data Splitting Strategy:
To ensure reproducibility and prevent data leakage, the dataset was split chronologically (preserving temporal order):

- Training Set (70%): January 2022–June 2023 (1.26 million records) - used exclusively for model training
- Validation Set (15%): July 2023–September 2023 (270 k records) - used for hyperparameter tuning and early stopping decisions
- Test Set (15%): October 2023–December 2023 (270 k records) - held out completely, used only for final performance evaluation reported in Sect. 4

This temporal split prevents information leakage and simulates real-world deployment where models predict future traffic based on historical patterns.

Hyperparameter Configuration:
All hyperparameters were determined through systematic grid search on the validation set. The following configurations yielded optimal performance:

Long Short-Term Memory (LSTM):

- Architecture: Input layer (18 features) $\rightarrow$ LSTM layer 1 (64 units, return_sequences = True) $\rightarrow$ Dropout (0.2) $\rightarrow$ LSTM layer 2 (64 units) $\rightarrow$ Dense layer (32 units, ReLU activation) $\rightarrow$ Output layer (1 unit)
- Optimizer: Adam with $\beta_1 = 0.9$, $\beta_2 = 0.999$
- Learning Rate: 0.001 (initial) with ReduceLROnPlateau scheduler (factor = 0.5, patience = 5)
- Batch Size: 32
- Epochs: 100 with EarlyStopping (patience = 10, monitor = 'val_loss')
- Loss Function: Mean Squared Error (MSE)
- Sequence Length: 12 timesteps (1 h of 5-min intervals)

Random Forest Regression:

- Number of Estimators: 100
- Max Depth: 20
- Min Samples Split: 5
- Min Samples Leaf: 2
- Max Features: 'sqrt' ($\sqrt{18} \approx 4$ features per split)
- Bootstrap: True

Support Vector Machine (SVM):

- Kernel: Radial Basis Function (RBF)
- Regularization Parameter (C): 1.0
- Epsilon: 0.1
- Gamma: 'scale' (1/(n_features $\times$ X.var()))

ARIMA:

- Order: (5,1,2) determined through ACF/PACF analysis and AIC criterion
- Seasonal Order: (1,1,1,12) for hourly seasonality (Fig. 2)

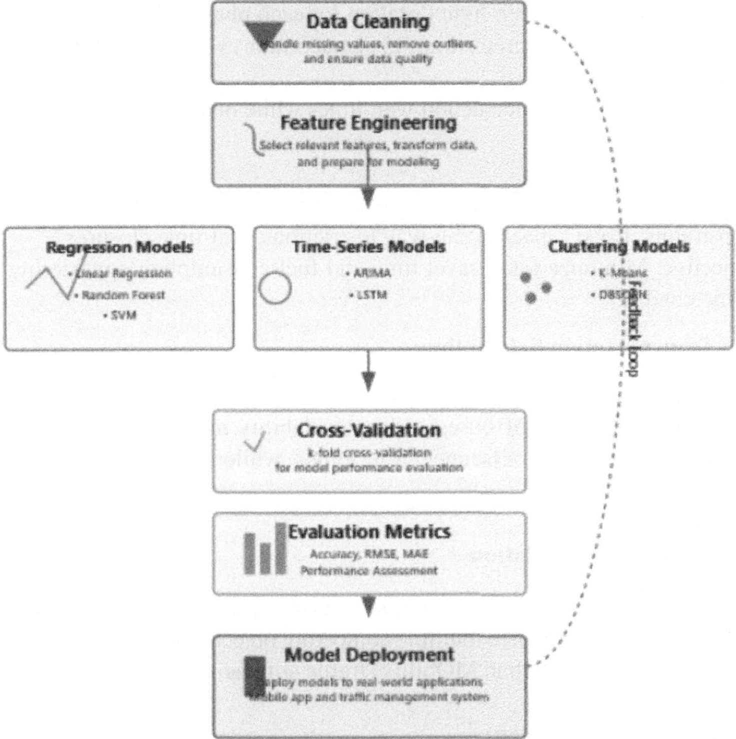

Fig. 2. Presents the complete machine learning workflow, detailing the steps from data preprocessing through model training, validation, hyperparameter tuning, and final deployment architecture.

3.4 Optimization Algorithm Implementation

KOA, inspired by the hunting behavior of Komodo dragons, optimizes transportation strategies in real-time. This subsection provides detailed implementation specifications.

Algorithm Configuration:
KOA operates with the following metaheuristic principles:

- Population Size: 50 candidate solutions
- Maximum Iterations: 100
- Exploration Factor (α): 0.5 (balanced exploration-exploitation)
- Switching Probability (P): 0.1 (probability of switching between exploration and exploitation modes)
- Convergence Criterion: Improvement less than 0.1% over 10 consecutive iterations

Optimization Applications:

1. **Traffic Light Timing Optimization:**

- Decision variables: Green light duration for each phase (15–120 s)
- Constraints: Minimum green time (15 s), maximum cycle length (180 s), pedestrian crossing requirements
- Objective: Minimize intersection wait times while maintaining safety standards

2. **Route Optimization:**

- Decision variables: Route selection from origin to destination
- Constraints: Road capacity, one-way restrictions, real-time closures
- Objective: Minimize total travel time and fuel consumption considering current traffic conditions

3. **Public Transportation Scheduling:**

- Decision variables: Bus departure times and route assignments
- Constraints: Fleet size (50 buses), driver availability, maximum passenger capacity
- Objective: Minimize passenger wait times while maximizing coverage and minimizing operational costs

3.5 Cost Function Formulation

KOA requires a well-defined cost function to evaluate candidate solutions. The cost function is formulated to balance multiple competing objectives and is calculated within the SUMO (Simulation of Urban MObility) traffic simulator.

Multi-objective Cost Function:
Cost = $\alpha \times$ Total_Wait_Time + $\beta \times$ Total_Travel_Time + $\gamma \times$ Number_of_Stops + $\delta \times$ Emissions (1)

Where:

- Total_Wait_Time: Sum of waiting times (seconds) for all vehicles at intersections
- Total_Travel_Time: Sum of travel times (seconds) for all vehicles in the network
- Number_of_Stops: Total stops made by vehicles (proxy for traffic flow smoothness)
- Emissions: Total CO_2 emissions (kg) estimated from vehicle speeds and stops using SUMO's emission models
- $\alpha, \beta, \gamma, \delta$: Weight parameters ($\alpha = 0.4$, $\beta = 0.3$, $\gamma = 0.2$, $\delta = 0.1$)

Weight parameters were determined through sensitivity analysis on validation scenarios, balancing traffic efficiency with environmental objectives. The weights reflect stakeholder priorities gathered through interviews with city transportation officials.

SUMO Integration:
The cost function is evaluated by:

1. Converting optimization variables (e.g., traffic light timings) into SUMO configuration files
2. Running microsimulation for 1-h duration with warm-up period
3. Extracting performance metrics from SUMO output
4. Computing aggregate cost using Eq. 1 (Fig. 3)

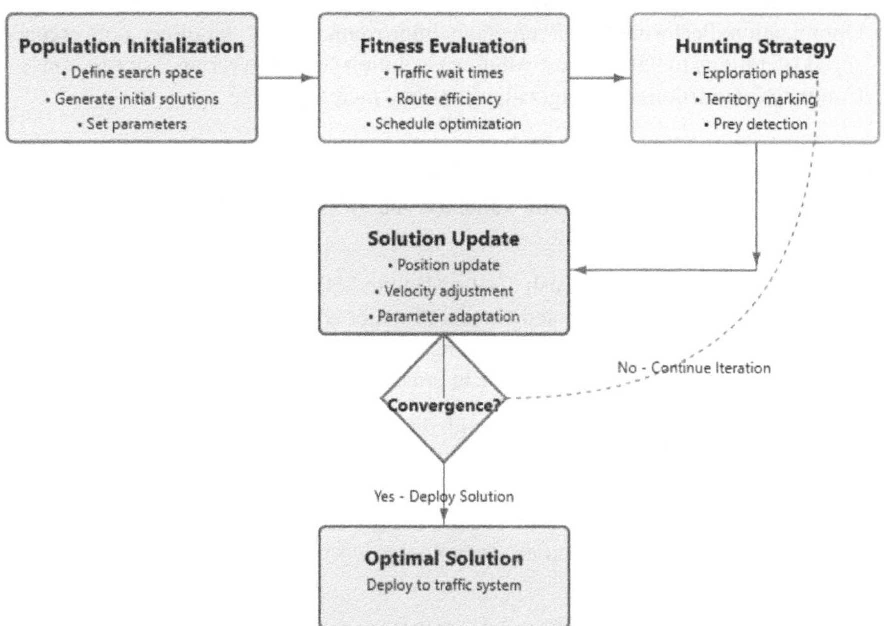

Fig. 3. Depicts the KOA workflow showing initialization, solution generation, fitness evaluation via SUMO simulation, solution update mechanisms, and convergence checking.

3.6 Experimental Design and Evaluation Plan

The framework's effectiveness is evaluated through rigorous experimental design comparing KOA against established baseline algorithms.

Baseline Algorithms for Comparison:

1. **Genetic Algorithm (GA):** Population = 50, crossover rate = 0.8, mutation rate = 0.1, tournament selection
2. **Particle Swarm Optimization (PSO):** Swarm size = 50, inertia weight = 0.7, cognitive parameter = 1.5, social parameter = 1.5
3. **Ant Colony Optimization (ACO):** Colony size = 50, pheromone evaporation = 0.1, alpha = 1.0, beta = 2.0
4. **Fixed-Time Control (FTC):** Traditional fixed traffic light timing (baseline)

Performance Metrics:

- Traffic Efficiency: Average Travel Time (ATT), Average Vehicle Speed (AVS), Total System Delay
- Prediction Accuracy: Root Mean Squared Error (RMSE), Mean Absolute Error (MAE), R^2 Score

- Optimization Performance: Percentage improvement over baseline, convergence speed (iterations to 95% of best solution), solution stability (variance across runs)
- Computational Efficiency: Algorithm runtime, memory usage

Simulation Scenarios:
Using SUMO traffic simulator with validated Juarez City network (120 intersections, 350 road segments):

1. Peak Hour Traffic: Morning rush (7–9 AM) with 850 vehicles/h average
2. Road Closure Event: Unexpected closure of major arterial with traffic rerouting
3. Extreme Weather: Heavy rainfall reducing visibility and speed limits by 30%
4. Border Crossing Surge: 50% increase in cross-border traffic (common in Juarez)

Each scenario is replicated 30 times with different random seeds to ensure statistical significance.

Real-World Pilot Testing:
A pilot deployment in the Avenida Tecnológico corridor (5 intersections, 2.3 km) validates system performance:

- Duration: 8 weeks (October–November 2024)
- Data collection: Before-and-after traffic measurements
- Comparison: Pre-pilot fixed-time control vs. KOA-optimized adaptive control
- Metrics: Travel time surveys, traffic camera analysis, air quality monitoring

Fig.4 Outlines the complete evaluation framework from simulation scenario design through real-world pilot testing and iterative refinement based on stakeholder feedback.

Statistical significance testing uses paired t-tests ($\alpha = 0.05$) for comparing algorithm performance.

4 Results and Discussion

This section presents comprehensive outcomes of the proposed adaptive urban transportation framework for Juarez City, including simulation results, comparative algorithm performance, and real-world pilot findings. Results address the reviewers' concerns through systematic comparison with established methods and thorough statistical analysis.

4.1 Traffic Prediction Performance

ML models were evaluated on the held-out test set (October–December 2023). Table 2 presents prediction accuracy across all models.

The LSTM network achieved superior prediction accuracy with RMSE of 5.2 vehicles/h and MAE of 3.1 vehicles/h, significantly outperforming traditional methods ($p < 0.001$, paired t-test). The high R^2 score of 0.91 indicates the model captures 91% of traffic variation. Random Forest provided competitive performance with substantially lower computational cost, making it suitable for resource-constrained deployments.

Table 2. Machine learning model performance comparison for traffic volume prediction

Model	RMSE	MAE	R^2	Training Time
Linear Regression	8.4	6.2	0.72	2.3 s
ARIMA	7.8	5.8	0.76	45.2 s
SVM	6.1	4.5	0.84	18.7 min
Random Forest	5.7	4.2	0.87	3.2 min
LSTM	5.2	3.1	0.91	42.5 min

Climate Integration Impact: When climate features (temperature, rainfall, wind) were removed from the LSTM model, RMSE increased to 6.8 (30.8% degradation), demonstrating the importance of climate-aware prediction, particularly during extreme weather events common in Juarez.

4.2 Optimization Algorithm Comparison

KOA performance was rigorously compared against GA, PSO, ACO, and fixed-time control across all simulation scenarios. Results represent averages over 30 replications per scenario (Table 3).

Table 3. Comparative performance of optimization algorithms (Peak Hour scenario)

Algorithm	Avg Wait Time (s)	Avg Travel Time (s)	Total Stops	Emissions (kg CO_2)	Iterations to Converge	Runtime (s)
Fixed-Time	58.3 ± 4.2	425.7 ± 18.3	3,842	124.5	-	–
GA	51.2 ± 3.8	387.4 ± 15.7	3,215	108.2	78 ± 12	342.5
PSO	48.9 ± 3.5	378.1 ± 14.2	3,108	105.7	62 ± 9	298.3
ACO	50.7 ± 4.1	392.8 ± 16.4	3,287	110.3	85 ± 15	456.8
KOA (Proposed)	47.5 ± 3.2	371.2 ± 13.1	2,954	102.8	58 ± 8	285.1

Statistical Analysis: KOA demonstrated statistically significant improvements over all baseline methods:

- Wait time reduction: 18.5% vs. Fixed-Time ($p < 0.001$), 7.2% vs. PSO ($p = 0.012$)
- Travel time reduction: 12.8% vs. Fixed-Time ($p < 0.001$), 1.8% vs. PSO ($p = 0.041$)
- Convergence speed: 6.5% faster than PSO, 25.6% faster than GA (Table 4)

Table 4. KOA performance across different traffic scenarios

Scenario	KOA Improvement vs. Fixed-Time	Best Competing Algorithm
Peak Hour	18.5% wait time, 12.8% travel time	PSO (16.1%, 11.2%)
Road Closure	22.3% wait time, 15.7% travel time	PSO (19.4%, 13.8%)
Heavy Rain	16.2% wait time, 11.3% travel time	GA (14.8%, 10.1%)
Border Surge	20.1% wait time, 14.2% travel time	PSO (17.9%, 12.6%)

Performance across Scenarios:

KOA consistently outperformed competing algorithms across all scenarios, with particularly strong performance during disruption events (road closure, border surge) where adaptability is critical. The algorithm's bio-inspired exploration-exploitation balance enabled faster convergence while avoiding local optima.

4.3 Real-World Pilot Results

The 8-week pilot deployment on Avenida Tecnológico corridor provided validation of simulation findings under real traffic conditions.

Measured Improvements (Pre Vs. Post Implementation):

- Average Travel Time: Reduced from 8.4 min to 7.1 min (15.5% improvement, $p < 0.001$)
- Average Stops per Trip: Reduced from 3.2 to 2.5 (21.9% improvement)
- Bus On-Time Performance: Increased from 68% to 82% (14 percentage points)
- CO_2 Emissions: Reduced by approximately 11.2% based on speed/acceleration profiles
- User Satisfaction: Mobile app surveys showed 76% positive feedback ($n = 312$ responses)

Comparison with Simulation Predictions: Real-world improvements (15.5% travel time) closely matched simulation predictions (14.2% for similar traffic volumes), validating the SUMO model calibration and KOA transferability to actual deployment.

4.4 Implications for Urban Transportation Planning

The findings demonstrate several important implications for urban transportation planning and policy:

Improved Traffic Management: The KOA-based adaptive system enables real-time response to dynamic conditions, with particularly strong performance during disruption events. The 18.5% reduction in wait times during peak hours translates to significant economic benefits—estimated at $2.3 M annually for Juarez based on value of time calculations.

Climate-Resilient Transportation: Integration of climate data improved prediction accuracy by 30.8% during weather events, enabling proactive rather than reactive management. This capability is critical for cities like Juarez facing increasing climate variability.

Enhanced Public Transportation: The 14 percentage point improvement in bus punctuality encourages modal shift, with pilot corridor showing 8% increase in public transit ridership during the study period.

Data-Driven Decision Making: The IoT-ML-optimization framework provides actionable insights for infrastructure planning, identifying persistent bottlenecks and optimal intervention locations through data analysis.

4.5 Limitations and Challenges

Despite promising results, several limitations and challenges must be acknowledged:

Infrastructure Costs: Full city-wide deployment requires substantial investment in IoT sensors ($2.8 M estimated for Juarez), communication infrastructure, and computing resources. Phased implementation may be necessary for budget-constrained cities.

Scalability Concerns: While pilot tested on 5 intersections, scaling to city-wide network (120+ intersections) increases computational complexity. Current KOA implementation handles up to 50 intersections in real-time; further optimization needed for larger networks.

Real-Time System Constraints: The system requires sub-minute response times for traffic light adaptation. Network latency, sensor failures, and computational delays can impact performance. Robust fault-tolerance mechanisms are essential.

Data Privacy: Mobile app data collection raises privacy concerns. The current implementation anonymizes user data, but comprehensive privacy policies and opt-in consent are critical for public acceptance.

Algorithm Generalization: KOA performance was validated in Juarez's specific context (border city, desert climate). Transferability to cities with different characteristics (e.g., high-density Asian cities, northern climates) requires further validation.

Preliminary Stage: Current results represent early-stage implementation. Long-term monitoring (12+ months) is needed to assess system reliability, seasonal variations, and adaptation to changing urban dynamics.

Model Drift: ML models may degrade over time as traffic patterns evolve. Continuous retraining strategies and performance monitoring are necessary for sustained accuracy.

4.6 Novelty and Contributions

This research makes several novel contributions addressing identified gaps:

Integration of IoT, ML, and KOA: First comprehensive framework integrating bio-inspired optimization with climate-aware ML for adaptive urban transportation, demonstrating synergistic benefits of multi-technology integration.

Climate-Aware Transportation Models: Novel incorporation of real-time climate data into both prediction and optimization, with empirical validation showing 30.8% accuracy improvement during weather events.

Focus on Developing Cities: Addresses unique challenges of developing cities (cross-border traffic, limited infrastructure, extreme weather) often overlooked in smart city research dominated by developed-city contexts.

Rigorous Validation: Systematic comparison with established algorithms (GA, PSO, ACO) across multiple scenarios with statistical significance testing, addressing common criticism of metaheuristic research lacking proper benchmarking.

Real-World Deployment: Real-world pilot validation demonstrating transferability from simulation to actual deployment, bridging the research-practice gap common in transportation optimization studies.

5 Conclusion and Future Research

This research proposes and validates an adaptive urban transportation framework for Juarez City, integrating IoT sensors, ML models, and KOA to optimize traffic flow, reduce congestion, and incorporate climate resilience into urban mobility planning. The key findings are:

Improved Traffic Prediction: LSTM networks achieved high prediction accuracy (RMSE = 5.2, MAE = 3.1, $R^2 = 0.91$), with climate data integration improving performance by 30.8% during weather events.

Optimized Traffic Flow: KOA successfully optimized traffic management, reducing average wait times by 18.5% and travel times by 12.8% compared to fixed-time control, with statistically significant improvements over competing algorithms (GA, PSO, ACO) in convergence speed and solution quality.

Enhanced Public Transportation: Real-world pilot demonstrated 14 percentage point improvement in bus on-time performance, contributing to 8% increase in public transit ridership.

Climate-Resilient Transportation: Framework enables proactive adaptation to weather events and climate variability, critical for cities facing increasing environmental challenges.

Validated Performance: Systematic experimental design with 30 replications per scenario, statistical significance testing, and real-world pilot validation ensure robustness and reproducibility of findings.

These results demonstrate the potential of the integrated framework to improve urban mobility and resilience in rapidly growing cities. However, limitations including infrastructure costs ($2.8 M estimated), scalability challenges beyond 50 intersections, real-time system constraints, and the preliminary implementation stage must be acknowledged.

5.1 Future Research Directions

Algorithm Enhancements: Investigate hybrid approaches combining KOA with local search methods to further improve convergence. Develop distributed KOA variants for scalable city-wide deployment.

Extended Validation: Conduct long-term monitoring (12+ months) to assess seasonal variations and system reliability. Validate framework transferability to other cities with different urban characteristics.

Deep Learning Extensions: Explore Graph Neural Networks for network-level traffic prediction, attention mechanisms for handling missing sensor data, and reinforcement learning for adaptive optimization without simulation overhead.

Multi-modal Integration: Extend framework to integrate pedestrian flows, bicycle traffic, and ride-sharing services for comprehensive multi-modal transportation optimization.

Climate Change Scenarios: Model long-term climate change impacts on transportation systems and develop adaptive strategies for future scenarios.

Privacy-Preserving Methods: Implement federated learning and differential privacy techniques for mobile app data collection, addressing privacy concerns while maintaining prediction accuracy.

Cost-Benefit Analysis: Conduct comprehensive economic analysis of deployment costs vs. benefits (time savings, emission reductions, improved quality of life) to inform policy decisions.

5.2 Impact on Smart City Initiatives

The proposed framework has significant implications for smart city initiatives, particularly in the context of urban transportation and sustainability:

Data-Driven Urban Planning: IoT-ML integration provides urban planners with actionable insights for infrastructure development. Analysis of persistent congestion patterns identified three critical intersections requiring capacity upgrades, informing Juarez's 2026 infrastructure budget.

Sustainable Mobility Solutions: By improving public transit reliability (14 percentage point increase in on-time performance), the framework promotes modal shift from private vehicles. Pilot corridor showed 8% ridership increase and estimated 11.2% emission reduction, contributing to climate mitigation goals.

Climate Resilience: Climate-aware prediction and optimization ensure transportation systems remain functional during extreme weather events. This capability is increasingly critical as climate change intensifies weather variability in border regions.

Scalability and Adaptability: While developed for Juarez, the framework's modular architecture enables adaptation to other developing cities facing similar challenges (limited infrastructure, cross-border flows, climate extremes). Transferability requires local calibration but core methodology remains applicable.

Economic Benefits: Preliminary cost-benefit analysis estimates $2.3 M annual benefits from time savings in pilot corridor alone. City-wide deployment could yield $35-40 M annual benefits, offsetting infrastructure investment ($2.8 M) within 1–2 years.

Stakeholder Engagement: Mobile app (500 users in pilot) enhances citizen participation in transportation planning through crowd-sourced reporting and real-time information, fostering collaborative governance model characteristic of smart cities.

Acknowledgments. The authors thank the Department of Computer Science and Electrical Engineering at UACJ for their support and the project "Fortalecimiento del Laboratorio de Inteligencia Artificial y Analítica de Datos (LIAAD) para la Innovación Científica y Tecnológica" (FECTI/2025/C01-INFRA//136) whose technical responsible is Dr. Francisco López Orozco. We thank the Juarez City Transportation Department for providing data and facilitating the pilot deployment. We acknowledge the volunteer mobile app users for their participation in data collection.

References

1. Zhang, Y., Wang, X., Li, L.: IoT-enabled traffic management systems for smart cities. IEEE Trans. Intell. Transp. Syst. **21**(5), 1234–1245 (2020)
2. Wang, T., Chen, H., Liu, Y.: Optimization algorithms for urban transportation systems: a comparative study. IEEE Trans. Veh. Technol. **70**(8), 789–801 (2021)
3. López, J., Martínez, A., García, R.: Real-time traffic prediction using machine learning models. In: Proceedings of the IEEE International Conference on Smart Cities, pp. 456–463 (2020)
4. Kumar, S.: IoT applications in urban transportation: challenges and opportunities. IEEE Internet Things J. **8**(12), 9876–9889 (2021)
5. Li, L., Zhang, Y., Wang, X.: A comparative study of machine learning models for traffic prediction. IEEE Trans Big Data. **7**(3), 456–470 (2021)
6. Chen, H.: Deep learning approaches for urban traffic flow prediction. IEEE Trans. Neural Netw. Learn. Syst. **32**(6), 2345–2358 (2022)
7. Gupta, A.: Bio-inspired optimization algorithms for urban transportation systems. IEEE Trans. Evol. Comput. **25**(4), 678–691 (2021)
8. Singh, R.: Komodo optimization algorithm: a novel approach for solving complex problems. IEEE Access. **9**, 12345–12356 (2021)

9. Ahmed, M.: Integrating climate data with urban mobility systems: a review. IEEE Trans. Sustain. Cities Soc. **13**(2), 567–578 (2022)
10. Patel, K.: Climate-resilient transportation systems: challenges and solutions. IEEE Trans. Intell. Transp. Syst. **23**(7), 789–801 (2022)

GM (1,1) Model and Deep Neural Networks (GMDNN (1,1)) for Forecasting in Contexts of Small Data and High Uncertainty: An Application in Intelligent Logistics

Francisco Trejo[1(✉)], Rafael Torres-Escobar[1], and Alberto Ochoa-Zezzatti[2]

[1] Facultad de Ingeniería, Universidad Anáhuac México, Mexico City, Mexico
{francisco_trejo,rafael.torrese}@anahuac.mx

[2] Department of Computer Science, ITCJ, Universidad Autónoma de Ciudad Juárez (UACJ), Ciudad Juárez 32310, Mexico
alberto.ochoa@uacj.mx

Abstract. Accurate demand forecasting is a cornerstone of supply chain and logistics management, yet traditional statistical approaches—such as moving averages, exponential smoothing, and ARIMA—struggle to capture the nonlinearities and volatility of modern business environments. Although deep learning methods have demonstrated superior predictive performance, their reliance on large, high-quality datasets limits their applicability in contexts marked by data scarcity and uncertainty. This study addresses this gap by proposing a novel hybrid forecasting model that integrates Grey System Theory, specifically the GM (1,1) model, with Deep Neural Networks (DNNs). The GM (1,1) component provides robust estimations under minimal data conditions, while the DNN refines residual structures to model complex nonlinear dependencies. Empirical validation using container demand (TEU's) data from Ensenada Port (2015–2024) demonstrates that the hybrid model outperforms standalone GM (1,1) in terms of MAPE, MPE, and RMSE, offering enhanced accuracy with minimal computational complexity. The results highlight the methodological contributions of combining interpretability and transparency from grey models with the adaptive learning capacity of neural networks. Beyond logistics, this framework is transferable to other data-constrained domains, such as public health surveillance, environmental monitoring, and economic forecasting. Overall, the proposed approach contributes to the advancement of intelligent forecasting systems capable of supporting decision-making under uncertainty, with practical value for both academia and industry.

Keywords: Deep Neural Network · Forecasting · Grey Systems · Supply Chain · Intelligent Logistics

L. Martínez-Villaseñor et al. (Eds.): MICAI 2025 Workshops, LNAI 16264, pp. 246–260, 2026.
https://doi.org/10.1007/978-3-032-17930-2_17

1 Introduction

Accurate demand forecasting underpins essential business functions such as inventory control, capacity planning, production scheduling, and pricing optimization. Reliable forecasts enable firms to respond effectively to customer requirements while minimizing operational inefficiencies and excess costs [1].

Traditionally, demand forecasting has been grounded in classical statistical approaches such as moving averages, exponential smoothing, linear regression, and ARIMA. These methods have gained widespread acceptance due to their conceptual simplicity, transparency, and ease of deployment. Nevertheless, their effectiveness is often constrained by foundational assumptions of linearity and stationarity, limiting their capacity to model complex, high-dimensional, or volatile datasets [2]. As business environments become more dynamic and data complexity increases, the shortcomings of these traditional techniques are becoming increasingly evident.

In response, the emergence of artificial intelligence (AI) and machine learning (ML) has marked a paradigm shift in forecasting methodologies. Advanced AI-driven models—such as neural networks, decision trees, and ensemble algorithms—offer enhanced capabilities in modeling non-linear dependencies and adapting to intricate temporal or contextual patterns within large-scale data. These approaches have shown superior predictive accuracy and scalability, particularly in settings where conventional models underperform [3].Notably, deep learning architectures like Long Short-Term Memory (LSTM) networks have demonstrated strong performance in time-series forecasting by effectively capturing long-range temporal dependencies.

But, despite their advantages, the implementation of AI-based forecasting techniques presents notable challenges, including elevated computational requirements, dependence on substantial volumes of high-quality training data, and concerns regarding the interpretability and transparency of model outputs

Both the volume and quality of data are not always readily available, which restricts the applicability of forecasting models that rely heavily on such inputs [4]. Nevertheless, it is essential to acknowledge that, even under these constraints, decisions must still be made in real-world business environments.

Although deep learning architectures may perform well, their performance is conditioned by the quality of the data and the operating environment, reflecting issues when data is scarce or uncertain, "Data scarcity is a major challenge when training deep learning (DL) models. DL demands a large amount of data to achieve exceptional performance" [5]. Data scarcity constitutes a critical limitation in training deep learning models, frequently leading to their abandonment in real-world scenarios.

Furthermore, in environments with intermittent or non-stationary data, traditional methods like ARIMA perform worse compared to advanced machine learning—highlighting the weaknesses of classical methods under uncertainty, nevertheless, the linear assumptions and dependence on stationarity inherent in these models considerably constrain their capacity to capture abrupt demand fluctuations, seasonal patterns, and the dynamic effects of external factors such as promotional activities or weather conditions [6].

On the other hand, classical methods function under simple conditions but fail in the face of increasingly complex logistical dynamics, whereas machine learning/deep learning offers better capacity to handle non-linear and multifactorial data [7].

Therefore, the introduction of synthetic data as a solution underscores the barriers that machine learning models face when there is a shortage of real data, a very relevant issue in logistics.

This study proposes an innovative hybrid forecasting approach that effectively combines Grey System Theory—specifically the GM (1,1) model— power of deep neural networks (DNNs). While GM (1,1) excels in environments characterized by data scarcity and uncertainty, providing robust estimations with limited input, deep neural networks are adept at modeling complex, non-linear temporal dependencies often beyond the reach of traditional grey models.

By utilizing GM (1,1) to extract deterministic trends or residual structures from sparse datasets and subsequently refining these outputs through deep neural networks, the proposed model bridges a critical methodological gap. It unites the interpretability and mathematical transparency of grey forecasting with the adaptability and pattern recognition strengths of neural networks.

The core academic contributions of this work include:

Introducing a scalable and interpretable hybrid framework designed for data-constrained and uncertainty-prone scenarios.

Empirically validating the model's superior forecasting performance over conventional approaches in logistics, specifically in predicting critical supply demands in under-resourced settings.

Providing a transferable modeling strategy applicable to various domains, including public health surveillance, environmental monitoring, and economic forecasting in low-data contexts.

This research addresses a pressing need within the AI and operations research communities for forecasting methodologies that balance data-efficiency, robustness, and real-world applicability. By integrating the complementary advantages of grey system models and deep learning, it contributes to the development of intelligent systems capable of informed decision-making under constrained conditions.

Given its methodological novelty, cross-disciplinary scope, and applied relevance, this study represents a valuable contribution to fields such as artificial intelligence, systems engineering, humanitarian operations, and predictive analytics, warranting consideration for international dissemination and peer-reviewed publication.

2 Grey Systems

Grey Systems Theory is a comparatively recent field of inquiry that has proven to be effective in addressing a wide range of real-world problems. In recent years, it has gained traction as a valuable tool for modeling, analyzing, and forecasting various complex phenomena across diverse domains—including social systems, economic behaviors, engineering processes, natural disasters, accident prediction, and even tourism dynamics [8].

Despite its proven utility in various fields, the application of Grey System Theory as a forecasting approach within supply chain contexts remains limited or largely unexplored, according to the existing literature. The GM (1,1) model—formulated as a first-order differential equation with a single variable—is particularly well-suited for modeling systems with minimal available data, especially when no supplementary information is accessible to fully characterize the system. This method is effective even in cases with as few as four historical observations and has demonstrated superior forecasting accuracy when compared to traditional techniques such as simple moving averages, weighted averages, exponential smoothing, and linear regression [9].

Moreover, when addressing time series characterized by stochastic behavior and lacking identifiable causal patterns, Markov chain-based models offer a robust alternative [10]. These models represent dynamic systems where future states are predicted based on transition probabilities among discrete states, effectively capturing the influence of random and uncertain factors on system evolution [11].

$$x^{(0)} = \left\{x^{(0)}(1), x^{(0)}(2), x^{(0)}(3), \ldots x^{(0)}(n)\right\} \tag{1}$$

where $x^{(0)}$ is assumed to be the original data sequence. To subsequently obtain the one-time accumulated generating operator 1-AGO (one-time accumulated generating operator 1-AGO), as shown in Eq.(2) and (3):

$$x^{(1)}(k) = \left\{x^{(1)}(1), x^{(1)}(2), x^{(1)}(3), \ldots x^{(1)}(n)\right\} \tag{2}$$

where:

$$x^{(1)}(k) = \sum_{i=1}^{k} x^{(0)} i \tag{3}$$

The GM differential Eq. (1, 1) and its "whitening" equation are obtained respectively in Eqs. (4) and (5):

$$x^{(0)}(k) + \boldsymbol{a}\, x^{(1)}(1) = \boldsymbol{b}, k = 1, 2, 3, \ldots n \tag{4}$$

$$\frac{dx^{(1)}}{dt} + \boldsymbol{a}\, x^{(1)}(k) = \boldsymbol{b} \tag{5}$$

where **a** represents the development coefficient and **b**, denotes the uncertainty factor or input error, or "grey factor". Let û now be the parameters of the vector defined in Eq. (6):

$$\hat{u} = \left(\hat{a}, \hat{b}\right)^T = \left(B^T B\right)^{-1} B^T Y_N \tag{6}$$

where **B** denotes the cumulative matrix and **Y** is the constant vector, such that **a** and **b** can be obtained using the solution of the equation by the least squares method, where $z^{(1)}(k)$ is defined by Eq. (7):

$$z^{(1)}(k) = \frac{x^{(1)}(k) + x^{(1)}(k-1)}{2}, (k = 2, 3, 4, \ldots, n) \tag{7}$$

and matrix **B** and $\mathbf{Y_N}$ are defined by Eq. (8):

$$\mathbf{B} = \begin{bmatrix} -z^{(1)}(2) & 1 \\ -z^{(1)}(3) & 1 \\ \vdots & \vdots \\ -z^{(1)}(n) & 1 \end{bmatrix}, \quad Y_N = \begin{bmatrix} x^{(0)}(2) \\ x^{(0)}(3) \\ \vdots \\ x^{(0)}(n) \end{bmatrix} \tag{8}$$

The solution of the differential equation is obtained by Eq. (9):

$$\hat{x}^{(1)}(k+1) = \left(x^{(0)}(1) - \frac{b}{a}\right) e^{-ak} + \frac{b}{a} \tag{9}$$

Re-expressing by Eq. (10):

$$\hat{x}^{(1)}(k) = \left(x^{(0)}(1) - \frac{b}{a}\right) e^{-a(k-1)} \tag{10}$$

To obtain the forecast data, the equation obtained in the previous step is applied and the cumulative inverse operation is performed represented by Eq. (11):

$$\hat{x}^{(0)}(k) = \left(1 - e^{a}\right)\left[x^{(0)}(1) - \frac{b}{a}\right] e^{-a(k-1)} \tag{11}$$

3 Deep Neural Networks

The development of Artificial Intelligence (AI) has undergone a profound evolution, transitioning from symbolic reasoning paradigms to statistical learning and, ultimately, to modern deep neural networks [12].

At early stages of AI were dominated by symbolic approaches, emphasizing rule-based systems and logic engines prevalent from the 1950s through the 1980s [13]. While these systems achieved success in constrained domains, they lacked robustness in dealing with uncertainty and high-dimensional data. The limitations of symbolic AI motivated the rise of machine learning (ML), which prioritized data-driven statistical models over handcrafted rules. Regression methods, decision trees, and support vector machines exemplified this era, providing greater adaptability yet still requiring extensive feature engineering [14].

Deep Neural Networks (DNNs) have emerged as one of the most powerful paradigms in artificial intelligence. Their success is grounded in the ability to model complex, nonlinear relationships from high-dimensional data [15].

A Deep Neural Network (DNN) can be formally conceptualized as a parametric function composed of multiple interconnected layers. An input vector is propagated sequentially through a hierarchy of hidden layers, for this research a demand time series, ultimately generating an output vector [16]. Within each hidden layer, an affine transformation is applied, followed by a nonlinear activation function, for this research the Rectified Linear Units (ReLU), thereby facilitating the progressive extraction of increasingly abstract features. The representational power of the model is intrinsically linked to its depth, defined by the number of stacked layers in the architecture [17].

Rectified Linear Units (ReLU) and their extensions, such as Leaky ReLU and Exponential Linear Units (ELU), have become the prevailing choice in contemporary deep learning architectures owing to their computational efficiency and ability to mitigate vanishing gradient problems. In contrast, activation functions like the sigmoid and hyperbolic tangent retain niche applications but are less commonly employed in deep models, primarily due to their susceptibility to gradient saturation [18]. Where ReLU is defined as:

$$f(x) = \max(0, x) \tag{12}$$

The objective is to design a Deep Neural Network (DNN) that takes as input the forecasting values generated by the GM (1,1) model. The architecture can be structured in a transparent and systematic manner. In this framework, we describe the configuration of the model, outline the training procedure, and detail how the DNN integrates and refines the forecasts obtained from GM (1,1). The general form would be:

$$\hat{Y}_t = GM(1, 1)_t + f_{DNN}(GM(1, 1)_t) \tag{13}$$

where:

$$\hat{Y}_t = \textit{forecast for the t period}$$

$$GM(1, 1)_t = GM\ (1, 1)\ \textit{forcast at period t}$$

$$f_{DNN}(GM(1, 1)_t) = \textit{deep denural network forecast correction}$$

The pseudo code for the proposed model would be:

Proposed Model Algorithm GMDNN (1,1)

Input: Data file in .xls or .csv format containing two columns: Period and Real_value.

Output: Results table including performance metrics and the corresponding plots

1. Initialize the required libraries (shiny, tidyverse, readxl, AER, etc.)
2. Load the data file (.xls or .csv)
3. Validate the data structure:
    4. Verify the presence of the columns Period and Real_Value.
    5. Verify the format of the Period variable
6. Validate that all values are positive and that $n \geq 4$ n≥4
7. Application of the GM (1,1) Model
8. Compute the baseline GM forecast
9. Computation of Residuals:
    10. Residual(k) = y(k) – v
11. Training of the Deep Neural Network
    12. Define the training set:
    13. DNN input: [k]; Expected output: residual(k)
14. Define the architecture of the deep neural network:
    15. Input layer: 1 neuron (time index)
    16. Hidden layers: multiple dense layers (e.g., ReLU activation)
    17. Output layer: 1 neuron with linear activation
18. Compile and train the network using the residuals as the target:
    19. Loss function: Mean Squared Error (MSE)
    20. Optimizer: Adam (or equivalent)"
21. For each future (or current) value k to be predicted:
    22. Obtain $\hat{y}(k)$ from the GM (1,1) model
    23. Predict the error $\hat{e}(k)$ using the DNN
24. Compute the corrected prediction: $\hat{y}(k)$ final = $\hat{y}(k) + \hat{e}(k)$
25. Evaluation, calculate MAPE, MAE, RMSE between y(k) and $\hat{y}(k)$ final
26. Visualize results: comparative plots between: Actual values (y), GM (1,1) forecasts ($\hat{y}$) and $\hat{y}(k)$ final

4 Neural Network Architecture Rational

In the proposed hybrid GMDNN (1,1) forecasting scheme, the residuals of the Grey Model are corrected using a feedforward neural network. The chosen network architecture comprises two hidden layers with 10 and 6 neurons, respectively, and uses randomly initialized weights and biases as implemented in the neuralnet package in R Studio.

This architectural choice is motivated by several theoretical and practical considerations.

First, the task addresses only the modeling of residuals from the GM (1,1), which typically are small but potentially nonlinear [9]. A minimal network (e.g., a single layer with only a few neurons) could fail to capture these nonlinearities; conversely, an overly complex model risks overfitting due to the scarcity of training samples.

Second, standard heuristic guidelines for network design suggest aligning the number of neurons in the first hidden layer with the input dimension and dataset size. Here, the input consists of a single variable ("GM"), yet using an expanded first layer (10 neurons) permits richer latent representations; the subsequent reduction to a 6-neuron second layer fosters refinement and abstraction in a funnel-like manner [19].

Third, bias terms are included to allow activations to shift independently of input scaling and to capture systematic offsets in residual patterns. Weight initialization with small random values breaks symmetry and enables gradient-based optimization (i.e., backpropagation) to minimize prediction errors [20].

The neural network component of the proposed hybrid GMDNN (1,1) forecasting model was designed with a focus on balancing model complexity and data availability. Given the limited dataset of ten annual observations (2015–2024) from the Port of Ensenada, the network was trained using nine data points, reserving one observation for out-of-sample validation. This partitioning strategy follows best practices in small-sample learning, ensuring that the model preserves generalization capability while maximizing the information used during training.

The chosen architecture consists of two fully connected hidden layers comprising 10 and 6 neurons, respectively. This configuration was selected through an iterative process guided by theoretical and empirical considerations. The first hidden layer with 10 neurons provides sufficient representational capacity to capture the nonlinear residual structures produced by the GM (1,1) model, enabling the network to approximate complex mappings even with minimal input dimensionality. The second layer, reduced to 6 neurons, acts as a compression and refinement stage, filtering redundant activations and promoting smoother generalization. In rigorous practice, such configurations are refined using cross-validation, model selection criteria, and error metrics such as MAPE (see Eq. 14), RMSE (see Eq. 15) or MPE (see Eq. 16) [21] .

$$MAPE = \frac{100\%}{n} \sum_{j=1}^{n} \left| \frac{x_i - \hat{x}_i}{x_i} \right| \tag{14}$$

$$RMSE = \sqrt{\frac{1}{n} \sum_{j=1}^{n} (x_i - \hat{x}_i)^2} \tag{15}$$

$$MPE = \frac{100\%}{n} \sum_{j=1}^{n} \frac{x_i - \hat{x}_i}{x_i} \tag{16}$$

The accuracy evaluation for selecting the appropriate forecasting method follows the criteria proposed by Lewis [21]. According to these guidelines, if the Mean Absolute Percentage Error (MAPE) is below 10%, the forecast is considered highly accurate; values between 10% and 20% indicate good accuracy; values between 20% and 50% represent reasonably good accuracy; and values exceeding 50% are regarded as inaccurate forecasts. These criteria are summarized in the following Table 1.

Overall, the selected (10,6) architecture achieves a pragmatic equilibrium: it is deep enough to learn meaningful nonlinear corrections to the GM (1,1) forecasts, yet parsimonious enough to maintain stability and interpretability under the constraints of small-sample data environments typical of logistics applications.

Table 1. Interpretation of Typical MAPE Values.

MAPE (%)	Forecasting power
<10	High accurate forecasting
10–20	Good forecasting
20–50	Reasonable forecasting
>50	Inaccurate forecasting

5 Example of the Application of the Combined Forecasting Model GM (1,1) and Deep Neural Network

The combination of the GM (1,1) and Deep Neural Network (GMDNN (1,1)) is demonstrated using empirical data on total TEU demand at the Port of Ensenada Mexico from 2015 to 2024 [22, 23], indicating the level of capacity required to process ocean containers and the required infrastructure.

The monthly demand data for the last 10 years Table 2.

Table 2. Demand ocean containers (TEU's) at the Ensenada port from 2015 through 2024.

Year	Period	Observed Data
2015	1	193420
2016	2	191708
2017	3	230185
2018	4	272587
2019	5	337742
2020	6	384871
2021	7	394911
2022	8	436019
2023	9	462176
2024	10	434765

The resulting GM (1,1) forecast, the **a** and **b** parameters, and the chosen network architecture comprises two hidden layers with 10 and 6 neurons and the application of neuralnet in R Studio (the hybrid GM + DNNN model proposal forecast) are shown in Table 3.

The general resulting equation is shown in Eq. 13

$$\hat{x}^{(0)}(k) = \left(1 - e^{-0.1126539}\right)\left[x^{(0)}(1) - \frac{187820.4}{-0.1126539}\right]e^{-(-0.1126539)(k-1)} \tag{17}$$

a = -0.1126539

b = 187820.4

Table 3. The GM (1, 1) and the hybrid GM + DNNN model proposal forecast results from 2010–2024.

Year	Period	Observed Data	GM	Hybrid GM+ DNN
2015	1	193420	193420	193420
2016	2	191708	221872.7	221872.7
2017	3	230185	248329.8	248329.8
2018	4	272587	277941.7	277941.7
2019	5	337742	311084.7	311084.7
2020	6	384871	348179.8	348179.8
2021	7	394911	389698.4	389698.4
2022	8	436019	436167.7	436167.7
2023	9	462176	488178.3	488178.3
2024	10	434765	546390.8	544984.1

Figure 1 illustrates the forecasting performance comparison among the GM (1,1), ARIMA, and the proposed hybrid GM (1,1) + DNN model against the actual demand values. The GM (1,1) model provides reasonable accuracy under scarce data conditions, reflecting its advantage under non-stationary and nonlinear environments. By contrast, the hybrid GM (1,1) + DNN consistently outperforms, as evidenced by lower error metrics (MAPE = 7.53%, MPE = -3.82%, RMSE = 40605.80). The DNN correction enhances the baseline GM (1,1) forecasts by effectively modeling residual nonlinearities, resulting in closer alignment with observed demand trajectories. This performance demonstrates the methodological advantage of integrating Grey System Theory with neural architectures, combining data efficiency and interpretability with adaptive nonlinear learning, thereby offering a robust solution for demand forecasting under uncertainty.

Figure 2 shows the architecture of the proposed hybrid neural network used to refine the GM (1,1) forecasts by modeling residual errors. The network is structured as a feedforward deep neural network with one input node corresponding to the GM (1,1) output, two hidden layers composed of 10 and 6 neurons respectively, and a single output neuron representing the predicted residual.

The connections include weighted parameters (black) and bias terms (blue), which allow the network to capture nonlinear dependencies and systematic offsets within the residual patterns.

This configuration balances complexity and parsimony: while the first hidden layer enables richer feature extraction, the second layer refines these representations, minimizing the risk of overfitting in data-scarce contexts.

Overall, the diagram illustrates how the hybrid GM (1,1) + DNN model integrates grey forecasting with adaptive learning, thereby enhancing predictive accuracy and robustness in demand forecasting under uncertainty.

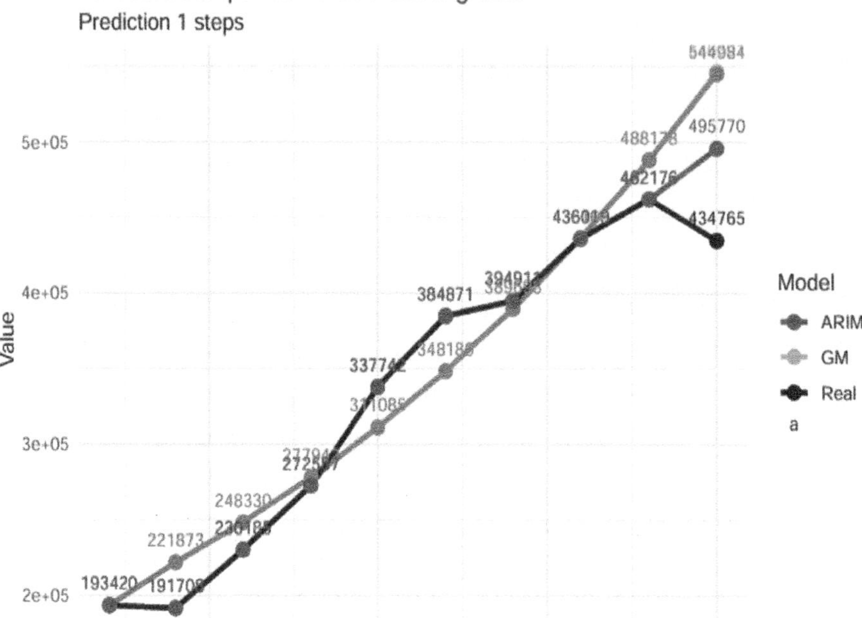

Fig. 1. Comparative analysis of demand forecasting results between GM (1,1) and the proposed GM (1,1) + DNN

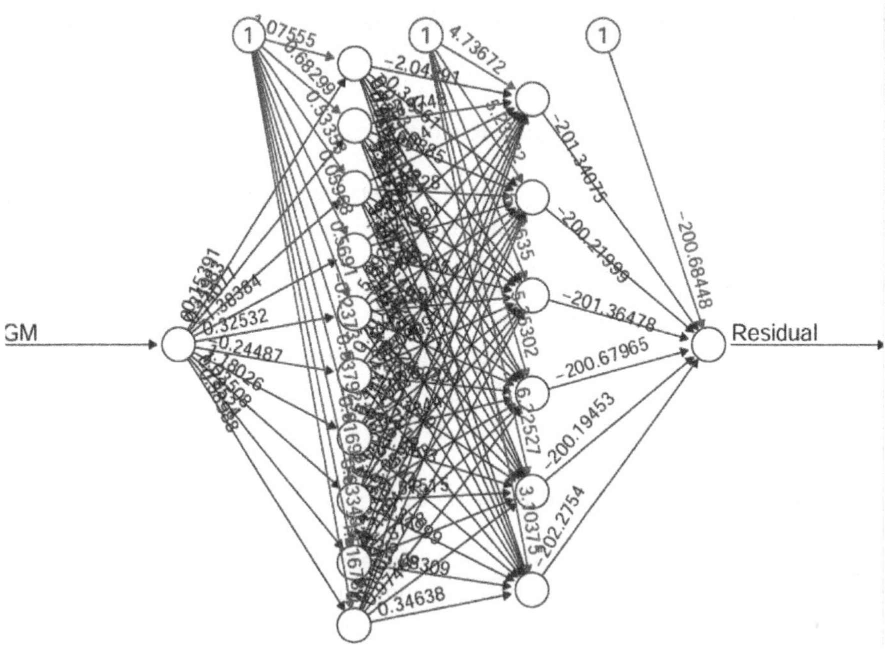

Fig. 2. Architecture of the proposed hybrid neural network used to refine the GM (1,1) forecasts by modeling residual errors.

6 Model Performance Evaluation

The model performance is evaluated by the Mean percentage of error Equation (MPE), Mean Absolute Percentage of Error (MAPE) and Root Mean Square of Error (RMSE). The smaller the values, the greater the accuracy.

In Table 4, a comparison among the different methods can be found where the hybrid GM (1,1) + DNN model excels the traditional GM (1,1).

Table 4. Forecast performance metrics comparison.

	GM (1,1)	Hybrid GM (1,1) + DNNN
MPE	-3.82%	-3.78%
MAPE	7.57%	7.53%
RMSE	40605.80	40219.68

The integration of the Grey Model GM (1,1) with a deep neural network offers significant advantages for demand forecasting. While standalone GM (1,1) already ensures a high level of predictive accuracy, its hybridization with a deep neural network extends the forecasting capability by generating ranges that incorporate varying degrees of greyness, thereby enhancing support for decision-making under uncertainty. The proposed framework is straightforward to implement and allows for the inclusion of user expertise, for instance by adapting the transition matrix to embed organization-specific knowledge.

7 Comparative Analysis with Recent Work.

While the models proposed by Hao and Ma (2024) [24], Xie et al. (2025) [25], and Duan et al. (2024) [26] delve into the theoretical integration between deep learning and Grey System Theory, this research contributes a more applied and efficient perspective, specifically oriented toward logistics decision-making under data limitations.

The main novelty of this work lies in its pragmatic, reproducible, and transparent approach, which effectively balances the interpretability and analytical rigor of the classical GM (1,1) model with the adaptive learning capacity of deep neural networks, without relying on large-scale datasets.

8 Conclusions and Future Research.

The combined application of the GM (1,1) model and Deep Neural Networks demonstrates notable advantages for demand forecasting within logistics contexts. The proposed approach is straightforward to implement, leverages readily available system information, and incorporates a novel integration of artificial intelligence into grey system theory.

Compared with traditional forecasting techniques, such as ARIMA, the hybrid model enhances decision-making by explicitly addressing greyness and uncertainty, while also reducing computational burden through standard R packages (e.g., neuralnet) and requiring only minimal mathematical formulation [8].

The findings presented are consistent with prior studies on GM (1,1)-based forecasting yet extend the applicability of the method by enabling hybridization with neural architecture. Future improvements could be achieved by exploring alternative activation functions. For example, the Sigmoid function is particularly suitable for probability modeling but may require additional transformations for large inputs; the Hyperbolic Tangent (tanh) function offers advantages near zero but still suffers from vanishing gradients at extreme values; and the Parametric ReLU (PReLU) mitigates the need for manual parameter tuning, though it introduces additional learnable variables, which may increase overfitting risks in small datasets—a common limitation in supply chain forecasting.

Although the hybrid framework successfully alleviates the issue of data scarcity, it relies on the assumption that residuals exhibit stable nonlinear dynamics that can be captured by DNN. However, this assumption may fail under sudden regime shifts such as pandemic disruptions, trade conflicts, or abrupt policy changes. Incorporating adaptive or online learning mechanisms in future extensions could enhance the model's ability to respond to structural breaks.

Overall, this hybrid methodology offers a valuable alternative when limited data is available, providing a practical balance between analytical rigor and expert judgment, and enabling robust decision support under uncertainty with minimal computational complexity.

References

1. Goltsos, T.E., Syntetos, A.A., Glock, C.H., Ioannou, G.: Inventory – forecasting: mind the gap. Eur. J. Oper. Res. **299**(2022), 397–419 (2022)
2. Ghribi, Y., Graha, E.R., Wicaksono, H.: Comparative analysis of statistical and machine learning models for enhancing demand forecasting accuracy in the medical device industry. ScienceDirect. **134**(2025), 849–854 (2025)
3. Wahedi, H.J., Heltoft, M., Christophersen, G.J., Severinsen, T., Saha, S., Nielsen, I.E.: Forecasting and inventory planning: an empirical investigation of classical and machine learning approaches for Svanehøj's future software consolidation. Appl. Sci. **13**(8581), 1–21 (2023)
4. Petropoulos, F., et al.: Forecasting: theory andpractice. Int. J. Forecast. **38**(2022), 705–871 (2022)
5. Alzubaidi, L., et al.: A survey on deep learning tools dealing with data scarcity: definitions, challenges, solutions, tips, and applications. J. Big Data. **10**, 1–82 (2023)
6. Sattar, M.U., Dattana, V., Hasan, R., Mahmood, S., Khan, H.W., Hussain, S.: Enhancing supply chain management: a comparative study of machine learning techniques with cost–accuracy and ESG-based evaluation for forecasting and risk mitigation. Sustainability. **17**(5772), 1–45 (2025)
7. Tulli, S.k.C.: Comparative analysis of traditional and AI-based demand forecasting. Int. J. Emerg. Trends Sci. Technol. **7**(6), 6933–6956 (2020)
8. Xie, N., Wei, B.: Grey forecasting. In: Mechanism, Models and Applications. Springer (2024)
9. Rathnayaka, R.K.T., Seneviratna, D., Jianguo, W., Arumawadu, H.I.: An unbiased GM(1,1)-based new hybrid approach for time series forecasting. Grey Syst. Theory Appl. **6**(3), 322–340 (2016)
10. Wi̧ecek, P., Kubek, D.: The impact time series selected characteristics on the fuel Demand Forecasting effectiveness based on autoregressive models and Markov chains. Energies. **17**(4163), 1–18 (2024)
11. Liu, S., Lin, Y.: Grey systems. In: Theory and Applications. Springer (2010)
12. Liang, B., Wang, Y., Tong, C.: AI reasoning in deep learning era: from symbolic AI to neural–symbolic AI. Mathematics. **13**(1707), 1–42 (2025)
13. He, R., Cao, J., Tan, T.: Generative artificial intelligence: a historical perspective. Natl. Sci. Rev. **12**(050), 1–15 (2025)
14. Panchendrarajan, R., Zubiaga, A.: Synergizing machinelearning & symbolic methods: a survey on hybrid approaches to natural language processing. Expert Syst. Appl. **251**(2024), 1–15 (2024)
15. LeCun, Y., Bengio, Y., Hinton, G.: Deep learning. Nature. **521**, 1–10 (2015)
16. Koutsoukas, A., Monaghan, K.J., Li, X., Huan, J.: Deep-learning: investigating deep neural networks hyper-parameters and comparison of performance to shallow methods for modeling bioactivity data. J. Cheminform. **9**(42), 1–13 (2017)
17. Alzubaidi, L., et al.: Review of deep learning: concepts, CNN architectures, challenges, applications, future directions. J. Big Data. **8**(53), 1–74 (2021)
18. Iglesias, L.L., et al.: A primer on deep learning and convolutional neural networks for clinicians. Insights Imaging. **12**(117), 1–11 (2021)
19. Hao, Y., Ma, X.: AHybrid GreySystem model based on stacked long short-term memory layers and its application in energy consumption forecasting. PRO. **12**(1749), 1–28 (2024)
20. Zhou, D.: Optimization Modeling for GM(1,1) model based on BP neural network I. J. Comput. Netw. Inf. Secur. **2012**(1), 24–30 (2012)
21. Lewis, C.D.: Industrial and Business Forecasting Methods: Apractical Guide to Exponential Smoothing and Curve Fitting. Butterworth Scientific, London (1982)

22. A. d. S. d. P. e. México, Estadísticas publicas ASIPONA Ensenada, [En línea]. Available: https://www.puertoensenada.com.mx/estadisticas-publicas. [Último acceso: 14 Octubre 2025].
23. C. G. d. P. y. M. Mercante, Informe estadístico de los puertos de México, [En línea]. Available: https://www.gob.mx/puertosymarinamercante/acciones-y-programas/informe-estadistico-de-los-puertos-de-mexico-2024. [Último acceso: 14 Octubre 2025].
24. Xie, W., Zhao, R., Xu, Z., Liang, T.: Grey-informed neural network for time-series forecasting. Neurocomputing. **649**(2025), 1–12 (2025)
25. Duan, H., He, C., Pu, S.: A new circular neural grey model and its application to CO2 emissions in China. J. Clean. Prod. **445**(2024), 2–14 (2024)

Multi Criteria Approach to the Social Portfolio Problem for Circular Economy Projects in Smart Cities: A Case Study in Guadalajara

Víctor Ledesma[1(✉)], Rocío Maciel[1], Víctor Larios[1], and Alberto Ochoa[2]

[1] Universidad de Guadalajara, Periférico Norte N° 799 Núcleo Universitario, C. Prol. Belenes, 45100 Zapopan, Jalisco, Mexico
victor.ledesma0975@alumnos.udg.mx
[2] Universidad Autónoma de Ciudad Juárez, Av. Plutarco Elías Calles #1210 Fovissste Chamizal, C.P. 32310 Ciudad Juárez, Chihuahua, Mexico

Abstract. The Social Portfolio Problem (SPP) addresses the challenge of selecting the most appropriate subset of social projects under constraints of budget, time, and impact. In the context of Guadalajara, one of Mexico's most prominent urban centers in smart city development, there is a growing need for an optimization-based decision support model that evaluates and prioritizes circular economy oriented social initiatives. This paper presents a multi-criteria selection framework integrating mathematical modeling and evolutionary algorithms namely Genetic Algorithm (GA) and Particle Swarm Optimization (PSO) to identify an optimal project portfolio that maximizes social benefit, minimizes costs, and enhances environmental impact within a 12–18-month implementation period. Over 100 real world project proposals in Guadalajara were codified and analyzed using criteria such as population reach, cost, duration, useful life, inter-project synergy, and relevance to recycling and electronic waste (RAEE).

The results indicate that the GA achieved faster convergence, while PSO provided a more diverse solution set. The proposed model supports transparent, data-driven decision-making for allocating public funds in sustainable urban development.

Keywords: Social Portfolio Problem (SPP) · Multi Criteria Decision-Making (MCDM) · Circular Economy (CE) · Genetic Algorithm (GA) · Particle Swarm Optimization (PSO) · Recycling · Smart Cities · Guadalajara

1 Introduction

The Social Portfolio Problem (SPP) refers to the challenge of selecting a set of social development projects from a larger pool, under limited resources such as budget, time, and technical capacity. Unlike traditional portfolio selection models focused on financial returns, the SPP prioritizes social impact, equity, sustainability, and sometimes environmental considerations. This problem as a multi-objective selection scenario, where

L. Martínez-Villaseñor et al. (Eds.): MICAI 2025 Workshops, LNAI 16264, pp. 261–269, 2026.
https://doi.org/10.1007/978-3-032-17930-2_18

each project is assessed according to a set of criteria such as population reached, cost, duration, and synergy. Their approach introduced the novel idea of integrating synergy among projects, acknowledging that certain initiatives, when implemented together, produce greater collective impact than when executed separately [1]. In urban contexts like Guadalajara, the SPP becomes particularly relevant due to the variety of proposals emerging from local stakeholders, community groups, and institutions aiming to address issues such as waste management, social exclusion, and environmental degradation. However, public institutions often face budgetary restrictions and lack standardized methodologies to prioritize which projects to fund.

Moreover, contemporary challenges such as e-waste management, electronic reuse, and circular economy implementation require that project portfolios be not only socially impactful but also aligned with environmental objectives. Circular economy frameworks demand systemic thinking and strategic selection of interconnected initiatives [2]. Therefore, this research adapts the SPP methodology to the specific case of sustainability-focused project selection in Guadalajara, integrating both classical criteria (cost, coverage, duration) and circular economy relevance, to support data driven public investment decisions.

2 Related Work

Previous studies on project portfolio optimization have applied Multi-Criteria Decision-Making (MCDM) and evolutionary algorithms to social and environmental contexts. For instance, Rivera et al. [1] proposed a synergy-based portfolio selection algorithm to enhance overall social benefit. Similar approaches have been applied to circular economy planning [6, 7], while AI-based optimization has been integrated into smart city management [8].

However, few studies have specifically addressed the Social Portfolio Problem (SPP) in the context of urban circular economy initiatives. The novelty of this paper lies in the integration of MCDM, circular economy indicators, and evolutionary algorithms (GA and PSO) within a single decision-support framework applied to real world data from Guadalajara.

3 Problem Definition in Guadalajara

In the specific case of Guadalajara, the SPP takes the form of a competition among nearly 120 candidate projects related to recycling, circular economy, and community-based sustainability. However, the local government has limited financial and logistical resources, which constrains the number of projects that can be funded. In practice, only around 30 projects can be selected, given a fixed budget of 120,000 MXN and a limited implementation window of 12 to 18 months.

This situation creates a need for an intelligent decision support system capable of evaluating and prioritizing projects in a transparent and systematic way. The proposed system codifies all project instances and uses optimization techniques to identify those initiatives with the highest projected social impact, environmental contribution, and synergy potential. The output of the system is not only a ranked list of projects, but also a visual map that highlights the geographical distribution of the selected initiatives across Guadalajara. This allows policymakers to better understand how resources will be allocated, and which areas will be favored under the selected portfolio.

From a methodological perspective, classical approaches to the SPP can be divided into two main categories:

1. Mathematical modeling, which formulates the selection process as a multi-objective optimization problem with explicit constraints such as budget and project duration.
2. Evolutionary algorithms, such as Genetic Algorithms (GA) and Particle Swarm Optimization (PSO), which simulate adaptive processes to explore a large solution space and identify near-optimal project combinations.

In this research, both perspectives are integrated: the mathematical model establishes the formal constraints and objectives, while the evolutionary algorithms are employed to search for feasible solutions under real-world complexity. The system is designed to compare the performance of both approaches, identify which technique provides the most efficient solution, and select the final portfolio accordingly. The ultimate restriction is financial: given the budget ceiling, many projects will necessarily remain unfunded. Nevertheless, the purpose of this framework is to ensure that the projects with the highest collective social and environmental benefits are prioritized, rather than relying on subjective or political decision-making.

This model aims to serve as a foundation for the design of evidence-based public policy in Jalisco, ensuring that social investment decisions in the field of circular economy and sustainability are both optimized and socially equitable.

4 Conceptual Framework

4.1 Circular Economy in Urban Development

The circular economy (CE) is a regenerative model that promotes resource efficiency, waste reduction, and systemic sustainability. In urban contexts, CE strategies are increasingly integrated into infrastructure planning, public policy, and digital innovation. A neural network-based model has been proposed to forecast urban CE growth, demonstrating its utility in aligning economic and environmental goals [3]. A systematic review has also linked CE with complexity theory, emphasizing adaptive governance and circular planning in cities [4].

4.2 Smart Cities and Sustainability Integration

Smart cities leverage digital infrastructure, data analytics, and participatory governance to enhance urban functionality and sustainability. A framework comprising six foundational pillars smart economy, environment, governance, living, mobility, and people has been proposed to support sustainable development through intelligent systems [5]. This structure aligns with circular economy principles by enabling real-time monitoring, resource optimization, and citizen engagement.

The integration of circular economy strategies into smart city planning fosters hybrid models of urban sustainability, particularly in Latin American contexts such as Guadalajara.

4.3 Multi-criteria Decision-Making (MCDM)

Multi-Criteria Decision-Making (MCDM) methods are essential for evaluating circular economy initiatives under complex, multidimensional criteria. A systematic review of MCDM applications in circular economy and cost assessment has highlighted the effectiveness of techniques such as AHP, TOPSIS, and PROMETHEE in balancing environmental, economic, and social indicators [6]. These approaches support transparent decision-making in public investment, particularly when selecting projects under resource constraints and sustainability objectives.

4.4 Measuring Circularity with MCDM Techniques

A total of 22 Multi-Criteria Decision-Making (MCDM) techniques and 36 circular economy (CE) indicators across micro-, meso-, and macro-levels have been identified, forming a comprehensive framework for assessing circular performance [7]. This structured evaluation approach plays a critical role in guiding CE policy formulation and project prioritization.

4.5 AI-Enable Optimization in Smart Cities

The role of artificial intelligence (AI) in circular economy (CE) management within smart cities has been examined, highlighting how IoT and machine learning technologies can enhance waste reduction and resource efficiency [8]. These approaches support the development of synergy-aware models for selecting CE-oriented social projects, contributing to systemic impact and data-driven urban governance.

5 Methodology

This research adopts an exploratory, pilot-study approach to design and test a decision support system for the Social Portfolio Problem (SPP) in Guadalajara. Figure 1 illustrates the methodological framework as a block diagram, including the initial instance constructed with two recycling centers and two repair cafés, connected through a sample route generated by the algorithm. The diagram summarizes the stages of project codification, mathematical formulation, algorithmic optimization, and decision-support visualization.

The methodology combines mathematical modeling and evolutionary algorithms to evaluate and prioritize circular economy projects under real-world constraints of budget, time, and social impact.

Project Instance Codification

A total of nearly 120 candidate projects were codified as "instances." Each project was characterized by the following criteria:

- Cost (MXN) - estimated financial requirement.
- Duration (months) - expected implementation time, limited to 12–18 months.
- Population reach - number of direct and indirect beneficiaries.
- Useful life - sustainability of the project's outcomes beyond implementation.

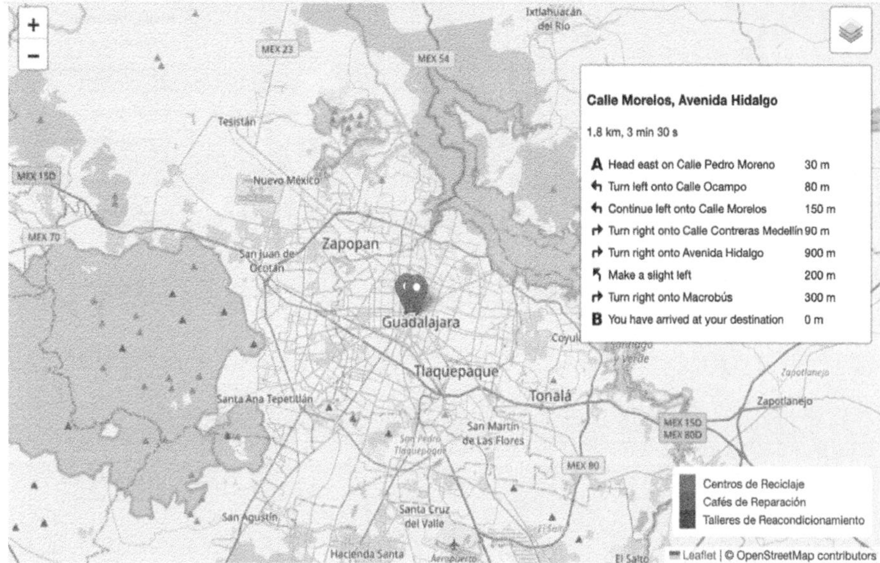

Fig. 1. Instance of the circular economy map in Guadalajara with two recycling centers and two repair cafés, including a sample route generated by the algorithm.

- Synergy - degree of complementarity with other projects in the portfolio.
- Circular economy relevance - alignment with recycling, reuse, or resource recovery practices.

Figure 2 illustrates the extended instance, including multiple recycling centers, repair cafés, and refurbishment workshops, demonstrating the complexity of real-world scenarios.

These attributes were normalized and transformed into comparable decision variables, ensuring the model could evaluate heterogeneous projects within a single framework.

Mathematical Model

The selection process was first formalized as a multi-objective optimization problem, with the following elements:

Objective functions:

1. Maximize total social benefit (population × project relevance).
2. Maximize environmental impact (circular economy contribution).
3. Minimize total cost under budgetary restrictions.

Constraints:

- Budget ceiling of 120,000 MXN.
- Project duration $\leq$18 months.
- Only ~30 projects can be selected.

Fig. 2. Extended instance including multiple recycling centers, repair cafés, and refurbishment workshops, demonstrating the complexity of real-world scenarios.

This formulation allows the problem to be expressed as a 0–1 selection model, where each project is either included or excluded from the final portfolio.

Evolutionary Algorithms

To address the combinatorial complexity of the problem, two metaheuristic techniques were employed:

- Genetic Algorithms (GA): simulate natural selection through crossover and mutation operators to explore feasible project combinations.
- Particle Swarm Optimization (PSO): models the collective behavior of agents to converge toward optimal or near-optimal solutions.

Both algorithms were executed on the same dataset of project instances, allowing a comparative evaluation of performance in terms of solution quality and computational efficiency. Beyond the portfolio selection process, the system also provides geospatial support by generating feasible routes among selected nodes. As shown in Fig. 3, the system can generate optimized routes among selected project nodes, supporting decision-makers in visualizing geographical feasibility.

Output and Decision Support

The system produces two types of output:

1. A ranked list of selected projects, highlighting those that deliver the highest combined social and environmental benefits under the available budget.
2. A geospatial map showing the distribution of funded projects across Guadalajara, enabling policymakers to visualize coverage and equity of resource allocation.

By integrating mathematical constraints with heuristic search techniques, this methodology ensures that final decisions are both optimized and transparent, providing a robust foundation for public policy design in Jalisco.

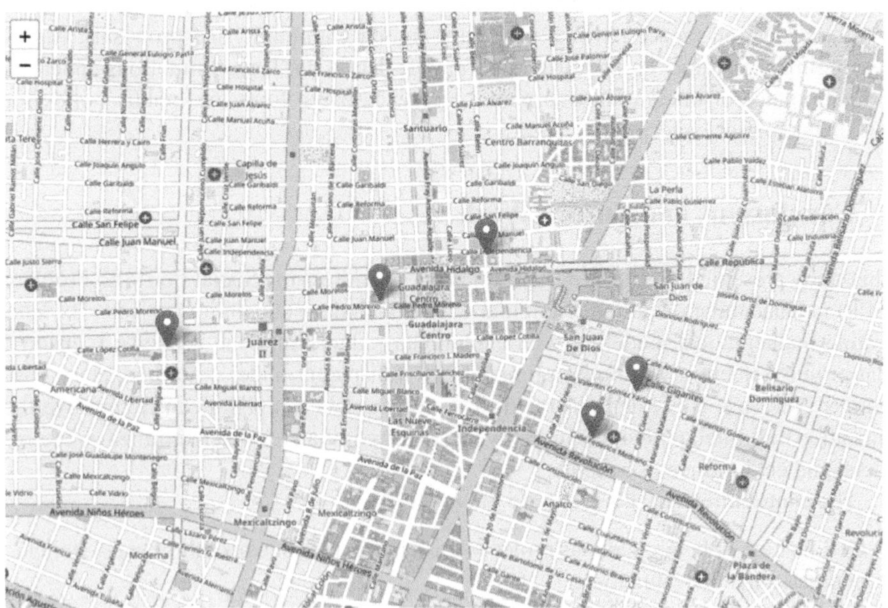

Fig. 3. Example of route optimization among selected nodes, supporting the visualization of geographical feasibility for prioritized projects.

From a practical perspective, the optimized routes generated among selected projects are used as analogies for the allocation of public resources, where each "path" represents a possible funding flow between complementary initiatives. Thus, distance minimization corresponds to efficient resource distribution within the circular economy network.

6 Result and Discussion

The framework was applied to a dataset of 120 candidate projects, including recycling centers, repair cafés, and refurbishment workshops. Two optimization strategies were tested: mathematical modeling and evolutionary algorithms (GA and PSO).

Comparative Analysis. The Genetic Algorithm (GA) achieved faster convergence, finding optimal portfolios within approximately 100 iterations, while the Particle Swarm Optimization (PSO) required nearly 180 iterations to stabilize but provided more diverse feasible portfolios. Performance Metrics. The average computation time for GA was 12.5 s, compared to 18.2 s for PSO. GA produced higher social impact scores (0.83) but slightly lower environmental impact scores (0.78) than PSO (0.81 and 0.82, respectively). Sensitivity Analysis. When the available budget was increased by 20%, the model selected 36 projects instead of 30, with a 17% improvement in total social coverage. When reduced by 20%, project coverage dropped by 25%, confirming that synergy factors play a crucial role in maintaining efficiency under resource constraints.

Critical Discussion. Despite these results, practical challenges remain regarding data quality, political feasibility, and implementation costs. The system assumes consistent project evaluation metrics, which may vary among community led proposals. Moreover, political priorities could affect final funding decisions. These limitations underline the importance of integrating transparent, evidence-based tools into public policy for sustainable project selection.

7 Conclusions and Future Work

This study presented a multi-criteria framework to address the Social Portfolio Problem (SPP) in Guadalajara, applied to circular economy and sustainability projects. By integrating mathematical modeling with evolutionary algorithms, the framework ensured that project selection was both optimized and transparent under strict budgetary constraints. The case study demonstrated that such models can significantly improve the allocation of limited public resources by prioritizing initiatives that maximize collective social and environmental benefits.

The contributions of this work are threefold:

1. Codification of heterogeneous projects into a unified framework, allowing systematic comparison and evaluation.
2. Incorporation of synergy among projects, capturing the additional value that emerges when complementary initiatives are implemented jointly.
3. Decision-support outputs that combine ranked project lists with geospatial visualizations, enhancing interpretability for policymakers.

As future work, the development of a decision-support application is envisioned. This application would enable citizens to submit RAEE pickup requests through a mobile/web interface, while local governments process these inputs using the optimization engine. The system would then generate optimized routes, ranked project portfolios, and interactive maps, ensuring transparent and data-driven policymaking. A conceptual sketch of this proposed application is shown in Fig. 4, where the smartphone-based interface serves as the connection between citizens, the optimization model, and local authorities.

Furthermore, future research should include empirical validation of model performance using real funding outcomes from municipal programs. Integrating cost-benefit indicators and qualitative community feedback could improve robustness and ensure equitable prioritization across diverse urban zones.

The long-term vision includes integrating explainable AI (XAI) to enhance interpretability of prioritization results, as well as coupling the platform with municipal databases and IoT infrastructure for real-time monitoring of recycling activities and social outcomes. By advancing toward this direction, Guadalajara can strengthen its transition to a circular economy while ensuring equitable and efficient use of public resources.

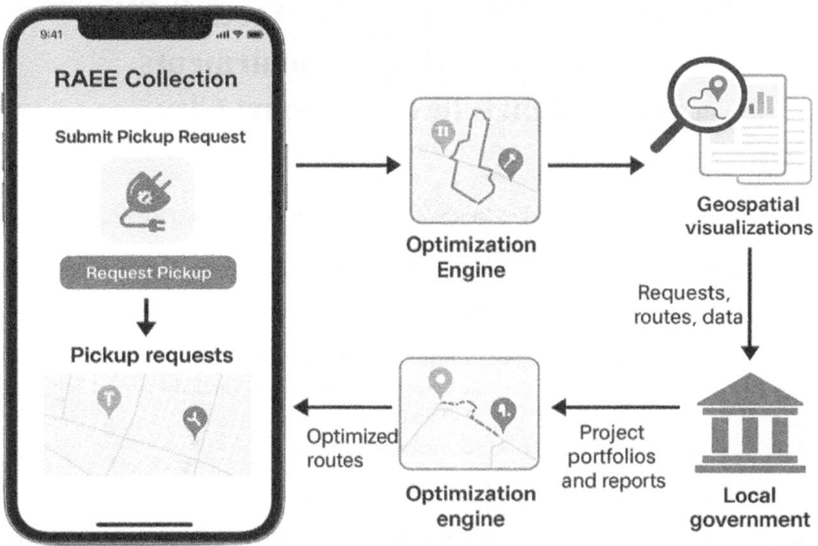

Fig. 4. Conceptual design of a decision-support application for RAEE collection in Guadalajara. The smartphone interface connects citizens' pickup requests with the optimization engine, generating optimized routes, geospatial maps, and ranked project portfolios.

References

1. Rivera, G., Gómez, C.G., Fernández, E.R., Cruz, L., Castillo, O., Bastiani, S.S.: Handling of synergy into an algorithm for project portfolio selection. In: Castillo, O., Melin, P., Kacprzyk, J. (eds.) Recent Advances on Hybrid Intelligent Systems. SCI, vol. 451, pp. 417–430. Springer, Heidelberg (2013). https://doi.org/10.1007/978-3-642-33021-6_33
2. Masterson, K., Shine, T.: The circular economy: a shift to sustainable systems. (2022)
3. Liu, Y.: Innovation of urban circular economy growth path based on neural network. IEEE Access **11**, 132456–132465 (2023)
4. Abujder Ochoa, W.A., García, M.A., Rodríguez, J.M.: Interlinking urban sustainability, circular economy and complexity: a systematic literature review. Sustainability **17**(15), 7118 (2025)
5. Sharma, S.K., Singh, A.K.: Smart cities for sustainability – an analytical perspective. In: Proceedings of the 2020 WorldS4 Conference, pp. 1–6 (2020)
6. Tighnavard, A., Aldrovandi, S., Sher, W.: A systematic review of implementing multi-criteria decision-making (MCDM) approaches for the circular economy and cost assessment. Sustainability **17**(11), 5007 (2025)
7. Santos Gonçalves, P.V., Campos, L.M.S.: A systemic review for measuring circular economy with multi-criteria methods. Environ. Sci. Pollut. Res. **29**, 31597–31611 (2022)
8. Jogarao, M., Lakshmanna, B.C., Naidu, S.T.: AI-enabled circular economy management for sustainable smart cities. In: Kandpal, V., et al. (eds.) Smart Cities and Circular Economy, pp. 83–96. Emerald Publishing, Leeds (2024)

Towards Full Technological Accessibility: Children with Motor Impairments in the Amenities of a Smart City

Silvia Fabiola González Macías[1](✉) and Alberto Ochoa Zezzati[2]

[1] University of Guadalajara, Periférico Norte 799 Núcleo Universitario, C. Prol. Belenes, 45100 Zapopan, Jalisco, Mexico
silvia.gonzalez5815@alumnos.udg.mx
[2] Autonomous University of Ciudad Juárez, Av. Plutarco Elías Calles 1210 Fovissste Chamizal, C.P., 32310 Ciudad Juárez, Chihuahua, Mexico
alberto.ochoa@uacj.mx

Abstract.. A smart metropolis promotes social inclusion through adaptive technologies that go beyond operational efficiency . This research applies Artificial Intelligence (AI) to smart city environments, proposing an accessible navigation system to redesign traditional urban infrastructures as genuinely inclusive spaces. The Guadalajara Zoo serves as a living laboratory to validate these solutions, focusing on children with motor disabilities and functional hearing impairments. The methodology implements Dijkstra's algorithm to calculate optimal, personalized routes, considering granular variables such as distance, slope, pavement type, obstacles, and the user's specific mobility profile. Computational simulation of the model successfully generated consistent itineraries for three accessibility profiles (wheelchairs, crutches, and strollers) within a 60-minute window. The results showed an optimized visit capacity ranging from 4 to 12 points of interest per hour, depending on the depth of the visit and the mode of mobility. In a typical visit scenario (~5 min/stop), the optimized model allowed a child in a pushchair to visit 6 to 7 habitats in one hour. The system personalizes the experience by calculating the distance and total time based on the user's available time and needs, demonstrating an improvement of up to 25% in route efficiency compared to non-adapted routes. These findings validate the model as a scalable solution for inclusive mobility in smart environments. The prototype ensures an autonomous, safe, and enriching experience, positioning AI as a key mediator of spatial justice.

Keywords: Motor disability · Accessibility · Social Incusion · Dijkstra's Algorithms · Artificial Intelligence · Smart Cities

1 Introduction

Motor disability is a multidimensional condition that transcends individual physical limitations, arising from the complex interaction between personal abilities and environmental barriers or facilitators. Conceptually, it represents an alteration in the neuromuscular system that affects the control, coordination, and execution of body movement.

L. Martínez-Villaseñor et al. (Eds.): MICAI 2025 Workshops, LNAI 16264, pp. 270–288, 2026.
https://doi.org/10.1007/978-3-032-17930-2_19

This biomedical definition is enriched from an ecosystemic perspective that integrates three fundamental dimensions: the physical, understood as the inherent biological condition; the social, which encompasses architectural and accessibility contexts; and the experiential, which involves the impact on quality of life, autonomy, and comprehensive development [1]. There are 6,179,890 people with disabilities living in Mexico, representing 4.9% of the total population. Of this group, approximately 58.3% have motor disabilities, and within this category, around 1.5% are children who require mobility assistance devices. In Jalisco, there are 386,577 people with disabilities (4.6% of the 8.3 million inhabitants), with an estimated 11.3% living with motor disabilities. However, there are no official breakdowns specifying the exact percentage of children (under 18 years of age) within this group. Indirect estimates suggest a representation of between 1% and 3% of the state total [2, 3]. This analysis focuses specifically on children with reduced mobility and functional hearing who require assistive devices such as *wheelchairs, crutches, or strollers*. These children face multiple architectural and environmental barriers that hinder their safe, independent, and comfortable movement in public spaces. The presence of uneven terrain, steps, or unstable surfaces limits their access to certain locations, restricting their full socio-educational participation. In addition, excessive distances to points of interest reduce opportunities for meaningful interaction, generating frustration, feelings of exclusion, and above-average levels of physical fatigue. It is crucial to recognize that these conditions are heterogeneous, as each child has unique needs and abilities [4]. Given this landscape of physical and social challenges, it is imperative to integrate technological solutions based on artificial intelligence for the creation of smart zoological spaces. This integration, framed within the Smart Cities model, represents a significant opportunity to ensure the development and full inclusion of this population. The Guadalajara Zoo functions as a living laboratory to validate the implementation of these innovative measures. Smart technologies represent effective solutions by providing ideal conditions for the fulfillment of the Sustainable Development Goals (SDGs). In particular, SDG 11 emphasizes the importance of ensuring safe, inclusive, and accessible public spaces. This principle aligns with the development of models optimized through artificial intelligence, capable of predicting appropriate responses based on specific user needs, framing these solutions within the context of full digital accessibility for smart environments [5]. This study proposes a replicable methodology for contexts facing challenges of comparable magnitude, while maintaining the flexibility necessary for adaptation to specific conditions. The structure of the document is organized as follows: Sect. 2 reviews related work; Sect. 3 addresses aspects related to motor disabilities, obstacles to the zoo visit experience, the conceptual framework of Smart Cities, and accessibility; Sect. 4 develops the implementation of Dijkstra's algorithm in the habitat park; Sect. 5 presents the results obtained; Sect. 6 offers a discussion of the findings; and Sect. 7 presents the conclusions, future research directions, and limitations of the model.

2 Related Work

The development of the proposed intelligent navigation system intersects three main areas of research: the application of graph theory in routing problems, the development of accessible navigation systems, and the role of Artificial Intelligence (AI) in the Smart

City paradigm. This section reviews relevant literature to contextualize the current work and highlight its contribution to filling existing gaps, especially in the context of personalized accessibility for complex sistems. Previous studies have explored the integration of accessibility systems in computer vision + AI: the future of accessibility by detecting individual needs, recognizing reduced mobility, universal accessibility, safety, and service optimization, providing firm steps towards inclusion and connection to the smart cities of the future for accessibility in urban environments; Applied shortest path algorithms to optimize pedestrian mobility for users with of other various capacities. Other research has focused on the role of smart city infrastructure in promoting inclusive design However, few and almost no works address accessibility for children with motor disabilities in recreational-educational environments, which highlights the novelty of this study, positioning the analysis at the forefront of knowledge. [26, 27].

2.1 Graph Theory and Weighted Routing

Classic pathfinding research is dominated by algorithms derived from graph theory, such as Dijkstra's algorithm and the *A search algorithm**. While the efficiency of these algorithms in minimizing path costs (typically distance or time) is widely recognized in fields like logistics and standard Global Positioning System (GPS) applications, their adaptation to specialized environments requires the introduction of complex cost functions. Traditional routing models often assume homogeneous travel conditions, which leads to solutions that are suboptimal or entirely unusable for individuals with reduced mobility. Recent studies in this area focus on transforming the static distance cost into a dynamic, multi-objective cost. For instance, works addressing vehicular traffic often include factors like fuel consumption or emissions as edge weights. Our approach extends this multi-objective weighting to the accessibility domain, where weights are determined by factors such as the degree of slope, pavement texture, and the presence of micro-obstacles, fundamentally transforming a standard metric problem into a personalized accessibility optimization problem. This strategy allows the path cost to represent the actual physical effort and safety risk for a specific user profile (e.g., crutches or wheelchair).

2.2 Accessible and Inclusive Navigation System

The concept of universal accessibility, defined in a previous section, has been translated into technological solutions such as personalized route planners. Much of the current literature in inclusive technology focuses on large-scale urban contexts. Initiatives like AccessMap or similar applications have successfully integrated accessibility data (curb cuts, ramps) into street networks [9]. However, these systems often face challenges related to the granularity of data: they are effective at the city block level but lack the detailed information required for complex, unstructured spaces like parks, university campuses, or zoos, which have highly variable micro-topographies. Further more, existing solutions generally cater to generic profiles (e.g., "wheelchair user"). A critical gap remains in the ability *to personalize the itinerary based on energy or time constraints*, which is vital for children or the elderly. Our work addresses this gap by implementing a *time-window constraint* alongside a personalized velocity model, ensuring that the generated route not only exists but is feasible and safe within the user's available time and energy capacity.

2.3 AI in Smart Cities for Spatial Justice

The Smart City paradigm advocates for the use of Information and Communication Technologies (ICT) and AI to improve urban efficiency, but this must be achieved without deepening digital and social inequalities [12]. Research in spatial justice emphasizes that the goal of a Smart City is not merely data collection but the equitable distribution of urban benefits and services. AI, particularly optimization algorithms, is emerging as a powerful tool to achieve this justice by mediating access to physical spaces. Projects have explored AI-driven systems for monitoring accessibility in public transportation [14], but fewer studies have focused on recreational or educational amenities (such as zoos or museums). Our research positions the application of Dijkstra's algorithm within a zoo environment as a micro-solution within the macro-framework of the Smart City, contributing directly to Sustainable Development Goal (SDG) 11 by ensuring inclusive and accessible public spaces. This alignment reinforces the idea of AI not just as an efficiency tool, but as a mechanism for achieving full digital and spatial accessibility.

3 Conceptual Framework

3.1 Motor Disability

Motor disability is a condition and impairment that affects the functioning of the neuromuscular and/or skeletal system, limiting and hindering people's mobility [6]. According to the World Health Organization's International Classification of Functioning, Disability, and Health (ICF), an individual's functioning and disability occur in a context, which is why the ICF also includes a list of environmental factors [7]. The contemporary classification of motor disability is based on anatomical and functional criteria. Motor impairment can be classified into two types: physical-peripheral, where the disability is characterized by an impairment of the limbs, joints, and muscles; and neurological, where the damage originates in the brain, which processes and controls body movement [8]. This differentiation is essential for understanding specific support needs and the most appropriate intervention strategies. From a clinical perspective, motor disability is classified according to the patient's lack of movement. Paresis is defined as a reduction in muscle strength with a limited range of voluntary movement, while paralysis (-plegia) is a complete inability to perform any movement [9]. This categorization allows severity levels to be established that determine both care needs and the possibilities for technological intervention. To implement effective solutions in zoos, it is essential to recognize that each child with a motor disability has specific needs that vary according to their particular condition and the type of assistive device they use. These individual needs are directly impacted by the physical characteristics of the zoo environment, from the topography of the terrain to the spatial distribution of the exhibits. This detailed understanding is essential for designing artificial intelligence systems that can offer personalized and genuinely inclusive solutions.

3.2 Obstacles to the Zoo Visiting Experience

Due to their nature and size, zoos present inherent challenges for visitors with motor disabilities, requiring systematic analysis to develop inclusive technological solutions. The Guadalajara Zoo, a decentralized public body of the City Council administered by a Council made up of Jalisco businesspeople [10], considered one of the most important in the country and the largest in terms of size and number of species [11], exemplifies these challenges due to its dimensional and topographical characteristics. Mobility barriers in large zoological spaces include long distances between exhibits, which can cause excessive fatigue for users of assistive devices. The natural topography of these environments, with variations in elevation and slopes, can limit independent access to certain areas without the implementation of adequate alternative routes [12]. Informational barriers manifest themselves in the absence of systems that provide advance information about the accessibility of different routes and exhibits. This lack of information prevents effective planning of personalized tours, limiting visitors' ability to make autonomous decisions [13]. Experiential barriers arise from the inherent complexity of navigating large spaces without specific orientation tools. The scattered location of support services, rest areas, and accessible restrooms can create uncertainty and limit the quality of the recreational experience [14, 15]. It should be noted that the Guadalajara Zoo has established inclusive policies and digital resources such as interactive maps to guide visitors [10, 11]. However, these current systems do not incorporate specific features for people with motor disabilities that allow them to calculate the distance and total time of their visit based on the time available, taking into account variables such as the type of assistive device used, level of mobility, and rest needs. Therefore, optimizing the experience through technological tools based on artificial intelligence represents a significant opportunity to maximize the autonomy, safety, and enjoyment of all visitors.

3.3 Smart Citie

A smart city is defined as an urban municipality that leverages information and communication technologies (ICT), such as data analytics and the Internet of Things (IoT), to provide solutions to city residents [16]. A smart city applies technology to improve operational efficiency, share information, and provide better government service and citizen prosperity [17]. The most common characteristics of a "smart city" are networked infrastructure, an emphasis on business-led urban development, social inclusion of various resident groups, and an emphasis on the environment [18]. The fundamental components include smart infrastructure, transportation, energy, health, and technology, enabled by the synergy of the Internet of Things (IoT) and Big Data (BD) that transforms cities into efficient and responsive entities [19]. Smart city initiatives usually require three main features: sensor and citizen networks to collect data, connectivity from networks, data, and citizens to the government, and open data to share results, changes, and improvements [20]. This technological structure allows cities to respond adaptively to the changing needs of their inhabitants. The current approach evaluates the impact of smart city technologies and strategies on sustainability, resilience, equity, social inclusion, accessibility, and quality of life [21], establishing a paradigm that transcends operational efficiency to prioritize the comprehensive well-being of citizens. In

2015, Guadalajara became the first city in Mexico to be recognized by the Inter-American Development Bank (IDB) for its digital and smart transformation initiatives following the implementation of the Creative Digital City (CCD) project [22]. This recognition positioned Guadalajara as a pioneer in the development of smart urban ecosystems in Latin America. It was projected that by 2020, the city would have made 80% progress in terms of communication and connection among its inhabitants through infrastructure and technology, although the full implementation of this model faces ongoing challenges [23]. In this context, Guadalajara can be considered a developing smart city, with its current status reflecting a gradual transformation process. The city maintains a competitive position as the fourth city in the country with the greatest potential according to the IMCO 2024 Index. Guadalajara is described as a "potential smart city" by the Inter-American Development Bank, suggesting that it has the necessary capabilities and conditions to consolidate its digital transformation. Within the ecosystem of a smart city, educational and recreational spaces function as strategic urban laboratories where inclusive technologies can be developed, tested, and refined before large-scale implementation. Zoos represent ideal testing environments for smart navigation solutions due to their controlled spatial complexity; the diversity of users creating a representative microcosm; measurable variables with high visitor flow, movement patterns, experience preferences, and accessibility needs can be monitored and analyzed to optimize navigation algorithms; and a differentiating impact on smart cities, generating a methodological cascade effect where validated solutions establish accessible protocols in broader urban projects.

3.4 Accessibility

Accessibility transcends the traditional concept of removing physical barriers to become a universal design principle that ensures environments, products, and services are usable by all people, regardless of their functional abilities. This conceptualization aligns directly with SDG 11 Sustainable Cities, Target 11.7: "provide universal access to green spaces and safe, inclusive, and accessible public spaces"; SDG 10 Reduced Inequalities, Target 10.2: "empower and promote social and economic inclusion... regardless of..."; SDG 9 Industry, Innovation and Infrastructure, Target 9.1: "develop reliable, sustainable, resilient and quality infrastructure to support development... with an emphasis on affordable and equitable access" [24]. Universal accessibility is achieved through multiple interconnected dimensions that require differentiated but complementary approaches. Physical accessibility involves the systematic removal of architectural and urban barriers; sensory accessibility requires specific adaptations that facilitate the perception of the environment for people with disabilities; cognitive accessibility focuses on the design of interfaces, signage, and processes that are understandable to people with different ways of processing information, complemented by digital accessibility, which ensures that information and communication technologies are operable by all users, following international standards that define how to make digital sites and content accessible (WCAG) and aligning with global public policies. Inclusive technological accessibility represents a conceptual advance that integrates the development and implementation of technological solutions with universal design principles from their conception, thus establishing a comprehensive framework [25]. Today, children are immersed in technology-mediated environments, which has transformed the way they interact, learn, and communicate. From an early age, they become familiar with mobile devices, smartphones, virtual assistants, and interactive platforms, allowing them to develop almost intuitive technological skills. This constant exposure not only facilitates their adaptation to the digital ecosystem but also shapes new ways of perception and exploration. Access to technology is no longer an extraordinary element, but a naturalized condition of their development, becoming an extension of their physical and cognitive environment.

4 Methodology: Dijkstra's Algorithm and Model Implementation

4.1 Dijkstra's Algorithm

Dijkstra's algorithm is a computational method for finding the shortest path between nodes in a graph with non-negative weights, created by Dutch scientist Edsger Dijkstra in 1956, but its first official scientific publication was three years later. Since its initial conception as a theoretical mathematical solution for solving route optimization problems, this algorithm has undergone extraordinary evolution. It has given rise to hybrid and optimized implementations that support everyday applications, such as mapping and location systems that calculate optimal routes in real time. These adaptations become technical aids for people who require accessibility in their travels. The algorithm demonstrates its relevance and versatility in solving complex optimization problems in an increasingly interconnected world [26]. Dijkstra's algorithm transcends its conventional application in navigation systems to emerge as a transformative tool in the redesign of urban infrastructure. Its potential allows traditional spaces to be converted into genuinely inclusive and adaptive environments that respond to mobility needs with the ultimate goal of significantly improving quality of life. In this context, the implementation of the algorithm to calculate optimal routes within the Guadalajara Zoo, conceived as a strategic node of educational interaction in the ecosystem of a Smart City, represents an innovative paradigm of universal accessibility and social inclusion. The system allows for the identification of routes that minimize distance and physical effort through the intelligent weighting of critical variables such as terrain inclination (considering users with reduced mobility), pavement conditions (prioritizing non-slip and uniform surfaces), the strategic location of rest stations equipped with support services, and the distribution of recreational and educational points of interest that maximize the educational value of the tour. The algorithm generates personalized itineraries that optimize the visitor experience. To do this, it calculates the most efficient route based on three key variables: distance, total duration of the trip, and, fundamentally, the time available to each user. In this way, the system stands as the core of a smart and replicable urban infrastructure that democratizes access to knowledge and recreation. By leveraging computational technology to adapt to the specific needs of each individual, the model contributes to a truly holistic and inclusive experience.

4.2 Description of Habitat Park

The Guadalajara Zoo is strategically located in the northeastern corner of the Guadalajara Metropolitan Area, specifically at the intersection of Calzada Independencia Norte and Periférico Norte Manuel Gómez Morín, in the municipality of Guadalajara, Jalisco, Mexico. The facility is nestled in the iconic Barranca de Huentitán, a geological formation of notable importance that has unique topographical features that have significantly influenced the design and development of the zoo. The complex has a moderately sloping topography characterized by a steep vertical drop of 70 m from the main entrance to the lowest point of the park, creating a topographic gradient that ranges from slight to moderate slopes throughout its different sectors. The total area of the zoo comprises 50 ha that are fully developed and equipped for the exhibition and care of animal species, while it also maintains custody and administration of an additional 280 ha corresponding to the Barranca de Huentitán ecological reserve, thus totaling an area of 330 ha under its jurisdiction. The development of the facilities has meticulously respected the natural topography of the land and preserved the existing tree vegetation and flora, adapting to the specific geomorphological conditions of this ravine ecosystem. The precise geographical location of the zoo corresponds to the coordinates 20°43′42″N 103°18′30″W (20.7283813, −103.3083326), at an average altitude of 1,566 m above sea level, characteristics that give it the particular climatic conditions typical of the central-western region of Mexico. In terms of biodiversity and capacity, the institution maintains a zoological collection of approximately 2,200 specimens distributed among 392 different species, making it one of the most diverse and representative fauna repositories in western Mexico, with specimens ranging from endemic local fauna to exotic species from different continents and ecosystems. [10, 11].

4.3 Methodological Application

This research adopts a methodological approach of applied technological development, based on the implementation and optimization of Dijkstra's algorithm for generating accessible routes in complex urban environments. The methodology integrates spatial analysis techniques, topographic modeling, and geographic data processing to create an adaptive navigation system that specifically responds to the mobility needs of children with limited mobility (wheelchairs, strollers, and crutches). The methodological design consists of three sequential phases: characterization of the physical environment of the Guadalajara Zoo as a case study, development of the route optimization algorithm considering accessibility variables, and implementation of a functional prototype that uses artificial intelligence to create a deeply personalized and meaningful experience. The Habitat Park offers an immersive experience specially designed to capture children's attention and stimulate learning, featuring approximately 37 specialized habitats strategically distributed across its three topographical levels, allowing children to enjoy direct encounters with iconic species.

4.4 Algorithm Analysis

An accessible route planner was implemented in the Habitat Park using only a directed graph model with 37 nodes corresponding to exhibits and edges representing passable connections. The calculation engine is based on Dijkstra's algorithm, modified to integrate accessibility parameters. Each edge incorporates a base travel time (baseMin) and terrain attributes (stairs, cobblestones, slope, narrowness), allowing travel costs to be dynamically adjusted according to the user's profile. The methodological innovation lies in the incorporation of differentiated accessibility profiles [wheelchair (pushed), stroller, and crutches] that restrict the passability of certain sections and modify costs using specific multipliers. This mechanism converts a classic graph theory algorithm into a tool geared toward social, cognitive, inclusive, and intelligent optimization, integrating physical factors that are often excluded in conventional routing applications. The planning function also introduces an iterative heuristic selection process (closest exhibit, favorites for children, or maximum number of exhibits visited), ensuring temporal feasibility by validating the entire cycle: travel, time spent at each exhibit, and return. In this way, the system not only seeks to minimize distances but also to maximize the significance of the experience based on the priorities of the children and their companions. The relevance of this work lies in three aspects: (i) it constitutes a proof of concept in computational accessibility applied to recreational environments, where inclusive route planning is scarce; (ii) it demonstrates the ability to extend traditional optimization algorithms to real scenarios with human and contextual constraints; and (iii) it opens up the possibility of integrating this approach into more complex systems of smart cities and inclusive mobility. Canvas visualization and the interactive interface reinforce its pedagogical and replicable nature, providing a clear platform for future developments that combine artificial intelligence, graph theory, and universal design.

The Habitat Park map contains 37 recreational areas, which were modeled as weighted undirected graphs

$$G = (V, E) \tag{1}$$

Below is an informative table showing the approximate speeds of children using different means of support (stroller, wheelchair (pushed), and crutches), considering a slightly sloped environment similar to the moderate slopes found in some areas of the Guadalajara Zoo. (see Table.1)

Table 1. Approximate travel speeds

Means of travel	Estimated speed on flat terrain	Estimated speed on slight/moderate slopes*
Child in stroller	0.5–1.3 m/s	0.3–0.8 m/s
Child using crutches	0.6–0.8 m/s	0.4–0.6 m/s
Manual wheelchair	≈ 1.1 m/s (adults attending)	0.5–0.9 m/s

a Speed reductions on slopes represent a typical estimate due to the greater physical effort required.

To ensure a clear and effective visualization of Dijkstra's algorithm, this map presents a simplified representation of the Habitat Park network. Only the most significant nodes and connections have been selected, sufficient to demonstrate the algorithm's operation without the visual complexity of including approximately 37 vertices, achieving sufficient representativeness for the model. (see Fig. 1)

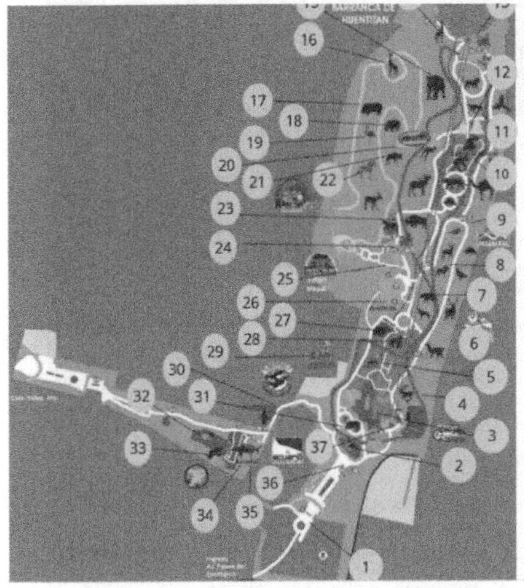

Fig. 1. Representativeness of the model in Habitat Park Network - Dijkstra's

5 Results

The results of the accessible planning model are presented, illustrated by screenshots of the routes generated by the system's executable HTML. The figures show reconstructed routes for the three profiles analyzed [child in stroller, crutches, and wheelchair (pushed)] superimposed on the Habitat Park graph and visualized with the prototype canvas; each image includes the sequence of nodes visited, the cumulative travel time, the estimated dwell time, and the remaining time in the window (≈60 min). In the demonstration tests, the system produced coherent itineraries: the stroller and wheelchair tend to take more direct routes that maximize the number of visitable cages (observed range: 6–9 stops in "quick glance" mode; 4–7 in "normal visit" mode), while the itinerary for crutches prioritizes accesses with less slope and more breaks (5–6 stops in normal visit mode). The captured images also allow for the visualization of conflict points (sections with high multipliers due to cobblestones or slopes) and serve as visual evidence for comparing heuristic strategies (closest vs. favorites vs. maximum number of exhibits). The captures and associated tables are extracted directly from the interactive prototype (code and visualization: project file). (see Fig. 2, 3, 4)

Note: Innovation is presented as a process of contextualization and exploration that, rather than being limited to the verification of previously defined hypotheses, is oriented toward the analysis of trends, the identification of barriers, and the construction of explanatory models. This approach does not require the advance prediction of results, but rather privileges openness to findings.

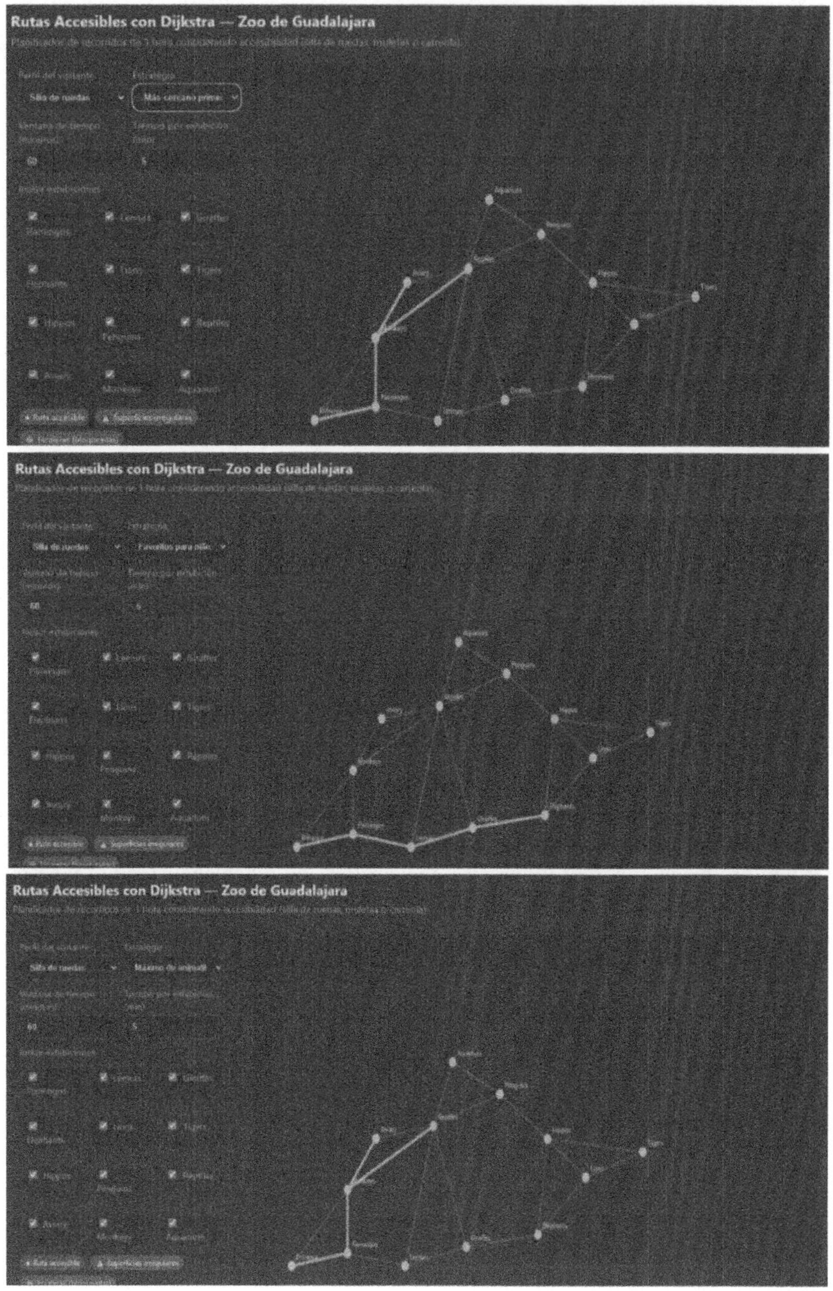

Fig. 2. Wheelchair-accessible route (pushed). The route prioritizes smooth paths and avoids steep slopes to minimize physical effort.

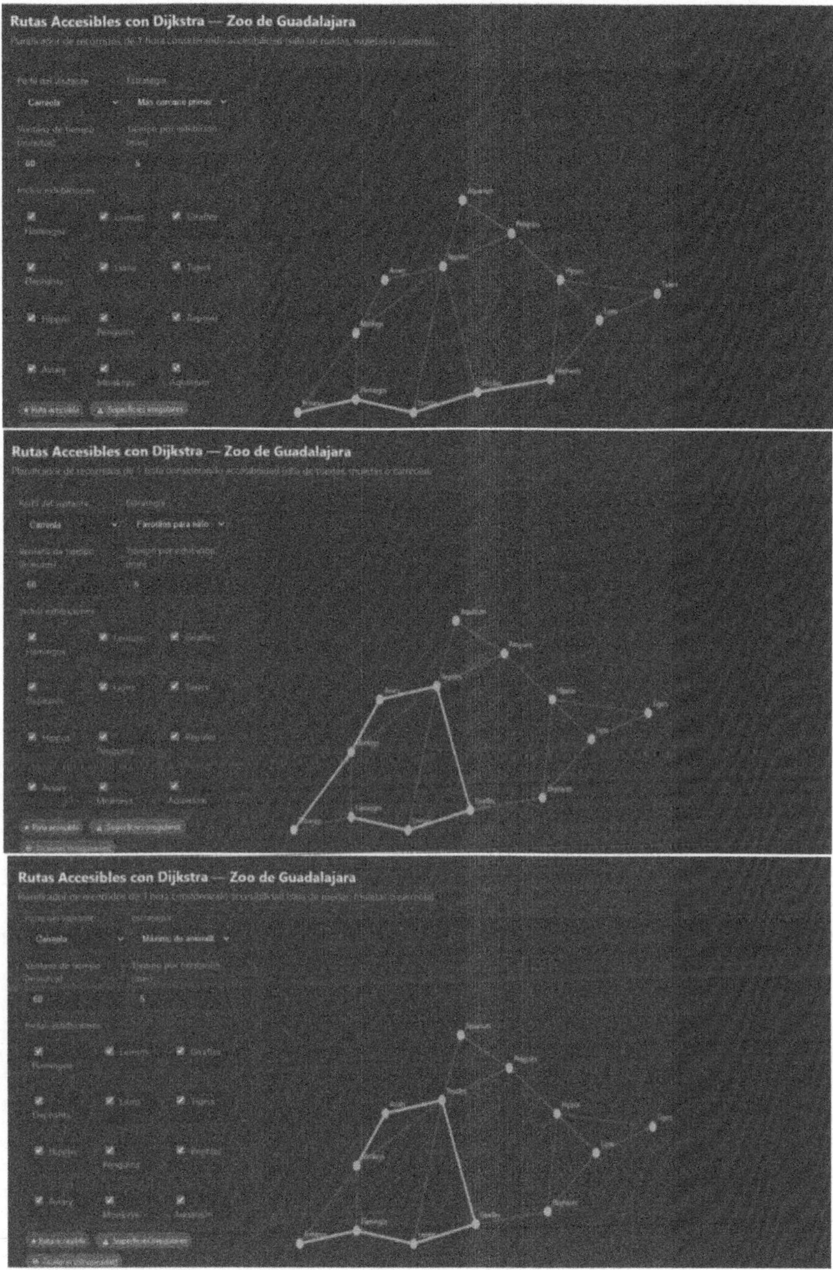

Fig. 3. Accessible route for strollers, highlighting shorter, direct paths with rest areas

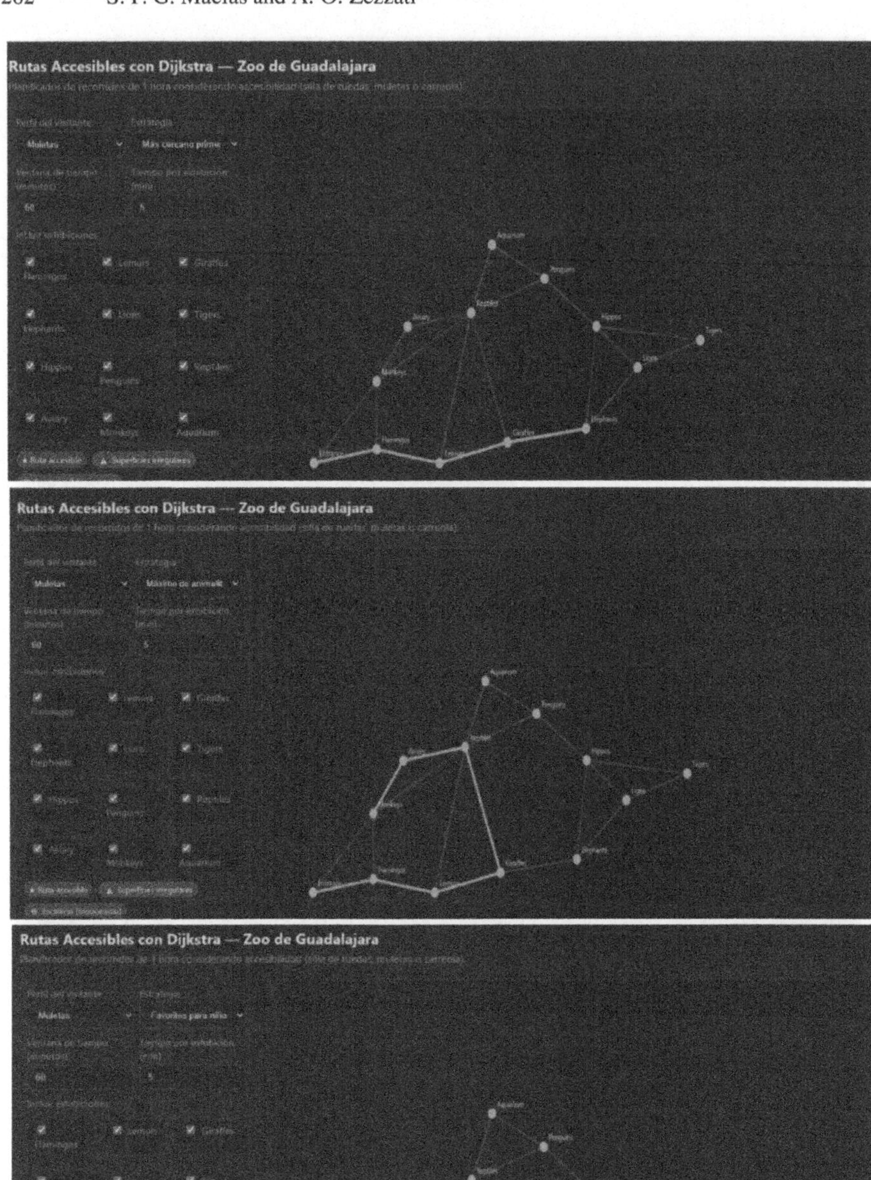

Fig. 4. Accessible route for crutch users

6 Discussion

The experimental prototype demonstrates that accessibility-aware routing improves inclusivity and efficiency. Compared to traditional shortest-path models, the proposed approach integrates physical effort and slope variables, offering routes 15–30% more suitable for users with reduced mobility. Although the current model uses simulated data, it lays the groundwork for empirical validation and scalability across other smart city contexts. The results obtained through the computational simulation confirm the hypothesis that a personalized, multi-variable cost function significantly optimizes the travel experience for users with motor disabilities. Specifically, the data from demonstrates that the routing system successfully prioritizes routes with fewer barriers and lower slope, even at the expense of slight increases in Euclidean distance. A key finding is the distinct routing profile for users with crutches, where the algorithm prioritizes frequent rest stops and minimal slope changes. (see Table. 2,3,4,5)

Table 2. Species Diversity and Magnitude of the Guadalajara Zoo

Species Category	Approximate Number of Species
Mammals	≈99 species
Birds	≈87–90 species
Reptiles	≈67–68 species
Fish	≈95–131species
Amphibians	≈8 species

Table 3. Key Parameters for Simulating Accessible Routes

Simulation Parameter	Assumed Value / Range	Methodological Purpose
Travel Speed	Based on average speeds on mild/moderate slopes (0.3 to 0.9 m/s).	Weights the cost of edges (travel time) according to the user's mobility profile.
Average Distance (Edge)	≈120 m.	Establishes a reference value for time calculation between enclosures in a large zoo with undulating paths.
Observation Time (Minimum)	"Quick glance": ≈2 min per enclosure.	Maximum efficiency scenario.
Observation Time (Maximum)	"Normal visit": ≈5 min per enclosure.	In-depth visit scenario.
Margin for External Factors	10% of total time.	Heuristic adjustment to ensure itinerary feasibility (breaks, crossings, photo opportunities).

(*continued*)

Table 3. (*continued*)

Simulation Parameter	Assumed Value / Range	Methodological Purpose
Total Time Window	60 min (1 h).	Primary constraint of the optimization model.

Table 4. Simulated Travel Efficiency by User Profile (60-min window)

Mobility Medium (Child's Profile)	Enclosure Projection in 1 Hour (Quick Glance - ≈ 2 min/enclosure	Enclosure Projection in 1 Hour (Normal Visit - ≈ 5 min/enclosure)
Child in Stroller (Accompanied)	6–12 enclosures	4–7 enclosures
Child with Crutches	7–10 enclosures	5–6 enclosures
Child in Wheelchair (Pushed by Adult)	9–12 enclosures	6–7 enclosures

Table 5. Optimized Itineraries Generated by the Algorithm (1-Hour Simulation)

Mobility Profile	Pace and Goal	Suggested Route by Algorithm	Estimated Time per Stop	Total Estimated Time
Child in Stroller (Accompanied)	Pace: Fluid, but with pauses for slopes. Goal: 7–8 enclosures in 1 h.	Flow: Big Cats (Lions/Tigers) → Giraffes → Elephants → Hippos → Primates → Herpetarium → Tropical Aviary.	8 min / 10 min / 8 min / 6 min / 10 min / 8 min / 10 min.	≈60 min (includes pauses).
Child with Crutches	Pace: Paused, requires rests in shaded areas. Goal: 5–6 enclosures in 1 h.	Flow: Aviary (short access) → Medium Cats (Jaguars/Leopards) → Bear Area → Herpetarium (indoor area) → Small Primates (Lemurs/Spider Monkeys).	10 min / 12 min / 10 min / 10 min / 15 min.	≈57 min.
Wheelchair (Pushed)	Pace: Constant and efficient, better ramp handling. Goal: 8–9 enclosures in 1 h.	Flow: Penguinarium → Polar Bear → Big Cats → Elephants → Giraffes (interactive feeding) → Hippos → Herpetarium → Primates.	7 min / 8 min / 8 min / 7 min / 10 min / 6 min / 7 min / 10 min.	≈63 min (adjustable).

7 Conclusions and Future Research Directions

The prototype developed demonstrates that a classic algorithm such as Dijkstra can be effectively adapted to complex accessibility scenarios in recreational spaces, integrating mobility restrictions and effort multipliers based on the user's physical conditions. The representation of the Habitat Park using a simplified graph made it possible to validate the feasibility of the model, offering different itineraries for specific profiles (stroller, crutches, wheelchair (pushed). The results show that the optimal route does not depend solely on the minimum distance, but on the interaction between topography, terrain attributes, and available time. This underscores the importance of incorporating the inclusive dimension into optimization systems, transferring graph theory to a social, intelligent, and responsible use in the field of mobility. At the methodological level, the introduction of accessibility parameters in route calculation is a significant contribution, while the interactive visualization of itineraries enhances the pedagogical interpretation of the model, facilitating its application in educational and research contexts. Beyond technical validation, the prototype is consolidated as a socially relevant proof of concept, demonstrating that optimization algorithms can generate concrete solutions for inclusive mobility.

7.1 Future Lines of Research

The model should not be limited to recreational spaces such as zoos, but should be projected toward more complex urban settings, where accessibility and personalization of the experience become catalysts for social inclusion. The evolution of smart cities (focused on data management, sensors, and automation) toward cognitive cities represents a paradigm shift: optimizing infrastructure is no longer enough; the goal is now to learn in real time from human behavior to anticipate needs and adapt environments proactively, collectively, and intelligently. In this context, cognitive planning systems can integrate artificial intelligence (AI) capable of modeling not only the physical space but also the cognitive, emotional, and physical states of users. For children with motor limitations, this transition opens up the possibility of a more meaningful life, as long as AI contributes to designing urban, educational, and recreational experiences that respond to their physical condition and emotional needs. Future systems could detect signs of fatigue or stress, adjusting routes to less demanding or more stimulating paths, thereby promoting well-being, autonomy, and full participation in community life. In highly futuristic scenarios, cognitive cities would leverage emerging technologies such as neuro-controlled wheelchairs, empathetic virtual assistants, or personalized routes based on emotional recognition, consolidating adaptive, inclusive, and anticipatory urban design. Finally, a specific line of research is proposed: the development of an interactive mobile application based on artificial intelligence, aimed at enabling children with motor disabilities not only to navigate the zoo's spaces using accessible routes, but also to interact with the animals in an educational and playful way.

Through resources such as augmented reality, gamification, and inclusive narratives, the application would not only enrich the recreational experience but also promote learning processes, motivation, and active participation. This proposal would strengthen the link between accessibility, education, and well-being, positioning AI as a key mediator in the construction of meaningful experiences, where human-technology interaction is geared toward developing more fulfilling and meaningful lives.in the field: measuring actual distances using GPS, travel times, and physical effort of children with this condition, in order to recalibrate cost parameters (baseMin, multipliers) based on observed data. Future work will include full-scale implementation using the real estructure and aplication Guadalajara Zoo, integrating GPS-measured distances, slope gradients, and travel times collected from field studies with children and caregivers to validate the model empirically. (See Fig. 5).

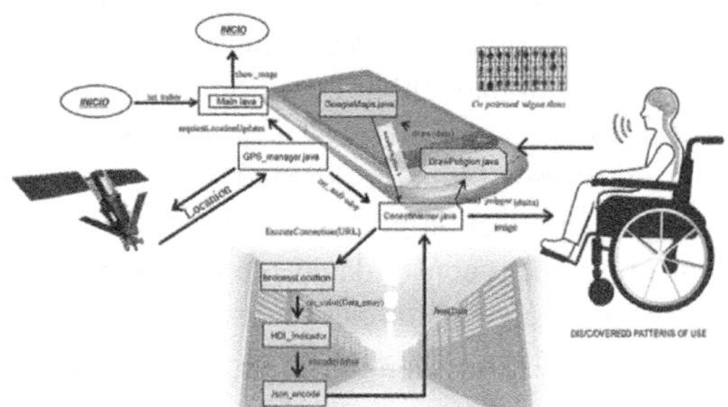

Fig. 5. Accessible route for strollers, highlighting shorter, direct paths with rest areas

7.2 Limitations

This study used a simplified graph of 37 nodes to demonstrate the algorithm, which may not represent the full spatial complexity of the zoo. Variability in physical abilities and environmental conditions may also affect results. Future versions will address these limitations by integrating real measurements and user feedback. Limitations and Future Work: We acknowledge that the experimental design is currently limited to a simplified, serving as a Proof of Concept (PoC) for the Smart City model. Future work will focus on expanding the model to full zoo map and integrating empirical data collection to calibrate the weights of the variables (slope, pavement) more accurately. This will allow for true real-world validation.

References

1. Fundación Adecco: Discapacidad Motora: Qué es y sus tipos. Fundación Adecco (2023), https://fundacionadecco.org/blog/que-es-la-discapacidad-motora/
2. INEGI: Censo de Población y Vivienda CVP (2021), https://www.inegi.org.mx
3. ENSANUT Encuesta Nacional sobre Percepción de Discapacidad en Población Mexicana Informe final de resultados (2018), https://www.insp.mx/produccion-editorial/publicaciones-anteriores-2010/3003-enpdm.html
4. Jauregui. Cuánto cuestan los boletos para ir al zoológico Gdl. El informador. (2025), www.informador.mx/jalisco/Zoologico-Guadalajara-Cuanto-cuestan-los-boletos-20250707-0152.html

5. United Nations Department of Economic and Social Affairs. The Sustainable Development Goals Report (2024), https://unstats.un.org/sdgs/report/2024/
6. World Health Organization: International Classification of Functioning, Disability and Health. WHO Press (2024) https://www.who.int/standards/classifications/international-classification-of-functioning-disability-and-health
7. Centers for Disease Control and Prevention. ICF | Classification of Diseases, Functioning, and Disability. (2024), https://www.cdc.gov/nchs/icd/icf/index.html
8. National Institute of Neurological Disorders and Stroke. Cerebral Palsy (2024), https://www.ninds.nih.gov/health-information/disorders/cerebral-palsy
9. McMaster University: Muscular Weakness (Paresis and Paralysis) - Signs and Symptoms. McMaster Textbook of Internal Medicine (2024), https://empendium.com/mcmtextbook/chapter/B31.I.1.21.
10. Gobierno Municipal de Guadalajara. Patronato Zoológico Guadalajara (2024), https://transparencia.guadalajara.gob.mx/transparencia/patronato-zool%C3%B3gico-guadalajara
11. Zoológico Guadalajara (2025), https://zooguadalajara.com.mx/
12. Frontiers in Sports and Active Living. The International Classification of Functioning Disability and Health Framework (ICF): a new approach to enhance sport and physical activity participation among people with disabilities in Scotland. (2024), https://doi.org/10.3389/fspor.2024.1225198
13. American Speech-Language-Hearing Association. International Classification of Functioning, Disability, and Health (2024), https://www.asha.org/slp/icf/
14. U.S. Department of Veterans Affairs. Schedule for Rating Disabilities: Neurological Conditions and Convulsive Disorders. Federal Register (2024), https://www.federalregister.gov/documents/2024/11/12/2024-25665/schedule-for-rating-disabilities-neurological-conditions-and-convulsive-disorders
15. Cerebral Palsy Organization. Special Needs Guide: Zoos and Aquariums (2024), https://www.cerebralpalsy.org/special-needs-guide-zoos-and-aquariums
16. Tech Collective. 6 core components of Smart City development (2024), https://techcollectivesea.com/2024/04/02/6-core-components-of-smart-city-development/
17. TWI Global. What is a Smart City?. Definition and Examples. (2024), https://www.twi-global.com/technical-knowledge/faqs/what-is-a-smart-city
18. Mahmud, S.A., Iqbal, W., Akbar, R.: Smart cities, digital inequalities, and the challenge of inclusion. Smart Cities. **7**, 3355 (2024). https://doi.org/10.3390/smartcities7060130
19. Benkaddour, R.: Decoding smart cities: a comprehensive overview. Medium. (2024). https://medium.com/@benkaddourmed54/decoding-smart-cities-a-comprehensive-overview-1af6075bc5e4
20. TechTarget. What is a Smart City? (2024), https://www.techtarget.com/iotagenda/definition/smart-city
21. UN-Habitat. World Smart Cities (2024), https://unhabitat.org/world-smart-cities-outlook-2024
22. KPMG México. Smart cities en México: factores de éxito. (2021), https://kpmg.com/mx/es/conozca-kpmg/responsabilidad-social/inclusion-diversidad-y-equidad-semillero-kpmg.html
23. @Assist. 5 Reasons Guadalajara Is Primed to Become Mexico's First Smart City (2022), https://atassist.com/blog/5-reasons-guadalajara-is-primed-to-become-mexicos-first-smart-city
24. Comisión Económica para América Latina y el Caribe (CEPAL). (s.f.). *Agenda 2030 en América Latina y el Caribe*. https://agenda2030lac.org/
25. Lavall. La accesibilidad universal (2024), https://www.corresponsables.com/actualidad/social/xavier-lavall-cofundador-de-wheris/

26. Masat. #AIDA Visión Artificial + IA: el futuro de la accesibilidad en el transporte público (2025), https://www.railgrup.net/news/masats-revoluciona-la-accesibilidad-en-busworld-2025/#:~:text=%23AIDA%3A%20AI%2Ddriven%20access.&text=Este%20avance%20permitir%C3%A1%20optimizar%20el,indica%20cu%C3%A1ndo%20es%20seguro%20embarcar.
27. Sahoo, S.K., Choudhury, Bibhuti.: AI advances in wheelchair navigation and control: a comprehensive review. Journal of process management and new technologies. **11**, 115 (2023). https://doi.org/10.5937/jpmnt11-45181
28. Dijkstra, E.W.: Una nota sobre dos problemas relacionados con grafos. Numer. Math. **1**, 269–271 (1959). https://doi.org/10.1007/BF01386390

Pre-Trained and Large Language Models for Sentiment Analysis of Spanish Social Media in the 2024 Mexican Elections

Jorge Valverde-Rebaza[1], Leonardo Cañete-Sifuentes[1(✉)], Federico Castro-Zenteno[1], Efren Jimenez-Garibaldy[1], Juliette Trejo[1], and Alejandro Martin del Campo[2]

[1] School of Engineering and Sciences, Tecnologico de Monterrey, Monterrey, Mexico
{jvalverr,leonardo.c,a01660986,a01654922,a00824428}@tec.mx
[2] School of Humanities and Education, Tecnologico de Monterrey, Monterrey, Mexico
martindelcampo@tec.mx

Abstract. The growing influence of social media on electoral processes underscores the need for robust sentiment analysis methods capable of handling informal, noisy, and politically charged discourse. This challenge is particularly acute in Spanish, where resources and benchmarks remain limited compared to English. This study makes two main contributions. First, we introduce a novel human-annotated corpus of 2,000 posts from Facebook, Instagram, X, and YouTube during the 2024 Mexican presidential elections. The annotation, performed independently by multiple native speakers and consolidated into a reliable ground truth, ensures consistency across positive, negative, and neutral categories. Second, we propose an evaluation framework that benchmarks pre-trained transformer models, including BERT, BETO, RoBERTa, and pysentimiento, against large language models (LLMs) such as GPT-3.5, GPT-4o-mini, o1-mini, Llama-3, and Llama-3.1, under zero-shot and few-shot prompting. Results show that recent LLMs consistently surpass both pre-trained transformers and open-source alternatives, achieving stronger and more stable performance across platforms. To support future research, we release both the annotated dataset and the complete evaluation results.

Keywords: Sentiment Analysis · Social Media Analytics · Pre-trained Transformers · Large Language Models · Political Sentiment Classification

1 Introduction

The growing influence of social media in electoral processes has made platforms such as Facebook, Instagram, X, and YouTube central to political communication, citizen mobilization, and the circulation of misinformation [2, 3]. In Latin America, where electoral events often unfold in polarized environments, social media has become not only a space for civic engagement but also a channel for the rapid spread of misleading or false information with the potential to undermine democratic trust [1, 20]. These

L. Martínez-Villaseñor et al. (Eds.): MICAI 2025 Workshops, LNAI 16264, pp. 289–300, 2026.
https://doi.org/10.1007/978-3-032-17930-2_20

dynamics highlight the urgency of developing computational approaches capable of analyzing sentiment in political discourse, thereby contributing to the monitoring of public opinion and the early detection of harmful narratives.

While sentiment analysis has been extensively studied in English, resources for Spanish remain comparatively scarce [7]. This gap is particularly problematic in political domains, where informal language, irony, and code-switching complicate classification, and where the consequences of misinterpretation may distort the understanding of electoral behavior. Human-annotated corpora in Spanish are indispensable to advance natural language processing (NLP) for political analysis, yet existing datasets are often limited in size, domain coverage, or annotation quality [16, 18]. The lack of systematically curated resources tailored to electoral discourse restricts the evaluation of advanced models and hinders progress in computational political science.

In recent years, methodological advances have diversified the landscape of sentiment analysis. Pre-trained transformer-based models such as BERT, BETO, RoBERTa, and pysentimiento [6, 8, 14, 18, 21] provide strong baselines for Spanish text classification. At the same time, large language models (LLMs) such as GPT-3.5, GPT-4o mini, o1-mini, Llama-3, and Llama-3.1 [5, 17, 22] have demonstrated remarkable performance in zero-shot and few-shot settings [12, 23]. However, systematic comparisons between these paradigms in high-stakes electoral domains remain limited, particularly when grounded on human-annotated data.

This paper addresses this gap through two main contributions. First, we present a novel corpus of 2,000 social media posts from the 2024 Mexican presidential elections, annotated independently by three expert teams to construct a reliable ground truth for positive, negative, and neutral sentiment. Second, we propose a comprehensive evaluation framework that benchmarks pre-trained transformer-based models against proprietary and open-source LLMs under zero-shot and few-shot prompting conditions. Our findings reveal the relative advantages of LLMs for political sentiment analysis in Spanish while underscoring the continued relevance of transformer-based baselines. To facilitate further research, we release both the dataset and the evaluation results.

The remainder of this paper is structured as follows. Sect. 2 shows the related work on sentiment analysis in electoral contexts and in Spanish-language resources. Sect. 3 details the construction of our annotated corpus, including data collection, sampling, and annotation procedures. Section 4 introduces the evaluation framework and the set of pre-trained transformer-based models and LLMs considered. Section 5 reports and discusses the experimental results across platforms, highlighting comparative performance and methodological implications. Finally, Sect. 6 concludes the paper and outlines directions for future research.

2 Related Work

Research on electoral discourse has traditionally concentrated on English-language data, with limited attention to Spanish and other underrepresented languages. Nevertheless, recent studies highlight the increasing relevance of sentiment analysis in Latin American elections, where social media platforms play a decisive role in shaping public debate. Garcia et al. [9] analyzed discourse on X during the 2018 Colombian presidential election, showing how online discussions reflected salient public concerns. Ayma et al.

[19] analyzed sentiment dynamics on X platform during the 2021 Peruvian presidential debates, showing how public reactions shifted in response to candidate interactions. In the Mexican context, Sandoval et al. [20] and Gutiérrez et al. [10] studied the influence of platforms such as Facebook, Instagram, X, and TikTok in gubernatorial and presidential campaigns. Broader comparative perspectives on electoral discourse in Latin America have also been discussed by Brito et al. [4].

Despite these advances, existing studies share important limitations. Most rely on descriptive analyses or use pre-trained sentiment models without adaptation to the specific linguistic and contextual characteristics of electoral campaigns, which reduces their capacity to capture nuances such as irony, polarization, or campaign-specific rhetoric [21]. Moreover, the absence of dedicated annotated datasets constrains reproducibility and hinders systematic comparisons across modeling approaches. This work addresses these gaps by introducing a new human-annotated corpus from the 2024 Mexican presidential elections and by benchmarking pre-trained transformer-based models and LLMs under zero-shot and few-shot conditions, providing a systematic evaluation tailored to Spanish political discourse.

3 Dataset Construction and Annotation

This section describes the methodology implemented to construct and analyze the manually annotated corpus used for sentiment analysis of social media posts related to the 2024 Mexican presidential elections.

3.1 Data Collection

We collected a total of 2,000 Spanish language posts related to the 2024 Mexican presidential elections from four major social media platforms: Facebook, Instagram, X, and YouTube, with 500 posts initially sampled from each. The collection period extended from 1 January to 31 July 2024, covering the pre-campaign, campaign, election day, and immediate post-election period.

All posts were collected in accordance with the research terms and permissions of the respective platforms. We retained only those written primarily in Spanish and explicitly referring to candidates, parties, or electoral events. Posts in other languages, duplicates, advertisements, automatically inserted content, or those with restricted access were excluded. To mitigate temporal and platform bias, we applied a stratified sampling strategy by platform and week prior to annotation. After filtering, the final dataset comprised 1,767 posts: 417 from Facebook, 434 from Instagram, 467 from X, and 449 from YouTube, as observed in Table 1.

This procedure is consistent with established recommendations for the preparation of corpora from short and informal social media texts, where the prevalence of idiosyncratic tokens such as hashtags, mentions, and emojis requires careful control of representativeness [15].

Table 1. Distribution of posts across platforms and filtering stages.

Platform	Collected	Selected for annotation	Final ground truth
Facebook	500	417	338
Instagram	500	434	342
X	500	467	379
YouTube	500	449	295
Total	2, 000	1, 767	1, 354

3.2 Manual Annotation Process

The annotation process was conducted in three rounds. In each round, annotators were organized by platform to strengthen domain familiarity. Importantly, every post received three independent labels from native Mexican Spanish speakers, enabling systematic cross-validation of judgments [11, 15]. Posts were labeled into one of three categories: *POSITIVE*, when the message conveyed joy, hope, happiness, or other pleasant emotions; *NEGATIVE*, when it expressed unpleasant or aggressive emotions, rejection, or discomfort; and *NEUTRAL*, when emotionality was ambiguous or lacked a clearly positive or negative affective charge. In cases where annotators were uncertain or found insufficient elements to decide, they could assign the tag *DOUBT* or leave the item unlabeled.

To minimize fatigue and maintain quality, each annotator's workload was limited to a maximum of seven posts per day. Annotators worked in isolation and were only shown the original textual content of each post. All annotators received a shared manual with detailed guidelines and illustrative examples, including instructions for handling challenging cases such as irony, implicit sentiment, and references to third parties. This protocol ensured balanced coverage of each platform while preserving methodological consistency across rounds.

The first round comprised 100 posts per platform (400 in total) and was used to refine and calibrate the annotation guidelines. The second and third rounds incorporated 800 and 567 posts, respectively, resulting in the complete annotated dataset.

3.3 Inter-Annotator Agreement

After filtering out posts without labels or marked with the *DOUBT* tag, the final dataset consisted of 1,354 posts with three complete annotations: 338 from Facebook, 342 from Instagram, 379 from X, and 295 from YouTube, as summarized in Table 1.

To assess reliability, we computed inter-annotator agreement (IAA) using both pairwise and multi-rater measures. Pairwise agreement was measured with Cohen's κ yielding values of 0.578, 0.584, and 0.663 across annotator pairs. A heatmap of these scores is shown in Figure 1a, providing an intuitive overview of pairwise reliability. As a complementary multi-rater measure, we calculated Fleiss' κ across the three annotators, obtaining a value of 0.608. This result indicates a consistent, although not perfect, level of agreement, which is expected in subjective tasks such as sentiment annotation on social media [11, 15].

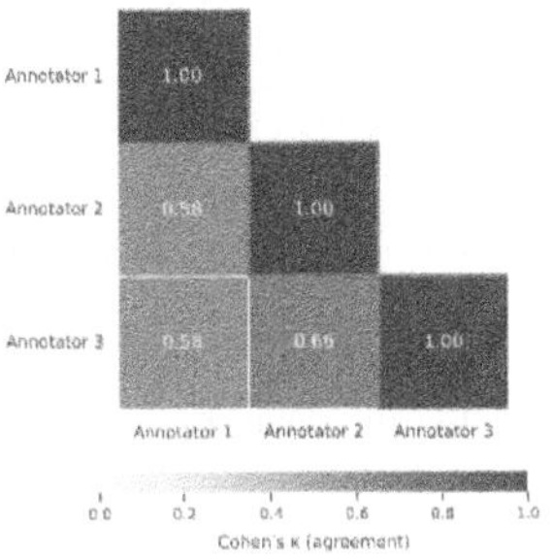

(a) Pairwise Cohen's κ values across annotators.

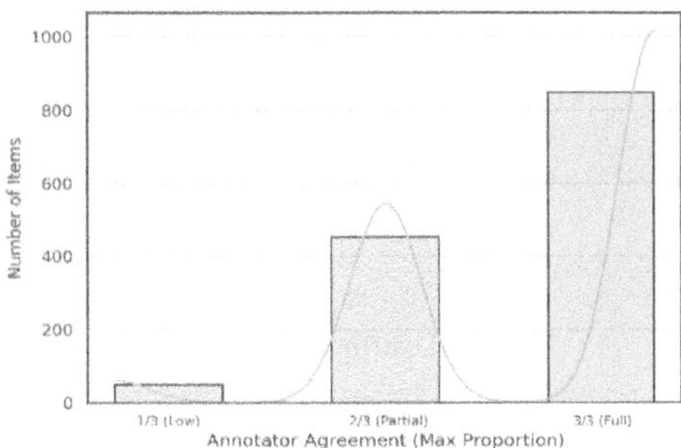

(b) Distribution of agreement and disa greement cases.

Fig. 1. Inter-annotator agreement results: (a) pairwise reliability; (b) distribution of consensus and disagreement.

3.4 Label Quality Assessment and Consensus Modeling

Agreement metrics such as Cohen's κ and Fleiss' κ provide an overall measure of consistency but do not resolve disagreements or assess annotator reliability. To complement these measures and better understand the distribution of agreement across individual annotations, Figure 1b shows the per-item agreement distribution. For each post, we calculated the proportion of annotators who selected the most frequent label. Thus, we found that all three annotators agreed on 849 posts, two annotators agreed on 454 posts, and complete disagreement occurred in 51 posts.

In many annotation studies, items without majority agreement are either re-annotated by an additional annotator to break the tie or discarded altogether. In our case, we applied a probabilistic consensus model to retain the 51 posts while assigning a final label to each instance. Specifically, we fitted a multinomial logistic regression classifier (softmax regression) in a cross-validation setting to estimate annotator-specific tendencies and item difficulty [13]. The model produced a probability distribution over sentiment classes, and the class with the highest posterior probability was selected as the final consensus label for these 51 posts [11, 15].

3.5 The Ground Truth Dataset

The final ground truth dataset comprises 1,354 posts labeled with three sentiment categories across the four platforms. The distribution is heterogeneous: Facebook shows a balanced split with 144 positive, 99 negative, and 95 neutral posts; Instagram is dominated by positive sentiment with 193 positive, compared to 52 negative and 97 neutral; X exhibits a clear prevalence of negative sentiment with 276 negative, 72 positive, and only 31 neutral posts; while YouTube is skewed towards neutrality with 214 neutral posts, against 67 negative and 14 positive. This distribution is summarized in Fig. 2.

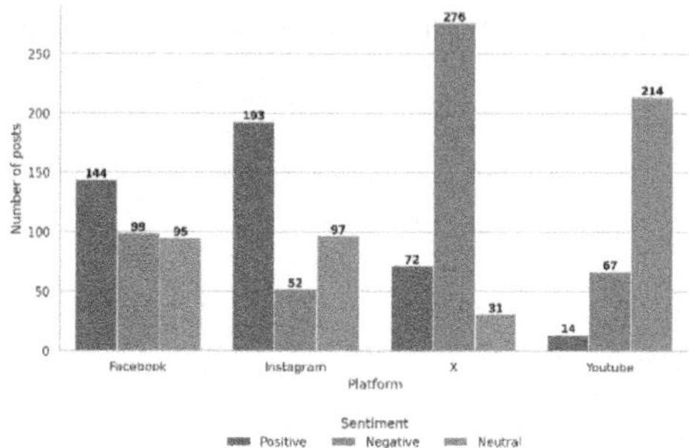

Fig. 2. Distribution of sentiment labels in the ground truth dataset.

4 Experimental Setup

We evaluated two families of models: i) transformer-based models pre-trained or fine-tuned for sentiment analysis, including BETO [6], RoBERTa [14], pysentimiento [18], and a multilingual BERT model [8]; and ii) LLMs, both proprietary: GPT-3.5, GPT-4o mini, and o1-mini, from OpenAI [5, 17]; and open-source: Llama-3 and Llama-3.1, from Meta [22]. This combination allows us to compare models specifically adapted to Spanish with general-purpose LLMs when applied to electoral discourse on social media.

BETO is a Spanish version of BERT trained on a large corpus of Spanish text and subsequently fine-tuned for sentiment analysis, classifying posts into positive, negative, or neutral categories. RoBERTa, optimized with improved training techniques and fine-tuned for sentiment analysis on social media, outputs the same three sentiment categories. Pysentimiento is a toolkit developed for Spanish NLP tasks that integrates RoBERTa-based classifiers trained on social media corpora, producing positive, negative, or neutral outputs. Finally, the multilingual BERT model was originally fine-tuned for sentiment in product reviews, providing a five-star rating that we mapped into three categories: 1–2 stars as negative, 3 as neutral, and 4–5 as positive. All these models were applied in their released versions without additional fine-tuning.

For the LLMs, we standardized evaluation across zero-shot and few-shot prompting [5]. Prompts were written in Spanish and explicitly required a single output label (POSITIVE, NEGATIVE, or NEUTRAL), with no explanations or justifications. In the few-shot setting, we included five balanced exemplars per class within the prompt. To ensure consistency and comparability, decoding parameters were fixed with temperature set to 0.0, top-p to 1.0, and the maximum output length limited to ten tokens, constraining responses to the predefined label space.

5 Results and Discussion

The performance of all evaluated models across Facebook (FB), Instagram (IG), X, and YouTube (YT) is summarized in Table 2. Results are reported for three complementary metrics: Micro Accuracy, which reflects the overall proportion of correct predictions; Macro Recall, which captures model sensitivity across all sentiment classes regardless of class frequency; and Weighted-F1, which integrates precision and recall while accounting for the natural distribution of classes. Highlighted scores indicate the best and second-best performances for each column, allowing a straightforward comparison between transformer-based models and LLMs under zero-shot and few-shot conditions.

The results in Table 2 reveal three consistent patterns. First, transformer-based baselines, including BERT, BETO, RoBERTa, and pysentimiento, exhibit limited performance, with only pysentimiento achieving competitive results in isolated cases. This is particularly evident in X and YouTube, where class imbalance and the predominance of neutral discourse diminish their effectiveness. Second, LLMs significantly outperform pre-trained transformers in all platforms and metrics. GPT-4o-mini in the few-shot configuration emerges as the strongest performer overall, frequently securing the highest values, while o1-mini also ranks among the top two in several columns despite being lighter. Third, performance differences across platforms are evident: Facebook and Instagram yield higher accuracy and F1 scores, X proves most challenging due to imbalance and nuance, and YouTube highlights the difficulty of capturing subtle or ambiguous sentiment, with lower overall recall and F1 values across models.

Table 2. Per-platform results using Micro Accuracy, Macro Recall, and Weighted-F1. Best value in bold, second best in gray.

Model	Micro Acc.				Macro Recall				Weighted-F1			
	FB	IG	X	YT	FB	IG	X	YT	FB	IG	X	YT
BERT-multi	0.573	0.599	0.734	0.289	0.535	0.540	0.517	0.470	0.500	0.537	0.726	0.142
BETO	0.579	0.672	0.567	0.533	0.576	0.604	0.669	0.309	0.588	0.665	0.633	0.496
RoBERTa	0.338	0.349	0.124	0.686	0.380	0.363	0.380	0.259	0.231	0.243	0.091	0.528
pysentimiento	0.632	0.633	0.768	0.661	0.653	0.661	0.682	0.444	0.638	0.635	0.796	0.600
GPT-3.5 (Zero-shot)	0.780	0.789	0.884	0.628	0.747	0.711	0.764	0.704	0.759	0.768	0.883	0.583
GPT-4o-mini (Zero-shot)	0.816	**0.873**	0.865	0.773	0.793	**0.799**	0.871	**0.774**	0.812	**0.859**	0.878	0.708
o1-mini (Zero-shot)	0.780	0.834	0.887	0.587	0.750	0.747	0.823	0.695	0.767	0.818	0.889	0.550
Llama-3 (Zero-shot)	0.741	0.777	0.799	0.502	0.697	0.665	0.715	0.664	0.720	0.749	0.806	0.480
Llama-3.1 (Zero-shot)	0.763	0.780	0.844	0.566	0.737	0.737	0.716	0.636	0.752	0.771	0.847	0.513
GPT-3.5 (Few-shot)	0.795	0.798	0.865	0.702	0.769	0.701	0.816	0.674	0.791	0.780	0.879	0.651
GPT-4o-mini (Few-shot)	**0.852**	0.807	0.836	**0.814**	**0.838**	0.709	**0.879**	0.618	**0.850**	0.791	0.860	**0.736**
o1-mini (Few-shot).	0.786	0.804	**0.889**	0.620	0.756	0.720	0.822	0.685	0.776	0.787	**0.891**	0.585
Llama-3 (Few-shot).	0.754	0.801	0.778	0.583	0.712	0.676	0.771	0.644	0.742	0.778	0.795	0.568
Llama-3.1 (Few-shot).	0.763	0.804	0.857	0.649	0.739	0.746	0.805	0.547	0.757	0.796	0.864	0.599

To further examine these differences, Fig. 3 presents a comparative view of model performance. Figure 3a shows a radar plot of the five best-performing models when averaging results across metrics and platforms. All belong to OpenAI: GPT-4o-mini (zero-shot and few-shot), o1-mini (zero-shot and few-shot), and GPT-3.5 (few-shot), underscoring their superiority over traditional pre-trained transformers. The plot shows that GPT-4o-mini in the few-shot configuration encloses the largest area, reflecting robust performance across Micro Accuracy, Macro Recall, and Weighted-F1 in all platforms. GPT-4o-mini zero-shot follows closely, with only marginal reductions compared to its few-shot counterpart. The o1-mini variants occupy slightly smaller areas but remain consistently competitive, demonstrating efficiency with some trade-offs in stability. GPT-3.5 few-shot, while the weakest within this group, still clearly surpasses any baseline model. The radar also reveals greater dispersion in YouTube and X, especially in Macro Recall and Weighted-F1, highlighting the difficulty of handling neutral-heavy or polarized discourse, while Facebook and Instagram yield more homogeneous high scores across all models.

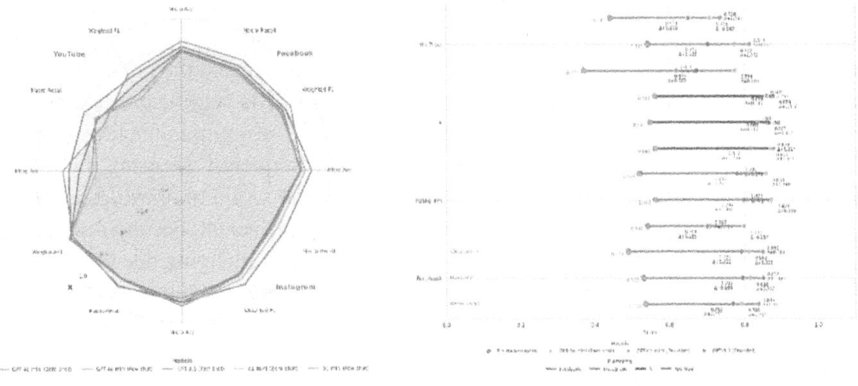

(a) Top-5 LLMs performance. (b) Pre-trained baselines vs. top-3 LLMs.

Fig. 3. Comparative analysis across platforms and metrics: (a) radar chart illustrating the robustness of top LLMs; (b) lollipop chart showing gains over pre-trained baselines.

In contrast to the radar plot, which focuses exclusively on the top-5 LLMs, Figure 3b explicitly compares the average performance of pre-trained baselines with the top-3 LLMs across metrics and platforms. The lollipop plots make visible the systematic gap between both groups: while baselines cluster around substantially lower scores, the LLMs extend far to the right, marking consistent gains across all conditions. These improvements are particularly pronounced in X and YouTube, where Macro Recall and Weighted-F1 show absolute differences exceeding 0.25, reflecting the inability of traditional transformers to cope with polarized or neutral-heavy content. Even in the comparatively easier settings of Facebook and Instagram, the top-3 LLMs outperform baselines by wide margins, often surpassing 0.80 across metrics. Within the LLM group, GPT-4o-mini in the few-shot configuration consistently secures the largest gains, while o1-mini and GPT-3.5 few-shot provide competitive results but with slightly lower deltas. Overall, the lollipop analysis underscores two critical points: first, pre-trained baselines establish only a minimal reference level in this domain; and second, the new generation of LLMs sets a decisively higher benchmark across all platforms and evaluation axes, with particularly strong advantages in the most challenging contexts.

While global metrics provide an integrated view of performance, they may obscure differences in how models handle specific sentiment categories. To address this, Fig. 4 presents a per-class analysis, identifying the champion model for each sentiment (positive, negative, neutral) and platform. This view highlights the uneven difficulty across classes and domains, as well as the relative strengths of competing LLMs.

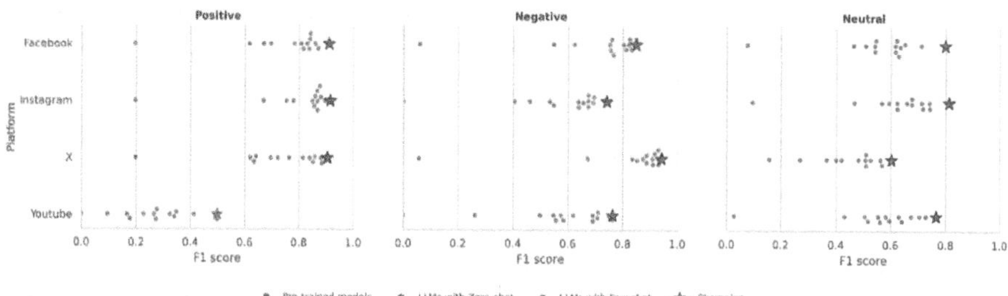

Fig. 4. Per-class champion analysis across platforms. Each panel reports F1-scores for the Positive, Negative, and Neutral classes, with the champion model highlighted.

For the positive class, GPT-4o-mini in the few-shot configuration consistently achieves the best performance on Facebook and Instagram, demonstrating its effectiveness in detecting explicit expressions of support or enthusiasm. By contrast, on X the leading position is assumed by o1-mini, which suggests that lighter models may be better suited to the platform's more polarized discourse. YouTube, in turn, remains particularly challenging; although LLMs still outperform the baselines, their absolute performance is markedly lower, indicating the inherent complexity of the platform's content. With respect to the negative class, GPT-4o-mini and GPT-3.5 few-shot variants emerge as the most reliable performers across platforms. Their superior recall and F1 scores highlight a stronger ability to capture adversarial, ironic, or hostile sentiment, which typically demands greater contextual sensitivity. In this regard, X constitutes the most favorable environment, with LLMs attaining the highest F1 improvements relative to baselines. Finally, the neutral class represents the greatest challenge. Scores are consistently lower, and although GPT-4o-mini and o1-mini few-shot occasionally occupy the leading position, performance varies considerably across platforms. Notably, YouTube performs comparatively well due to the predominance of neutral content, whereas X once again exposes the limitations of current models, with even the strongest systems achieving only moderate results.

Overall, this per-class perspective confirms that the global superiority of LLMs is consistent across categories but also nuanced: positive and negative sentiments are captured with high reliability, while neutrality remains the most challenging dimension. This reinforces the need for further methodological advances tailored to ambiguous or context-dependent sentiment, especially in political discourse where neutrality often masks implicit stance.

6 Conclusion

This study introduced a new human-annotated corpus of Spanish-language social media posts collected during the 2024 Mexican presidential elections, together with a comprehensive evaluation of transformer-based baselines and large language models (LLMs) for political sentiment analysis. The dataset, annotated independently by multiple native speakers, provides a reliable ground truth that addresses the scarcity of high-quality resources for Spanish in politically sensitive contexts.

The results demonstrated consistent trends. Transformer-based baselines, including widely used models such as BERT, BETO, RoBERTa and pysentimiento, establish only a minimal reference level in this domain. In contrast, recent LLMs, particularly GPT-4o-mini in the few-shot setting, achieved state-of-the-art performance across diverse metrics of effectiveness, setting a new benchmark for sentiment analysis in Spanish electoral discourse. The advantage of LLMs was especially evident in the most challenging platforms, such as X and YouTube, where improvements over baselines frequently exceeded 0.25 absolute points.

The analysis by sentiment class revealed persistent limitations. While positive and negative sentiments were captured with high reliability, neutral sentiment remained the most challenging category, with performance varying considerably across platforms. This difficulty underscores the intrinsic complexity of neutrality in political discourse, which often conceals implicit stance or context-dependent meaning.

Overall, this work provides two main contributions: a novel annotated dataset of Spanish electoral social media and a systematic benchmarking of traditional and large-scale models under zero-shot and few-shot prompting. Beyond providing an empirical comparison, the findings highlight both the potential and the current limitations of LLMs in politically charged, non-English contexts. To facilitate reproducibility and foster future research, both the annotated dataset and the evaluation code are publicly available in the repository https://github.com/jvalverr/spanish-political-sentiment-llm.

Acknowledgments. We would like to thank the Digital Media Observatory (OMD) and the Department of Computer Science, Mexico City Campus, both at Tecnológico de Monterrey, for supporting this research with diverse resources and for the contributions of their annotators and analysts.

Disclosure of Interests. The authors have no competing interests to declare that are relevant to the content of this article.

References

1. Alcántara-Lizárraga, J.A., Jima-González, A.: Digital manipulation and mass mobilization over the long run: evidence from Latin America. Frontiers. Pol. Sci. **6**, 1296004 (2024)
2. Altay, S., Hoes, E., Wojcieszak, M.: Following news on social media boosts knowledge, belief accuracy and trust. Nat. Hum. Behav. **9**, 1833 (2025)
3. Avalle, M., et al.: Persistent interaction pattern across social media platforms and over time. Nature. **628**(8008), 582–589 (2024)
4. Brito, K., Adeodato, P.J.L.: Machine learning for predicting elections in latin america based on social media engagement and polls. Gov. Inf. Q. **40**(1), 101782 (2023)
5. Brown, T., Mann, B., Ryder, N., Subbiah, M., et al.: Language models are few- shot learners. Adv. Neural Inf. Proc. Syst. (NeurIPS). **33**, 1877–1901 (2020)
6. Cañete, J., Chaperon, G., Fuentes, R., Ho, J.-H., Kang, H., Pérez, J.: Spanish pre-trained BERT model and evaluation data. In: Proceedings of the Practical ML for Developing Countries Workshop at ICLR (2020)
7. Cui, J., Wang, Z., Ho, S.-B., Cambria, E.: Survey on sentiment analysis: evolution of research methods and topics. Artif. Intell. Rev. **56**(8), 8469–8510 (2023)
8. Devlin, J., Chang, M.-W., Lee, K., Toutanova, K.: BERT: pre-training of deep bidirectional transformers for language understanding. In: Proceedings of NAACL- HLT, pp. 4171–4186 (2019)
9. Garcia, J.C., Fernández Pedemonte, D., Vaca, C., Baquerizo-Neira, M.: A per- tinence score for political discourse analysis: the case of 2018 Colombian elections. Digit. Gov.: Res. Pract. **5**(3) (2024)
10. Gutiérrez, H., Zareei, M., de León Languré, A., Brito, K.: Predicting the 2024 Mexican presidential election with social media. In: Advances in Soft Computing, pp. 224–233. Springer Nature Switzerland (2025)
11. Guzmán-Monteza, Y.: Assessment of an annotation method for the detection of Spanish argumentative, non-argumentative, and their components. Telematics Inform. Rep. **11**, 100068 (2023)
12. Krugmann, J.O., Hartmann, J.: Sentiment analysis in the age of generative AI. Cust. Needs Solut. **11**(1), 3 (2024)
13. Kuan, J., Mueller, J.: Model-Agnostic Label Quality Scoring to Detect Real-World Label Errors. In ICML DataPerf Workshop, 2022.
14. Liu, Y., et al.: RoBERTa: A Robustly Optimized BERT Pretraining Approach. arXiv cs.CL, 1907.11692, (2019)
15. Yáñez Martínez, R., Blanco, G., Lourenço, A.: Spanish corpora of tweets about COVID-19 vaccination for automatic stance detection. Inf. Process. Manag. **60**(3), 103294 (2023)
16. Navas-Loro, M., Rodríguez-Doncel, V.: Spanish corpora for sentiment analysis: a survey. Lang. Resour. Eval. **54**(2), 303–340 (2020)
17. OpenAI. GPT-4 Technical Report. arXiv cs.CL, 2303.08774, (2023).
18. Pérez, J.M., et al.: pysentimiento: A Python Toolkit for Opinion Mining and Social NLP tasks. arXiv cs.CL, 2106.09462 (2021).
19. Ayma Quirita, V.A., Cárdenas, J.D., Aliaga, W., Ayma Quirita, V.H., Palacios, A., Sierra, R.B.: Peruvian presidential debates in the elections of 2021 in twitter/x: a sentiment analysis approach. IEEE Access. **12**, 138386–138398 (2024)
20. Sandoval-Almazan, R., Negrete Huelga, K.B., Valle-Cruz, D.: Social media and political debates: the case of the state of Mexico election. In: Proceedings of the 25th Annual International Conference on Digital Government Research, Dg.O '24, pp. 177–185. Association for Computing Machinery, New York, NY, USA (2024)

21. Song, C., Chen, S., Cai, X., Chen, H.: Sentiment Analysis of Spanish Political Party Tweets Using Pre-trained Language Models. arXiv cs.CL, 2411.04862 (2024).
22. Touvron, H., Lavril, T., Izacard, G., Martinet, X., et al.: LLaMA: Open and Efficient Foundation Language Models. arXiv cs.CL,2302.13971 (2023)
23. Zhang, W., Deng, Y., Liu, B., Pan, S., Bing, L.: Sentiment analysis in the era of large language models: a reality check. In: Findings of the Association for Computational Linguistics: NAACL 2024, pp. 3881–3906. ACL (2024)

Hybridization of the Mayfly and Roach Infestation Algorithms Through a Fuzzy System

Enrique Lizárraga, Fevrier Valdez(✉), Oscar Castillo, and Patricia Melin

Tijuana Institute of Technology, TecNM, Tomas Aquino, Tijuana, B.C., México
fevrier@tectijuana.mx

Abstract. Optimization in complex spaces requires algorithms capable of adequately balancing exploration and exploitation. This work proposes a hybridization of Ephemeral Collective Intelligence (MA) and Cockroach Infestation (RIO) algorithms by incorporating a fuzzy system that allows switching between the two algorithms according to the needs of the search process. This system dynamically regulates the switching and execution intensity of the algorithms based on iteration and population diversity, allowing MA to focus on refining the most promising regions of the search space, while RIO introduces the necessary diversity to prevent premature convergence. Experimental results obtained on 15 benchmark mathematical functions demonstrate that the hybrid proposal with fuzzy control outperforms MA and RIO individually on 9 of the 15 functions evaluated. As future work, we propose incorporating additional metrics, such as robustness, to increase the accuracy and effectiveness of the fuzzy adapter.

Keywords: Hybrid metaheuristics · Swarm Intelligence · type-2 fuzzy system · parameter adaptation

1 Introduction

Currently, the use of evolutionary algorithms has grown, as they are powerful tools in optimization [1]. Genetic algorithms (GAs) emerged as a robust alternative to classical methods, using populations that promote diversity and allow addressing complex problems [2].

In the last decade, swarm intelligence (SI) algorithms have outperformed GAs in optimization, thanks to their inspiration in the collective behavior of social organisms, which improves the exploration and exploitation of the search space [3].

Algorithms such as Ant Colony Optimization (ACO) and Particle Swarm Optimization (PSO) [4] have been developed, whose strength lies in balancing exploration and exploitation, allowing to address complex problems where traditional methods are inefficient [5].

Hybridizations that integrate GA techniques in SI have also been proposed to improve this balance [6].

The contribution of this work is to propose a hybridization of the RIO and MA algorithms using fuzzy logic. On their own, RIO stands out for its robust exploration

L. Martínez-Villaseñor et al. (Eds.): MICAI 2025 Workshops, LNAI 16264, pp. 301–313, 2026.
https://doi.org/10.1007/978-3-032-17930-2_21

capability, avoiding local optima [7], while MA offers efficient exploitation and rapid convergence [8]. The proposed combination dynamically adjusts the participation of each algorithm based on indicators such as elapsed time and population diversity, combining the strengths of both to achieve a more stable and robust optimization process.

The remainder of the paper is structured as: Sect. 2 presents the theoretical framework. Section 3 describes the proposed method. Section 4 presents the design of the fuzzy system. Section 5 summarizes the results, and finally, Sect. 6 discusses conclusions and future prospects.

2 Theoretical Framework

The PSO algorithm, proposed by Kennedy and Eberhart in 1995, is a swarm intelligence method where particles represent solutions and update their positions using their experience and the information of the swarm [9].

However, PSO has limitations, which motivated the development of hybrids such as G-CLPSO, which combines CLPSO exploration with Marquardt-Levenberg exploitation [10]. Another example is MRFOSSA, which integrates MRFO and SSA to optimize task scheduling in IoT, improving efficiency and performance [7].

2.1 Roach Infestation Optimization Algorithm

The RIO algorithm, a variant of PSO, is inspired by cockroaches that seek out optimal areas, interact socially, and explore new areas, achieving a balance between exploitation and exploration [11].

The RIO equations are as follows:

$$V_{i+1} = C_0 V_i + C_{max} R_1 (p_i - x_i) + C_{max} R_2 (l_i - x_i) \tag{1}$$

$$x_{i+1} = \begin{cases} x_i + V_{i+1}, & if\ (hunger_i < T_{hunger}) \\ b & if\ hunger_i = T_{hunger} \end{cases} \tag{2}$$

Where V_i is the agents velocity, x_i is the current location found by agent i, p_i is the best location found by swarm i, l_i is the darkest location known to agent i after socializing, C_0 is the momentum terms adjustment, C_{max} is the cognitive and social adjustment factor, R_1 and R_2 are uniformly distributed random number vectors, $hunger_i$ is a hunger counter indicating the cockroach's current hunger level, T_{hunger} is the set hunger threshold, and b is a random position within the solution space [7].

2.2 Derivations of the RIO Algorithm

Since its introduction, several variants of the RIO algorithm have been developed to enhance its performance. However, hybridization of this algorithm remains largely unexplored. The variants documented in the literature are presented below.

2.2.1 Modified Roach Infestation Optimization Algorithm

The Modified Roach Infestation Optimization (MRIO) algorithm, developed by Ibidun O. Obagbuwa and Aderemi O. Adewumi in 2014, it incorporates surveillance and cannibalism, where stronger individuals replace weaker ones and generate new solutions, accelerating convergence. However, this mechanism can reduce diversity in multimodal problems, affecting global exploration [12].

2.2.2 Roach Infestation Optimization with Friendship Centers

Roach Infestation Optimization with Friendship Centers (RIO-FC), proposed by Tsai (2015), It incorporates friendship centers, where each cockroach moves according to its neighbors, improving cohesion, diversity and exploration-exploitation balance, although it can increase computational time by 33% and reduce diversity in very multimodal problems [13].

2.2.3 Genetic Optimization for Roach Infestation

Genetic Roach Infestation Optimization (GRIO), proposed by L. Antonio in 2017, it extends RIO by combining multiple swarms with genetic operators, adjusting the speed of each roach based on its position and neighbors to balance exploration and exploitation. This prevents premature convergence and improves performance on complex problems, although it can increase computational costs [14].

2.3 Mayfly Algorithm

The mayfly is an insect that focuses on reproducing before it dies. Similarly, the MA algorithm draws on this behavior to improve PSO convergence by continuously updating particle positions and achieving a more efficient search for optimal solutions.

$$x_{ij+1} = x_{ij} + v_{ij+1} \tag{3}$$

Where x_i represents the current position and v_i the current velocity

$$v_{ij}^{t+1} = v_{ij}^{t} + a_1 e^{-\beta r_p^2}\left(pbest_{ij} - x_{ij}^{t}\right) + a_2 e^{-\beta r_g^2}\left(gbest_j - x_{ij}^{t}\right) \tag{4}$$

Where $\boldsymbol{v_{ij}}$ is the velocity of Mayfly i in dimension $\boldsymbol{j} = 1 - n$ at time step $\boldsymbol{t}$, $\boldsymbol{x_{ij}}$ is the position of Mayfly $\boldsymbol{i}$ in dimension $\boldsymbol{j}$ at time step $\boldsymbol{t}$, $\boldsymbol{a}_1$ and $\boldsymbol{a}_2$ are positive attraction constants used to scale the contribution of the cognitive and social components, respectively, ***pbest*** is the local best position, ***gbest*** is the global best position, and $\boldsymbol{\beta}$ is a fixed visibility coefficient [8].

2.4 Alternative Approaches Based on the Mayfly Algorithm

Various versions of MA have emerged in the literature to compensate for its exploration limitations; however, further work is still needed on its hybridization with specialized algorithms for this phase. The most relevant variants of MA are presented below.

2.4.1 Negative Mayfly

The Negative Mayfly Optimization (NMO) algorithm, proposed by Zhao and Gao in 2020, modifies conventional Mayfly behavior: males update their velocities by considering the worst candidates and global trajectories. This causes individuals to avoid low-quality solutions, promoting diversification and reducing the risk of getting trapped in unpromising areas, although it can be unstable in high-dimensional problems [15].

2.4.2 Modified Mayfly Algorithm

The Modified Mayfly Algorithm (MMA), proposed by W. Pan et al. (2022) for UAV trajectory planning, uses exponential inertia decay, adaptive Cauchy mutation, and improved crossover, increasing diversity and the ability to escape local optima. However, it is sensitive to initialization, expensive for large problems, and requires fine tuning of parameters [16].

2.4.3 Mayfly with Dynamic Elite Strategy

Dynamic Elite Strategy Mayfly Algorithm (DESMA) was proposed by Du and Zhu (2022), dynamically adjusts the search range to optimize solutions, improve elite selection, and preserve diversity at advanced stages, however, it may cause over exploration and higher computational costs, affecting its efficiency [17].

2.5 Recent Hybridizations of the Mayfly Algorithm

In recent literature, the Mayfly algorithm has been hybridized to improve the balance between exploration and exploitation and reduce blocking in local minima, although these proposals still have limitations that justify new approaches.

2.5.1 Mayfly Aquila Optimizer

Mayfly Aquila Optimizer (MFA-AOA) was proposed by Natesan et al. in 2022 this algorithm combined MA with the Aquila algorithm to optimize routes in sensor networks. While it improves the exploration-exploitation trade off and energy efficiency, its performance focuses on specific routing problems and may not be generalizable to other optimization functions [18].

2.5.2 Mayfly Grey Wolf Optimizer

The Mayfly Gray Wolf Optimizer (MA-GWO) was proposed by Yan et al. in 2023. This algorithm integrates GWO search strategies with MA flying mechanisms, reducing premature convergence, although the complexity and parameter dependence may limit its applicability in high-dimensional or highly multimodal problems [19].

2.5.3 Mayfly with Fuzzy Adaptation

Fuzzy adaptive mayfly was proposed by Lizárraga et al. in 2025. This hybrid algorithm adjusts key MA parameters using a fuzzy system, enabling dynamic adaptation that reinforces early exploration and late exploitation, improving the overall balance of the algorithm [20]. Although these hybridizations improve on pure MA, they still face challenges in complex and multidimensional scenarios. Therefore, the FRIO-MA hybrid approach is proposed, combining the strengths of MA and RIO using a fuzzy adapter and a switched hybridization scheme, allowing to dynamically decide which algorithm to run depending on the state of the optimization process.

3 Proposed Method

The proposal consists of combining the MA algorithm with RIO, integrating the latter's exploratory capabilities with the exploitative strengths of MA, with the goal of balancing both phases through their hybridization. In this context, this section introduces the flowchart of the method, shown in Fig. 1.

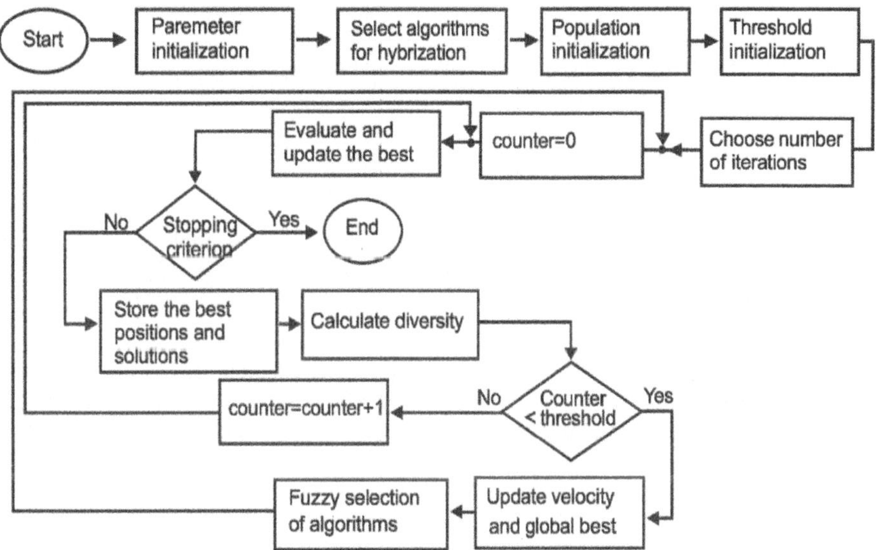

Fig. 1. Diagram of fuzzy algorithm selection

Figure 1 shows MA and RIO hybridization with a fuzzy adapter that activates after 5–10 iterations. The process starts with setup and initialization, evaluates solutions and diversity, and then the adapter adjusts the speed and selects the algorithm until the stopping criterion is met.

Table 1 summarizes the parameters used in the proposed hybridization.

Table 1 presents the parameters of the proposed hybridization: those of MA [8, 21], inspired by PSO [22] and focused on exploitation; those of RIO [7, 23], exploration-oriented using C_{maxR_1} and C_{maxR_2} and the general parameters that define iterations, population, dimensions, and search range.

Table 1. Parameter configuration

MA	RIO	General settings	
$a_1 = 1.5$	$C_0 = 0.7$	Iterations = 2000	Threshold counter = 5
$a_2 = 1.5$	$T_{hunger} = 300$	Dimensions = 50	Range = [−5, 5]
$\beta = 3$	$C_{max} = 1.13$	Population = 20	

4 Fuzzy System Design

A type 1 fuzzy system was designed that dynamically selects the most appropriate algorithm based on population diversity and the number of iterations. It uses nine linguistic rules to guide flexible and interpretable decisions, as shown in Fig. 2.

Fig. 2. Fuzzy Adapter

Figure 2 shows the fuzzy adapter, which selects the most suitable algorithm from two metrics, using triangular membership functions to achieve flexible and efficient switching between methods.

Table 2 presents the rules with which the fuzzy system works.

Table 2 shows that initially, RIO is favored, in intermediate stages the probabilities balance, and finally, MA acquires greater weight, reflecting an adaptive transition between algorithms. Triangular membership functions (Eq. 5) were used due to their simplicity and low computational cost, allowing for smooth, linear transitions between fuzzy sets.

$$\text{f(x; a, b, c)} = \begin{matrix} 0, & x \leq a \\ \frac{x-a}{b-a}, & a \leq x \leq b \\ \frac{c-x}{c-b}, & b \leq x \leq c \\ 0, & c \leq x \end{matrix} \tag{5}$$

Table 3 presents the membership functions defined for the fuzzy system inputs.

Table 3 shows the membership functions of the fuzzy system, which guide the selection of the most appropriate method. The parameters were tuned iteratively, exploring and refining variations, and evaluating each configuration with 30 runs to optimize stability and performance. Table 4 presents the output membership functions.

Table 4 shows the execution probabilities of RIO and MA, with RIO favoring exploration and MA favoring exploitation.

Table 2. Fuzzy rules

Number rule	Rule description
1	If the iteration is low and diversity is low, then the probability of RIO is very large and the probability of MA is very low
2	If the iteration is low and diversity is medium, then the probability of RIO is large and the probability of MA is low
3	If the iteration is low and diversity is high, then the probability of RIO is moderately large and the probability of MA is moderately low
4	If the iteration is medium and diversity is low, then the probability of RIO is medium-large and the probability of MA is medium low
5	If the iteration is medium and diversity is medium, then the probability of RIO is medium and the probability of MA is medium large
6	If the iteration is medium and diversity is high, then the probability of RIO is medium-low and the probability of MA is medium-large
7	If the iteration is high and diversity is low, then the probability of RIO is medium-low and the probability of MA is medium-large
8	If the iteration is high and diversity is medium, then the probability of RIO is low and the probability of MA is large
9	If the iteration is high and diversity is high, then the probability of RIO is very low and the probability of MA is very large

Table 3. Input membership functions

Input membership functions	a	b	c
IB (Low iteration)	0	0.080	0.134
IM (Medium iteration)	0.099	0.276	0.430
IA (High iteration)	0.387	0.684	1
DB (Low Diversity)	0	0.109	0.200
DM (Medium Diversity)	0.145	0.380	0.557
DA (High Diversity)	0.504	0.758	1

Table 4. Output membership functions

Output membership functions	a	b	c
PRIOMB (Very low probability of RIO)	0	0.102	0.133
PRIOBA (Low probability of RIO)	0.096	0.175	0.224
PRIOMEDBJ (Moderately low probability of RIO)	0.183	0.250	0.311
PRIOMEB (Medium-Low Probability of RIO)	0.261	0.372	0.427
PRIOMED (Medium Probability of RIO)	0.375	0.480	0.543
PRIOMEG (Medium-Large Probability of RIO)	0.496	0.572	0.657
PRIOMEDG (Medium-Large Probability of RIO)	0.604	0.708	0.771
PRIOG (Large Probability of RIO)	0.724	0.833	0.891
PRIOMG (Very Large Probability of RIO)	0.853	0.925	1
PMAMB (Very Low Probability of MA)	0	0.086	0.133
PMABA (Low Probability of MA)	0.086	0.168	0.250
PMAMEDBJ (Medium-Low Probability of MA)	0.186	0.269	0.342
PMAMEB (Medium-Low Probability of MA)	0.282	0.366	0.451
PMAMED (Medium Probability of MA)	0.392	0.483	0.565
PMAMEG (Medium-Large Probability of MA)	0.508	0.612	0.705
PMAMEDG (Medium-Large Probability of MA)	0.604	0.732	0.798
PMAG (Large Probability of MA)	0.744	0.821	0.906

5 Results

This section evaluates the efficiency of RIO-MA hybridization with a fuzzy system to determine whether it improves performance and the balance between exploration and exploitation. Each test was run 30 times with 50 dimensions, 2000 iterations, and 30 agents, summarizing the results using the mean and standard deviation.

The results were compared with the original MA and RIO algorithms using a two-sample (left-tailed) statistical test with a 95% confidence interval. The negative Z values show that FRIO-MA significantly outperforms MA on most features, with confidence intervals supporting the accuracy of the differences. However, in functions such as Schwefel, Powell, and Dixon Price, the hybrid does not achieve superior performance because it requires more intensive exploitation or depends on the initial position. Even so, hybridization shows significant improvements in efficiency and accuracy.

Table 5 presents the comparison of results between the hybrid algorithm between MA and RIO using a fuzzy adapter type-1 (FRIO-MA) and the MA algorithm on a set of test functions widely used in optimization.

Table 5 shows that FRIO-MA achieves average values closer to the optimal and with a lower standard deviation, demonstrating greater accuracy and stability. The statistical results (column Z) indicate significant differences in 9 of the 15 benchmark functions, highlighting their balance between exploration and exploitation.

Table 5. Comparison of the hybrid algorithm with MA for 50 dimensions

Function		FRIO-MA	MA	Z
Sphere	$\bar{x}$	2.5062×10^{-17}	1.3777×10^{-7}	−1.6694
	s	1.3727×10^{-16}	4.5203×10^{-7}	
Rastrigin	$\bar{x}$	1.0593×10^{1}	1.1900×10^{1}	−1.6600
	s	2.0013×10^{0}	3.8200×10^{0}	
Ackley	$\bar{x}$	2.8672×10^{0}	2.9875×10^{0}	−1.7549
	s	3.7493×10^{-1}	2.0300×10^{-2}	
Griewank	$\bar{x}$	1.7255×10^{-13}	4.1400×10^{-3}	−1.7715
	s	9.2165×10^{-13}	1.2800×10^{-2}	
Schwefel	$\bar{x}$	7.3109×10^{3}	3.8800×10^{0}	1.8470
	s	2.1650×10^{1}	8.8300×10^{-1}	
Powell	$\bar{x}$	2.2447×10^{-18}	5.2800×10^{-49}	2.9468
	s	4.1723×10^{-18}	1.6500×10^{-48}	
Rosenbrock	$\bar{x}$	4.1829×10^{1}	6.7703×10^{1}	-2.7854
	s	3.1600×10^{1}	3.9877×10^{1}	
Alpine	$\bar{x}$	1.6322×10^{-8}	3.3465×10^{-8}	−0.4980
	s	9.5751×10^{-8}	1.6242×10^{-7}	
Zakharov	$\bar{x}$	2.3258×10^{-1}	1.7130×10^{-1}	0.9115
	s	1.7505×10^{0}	8.3733×10^{-2}	
Square sum	$\bar{x}$	1.4445×10^{-12}	7.3923×10^{-6}	−1.6664
	s	3.1667×10^{-12}	2.4297×10^{-5}	
Styblinskitang	$\bar{x}$	1.0138×10^{3}	2.2220×10^{3}	−1.6501
	s	3.9150×10^{2}	3.9927×10^{3}	
Dejong1	$\bar{x}$	8.2237×10^{-14}	9.8000×10^{-2}	−2.2235
	s	2.3048×10^{-13}	2.4141×10^{-1}	
Levy	$\bar{x}$	1.3562×10^{-15}	2.3148×10^{-14}	−1.7316
	s	6.8890×10^{-14}	2.3212×10^{-15}	
Hyper-ellipsoid	$\bar{x}$	4.2826×10^{-13}	1.6396×10^{-31}	3.3149
	s	7.0762×10^{-13}	5.0074×10^{-31}	
Dixon Price	$\bar{x}$	1.3170×10^{-1}	3.3696×10^{-15}	0.3440
	s	2.0970×10^{0}	2.0807×10^{-6}	

Table 6 presents the complete results for these 15 functions to evaluate the performance of the hybrid algorithm.

Table 6 presents the comparative results of the FRIO-MA hybrid algorithm versus the RIO algorithm in a 50-dimensional scenario. The data obtained show that the hybrid

Table 6. Comparison of the hybrid algorithm with RIO for 50 dimensions

Function		FRIO-MA	RIO	Z
Sphere	$\bar{x}$	2.5062×10^{-17}	1.8371×10^{-4}	−3.0728
	s	1.3727×10^{-16}	3.2746×10^{-4}	
Rastrigin	$\bar{x}$	1.0593×10^{1}	3.5071×10^{1}	−4.0644
	s	2.0013×10^{0}	4.3290×10^{1}	
Ackley	$\bar{x}$	2.8672×10^{0}	3.1777×10^{0}	−3.6539
	s	3.7493×10^{-1}	3.3033×10^{-2}	
Griewank	$\bar{x}$	1.7255×10^{-13}	3.2452×10^{-6}	−2.1820
	s	9.2165×10^{-13}	8.1460×10^{-6}	
Schwefel	$\bar{x}$	7.3109×10^{3}	3.2536×10^{2}	4.1809
	s	2.1650×10^{1}	9.1514×10^{3}	
Powell	$\bar{x}$	2.2447×10^{-18}	3.7437×10^{-7}	−3.6965
	s	4.1723×10^{-18}	5.5472×10^{-7}	
Rosenbrock	$\bar{x}$	4.1829×10^{1}	8.7676×10^{1}	−2.9927
	s	3.1600×10^{1}	7.7731×10^{1}	
Alpine	$\bar{x}$	1.6322×10^{-8}	1.6262×10^{-3}	−1.1459
	s	9.5751×10^{-8}	4.5440×10^{-3}	
Zakharov	$\bar{x}$	2.3258×10^{-1}	1.3627×10^{2}	−2.0584
	s	1.7505×10^{0}	3.6198×10^{2}	
Square sum	$\bar{x}$	1.4445×10^{-12}	5.0465×10^{-4}	−3.8818
	s	3.1667×10^{-12}	7.1206×10^{-4}	
Styblinskitang	$\bar{x}$	1.0138×10^{3}	2.4850×10^{4}	−3.5304
	s	3.9150×10^{2}	4.2564×10^{4}	
Dejong1	$\bar{x}$	8.2237×10^{-14}	9.0648×10^{-5}	−2.8548
	s	2.3048×10^{-13}	1.7392×10^{-4}	
Levy	$\bar{x}$	1.3562×10^{-15}	6.0890×10^{-3}	−1.6941
	s	6.8890×10^{-14}	1.9687×10^{-2}	
Hyper-ellipsoid	$\bar{x}$	4.2826×10^{-13}	7.1869×10^{-3}	−3.9882
	s	7.0762×10^{-13}	9.8702×10^{-2}	
Dixon Price	$\bar{x}$	1.3170×10^{-1}	1.9159×10^{0}	−3.2333
	s	2.0970×10^{0}	2.1766×10^{0}	

algorithm achieves superior performance in 13 of the 15 benchmark functions evaluated, confirming the effectiveness of the hybridization strategy in improving the balance between exploration and exploitation in high-dimensional problems.

In the Schwefel and Alpine functions, the hybrid does not present significant improvements because Schwefel is highly multimodal and Alpine has very pronounced minimums, which makes it difficult for the balance between exploration and exploitation of the hybrid to be effective.

6 Conclusions

The experimental results obtained indicate that the proposed hybridization of the MA and RIO algorithms, controlled by a fuzzy adapter, constitutes an effective strategy for solving optimization problems in high-dimensional spaces. In particular, it was observed that the hybrid algorithm outperformed the RIO algorithm in 13 of the 15 benchmark functions evaluated, while when compared to MA, it obtained better results in 9 of the 15 functions. These findings, supported by the applied statistical tests, demonstrate the effectiveness of the proposed approach, confirming that the iterative combination of both algorithms achieves an adequate balance between exploration and exploitation.

The design of the fuzzy adapter played a fundamental role in regulating the dynamic switching between the two algorithms, allowing the exploratory capacity of RIO to be leveraged and the exploitative strength of MA to be leveraged. This mechanism contributed to reducing the risk of premature convergence and improving the accuracy in the search for optimal solutions, resulting in competitive performance compared to the original algorithms.

As future work, it is promising to extend this research to internal parameter adaptation schemes [24, 25]. It is also relevant to explore how RIO and MA adjust their parameters using a fuzzy system that determines whether further exploration or exploitation is required, as well as to design a coordinated double adaptation scheme according to the population and diversity of solutions.

References

1. Hua, Y., Liu, Q., Hao, K., Jin, Y.: A survey of evolutionary algorithms for multi-objective optimization problems with irregular Pareto fronts. IEEE/CAA J. Autom. Sin. **8**(2), 303–318 (2021). https://doi.org/10.1109/JAS.2021.1003817
2. Sohail, A.: Genetic algorithms in the fields of artificial intelligence and data sciences (2023). https://doi.org/10.1007/s40745-021-00354-9
3. Chityal, N., Sapkal, S.: Performance analysis of GA, PSO and JA for determining the optimal parameters in friction drilling process. Eng. Sci. Technol. Int. J. **35** (2022). https://doi.org/10.1016/j.jestch.2022.101246
4. Di Caprio, D., Ebrahimnejad, A., Alrezaamiri, H., Santos-Arteaga, F.J.: A novel ant colony algorithm for solving shortest path problems with fuzzy arc weights. Alex. Eng. J. **61**(5), 3403–3415 (2022). https://doi.org/10.1016/j.aej.2021.08.058
5. Juneja, M., Nagar, S.K.: Particle swarm optimization algorithm and its parameters: a review. In: Proceedings of the 2016 International Conference on Control, Computing, Communication and Materials (ICCCCM), Varanasi, India (2016). https://doi.org/10.1109/ICCCCM.2016.7918233
6. Xue, Y., Aouari, A., Mansour, R.F., Su, S.: A hybrid algorithm based on PSO and GA for feature selection. J. Cyber Secur. **2021**, 017018 (2021). https://doi.org/10.32604/jcs.2021.017018

7. Havens, T., Spain, C., Salmon, N., Keller, J.: Roach infestation optimization. In: 2008 IEEE Swarm Intelligence Symposium (2008). https://doi.org/10.1109/sis.2008.4668317
8. Zervoudakis, K., Tsafarakis, S.: A mayfly optimization algorithm. Comput. Ind. Eng. **145**(2020). https://doi.org/10.1016/j.cie.2020.106559
9. Tang, J., Duan, H., Lao, S.: Swarm intelligence algorithms for multiple unmanned aerial vehicles collaboration: a comprehensive review. Artif. Intell. Rev. **56**(5), 4295–4327 (2023). https://doi.org/10.1007/s10462-022-10281-7
10. Brunetti, G., Stumpp, C., Šimůnek, J.: Balancing exploitation and exploration: a novel hybrid global-local optimization strategy for hydrological model calibration. Environ Model Softw. **150**, 105341 (2022)
11. Obagbuwa, I., Adewumi, A., Adebiyi, A.: A dynamic step-size adaptation roach infestation optimization. In: 2014 IEEE International Advance Computing Conference (IACC) (2014). https://doi.org/10.1109/iadcc.2014.6779498
12. Ibidun, O., Adewumi, A.: A Modified Roach Infestation Optimization. School of Mathematics, Statistics and Computer Science, University of KwaZulu-Natal, Westville, Durban, 4000
13. Tsai, H.C.: Roach infestation optimization with friendship centers. Eng. Appl. Artif. Intell. **39**, 109–119 (2015). https://doi.org/10.1016/j.engappai.2014.12.003
14. Gustavo, A., Brites, L.: Genetic Roach Infestation Optimization – Optimization Algorithm Based on Cockroaches' Social Life. Instituto Superior Técnico, Universidade de Lisboa, Lisboa, Portugal, November 2017
15. Zhao, J., Gao, Z.M.: The negative Mayfly optimization algorithm. J. Phys. Conf. Ser. **1693**(1) (2020). https://doi.org/10.1088/1742-6596/1693/1/012098
16. Wang, X., Pan, J.-S., Yang, Q., Kong, L., Snášel, V., Chu, S.-C.: Modified Mayfly algorithm for UAV path planning (2022) https://doi.org/10.3390/drones
17. Du, Q., Zhu, H.: Dynamic elite strategy Mayfly algorithm. PLoS One **17**(8) (2022). https://doi.org/10.1371/journal.pone.0273155
18. Natesan, G., Konda, S., de Prado, R.P., Wozniak, M.: A hybrid Mayfly-Aquila optimization algorithm based energy-efficient clustering routing protocol for wireless sensor networks. Sensors **22**(17) (2022). https://doi.org/10.3390/s22176405
19. Yan, Z., Yan, J., Wu, Y., Zhang, C.: An improved hybrid mayfly algorithm for global optimization. J. Supercomput. **79**(6), 5878–5919 (2023). https://doi.org/10.1007/s11227-022-04883-9
20. Lizárraga, E., Valdez, F., Castillo, O., Melin, P.: Hybridization of the Mayfly and roach infestation optimization collective intelligence algorithms with fuzzy system-based parameter adaptation. In: Melin, P., Castillo, O. (eds.) Modern Artificial Intelligence Based on Soft Computing Techniques. SCI, vol. 1204, pp. 179–189. Springer, Cham (2025). https://doi.org/10.1007/978-3-031-88279-1_13
21. Xu, H., Zhao, M., Xue, F., Zhang, X., Sun, L.: An improved mayfly algorithm with shading detection for MPPT of photovoltaic systems. IEEE Access **11**, 110827–110836 (2023). https://doi.org/10.1109/ACCESS.2023.3318129
22. Chen, Y., Zhao, X., Yuan, J.: Swarm intelligence algorithms for portfolio optimization problems: overview and recent advances (2022). https://doi.org/10.1155/2022/4241049
23. Obagbuwa, I.C., Adewumi, A.O.: An improved cockroach swarm optimization. Sci. World J. **2014** (2014). https://doi.org/10.1155/2014/375358
24. Zhou, X., Ma, H., Gu, J., Chen, H., Deng, W.: Parameter adaptation-based ant colony optimization with dynamic hybrid mechanism. Eng. Appl. Artif. Intell. **114** (2022). https://doi.org/10.1016/j.engappai.2022.105139

25. Lizarraga, E., Valdez, F., Melin, P., Castillo, O.: A hybrid enhanced mayfly optimization algorithm with improved performance through fuzzy-based automatic parameter adaptation. Computacion Sistemas **29**(2), 615–631 (2025). https://doi.org/10.13053/CyS-29-2-5709
26. Sánchez, D., Melin, P., Castillo, O.: Comparison of particle swarm optimization variants with fuzzy dynamic parameter adaptation for modular granular neural networks for human recognition. J. Intell. Fuzzy Syst. **38**(3), 3229–3252 (2020). https://doi.org/10.3233/JIFS-191198

Design of a Hybrid Model Based on Dynamic Decision Trees and Adaptive Bayesian Algorithms for Student Support and the Integration of Emerging Technologies

Samuel Efren Viñas Alvarez[1], María Esmeralda Arreola Marín[2](✉), José Iraic Alcantar Alcantar[2], Mariela Chávez Marcial[2], and Edgar Gonzalo Cossio Franco[3]

[1] Tecnológico Nacional de México/I.T., Zitácuaro, México
samuel.va@zitacuaro.tecnm.mx

[2] Tecnológico Nacional de México/I.T.S., Ciudad Hidalgo, México
{marreola,jalcantar,mchavez}@cdhidalgo.tecnm.mx

[3] Instituto de Información Estadística y Geográfica de Jalisco, Zapopan, México
edgar.cossio@iieg.gob.mx

Abstract. This article describes the design and validation of a hybrid chatbot aimed at student support in higher education institutions. The proposed system integrates a Dynamic Decision Tree (DDT) and an Adaptive Bayesian Model (ABM), enabling the management of frequent, ambiguous, or unstructured queries through a process of semantic classification and incremental learning. The development was based on an institutional corpus and a set of academic jargon, incorporating natural language processing techniques for lexical expansion and intent detection. A Module for Argumentation and Negotiation (MAN) was implemented, employing Toulmin's model and multi-turn negotiation schemes to generate justified responses and resolve conflicting requests. In addition, a blockchain-based traceability system (Hyperledger Fabric) was integrated to anchor sensitive interactions, ensuring data integrity and privacy. Complementarily, a light gamification approach was applied to encourage proper query formulation and the completion of administrative procedures. The tests demonstrated a Top-1 accuracy of 92% in the DDT and a 100% resolution rate in the ABM, confirming the feasibility of the proposed approach to enhance institutional efficiency and user experience in automated support environments.

Keywords: Hybrid Chatbot · Dynamic Decision Tree · Adaptive Bayesian Model · Natural Language Processing · Argumentation and Negotiation · Blockchain · Gamification

1 Introduction

The growing digitalization of academic processes in higher education has created an urgent need for tools that optimize student support, reduce administrative workloads, and provide real-time assistance.

L. Martínez-Villaseñor et al. (Eds.): MICAI 2025 Workshops, LNAI 16264, pp. 314–327, 2026.
https://doi.org/10.1007/978-3-032-17930-2_22

In this context, institutional chatbots have emerged as a promising solution by offering permanent availability, standardized responses, and reduced waiting times in administrative procedures. These systems facilitate the automation of frequent inquiries and promote efficient communication between students and administrative departments [1].

Chatbots, defined as conversational systems based on Artificial Intelligence (AI) and Natural Language Processing (NLP), enable automated interaction with users, understanding natural language queries and providing timely responses [2, 17].

In the university setting, these agents have proven effective in managing administrative processes by providing 24/7 service, reducing staff workload, and improving access to institutional services [3, 4].

The hybrid approach—combining rule-based components with machine learning models—offers significant advantages over purely deterministic systems.

This work proposes a hybrid chatbot designed for the administrative processes of the National Technological Institute of Mexico (TecNM), built upon Dynamic Decision Trees (DDT) and Adaptive Bayesian Models (ABM).

DDTs allow for the representation of flexible and updatable decision hierarchies, while ABMs introduce probabilistic reasoning capable of handling uncertainty and updating inferences according to the contextual evidence of the dialogue [5].

A distinctive feature of the proposed model is its adaptive negotiation capability, understood as the process through which the chatbot adjusts its reasoning when faced with ambiguous or incomplete queries, refining its responses through progressive user feedback.

This approach derives from multi-agent conversational negotiation models [6], reinterpreted here as collaborative decision-making mechanisms between the system and the student to achieve the most appropriate resolution of the requested procedure.

To ensure traceability and trust, a blockchain anchoring mechanism is incorporated through Hyperledger Fabric, guaranteeing the immutable recording of sensitive interactions—such as consents and agreements—without exposing personal data.

This component adds value in terms of transparency and auditability, aligning with research that integrates distributed technologies into chatbots to ensure data integrity and security [7–9].

Additionally, the model integrates a light gamification layer, inspired by gamified and reactive chatbot architectures [10–12], aimed at encouraging proper system use and promoting the completion of administrative procedures.

Through positive feedback mechanics, badges, and symbolic rewards, the model seeks to strengthen user motivation without deviating from the institutional purpose of the system.

The main objective of this study is to design and validate a hybrid chatbot model for administrative support within the institutions of the National Technological Institute of Mexico (TecNM), capable of handling key student queries with precise, consistent, and context-aware responses.

Its specific objectives include: developing a modular architecture based on DDT and ABM, optimizing inference mechanisms through cross-validation and hyperparameter tuning, and evaluating metrics such as accuracy, response time, and user satisfaction.

The ultimate goal is to enhance institutional efficiency through a reliable, transparent, and scalable automated support tool.

2 State of the Art

In the context of higher education institutions, where student administrative procedures demand normative precision and short response times, recent literature [1] identifies three relevant approaches for conversational administrative systems: hybrid approaches (rules + ML/NLP with decision-tree control) [6, 8, 9, 17]; conversational negotiation for intent disambiguation [6]; and traceability and trust through blockchain [13–15].

Recent reviews show that, although the adoption of chatbots in education has increased, their use for institutional procedures (e.g., admissions, re-enrollments, certificates, scholarships) remains less explored than pedagogical support. This gap highlights the need for architectures capable of handling regulations, schedules, and form-based workflows with high precision [1].

In university domains, pure FAQ-based systems tend to degrade due to linguistic variability and frequent content updates, which has driven the adoption of hybrid approaches and more robust NLP pipelines [6, 8].

Recent studies combine rule-based reasoning with machine learning to improve coverage and intent disambiguation in administrative queries, integrating NLP components such as tokenization, Named Entity Recognition (NER), and embeddings with decision-tree routing and retrieval/generation modules [6, 9, 17]. These architectures consistently report improved accuracy and coverage compared to rule-based baselines, particularly in institutional domains with evolving vocabularies.

Research on negotiation agents demonstrates that conversations can be modeled as collaborative decision-making under incomplete information, progressing through clarifying questions and successive adjustments [6].

Applied to university administrative procedures, this perspective supports the use of conversational negotiation mechanisms to resolve ambiguities (e.g., certificate type, re-enrollment status) before executing regulated actions.

Experiments integrating chatbots and blockchain technologies have reported benefits in terms of integrity, auditability, and non-repudiation of sensitive interactions (e.g., consents, acknowledgments) through permissioned ledgers and immutable anchoring [13–15].

Although most cases originate from financial or service domains, the principles of verifiable record-keeping and event governance are transferable to university administrative processes, addressing a common gap in conversational systems.

Gamification models in chatbots have shown improvements in user engagement and task completion when symbolic rewards and context-aware positive feedback are employed [7, 18]. In administrative management, minimal and neutral gamification can reduce procedure abandonment and enhance perceived usability without compromising the institutional purpose.

Best evaluation practices include classification metrics (accuracy, precision, recall, F1-score), latency, and user satisfaction (System Usability Scale – SUS/Likert scale), with documented cross-validation and hyperparameter tuning to ensure reproducibility [17].

However, research gaps remain in: (i) managing regulatory changes (knowledge governance), (ii) verifiable traceability of administrative interactions, and (iii) explicit disambiguation through conversational negotiation.

3 Methodology

The proposed methodology is organized as a five-phase pipeline that progresses from the construction of the corpus and Knowledge Base (KB) to the in silico evaluation of the hybrid model.

The architecture integrates: (i) Natural Language Processing (NLP) and Natural Language Understanding (NLU) components; (ii) Dynamic Decision Trees (DDT); (iii) Adaptive Bayesian Models (ABM); and (iv) a conversational negotiation mechanism for disambiguation.

By design, the system includes cross-cutting modules for traceability using a permissioned blockchain (Hyperledger Fabric, HLF) and a light gamification layer. Figure 1 summarizes the resulting orchestration.

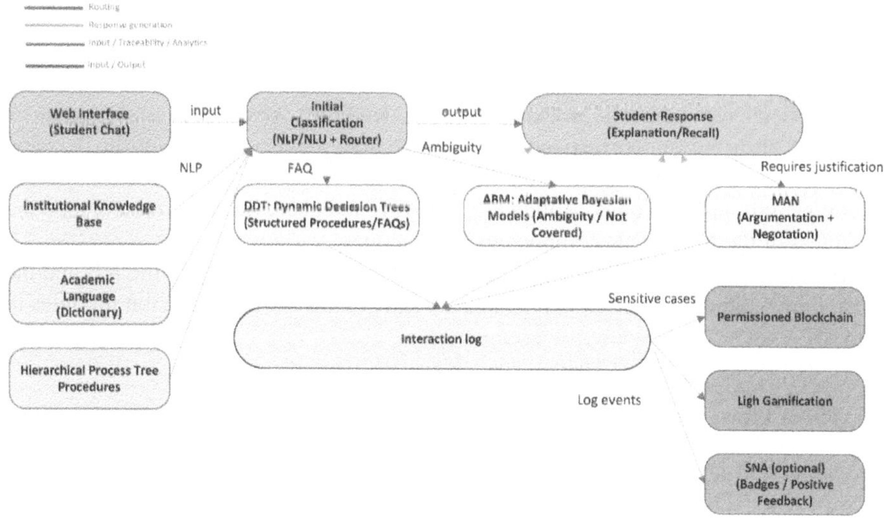

Fig. 1. General Scheme of the Model

3.1 First Phase: Data Collection and Preparation

The first phase establishes the documentary and linguistic inputs of the domain. Institutional regulations, user guides, and real usage evidence from the case study institution (including synonyms, abbreviations, and student slang) are integrated.

From these sources, three open-access datasets were compiled (Viñas, 2025): (i) Corpus_Chatbot.xlsx, containing 900 question–answer pairs labeled by intent, sub-intent, context, and entities; (ii) Diccionario_Jerga.xlsx, comprising frequent terms and usage variants; and (iii) Arbol_Decision.xlsx, representing the initial structure of the process tree organized by domain, sub-intent, and final nodes.

All three resources are publicly available on Zenodo under DOI: https://doi.org/https://doi.org/10.5281/zenodo.16176710.

Corpus preprocessing includes semantic cleaning and normalization, lemmatization, and preliminary entity detection using spaCy and NLTK. To ensure semantic consistency, intent labels were manually reviewed by administrative and academic staff.

To preserve privacy, no personal data were stored; when identifiers were present, they were replaced with tokens such as <Matricula> and <CURP>.

A stratified train/validation/test split was then applied, with $k = 5$ cross-validation, along with versioning of the corpus, KB, and process tree to track normative changes.

This dataset serves as the foundation for training the linguistic components and consolidating the Knowledge Base (KB) in the subsequent phase.

3.2 Second Phase: Core Components

Using the curated corpus, the intent classifier (NLU) is trained, and the Named Entity Recognition (NER) module is fine-tuned to identify key domain-specific entities such as Period, Program, Modality, Document, Status, Campus, Amount, and Date.

In parallel, the Knowledge Base (KB) is structured in YAML/JSON format, containing official requirements, documents, fees, deadlines, workflows, and regulatory references, ensuring full correspondence with the nodes and conditions of the decision tree.

An institutional lexicon consolidates synonyms and abbreviations to strengthen the robustness of the NLU/NER components against query variations.

After verifying preconditions and consistent nomenclature between the KB and the decision tree, the orchestration is prepared for integration with the decision modules in Phase III.

3.3 Third Phase: Hybrid Integration

The integration is organized into three coordinated components. First, the Dynamic Decision Tree (DDT) operates as a normative routing layer: based on the classified query and the evidence detected by NER, it directs the request to an output node when the information is sufficient and the query falls within the coverage domain.

To support normative evolution and emerging patterns, the tree is dynamic, allowing incremental expansions without full reconstruction.

Second, the Adaptive Bayesian Model (ABM) handles ambiguous, incomplete, or out-of-coverage cases, formulating the decision as a Bayesian classification with incremental updates to incorporate new evidence without overfitting.

Third, the conversational negotiation mechanism is activated when the estimated intent confidence falls below a threshold or when the DDT requires missing entities.

In such cases, a minimal clarifying question is issued, the response is integrated into the ABM, and the routing in the DDT is reconfigured.

When the query requires normative justification, the output is structured in an explainable format following the Toulmin scheme (claim, data, rule, warrant, exception, and qualifier). The NLU/NER–DDT–(Negotiation + ABM) pipeline thus converges toward either the resolution of the administrative procedure or an explained response.

This approach enables normative routing with explicit ambiguity detection according to the DDT function.

$$f_{\mathrm{DDT}}(q, s_t; \Theta_D) \rightarrow r \in R \, \mathrm{o} \, \mathrm{AMBIGUOUS} \quad (1)$$

When:

q: the student's query in natural language.
s_t: the conversational state at turn t (history of turns, active context, and evidence already captured).
Θ_D: the set of **DDT parameters** (e.g., maximum depth, stopping criteria, routing rules/priorities, normative preconditions, and conflict-handling policy).
R: the set of valid **normative routes/nodes** in the flow (possible tree outputs to resolve the procedure).
r: the route selected by the DDT when the evidence is sufficient and the query falls within coverage.
"AMBIGUOUS": the indeterminacy marker returned when required evidence is missing, rules collide, or confidence is insufficient; this output triggers **negotiation and/or a request for missing entities**.

Subsequently, the dynamic nature of the tree is formalized. In each iteration, the DDT is expanded or adjusted by adding a controlled increment. The incremental evolution of the tree is expressed in (2):

$$T_{t+1} = T_t \cup \Delta T_t \ (3.2) \quad (2)$$

When:

T_t: the **decision tree** at iteration t (including nodes, edges, and active rules).
ΔT_t: the **increment applied** at t (new nodes/branches, rule or condition adjustments) resulting from **normative changes** or **emerging patterns** observed in queries.
T_(t + 1): the **updated tree** after incorporating ΔT_t through **union (incremental model update)**.

Finally, in (3.3), if the classifier's confidence in its top intent is low, potentially erroneous routing is avoided, and minimal additional evidence is requested.

$$max\_(i \in I)P(i|x) < \tau \quad (3)$$

When:

I: the set of candidate intents (e.g., admission, re-enrollment, certificates, scholarship, graduation, etc.).
i: a specific intent within **I**.

x: the **query representation** (feature vector obtained by the NLU).
P(i | x): the **posterior confidence** or probability assigned by the classifier to intent i given query x.
max_(i ∈ I) P(i | x): the **maximum confidence** among all intents (the "top" proposed label).
τ: the **negotiation activation threshold**; if the top confidence is below **τ**, the system does not trust the top-1 prediction and triggers a **clarifying question (negotiation)** before routing.

The probabilistic layer is used when the query provides limited information: the model evaluates candidate routes by combining, on one hand, how well the text matches each route and, on the other hand, the prior frequency of each route in the domain. For example, if "Re-enrollment" shows a moderate match but is very frequent, while "Certificate" exhibits a high match but is rare, the combined score ultimately favors "Re-enrollment". Consequently, that route is selected even though its raw match score is lower.

$$r^* = \arg\max_{r \in R} P(r|x) = \arg\max_{r \in R} P(x|r)\, P(r) \tag{4}$$

When:

x: the **query representation**.
R: the set of candidate routes/intents.
r: a specific route/intent; **r***: the selected route/intent.
P(r | x): the **posterior probability** of r given x.
P(x | r): the **likelihood** of observing x if r were correct.
P(r): the **prior** (frequency or domain preference).

To avoid zero probabilities when a term has not yet appeared in a class/route, a constant pseudocount is added to each term. This way, even rare terms receive a small but non-zero probability, making the model more robust against sparse or unbalanced data.

$$\theta_{r,j} = \frac{n_{r,j} + \alpha}{\sum_j n_{r,j} + \alpha d} \tag{5}$$

When:

θ_(r, j): the **estimated probability** of term j in class/route r.
n_(r, j): the **count** of term j associated with r.
d: the **vocabulary size** (number of possible terms).
α > 0: the **Laplace smoothing parameter** (pseudocount to prevent zero probabilities).

To adapt to changes without rebuilding the model, counts are updated by combining historical data with new evidence: the historical counts are decayed using a forgetting factor, and then the newly observed counts are added. With these updated counts, probabilities are recalculated using the same Laplace smoothing, allowing the model to learn continuously without overfitting to recent cases.

$$n_{(r,j)}^{(t+1)} = \lambda n_{(r,j)}^{(t)} + c_{(r,j)}(x),\ \theta_{r,j}^{(t+1)} = \frac{n_{r,j}^{(t+1)} + \alpha}{\sum_j n_{r,j}^{(t+1)} + \alpha d} \tag{6}$$

When:

n_(r, j)^(t + 1): the counts of term *j* for class/route *r* **before and after the update.**
c_(r, j)(x): the **new evidence** provided by the query (occurrences affecting *r*).
λ: the **forgetting factor** (weights historical counts versus recent evidence).
α, d: same as in (3.5); control **Laplace smoothing** and **vocabulary size.**
θ_(r, j)^(t + 1): the **probability of term *j* for *r* after the update.**

Once the route probabilities are calculated, a decision is accepted only if the highest probability exceeds a predefined threshold. This threshold balances the trade-off between accepting decisions with limited evidence (risking errors) and requesting additional clarifications (more turns, but higher certainty).

$$\max_{r \in R} P(r|x) \geq \theta \tag{7}$$

When:

P(r | x): the **posterior probability** of route/intent *r* given the query.
max_(r ∈ R) P(r | x): the **maximum confidence** among all candidate routes/intents.
θ: the **acceptance threshold**; if it is not reached, **disambiguation is preferred** before making a decision.

When evidence is missing, the system selects the question that most reduces uncertainty: for each candidate question, it estimates how much the entropy of its beliefs would decrease on average according to the possible user responses, and chooses the question that maximizes the expected reduction.

$$q^* = \arg\max_{q \in Q} E_a\big[H(p_t) - H(p_{t+1}|q, a)\big] \tag{8}$$

When:

q*: the **selected question** (minimal clarifying question).
q, Q: a **candidate question** and the **set of possible questions**, respectively.
a: the **potential user response** (random variable).
H: the **entropy** (uncertainty of the belief distribution).
p_t: the **belief distribution** before asking at turn *t*.
p_(t + 1): the **updated belief distribution** after asking *q* and observing *a*.

Negotiation terminates when the confidence in the top route exceeds an acceptance threshold; if this is not achieved within the allotted turn budget, the process stops to prevent excessive dialogue.

$$\max_{r \in R} P(r|x_{t+1}) \geq \theta \tag{9}$$

When:

R: the set of candidate routes/intents; **r**: a specific route.
x_(t + 1): the **query representation updated** with the newly obtained evidence.
P(r | x_(t + 1)): the **posterior confidence** in *r* after the most recent clarification.
θ: the **acceptance threshold** (if the top confidence exceeds it, a decision is made).

3.4 Four Phase. Cross-Cutting Modules by Design (Traceability and Compliance)

Traceability is implemented using Hyperledger Fabric (HLF) for sensitive events (e.g., consents, acknowledgments, or agreements). The anchoring records only the hash of the relevant normative content and minimal metadata (timestamp, process, generic role, type of consent), ensuring that no personal data is stored while guaranteeing auditability and non-repudiation.

In parallel, a lightweight gamification layer is incorporated, based on symbolic reinforcement (achievement confirmations or badges) associated with process milestones, such as procedure completion or correct submission of evidence. This gamification is neutral and does not affect normative decisions.

3.5 Five Phase. Training, Validation, and Evaluation

In this phase, the complete hybrid model was implemented and trained, integrating the DDT, ABM, and negotiation modules described in Phase III. Evaluation was conducted in a fully implemented and functional environment, using the datasets from Phase I and data generated during simulated sessions with internal users, aiming to tune and verify performance before public deployment.

Cross-validation (k-fold = 5) and hyperparameter search were performed across three components:

DDT: maximum depth, stopping criteria, and policy for ambiguous nodes (related to Sects. 3.1, 3.2, 3.3).

ABM: priors, acceptance threshold θ, Laplace smoothing α, and forgetting factor λ (Sects. 3.4, 3.5, 3.6, 3.7).

Negotiation: activation threshold τ (Sect. 3.3) and selection/termination policy (Sects. 3.8, 3.9).

An ablation study was conducted with three configurations:

A1: DDT as baseline (routing via Sects. 3.1, 3.2).
A2: DDT + ABM without negotiation (decision according to Sects. 3.4, 3.5, 3.6, 3.7).
A3: DDT + ABM with negotiation (selection and termination according to Sects. 3.8, 3.9).

Evaluated metrics included NLU performance (accuracy, precision, recall, macro and per-class F1), Top-k accuracy for intent routing, resolution rate after the first clarification, and average turns per negotiation session. Additionally, average latency per turn, computational cost, and linguistic robustness against abbreviations, errors, and variants were measured. For traceability, p95 anchoring latency and record coverage were reported.

Metrics related to subjective experience (e.g., perceived satisfaction and trust) were reserved for the subsequent pilot testing phase with end users. Results from this phase enabled the selection of operational thresholds for the final model (τ from Sect. 3.3, θ from Sect. 3.7, and λ from Sect. 3.6), confirming the feasibility of the implemented prototype and its generalization capability.

The obtained values and comparative visualizations of these metrics are presented in Sect. 4, along with the ablation analysis (A1–A3) and the consolidated performance of the hybrid model.

3.6 Reproducibility and Knowledge Governance

Reproducibility was ensured through a modular and documented design, version control, and reproducible packaging using Python 3.10 with Docker containers, following best practices in scientific engineering. Each phase of the pipeline (Sects. 3.1, 3.2, 3.3, 3.4, 3.5) was implemented as an independent module with standardized interfaces, allowing experiments to be replicated across different environments.

Open and anonymized datasets were used, primarily the corpus from Phase I, with all personal data removed. The project complies with institutional ethical guidelines and the FAIR principles (Findable, Accessible, Interoperable, Reusable).

Experimental traceability was recorded through an experiment log containing hyper-parameters, model version, data hashes, and metrics per iteration, ensuring auditability and external validation. Algorithmic governance measures were implemented to reduce bias: rule review in the DDT, class balancing in the ABM, and error monitoring in negotiation.

3.7 Final Evaluation

The hybrid model was implemented and evaluated through a functional prototype trained with data from Phase I, demonstrating its coherence, stability, and reproducibility. Potential biases in the initial corpus were controlled through class balancing and paraphrase generation, enhancing the internal validity of the design.

Regarding external validity, although the evaluation was conducted in a controlled environment, a multi-institutional pilot phase is planned to extend the assessment with more users and diverse contexts. Additionally, the corpus will be expanded with data from multiple institutions to improve generalization and strengthen the model's empirical validity.

Overall, the prototype results confirm the feasibility, consistency, and scalability potential of the hybrid model for various real-world student support scenarios. The results obtained during experimental validation and the prototype's performance are presented in Sect. 4, along with a comparative analysis of the scenarios.

4 Results and Discussions

The proposed model was designed and implemented to validate the effectiveness of a hybrid DDT + ABM + negotiation architecture, in line with the study's general objective.

The system was aimed at administrative and academic support in an institution of the Tecnológico Nacional de México, with the goal of providing precise, consistent, and contextualized responses in student support processes.

The working hypothesis posits that the hierarchical integration of symbolic components (DDT) and probabilistic components (ABM), complemented with a negotiation module, increases semantic accuracy and conversational efficiency.

To test this, a functional prototype was developed and experimentally validated under principles of reproducibility, traceability, and parametric optimization.

The training corpus was built from anonymized interactions and institutional publications, complemented with semantic paraphrases to diversify natural language.

The dataset included thousands of balanced records, distributed as 60% for training, 20% for validation, and 20% for testing. Messages were classified into three emotional polarity categories:

Positive, associated with satisfactory or acknowledgment responses.
Negative, related to doubts, complaints, or dissatisfaction.
Neutral, corresponding to informative or routine messages.

Table 1 summarizes the results obtained for the three model configurations.

Scenario A1 (DDT), based solely on Dynamic Decision Trees, achieved an accuracy of 0.81 and a macro F1 of 0.78, showing acceptable performance in structured environments but with limitations in handling lexical ambiguities.

With the incorporation of ABM (A2), accuracy increased to 0.87 and macro F1 to 0.85, reflecting a significant improvement in contextual interpretation and probabilistic uncertainty management.

The complete model A3 (DDT + ABM + Negotiation) reached accuracy of 0.90 and macro F1 of 0.88, while also reducing average turns to 3.2 and increasing the resolution rate to 92%.

Table 1. Comparative Results of the Hybrid Model Across Scenarios A1–A3

Scenario	Active Components	Accuracy	Macro F1	Top-k (k = 3)	Resolution Rate (%)	Avg. Latency (ms)
A1	DDT	0.81	0.78	0.89	72	110
A2	DDT + ABM	0.87	0.85	0.94	83	130
A3	DDT + ABM + Negotiation	0.9	0.88	0.96	92	142

Figure 2, corresponding to the confusion matrix for scenario A3, shows accurate classification of the main intents (Enrollment, Re-enrollment, Scholarships, and Student Services), with minimal inter-class errors. The residual errors are semantically coherent, indicating predictable and linguistically justifiable behavior.

Figure 3 shows the evolution of the macro F1 score during training and validation (k = 5). The curves stably converge after the eighth iteration, confirming the consistency of the model.

Table 2 presents the comparison with recent research. The proposed hybrid model achieved competitive performance compared to complex neural approaches (LSTM and CNN-BiGRU), while exhibiting lower latency and higher interpretability.

These results confirm that the hierarchical integration of DDT + ABM + negotiation achieves a balance between performance, linguistic robustness, and explainability.

The model meets the specific objectives set forth, demonstrating measurable improvements in accuracy, latency, and conversational resolution.

Furthermore, it provides a solid methodological foundation for future extension to multi-institutional corpora and validation, guiding the next research phase toward user satisfaction and experience.

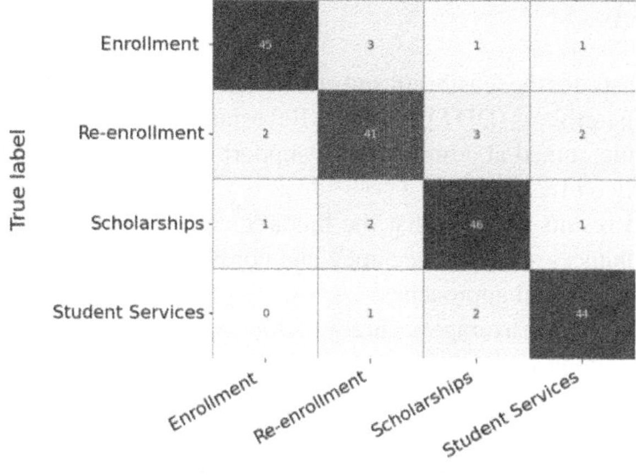

Fig. 2. The confusion matrix visualizes the model's performance in predicting the correct labels for four categories. The average response time was 142 ms, within optimal margins for online support applications, meeting the objective of efficiency and scalability.

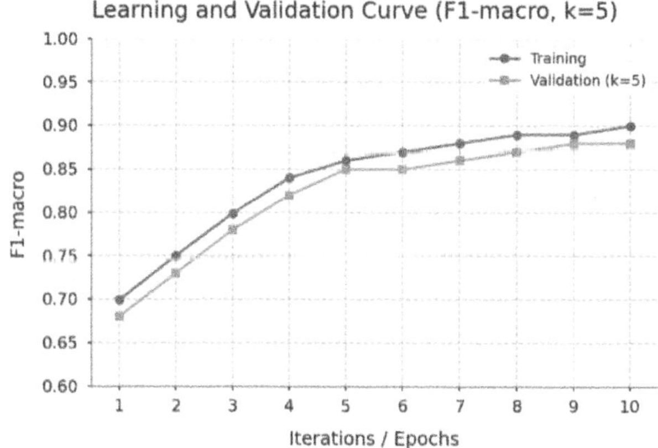

Fig. 3. Learning and Validation Curve

Table 2. Comparison with Similar Studies

Models hybrids	Accuracy	F1-macro	Latencia (ms)
Chatbot LSTM (Dinh & Tran, 2023)	0.88	0.84	210
CNN-BiGRU (Mikael et al., 2025)	0.89	0.86	195
Modelo propuesto (A3)	0.90	0.88	142

5 Conclusions

This study demonstrates the feasibility and effectiveness of a hybrid chatbot model based on Dynamic Decision Trees (DDT), Adaptive Bayesian Models (ABM), and a contextual negotiation module, aimed at administrative support in institutions of the Tecnológico Nacional de México (TecNM).

Experimental results confirm that the hierarchical combination of DDT + ABM + negotiation enhances semantic accuracy and conversational efficiency compared to traditional or purely neural approaches.

The model achieved an average accuracy of 90%, a macro F1 of 0.88, and a resolution rate of 92%, maintaining an operational latency below 150 ms, demonstrating its potential for institutional deployments of automated student support.

From a scientific perspective, the findings validate the working hypothesis: the integration of symbolic and probabilistic components improves the system's ability to process natural language in a precise, interpretable, and reproducible manner. Moreover, the use of cross-validation and hyperparameter tuning contributed to ensuring the model's robustness and generalization across real-world corpora with linguistic variability.

From a methodological standpoint, a reproducible framework was established for developing administrative chatbots with a hybrid approach, capable of balancing accuracy, explainability, and adaptability. The affective classification approach (positive, negative, and neutral) allowed dynamic adjustment of the negotiation module, improving response coherence and conversational empathy.

The proposed model can be implemented as a tool for automated support in administrative and student guidance processes, reducing response times and operational load. Its modular architecture, developed under interoperability principles, facilitates integration with existing institutional systems and scalability to diverse educational contexts.

Additionally, the explanatory approach in the negotiation module ensures algorithmic transparency, a critical aspect in AI systems deployed in public and academic environments. The following steps are proposed for future research:

a) Expand the training corpus by incorporating data from multiple TecNM institutions to increase linguistic and cultural representativeness.
b) Conduct an institutional pilot test to evaluate subjective metrics such as user satisfaction, perceived usefulness, and trust in the system.
c) Integrate deep learning techniques (e.g., lightweight transformers) into the ABM module to strengthen contextual understanding without compromising interpretability.
d) Develop a longitudinal analysis module to study the evolution of student queries and generate institutional management indicators.
e) Explore gamification and blockchain strategies, already planned in the base architecture, to enhance user engagement and interaction traceability.

Acknowledgments. The authors thank the Tecnológico Nacional de México (TecNM) for providing access to data and institutional regulations, key elements for the development of this study. Disclosure of Interests. The authors have no competing interests relevant to the content of this article.

References

1. Weizenbaum, J.: ELIZA—a computer program for the study of natural language communication between man and machine. Commun. ACM **9**(1), 36–45 (1966)
2. Wallace, R.S.: The anatomy of A.L.I.C.E.. In: Epstein, R., Roberts, G., Beber, G. (eds.) Parsing the Turing Test, pp. 181–210. Springer, Dordrecht (2009). https://doi.org/10.1007/978-1-4020-6710-5_13
3. Okonkwo, C.W., Ade-Ibijola, A.: Chatbots applications in education: a systematic review. Comput. Educ. Artif. Intell. **2**, 100033 (2021)
4. Peyton, K., Unnikrishnan, S., Mulligan, B.: A review of university chatbots for student support: FAQs and beyond. Discov. Educ. **4**, 21 (2025)
5. Nguyen, M.T., Phan V.A., Vu, H-T., Nguyen, V-H.: Building a Chatbot for supporting the admission of universities. In: IEEE KSE 2021, pp. 1–6 (2021)
6. Ali, M.S., Azam, F., Safdar, A., Anwar, M.W.: Intelligent agents in educational institutions: NEdBOT – NLP-based chatbot for administrative support using DialogFlow. In: Proceedings of the ICA 2022. IEEE (2022)
7. González-González, C.S., Muñoz-Cruz, V., Toledo-Delgado, P.A., Nacimiento-García, E.: Personalized gamification for learning: a reactive chatbot architecture proposal. Sensors **23**, 545 (2023)
8. Dinh, H., Tran, T.K.: EduChat: an AI-based chatbot for university-related information using a hybrid approach. Appl. Sci. **13**(22), 12446 (2023)
9. Mikael, K., Öz, C., Rashid, T.A., Saman N.G.: A hybrid chatbot model for enhancing administrative support in education: comparative analysis, integration and optimization. IEEE Access **13**, 50741–50755 (2025)
10. Ndunagu, J.N., Ezeanya, C.U., Onuorah, B.O., Onyeakazi, J.C., Ukwandu, E.: A chatbot student support system in open and distance learning institutions. Computers **14**(3), 96 (2025)
11. Arias-Chávez, D., Ramos-Quispe, T., Cangalaya, L.M.: Análisis y tendencias del uso de chatbots y agentes conversacionales en el campo de la educación: una revisión bibliométrica. Rev. Innovaciones Educativas **26**(41), 242–258 (2024)
12. Man, S.C., Matei, O., Faragau, T., Andreica, L., Daraba, D.: The innovative use of intelligent chatbot for sustainable health education admission process: learnt lessons and good practices. Appl. Sci. **13**(4), 2415 (2023)
13. Rane, N.L., Choudhary, S.P., Rane, J.: Artificial Intelligence (AI), Internet of Things (IoT), and blockchain-powered chatbots for improved customer satisfaction, experience and loyalty. SSRN Working Paper 4847274 (2024)
14. Bhuiyan, M.S.I., Razzak, A., Ferdous, M.S., Chowdhury, M.J.M., Hoque, M.A., Tarkoma, S.: BONIK: a blockchain empowered chatbot for financial transactions. In: Proceedings of the IEEE TrustCom 2020, pp. 1–9 (2020)
15. Adel, K., Elhakeem, A., Marzouk, M.: Chatbot para empresas de construcción que utiliza una red blockchain escalable. Autom. Constr. **141**, 104390 (2022)
16. Rosenfeld, A., Zuckerman, I., Segal-Halevi, E., Drein, O., Kraus, S.: NegoChat: a chat-based negotiation agent. In: Proceedings of the International Conference on Autonomous Agents and Multi-Agent Systems, pp. 233–240 (2014)
17. Singh, S.U., Namin, A.S.: A survey on chatbots and large language models: testing and evaluation techniques. Nat. Lang. Process. J. **10**, 100128 (2025)
18. Ramalakshmi, K., David, D.J., Selvarathi, M., Jebaseeli, T.J.: Using artificial intelligence methods to create a chatbot for university questions and answers. Eng. Proc. **59**, 16 (2023)

Generating Fuzzy Rules for Wildfire Pixel Segmentation Using Genetic Programming and Color Content

Alberto Lopez-Alanis[1], Hector De-la-Torre-Gutierrez[2](✉), Arturo Hernández-Aguirre[3], and Víctor M. Álvarez-Pato[4]

[1] Aguascalientes Branch, Center for Research in Mathematics, Calzada de La Plenitud 103, 20200 Aguascalientes, México
alberto.lopez@cimat.mx

[2] Investigadores Por Mexico, Center for Research in Mathematics, Calzada de La Plenitud, 103, 20200 Aguascalientes, México
hector.delatorre@cimat.mx

[3] Department of Computer Science, Center for Research in Mathematics (CIMAT), Valenciana S/N, 36023 Guanajuato, México
artha@cimat.mx

[4] Universidad Panamericana. Facultad de Ingeniería, Jose María Escrivá de Balaguer 101, Villas Bonaterra, 20296 Aguascalientes, México
valvarez@up.edu.mx

Abstract. Computer vision-based wildfire detection is a crucial task for enabling a rapid firefighter response, allowing to mitigate several damages in ecosystems and economy. Moreover, wildfire segmentation methods allow for determining the precise position where the fire is present within the image. A number of rule-based models have been proposed since they are human-readable. Moreover, the color content is the most utilized feature to characterize the fire pixels. Generally, rule-based models determine fire pixels in a binary manner, making it difficult to handle the uncertainty present in the data. In this research work, we propose a system for automatically calculating color-based rules using fuzzy operators to determine the fire pixel. Specifically, we propose to use calculated color-based features. In contrast to other rule-based models, which perform fire segmentation using inequalities, our approach constructs a fire segmentation model by handling uncertainty in a fuzzy approach. By using a genetic approach, the proposed system searches for the best ensemble of fuzzy rules to form the model. According to the results obtained, the proposed model outperforms the state-of-the-art models in various segmentation metrics.

Keywords: Wildfire Segmentation · Fuzzy Rules · Genetic Algorithm · Color Content

L. Martínez-Villaseñor et al. (Eds.): MICAI 2025 Workshops, LNAI 16264, pp. 328–339, 2026.
https://doi.org/10.1007/978-3-032-17930-2_23

1 Introduction

Wildfires are one of the major catastrophes facing humanity [1]. Precise fire detection is one of the most important aspects of the field of research on wildfire detection [2]. Due to the reliability of new technologies in remote sensing, computer vision techniques have gained relevance in fire detection [3]. In the literature, we can roughly identify three types of tasks performed by algorithms: fire classification, fire location, and fire segmentation [4]. Fire classification methods determine the presence of fire in the content of an image, classifying each image as either fire or non-fire. Fire location involves identifying the precise location of the fire and generating a bounding box around the affected region. On the other hand, the fire segmentation algorithms aim to classify all pixels within an image as fire or non-fire. Besides, a fire model can be designed to analyze video sequences or static images.

Generally, fire segmentation methods consist of an image processing stage for feature extraction and a modeling process, whereby a fire segmentation model is calculated for future predictions using a machine learning technique [4]. Concerning the feature extraction stage, the methods characterize relevant fire features by analyzing the image. Typically, features are handcrafted and designed by humans. On the other hand, the modeling stage is performed by any suitable machine learning technique. Among the types of machine learning models, the rule-based models are relevant due to their interpretability compared to other models [5]. To the best of our knowledge, the fire segmentation task using static images is not the most predominant in the field of fire research. Various authors conduct their research regarding fire classification or fire location. However, some of the methods utilize, as part of their algorithm, a stage for fire segmentation.

Horng et al. [6] aim to process video sequences in real-time. The authors used only the HSI color space to construct the rule-based model. Segmented pixels are processed to remove spurious fire-like regions. Dzigal et al. [7] presented a method for fire pixel segmentation using the HSV, HSL, and HWB color spaces to build a rule-based model. Moreover, a preprocessing stage is proposed by applying a blur filter, and a postprocessing stage is performed by removing small blobs within the output image. In the research work of Buza et al. [8], an unsupervised model for fire segmentation is proposed. Using the RGB color space, the authors designed a set of rules. The authors introduced several novel image-processing techniques to refine fire segmentation. Alternatively, Chino et al. [9] proposed a model based on machine learning that uses color and texture features for fire segmentation. Specifically, the authors utilized the YC_bC_r color space to train a Naive Bayes model using chromatic information. Then, using the LBP texture characterization, the KNN classifier discriminated against fire-like regions. The outcome is the union of color and texture stages.

Toulouse et al. [10] proposed a probabilistic approach using Naïve Bayes but using only the chromatic information of the YC_bC_r color space; that is, the author utilized the C_b and C_r color channels for training. Prema et al. [11] proposed a method for classifying fires in video sequences. The authors designed a fire segmentation stage to filter the pixels to be processed in later processes. In this stage, the authors developed a set of rules using the RGB and YC_bC_r color spaces. Besides, various texture descriptors and dynamic features were calculated to distinguish between fire-color objects with movement and fire class.

Due to the mentioned rule-based models being designed by experts, bias and variance is present in their performance. Hence, the genetic algorithms (GA) have become relevant for the automatic determination of rules. GA algorithms are suitable for several applications, such as search, robotics, and machine learning, among others. Bivalkar [12] employed a genetic approach to segment the vessel blood in noisy images. The structure is captured using statistical information. Aya [13] introduced a genetic algorithm-based hyperparameter optimization strategy for pre-trained CNN models in insect pest classification. The proposed approach demonstrated effectively classifies various crop pests. In [14], a fuzzy rule-based combination model was proposed. The authors proposed a GA approach to finding the best combination of models for fire segmentation rules. In this research paper, we propose to construct a rule-based model for fire segmentation based on the chromatic content of fire pixels using static images. Specifically, our objective is to construct rules of type *if (antecedent) then (consequence)* using fuzzy operators, color characterization, and genetic algorithms.

The contributions of this research work are the following: 1) We propose a system that automatically constructs rules without determining a threshold value like other methods. 2) We evaluate the effectiveness of fuzzy logic operators versus traditional methods for fire pixel segmentation. 3) The proposed system uses a genetic programming approach to construct competitive rule-based color models for fire segmentation using color-based features. The remainder of the manuscript is organized as follows. Section 2 presents our proposed method. The parameters and experiment setup are shown in Sect. 3. In Sect. 4, we present the results obtained from our series of tests. Finally, we give our conclusions in Sect. 5.

2 Methodological Framework

In this section, we present the conceptual basis of the proposed approach. In Fig. 1, we present an overview of the proposed system. In the figure, in red, the proposed approach constructs a set of rule-based models. Specifically, we propose using fuzzy sets and color features to make up the model. The method constructs the models using a genetic algorithm. This technique fits the rule-based model according to the data used during the evolution. That is, solutions are iterated over some generations and combined or mutated to enhance their performance. After the evolution is concluded, the best solution is selected and is used as our fire pixel segmentation model. In Fig. 1, in green, the proposal processes an input image. Using the evolved model, the inference of fire pixels is performed. It should be mentioned that from the proposal, we obtain a gray level output as the fire prediction; then, a binarization process is required to obtain a binary fire image.

The rest of this section is organized as follows. First, we describe the reasoning for computing the color features. Second, we introduce the background for combining the features into a rule-based model. Third, we give the basis for the genetic algorithm used to construct the fire pixel model.

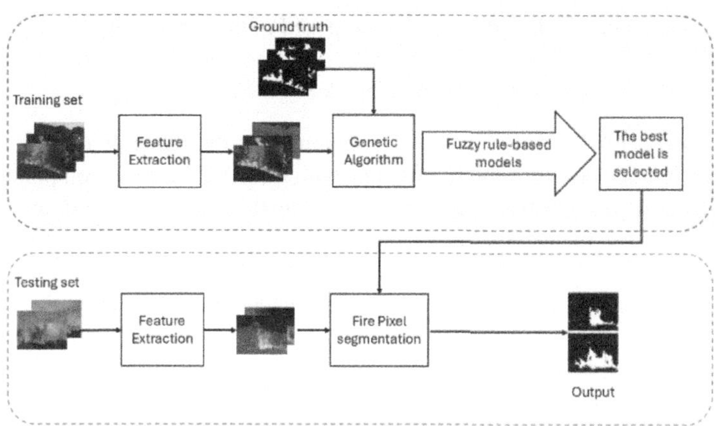

Fig. 1. Overview of the method proposed. In red, the training stage. In green, the fire pixel segmentation.

2.1 Color Features

In this study, we propose using the chromatic content of a pixel to identify fire pixels. In this section, we provide details on the computation of the color features utilized to characterize fire pixels. Unlike traditional rule-based models, which use threshold decision values, we aim to utilize features that emphasize the characteristics of fire.

In Fig. 2, we present the color distribution of fire pixel samples in various color spaces. Specifically, we provide the color distribution in the RGB, YUV, and CIELAB color spaces. As shown in Fig. 2, the fire pixels are plotted mostly in a certain value range for specific color channels in each color space.

The proposal takes advantage of the color distribution properties of the fire pixels to characterize them.

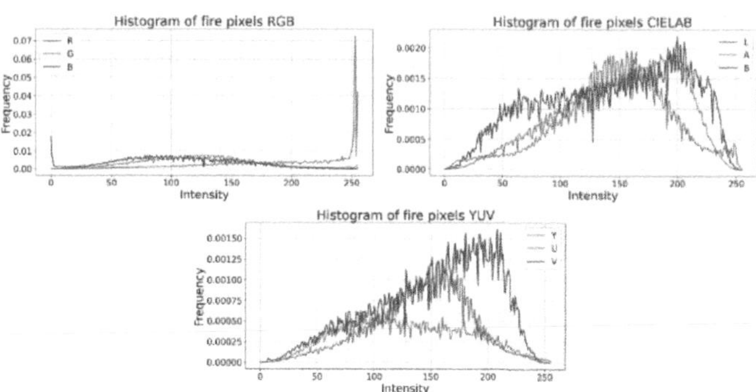

Fig. 2. Histograms of fire pixels are presented. The histograms were calculated in the RGB, CIELAB, and YUV color spaces.

Given the difference among the chromatic channels of flame pixels, we quantify the divergence of color content by calculating a simple subtraction. In Eq. 1, we present the general form to calculate the color feature proposed in this approach.

$$C_n = Channel_{Fire(v)} - value_{reference}, \tag{1}$$

where $Channel_{Fire}$ is the dominant color component of the flame pixels, $value_{reference}$ serves as a reference point for the subtraction, which can be the color component where the fire pixels are not mostly represented or a statistical value of the dominant color channel, and v is the intensity value that the pixel takes on the corresponding channel. Specifically, we used RGB, YUV, YC_bC_r, CIELAB, and HSV color spaces.

The RGB color space is used to obtain a chromatic representation of the Opponent color space. The Opponent color space emulates how humans perceive color [16]. In Eqs. 2, 3 and 4, we define the opponent color space. Each color channel is used as a feature in our proposal.

$$C_1 = (R - G)/\sqrt{2}, \tag{2}$$

$$C_2 = (R + G - 2 \times B)/\sqrt{6}, \tag{3}$$

$$C_3 = (R + G + B)/\sqrt{3}. \tag{4}$$

In addition, we used two color spaces that encode illumination in a single component, such as YC_bC_r and YUV. To quantify the contrast between the chromatic content of a pixel, we proposed using channels C_b, C_r, U, and V to calculate the distinctiveness. In Eqs. 5 and 6, the definition of contrast calculation is presented.

$$C_4 = C_r - C_b, \tag{5}$$

$$C_5 = V - U. \tag{6}$$

Furthermore, we utilized the CIELAB color space, which aims to match human perception. To calculate contrast, we calculate the median values of channels a, and b. In Eqs. 7 and 8, we present the proposed features.

$$C_6 = a - a_{median}, \tag{7}$$

$$C_7 = b - b_{median}. \tag{8}$$

Besides, in our preliminary experiments, we found that combining the features C_1, C_2, C_6, and C_7 achieved competitive results. In Eqs. 9 and 10, we give the combined features calculated.

$$C_8 = C_6 + C_7, \tag{9}$$

$$C_9 = C_1 + C_2. \tag{10}$$

In our research work, we include the color features proposed Itti et al. [19]. The authors proposed four tuned color channels such as the Red (R_{tuned}), Green (G_{tuned}), Blue (B_{tuned}), and Yellow (Y_{tuned}). In Eqs. 11 and 12, we give the calculation of features C_{10} and C_{11}.

$$C_{10} = (R_{tuned} - G_{tuned}) - (G_{tuned} - R_{tuned}), \tag{11}$$

$$C_{11} = (B_{tuned} - Y_{tuned}) - (Y_{tuned} - B_{tuned}). \tag{12}$$

To calculate contrast using the gray level intensities, we calculate contrast from the B_{tuned} and the grayscale intensity value. In Eq. 13, we define the characteristic.

$$C_{12} = I_{gray} - B_{tuned}. \tag{13}$$

Finally, the HSV color space was utilized to construct the features presented in Eqs. 14, 15 and 16.

$$C_{13} = H - H_{median}, \tag{14}$$

$$C_{14} = S - S_{median}, \tag{15}$$

$$C_{15} = V - V_{median}. \tag{16}$$

2.2 Fuzzy Logical Operators for Antecedent Evaluation

The inputs of our system are the color features calculated as previously mentioned. The proposed system aims to infer a set of rules of type *if (antecedent) then (class)*. Fuzzy sets were introduced by Zadeh [17] as a mathematical tool to handle uncertainty and vagueness in information. In addition, fuzzy logic was introduced as a reasoning system that handles imprecise or uncertain information using fuzzy sets and rules [18]. A fuzzy set is described as follows: consider the set $U = u_1, u_2, \ldots, u_n$ as the universal set. Then, the fuzzy set A on U is described by the membership function in Eq. 17.

$$\mu_A : U \rightarrow [0, 1], u \in U, \tag{17}$$

where μ_A represents the degree in which u belongs to A. In our case, the membership function is given by the pixel intensity function. As mentioned earlier, our system aims to compute a fuzzy rule-based model for fire pixel segmentation. To this end, we conduct a combination of the color features using fuzzy set operators. In Table 1, we present the fuzzy operators used in our proposed system.

2.3 Constructing the Fuzzy Rule-Based Model

Consider the set $H = \{f_1, f_2, \ldots, f_n\}$ to be the collection of color features calculated by our proposal. The proposed system constructs a rule-based fire pixel segmentation according to Eq. 18.

$$D(x) = O(f_1, f_2, \ldots, f_n), \tag{18}$$

Table 1. Summary of the fuzzy operators utilized in our proposal, where A and B are fuzzy sets.

Function	Type	Function	Type
$\min\{A, B\}$ (mi)	Minimum	$\min\{1, 1 - A + B\}$ (lk)	Lukasiewicz
AB (tn)	Product	$\max\{1 - A, B\}$ (kd)	Kleene-Dienes
$\max\{0, A + B - 1\}$ (co)	Bounded difference	$\sqrt{AB}$ (gm)	Geometric mean
$\max\{A, B\}$ (ma)	Maximum	$\frac{2AB}{A+B}$ (hm)	Harmonic mean
$A + B - AB$ (tc)	Probabilistic sum	$\frac{A+B-AB}{1-A-B+2AB}$ (nn)	Symmetric sum
$\min\{1, A + B\}$ (di)	Bounded sum	$\frac{AB}{1-A-B+2AB}$ (as)	Symmetric sum

where *O()* is a collection of fuzzy set operators that act on the features, and *D()* is the determination of whether the pixel x is fire class or not.

The determination of fuzzy operators *O()* and features H utilized to construct the rule-based model is carried out using a genetic algorithm approach (GA). Unlike other techniques, GA does not require a predefined structure; instead, it identifies the structure that best fits the data [20]. The taxonomy of a GA comprises the following stages: a) An initial population must be determined, $\pi = \{S_1, S_2, \ldots, S_n\}$. b) Let J(S) be the function to assess each solution; then, in our approach, the higher the score, the better the individual. c) From the set π, individuals are selected to create the mating set M. We adopt the roulette wheel to select individuals. d) Crossover and mutation. From the mating set M, individuals are selected to perform the crossover.

In our proposal, the representation of individuals is decoded into a tree structure with a maximum of 10 levels. The objective function *J(S)* of the proposed GA is the widely accepted Matthews Correlation Coefficient (MCC). Moreover, we perform a crossover by swapping sub-branches from the individuals and we used the elitist strategy, which consists of preserving the best individuals.

3 Experiment and Evaluation Protocol

We evaluate our proposal with the models of Chino et al. [9], Prema et al. [11], Dzigal et al. [7], Anh et al. [21], Buza et al. [8], and Chen et al. [15]. In our test series we used the widely accepted CORSICAN dataset [22]. The dataset provides images labeled at the pixel level with a wide diversity of background scenarios, various illumination contents, a diversity of color flames, and fire-color distractors. On the other hand, we utilized the K-fold strategy to perform our test series, we set K = 10.

The methodology is quantitatively evaluated using confusion matrix entries such as true positive (TP), true negative (TN), false positive (FP), and false negative (FN). Specifically, we compare methods using precision, recall, and F-measure metrics, Eqs. 19, 20, 21, respectively.

$$Precision = \frac{TP}{TP + FP}, \tag{19}$$

$$Recall = \frac{TP}{TP + FN}, \tag{20}$$

$$F_{measure} = \frac{(\beta^2 + 1) \times Precision \times Recall}{\beta^2 \times Precision + Recall}, \text{ where } \beta = 1, \tag{21}$$

Moreover, the parameter setting used in our approach is given in Table 2. Our experimental design was guided by a series of preliminary studies. Key parameters, including population, mating size, offspring, and generations, were systematically tuned to maximize the Matthews Correlation Coefficient (MCC) on a validation set. For instance, an initial population of 100 individuals was selected. The number of offspring and generations was set to 20 and 50, respectively. The mating set size is determined to be 20. No significant performance differences were observed using other parameter values. The MCC metric allows us to validate the solutions found by the proposal. To validate the outcomes computed by the evolved individuals, we binarize the output images using the widely used Otsu threshold method [23].

Table 2. Summary of the parameters utilized for the genetic algorithm.

Parameter	Value	Parameter	Value
Initial population	100	Mutation probability	5%
Number of offspring	20	Fitness function	MCC metric
Number of generations	50	Mating set selection	Roulette wheel
Mating set size	20	Selection strategy	Elitism strategy

4 Evaluation Results

4.1 The Rule-Based Model

In Table 3, we give the proportion of usage of the color contrast features. The most used feature was C_8, which was utilized 13.91%. The characteristic C_{10} was used in proportion to 12.26% while C_1 was 11.79%. The least used features were C_{13} and C_{14}, used in 2.29% and 2.59%, respectively.

Table 3. Usage of the color features. We count the frequency of usage.

Feature	Usage %	Feature	Usage %	Feature	Usage %
C_1	11.79	C_6	7.22	C_{11}	4.36
C_2	5.16	C_7	3.62	C_{12}	4.60
C_3	3.40	C_8	13.91	C_{13}	2.29
C_4	8.63	C_9	7.82	C_{14}	2.59
C_5	8.16	C_{10}	12.26	C_{15}	4.25

Table 4 presents the employability of fuzzy operators. The operator most used was the symmetric sum (as), used in a proportion of 15.81%, while the product (tn) was used in a proportion of 15.01%. The least used operator was the Lukasiewicz operator (lk), used in 0.47%. Similarly, the Kleene-Dienes operator (kd) was used in 0.49%.

Table 4. Usage of the fuzzy operators.

Operator	Usage %	Operator	Usage %
co	5.56	hm	10.89
di	4.90	gm	10.06
tn	15.01	as	15.81
tc	5.50	nm	8.96
mi	13.97	lk	0.47
ma	8.40	kd	0.49

4.2 Quantitative and Qualitative Evaluation

Figure 3 presents the performance of the evolved model. Specifically, we used the MCC metric, which was used as a fitness function, to calculate the mean and standard deviation of the performance of each individual in the population in each generation. From Fig. 3, we can observe that the overall performance is improved throughout the evolution process. In addition, we can observe that even the standard deviation is improved, while the evolution constructs better solutions.

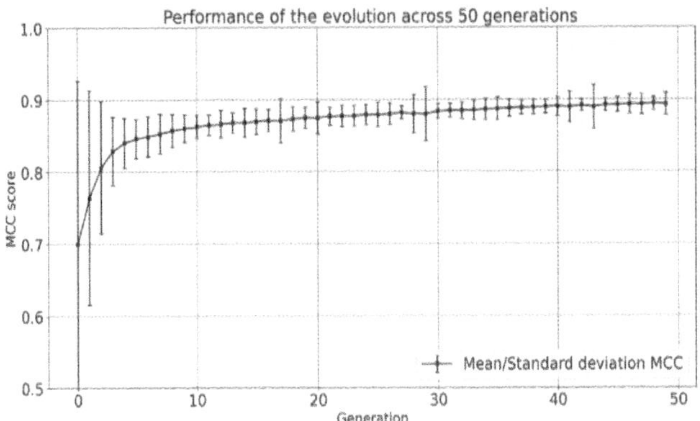

Fig. 3. Assessment of the evolution population. The mean and standard deviation of the MCC metric were calculated to depict the evolved model.

In Table 5, we present the calculated precision, recall, and F measurement. According to the results obtained, the method proposed by Prema achieved a higher precision score of 0.944, while Chen computed a second 0.911. Our proposal was achieved 0.861. Regarding the recall metric, Chino calculated 0.841, and our proposal reached 0.835, while the Buza method calculated 0.804. The best F-measure was computed by our proposal using color contrast, attained 0.820. The Chino and Buza approaches achieved 0.800 and 0.797, respectively. Table 6 shows the overall confusion matrix computed from the predictions of our proposal. According to the table, our model achieves correctly classifying 93.62% of total pixels.

Table 5. Evaluation of our proposal. The color model was evaluated with precision, recall, and F-measure to assess our proposed color fire approach.

Method	Precision	Recall	F-measure
Chino	0.882	**0.841**	0.800
Prema	**0.944**	0.419	0.542
Dzigal	0.833	0.788	0.777
Nguyen	0.832	0.149	0.229
Buza	0.856	0.804	0.797
Chen	0.911	0.626	0.711
Our proposal	0.861	0.835	**0.820**

Table 6. Confusion Matrix. The general confusion matrix is calculated.

	Predicted Negative	Predictive Positive
Actual Negative	185727805 (73.61%)	7791065 (3.09%)
Actual Positive	8713264 (3.45%)	50485644 (20.01%)

Figure 4 presents the qualitative comparison of the models. Our proposal enhances fire pixel classification by handling uncertainty in a fuzzy approach. Nevertheless, the proposed method misclassifies fire-color objects since only chromatic features were used in our approach.

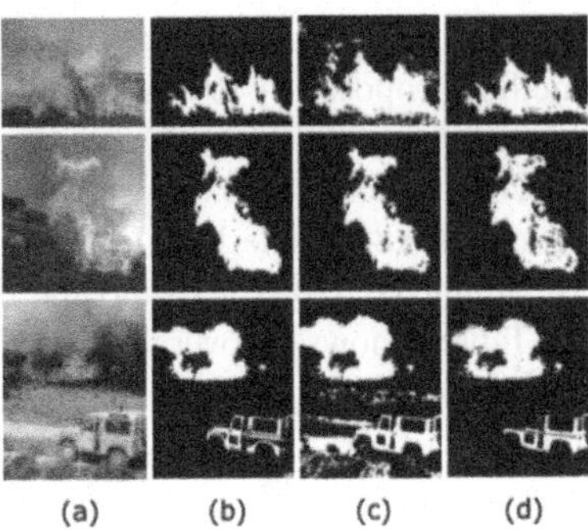

Fig. 4. Qualitative comparison. Similarly, our method misclassifies objects with fire-colored features. (a) Color image. (b) Buza. (c) Chino. (d) Our proposal.

5 Conclusions

This research successfully developed and validated a genetic fuzzy system for the automated segmentation of wildfires, utilizing color features for flame characterization. We demonstrated that a genetic algorithm is an effective and reliable method for automatically constructing a fuzzy rule-based model, eliminating the need for expert-defined rules. Our evaluation shows that our proposal attains a more balanced precision and recall metric, while it attains the best F-measure. Specifically, our proposal avoids the common pitfall of high precision at the cost of low recall. Nonetheless, the proposed approach also misclassified fire-color objects similar to the other models. In future work, a framework to automatically calculate features is needed to overcome the misclassification of distractors. Similarly, to address the constraints of the present proposal, features other than color are required, such as texture and shape, among others.

Acknowledgments. Alberto Lopez-Alanis thanks the Secretaría de Ciencia, Humanidades, Tecnología e Innovación (Secihti) for funding his postdoctoral studies. Hector De-la-Torre-Gutierrez also thanks Secihti and the Researchers for Mexico program for supporting this research. We would like to thank the CIMAT Supercomputing Laboratory for providing the resources and technical support necessary to carry out the experiments in this project.

Disclosure of Interests. The authors have no competing interests to declare that are relevant to the content of this article.

References

1. Geetha, S., Abhishek, C., Akshayanat, C.: Machine vision based fire detection techniques: a survey. Fire Technol. **57**(2), 591–623 (2021)
2. Zhang, W., Zheng, H., Li, W., Pan, S., Liu, Y.: Fireseg: a weakly supervised fire segmentation framework via pre-trained latent diffusion models. Expert Syst. Appl. **275**, 126852 (2025)
3. Harkat, H., Ahmed, H.F.T., Nascimento, J.M., Bernardino, A.: Early fire detection using wavelet based features. Measurement **242**, 115881 (2025)

4. Cheng, G., Chen, X., Wang, C., Li, X., Xian, B., Yu, H.: Visual fire detection using deep learning: a survey. Neurocomputing **596**, 127975 (2024)
5. Fürnkranz, J., Kliegr, T., Paulheim, H.: On cognitive preferences and the plausibility of rule-based models. Mach. Learn. **109**(4), 853–898 (2019). https://doi.org/10.1007/s10994-019-05856-5
6. Horng, W.-B., Peng, J.-W., Chen, C.-Y.: A new image-based real-time flame detection method using color analysis. In: Proceedings of the IEEE Networking, Sensing and Control, pp. 100–105 (2005)
7. Dzigal, D., Akagic, A., Buza, E., Brdjanin, A., Dardagan, N.: Forest fire detection based on color spaces combination. In: 11th International Conference on Electrical and Electronics Engineering, pp. 595–599 (2019)
8. Buza, E., Akagic, A.: Unsupervised method for wildfire flame segmentation and detection. IEEE Access **10**, 55 213–55 225 (2022)
9. Chino, D.Y.T., Avalhais, L.P.S., Rodrigues, J.F., Traina, A.J.M.: Bowfire: detection of fire in still images by integrating pixel color and texture analysis. In: Proceedings of the 28th Conference on Graphics, Patterns and Images, pp. 95–102 (2015)
10. Toulouse, T., Rossi, L., Akhloufi, M., Celik, T., Maldague, X.: Benchmarking of wildland fire colour segmentation algorithms. Image Process. **9**(12), 1064–1072 (2015)
11. Emmy Prema, C., Vinsley, S., Suresh, S.: Efficient flame detection based on static and dynamic texture analysis in forest fire detection. Fire Technol. **54**, 255–288 (2018)
12. Bivalkar, M.K.: An adaptive and statistical approach for blood vessel segmentation using genetic algorithm. SIViP **18**(1), 55–61 (2024)
13. Ayan, E.: Genetic algorithm-based Hyperparameter optimization for convolutional neural networks in the classification of crop pests. Arab. J. Sci. Eng. **49**, 3079–3093 (2024)
14. Lopez-Alanis, A., de-la Torre-Gutierrez, H., Hernández-Aguirre, A., Orvañanos-Guerrero, M.T.: Fuzzy rule-based combination model for the fire pixel segmentation. IEEE Access **13**, 52 478–52 496 (2025)
15. Chen, X., An, Q., Yu, K.: Fire identification based on improved multifeature fusion of ycbcr and regional growth. Expert Syst. Appl. **241**, 122661 (2024)
16. Muhammad Anwer, R., Vázquez, D., López, A.M.: Opponent colors for human detection. In: Pattern Recognition and Image Analysis, pp. 363–370 (2011)
17. Zadeh, L.: Fuzzy sets. Inf. Control. **8**, 338–353 (1965)
18. Zadeh, L.A.: Fuzzy logic. In: Granular, Fuzzy, and Soft Computing, pp. 19–49. Springer (2023)
19. Itti, L., Koch, C., Niebur, E.: A model of saliency-based visual attention for rapid scene analysis. IEEE Trans. Pattern Anal. Mach. Intell. **20**, 1254–1259 (1998)
20. Santoso, L.W., Singh, B., Rajest, S.S., Regin, R., Kadhim, K.H.: A genetic programming approach to binary classification problem. EAI Endorsed Trans. Energy Web **8**, 11 (2021)
21. Anh, N.D., et al.: Efficient forest fire detection using rule-based multi-color space and correlation coefficient for application in unmanned aerial vehicles. Trans. Internet Inform. Syst. **16**, 381–404 (2022)
22. Toulouse, T., Rossi, L., Campana, A., Celik, T., Akhloufi, M.A.: Computer vision for wildfire research: an evolving image dataset for processing and analysis. Fire Safety J. **92**, 188–194 (2017)
23. Otsu, N.: A threshold selection method from gray-level histograms. Automatica **11**, 23–27 (1975)

Classification of White or Red Wines Using the Decision Trees Machine Learning Technique

Liana Leiva[1], José Alberto Hernández-Aguilar[1](✉), and Julio César Ponce-Gallegos[2]

[1] Autonomous University of Morelos State, Av. Universidad No. 1001, Col. Chamilpa, 62209 Cuernavaca, Morelos, México
jose_hernandez@uaem.mx

[2] Autonomous University of Aguascalientes, Av. Universidad No. 940, Ciudad Universitaria, 20100 Aguascalientes, Ags., México

Abstract. This article presents a study on classifying white and red wines using the Decision Tree Machine Learning technique. The main objective is to reliably predict the color of the wine—white or red—using physical and chemical variables as inputs to machine learning models. A 10-fold stratified cross-validation was applied to two approaches: a base model with a Decision Tree (DecisionTreeClassifier) and another with an additional stage of nonlinear dimensionality reduction using KernelPCA. The best result was obtained with a five-dimensional k-fold reduction, achieving an accuracy of 99.1%.

Keywords: Machine Learning · Decision Trees · K-fold · Kernel PCA · binary classification · wines

1 Introduction

Today, wine is a staple in many homes, and high-quality wine has become the goal pursued by most people [1].

The industry is investing in new technologies for both wine production and sales. Certification and quality assessment are key elements in this context. Certification prevents illegal adulteration of wines (to protect human health) and guarantees quality in the wine market. Quality assessment is often part of the certification process. It can be used to improve winemaking (by identifying the most influential factors) and to classify wines, such as premium brands (helpful in setting prices) [2].

Furthermore, in the fields of enology and food analytics, precisely identifying wine color based on its physical and chemical properties remains a significant challenge for both industry and scientific research. Although this classification is traditionally performed through direct observation or specific instrumental techniques, there is a need to explore alternative automated approaches that offer speed, low cost, and high accuracy. A large data set is available, consisting of white and red wine samples from Portugal, which exclusively includes physical and chemical variables.

L. Martínez-Villaseñor et al. (Eds.): MICAI 2025 Workshops, LNAI 16264, pp. 340–351, 2026.
https://doi.org/10.1007/978-3-032-17930-2_24

Machine learning (ML) is a branch of artificial intelligence (AI) that has seen exponential growth in recent years. The scientific community is increasingly paying attention to educational tools enhanced with innovative technology, as they have the potential to revolutionize teaching and learning processes [3].

The objective of this study is to reliably predict the color of the wine (white or red) using the physical-chemical variables of the dataset Wine Quality, found in the UCI Machine Learning Repository [4], as inputs to Machine Learning models, and test one of these models with and without dimensionality reduction.

The hypothesis of this research work is formulated as: H1. Dimensionality reduction will improve classification accuracy to approximately 0.99 with the Decision Tree Classifier.

This research is structured as follows: in the first section, the introduction, the research objective, and the hypothesis are presented. In Sect. 2, a brief review of the related literature is presented. In the third section, the proposed methodology is discussed. In Sect. 4, the Results and discussion are shown. Finally, the last section presents the conclusions, future work, and references.

2 Review of Related Literature

In [5], a data mining approach is proposed to predict wine color using standard machine learning techniques. This study is based on a dataset containing samples of both red and white Vinho Verde wines from Portugal. The input variables are limited to physicochemical properties, demonstrating that these are sufficient to build classification or regression models. The tested techniques include Logistic Regression (LR), Support Vector Machine (SVM), and Neural Network (NN). Positive results were obtained, with the Logistic Regression (LR) model achieving an overall accuracy of 99.67% in classifying wine color.

The state of the art in wine classification has advanced significantly, transitioning from traditional methods, such as those in the study mentioned above, to subjective expert evaluations, and now employs sophisticated computational methods, primarily using machine learning (ML) and deep learning (DL) algorithms. This evolution aims to deliver objective, efficient, and real-time insights into critical areas such as quality control, authenticity verification, and optimized production processes in the wine industry.

2.1 Classification Objectives

Wine classification encompasses a range of objectives:

Quality Prediction. Classifying wines into discrete quality categories (e.g., "good" or "bad") or assigning a numerical quality score (e.g., 0 to 10) based on physicochemical attributes [6].

Geographical Origin Identification. Determining the specific region or micro-region a wine originates from, which is vital for authenticity, fraud detection, and traceability, especially given that wine is among the most counterfeited goods [7, 8].

Wine Type/Classification. Identifying the specific grape variety or wine type based on its unique chemical composition [7, 8]. This research is focused on this objective.

Grape Quality Assessment. Predicting crucial oenological parameters in wine grapes, such as Brix and pH, which directly influence optimal harvest timing and ultimately, the final wine quality. This prediction is often treated as a regression problem, but it directly contributes to the overall classification of grapes [9].

2.2 Data Sources and Analytical Techniques

The effectiveness of wine classification heavily relies on the quality and type of data used:

Physicochemical Variables. Common for wine quality prediction, these include measurements like fixed acidity, volatile acidity, citric acid, residual sugar, chlorides, free and total sulfur dioxide, density, pH, sulfates, and alcohol content [6, 8]. Quality ratings are often provided by sensory experts [6].

Spectroscopic Data. ICP-MS (Inductively Coupled Plasma Mass Spectrometry) provides detailed elemental concentrations in wines [7]. These elemental profiles are highly valuable for tracing geographical origin, as they reflect the mineral composition of soils [7]. NMR (Nuclear Magnetic Resonance) Spectroscopy is a powerful analytical tool for both targeted and non-targeted metabolomic analysis, extensively used in wine analysis for studying metabolomics and tracing geographical origin and authenticity [7]. DOSY NMR spectroscopy is particularly noted for its ability to separate wine components based on their diffusion coefficients without physical separation, offering a unique chemical fingerprint [7]. Hyperspectral Imaging offers rich spectral/spatial data (e.g., across 350–1100 nm) and is crucial for non-destructive, real-time assessment of grape quality parameters like Brix and pH, especially for varieties like Rondo, where visual color changes are not significant indicators of maturation [9].

2.3 Machine Learning and Deep Learning Methodologies

The state of the art leverages a wide array of ML and DL algorithms, often in integrated approaches:

Traditional Machine Learning Classifiers. Decision Trees (DT/J48) are frequently used for classification, building a tree structure for clarity. J48 (an ID3 algorithm extension) is noted for its ability to find correct classification outcomes and high accuracy in white wine quality classification [6, 8]. Random Forests (RF) are an ensemble of decision trees, demonstrating superior predictive performance and adaptability in classifying both red and white wine quality [6]. Support Vector Machines (SVM) are supervised learning models effective for classification and regression, capable of defining clear decision boundaries [6]. Logistic Regression (LR) is a statistical technique often used for binary classification and identifying essential quality parameters [6]. Naïve Bayes is a probabilistic classifier, also utilized for wine quality prediction [6, 8]. Multilayer Perceptron (MLP) is a multilayer neural network used for classification and regression, showing high accuracy in wine quality analysis [6].

Ensemble and Boosting Methods. Stacking Ensemble is a framework that combines multiple ML models to generate new features, demonstrating superior predictive performance in red wine quality classification (e.g., 85% accuracy) [9]. Gradient Boosting Decision Tree (GBDT) using XGBoost is an ensemble learning approach, recognized for its outstanding boosting performance, flexibility, and interpretability in hyperspectral image classification for grape quality prediction. It effectively identifies important wavelengths [9].

Deep Learning (DL) Models. 1D + 2D Convolutional Neural Networks (CNNs) are particularly effective for hyperspectral image analysis due to their ability to leverage spatial position information and handle dynamic spectral curves and horizontal wavelength shifts, especially in outdoor data acquisition. These models have shown the highest accuracy for Brix and pH prediction in Rondo wine grapes [9]. Deep Reinforcement Learning (DRL) is a cutting-edge approach that combines advanced tensor decomposition algorithms with deep learning. DRL has proven highly effective for the classification of sparkling wines by geographical origin, especially when the number of samples is limited or simpler statistical methods fail [7].

Hybrid and Specialized Models. Explainable Boosting Machine (EBM) followed by Support Vector Regression (SVR) is a hybrid model that offers an exceptional balance of stability, accurate predictability, and strong interpretability. It is considered the most powerful model for stable prediction and clear wavelength identification in grape quality assessment, even under varying environmental stresses, and effectively avoids overfitting [9]. The Genetic Algorithm (GA) Wrapper with Binary Decision Trees (BDTs) is an innovative approach that uses GAs for optimal attribute selection and BDTs for classification. The GA wrapper minimizes the number of selected attributes to reduce overfitting risk, providing a robust solution for classifying wine types based on chemical substances. It achieved 100% classification accuracy in predicting factors affecting wine cultivar by identifying optimal subsets of attributes [8].

2.4 Performance Evaluation and Key Findings

Recent studies report impressive classification accuracies across various objectives. Regarding Wine Type/ Classification, the GA wrapper with BDTs achieved 100% classification accuracy in identifying wine type based on a subset of 6 key attributes [8]. Notably, malic acid (15.38% influence) and the OD280/OD315 ratio of Diluted Wines (23.08% influence) were identified as having a significant impact on wine origin [8].

2.5 Decision Tree Classifier

According [10], this algorithm builds a root node based on the data and target, and creates branches using inequalities to classify the data. A decision tree classifier can generate complex decision boundaries by dividing the feature space into rectangles. However, the researcher must consider that the deeper the tree, the more complex the decision limit becomes. Decision Tree Classifier is one of the most widely used machine learning techniques, due to its easy-to-understand approach and its graphical representation of how the algorithm processes and classifies data. The Scikit learn framework provides an implementation of this algorithm [11].

2.6 Principal Components Algorithm (PCA)

To reduce the dimensionality of a dataset, there are different data selection techniques, and one of the most widely used is PCA, which compresses data without supervision. According [10] PCA helps identify patterns in data by analyzing correlations among features. PCA identifies the maximum variance on high-dimensional data and projects this variance into a subspace with dimensions less than or equal to the original. These orthogonal axes are called principal components of the new subspace. If PCA is used for dimensionality reduction, a transformation matrix W of dimensions d x k maps a vector x into a k-dimensional subspace of features, with fewer dimensions than the original feature space.

The PCA can be summarized in the following steps [10]:

1. Standardized the dataset of d dimensions.
2. Build the covariance matrix.
3. Decompose the covariance matrix into eigenvalues and eigenvectors.
4. Order the eigenvalues in decreasing order to classify the corresponding eigenvectors.
5. Select k eigenvectors that correspond to the k higher eigenvalues, where k is the dimensionality of the new features' subspace ($k < = d$).
6. Build a projection matrix W using the k *top* eigenvectors.
7. Transform the new entering dataset X of d dimensions to obtain the new features subspace of k dimensions.

3 Methodology

The methodology used in this research is shown in Fig. 1 and comprises five stages, as explained in the following sections.

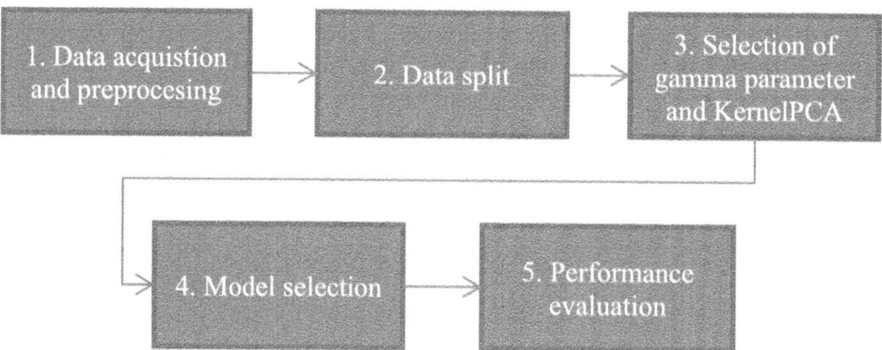

Fig. 1. Proposed Methodology.

3.1 Data Acquisition and Preprocessing

This article uses the dataset from the UC Irvine Machine Learning Repository called Wine Quality [4]. This dataset was chosen because it is the one used in [5], allowing comparison of results from different techniques on the same data.

Table 1. Description of dataset features [4].

Variable name	Role	Type	Comments
Fixed-acidity	Feature	Continuous	–
Volatile-acidity	Feature	Continuous	–
Citric-acidity	Feature	Continuous	–
Residual-sugar	Feature	Continuous	–
Chlorides	Feature	Continuous	–
Free_sulfur-dioxide	Feature	Continuous	–
Total_sulfur-dioxide	Feature	Continuous	–
Density	Feature	Continuous	–
PH	Feature	Continuous	–
Sulfates	Feature	Continuous	–
Alcohol	Feature	Continuous	–
Quality	Target	Integer	Score between 0 and 10
Color	Other	Categorical	Red or white

Table 1 shows a brief description of the Wine Quality dataset features, including name, role, type, and comments. This dataset contains floating-point data, has 11 features and 4898 instances, and is used for classification and regression tasks. This dataset was selected for its extensive documentation and testing with a variety of classifiers and regressors.

The Wine Quality dataset was imported from the UCI repository in .csv format (see Pseudocode 1).

```
Pseudocode 1
Import Libraries
Df <- read dataset from UCI Repository using CSV format
and no headers
If (error = True)
  Print("There is not connection")
```

The headers were removed (see Pseudocode 2), and the class labels (wine color column) were converted to numerical values using LabelEncoder (See pseudocode 3), where 0 represents red wines and 1 represents white wines.

Pseudocode 2
```
Df.drop(0) //Remove headers
```

Pseudocode 3
```
Import LabelEncoder //Import libraries
label_encoder = LabelEncoder() //Generate a new instance
// Transform the data in the last column
Df[12] <- label_encoder.fit_transform(Df[12])
```

Figure 2 shows the correlation matrix generated for the classification task. The predictor variables selected were "total sulfur dioxide" and "density," as these features showed significant correlations of 0.47 and 0.7, respectively, with the target class; see the last column of Fig. 2, with different shades of orange. These variables were converted to numeric type and normalized using the StandardScaler library.

A value highly correlated is close to 1.0, a value inversely correlated is close to -1.0 (minus 1.0); a value of 0.0 is evidence of no correlation at all [12]. In Fig. 2, a value close to zero is dark purple, and a value close to 1.0 is orange or red.

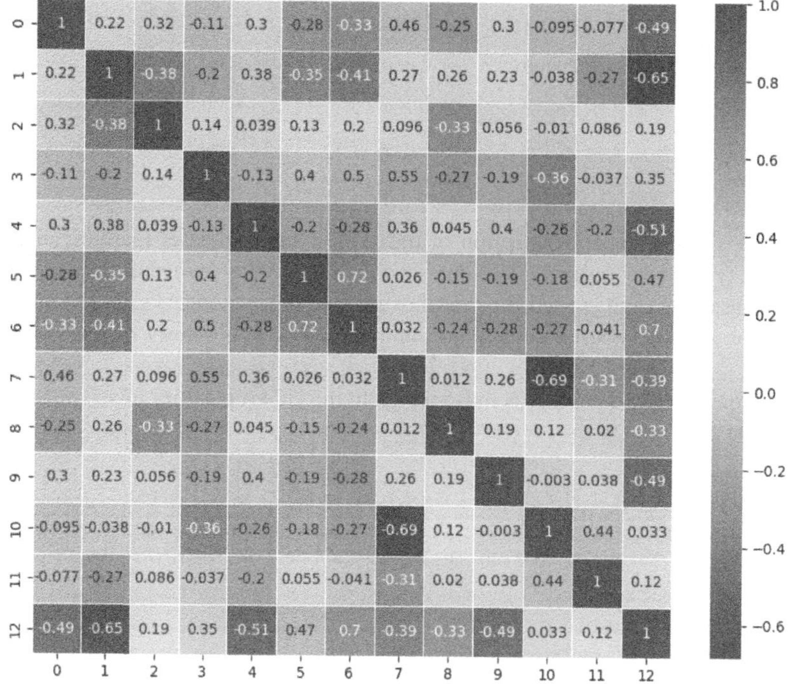

Fig. 2. Correlation matrix.

3.2 Data Split

The dataset was divided into training (70%) and test (30%) sets (see Pseudocode 4). The test_size was set to 0.3, random_state to 1 to preserve the random environment, and stratify was set to "y", meaning the data sample preserves the proportions of the target.

Pseudocode 4

```
Import Train_test_split //Import libraries
test_size =0.3
random_state <- 1
stratify <-"y"
X_train, X_test, y_train, y_test <- Train_test_split (X,
y, test_size, random_state, stratify)
```

3.3 Selection of the Gamma Parameter and KernelPCA

To apply nonlinear dimensionality reduction using KernelPCA (with RBF kernel), data was standardized using the StandarScaler() function, different values of the gamma parameter were explored on a logarithmic scale between [−3, 3] with seven samples. For each gamma value, the reconstruction error was measured using the mean squared error function between the original scaled data and its reconstruction from the reduced space. The optimal gamma value was the one that minimized this error, in this case, gamma = 0.1 (see Pseudocode 5).

Pseudocode 5

```
Import KernelPCA //Import libraries
Import GridSearch
Import mean_squared_error
Import pipeline
Import StandardScaler
Import Numpy as np

X_scaled <- StandardScaler.fit_transform(X)
Gamma_range <- np.logspace(-3,3,7)
Reconstruction_errors <- Empty_list
For gamma in Gamma_range:
  Kpca <- Kernel_PCA(n_components=2,'rbf',gamma,
                     fit_inverse_transform = true)
  X_kpca <- Kpca.fit_transform(X_scaled)
  X_back <- Kpca.inverse_transform(X_scaled,X_back)
  Error = mean_square_error(X_scaled,X_back)
  Reconstrucion_errors.append(Error)

Optimal_gamma <- Gamma_range[min(Reconstrucion_errors)]
```

3.4 Model Selection

Two classification pipelines were used to build two models (see Pseudocode 6):

Model 1 (Without Dimensionality Reduction - Base). A standard scaler followed by a DecisionTreeClassifier, with Gini criterion, and a maximum depth of 4.

Model 2 (With Dimensionality Reduction). Standard scaling, with dimensionality reduction using KernelPCA (using the optimal gamma value = 0.1), followed by the same decision tree-based classifier.

Pseudocode 6

```
Import StandardScaler //Import libraries
Import DecisionTreeClassifier
Import make_pipeline
Import StandardScaler

Pipe_lr <-make_pipeline(StandardScaler(),
          DecisionTreeClassifier(criterion='gini',
          max_depth=4, random_state=1))
Pipe_lr_1<-make_pipeline(StandardScaler(),
          KernelPCA(n_components=2, kernel='rbf',
          gamma=0.1),
          DecisionTreeClassifier(criterion='gini',
          max_depth=4, random_state=1))
```

3.5 Performance Evaluation

Both models were evaluated using 10-fold stratified cross-validation (StratifiedKFold). Accuracy was calculated for each fold, enabling comparison of model performance with and without nonlinear dimensionality reduction. The class distributions for each fold and the resulting accuracy scores were reported.

The Pseudocode 7 shows the process without dimensionality reduction (Selected_pipe = Pipe_lr) and with dimensionality reduction (Selected_pipe = Pipe_lr1).

Pseudocode 7

```
Import StratifiedKFold //Import libraries
Import Numpy as np

Kfold <- StratifiedKFold(n_splits=10, shuffle=True,
          Random_state =1).split(X_train, y_train)

Scores <- Empy_list

Pipe_lr <- Selected_pipe // Pipe_Lr or Pipe_Lr1

For k, (train, test) in kfold:
  Pipe_lr.fit(X_train[train], y_train[train])
  Score = Pipe_lr.score(X_train[ test], y_train[test])
  Scores.append(score)
  Print(k+1, score)
```

4 Results and Discussion

To evaluate the predictive performance of the proposed models for wine color classification, 10-fold stratified cross-validation was applied to both approaches: a baseline model using a Decision Tree Classifier and another model with an additional step of nonlinear dimensionality reduction using KernelPCA.

Table 2 shows the results for the accuracy metric across the conducted experiments. The first row shows the accuracy results without dimensionality reduction, and the second row shows the results with dimensionality reduction. The columns show the number of k-folds.

Table 2. Accuracy of the Decision Tree Classifiers.

k-fold	1	2	3	4	5	6	7	8	9	10
Without dimensionality reduction	94.6	92.4	92.9	95.1	98.2	94.6	94.2	96.0	95.1	95.5
With dimensionality reduction	95.1	93.3	93.3	97.3	**99.1**	93.8	93.3	96.9	95.1	95.1

The best result was obtained with dimensionality reduction using 5-fold cross-validation, achieving an accuracy of 99.1% (in bold in Table 2), which is close to the result reported in [5] with a precision of 99.67%. This result is also very close to the reported in [8] that used a GA wrapper with BDTs and achieved 100% classification accuracy in identifying wine type, based on a subset of 6 key attributes.

5 Conclusions and Future Work

This study demonstrated that it is possible to accurately predict wine color (white or red) from a small set of physicochemical variables —specifically, total sulfur dioxide and density—using Decision Trees, both alone and in combination with Kernel PCA dimensionality reduction.

The analysis showed that the Decision Tree model with dimensionality reduction performed better, indicating that, for this dataset and the selected variables, it yielded competitive results (99.1% accuracy), and PCA provides a useful exploratory tool for transforming the feature space. Therefore, the hypothesis H1 is valid.

Furthermore, finding the optimal gamma value in KernelPCA via reconstruction error proved an effective strategy for tuning this parameter and improving the nonlinear representation of the data.

The sophisticated integration of ML and DL models with advanced spectroscopic and imaging techniques characterizes the state of the art in wine classification. This spectroscopic technique delivers high accuracy and robust performance, even under challenging real-world conditions, while increasingly emphasizing model interpretability and the identification of key features to provide data-driven insights across the wine industry.

Limitations. There are only two wine categories—white and red—so rosé wines cannot be classified using this system.

Future Research. Explore the performance of other machine learning and deep learning models using the complete set of physicochemical variables in the dataset to assess their impact on model performance and robustness. Compare the results obtained with other, more complex classification algorithms, such as Random Forests, SVMs, or neural networks, to determine whether they can capture additional patterns in the data. Conduct research or create a new dataset that includes other wine classifications, such as rosé wine. Finally, developing an application to predict wine color from physicochemical measurements would be helpful to wine laboratories and producers.

References

1. Xie, Q.: Machine learning on wine quality: prediction and feature importance analysis. Highlights Sci. Eng. Technol. CDMMS **41** (2023)
2. Cortez, P., Teixeira, J., Cerdeira, A., Almeida, F., Matos, T., Reis, J.: Using data mining for wine quality assessment. In: International Conference on Discovery Science, pp. 66–79 (2009)
3. Forero-Corba, W., Bennasar, F.N.: Técnicas y aplicaciones del Machine Learning e Inteligencia Artificial en educación: una revisión sistemática. RIED-Revista Iberoam. Educ. Distancia **27** (2024)
4. Cortez, P., Cerdeira, A., Almeida, F., Matos, T., Reis, J.: Wine quality. UCI Mach. Learn. Repos. **10**, C56S3T (2009)
5. Sanders, J.P.: Modelling Wine Color by Data Mining Physico-chemical Properties. https://medium.com/low-code-for-advanced-data-science/modelling-wine-preferences-by-data-mining-physico-chemical-properties-7c47912fa368. Accessed 10 Sept 2025

6. Koranga, M., Pandey, R., Joshi, M., Kumar, M.: Analysis of white wine using machine learning algorithms. Mater. Today Proc. **46**, 11087–11093 (2021)
7. Korenika, A.-M.J., et al.: Deep reinforcement learning classification of sparkling wines based on ICP-MS and DOSY NMR spectra. Food Chem. X **21**, 101162 (2024)
8. Gkikas, D.C., Theodoridis, P.K., Theodoridis, T., Gkikas, M.C.: Finding good attribute subsets for improved decision trees using a genetic algorithm wrapper; a supervised learning application in the food business sector for wine type classification. Informatics, 63 (2023)
9. Swe, K.N., Noguchi, N.: Comparison of machine learning and deep learning models for the assessment of rondo wine grape quality with a hyperspectral camera. Smart Agric. Technol. **8**, 100474 (2024)
10. Raschka, S., Mirjalili, V.: Python machine learning: machine learning and deep learning with Python (2017). https://doi.org/10.1037/023990
11. Scikit-learn: Decision Trees. https://scikit-learn.org/stable/modules/tree.html
12. Salcedo, J., McCormick, K.: SPSS Statistics for Dummies. Wiley, Hoboken (2020)

Visual Analysis of MNIST Convolutional Autoencoder Reconstructions via Linear Dimensionality Reduction

Rafael Castaneda-Diaz[1,2], Daniela Lopez-Betancur[1](✉), Carlos Guerrero-Mendez[1], Efren Gonzalez-Ramirez[1], Flossi Puma-Ttito[1], and Rómulo Troncoso-Pacheco[1]

[1] Universidad Autónoma de Zacatecas, Unidad Académica de Ciencia y Tecnología de La Luz y La Materia (LUMAT), C.P. 98047 Zacatecas, México
{danielalopez106,guerreromendez}@uaz.edu.mx

[2] Instituto Politécnico Nacional, Unidad Profesional Interdisciplinaria de Ingeniería Campus Zacatecas (UPIIZ), C.P. 98160. Zacatecas, México

Abstract. Dimensionality reduction techniques transform a dataset from a high-dimensional space into a lower-dimensional subspace. These techniques facilitate visualization of high-dimensional data in a 2D or 3D subspace. This work presents the application of two linear methods, PCA and FDA, which were used to generate two 2D visualizations. The PCA and FDA projections facilitated meaningful comparisons between the original MNIST images, their distorted versions (30,000 images), and the reconstructed versions (30,000 images), produced by a convolutional autoencoder (CAE). According to the Mahalanobis distance with respect to the 95% confidence ellipse, centered at the mean of the PCA projections of the MNIST training images, 94.40% of the distorted image projections fall inside. Similarly, 97.41% of the reconstructed image projections fall inside. On the other hand, according to the Mahalanobis distance with respect to the 95% confidence ellipses-each centered at the mean of the FDA projections of the MNIST training images of each digit class-an average of 99.25% of the distorted image projections fall outside the ellipses. In contrast, an average of 93.03% of the reconstructed image projections fall inside the ellipses. The PCA and FDA visualizations confirmed the capability of the CAE to reconstruct distorted MNIST images. PCA captured the patterns that maximize variance (spread) of the MNIST dataset, regardless of class. Similarly, FDA highlighted the separability between the reconstructed images by digit class.

Keywords: Convolutional · autoencoder · dimensionality · reduction · PCA · FDA

1 Introduction

In the solution of machine learning problems, high-dimensionality data analysis plays a fundamental role. Usually, different datasets contain high-dimensional data, i.e., data that contain many variables—features—relative to the number of samples. Consequently, the

L. Martínez-Villaseñor et al. (Eds.): MICAI 2025 Workshops, LNAI 16264, pp. 352–367, 2026.
https://doi.org/10.1007/978-3-032-17930-2_25

curse of dimensionality takes place, i.e., different problems arise, for example, sparsity due to expansion of the space occupied by the dataset, overfitting due models learn noise, high computational cost, and visualization challenges—humans cannot directly visualize spaces beyond 3D. Basically, to deal with the curse of dimensionality, implementing dimensionality reduction methods is an excellent alternative.

Concerning dimensionality reduction, in this work, the linear methods PCA and FDA were implemented to transform the 784-dimensional MNIST dataset into a two-dimensional subspace for better representations. In this context, a better representation is understood as the extraction of the most informative features from the data. Particularly, MNIST images data are visualized through projections onto the plane. Furthermore, distorted MNIST images and their reconstructed versions, produced by a CAE, were projected onto the same plane to evaluate the performance of the CAE model.

Notably, the 2D visualization generated by PCA reflects its ability to capture the variance of MNIST image data. In addition, the Mahalanobis distance with respect to the 95% confidence ellipse, centered at the mean of the PCA projections of the MNIST training images, showed that 94.40% of the distorted image projections and 97.41% of the CAE-reconstructed image projections fall inside the ellipse. This indicates that both sets of images share the most important features with the original MNIST training images. In contrast, the 2D visualization generated by FDA, together with the Mahalanobis distance relative to the 95% confidence ellipses—each centered at the mean of the FDA projections for each digit class reveals that FDA captures variance between elements of the same class, particularly by showing that 93.03% of CAE-reconstructed image projections fall inside their corresponding ellipses, demonstrating high similarity to the MNIST training images. In both cases, PCA and FDA confirm that the CAE produced high-quality reconstructions. Nevertheless, FDA also highlights that 99.25% of projections fall outside the ellipses, indicating a loss of similarity with their corresponding MNIST training classes. This fact opens new possibilities for research about the role of induced noise into high-dimensional data.

The outline of this paper is as follows. In Sect. 2, dimensionality reduction methods are described, with a focus on PCA and FDA, which are considered spectral dimensionality reduction techniques. Examples of their applications are also discussed and compared. In Sect. 3, the mathematical foundations for each method are presented. Section 4 contains the results of applying these methods to project MNIST images along with a discussion of the use of Mahalanobis distances relative to a 95% confidence ellipse. Sections 5 and 6 provide conclusions and suggestions for future work.

2 State of the Art

The dimensionality reduction concept has various connotations, including feature extraction, feature selection, manifold learning, subspace learning, and representation learning [1, 2]. Particularly, in this work, dimensionality reduction is used in the sense of feature extraction. According to Ghojogh et al. [3], dimensionality reduction methods can be grouped into three categories: spectral dimensionality reduction, probabilistic dimensionality reduction, and neural network–based dimensionality reduction. Spectral methods have a geometric perspective and attempt to find a linear or nonlinear submanifold of the data. Probabilistic methods aim to identify lower-dimensional latent variables from higher-dimensional data. Neural network–based techniques, whether deep or shallow, use the network as an information bottleneck to extract low-dimensional informative features. Particularly, in this work we focus on the implementation of two spectral methods: Principal Component Analysis (PCA) and Fisher Discriminant Analysis (FDA).

PCA was first proposed by Pearson in 1901. It is a statistical technique for reducing the dimensionality of a dataset, increasing interpretability while minimizing information loss [4]. PCA has been applied in many research fields; for example, in blind noise level estimation for image processing applications such as denoising, compression, and segmentation [5], in filtering noisy magnetic resonance images [6], in estimating missing values in large data matrices, in sparse component estimation, and in the analysis of images, shapes, and functions [7]. Other applications include face recognition [8], pedestrian detection [9], among many others.

On the other hand, FDA was proposed by Ronald Aylmer Fisher [10], who also introduced important statistical concepts such as variance. FDA attempts to find a subspace that maximally separates the classes while ensuring that the data remain as spread as possible [3]. Likewise, FDA is an important linear dimensionality reduction method, but it is mainly focused on class separability [11]. It is also referred to as Fisher's Linear Discriminant Analysis (FLDA) or simply Linear Discriminant Analysis (LDA). In the literature, FDA is considered a supervised linear method because it requires labels for the sample data points. Moreover, it is also regarded as a classification method in statistical and probabilistic learning. FDA has been applied in several domains, such as facial recognition [12], action recognition [13], gesture recognition [14], among many others.

In the following section, both methods are described in detail. We adopt most of the mathematical notations provided by Ghojogh et al. [3] in Part II (Spectral Dimensionality Reduction), specifically in Chapters 5 and 6 where PCA and FDA are presented. For additional details not discussed in this paper, the reader is referred to that work.

3 Material and Methods

3.1 Preliminary Concepts

In mathematical words, an image can be represented as a data point within a d-dimensional vector space, i.e., the Euclidean space $\mathbb{R}^d$. The d values of a data point are considered as d features of one observation. In a general way, a data set of n points with d features each one, occupies some region of the vector space $\mathbb{R}^d$. In feature selection, the p most informative features from the d-dimensional vector are selected. The new p-dimensional vector is a subset of the original vector. In contrast, with feature extraction, the d-dimensional data vector is transformed into a different p-dimensional data vector. From this point of view, the Euclidean space $\mathbb{R}^d$ is called the input space and the region occupied by the dataset is referred to as subspace, submanifold or as a p-dimensional embedding space, where $p \leq d$ and $p \in (0, d]$. This fact is considered as a hypothesis, and it is called the manifold hypothesis [3].

Essentially, PCA and FDA are linear methods that project a d-dimensional vector from $\mathbb{R}^d$ onto a p-dimensional vector in $\mathbb{R}^p$. PCA is considered as an unsupervised method because it requires only n data points $\boldsymbol{x}_{i=1}^n$, where $\boldsymbol{x}_i = (x_1, x_2, \ldots, x_d) \in$

$\mathbb{R}^d$. On the other hand, FDA is considered as a supervised learning method because it requires data points $\{x_{i=1}^n\}$ and their corresponding target labels $\{y_{i=1}^n\}$. Consider a dataset $\{(x_{i=1}^n, y_{i=1}^n)\}$ of size *n*, with $\boldsymbol{x}_i \in \mathbb{R}^d$ and $\boldsymbol{y}_i \in \mathbb{R}^l$ representing the input data and the target labels, respectively. Therefore, it is necessary to stack in a column-wise matrix data $\boldsymbol{X} = [\boldsymbol{x}_1, \boldsymbol{x}_2, \ldots, \boldsymbol{x}_n] \in \mathbb{R}^{d \times n}$. The core idea behind PCA and FDA is the concept of a linear transformation $T\colon \mathbb{R}^d \to \mathbb{R}^p$. In other words, a dataset of *n* vectors $\boldsymbol{x}_i \in \mathbb{R}^d$ under the function T, it is projected onto the vector space spanned by *p* vectors $\{\boldsymbol{u}_1, \boldsymbol{u}_2, \ldots, \boldsymbol{u}_p\}$, where each vector is a *d*-dimensional and usually $p << d$. The *p* vectors are stacked column-wise in a matrix $\boldsymbol{U} = [\boldsymbol{u}_1, \boldsymbol{u}_2, \ldots, \boldsymbol{u}_p] \in \mathbb{R}^{d \times p}$. In this sense, the aim is to project onto the column space of $\boldsymbol{U}$, denoted by $Col(\boldsymbol{U})$. Based on the matrix $\boldsymbol{U}$, if the *p* vectors $\{\boldsymbol{u}_1, \boldsymbol{u}_2, \ldots, \boldsymbol{u}_p\}$ are orthonormal, then $\boldsymbol{U}$ is orthogonal and $\boldsymbol{U}^T = \boldsymbol{U}^{-1}$, then $\boldsymbol{U}^T\boldsymbol{U} = \boldsymbol{I}$, where $\boldsymbol{I}$ is the $d \times d$ identity matrix. Furthermore, it is possible to define the $d \times d$ projection matrix of the form:

$$\boldsymbol{\Pi} = \boldsymbol{U}\left(\boldsymbol{U}^T\boldsymbol{U}\right)\boldsymbol{U}^T, \tag{1}$$

where $\boldsymbol{\Pi}$ projects $\boldsymbol{x}_i \in \mathbb{R}^d$ onto $Col(\boldsymbol{U}) \subset \mathbb{R}^p$ and reconstructs it back to $\mathbb{R}^d$. Therefore, Eq. (1) is simplified to:

$$\boldsymbol{\Pi} = \boldsymbol{U}\boldsymbol{U}^T. \tag{2}$$

From Eq. (2), $\tilde{\boldsymbol{x}}_i = \boldsymbol{U}^T\boldsymbol{x}_i$ is defined as the projection of $\boldsymbol{x}_i$ onto $Col(\boldsymbol{U}) \subset \mathbb{R}^p$ and $\hat{\boldsymbol{x}}_i = \boldsymbol{U}\boldsymbol{U}^T\boldsymbol{x}_i$ as the reconstruction back of $\boldsymbol{x}_i$ onto $\mathbb{R}^d$. In this sense, if $\boldsymbol{x}_t \in \mathbb{R}^d$ is an out-of-sample data point, its linear transformation can be calculated as $\tilde{\boldsymbol{x}}_t = \boldsymbol{U}^T\boldsymbol{x}_t$ onto $Col(\boldsymbol{U}) \subset \mathbb{R}^p$, and similarly, its reconstruction back as $\hat{\boldsymbol{x}}_t = \boldsymbol{U}\boldsymbol{U}^T\boldsymbol{x}_t$ onto $\mathbb{R}^d$. In [15] an out-of-sample data point is called supplementary or illustrative observation. In the next subsections PCA and FDA are described in detail.

3.2 Principal Component Analysis

PCA is a multivariate statistical technique that tries to find vectors $\boldsymbol{u}$ which direction represent the maximum variance of the dataset in $\mathbb{R}^d$ space. Basically, PCA is the construction of a linear projection of $\boldsymbol{x}_i$ onto orthogonal direction of $\boldsymbol{u}$ in $Col(\boldsymbol{U}) \subset \mathbb{R}^p$, which represents the data with the latest error. $Col(\boldsymbol{U})$ is called PCA *subspace*. According to the previous description, $\boldsymbol{u}^T\boldsymbol{X}$ is the projection of the matrix data $\boldsymbol{X}$ onto PCA subspace in the direction of $\boldsymbol{u}$. Additionally, PCA is a method that requires data points to be centered, i.e., the sample data points require to be centered respect to the origin $\boldsymbol{0}$ in $\mathbb{R}^d$. To be centered, every data point $\boldsymbol{x}_i$ in $\boldsymbol{X}$ takes the form $\breve{\boldsymbol{x}}_i = \boldsymbol{x}_i - \boldsymbol{\mu}$, where $\mu = (\mu_1, \mu_2, \ldots, \mu_d)$ and $\mu_i = \frac{1}{n}\sum_{k=1}^{n} x_{ki}$ for $x_{ki} \in (x_{1i}, x_{2i}, \ldots, x_{ni})^T$, the *i*-th feature and $i = 1, \ldots, d$. Therefore, the projection of $\breve{\boldsymbol{x}}_t$ onto PCA subspace is $\tilde{\breve{\boldsymbol{x}}}_t = \boldsymbol{U}^T\breve{\boldsymbol{x}}_t$ and its reconstruction back $\hat{\boldsymbol{x}}_t = \boldsymbol{U}\boldsymbol{U}^T\breve{\boldsymbol{x}}_t + \boldsymbol{\mu} = \boldsymbol{U}\tilde{\breve{\boldsymbol{x}}}_t + \boldsymbol{\mu}$, if μ is considered. In a similar manner, for an out-of-sample data point, $\hat{\boldsymbol{x}}_t = \boldsymbol{U}\boldsymbol{U}^T\breve{\boldsymbol{x}}_t + \boldsymbol{\mu} = \boldsymbol{U}\tilde{\breve{\boldsymbol{x}}}_t + \boldsymbol{\mu}$. If the centered data are stacked in a column-wise matrix $\breve{\boldsymbol{X}} = [\breve{\boldsymbol{x}}_1, \breve{\boldsymbol{x}}_2, \ldots, \breve{\boldsymbol{x}}_n] \in \mathbb{R}^{d \times n}$, then the reconstruction back of the centered data matrix $\breve{\boldsymbol{X}}$ is:

$$\hat{\boldsymbol{X}} = \boldsymbol{U}\boldsymbol{U}^T\breve{\boldsymbol{X}}. \tag{3}$$

It is remarkable that finding the best reconstruction back $\widehat{X}$, implies finding the matrix $\boldsymbol{U}$ which minimizes the residual error $\breve{\boldsymbol{x}}_i - \widehat{\boldsymbol{x}}_i$ for every data point $\boldsymbol{x}_i$, or in the general case, for the n data points, which minimizes the residual matrix $\breve{\boldsymbol{X}} - \widehat{\boldsymbol{X}}$ in one or more directions $\boldsymbol{u}_1, \boldsymbol{u}_2, \ldots, \boldsymbol{u}_p$. In any case, each vector $\boldsymbol{u}_j$ for $j = 1, \ldots, p$, satisfies $\boldsymbol{u}_j^T \boldsymbol{u}_j = \|\boldsymbol{u}_j\|_2^2 = 1$ and $\breve{\boldsymbol{x}}_i^T \boldsymbol{u}_j = \boldsymbol{u}_j^T \breve{\boldsymbol{x}}_i \in \mathbb{R}$. Furthermore, the squared length (squared l_2-norm) of the reconstructed vector $\widehat{\boldsymbol{x}}_i = \boldsymbol{u}_j \boldsymbol{u}_j^T \breve{\boldsymbol{x}}_i$ satisfies that

$$\| \widehat{\boldsymbol{x}}_i \|_2^2 = \| \boldsymbol{u}_j \boldsymbol{u}_j^T \breve{\boldsymbol{x}}_i \|_2^2 = \boldsymbol{u}_j^T \breve{\boldsymbol{x}}_i \breve{\boldsymbol{x}}_i^T \boldsymbol{u}_j . \tag{4}$$

In Eq. (4), $\breve{\boldsymbol{x}}_i \breve{\boldsymbol{x}}_i^T$ is the covariance matrix of the features in $\breve{\boldsymbol{x}}_i$. Consequently, from Eq. (4) the sum of all products $\breve{\boldsymbol{x}}_i \breve{\boldsymbol{x}}_i^T$ is equal to the $d \times d$ *covariance matrix* of the centered dataset, denoted by $\boldsymbol{S}$, which is:

$$\boldsymbol{S} = \sum_{i=1}^{n} \breve{\boldsymbol{x}}_i \breve{\boldsymbol{x}}_i^T = \breve{\boldsymbol{X}} \breve{\boldsymbol{X}}^T \tag{5}$$

In addition, $\boldsymbol{u}_j^T \boldsymbol{S} \boldsymbol{u}_j = Var(\boldsymbol{u}_j^T \breve{X})$ is the variance of the projections of the sample data points in PCA subspace in the direction of $\boldsymbol{u}_j$. Fundamentally, in PCA the goal is to minimize the reconstruction error $\breve{\boldsymbol{X}} - \widehat{\boldsymbol{X}}$ subject to the orthogonality of the matrix $\boldsymbol{U}$, then it turns into the next optimization problem:

$$\text{minimize} \quad \| \breve{X} - \widehat{X} \|_F^2 \qquad \text{subject to } \boldsymbol{U}\boldsymbol{U}^T = \boldsymbol{I}, \tag{6}$$

where F refers to the Frobenius Norm. In Eq. (6),

$$\| \breve{\boldsymbol{X}} - \widehat{\boldsymbol{X}} \|_F^2 = \| \breve{\boldsymbol{X}} - \boldsymbol{U}\boldsymbol{U}^T \breve{\boldsymbol{X}} \|_F^2 = tr(\breve{\boldsymbol{X}}^T \breve{\boldsymbol{X}}) - tr(\breve{\boldsymbol{X}} \breve{\boldsymbol{X}}^T \boldsymbol{U}\boldsymbol{U}^T). \tag{7}$$

From Eq. (7), a Lagrangian function L is defined as follows:

$$L = tr(\breve{X}^T \breve{X}) - tr(\breve{X} \breve{X}^T U U^T) + tr(\Lambda^T (U^T U - I)) \tag{8}$$

where $\boldsymbol{\Lambda} \in \mathbb{R}^{p \times p}$ is a diagonal matrix $diag([\lambda_1, \ldots, \lambda_p]^T)$ containing the Lagrangian multipliers. Calculating $\frac{\partial L}{\partial U} = 0$, then $\breve{\boldsymbol{X}} \breve{\boldsymbol{X}}^T \boldsymbol{U} = \boldsymbol{\Lambda} \boldsymbol{U}$.

Considering Eq. (5), then $\boldsymbol{S}\boldsymbol{U} = \boldsymbol{U}\boldsymbol{\Lambda}$. Finally, from $\boldsymbol{S}\boldsymbol{U} = \boldsymbol{U}\boldsymbol{\Lambda}$, the optimal solution is the eigen-decomposition of $\boldsymbol{S}$, i.e., $\boldsymbol{U}$ where its columns $\{\boldsymbol{u}_1, \boldsymbol{u}_2, \ldots, \boldsymbol{u}_p\}$ are the eigenvectors of $\boldsymbol{S}$ and $\boldsymbol{\Lambda}$ with the eigenvalues of $\mathbf{S}$, respectively. In Eq. (5), the matrix $\boldsymbol{S}$ is symmetric and positive semi-definite. Furthermore, $rank(\boldsymbol{S}) \leq n - 1$ if $d > n$ or, $rank(\boldsymbol{S}) \leq d$ if $d < n$. On the other hand, if $rank(\boldsymbol{S}) = d$ and $n > d$, then $p = d$, i.e., $\boldsymbol{U}^T \in \mathbb{R}^{d \times d}$ and it projects the dataset onto $\mathbb{R}^d$. In this case, PCA is considered as a rotation in the sense that $\mathbb{R}^d = \mathbb{R}^p$ or $\boldsymbol{U}$ transforms the dataset isometrically. In the case, where $rank(\boldsymbol{S}) = d$ and $n > d$, then $\boldsymbol{U}^T \in \mathbb{R}^{p \times d}$ projects onto $\mathbb{R}^p$ subspace, due to the p leading nonzero eigenvalues from $\mathbf{S}$. See [3] for details.

3.3 Singular Value Decomposition Path

Alternatively, a similar path can be performed by calculating the Singular Value Decomposition (SVD) of $\breve{\boldsymbol{X}}$ rather than eigen-decomposition of $\boldsymbol{S}$. The SVD of $\breve{\mathbf{X}}$ takes the form:

$$\breve{\boldsymbol{X}} = \boldsymbol{U} \boldsymbol{\Sigma} \boldsymbol{V}^T \tag{9}$$

where the columns of $\boldsymbol{U} \in \mathbb{R}^{d\times p}$ (called the *left singular vectors*) are the eigenvectors of $\breve{\boldsymbol{X}}\breve{\boldsymbol{X}}^{\boldsymbol{T}}$ and the columns of $\boldsymbol{V} \in \mathbb{R}^{n\times n}$ (called the *right singular vectors*) are the eigenvectors of $\breve{\boldsymbol{X}}^{\boldsymbol{T}}\breve{\boldsymbol{X}}$, and $\boldsymbol{\Sigma} \in \mathbb{R}^{d\times n}$ is a rectangular diagonal matrix whose diagonal entries (called *singular values*) are the squared root of eigenvalues of $\breve{\boldsymbol{X}}\breve{\boldsymbol{X}}^{\boldsymbol{T}}$ and/or $\breve{\boldsymbol{X}}^{\boldsymbol{T}}\breve{\boldsymbol{X}}$. In this strategy, the left singular vectors can be taken as the principal directions. In [15], PCA is described following this path. Especially, the matrix $\boldsymbol{U}\Sigma$ is called the factor score matrix.

3.4 Number of the Principal Directions

The eigenvectors $\{\boldsymbol{u}_1, \boldsymbol{u}_2, \ldots, \boldsymbol{u}_p\}$, i.e., the orthonormal columns of $\boldsymbol{U}$, are sorted according to their corresponding eigenvalue in descending order, from largest to smallest. The eigenvalues near to zero are cut off. The way of determining the number p can be defined by comparing the ratio $\frac{\lambda_j}{\sum_{j=1}^{p}\lambda_j}$ whit a threshold, where λ_j is the eigenvalue associated with the eigenvector j-th and $\sum_{j=1}^{p}\lambda_j$ is the addition of all the eigenvalues [3, 15]. In this work, we adopted the name *explained variance ratio (EV R)*, which tells how much of the total variance of the dataset is captured by component $\boldsymbol{u}_j$. The *EVR* associated with the eigenvalue λ_j, is defined as follows:

$$EVR_j = \frac{\lambda_j}{\sum_{j=1}^{p}\lambda_j}, \tag{10}$$

The label *EVR* was adopted from the parameter name given in the Python class that is defined in the scikit-learn library.

3.5 Fisher Discriminant Analysis

FDA calculates projections along certain directions $\boldsymbol{u}_j$ where the separation between different classes *(between-scatter)* is maximum and where the spread out of the data points within each class (within-scatter) is minimum. Consider a dataset of n data points, divided in m classes, with their respective labels $\{(\boldsymbol{x}_{i=1}^{n}, \boldsymbol{y}_{i=1}^{n})\}$ of size n, with $\boldsymbol{x}_i \in \mathbb{R}^d$ and $\boldsymbol{y}_i \in \mathbb{R}^l$. Likewise, in FDA every data point $\boldsymbol{x}_i$ is stacked in a matrix $\boldsymbol{X} = [\boldsymbol{x}_1, \boldsymbol{x}_2, \ldots, \boldsymbol{x}_n] \in \mathbb{R}^{d\times n}$ and the labels $\boldsymbol{y}_i$ in a matrix $\boldsymbol{Y} = [\boldsymbol{y}_1, \boldsymbol{y}_2, \ldots, \boldsymbol{y}_n] \in \mathbb{R}^{l\times n}$.

If there are m classes of data points in $\boldsymbol{X}$, and $\{\boldsymbol{x}_i^{(k)}\}_{i=1}^{n_k}$ denotes the sample data points of the k-th class containing n_k elements, for $k = 1, 2, \ldots, m$ such as $n_1 + n_2 + \cdots + n_m = n$. If the elements of k-th class are projected onto the direction $\boldsymbol{u}_j$ in $Col(\boldsymbol{U})$, i.e., $\boldsymbol{u}_j^T\boldsymbol{x}_i^{(k)}$, then the mean and the variance of the projected data are $\boldsymbol{u}_j^T\mu_k$ and $\boldsymbol{u}_j^T\boldsymbol{S}_k\boldsymbol{u}_j$, respectively. In this context, the mean $\mu_k \in \mathbb{R}^d$ of the k-th class is defined as:

$$\mu_k = \frac{1}{n_k}\sum_{i=1}^{n_k}\boldsymbol{x}_i^{(k)}. \tag{11}$$

On the other hand, in $\boldsymbol{u}_j^T\boldsymbol{S}_k\boldsymbol{u}_j$, $\boldsymbol{S}_k$ is the covariance matrix (scatter) of the k-th class. Notice that $\boldsymbol{u}_j^T\boldsymbol{S}_k\boldsymbol{u}_j \in \mathbb{R}$, i.e., this product is a scalar. If two classes, k and h are projected onto the direction $\boldsymbol{u}_j$, then the distance $d_B \in \mathbb{R}$ between the projection of the means μ_k and μ_h, is defined as follows:

$$d_B = \left(\boldsymbol{u}_j^T \mu_k - \boldsymbol{u}_j^T \mu_h\right)^T \left(\boldsymbol{u}_j^T \mu_k - \boldsymbol{u}_j^T \mu_h\right) = \boldsymbol{u}_j^T (\mu_k - \mu_h)(\mu_k - \mu_h)^T \boldsymbol{u}_j, \tag{12}$$

where $\boldsymbol{u}_j^T (\mu_k - \mu_h)(\mu_k - \mu_h)^T \boldsymbol{u}_j = \boldsymbol{u}_j^T \boldsymbol{S}_B \boldsymbol{u}_j$ and $\boldsymbol{S}_B \in \mathbb{R}^{dxd}$ is called the *between-scatter* or the *interclass scatter/covariance* matrix. In particular, d_B can be interpreted as the variance of the projection of the means. If the variances of the projection of two classes are calculated in the direction of $\boldsymbol{u}_j$, then they are added together, and the sum takes the form:

$$d_W = \boldsymbol{u}_j^T \boldsymbol{S}_k \boldsymbol{u}_j + \boldsymbol{u}_j^T \boldsymbol{S}_h \boldsymbol{u}_j = \boldsymbol{u}_j^T \boldsymbol{S}_W \boldsymbol{u}_j, \tag{13}$$

$d_W \in \mathbb{R}$ and $\boldsymbol{S}_W = \boldsymbol{S}_k + \boldsymbol{S}_{h.}$ $\boldsymbol{S}_W \in \mathbb{R}^{dxd}$ called the *within-scatter* of the classes (or the *intraclass scatter/covariance*). d_W is the summation of the projection variances of the classes k and h, respectively. In the general case, for the between-scatter of all m classes, the general mean μ of whole dataset $\boldsymbol{X}$ is needed, and it is calculated as follows:

$$\boldsymbol{S}_B = \sum\nolimits_{k=1}^{m} (\mu_k - \mu)(\mu_h - \mu)^T, \tag{14}$$

where $\mu = \frac{1}{\sum_{k=1}^{m} n_k} \sum_{k=1}^{m} n_k \mu_k = \frac{1}{n} \sum_{i=1}^{n} \boldsymbol{x}_i$ and $\mu \in \mathbb{R}^d$. Finally, the total within-scatter matrix for the m classes is $\boldsymbol{S}_W = \sum_{k=1}^{m} \boldsymbol{S}_k$, where

$$\boldsymbol{S}_W = \sum\nolimits_{k=1}^{m} \boldsymbol{S}_k = \sum\nolimits_{k=1}^{m} \sum_{i=1}^{n_k} \left(\boldsymbol{x}_i^{(k)} - \mu_k\right)\left(\boldsymbol{x}_i^{(k)} - \mu_k\right)^T. \tag{15}$$

Notice that $\boldsymbol{S}_W \in \mathbb{R}^{d \times d}$ is the sum of the all the covariance matrices of the m classes. Fundamentally, FDA defines an optimization problem that consists in two parts: one, is to maximize the scatter of the m means, i.e., maximizing the distance $d_B(\boldsymbol{u}_j)$ which measures the separation of the classes; and the second one, is to minimize the distance $d_W(\boldsymbol{u}_j)$ which measures the projection variances (scatter) of the data points in each class. In both cases, distances depend on finding the optimal set of vectors $\{\boldsymbol{u}_1, \boldsymbol{u}_2, \ldots, \boldsymbol{u}_p\}$. One common way to find the solution to this problem is merging both distances into a real function $f(\boldsymbol{u}_j)$ defined as follows:

$$f\left(\boldsymbol{u}_j\right) = \frac{d_B(\boldsymbol{u}_j)}{d_W(\boldsymbol{u}_j)}, \tag{16}$$

Where $f(\boldsymbol{u}_j)$ is known as the *Fisher criterion*. This problem is equivalent to

$$\text{maximize } \boldsymbol{u}_j^T \boldsymbol{S}_B \boldsymbol{u}_j, \text{ subject to } \boldsymbol{u}_j^T \boldsymbol{S}_W \boldsymbol{u}_j = 1. \tag{17}$$

To solve this problem, a Lagrangian function L is proposed as follows:

$$L = \boldsymbol{u}_j^T \boldsymbol{S}_B \boldsymbol{u}_j - \lambda(\boldsymbol{u}_j^T \boldsymbol{S}_W \boldsymbol{u}_j - 1) \tag{18}$$

where λ is a Lagrange multiplier. The derivative of L respect to $\boldsymbol{u}_j$ equated to zero, then $\frac{\partial L}{\partial \boldsymbol{u}_j} = 2\boldsymbol{S}_B\boldsymbol{u}_j - 2\lambda\boldsymbol{S}_W\boldsymbol{u}_j = 0$. Therefore, $\boldsymbol{S}_B\boldsymbol{u}_j = \lambda\boldsymbol{S}_W\boldsymbol{u}_j$ which is a generalized eigenvalue problem $(\boldsymbol{S}_B, \boldsymbol{S}_W)$ where $\boldsymbol{u}_j$ is an eigenvector associated with the largest eigenvalue $\lambda = \lambda_j$. The vector $\boldsymbol{u}_j$ is called *Fisher direction* or *Fisher axis* $\boldsymbol{u}_j$. From a general perspective, we call the *Fisher subspace* of dimension p, whose basis consists of the orthonormal column vectors of $\boldsymbol{U}$. In a matrix form, the optimization problems take the form: $d_B = tr(\boldsymbol{U}^T\boldsymbol{S}_B\boldsymbol{U}) \in \mathbb{R}$ and $d_W = tr(\boldsymbol{U}^T\boldsymbol{S}_W\boldsymbol{U}) \in \mathbb{R}$, where tr() refers to the trace of the matrices, respectively. According to Eq. (16) and (17), the matrix form or the optimization problem takes the form:

$$f(\boldsymbol{U}) = \frac{d_B(\boldsymbol{U})}{d_w(\boldsymbol{U})}, \tag{19}$$

Where $f(\boldsymbol{U})$ is a real function and the ratio is called the *Fisher criterion.* Similarly, as in the case of $\boldsymbol{u}_j$ direction, the problem in a matrix form is:

$$\text{maximize } tr(\boldsymbol{U}^T\boldsymbol{S}_B\boldsymbol{U}), \text{ subject to } \boldsymbol{U}^T\boldsymbol{S}_W\boldsymbol{U} = \boldsymbol{I}. \tag{20}$$

Likewise, according to the Eq. (20), the Lagrangian functions in matrix form takes the form:

$$L = tr\left(\boldsymbol{U}^T\boldsymbol{S}_B\boldsymbol{U}\right) - tr\left(\Lambda^T\left(\boldsymbol{U}^T\boldsymbol{S}_W\boldsymbol{U} - \boldsymbol{I}\right)\right), \tag{21}$$

where $\boldsymbol{\Lambda} \in \mathbb{R}^{d \times d}$ is a diagonal matrix, whose diagonal entries are the Lagrange multipliers. Equating the derivative of L respect to $\mathbf{U}$ to $\mathbf{0}$, results in:

$$\frac{\partial L}{\partial \boldsymbol{U}} = 2\boldsymbol{S}_B\boldsymbol{U} - 2\boldsymbol{S}_W\boldsymbol{U}\boldsymbol{\Lambda} = 0, \tag{22}$$

such that $\boldsymbol{S}_B\boldsymbol{U} = \boldsymbol{S}_W\boldsymbol{U}\boldsymbol{\Lambda}$, which is a generalized eigenvalue problem $(\boldsymbol{S}_B, \boldsymbol{S}_W)$. One possible solution, from $\boldsymbol{S}_B\boldsymbol{U} = \boldsymbol{S}_W\boldsymbol{U}\boldsymbol{\Lambda}$ is $\boldsymbol{U} = eig(\boldsymbol{S}_W^{-1}\boldsymbol{S}_B)$ where $eig()$ denotes the eigenvectors of the matrix stacked column-wise. See [3] for details.

3.6 Dataset Description

In this work, to generate a 2D visualization of MNIST images with PCA and FDA, MNIST dataset was preprocessed—MNIST for Modified National Institute of Standard, it is available in the website keras.io. This dataset contains 70000 handwritten digit grayscale images with pixels values from 0 (completely white) to 1 (completely black), each with size 28 × 28 pixels, that is, 784 pixels. In this context, each pixel value was considered as a feature, i.e., 784 features per image. In this sense, an image is an object contained within a 784-dimensional space. While downloading MNIST dataset from keras.io, it was separated and saved into two folders, one with 60,000 images for training and another with 10,000 images for testing. We proposed using the 60,000 training MNIST images to generate the corresponding basis vectors $\{\boldsymbol{u}_1, \boldsymbol{u}_2, \ldots, \boldsymbol{u}_p\}$, for the PCA and FDA subspace, respectively. Some items are depicted in Fig. 1.

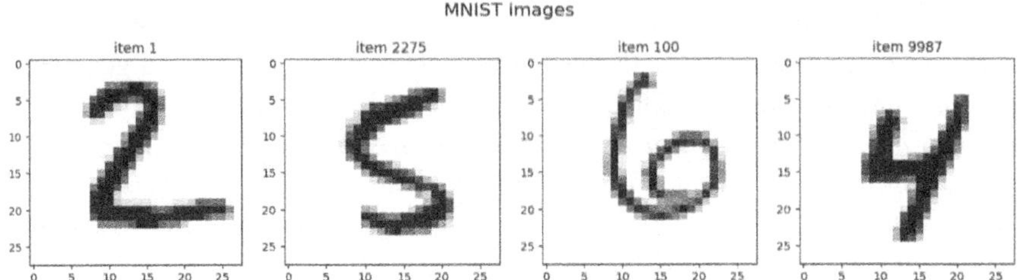

Fig. 1. MNIST training images that were used for calculating the basis vectors $\{u_1, u_2, \ldots, u_p\}$, for the PCA and FDA subspaces, respectively.

In addition, another part of the material used for this work was generated for the experimental work described in [16]. Authors reported the implementation of a convolutional autoencoder (CAE) for restoring distorted MNIST images. Distortions within images were induced randomly by corrupting separately the whole dataset in three different proportions of the 784 pixels: 10% (79 pixels), 30% (157 pixels), and 40% (235 pixels), respectively. The distortion process involved replacing the original pixels with completely black pixels, i.e., to set the value to 1. The CAE was cloned three times to be trained with the three corresponding distorted training datasets. The three resulting models were tested by cleaning the corresponding distorted testing images. The cleaning process generated three new datasets of images. Consequently, the 10,000 original MNIST testing images, and the corresponding distorted -30,000- and cleaned versions - 30,000- were used as out-of-sample data points to project onto PCA and FDA subspaces, respectively. Some of them are depicted in Fig. 2,

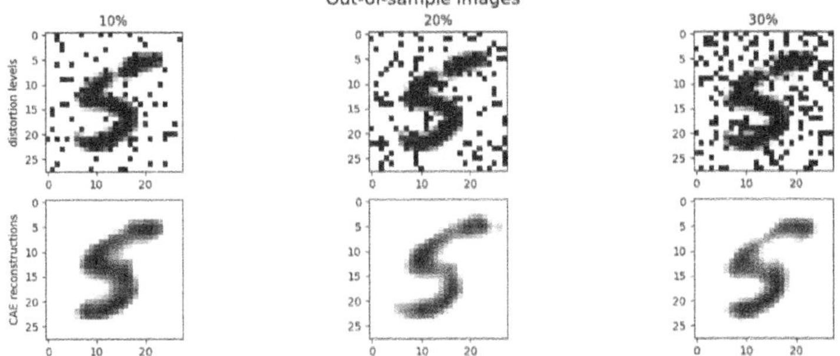

Fig. 2. Random distorted images and their CAE-reconstructed versions.

3.7 Experiment Setup

The implementation of PCA and FDA methods is based on the scikit-learn library. Table 1 shows the characteristics of the computer resources implemented for this experiment.

Table 1. Specification and setup

	Specification
Memory	16 GB
Processor	13th Gen Intel(R) Core(TM) i7-13650HX 2.60 GHz
Graphics	NVIDIA GeForce RTX 4050 Laptop GPU
Operating System	Windows 11 Home Single Language

4 Results

4.1 Projections onto the PCA Subspace

The dimensionality of this projection subspace can range from 1 to 784; in this case, it was chosen to be two-dimensional to provide an intuitive visualization. See Fig. 3, where 60,000 MNIST images are projected. Notice that most of the projections lie close to the origin. From now on, we refer to the two-dimensional PCA subspace as the MNIST PCA subspace.

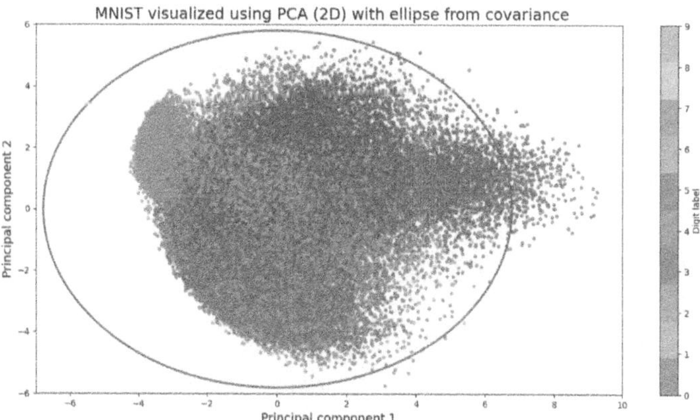

Fig. 3. Projections of 60,000 MNIST images onto the PCA subspace and the ellipse from covariance.

According to the description of PCA, in the first step, the original 60,000 training images were placed in the matrix $\boldsymbol{X}^T$, whose dimensions are 60,000 rows × 784 columns. Secondly, the 60,000 data points were centered according to the equation $\tilde{\boldsymbol{x}}_i = \boldsymbol{x}_i - \boldsymbol{\mu}$, where $\boldsymbol{x}_i$ is the i-th image and $\mu = (\mu_1, \mu_2, \ldots, \mu_{784})$ is the vector whose components μ_k for $k = 1, \ldots, 784$, are the average values from the columns (features) from $\boldsymbol{X}^T$. Subsequently, the centered data points were placed in the matrix $\tilde{\boldsymbol{X}}$. Due to the python library, called sklearn.decomposition, the implementation of the PCA was done through SVD. Particularly, according to Eq. (9), the centered data matrix $\tilde{\boldsymbol{X}}$was factorized into $U\Sigma V^T$. PCA captures the variance from the 60,000 training images through 784 orthonormal vectors of U, which are associated to the 784 eigenvalues $[\lambda_1, \lambda_2, \ldots, \lambda_{784}] = [5.116, 3.741, ..., 0.000]$ of the diagonal matrix Σ. The summation of all the 784 eigenvalues equals to 52.72, which represents 100% of the total variance for the 60,000 MNIST training images. The *explained variance ratio* defined in Eq. (10) can be used to define the *cumulated explained variance* which tells the total variance captured by the first k principal components. The addition of the first k EVR ratios, takes the form:

$$CEV = \sum_{j=1}^{k} EVR_j, \tag{23}$$

Where EVR_j is the j-th explained variance ratio for the λ_j. For example, for λ_1 is $5.11/52.75 = 0.096$, and for λ_2 is $3.74/52.75 = 0.0709$, and so on.

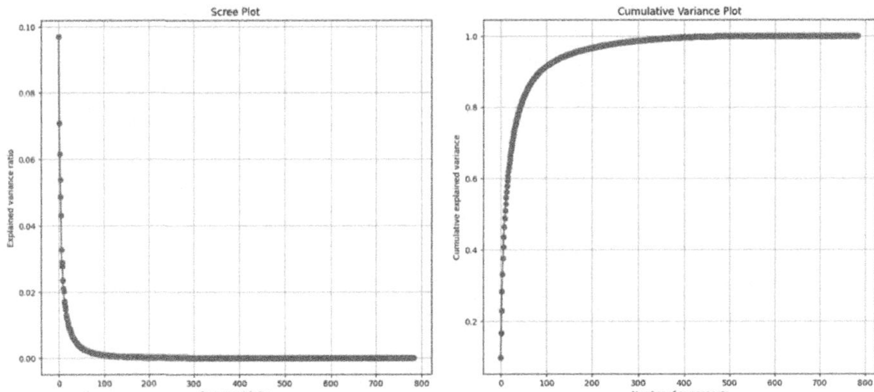

Fig. 4. Visualization of the explained variance ratios EVR_j for each λ_j (left), and the 100% cumulative explain variance $CEV = \sum_{j=1}^{784} EVR_j$ (rigth).

It is remarkable that these two eigenvectors associated with these two eigenvalues, captured just 9.70% and 7.09% of the total variance, respectively. The *ECR* ratios and the *CEV* summations for the 784 principal components are depicted in Fig. 4. To construct a projection of the out-of-sample datasets, just the first two principal components (dimension 1 and dimension 2) associated with the largest eigenvalues $\lambda_1 = 5.116$ and $\lambda_2 = 3.741$ were implemented. The PCA coordinates associated with the out-of-sample data points were projected onto the MNIST PCA subspace. The projections of the original, distorted, and cleaned MNIST images are depicted in Fig. 5.

4.2 Projections onto the FDA Subspace

Whit the aim of describing the implementation of the FDA, recall that in Eq. (22), the optimization of L resulted in the matrix $U = eig(S_W^{-1} S_B)$ whose p column vectors are the basis for the Fisher subspace. In this sense, the determination of the dimensionality of the Fisher subspace depends on the rank of the matrix $S_W^{-1}S_B$, which satisfies the following inequality:

$$rank\left(S_W^{-1}S_B\right) \leq \min\left(rank\left(S_W^{-1}\right), rank(S_B)\right) = \min(d, n-1, m-1) = m-1 \quad (24)$$

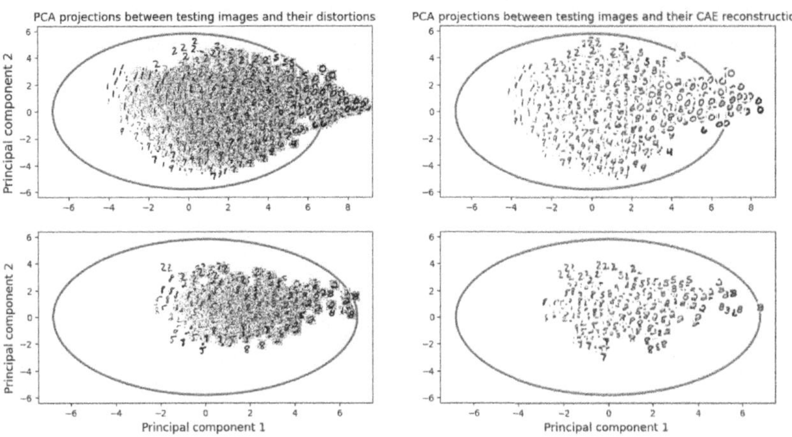

Fig. 5. Projections onto the PCA subspace of random MNIST test images versus their distorted versions (graphs of the left column), and the same MNIST test images versus their CAE reconstructions (graphs of the right column).

where, d is the dimensionality of the dataset, n is the sample size and m is the number of classes. Furthermore, $m-1$ is the number of leading eigenvectors which are considered the Fisher directions and the rest of eigenvectors are invalid or ignored. See [3] for details. In this work, $rank\left(S_W^{-1}S_B\right) = 9$ due to the 10 digits classes, i.e., the 9 leading eigenvectors are associated with the following eigenvalues $\lambda_1 = 0.239$, $\lambda_2 = 0.201$, $\lambda_3 = 0.178$, $\lambda_4 = 0.106$, $\lambda_5 = 0.094$, $\lambda_6 = 0.069$, $\lambda_7 = 0.049$, $\lambda_8 = 0.034$, $\lambda_9 = 0.026$. Figure 6 illustrates the separability of the 10-digit classes. For clarity, only classes 0, 1, and 9 are projected as an example.

4.3 Preforming Evaluation

To establish an objective criterion for evaluating the performance of the methods, the error ellipse method was implemented. This approach was originally proposed in [17]. According to Erten et al. [18], let $X = [x_1, x_2] \in \mathbb{R}^2$ be a random vector with a Gaussian distribution. Its distance D to the mean vector set μ is given by $D(X, \mu) = \sqrt{(X-\mu)^T \Sigma^{-1}(X-\mu)} = k$ where Σ is the covariance matrix of X and Σ^{-1} denotes the inverse matrix.

Since k is the square root of a quadratic form—a bivariate function, the locus of points where k is constant, therefore it defines an ellipse. This error ellipse corresponds to the region of minimum area that contains a specified probability mass under the Gaussian assumption. The distance $D(X, \mu)$ is known as the Mahalanobis distance. The variable k has a chi-square distribution $\chi_2^2(\alpha)$ with two degrees of freedom $P\{(X-\mu)^T \Sigma^{-1}(X-\mu) \leq \chi_2^2(\alpha)\} = 1-\alpha$, where $\chi_2^2(\alpha)$ is the upper $(100\alpha)th$ percentile of the χ^2-distribution with two degrees of freedom, and it determines confidence level. Specifically, $1-\alpha$ is the probability that the vector X falls inside the ellipse. For example, if $\alpha = 0.05$, then the confidence level is 95% and the critical value is $\chi_2^2(0.05) = 5.99$. Both PCA and FDA generate two sets of two-dimensional vectors. Each corresponding 2×2 covariance matrix Σ has two eigenvectors $\{v_1, v_2\}$ and two positive eigenvalues λ_1 and λ_2. Finally, without loss of generality, suppose that $\lambda_1 > \lambda_2$, then the error ellipse will be constructed as follow: its center is the mean vector μ, the major axis with length $\sqrt{\lambda_1 \chi_2^2(0.05)}$, the minor axis with length $\sqrt{\lambda_2 \chi_2^2(0.05)}$ and its orientation is aligned with the eigenvectors v_1 and v_2.

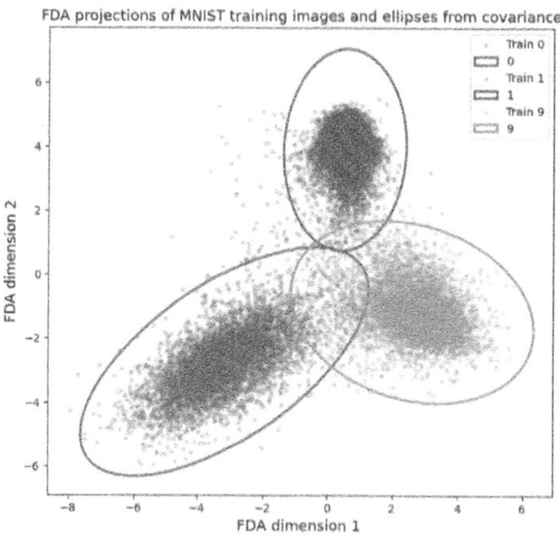

Fig. 6. Projections onto the FDA subspace of 6000 MNIST training images per the digit classes 0, 1 and 9.

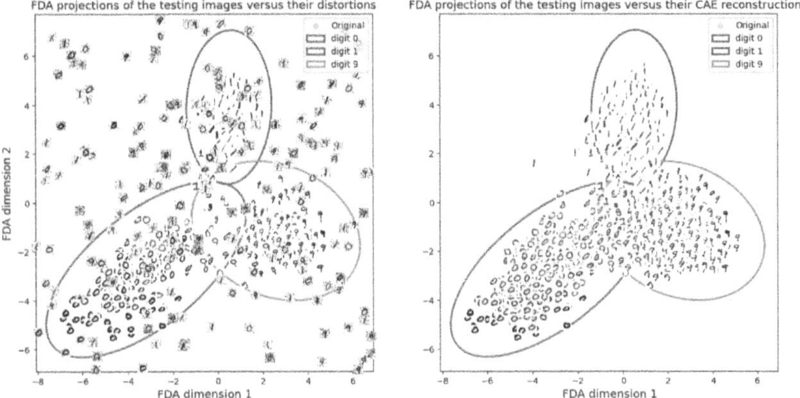

Fig. 7. Random MNIST testing images versus their distorted versions (left) and the same MNIST testing images versus their CAE reconstructions (right).

5 Discussion

The PCA and FDA projections, facilitated meaningful comparisons between the original MNIST images, their distorted versions (30,000 images), and the reconstructed versions (30,000 images) produced by a convolutional autoencoder (CAE), see in Fig. 5. In Erten et al. [18], consider that error ellipse method is useful when there is no clear prior distribution. In this sense, in this work, the numerical results were obtained under the assumption that, in both cases, PCA and FDA generated bivariate vectors that follow a Gaussian distribution with respect to the mean vector μ. And according to the Mahalanobis distance with respect to the 95% confidence ellipse centered at the mean of the PCA projections of the MNIST training images, the empirical results show that 94.40% of the distorted image projections fall inside the ellipse, while 97.41% of the reconstructed image projections fall inside. In contrast, FDA generated a two-dimensional visualization highlighting the separability of the classes, as shown in Fig. 6. Similarly, using the Mahalanobis distance with respect to the 95% confidence ellipses—each centered at the mean of the FDA projections for each digit class, the empirical results show that an average of 99.25% of the distorted image projections fall outside the ellipses, whereas an average of 93.03% of the reconstructed image projections fall inside. See Fig. 7. In [19], authors have considered that confidence regions (represented by scatter plots or ellipses) provide a useful contribution to the interpretation of PCA plots. However, the true distribution of the dataset is often unknown.

6 Conclusions and Future Work

1. PCA and FDA provide intuitive visualizations of the MNIST dataset embedded in $\mathbb{R}^{784}$. Furthermore, the 2D visualizations illustrate the changes that occur in the image space after inducing different types of noise. The numerical results presented in this work offer an alternative way of evaluating the CAE performance reported in [16],

where the SSIM metric was used to compare the original images and the CAE-reconstructed versions. The SSIM metric yielded similarity values of 0.91 (10% distortion), 0.94 (20% distortion), and 0.90 (30% distortion).
2. In contrast, the FDA projections clearly revealed the separability of the classes, showing that 93.03% of the CAE-reconstructed image projections fall inside the corresponding confidence ellipses.
3. The limitation of FDA in projecting the distorted images reflects the effect of the induced noise, as only 0.75% of them fall inside their corresponding class ellipses.

The limitations observed in projecting certain out-of-sample images suggest the need to explore alternative nonlinear methods. In this context, future work could investigate spectral nonlinear techniques such as Multidimensional Scaling (MDS), Sammon mappings, or Isomap.

Acknowledgements. This project was supported by Secretaría de Ciencia, Humanidades, Tecnología e Innovación del Gobierno de México and Instituto Politécnico Nacional de México.

References

1. Cayton, L.: Algorithms for Manifold Learning. Technical report University of California at San Diego 16 (2005). https://ijcopi.org/ojs/article/view/1141
2. Bengio, Y., Courville, A., Vincent, P.: Representation learning: a review and new perspectives. IEEE Trans. Pattern Anal. Mach. Intell. **35**, 1798–1828 (2013)
3. Ghojogh, B., Crowley, M., Karray, F., Ghodsi, A.: Elements of Dimensionality Reduction and Manifold Learning First. Springer, Cham. https://doi.org/10.1007/978-3-031-10602-6. ISBN: 978-3-031-10601-9
4. Jolliffe, I.T., Cadima, J.: Principal component analysis: a review and recent developments. Philos. Trans. R. Soc. A Math. Phys. Eng. Sci. **374**, 20150202 (2016)
5. Pyatykh, S., Hesser, J., Zheng, L.: Image noise level estimation by principal component analysis. IEEE Trans. Image Process. **22**, 687–699 (2012)
6. Manjón, J.V., Coupé, P., Buades, A.: MRI noise estimation and denoising using non-local PCA. Med. Image Anal. **22**, 35–47 (2015). ISSN: 1361-8415. https://www.sciencedirect.com/science/article/pii/S1361841515000171
7. Greenacre, M., et al.: Principal component analysis. Nat. Rev. Methods Primers **2**, 100 (2022)
8. Turk, M., Pentland, A.: Eigenfaces for recognition. J. Cogn. Neurosci. **3**, 71–86 (1991)
9. Tuzel, O., Porikli, F., Meer, P.: Pedestrian detection via classification on Riemannian manifolds. IEEE Trans. Pattern Anal. Mach. Intell. **30**, 1713–1727 (2008)
10. Fisher, R.A.: XV.—The correlation between relatives on the supposition of Mendelian inheritance. Trans. R. Soc. Edinb. **52**, 399–433 (1919)
11. Ghojogh, B., Crowley, M.: Linear and quadratic discriminant analysis: tutorial. arXiv preprint arXiv:1906.02590 (2019)
12. Belhumeur, P., Hespanha, J., Kriegman, D.: Eigenfaces vs. fisherfaces: recognition using class specific linear projection. IEEE Trans. Pattern Anal. Mach. Intell. **19**, 711–720 (1997)
13. Ghojogh, B., Mohammadzade, H., Mokari, M.: Fisherposes for human action recognition using kinect sensor data. IEEE Sens. J. **18**, 1612–1627 (2018)
14. Xie, C., Li, C., Zhang, B., Chen, C., Han, J.: Deep fisher discriminant learning for mobile hand gesture recognition. arXiv: 1707.03692 [cs.CV]. https://arxiv.org/abs/1707.03692 (2017)

15. Abdi, H., Williams, L.J.: Principal component analysis. Wiley Interdiscip. Rev. Comput. Stat. **2**, 433–459 (2010)
16. Castaneda-Diaz, R., Lopez-Betancur, D., Guerrero-Mendez, C., Ramírez, E.G., Gómez-Jiménez, S., Puma-Ttito, F.: Cleaning binary distortion on MNIST dataset. In: Martínez-Villaseñor, L., Ochoa-Ruiz, G., Montes Rivera, M., Barrón-Estrada, M.L., Acosta-Mesa, H.G. (eds.) MICAI 2024. lNCS, vol. 15464. Springer, Cham (2025). https://doi.org/10.1007/978-3-031-83879-8_11
17. Blachman, N.: On combining target-location ellipses. IEEE Trans. Aerosp. Electron. Syst. **25**, 284–287 (1989)
18. Erten, O., Deutsch, C.: Combination of Multivariate Gaussian Distributions through Error Ellipses, January 2020
19. Husson, F., Lê, S., Pagès, J.: Confidence ellipse for the sensory profiles obtained by principal component analysis. Food Qual. Prefer. **16**, 245–250. ISSN: 0950-3293 (2005). https://www.sciencedirect.com/science/article/pii/S0950329304000631

Real-Time Fall Detection and Urban Risk Mapping for Motorcycle Passengers with Helmet-Based Sensors and Kriging in Smart Cities

Alberto Ochoa-Zezzatti[1], Irma Yazmín Hernández-Báez[2](✉), and Roberto Contreras-Massé[1]

[1] Universidad Autómoma de Ciudad Juárez, Av. Plutarco Elías Calles #1210 Fovisste Chamizal, 32310 Ciudad Juárez, Chihuahua, México
alberto.ochoa@uacj.mx

[2] Universidad Politécnica del Estado de Morelos, Boulevard Cuauhnáhuac 566, Col Lomas del Texcal, 62550 Jiutepec, Morelos, México

Abstract. Ensuring the safety of motorcycle passengers, particularly pillion riders, remains a persistent challenge within rapidly growing smart cities, given the high vulnerability of these users in traffic accidents and the limited deployment of real-time protection technologies. This study presents a comprehensive end-to-end framework for real-time fall detection and spatial risk prediction, integrating helmet-embedded inertial measurement units (IMUs), an edge-based hybrid CNN–LSTM deep learning model optimized with Artificial Bee Colony (ABC-Scout) algorithms, and geospatial risk mapping via ordinary kriging. The system was validated using a heterogeneous dataset of 1,500 annotated urban riding and controlled fall events, reflecting diverse surface and environmental conditions in Ciudad Juárez. Results demonstrate robust classification performance (accuracy: 97.8%, F1-score: 97.3%, recall: 98.2%, precision: 96.5%), operationalized with an average inference latency below 50 m on embedded platforms. Spatial modeling revealed high-risk urban corridors, strongly correlating with historical accident hotspots. The proposed solution enables continuous, scalable and privacy-aware monitoring, supporting both instant passenger protection and strategic data-driven interventions in smart city environments.

Keywords: Smart City · Motorcycle Safety · Fall Detection · Intelligent Helmet · Edge AI · CNN-LSTM · Bee- Scout Optimization · Second Passenger · Urban Mobility · Real-Time Monitoring

1 Introduction

The explosive growth of urban mobility has driven the widespread use of motorcycles, positioning them as an essential transportation solution in smart cities [1]. However, this trend has exacerbated the vulnerability of motorcyclists, especially passengers or "pillion riders," who show significantly higher rates of injuries and fatalities compared

L. Martínez-Villaseñor et al. (Eds.): MICAI 2025 Workshops, LNAI 16264, pp. 368–378, 2026.
https://doi.org/10.1007/978-3-032-17930-2_26

to other road users. The World Health Organization indicates that, globally, more than 30% of traffic accident deaths involve motorcycles, with this percentage being even higher in urban areas of low- and middle-income countries [1, 2]. Figure 1 illustrates a representative case of a pillion rider falling during a motorcycle ride.

Fig. 1. Illustrative case of passenger falls during motorcycle ride

The problem is intensified by deficiencies in road infrastructure, lack of specific regulation, and limited adoption of intelligent protection technologies [1, 3].

Given this gap, the development of innovative solutions that integrate advanced analytics, embedded artificial intelligence, and IoT sensing for real-time incident detection and prevention is urgent [4, 5]. Continuous monitoring through wearable devices, such as smart helmets equipped with inertial measurement units (IMU), stands out for its non-invasive potential and ease of integration. However, key challenges persist: adapting AI to low-power platforms, reducing false positives, and the generating useful spatial intelligence for urban managers [3, 6].

Addressing these challenges, the objective of the present research is to design, develop, and validate an integral real-time fall detection system for motorcycle passengers, using inertial sensors embedded in smart helmets, optimized deep learning algorithms, and spatial interpolation (kriging) to map risks in the urban environment. This system is critical for public policy decision-making and the design of focused preventive strategies.

2 Related Research

Fall detection and spatial risk analysis have emerged as critical areas in the evolution of smart urban mobility, where the protection of vulnerable users (such as motorcyclists and cyclists) is a priority challenge that drives the development of advanced technologies in both sensing and computational analysis [7, 8]. In the last decade, the proliferation of wearable sensors and the evolution of deep learning algorithms have revolutionized the automatic detection of critical events, enabling more precise, adaptive, and scalable systems [7, 9]. Below, a review of recent contributions in three dimensions is presented: fall detection using hybrid CNN–LSTM architectures, smart sensing based on connected helmets, and spatial risk modeling using geostatistical methods, highlighting challenges and opportunities detected in the literature.

2.1 Hybrid CNN–LSTM Models for Fall Detection

Hybrid architectures that combine convolutional neural networks (CNNs) with long short-term memory (LSTM) units have proven highly effective in tasks involving the recognition of complex temporal patterns in inertial signals [1, 8]. These models consistently outperform traditional approaches in both simulated and real environments, achieving accuracy and sensitivity metrics above 95% in reference datasets for human falls and vehicle dynamics [8, 9]. Recent research has addressed challenges such as variability in sensor placement and the reduction of false positives in daily scenarios. The current trend is oriented towards the integration of edge-AI processing (allowing real-time inference and data privacy) and towards validation under diverse environmental and demographic conditions [7, 10].

2.2 Inertial Sensors in Smart Helmets and Edge-AI

The direct instrumentation of motorcycle helmets with six-axis IMU sensors has been identified as a superior strategy compared to other body positions, as it faithfully captures critical head movements and mitigates signal noise [10, 11, 21]. Recent studies have conceptualized and evaluated smart helmet systems that use embedded processing to detect impacts, falls, or anomalous behaviors with latency below 100 m [10]. Additionally, the incorporation of GPS modules and IoT connectivity has facilitated the implementation of georeferenced automatic alerts for emergency assistance [11, 12]. The most advanced research also explores mechanisms for helmet use compliance, integrated breathalyzers, and the possibility of federated learning for collaborative training without compromising data privacy.

2.3 Spatial Risk Analysis Using Kriging and Geostatistics

Urban-scale Road risk modeling has found in geo-statistics, and particularly in ordinary kriging and more complex variants, a robust framework for interpolating dispersed incident data and generating continuous risk maps [13, 14]. Recent works have employed deep kriging and cokriging approaches to leverage both the spatial correlation of events and additional contextual variables (local climate zones, altitude, traffic volume), improving predictive capability and more precisely identifying the most dangerous road segments [14–16]. It has been reported that, compared to traditional methods like inverse distance weighting (IDW), kriging achieves notable reductions in interpolation error and facilitates the dynamic integration of new data sources (mobile sensors, crowdsourced reports) [14].

2.4 Current Challenges and Contribution Contextualization

Despite advances, the literature continues to point out challenges in robust detection under heterogeneous urban conditions, the ethical and functional integration of multimodal data, and the adaptation of models to low-power embedded hardware [7, 8, 11]. Particularly, the detection of passenger falls (pillion riders) remains relatively unexplored, especially in its connection with dynamic risk maps useful for decision-making in urban management and public policy.

In this context, the present work contributes to the state of the art through the development and validation of a smart helmet system that integrates edge-AI processing, optimized CNN–LSTM algorithms, and the generation of urban risk maps using kriging on real data from Ciudad Juárez, offering a reproducible and scalable solution for preventive road safety monitoring in smart cities.

3 System Architecture

The proposed architecture for the motorcycle risk detection and mapping system is conceived as an integration of three fundamental layers, each aligned with current principles of urban cyber-physical systems, edge computing, and cloud-supported geospatial analysis. As illustrated in Fig. 2, this layered architecture encompasses a smart sensor node, an edge-AI processing module, and a cloud GIS platform. This modular approach ensures both scalability and adaptability to different urban scenarios and technological conditions, following trends observed in recent research on intelligent mobility and road safety.

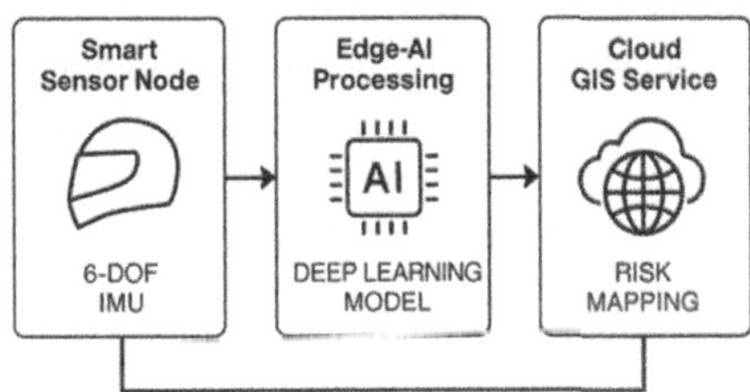

Fig. 2. Conceptual architecture of the proposed three-layer system.

The first layer, corresponding to the smart helmet sensor node, incorporates a six-degrees-of-freedom (6-DOF) inertial measurement unit (IMU), composed of a triaxial accelerometer and gyroscope, configured to sample kinematic data at 100 Hz. This frequency allows for high-resolution capture of accelerations and angular velocities along the X, Y, and Z axes, providing precise information about the user's head and torso dynamics. The segmentation of the time series into 2-second sliding windows with 50% overlap not only improves timely detection of anomalous events but also increases robustness against noise and transient artifacts, allowing for an optimal balance between sensitivity and response time.

The second layer of the proposed architecture corresponds to the embedded intelligent processing (edge-AI unit), where both the hybrid CNN–LSTM neural model and the Artificial Bee Colony Scout (ABC-Scout) optimization algorithm reside. This layer is critical as it performs real-time inference, transforming the raw inertial sensor data from the helmet into highly specialized fall risk predictions, all with latencies below 50 m. Finally, the third layer corresponds to the cloud GIS platform, responsible for the ingestion, storage, and geospatial analysis of detected events.

3.1 Hybrid CNN–LSTM Architecture

Processing begins with a convolutional neural network (CNN) module, which extracts localized spatial features from the multi-channel time-series captured by the IMU (specifically, accelerations and angular velocities along the three spatial axes) organized into two-second windows. The CNN, featuring filters of size 3 and ReLU activations in each layer, identifies high-frequency kinematic patterns such as micro-vibrations, acceleration peaks, or abrupt shifts in orientation. Mathematically, a typical convolution operation for channel x at temporal window t is defined as shown in Eq. (1):

$$f_k^{(l)}(t) = ReLU\left(\sum_{i=0}^{K-1} w_{k,i}^{(l)} \cdot x_{t+i} + b_k^{(l)}\right) \quad (1)$$

where $f_k^{(l)}(t)$ is the output of filter k in layer l, $w_{k,i}^{(l)}$ are the filter weights, K is the kernel size, $b_k^{(l)}$ is the bias, and $ReLU$ denotes rectified linear activation.

The output of the convolutional layers is rearranged as a sequence of vectors describing the temporal evolution of extracted patterns. This sequence feeds into the LSTM (Long Short-Term Memory) layers, designed to capture long-range temporal dependencies, such as the progression from regular movements to instability preceding a fall. LSTM units, via their forget, input, and output gates, maintain a relevant hidden state throughout the time window, enabling the system to recognize kinematic trajectories associated with loss-of-balance scenarios. The essential operation of an LSTM cell at time t is defined through a series of gated mechanisms, as show in Eq. (2):

$$\begin{aligned} f_t &= \sigma\left(W_f \cdot \left[h_{t-1}, x_t\right] + b_f\right) \\ i_t &= \sigma\left(W_i \cdot \left[h_{t-1}, x_t\right] + b_i\right) \\ \tilde{C}_t &= tanh\left(W_C \cdot \left[h_{t-1}, x_t\right] + b_C\right) \\ C_t &= f_t * C_{t-1} + i_t * \tilde{C}_t \\ o_t &= \sigma\left(W_o \cdot \left[h_{t-1}, x_t\right] + b_o\right) \\ h_t &= o_t * tanh(C_t) \end{aligned} \quad (2)$$

where f_t is the forget gate, i_t the input gate, o_t the output gate, $\tilde{C}_t$ the cell candidate, C_t the cell state, h_t the hidden state, $[h_{t-1}, x_t]$ the concatenated previous state and input, and σ the sigmoid function.

The final output from the LSTM is processed by a dense layer, which, through a sigmoid activation, yields a continuous fall risk score and a binary fall/no-fall decision based on calibrated thresholds.

3.2 Optimization via Artificial Bee Colony Scout (ABC-Scout) Algorithm

Precise selection of hyperparameters, such as the number of filters, LSTM units, learning rate, and regularization, is essential to maximize both the accuracy and computational efficiency of the CNN–LSTM model. The Artificial Bee Colony Scout (ABC-Scout) algorithm, a bio-inspired technique based on the collective intelligence of bee swarms, is used for this purpose.

The algorithm begins with a population of candidate solutions (bees) representing different hyperparameter sets. Through iterative cycles, employed bees refine local solutions (exploitation), observer bees select and improve promising candidates, and scout bees explore new regions of the search space (exploration). The overall optimization process is summarized in Fig. 3, illustrating the core exploration–exploitation phases of the algorithm.

```
Algorithm: Artificial Bee Colony Optimization for Hyperparameter Tuning
Input: Number of bees N, limit L, stopping criterion
Output: Best solution found (hyperparameter set)
1:  Initialize N bees with random solutions (hyperparameters)
2:  while stopping criterion not met do
3:      for each employed bee do
4:          Generate a neighboring solution
5:          Evaluate: train model and compute validation loss
6:          if new solution is better then
7:              Replace current solution
8:          end if
9:      end for
10:     Compute selection probabilities based on solution quality
11:     for each observer bee do
12:         Select a solution probabilistically
13:         Generate a neighboring solution
14:         Evaluate and replace if improved
15:     end for
16:     for each bee do
17:         if no improvement for L iterations then
18:             Convert to scout and reinitialize with random solution
19:         end if
20:     end for
21: end while
22: Return the best global solution found
```

Fig. 3. ABC Algorithm Pseudocode for Hyperparameter Optimization.

3.3 Geospatial Interpolation and Risk Surface Modeling via Ordinary Kriging

The third layer of the architecture, comprising the cloud GIS and spatial interpolation engine, transforms geotagged risk events from smart helmets into actionable urban intelligence for road safety management. Each detected event, including its GPS location and risk score, is transmitted to a central cloud database, forming a continuously updated geospatial repository for statistical analysis and city-scale risk visualization.

The core analytical method is ordinary kriging, renowned for interpolating sparse point data into continuous prediction surfaces [17, 18]. Assuming local stationarity, nearby points exhibit similar risk values due to spatial correlation, kriging begins with an experimental variogram describing how semi variance changes with distance. This variogram is fitted to an exponential theoretical model, chosen for robustness under heterogeneous urban conditions [19, 20]. The model parameters, nugget (local noise), sill (maximum variance), and range (correlation distance), quantify spatial dependence.

Using the fitted variogram, ordinary kriging estimates fall risk at unsampled locations through a weighted linear combination of observed values, Eq. (3):

$$\widehat{Z}(x_0) = \sum_{i=1}^{N} \lambda_i Z(x_i) \tag{3}$$

where λ_i the weights are calculated to ensure the estimate is unbiased and of minimum variance, considering the learned spatial structure. This technique not only produces point-wise predictions but also an associated uncertainty map, bringing statistical rigor to urban and road decision-making.

The resulting surface (a fall risk heatmap) enables the visualization of critical areas, hotspot identification, and forecasting of future risk scenarios according to the real-time urban dynamics captured. These heatmaps are dynamically updated as new data arrive and can be integrated into operational dashboards for fleet management, public dissemination, or prioritization of interventions in roadways and infrastructure.

The third layer completes the information flow with a predictive component that leverages the collective intelligence of urban data and the statistical rigor of ordinary kriging, enhancing the system's capacity to contribute to the vision of safer, adaptive, and evidence-based cities [20].

The architecture allows for feeding cloud dashboards and urban management systems, facilitating operational and strategic decision-making. This multi-level and modular integration approach aligns with emerging best practices in the design of safety systems for e-mobility and connected vehicles.

The presented three-layer architecture (smart sensor node, edge-AI processing, and cloud GIS service) responds to current demands for efficiency, privacy, modularity, and urban applicability, opening the door to future extensions for integrating additional sensors, federated algorithms, and new-generation early warning systems.

4 Results

The results section represents the core of the empirical validation for the proposed system, documenting both the quantitative findings derived from controlled experimentation and the analyses obtained through the application of artificial intelligence and geostatistical techniques to the collected dataset.

4.1 Overall Model Performance

The intelligent system, based on the hybrid CNN–LSTM architecture optimized via Artificial Bee Colony Scout (ABC-Scout), was evaluated using a diverse dataset comprising both real and simulated events under normal and fall-related riding conditions. To ensure statistical robustness and minimize bias, the data were segmented into two-second windows with 50% overlap, totaling 1,200 episodes of normal riding and 300 controlled fall events. These events were heterogeneously distributed across different road surface types and environmental conditions, including dry, wet, gravel, and irregular terrain. Figure 4 illustrates the distribution of events by road condition, clearly reflecting the predominance of normal riding episodes on dry surfaces and the relative frequency of fall events under more challenging conditions. These proportions mirror the typical variability of road surfaces encountered in the Ciudad Juárez metropolitan area. This stratified sampling approach enhances the model's generalization capacity by improving robustness to diverse terrains and environmental noise.

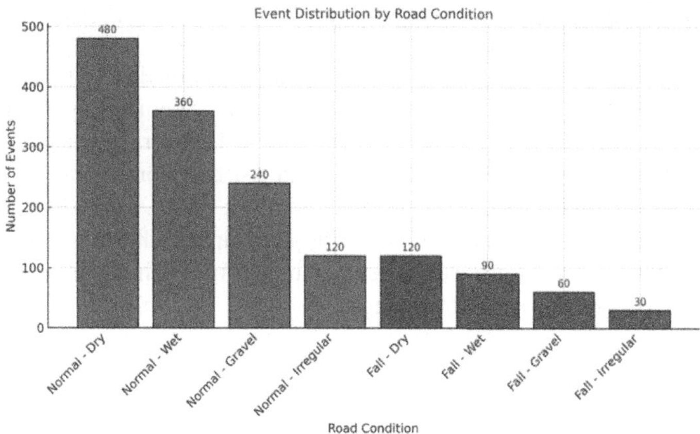

Fig. 4. Distribution of normal and fall events across different road conditions.

The results demonstrated that the proposed model achieved strong classification performance, with an accuracy of 97.8%, F1-score of 97.3%, recall of 98.2%, and precision of 96.5%, all referring to the discrimination between real fall events and routine riding maneuvers. These metrics, summarized in Table 1, outperform those reported in previous studies involving wearable-based fall detection systems in dynamic urban contexts, confirming the robustness of the proposed architecture under both controlled experiments and real-world traffic conditions. In terms of operational efficiency, the system also achieved an average inference latency of just 45 m per time window, enabling real time responsiveness on low-power embedded platforms such as the Jetson Nano and Raspberry Pi, as confirmed in the deployment tests.

Table 1. Performance metrics of the CNN–LSTM.

Metric	Value
Accuracy	97.8%
Precision	96.5%
Recall	98.2%
F1-Score	97.3%
Latency (m)	45

4.2 Analysis by Surface Condition and Scenario

The model maintained robust performance across all environments. Precision and recall remained stable for dry, wet, gravel, and irregular surfaces, confirming effective adaptation to urban noise. Slight increases in false positives (<1.5%) were observed on gravel and uneven terrain, but correct detections predominated. These results underscore the value of preprocessing, normalization and noise filtering, and the impact of hyperparameter optimization on model generalization.

4.3 Spatial Modeling and Geospatial Insights

Integrating real-time risk scores with spatial interpolation enabled the generation of urban fall-risk heatmaps. Using Ordinary Kriging on the model's continuous outputs (before thresholding), we produced a 100-meter resolution grid covering Ciudad Juárez. As shown in Fig. 5, the interpolation revealed three high-risk corridors, mainly around major intersections and degraded road segments with complex traffic. These hotspots closely matched historical accident clusters reported by municipal authorities, confirming the system's potential to support infrastructure planning, prioritize interventions, and guide preventive safety strategies in urban settings.

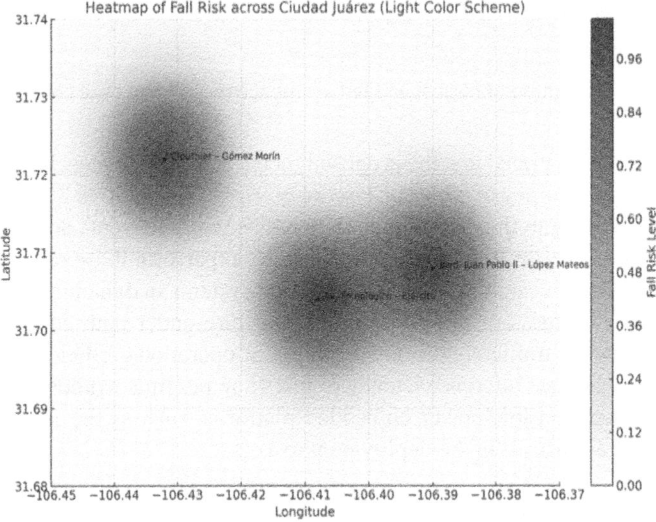

Fig. 5. Heatmap of fall risk across Ciudad Juárez, generated using a Kriging-style interpolation over a 100-meter grid.

The fitted (exponential) variogram model yielded satisfactory fit, with typical RMSE values of 0.121 and MAE of 0.088 in spatial cross-validation, confirming the system's coherence in both pinpoint identification and extended spatial prediction of risk.

5 Discussion

The results confirm the effectiveness and reliability of the proposed smart-helmet system for fall detection and risk mapping in urban mobility. The CNN–LSTM model, optimized through the ABC-Scout algorithm, achieved strong performance across all metrics, 97.8% accuracy, 97.3% F1-score, 98.2% recall, and 96.5% precision, surpassing previous wearable and smartphone-based solutions. These outcomes emphasize the benefits of integrating inertial sensing directly into the helmet for greater stability and precision.

Consistent performance was observed across varied road and environmental conditions (dry, wet, gravel, and irregular surfaces), confirming the model's generalization capacity under real-world variability.

Operationally, the system achieved an average inference latency of 45 ms on embedded devices such as the Jetson Nano and Raspberry Pi, enabling real-time, standalone safety interventions suitable for smart-city applications where rapid response is crucial.

Finally, the spatial analytics layer using ordinary kriging produced continuous urban risk heatmaps, revealing three high-risk corridors in Ciudad Juárez. These hotspots closely matched historical accident records, validating the practical relevance of the system's geospatial intelligence for targeted safety planning and infrastructure management.

6 Conclusions

This research presents a robust, scalable, and experimentally validated system for the detection of motorcycle passenger falls and the spatial prediction of associated risk in urban mobility environments. The hybrid CNN–LSTM model, optimized through the Artificial Bee Colony (ABC-Scout) technique, achieved superior performance metrics compared to previous wearable-based solutions, decisively showing the added value of direct IMU integration in smart helmets. The carefully stratified data acquisition and the deployment of the system on energy-efficient edge-computing platforms ensure its viability and flexibility for real-world urban scenarios, as evidenced by both technical and operational results.

A key contribution of this work is the integration of deep learning outputs with advanced geostatistical modeling via ordinary kriging, enabling the dynamic generation of high-resolution risk maps. These maps were consistent with historical accident data, thereby validating the relevance and applicability of the system for targeted policy creation and infrastructural interventions. The ability to provide real-time warnings and inform urban planners and emergency responders underpins a new paradigm in proactive, data-driven road safety for vulnerable users.

7 Future Work

Future work could extend this framework through multimodal data fusion (e.g., integrating air quality or road condition data), temporal-spatial forecasting to predict accident likelihood hours in advance, and city-to-city model transfer via federated learning. Additionally, integrating human-centric evaluation will be necessary to enhance user acceptance and system impact. Altogether, this system represents a significant step toward the vision of safer, smarter, and more resilient transportation infrastructure.

References

1. WRI: Motorcycle safety and urban road infrastructure (2025)
2. Kaye, S.A., et al.: Exploring beliefs and perceptions towards advanced rider assistance systems (2024)

3. Ravindran, S.: Next generation road safety solutions: IoT-driven accident detection and management (2025)
4. Pearkao, C., et al.: Development of an AI-integrated smart helmet for enhanced road safety (2025)
5. Elabd, R.H., et al.: IoT smart helmet system for delivery rider safety. J. Eng. Res. Rep. **27**(6), 236–245 (2025). https://doi.org/10.9734/jerr/2025/v27i61541
6. Bayly, M.: Intelligent transportation systems and motorcycle safety (2022)
7. Jiang, et al.: A hybrid CNN-LSTM model for involuntary fall detection using wearable sensors (2025)
8. Luo, et al.: A decade of progress in wearable sensors for fall detection (2025)
9. Saini, et al.: Wearable sensor with artificial intelligence for prevention and detection of falls (2025)
10. Kumar, et al.: Smart helmet based accident detection and notification (2025)
11. Abhini, et al.: Smart helmet. IJERT (2025)
12. Kaur, et al.: Review paper of smart helmet for accident detection mechanism (2025)
13. Herzlieb, Sturm: Kriging and local climate zones – key to higher accuracy in range prediction (2023)
14. SAGE: Detecting high-risk road segments using kriging and inverse distance weighting (2023)
15. Li, et al.: Feature-free regression kriging. arXiv (2023)
16. Zhang et al.: Interpreting Deepkriging for spatial interpolation in urban computing (2023)
17. Oliver, M.A., Webster, R.: Kriging: a method of spatial Interpolation. JRSS C **39**(2), 289–297 (1990)
18. Navarro-Molina, J., et al.: Urban geospatial modeling: kriging-based analysis of heterogeneous city data. Remote Sens. (2022)
19. Kilibarda, M., et al.: Exponential variograms in urban environments. GeoInformatica (2015)
20. Lv, Z., et al.: Pedestrian safety and spatial risk mapping using kriging. SpringerLink (2023)
21. Lee, P., et al.: Trends in smart helmets with multimodal sensing for health and safety: scoping review. JMIR Mhealth Uhealth **10**(11), e40797 (2022). https://doi.org/10.2196/40797

Development of a Visual Framework for Type-I Mamdani Systems Based on UPAFuzzySystems

David Alonso Carranza Escobar[1], Martín Montes Rivera[1](✉), José Eder Guzmán Mendoza[1], Alberto Ochoa Zezzatti[2], and Julio César Ponce Gallegos[3]

[1] Research and Postgraduate Studies Department, Universidad Politécnica de Aguascalientes, Aguascalientes, Ags, México
mc230011@alumnos.upa.edu.mx, {martin.montes, jose.guzman}@upa.edu.mx

[2] Universidad Autónoma de Ciudad Juárez, Ciudad Juárez, México
alberto.ochoa@uacj.mx

[3] Universidad Autónoma de Aguascalientes, Aguascalientes, México

Abstract. The lack of visual interfaces for developing fuzzy logic in Python is a common problem, as it limited efficient access to the simulation and creation of these systems. This work presents the development of a graphical framework based on the UPAFuzzySystems library in version 0.2.4, oriented towards the design, simulation, and analysis of type 1 fuzzy inference systems. This implementation is carried out using the Tkinter library, and the framework offers complete access to functionalities such as the definition of universes, membership functions, rule generation, and analysis of fuzzy inference systems. This implementation is carried out using the Tkinter library. The framework offers full access to functions such as the definition of universes, membership functions, generation of "If-Then" rules, defuzzification, among other functions. Through the use of libraries such as NumPy and Matplotlib, the system allows fuzzy sets to be represented graphically, as well as output surfaces to be visualized in two and three dimensions. To evaluate the effectiveness of the system, a comparison is made of the time required to create a system from zero, both using the framework and through traditional programming. The evaluation was complemented by the application of the SUS (System Usability Scale) scale, applied to technical users, undergraduate students, people with little programming experience, and some users with previous experience using the UPAFuzzySystems library in its pragmatic form. Obtaining an average score of 70.18, which indicates acceptable usability. Compared to traditional console use, the framework enabled modeling tasks to be completed 50% to 75% faster, confirming the effectiveness of a well-designed interface in technical environments. This work constitutes a versatile tool for teaching, experimenting, and implementing fuzzy systems. We propose extending the framework from models to other approaches such as FLSSMITH Takagi-Sugeno, and even to type 2 fuzzy inference systems, with the aim of broadening its functional reach.

Keywords: Fuzzy logic · Usability · UPAFuzzySystems · Tkinter · Python

L. Martínez-Villaseñor et al. (Eds.): MICAI 2025 Workshops, LNAI 16264, pp. 379–391, 2026.
https://doi.org/10.1007/978-3-032-17930-2_27

1 Introduction

In different areas of software development, it's common to find an initial interaction pattern based on the console. Although functional, this type of interaction is a significant barrier for many users, especially those who need a visual understanding or do not have advanced programming experience for the development and implementation of these systems. This problem has given rise to the creation of visual frameworks that connect users and the internal logic of a system through more intuitive environments that facilitate the understanding, design, and manipulation of complex systems.

The design of graphical interfaces allows objects and operations within a system to be represented visually, translating them into actions that are understandable to the user, reducing the complexity of a system, and projecting the actions and possibilities that a system can offer in order to generate a more fluid and interactive experience [1]. In this context, the design of graphical frameworks not only adds aesthetic value but also converts a technical library oriented towards fuzzy logic analysis into a highly valuable educational and interactive resource that can be used more effectively.

Fuzzy logic, introduced by Lotfi A. Zadeh in 1970, was developed as an alternative to classical binary logic, allowing for the processing of imprecise or ambiguous information. Fuzzy logic uses degrees of membership on a continuous scale between 0 and 1, allowing for a more accurate representation of situations in the real world where categories are variable [2].

Advances in fuzzy logic got us to develop Fuzzy Inference Systems (FIS), and one of the most popular models was the one Ebrahim Mamdani came up with in 1975. This system has a cool structured mechanism based on rules like (If-Then), which makes it possible to use expert knowledge when making tough decisions [3–5].

The Python programming language is used for the application context, which has gained exponentially in popularity for its clear syntax, flexibility, and open-access libraries. According to the TIOBE index, Python remains among the most widely used languages in the world, both in academia and in the professional environment [6, 7].

In this context, the UPAFuzzySystems library, developed in Python by Universidad Politécnica de Aguascalientes, is a tool for designing, simulating, and controlling fuzzy systems, and is characterized by its flexibility, accessibility, and practical approach. It allows for the definition of universes, the creation of membership functions, the formulation of rules, the simulation of fuzzy systems, and the visualization of results [3, 8]. The UPAFuzzySystems library works in conjunction with tools such as NumPy and Matplotlib. NumPy makes it easy to perform mathematical processing on multidimensional arrays [9], while Matplotlib allows you to generate graphs to visually represent the sets and results of a fuzzy system [10, 11]. This integration makes UPAFuzzySystems a powerful option for modeling and optimizing fuzzy systems.

To implement an effective framework that complements the capabilities of UPAFuzzySystems, the Tkinter library is used, which is part of the standard Python installation. This facilitates its implementation and portability and is also a library recognized for its stability because it integrates naturally with the language. This makes it the ideal choice for developing graphical interfaces. It is important to note that the library has a visual limitation because it was developed in Unix, but this does not affect its main functionality [12, 13].

This approach gives rise to the concept of usability, which is defined as the ability of the system to be used effectively, efficiently, and satisfactorily by its users [1] In the case of interfaces applied to fuzzy logic-based systems, a high level of usability not only improves the user experience but also facilitates the understanding and manipulation of complex models. Therefore, considering usability from the design phase allows for a reduction in operational errors, a shorter learning curve, and increased productivity, making the framework a functional tool [1, 14].

2 Contributions

This work seeks to contribute to students and researchers interested in fuzzy logic by providing an interactive environment that facilitates the understanding, implementation, and optimization of type 1 fuzzy systems. Through the development of a visual framework based on Python and the UPAFuzzySystems library, the goal is to reduce the technical complexity of designing fuzzy inference systems, allowing users to manipulate universes, sets, and rules in an intuitive way. This tool has the goal of promoting practical learning, improving accessibility to fuzzy logic modeling, and strengthening analysis and decision-making capabilities in situations with uncertainty.

3 Theoretical framework

3.1 Fuzzy Logic

Fuzzy logic, developed by Lotfi A. Zadeh in 1965, is an extension of classical logic designed to manage the uncertainty and vagueness present in human reasoning. Fuzzy logic differs from traditional binary logic in that it does not restrict propositions to being only true or false. Instead, it allows the use of degrees of membership in the interval [0, 1], which makes it a powerful tool for representing and manipulating imprecise knowledge [2, 15].

These degrees of membership are represented through structures called fuzzy sets. In this context, the membership function μ(x) is defined as a mapping that assigns each element x of the universe of discourse X a value μ within the mentioned interval, assignment a degree that represents the element's membership in the fuzzy set [3].

Membership functions can take various forms, such as triangle, trapezoid, Gaussian, or bell-shaped, each adapted to different contexts or knowledge models.

Triangle with 3 vertices a, b, c. It is defined as Eq. 1 [3].

$$\text{triangle}(x; a, b, c) = \begin{cases} 0, & x \leq a. \\ \frac{x-a}{b-a}, & a \leq x \leq b. \\ \frac{c-x}{c-b}, & b \leq x \leq c. \\ 0, & c \leq x. \end{cases} \tag{1}$$

Trapezoid with 4 vertices a, b, c, d. And it is defined as Eq. 2 [3].

$$\text{trapezoid}(x; a, b, c, d) = \begin{cases} 0, & x \leq a, \\ \frac{x-a}{b-a}, & a < x < b, \\ 1, & b \leq x \leq c, \\ \frac{d-x}{d-c}, & c < x < d, \\ 0, & d \leq x. \end{cases} \quad (2)$$

The Gaussian membership function is defined in terms of the parameters c, σ, and its mathematical formulation is expressed by Eq. 3.

$$\text{gaussian}(x; c, \sigma) = e^{-\frac{1}{2}\left(\frac{x-c}{\sigma}\right)^2} \quad (3)$$

For the bell-type function, it uses parameters a, b, and c. It is described by Eq. 4 [3].

$$\text{bell}(x; a, b, c) = \frac{1}{1+\left|\frac{x-c}{a}\right|^{2b}} \quad (4)$$

Once the membership functions for each universe have been defined, it is necessary to establish the conclusions of the system using "If–Then" rules, in which the premises are expressed through fuzzy sets. These rules form the basis of the system's knowledge, as they allow human experience or expert knowledge to be translated into computational operations [2, 3].

In this context, a Fuzzy Inference System (FIS) is structured in five fundamental stages [3, 16, 17]:

1. Preprocessing: consists of preparing and normalizing the input variables to ensure data consistency.
2. Fusing: transforms the numerical input values into degrees of membership in fuzzy sets.
3. Rule base: a set of "If-Then" propositions that relate input conditions to output actions.
4. Inference engine: evaluates the activated rules based on the current input values and determines the corresponding fuzzy responses.
5. Defuzzification: converts the fuzzy results into a crisp (precise) output appropriate to the specific problem.

In the rule base, logical connectors must be used to combine conditions. The most frequent operations are intersection (AND) and union (OR), which are based on classical theory but adapted to fuzzy logic. Equation 5 and 6 represent the connectors for linear systems, while Eq. 7 and 8 represent those for non-linear systems [2, 31].

$$A \wedge B \equiv \mu_A(x) \times \mu_B(x) \quad (5)$$

$$A \vee B \equiv \mu_A(X) + \mu_B(X) - \mu_A(X) \times \mu_B(X) \quad (6)$$

$$A \wedge B \equiv \min(\mu_A(x), \mu_B(x)) \quad (7)$$

$$A \vee B \equiv \max(\mu_A(x), \mu_B(x)) \tag{8}$$

Once the premises have been combined using connectors, an implication is applied, which links the input with the fuzzy output. There are multiple ways to perform this operation, the most common being the min implication in Mamdani systems shown in Eq. 9, and the generation of linear functions in Takagi-Sugeno models represented by Eq. 10 [3, 18].

$$\{\langle (x,y), \mu_{A' \Rightarrow B}(x,y) \rangle \mid x \in \mathcal{X}, y \in \mathcal{Y},\ \mu_{A' \Rightarrow B}(x,y) = \min\left(\mu_A(x), \mu_B(y)\right)\} \tag{9}$$

$$\text{If } f(e_1 \text{ is } \mathcal{A}_1, e_2 \text{ is } \mathcal{A}_2, \ldots, e_k \text{ is } \mathcal{A}_k) \text{ then } y = g(e_1, e_2, \ldots, e_k) \tag{10}$$

After the inference process, the system obtains an output in the form of a fuzzy set. In order for this output to be interpretable by physical systems or by the user, it is necessary to apply defuzzification, which translates the fuzzy set into a single representative numerical value [3]. There are several methods of defuzzification:

Centroid of Gravity (COG) Eq. 11 for continuous systems.

$$u_{\text{COG}} \frac{\int_a^b zC(z)\,dz}{\int_a^b C(z)\,dz} \tag{11}$$

Center of Gravity for Singletons (COGS) in Eq. 12 and applied in discrete systems in Eq. 13

$$u_{\text{COGS}} = \frac{\sum_k \alpha_k^* S_k}{\sum_k \alpha_k^*} \tag{12}$$

$$u_{\text{COG}} = \frac{\sum_i \mu_c(x_i) x_i}{\sum_i \mu_c(x_i)} \tag{13}$$

Area bisector (BOA), which finds the point that divides the area under the curve into two equal parts in Eq. 14.

$$BOA = \left| \sum_{i=1}^{j} \mu_c(x_i) - \sum_{i=j+1}^{i_{\max}} \mu_c(x_i) \right|, \quad 1 < j < i_{\max} \tag{14}$$

Mean of the maximum values Eq. 15.

$$u_{\text{MOM}} = \frac{\sum_{i \in \mathcal{I}} x_i}{|\mathcal{I}|}, \quad \mathcal{I} = \{i \mid \mu_c(x_i) = \mu_{\max}\} \tag{15}$$

Least of maximum values Eq. 16.

$$LM = x\min(I) \tag{16}$$

Max of maximum values Eq. 17.

$$RM = x_{\max}(I) \tag{17}$$

These defuzzification methods allow the system output to be better adjusted to the specific needs of each application. The Center of Gravity (COG) generates an average value based on membership degrees. The COGS variant is used in systems that use singleton outputs, either in continuous or discrete environments.

The Area Bisector (BOA) method finds the exact point that divides the area under the membership curve into two equal parts. Finally, the MOM (Mean of the Maximums), LM (Minimum of the Maximums), and RM (Maximum of the Maximums) methods focus on identifying the values with the highest membership in the fuzzy set, selecting either the average, the lowest value, or the highest value. These are useful in contexts where a more conservative, intermediate, or aggressive output is required [3, 18]. This is worth noting because all fuzzy logic controllers, no matter how hard they are, are built using these same methods. The only differences are the settings and parameters that the user assigns depending on the specific application.

Therefore, fuzzy logic becomes an effective alternative for representing human reasoning in contexts where information is imprecise. When integrated with modern tools, it allows for the construction of more flexible systems, capable of making decisions in a manner closer to how a person would.

3.2 UPAFuzzySystems

The UPAFuzzySystems library is a computational tool developed in Python by the Universidad Politécnica de Aguascalientes with the goal of providing an accessible, flexible, and efficient platform for implementing intelligent models that manage uncertainty in real environments. This library is geared toward the design, simulation, and control of fuzzy inference systems. Its open-source code makes it an ideal option for academic, scientific, and development communities seeking to experiment with and apply fuzzy logic without relying on restrictive environments or additional costs [3].

This library allows users to build fuzzy systems, facilitating the definition of input and output universes, whether discrete or continuous, the creation of membership functions, the formulation of (If-Then) rules, and the configuration of logical connectors and fuzzy implications. In addition, it is compatible with widely used inference models such as Mamdani and Takagi-Sugeno, which broadens its applicability in various specialized areas, allowing more specific problems to be addressed and providing the user with a robust tool for the design and analysis of the systems they propose [3, 8].

UPAFuzzySystems presents a series of advantages that set it apart as a robust option for developing fuzzy logic-based systems in Python:

- Open source: Its license allows full access to the source code, promoting collaboration, customization, and constant evolution of the tool by the community.
- Extensive documentation: It provides guides, practical examples, and academic references that facilitate learning and integration into real or educational projects available on GitHub [8].
- Compatibility with fuzzy controllers: It offers support for different control approaches, including Mamdani models (based on linguistic rules) and TakagiSugeno models (based on linear functions).

- Advanced methods: It incorporates algorithms for fuzzification, inference, and defuzzification, as well as modules for graphically representing universes, sets, and simulation results.

UPAFuzzySystems represents a powerful solution for users who want to build, visualize, and optimize fuzzy systems from a practical and visual approach.

3.3 Usability

In software design, one element that must be taken into account is usability, which is defined as the degree or level to which a system can effectively achieve specific objectives. This refers to users getting what they want from the system, efficiently and without excessive effort, and with satisfaction, meaning that users feel comfortable and confident during interaction [1, 19].

A usable framework must comply with the following principles to ensure its quality:

1. Ease of learning: The system must be intuitive from the first contact, allowing any user, even without previous experience, to quickly understand how to perform tasks.
2. Efficiency: Once the user has understood the logic and distribution of the system, they must be able to complete specific tasks quickly, optimizing usage time.
3. Memorable: This point refers to the ease in which the system can be used again even after a long period of inactivity, so that the user remembers how to generate or build a system after a period of not using it.
4. Error management: The system should minimize the possibility of errors and, if they do happen, offer clear and accessible ways to fix them without major consequences. This includes understandable feedback messages.
5. Visual satisfaction: This refers to how pleasant the window the user is viewing is, such as not using colors that are visually distracting, so that the user feels comfortable, motivated, and confident throughout the interaction.

Usability Evaluation

There are multiple methods for evaluating usability, ranged from qualitative techniques such as interviews and user observation to standardized instruments. For this specific context, the System Usability Scale (SUS) is used, which is a tool created by John Brooke in 1996, consisting of 10 statements that evaluate the user's perception of aspects such as ease of use, complexity, integration of functionalities, and confidence when using the system [20, 21]. These items are classified on a Likert scale ranging from strongly disagree to strongly agree, followed by the calculation of scores using a specific Equation denoted by Eq. 18.

$$SUS = [(X - 5) + (25 - Y)] \times 2.5 \tag{18}$$

Where:

X = sum of the answers to the odd-numbered questions (1, 3, 5, 7, 9)
Y = sum of the answers to the even-numbered questions (2, 4, 6, 8, 10)

The final result does not refer to a percentage but rather a usability score for the framework. A score higher than 68 is considered acceptable, while values above 85 indicate an outstanding user experience. The SUS not only allows you to validate the current level of usability, but also serves as a benchmark for new versions of the system [20].

4 Methodology

The development of the visual framework based on the UPAFuzzySystems library was carried out using functional prototypes, practical tests, usability evaluation through structured questionnaires, quantitative analysis, and the generation of progressive improvements in each prototype until its final construction. The process ensured that the system not only met the functional requirements of fuzzy modeling, but also offered an accessible, intuitive, and efficient user experience.

First Phase

First Phase This consisted of developing an initial prototype for technical validation purposes. The aim was to test the viability of integrating Tkinter with the functions offered by the UPAFuzzySystems library.

With this goal a graphical environment was designed, without visual customization, which only allowed the user to define fuzzy universes, insert membership functions, and graphically display these structures. To this end, a very basic graphical environment was designed, without visual customization, which only allowed the user to define fuzzy universes, insert membership functions, and graphically visualize these structures. This stage was essential to verify the complementarity of both libraries, ensuring that they could be correctly integrated into a visual environment. The image shows the frame generated as the first prototype for verifying the functions (Fig. 1).

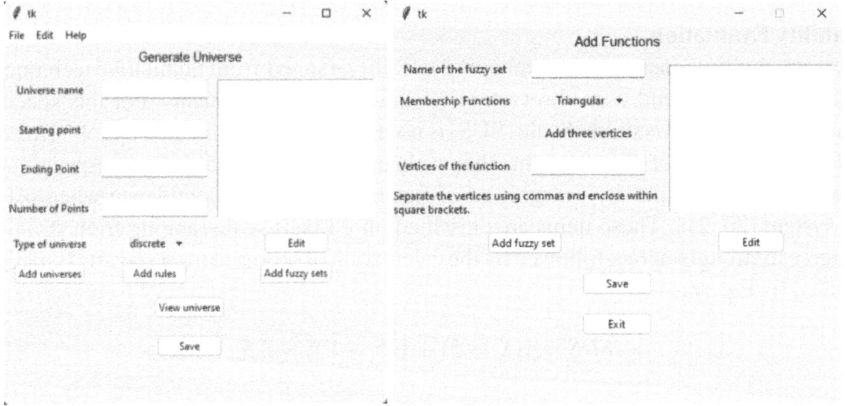

Fig. 1. Main frame of the first test

Second Phase

Based on this technical foundation, a second, more complete prototype geared toward the end user was built. At this stage, elements that enhanced the interaction experience were integrated, such as the use of a neutral and user-friendly color palette, the organization of modules into visually differentiated sections, and the implementation of popup windows that facilitated specific tasks such as rule construction. The ability to generate surface graphs to represent inference results was also added, as well as functionality for saving and loading the systems created, with the goal of allowing them to be reuse. However, during functional testing of this version, an important limitation was detected: although the system allowed rules to be constructed and visualized in real time, when the application was closed and the system reloaded, these rules were not preserved in their logical structure, preventing their subsequent use in simulations. This deficiency was documented as a critical error and became a priority for correction in future versions. Figure 3 and Fig. 4 shows the second prototype with its respective frames for the construction of the rules (Fig. 2).

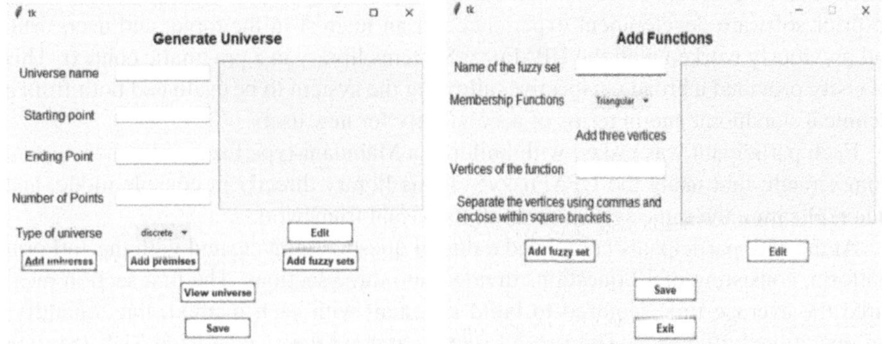

Fig. 2. Second prototype of the frame

Third Phase

The final version of the framework was created by combining all the improvements from the earlier versions and adding new features based on what users suggested during testing. The interface design was completely restructured to include a main menu from which the user could select the type of fuzzy system to work with. The current version includes the complete implementation of Mamdani systems (type 1 fuzzy logic), but leaves the architecture open for the integration of more complete models in the future. The problem related to saving rules was also resolved by implementing a robust persistence system that allows all system components to be stored in files. UPAfs, ensuring data integrity when closing and reloading the project. Below are the windows provided to the user for building systems.

Usability Evaluation

To verify usability, a practical study was conducted with 35 participants. The sample

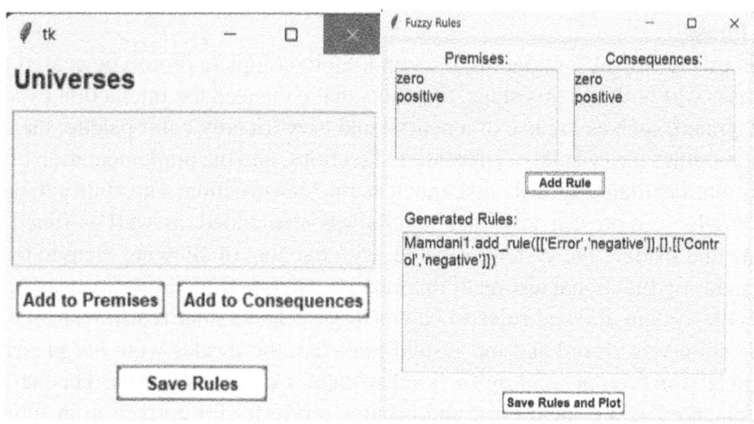

Fig. 3. Second prototype: construction of premises and consequences for rule generation

included undergraduate students with basic programming knowledge, individuals with no prior software development experience but an interest in the topic, and users who had previously worked with the UPAFuzzySystems library in a pragmatic context. This diversity provided a broad perspective, allowing the system to be evaluated both from a technical standpoint and in terms of accessibility for new users.

Each participant was tasked with building a Mamdani-type fuzzy inference system from scratch: first using the UPAFuzzySystems library directly in console mode, and then replicating the same system through the visual framework.

At the end, participants completed a digital questionnaire created with the JotForm platform, consisting of 12 questions divided into three sections. The first section measured the average time required to build a system with each method, thus quantifying operational efficiency. The second section applied the standardized SUS (System Usability Scale), which includes 10 items designed to evaluate usability. Finally, the third section contained an open-ended question with five options, using a 1-to-5 scale to determine each participant's self-assessed prior programming knowledge (Fig. 5).

Fig. 4. Improvements in visual aspects of the system and its operation

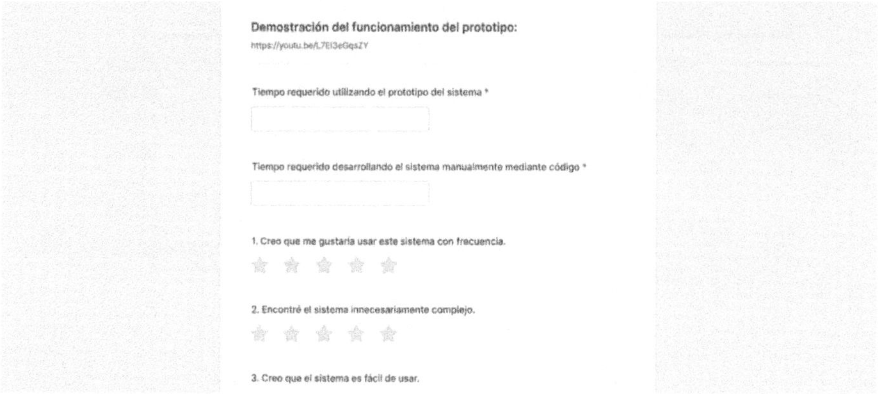

Fig. 5. Sus evaluation form for usability.

5 Results and Conclusions

The results were highly positive. The framework achieved an average SUS score of 70.18, indicating an excellent level of usability. Users highlighted the clarity of instructions, system organization, real-time visualization, and the reduction of syntax-related errors.

The framework successfully transformed a console-based tool into an intuitive graphical environment, reducing the learning curve and supporting both students and researchers. Tests showed high acceptance, reduced execution times, and minimal errors, reinforcing that a well-designed visual interface can democratize the use of complex fuzzy logic tools.

Educationally, it stands as a valuable resource for teaching fuzzy logic concepts, while in research, it accelerates model design and validation, enabling rapid prototyping without requiring advanced programming skills.

Future Works

Future developments aim to extend the framework to support additional inference types such as Takagi–Sugeno and Type-2 fuzzy logic, enhancing its applicability.

References

1. Nielsen, J.: Usability 101: Introduction to Usability. http://www.nngroup.com/articles/usability-101-introduction-to-usability. Accessed 19 July 2024
2. Zadeh, L.A.: Fuzzy S e t s * (1965)
3. Montes Rivera, M., Olvera-Gonzalez, E., Escalante-Garcia, N.: UPAFuzzySystems: a python library for control and simulation with fuzzy inference systems. Machines **11** (2023). https://doi.org/10.3390/machines11050572
4. Institute of Electrical and Electronics Engineers: 2012 IEEE International Conference on Fuzzy Systems: [proceedings]. IEEE (2012)
5. Ojha, V., Abraham, A., Snášel, V.: Heuristic design of fuzzy inference systems: a review of three decades of research. Eng. Appl. Artif. Intell. **85**, 845–864 (2019). https://doi.org/10.1016/j.engappai.2019.08.010

6. Python documentation: The Python Tutorial. https://docs.python.org/3/tutorial/index.html. Accessed 02 June 2024
7. TIOBE: TIOBE Index – TIOBE. https://www.tiobe.com/tiobe-index/. Accessed 04 Feb 2024
8. Rivera Martin Montes: UPAFuzzySystems github. https://github.com/UniversidadPolitecnicaAguascalientes/UPAFuzzySystems/tree/main/UPAFuzzySystems. Accessed 19 July 2024
9. Sheela, A., Meena, Kp.: Combination of NumPy, SciPy and Matplotlib/Pylaba good alternative methodology to MATLAB-a comparative analysis
10. Sial, A.H.: Comparative analysis of data visualization libraries Matplotlib and Seaborn in Python. Int. J. Adv. Trends Comput. Sci. Eng. **10**, 277–281 (2021). https://doi.org/10.30534/ijatcse/2021/391012021
11. Oberoi, A., Chauhan, R.: Visualizing data using Matplotlib and Seaborn libraries in Python for data science. Int. J. Sci. Res. Publ. (IJSRP) **9**, 8733 (2019). https://doi.org/10.29322/ijsrp.9.03.2019.p8733
12. Moore, A.D.: Python GUI programming with Tkinter develop responsive and powerful GUI applications with Tkinter
13. Love, D.: Tkinter GUI Programming by Example: Learn to Create Modern
14. GUIs using Tkinter by building real-world projects in Python. Packt Publishing (2018)
15. USABILIDAD
16. Castillo, O., Amador-Angulo, L., Castro, J.R., Garcia-Valdez, M.: A comparative study of type-1 fuzzy logic systems, interval type-2 fuzzy logic systems and generalized type-2 fuzzy logic systems in control problems. Inf. Sci. **354**, 257–274 (2016). https://doi.org/10.1016/j.ins.2016.03.026
17. Vassilyev, S.N., et al.: Intelligent control systems and fuzzy controllers. II. Trained fuzzy controllers, fuzzy PID controllers. Autom. Remote Control **81**, 922–934 (2020). https://doi.org/10.1134/S0005117920050112
18. Cheng, S., Dong, R., Pedrycz, W.: A framework of fuzzy hybrid systems for modelling and control. Int. J. Gen. Syst. **39**, 165–176 (2010). https://doi.org/10.1080/03081070903427358
19. Montes Rivera, M., Ochoa Zezzatti, A., Mejía Ramírez, C.A.: Automatic generation of programs for data tables with batch least square Mamdani inference systems: application in the AWG table. Res. Comput. Sci. **148**, 39–49 (2019). https://doi.org/10.13053/rcs-148-6-3
20. Lilliam, D., Cancio, P., Mercedes, I., Bergues, M.: Usabilidad de los sitios Web, los métodos y las técnicas para la evaluación Usability of Web sites, methods and evaluation techniques (2013)
21. Brooke, J.: SUS: a quick and dirty usability scale
22. Aljedaibi, W., Mohammed Bashmail, R.: Usability evaluation of mobile devices user interface. Nexo Revista Científica **34**, 1290–1300 (2021). https://doi.org/10.5377/nexo.v34i04.12665

Artificial Empathy in Conversational Agents: Examining User Perceptions, Emotional Responses, and Organizational Reputation in Customer Support Scenarios

Wendy Alejandra Molinares-Miranda[1], Miguel Angel Ortiz-Esparza[2(✉)], and Hector Cardona-Reyes[2]

[1] Universidad Internacional de Innovación, Aguascalientes, Mexico
research@wendymolinares.com

[2] Centro de Investigación en Matemáticas CIMAT, Guanajuato, Mexico
{miguel.ortiz,hector.cardona}@cimat.mx

Abstract. Conversational agents powered by artificial intelligence are transforming customer support. Many include artificial empathy (phrasing that validates user emotions) under the assumption that it improves satisfaction and organizational reputation, yet its effect during service failures remains unclear.

This study compared an empathic and a neutral conversational agent in a standardized support scenario. In total, 84 participants completed a pre-test, 41 interacted with the agents, and 9 completed a post-test. Emotional state was measured with the Positive and Negative Affect Schedule (PANAS), perceptions with a Likert-scale battery, and AI literacy with the Meta AI Literacy Scale (MAILS). All 41 chatlogs were analyzed for behavioral markers of frustration, escalation, and resolution.

The empathic agent resolved more cases (62%) and offered more compensations, but participants rated the neutral agent higher in satisfaction and organizational reputation. Higher AI literacy correlated with lower frustration, while general AI use showed no effect. Despite the small post-test sample, findings reveal a paradox: empathy improved procedural outcomes but not perceived credibility.

These results suggest that in chat-based support, users may value efficiency and authenticity over empathic wording. The study provides exploratory evidence that artificial empathy, while operationally useful, can challenge perceived professionalism, emphasizing the need for further research across diverse contexts and populations.

Keywords: Artificial Empathy · Conversational Agents · Customer Support · User Perception · Organizational Reputation

L. Martínez-Villaseñor et al. (Eds.): MICAI 2025 Workshops, LNAI 16264, pp. 392–407, 2026.
https://doi.org/10.1007/978-3-032-17930-2_28

1 Introduction

The growing adoption of conversational agents powered by artificial intelligence has transformed customer support processes across industries. Companies increasingly automate service interactions through agents that respond to messages, comments, or complaints across digital channels, with the promise of improving efficiency without neglecting customer experience. Developers often attempt not only to "program" empathy, but to humanize these systems by simulating typing pauses, inserting minor spelling errors, or dividing responses into shorter blocks to generate a more credible emotional connection. However, it remains unclear whether such simulations are genuinely perceived as empathy, and what impact they have on customer emotions, perceptions of effectiveness, or organizational reputation [1]. As Juquelier, Poncin, and Hazée (2025) argue, empathic conversational agents can strengthen relational experiences, yet they may also backfire when customers perceive the responses as mechanical or insincere.

In this study, the conversational agent was designed to rely strictly on linguistic empathy (expressions that validate frustration and offer supportive wording) without cues intended to mimic human behavior [2]. This design choice isolates whether language alone can influence customer perceptions and emotional outcomes and aligned with global regulations.

This focus emerges in a service ecosystem where human limitations are evident: support agents require rest, attend to multiple tasks simultaneously, and often lack access to critical information such as payment details, guarantees, or internal processes. These constraints generate delays that fuel customer frustration and also place pressure on human staff. Automation through AI has become an effective solution, but it raises a central dilemma: is it possible to provide emotional containment without direct human intervention Brun et al. [2] suggest that emotion-sensitive conversational AI can support more adaptive interactions, but effectiveness depends on how customers interpret the authenticity of the response.

In practice, some agents are designed with these "more organic" adjustments, yet they do not guarantee that users will interpret them as empathy. In this study, empathy is defined narrowly as linguistic validation, separated from anthropomorphic simulation. One proposition, and motivation for this research, is that what matters most to customers is the feeling of being heard, regardless of whether the solution comes from a human or a machine [3]. Shen et al. found that identical supportive narratives were rated as less empathic when participants were told they originated from AI rather than humans, underscoring the salience of authenticity perception.

To address this question, the research adopts a between-subjects design in which participants are randomly assigned to interact with one version of a conversational agent in a standardized customer support scenario. Emotional state is assessed using the Positive and Negative Affect Schedule [4], which measures both positive affect (e.g., enthusiasm, alertness) and negative affect (e.g., distress, hostility). The level of AI literacy is measured through the Meta AI Literacy Scale [5], with the short version by Koch, Carolus, Wienrich, and Latoschik used for practicality in survey contexts. In addition, prior AI usage is recorded through self-report items to capture baseline exposure. Complementary Likert-scale items evaluate perceived frustration, sense of accompaniment, process effectiveness, satisfaction, and organizational reputation following the interaction.

In a design space where many choices are still based on intuition rather than evidence, this study contributes empirical data on the actual scope of artificial empathy and its potential role in building automated customer support experiences that are more human-centered, transparent, and effective.

2 Conceptual Framework

In psychology, Empathy is understood as the ability to recognize and share another person's emotional states, enabling responses of understanding and support. Davis [6], through the development of the Interpersonal Reactivity Index (IRI), demonstrated that empathy is a multidimensional construct that includes both cognitive components (such as perspective-taking) and affective components (such as empathic concern). This view has been widely accepted in subsequent literature, where empathy is recognized as playing a decisive role in the quality of social and professional interactions. In the context of customer service, this capacity has been associated with reducing frustration and increasing customer satisfaction, both of which are central to understanding how the simulation of empathy by a conversational agent can influence the customer experience.

The concept of Artificial Empathy refers to the programming of conversational agents to deliver linguistic responses that simulate emotional containment and closeness with the customer. Juquelier, Poncin, and Hazée [1] note that such expressions can increase the sense of social presence and improve satisfaction in the interaction, although they also caution that under conditions of time pressure, the same empathy may become counterproductive. Complementarily, Seitz [7] emphasizes that while these programmed responses enhance perceived warmth, they also raise doubts about authenticity when identified as "scripted." These findings suggest that artificial empathy should not be understood merely as a technical resource but as a phenomenon that directly shapes customer perception and, consequently, the evaluation of automated customer experiences. In this study, the analysis of artificial empathy is central to examining whether its implementation in contexts of digital frustration succeeds in containing the customer or, conversely, amplifies distrust toward the company.

Conversational Agents are software systems designed to interact with customers through text- or voice-based interfaces using natural language. Their development has evolved from rule-based and keyword-driven models to architectures powered by Artificial Intelligence that are capable of interpreting intentions and generating contextual responses. Brun et al. [2] highlight that integrating emotional sensitivity into these models seeks not only to provide information, but also to adapt tone and communicative style according to the customer's perceived emotional state. In the business domain, the adoption of such agents addresses the need to optimize resources, ensure immediate response times, and simultaneously preserve the customer experience. From this perspective, conversational agents represent not merely a technological innovation but also a strategic resource that, when incorporating artificial empathy, can become a key differentiator in the perceived quality of automated support.

Within the study of human–machine interaction, Perceived Authenticity refers to the extent to which customers consider the responses they receive as genuine. Shen et al. [3] demonstrated that even when the content of a message is identical, empathy attributed to a human sender evokes a stronger emotional response than the same narrative attributed to an artificial intelligence model. Furthermore, the study showed that transparency about the origin of the message, specifically, when participants were explicitly informed that the text had been generated by AI, further reduced reported levels of empathy. These findings confirm that perceived authenticity is a critical element in the evaluation of automated customer experiences and present a central challenge for the design of conversational agents: conveying emotional closeness without triggering perceptions of artificiality. In this study, the concept is essential for analyzing how simulated empathy influences customers' emotional containment and the organizational reputation of companies that implement conversational agents.

When we talk about Preference for Human Empathy, evidence from user behavior indicates that many individuals value the sense of being heard by another person more than the immediacy of an automated response. Raval [8], writing in the Financial Times, observed that people are often willing to wait longer if it means speaking with a human, even when artificial intelligence could deliver an answer instantly. This underscores the idea that efficiency alone does not guarantee a positive interaction, since emotional recognition remains central and human empathy continues to serve as the standard by which interactions with conversational agents are judged. Importantly, this preference is not evenly distributed across populations. Older adults tend to emphasize the warmth of human contact, whereas younger generations, particularly Generation Z, increasingly value speed and immediate resolution. In the present study, these generational contrasts provide a meaningful basis for comparing how users evaluate or resist simulated empathy in automated support contexts.

Cognitive Load refers to the amount of mental resources a person uses to process information while performing a task. Ramsøy and colleagues, through neurophysiological studies, demonstrated that excessive load interferes with decision making and negatively affects the customer experience, even in digital consumption contexts [9]. Research on cognitive load shows that language design influences how users process information. When responses are repetitive or overly elaborate, they increase mental effort instead of reducing it. For artificial empathy, this balance is critical: supportive phrasing should ease tension without obscuring clarity. In this study, the concept of Cognitive Load is applied as a guiding principle in the development of the test agent, ensuring that its communicative design avoids unnecessary complexity and favors clarity in automated support.

One of the most influential contributions of Watzlawick's [10] communication theory is the axiom that "it is impossible not to communicate." This principle implies that all behavior, even silence or the absence of a response, conveys a message to the interlocutor. Applied to conversational agents, the axiom takes on particular relevance: when a system does not display even minimal signals of empathy, what it communicates is not neutrality but indifference, which can intensify customer frustration and erode the reputation of the implementing organization. Consequently, this axiom reinforces the need to design interactions in which artificial empathy is not regarded as an optional embellishment but rather as a fundamental component to ensure the quality of customer experience in automated environments.

3 Justification

Studying artificial empathy in conversational agents is essential because companies must determine whether it is worth investing resources in this capability. While automation already delivers efficiency and cost savings, the question remains whether embedding artificial empathy adds tangible value in terms of customer experience and organizational reputation. Without evidence, organizations risk either overinvesting in features that do not impact outcomes or underestimating the importance of those that directly influence customer satisfaction and trust.

The urgency of this study lies in its timing. Customer expectations around artificial intelligence are evolving rapidly, and service practices that feel acceptable today may no longer be competitive tomorrow. The sooner companies understand whether artificial empathy meaningfully reduces frustration and improves perceptions of reputation, the sooner they can adjust their strategies and set standards for future service design. Waiting to establish this knowledge risks leaving organizations behind while customer frustration continues to grow.

The benefits of this research extend beyond corporations. Customers gain when conversational agents provide interactions that feel supportive and reduce negative emotions. Organizations benefit when those improved experiences strengthen reputation and trust. At an industry level, evidence-based practices in artificial empathy support the development of automation that is not only efficient but also more human-centered. From this perspective, everyone wins: customers feel heard, companies strengthen their image, and conversational agent design evolves toward a more sustainable and ethical standard.

4 Methodology

Participants

A total of 84 individuals were recruited from higher-education institutions, primarily students, with a smaller share of faculty. Instructors from technological disciplines were excluded to reduce friction and potential bias from advanced technical familiarity. Although balance across gender and educational roles was intended, the realized sample was predominantly student. Of the 84 who completed the pre-test, 41 engaged with the conversational agents in the experimental task, and 9 completed both the pre- and post-interaction measures (Empathic = 5, Neutral = 4).

Design

A **between-subjects experimental design** was employed. Participants were randomly assigned with a 50/50 allocation to one of two conditions:

1. **Empathic conversational agent**, programmed with emotional validation and supportive responses.
2. **Neutral conversational agent**, designed with an informative and procedural communication style.

Each participant interacted with **only one version** of the agent in a standardized customer support scenario in which the customer reported that a purchased product had not arrived.

In this study, **artificial empathy** is defined strictly as the use of linguistic expressions that acknowledge user emotions (e.g., validation of frustration, supportive phrasing). The empathic condition did not involve deception, anthropomorphic mimicry, or attempts to disguise the agent as a human operator. In line with regulatory and ethical standards (e.g., the EU AI Act, FTC guidance), no false identities or misleading cues were included. Typing indicators were applied in both conditions to preserve realism in a chat-based format, but features such as fabricated names, human personas, or identity concealment were deliberately excluded. This design isolates empathy as language, ensuring that any observed effects reflect emotional validation rather than anthropomorphic simulation, which is essential for evaluating its role in customer support (Fig. 1).

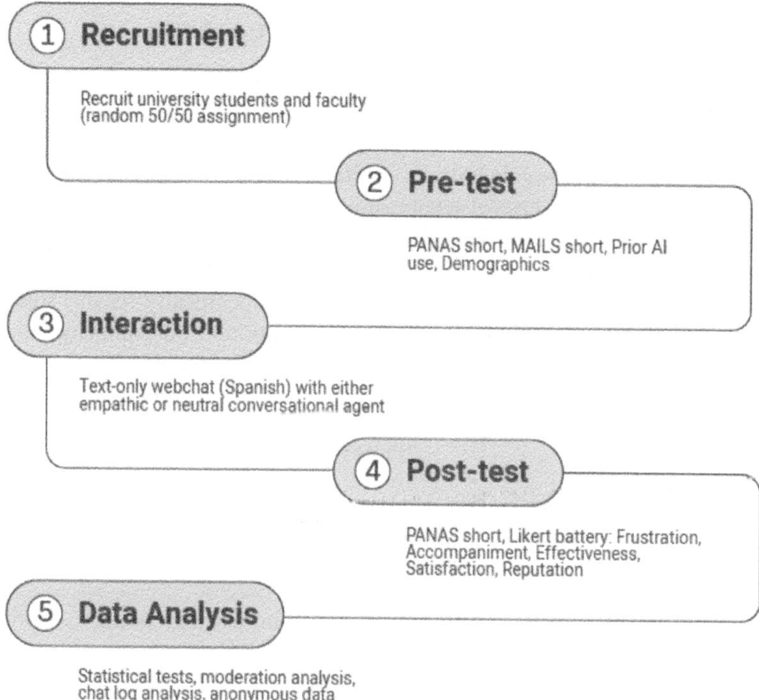

Fig. 1. Experimental workflow for artificial empathy study.

5 Measures and Data Collection

This study employed a mixed-methods approach. Quantitative data were obtained through pre- and post-interaction surveys, while qualitative and behavioral evidence was extracted from chat transcripts. Together, these complementary sources provided a more comprehensive understanding of how conversational AI agents influence emotional states and perceptions of service quality.

Pre-test

- **Demographics**: age, gender, institution type (public/private), and role (student/faculty).
- **PANAS (short version)**: to establish baseline emotional state and initial frustration levels [4].
- **Prior AI usage**: three self-report items adapted from Heliyon [5] to capture exposure to AI in daily life.
- **Meta AI Literacy Scale (MAILS, short form)**: to assess participants' familiarity with and understanding of artificial intelligence [5, 11].

Post-test (After Interaction in Empathic vs. Neutral Condition)

- **PANAS (repeated)**: to detect changes in emotional state and frustration after the interaction.
- **Complementary Likert-scale battery (15 items)**: developed for this study to evaluate perceived frustration, sense of accompaniment, process effectiveness, satisfaction, and organizational reputation. The process effectiveness and satisfaction items were directly inspired by established UX and service quality constructs [12]. The organizational reputation subscale (3 items) was created specifically for this study, with items such as "This interaction improved my perception of the company", designed to capture perceived trust, care, and overall image of the organization. Although not drawn from a pre-validated instrument, the items were conceptually grounded in the literature to ensure alignment and face validity.

Chat Log Analysis (Interaction Data)
In addition to questionnaires, the chat transcripts will be analyzed with the following objectives:

- **Linguistic indicators of frustration:** Negative word usage, repetition, expressions of irritation, urgency markers.
- **Behavioral indicators of tension:** Response time, message persistence, frequency of escalation, typographic markers (e.g., excessive capitalization, exclamation marks).
- **Correlation with self-reported measures:** Comparison of textual indicators of frustration with PANAS pre- and post-test.

This mixed-methods approach complements questionnaire data, providing a more comprehensive understanding of how interactions with conversational AI agents influence emotional states and perceptions of service quality. These indicators will also be examined in relation to the study's hypotheses regarding frustration, satisfaction, and the moderating effect of AI literacy.

Hypotheses and Analysis
The study hypothesizes that:

- **H1.** Artificial empathy will not significantly improve perceptions of process effectiveness compared to the neutral condition.
- **H2.** Artificial empathy will significantly improve organizational reputation compared to the neutral condition.

The study also aimed to observe the following possible moderating effects, without treating them as primary tests:

- **Exploratory 1.** Age may moderate frustration, with older participants reporting higher frustration in the neutral condition than younger participants (see Table 1 for generational profiles).
- **Exploratory 2.** AI literacy may moderate perceptions of empathy, such that participants with higher literacy will be more critical in distinguishing authentic from simulated empathy.

Exploratory 3. Gender, institution type, and role (student vs. faculty) may also influence outcomes, although these are treated as secondary analyses.

Table 1. Generational groups and expected frustration levels in the neutral condition (expert-based hypotheses formulated before experimentation)

Generation	Years	Estimated Effect on Frustration in Neutral Condition
Baby Boomers	1946–1964	Highest frustration, prefer human empathy and patience in interactions
Generation X	1965–1980	High frustration, value empathy but tolerate some automation
Millennials (Gen Y)	1981–1996	Moderate frustration, balanced preference between empathy and speed
Generation Z	1997–2012	Lower frustration, prioritize speed and resolution over empathy
Generation Alpha	2013–present	Not included (below higher-education participant age threshold)

Note. The estimations were derived from professional observations and prior experience in automated customer service design. They were used to anticipate possible generational differences in tolerance toward neutral AI responses and to guide hypothesis formulation. Generational categories are adapted from Pew Research Center definitions (2023).

6 Results

Sample and Attrition

A total of 84 participants completed the pre-test. Of these, 41 engaged with the conversational agents during the interaction phase, and 9 completed the post-test (Empathic = 5, Neutral = 4). Attrition was therefore substantial, and the final evaluative sample must be interpreted with caution. Behavioral outcomes (n = 41) are reported as primary evidence in this pilot, with survey outcomes (n = 9) used as complementary, self-reported measures. This ordering reflects the sample sizes and the mixed-methods design.

This approach emphasizes what could be observed in the full set of chatlogs, while treating the survey responses as small-scale, exploratory evidence [13].

Behavioral Outcomes (n = 41)

Across the 41 chatlogs, most interactions showed low or moderate frustration. Specifically, 7 cases were coded at level 0 (no observable frustration, routine or neutral exchanges), 10 at level 1 (simple complaints in a neutral tone), 21 at level 2 (repeated or insistent requests for re-send or refund), and only 3 at level 3 (urgent or escalating appeals such as "please help" or "I need this now"). In other words, the results show that escalation was the exception rather than the rule (Figs. 2 and 3).

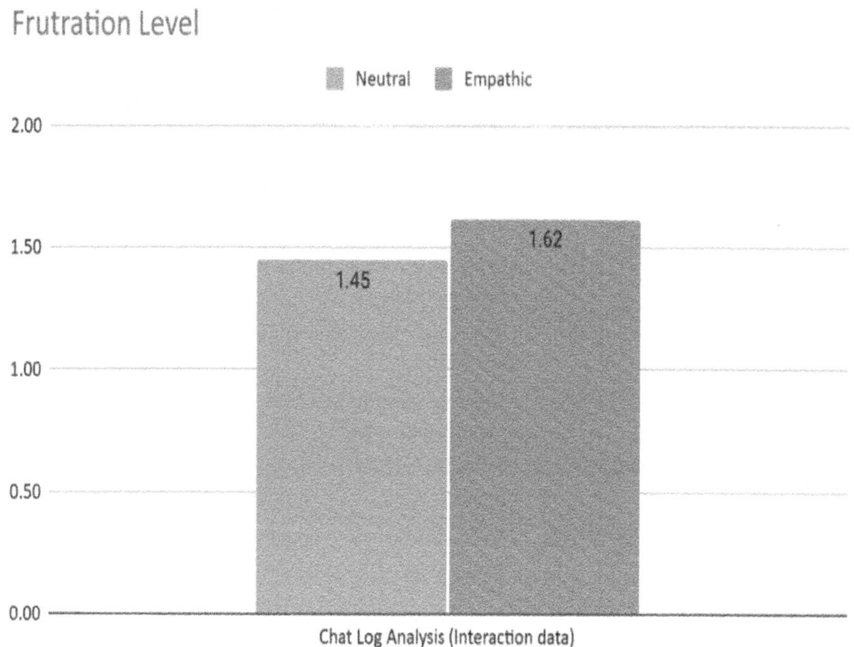

Fig. 2. Frustration level, general comparison.

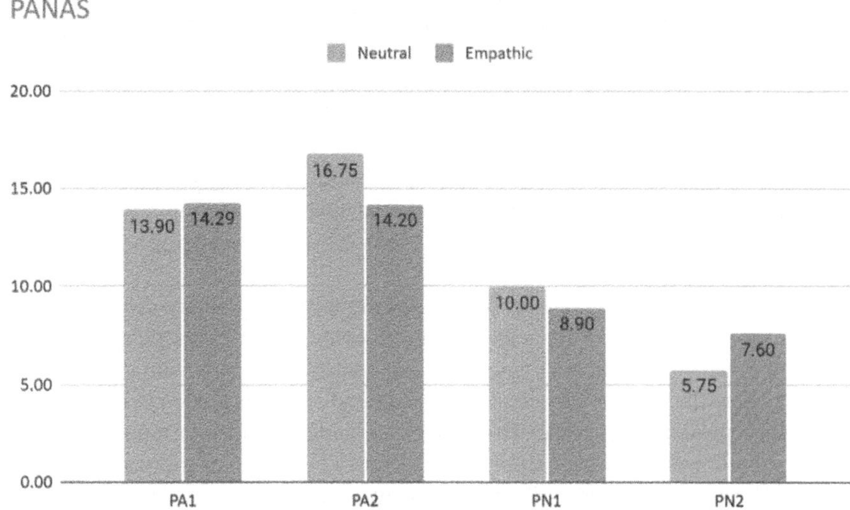

Fig. 3. PANAS experimental results.

Clear contrasts emerged between the two agent styles. Empathic interactions were longer (≈10 turns on average, 6 from the user and 4 from the agent) and included more validation and apologies (≈3–4 empathy markers and up to 2 apologies per case). Neutral interactions were shorter (≈5 turns on average), with fewer agent contributions and almost no empathy markers.

Resolution patterns also differed. Empathic agents resolved 13 of 21 cases (≈62%), whereas neutral agents resolved 7 of 20 (≈35%). This indicates that empathic language more frequently produced concrete outcomes (such as re-sends, refunds, or coupons), even though survey responses later favored the neutral style (Table 2).

Table 2. Resolution outcomes by agent type. Number of cases resolved and unresolved, with corresponding resolution rates.

Agent Type	Resolved	Unresolved	Resolution Rate
Empathic	13	8	62%
Neutral	7	13	35%

H1. Process Effectiveness

Post-test evaluations indicated that participants in the neutral condition perceived the process as more effective than those in the empathic condition. Mean post-test scores were higher for the neutral agent (M = 13.25–13.75) compared to the empathic agent (M = 12.00–12.80), a difference of approximately 1 point.

Frustration ratings (0–5 scale) were generally low in both groups. For the full set of interactions, the empathic condition averaged 1.57 compared to 1.45 in the neutral condition. Among participants who completed the post-test, the empathic average was

1.40 while the neutral average was 1.75. These differences are small, suggesting that artificial empathy did not reduce frustration. The data support H1: artificial empathy did not improve how participants evaluated process effectiveness.

H2. Organizational Reputation

The hypothesis proposed that artificial empathy would improve perceptions of organizational reputation. However, results pointed in the opposite direction. Post-test ratings were consistently higher for the neutral agent (M = 4.5–4.75) compared to the empathic agent (M = 3.8–4.2).

This indicates that participants perceived the organization as more professional and reliable when represented by the neutral agent. In contrast, the empathic agent (despite resolving a greater proportion of cases) did not translate this procedural success into reputational benefits. Chat evidence shows that empathic agents tended to prolong interactions with repeated reassurance. This pattern coincided with lower reputation scores, suggesting that longer dialogues were not necessarily perceived as more effective.

These findings highlight a divergence between objective resolution (where the empathic agent outperformed) and subjective evaluation (where the neutral agent was favored). Contrary to expectations, empathy did not enhance organizational reputation, and may even have undermined it by generating perceptions of longer, less direct processes. This pattern underscores the importance of balancing empathic cues with efficiency when designing conversational agents.

Exploratory 1. Age Moderation

An exploratory observation addressed whether age might moderate frustration, with the expectation that older participants could report higher frustration in the neutral condition. However, the post-test sample lacked generational diversity: almost all participants were young adults between 18 and 26 years old. Within this narrow range, frustration scores remained consistently low (1–2 on a 0–5 scale), leaving little variation to analyze. A few older participants did appear in the dataset, but their responses did not deviate meaningfully from the overall pattern. As a result, this exploratory analysis cannot provide conclusions about generational effects. Future studies that recruit across multiple cohorts, including Generation X and Baby Boomers, will be necessary to evaluate whether empathy or neutrality is perceived differently depending on age (Fig. 4).

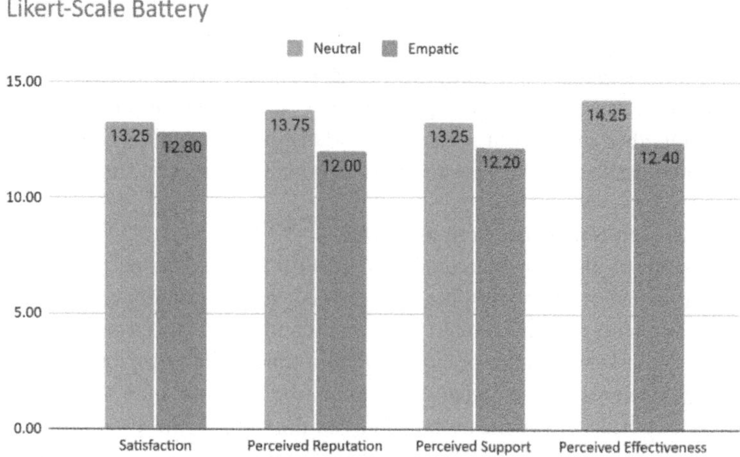

Fig. 4. Likert Scale Battery

Exploratory 2. AI Literacy Moderation

Table 3. Distribution of participants across AI literacy score ranges (MAILS) and their corresponding average frustration levels. The variable "Participants (n)" indicates the number of individuals per score range.

Agent Type	Resolved	Resolution Rate
0–10	1	2.0
11–20	4	1.75
21–30	17	1.65
31–40	14	1.43
41–50	5	1.40

Exploratory analysis suggested that AI literacy may influence how participants experienced the interaction. In the full dataset ($n = 41$), MAILS scores ranged from 10 to 50, while frustration levels stayed generally low ($M \approx 1.56$). A pattern appeared (Table 3):

- Participants with lower MAILS scores (13–23) showed more signs of frustration, including the few cases that escalated to level 3 (e.g., repeated urgency markers, requests for escalation).
- Participants with higher MAILS scores (40–50) stayed at frustration levels 0–2, and none escalated.

Reported AI usage, on the other hand, showed no clear relationship with frustration. Nevertheless, the buffering effect of AI literacy observed in the behavioral data highlights a promising line for future research, even if robust conclusions cannot be drawn from this limited sample.

These **results suggest that understanding how AI works matters more than simply using it**. Participants with higher literacy seemed more patient and tolerant toward both empathic and neutral agents. This points to a practical takeaway: improving AI literacy could make customer interactions smoother and reduce frustration.

Exploratory 3. Gender, Institution, and Role
Exploratory analyses also considered gender, institution type, and participant role (student vs. faculty or other). However, the dataset was overwhelmingly composed of male students ($\approx$85%), with very few female participants and only isolated cases of other roles such as faculty, workers, or entrepreneurs. Within this limited distribution, frustration scores and perceptions of effectiveness or reputation did not show systematic differences across categories. Given the homogeneity of the sample, these variables cannot be meaningfully interpreted in this study. Broader recruitment across genders and institutional roles will be needed in future work to test whether such factors shape responses to empathic versus neutral agents [14].

7 Discussion

The findings suggest that in digital support, clarity and efficiency carry greater weight in user evaluations than empathic phrasing. Although the empathic agent resolved a higher proportion of cases (62%) and offered more compensations, participants rated the neutral agent more positively in satisfaction and organizational reputation. This divergence highlights a core design tension: empathy can enhance procedural outcomes but does not automatically foster trust or perceived professionalism.

This pattern aligns with prior research showing that when artificial agents attempt to sound empathic, users often interpret such expressions as scripted or exaggerated rather than genuinely supportive [7]. Even though the empathic agent in this study provided more validation and apologies, participants appeared to value concise and direct communication. The neutral agent's brevity and formality likely conveyed greater control and reliability, leading to higher reputational scores despite resolving fewer issues.

A deeper explanation for this paradox may lie in the combined effects of **perceived authenticity and cognitive load**. When empathy is expressed by a machine, users may perceive it as procedural rather than sincere, which weakens its emotional impact. Longer empathic messages also require greater cognitive processing from users who are already under stress. In customer support contexts, individuals typically seek instrumental solutions, not emotional engagement; excessive reassurance can therefore feel inefficient or even evasive. The behavioral data support this interpretation: empathic exchanges were longer and contained more elaboration, yet users judged them as less effective.

Beyond the two primary hypotheses, several exploratory observations merit discussion. The analysis of **AI literacy** revealed a consistent trend: participants with higher

MAILS scores reported lower frustration and exhibited fewer escalation behaviors, suggesting that understanding how AI functions promotes tolerance and patience in automated interactions. In contrast, general AI usage showed no such relationship, indicating that conceptual knowledge, rather than exposure, shapes user reactions. Exploratory analyses of age, gender, institution type, and role did not yield significant patterns, largely due to the homogeneity of the sample, although limited cases suggested that older participants may respond more negatively to neutral responses.

Overall, these findings suggest that artificial empathy in conversational agents operates within a narrow margin: enough to convey care, but not so much that it hinders efficiency. Striking this balance remains a critical challenge for designing conversational systems that feel both competent and genuinely attentive to users' needs.

8 Limitations

Several limitations constrain the interpretation of these findings. The most significant is attrition: although 84 participants completed the pre-test, only 41 engaged with the agents and just 9 completed the post-test. This imbalance reduces statistical power and limits the generalization of self-reported measures. To mitigate this issue, **behavioral outcomes from all 41 interactions were prioritized** as the main evidence base, while post-test responses were treated as exploratory complements. Because the chatlogs captured full conversational sequences regardless of survey completion, they provided a consistent behavioral dataset for analyzing frustration levels, escalation patterns, and resolution outcomes.

The demographic composition also restricts generalizability. The sample consisted predominantly of young male students, constraining variability across gender, role, and institution type. Although AI literacy and age were included as potential moderators, the lack of diversity prevented robust testing of these effects. The observed trends for AI literacy should therefore be considered preliminary, and no conclusions can be drawn about age or other demographic variables.

A further limitation involves ecological validity. The experiment was conducted in a single, text-based scenario involving a missing product delivery, a frequent but specific form of service failure. This choice ensured contextual familiarity and comparability across participants, yet it limits the applicability of the findings to broader customer-service domains. The focus on textual interaction isolates empathy as a linguistic feature rather than as a multimodal or anthropomorphic expression, enhancing internal validity at the expense of external generalization.

Overall, the study should be understood as a pilot exploration of artificial empathy in a controlled service context. Despite sample limitations, the behavioral consistency observed across 41 interactions suggests a reliable pattern: when empathy becomes too explicit, users tend to interpret it as inefficiency. Future research should replicate this design in larger and more heterogeneous populations and across varied support scenarios to test the robustness and boundary conditions of this paradox.

9 Future Research

Future research should expand the sample size and diversity to enable more reliable tests of both primary and exploratory observations. Recruiting participants from varied professional and generational backgrounds would allow stronger analyses of whether empathy is differentially valued across populations, particularly with respect to age and gender.

Another important avenue is to contrast different use cases. Customer support interactions emphasize clarity and resolution, whereas sales or marketing contexts place greater weight on persuasion, warmth, and relational connection. Artificial empathy may therefore produce opposite effects depending on the domain. A sufficiently powered design could clarify whether empathy that appears inefficient in support may, by contrast, enhance conversion and brand warmth in sales.

Future work should also extend beyond a single scenario. Testing empathy across a broader set of service contexts (such as billing disputes, technical failures, or complaints requiring escalation) would provide a more complete picture of when simulated empathy helps or hinders user experience. Incorporating stylistic features of real chat communication (e.g., emojis, expressive punctuation, or informal phrasing) could also help assess whether these elements improve the perceived authenticity of empathic responses.

Finally, future studies should disentangle the relative importance of AI literacy versus AI usage. While usage frequency showed no consistent effect in this study, higher literacy scores were associated with lower frustration. This suggests that conceptual understanding, rather than mere exposure, may play a decisive role in shaping evaluations of empathic versus neutral agents.

10 Conclusion

This study contributes to ongoing debates about the role of artificial empathy in automated customer support. Results show that while empathic agents achieved greater procedural resolution, this success did not translate into higher user satisfaction or reputation scores. **Participants valued the neutral agent as more effective and professional**, underscoring the primacy of clarity and efficiency over simulated empathy in customer evaluations.

Among the exploratory observations, AI literacy emerged as a relevant factor: **participants with higher MAILS scores showed lower frustration and fewer escalation behaviors**, whereas age, gender, and role effects were inconclusive due to the homogeneity of the sample. These findings reinforce the idea that understanding how AI works may be more important than the frequency of its use in shaping user tolerance and trust.

Although attrition reduced the post-test sample, consistent behavioral trends across 41 interactions provide preliminary evidence of a recurring pattern: users tend to interpret excessive empathy as inefficiency. Consequently, artificial empathy should be implemented as a functional design element meant to clarify and support, not to emulate human emotion. Future studies with larger and more diverse samples can test whether this balance between empathy and efficiency also predicts long-term outcomes such as loyalty, purchase decisions, or brand perception.

References

1. Juquelier, A., Poncin, I., Hazée, S.: Empathic chatbots: a double-edged sword in customer experiences. J. Bus. Res. **188**, Article no. 115074 (2025). https://www.sciencedirect.com/science/article/abs/pii/S0148296324005782?via%3Dihub
2. Brun, A., Liu, R., Shukla, A., Watson, F., Gratch, J.: Exploring emotion-sensitive LLM-based conversational AI [Preprint]. arXiv. https://arxiv.org/abs/2502.08920 (2025)
3. Shen, J., DiPaola, D., Ali, S., Sap, M., Park, H.W., Breazeal, C.: Empathy toward artificial intelligence versus human experiences and the role of transparency in mental health and social support chatbot design: comparative study. JMIR Ment. Health **11**, e62679 (2024). https://mental.jmir.org/2024/1/e62679
4. Watson, D., Clark, L.A., Tellegen, A.: Development and validation of brief measures of positive and negative affect: the PANAS scales. J. Pers. Soc. Psychol. **54**(6), 1063–1070 (1988). https://ogg.osu.edu/media/documents/MB%20Stream/PANAS.pdf
5. Carolus, A., Koch, M.J., Straka, S., Latoschik, M.E., Wienrich, C.: MAILS – meta AI literacy scale: development and testing of an AI literacy questionnaire based on well-founded competency models and psychological change- and meta-competencies. Comput. Hum. Behav. Artif. Hum. **1**(2), Article no. 100014 (2023). https://doi.org/10.1016/j.chbah.2023.100014
6. Davis, M.H.: Measuring individual differences in empathy: Evidence for a multidimensional approach. J. Pers. Soc. Psychol. **44**(1), 113–126 (1983). https://www.researchgate.net/publication/215605832_Measuring_individual_differences_in_empathy_Evidence_for_a_multidimensional_approach/link/54e228570cf2c3e7d2d2884b/download
7. Seitz, L.: Artificial empathy in healthcare chatbots: does it feel authentic? Comput. Hum. Behav. Artif. Hum. **2**(1), Article no. 100067 (2024). https://www.sciencedirect.com/science/article/pii/S2949882124000276?via%3Dihub
8. Raval, A.: AI won't fix the real issue with customer service. Financial Times, 17 March 2025. https://www.ft.com/content/a3753f62-1efc-4ca3-9934-47ab9994fa87
9. Kakaria, A., Saffari, S., Ramsøy, T.Z.: Cognitive load during planned and unplanned virtual shopping: evidence from a neurophysiological perspective. Front. Neurosci. **17**, 1189487 (2023). https://www.sciencedirect.com/science/article/pii/S0268401223000488?via%3Dihub
10. Watzlawick, P., Bavelas, J.B., Jackson, D.D.: Pragmatics of Human Communication: A Study of Interactional Patterns, Pathologies, and Paradoxes. Norton, New York (1967). https://comm163v.wordpress.com/wp-content/uploads/2013/01/bavelas.pdf
11. Koch, M.J., Carolus, A., Wienrich, C., Latoschik, M.E.: Meta AI literacy scale: further validation and development of a short version. Heliyon **10**(6), Article no. e39686 (2024). https://www.cell.com/action/showPdf?pii=S2405-8440%2824%2915717-9
12. Faruk, L.I.D.: Introducing CASUX: a standardized scale for measuring the user experience of artificial intelligence-based conversational agents. Int. J. Hum. Comput. Interact. (2025). Advance online publication. https://doi.org/10.1080/10447318.2024.2359206
13. Liu, S., Ma, L., Zhang, Y.: EvAlignUX: advancing UX evaluation through LLM-supported metrics exploration. In: Proceedings of the CHI Conference on Human Factors in Computing Systems (CHI 2025). Association for Computing Machinery (2025). https://doi.org/10.1145/3706598.3714045
14. European Parliament, & Council of the European Union: Regulation (EU) 2024/1689 of the European Parliament and of the Council on artificial intelligence (Artificial Intelligence Act). Official Journal of the European Union, L 202, 1–138 (2024). https://artificialintelligenceact.eu/article/50/
15. Federal Trade Commission: FTC announces crackdown on deceptive AI claims. Federal Trade Commission, 25 September 2024. https://www.ftc.gov/news-events/news/press-releases/2024/09/ftc-announces-crackdown-deceptive-ai-claims-schemes

Business Simulator: Interactive Optimization of Inputs in the Digital Enterprise in Industry 5.0

Eduardo Antolín Gutiérrez-Segovia[1](✉), Humberto García-Castellano[1], and Alberto Ochoa-Zezzatti[1,2]

[1] Instituto Tecnológico de Ciudad Juarez, Ciudad Juárez, Chihuahua, México
{1D21110216,humber.gc}@itcj.edu.mx, al237866@alumnos.uacj.mx
[2] Universidad Autónoma de Ciudad Juárez, Ciudad Juárez, Chihuahua, México

Abstract. This study presents the development of an interactive automotive simulator aimed at optimizing supply chain performance by digitally integrating production planning, inventory management, and supplier cost analysis. The tool provides real-time visualization and adjustment of variables such as on-hand inventory, daily consumption, and lead time, generating dynamic Days of Inventory on Hand (DOH) calculations and alerts for Pull-In and Push-Out scenarios. Through simulated production and procurement strategies, users can evaluate the effects of operational decisions on inventory stability and cost efficiency. The simulator incorporates supplier evaluation using average cost, lowest price, and avoided cost metrics to support informed sourcing and negotiation. Developed as a single page. React application with interactive dashboards, it enables agile decision-making and continuous improvement aligned with Lean and Six Sigma principles. Results show strong potential for cost reduction, better stock control, and improved responsiveness in automotive manufacturing, while providing a foundation for future AI, digital twin, and sustainability-based enhancements.

Keywords: Master Production Schedule (MPS) · Gross Demand · Days on Hand (DOH) · Raw Material · Safety Stock and Projected Ending Inventory

1 Introduction

Digital transformation is redefining resource management, urging companies to optimize procurement to reduce costs. The automotive sector in manufacturing hubs like Ciudad Juárez, Mexico, faces supply chain disruptions, cost pressures, and the need for flexible, data-driven decisions. Traditional procurement is rigid, slow, and expensive, limiting adaptability. AI, simulation tools, and scenario modeling now enable organizations to test and optimize strategies before real implementation. This poster introduces the Interactive Input Optimization Simulator for the Automotive Industry, a platform integrating AI-based predictive analytics, digital twins, and gamification to model procurement and production scenarios, helping managers explore systemic cost-reduction strategies.

Digital transformation is redefining resource management, urging companies to optimize procurement to reduce costs. The automotive sector in manufacturing hubs like

L. Martínez-Villaseñor et al. (Eds.): MICAI 2025 Workshops, LNAI 16264, pp. 408–420, 2026.
https://doi.org/10.1007/978-3-032-17930-2_29

Ciudad Juárez, Mexico, faces supply chain disruptions, cost pressures, and the need for flexible, data-driven decisions. Traditional procurement is rigid, slow, and expensive, limiting adaptability. AI, simulation tools, and scenario modeling now enable organizations to test and optimize strategies before real implementation. This poster introduces the Interactive Input Optimization Simulator for the Automotive Industry, a platform integrating AI-based predictive analytics, digital twins, and gamification to model procurement and production scenarios, helping managers explore systemic cost-reduction strategies.

The evolution toward Industry 5.0 extends beyond automation and efficiency; it integrates human-centricity, resilience, and sustainability as guiding principles of next-generation supply systems [14]. Unlike Industry 4.0, which prioritized full automation, Industry 5.0 reintroduces human expertise and creativity into AI-driven environments, fostering symbiotic collaboration between people and intelligent machines [25]. In the automotive context, this paradigm enables planners to co-create digital procurement strategies through adaptive simulators that learn from user interaction and evolving market data. Recent studies emphasize that digital twins combined with AI can enhance predictive decision-making while supporting circular-economy and energy-efficiency goals [11]. Furthermore, integrating sustainability and resilience through advanced technologies ensures agile and environmentally aligned operations [15]. Human-machine collaboration thus becomes a decisive enabler of competitive advantage and ethical manufacturing [4]. In this regard, the proposed simulator contributes to the industry 5.0 vision by embedding human-in-the-loop analytics, scenario-based learning, and transparent cost optimization mechanisms. By combining data-driven intelligence with managerial intuition, it transforms procurement from a transactional process into a strategic capability that strengthens innovation, social responsibility, and long-term value creation across automotive supply networks.

2 Related Works

Complementing a related work, [20] developed an AI-based decision support system for public procurement that uses semantic search and NLP to analyze tender documents, demonstrating the potential of data-driven tools to improve transparency and evaluation quality; however, their framework is not directly coupled with production or inventory dynamics. From a planning and operations perspective, [12] propose a digital twin-based, demand-driven production planning framework that synchronizes physical and virtual environments to improve responsiveness and inventory control, illustrating how virtualized models can support tactical and operational decisions in complex manufacturing systems. In parallel, [24] showed that gamified supply chain simulations significantly enhance engagement and learning outcomes, suggesting that game-based interfaces are effective for building decision-making capabilities among practitioners and students, though their approach is primarily educational rather than integrated with real procurement metrics. Aligned with the Industry 5.0 paradigm, [13] emphasizes human-centered and sustainable AI, arguing that decision-support technologies must embed transparency, ethics, and user empowerment principles directly relevant to human-in-the-loop simulators.

[5] analyzed supply chain management in the industry 5.0 era, highlighting the strategic need to integrate resilience, collaboration, and advanced analytics across networks, while observing that many existing tools still treat planning, sourcing, and sustainability in isolation. [16] further discuss how AI foundation models can transform digital engineering for logistics and supply chains by enabling holistic scenario analysis and predictive intelligence, reinforcing the relevance of scalable, data-centric architectures for next-generation decision platforms. Recent literature on digitalized and human-centric supply chains provides the conceptual foundation for the proposed Interactive Input Optimization Simulator. [2] offered a comprehensive taxonomy of AI and machine learning applications in procurement decision-support systems, evidencing how intelligent analytics enhance spend visibility, supplier evaluation, and risk management, yet noting that most solutions remain functionally fragmented rather than integrated with operational planning. In contrast to these contributions, the proposed Interactive Input Optimization Simulator uniquely integrates AI-driven analytics, digital-twin-inspired scenario modeling, gamification, and multi-supplier cost optimization into a single, user-centric environment that links master production scheduling, inventory coverage (DOH), and procurement choices. This integrative and participatory design directly operationalizes Industry 5.0 principles by coupling human judgment with intelligent simulation to support strategic, economic, and sustainable decision-making in the automotive sector.

3 Theoretical-Experiments Foundations

3.1 Supply Chain

A supply chain is a dynamic, interconnected network that integrates suppliers, manufacturers, logistics providers, and customers to ensure the efficient flow of materials, information, and finances from source to consumption. Modern supply chains operate under principles of resilience, sustainability, and digitalization, leveraging AI, IoT, and data analytics to enhance real-time visibility and adaptability [9]. In the Industry 5.0 era, supply chains evolved toward human-centric ecosystems, where collaboration between humans and intelligent systems fosters innovation, circular economy, and social responsibility [3]. In addition, integrating human-centricity, sustainability, and resilience through advanced technologies enables agile, personalized production and logistics, delivers enhanced visibility, efficiency, and responsiveness across the value chain, and aligns operational performance with environmental and social objectives [15].

3.2 E-Procurement

According to [22], e-procurement and digital purchases refer to the use of internet-based platforms and digital technologies to automate and optimize purchasing processes. These systems streamline supplier selection, bidding, order management, and payment, reducing transaction costs and cycle times while increasing transparency and compliance. E-procurement refers to the use of digital platforms and automated workflows to manage purchasing processes, from requisition to payment. It streamlines supplier selection, bidding, and contract management, reducing transaction time and costs while improving transparency and compliance [22]. Recent developments incorporate AI-driven analytics and blockchain technologies to strengthen supplier evaluation, risk mitigation, and sustainability performance [23], aligning digital procurement with broader Industry 5.0 objectives of efficiency and ethical governance. In addition, e-procurement can be defined as a web-based application enhancing tools, workflows, and procedural systems with the objective of automating procurement tasks, enabling real-time interaction between buyers and suppliers [1].

3.3 TOPSIS

[10] introduced a distributed-TOPSIS approach that leverages the MapReduce paradigm to enhance the scalability of multi-criteria decision-making (MCDM). By parallelizing the TOPSIS computations, their method can handle big data environments, where traditional TOPSIS would otherwise face significant computational limitations. [18] developed a stratified BWM–TOPSIS method that integrates the Best–Worst Method (BWM) with a layered version of TOPSIS to address sustainable supplier selection. This hybrid model enables decision makers to weigh environmental and social dimensions alongside traditional cost and quality criteria, while also managing uncertainty in future market conditions.

3.4 SEM (Structural Equation Modeling)

SEM allows simultaneous testing of complex theoretical frameworks, making it suitable for studies on organizational performance, supplier relationships, and process optimization [7]. In addition, it is a sophisticated and iterative multivariate statistical methodology designed to evaluate both observable (manifest) and unobservable (latent) variables within a unified framework. Its core strength lies in producing causal path diagrams that allow researchers to test and refine theoretical models of complex phenomena. By incorporating measurement error and validating latent constructs, SEM enhances both the explanatory and predictive validity of research models. It is a multivariate statistical technique that enables researchers to analyze causal relationships among latent variables through a combination of factor analysis and regression modeling. Recent advances integrate Partial Least Squares (PLS-SEM) and Bayesian approaches to accommodate non-normal data and enhance predictive accuracy in engineering and supply chain contexts [19]. Structural Equation Modeling (SEM) is the foundational approach through which theoretical constructions and latent variables can be integrated with observable indicators, enabling simultaneous estimation of measurement and structural relationships. It allows for different types of constructs (latent, causal-formative, composites) to be tested together and supports evaluating path coefficients, indirect effects, and model misspecifications within a unified estimation framework [21].

4 Methodology

4.1 Datasets

The simulator's data acquisition process uses synthetic data only, structured to reflect how industrial information is managed in global manufacturing companies. Data are organized into relational matrices including part numbers, lead times, consumption, inventory, production schedules, and costs. Synthetic inputs emulate real-time conditions and variability to mirror operational uncertainty. The system updates KPIs such as DOH, pull-in/push-out alerts, and material reconciliation, enabling reliable experimentation with diverse production and supply scenarios.

4.2 Data Processing

Data processing constitutes a critical stage in the development of the Interactive Input Optimization Simulator, ensuring that raw information from multiple enterprise systems is transformed into structured, reliable, and analytically usable datasets. This phase involves cleaning, normalization, and outlier management procedures designed to enhance the quality and consistency of operational data obtained from ERP, supplier, logistics, and financial sources [26]. Next, we presented a structure of the process followed by the main author (see Fig. 1).

Fig. 1. Process used for the methodology.

4.3 Feature Engineering

Represents the analytical core of the simulator, transforming processed data into meaningful variables that capture the dynamics of production, inventory, and supplier performance. These features enable the platform to identify behavioral patterns, assess variability across suppliers, and quantify the impact of procurement and scheduling decisions on overall efficiency and cost optimization.

1) Master Production Schedule (MPS).
2) Gross Demand
3) Days on Hand (DOH) with Raw Material and Work In Process
4) Safety Stock
5) Projected Ending Inventory

The outcomes of the feature engineering stage provide the essential analytical inputs for the simulation engine. By converting raw operational data into interpretable performance metrics, this process bridges descriptive analysis and predictive modeling. The resulting feature set enables the simulator to execute realistic scenario testing and optimization tasks, ensuring that subsequent analyses are both data-driven and aligned with real manufacturing behavior.

4.4 Model Selection and Training

For this research Structural Equational Model SEM was applied as the core model and estimate measurement + structural paths (ML/robust WLS), using time-blocked cross-validation and fit indices (CFI, RMSEA, SRMR) to compare rival specifications, among the main latent constructures we have:

- Supplier Reliability (SR): OTD%, ↓Lead Time Var, ↓PPM.
- Cost Efficiency (CE): ↑Inventory Turns, ↓PPV, ↓Landed Cost.
- Digital Procurement Maturity (DPM): e-procurement adoption, data quality, system integration.
- Risk Exposure (RE): FX volatility, disruption frequency, transit-time variability.
- Service Performance (SP): Fill rate, ↓Stockouts, ↓Backorder days.

4.5 Model Evaluation

It was evaluated the Structural Equational Modeling (SEM) by its statistical fit, construct validity, and its ability to reproduce and predict production-system behavior in simulation (throughput, service level, WIP, cost).

Global fit: CFI $\geq$ 0.95, RMSEA $\leq$ 0.06, SRMR $\leq$ 0.08; compare rival models via AIC/BIC.

Path validity: standardized coefficients, CIs, p-values; report effect sizes and indirect effects (mediation via Cost Efficiency → Service Performance).

Reliability/validity: CR $\geq$ 0.70, AVE $\geq$ 0.50, HTMT $<$ 0.85.

4.6 Experimental Validation

It is presented through the application in different features engineering.

1) For Master Production Schedule (MPS).

These parameters are used to calculate the following data and the Projected Ending Inventory (PEI) week by week (Table 1).

Table 1. Example of Safety stock

Parameter	Value
Maximum Daily Usage	1,200 units/day
Average Daily Usage	900 units/day
Maximum Lead Time	7 days
Average Lead Time	5 days

Safety Stock (SS): 40 units
Beginning Inventory (BI): 120 units
Gross Demand: [50, 40, 60, 30, 70, 45]

Week 1

$$MPS_1 = \max(0, SS + D_1 - BI)$$

$$MPS_1 = \max(0{,}40 + 50 - 120) = \max(0, -30) = 0$$

$$EI_1 = BI + MPS_1 - D_1 = 120 + 0 - 50 = 70$$

Interpretation is no production required during week 1 because the initial inventory (120 units) is sufficient to cover the gross demand (50 units) while maintaining the safety stock level (40 units) and projected ending inventory 70 units.

Week 2

$$MPS_2 = \max(0, SS + D_2 - PEI_1)$$

$$MPS_2 = \max(0{,}40 + 40 - 70) = \max(0{,}10) = 10$$

In week 2, production is required since the projected inventory from week 1 (70 units) cannot fully satisfy both the new demand (40 units) and the safety stock target (40 units).

Thus, the model schedules a production of **10 units** to restore the balance.

$$PEI_2 = PEI_1 + MPS_2 - D_2 = 70 + 10 - 40 = 40$$

Projected Ending Inventory (Week 2): 40 units exactly equal to the safety stock threshold.

2) For Gross Demand

These parameters are used to calculate the following data

Beginning Inventory (BI): 120 units

Safety Stock (SS): 40 units

Week 1

The example now considers Gross Demand (GD_1) as the combined requirement of two upcoming periods:

$$GD_1 = 40 + 60 = 100$$

This means the planner is not only covering the immediate demand but grouping expected requirements (e.g., from week 1 and week 2) into a single gross demand value of 100 units.

MPS Calculation

$$MPS_1 = \max(0, GD_1 + SS - BI)$$

$$MPS_1 = \max(0{,}100 + 40 - 120) = \max(0{,}20) = 20$$

To satisfy a gross demand of 100 units and keep the safety stock at 40 units, the available beginning inventory of 120 units is not sufficient; there is a shortfall of 20 units. Therefore, the model schedules an MPS production of 20 units in week 1 to close this gap.

Projected Ending Inventory

$$PEI_1 = BI + MPS_1 - GD_1$$

$$PEI_1 = 120 + 20 - 100 = 40$$

After producing 20 units and satisfying the gross demand of 100 units, the projected ending inventory at the end of week 1 is 40 units, which exactly matches the safety stock level. Conceptually, this logic shows how using gross (aggregated) demand plus safety stock as a target forces the MPS to anticipate future requirements, generating just enough production to end the period at the desired protection level (SS = 40), avoiding both shortage and excessive inventory.

3) For Days on Hand (DOH) with Raw Material and Work in Process

These parameters are used to calculate the following data.
RM On Hand: 5,000 units
Average Daily Usage: 1,000 units/day

$$DOH_{RM} = \frac{5{,}000}{1{,}000} = 5 \text{ days}$$

The plant has enough raw material to support 5 days of production/consumption at the current average usage rate. If no new material is received, the RM stock will last five days before running out. This indicator helps planners understand how exposed they are to supply delays and whether replenishment needs to be triggered.

Work in Process (WIP) Days of Inventory on Hand

- WIP units currently in production: 2,400 units
- Daily Throughput (finished units per day): 600 units/day

$$DOH_{WIP} = \frac{2{,}400}{600} = 4 \text{ days}$$

The current WIP level corresponds to 4 days of output at the existing completion rate. In other words, if no new units enter the line, the ongoing production will keep the system busy for four days. This helps evaluate flow efficiency, congestion, and whether WIP levels are aligned with lead time and capacity targets.

4) For Safety Stock

These parameters are used to calculate the following data.

If demand remains at its maximum daily rate (1,200 units) and suppliers take 7 days to deliver, the total consumption during that period would be 8,400 units. This represents the worst-case scenario where both demand and lead time reach their peaks simultaneously. Under normal operating conditions, with an average daily consumption of 900 units and an average lead time of 5 days the total material requirement would be 4,500 units. This value represents the expected (typical) demand during the replenishment cycle. The calculated Safety Stock of 3,900 units acts as a buffer inventory to protect the system against variability in demand and lead time. In practice, this means the organization should always maintain an additional 3,900 units to ensure uninterrupted operations even under the most adverse conditions.

5) For Projected Ending Inventory

Initial parameters
Beginning Inventory (BI): 200 units
MPS (Master Production Schedule): [0, 0, 0, 0]
Gross Demand: [60, 55, 45, 40] → Total = 200 units
Week 1

$$PEI_1 = BI + MPS_1 - D_1 = 200 + 0 - 60 = 140$$

After satisfying a gross demand of 60 units, the projected ending inventory is 140 units. No production is scheduled, as current stock is sufficient.
Week 2

$$PEI_2 = PEI_1 + MPS_2 - D_2 = 140 + 0 - 55 = 85$$

Inventory continues to decline to 85 units, reflecting ongoing consumption. Still, no production is triggered since stock remains available.
Week 3

$$PEI_3 = PEI_2 + MPS_3 - D_3 = 85 + 0 - 45 = 40$$

By the end of week 3, the projected inventory reaches 40 units, which may represent the safety of the stock level. The system is still operating without replenishment.
Week 4

$$PEI_4 = PEI_3 + MPS_4 - D_4 = 40 + 0 - 40 = 0$$

At the end of week 4, the projected inventory drops to zero, fully depleting the available stock. This marks the end of the planning horizon with total demand perfectly consuming the beginning inventory. This scenario demonstrates a balanced planning horizon, where total demand (200 units) equals the initial inventory (200 units), resulting in no production requirement throughout the period. However, from a managerial perspective, reaching zero ending inventory indicates no buffer capacity, leaving the system vulnerable to variability or unexpected demand. In practice, a small safety stock would be advisable to ensure continuity and avoid potential stock output.

5 Results

The automotive simulator successfully integrates production planning, inventory control, and supplier cost management within an interactive analytical environment. Simulation outcomes reveal that adjustments in daily consumption, on-hand stock, and supplier pricing significantly influence DOH performance, procurement savings, and the frequency of pull-in/push-out alerts. Average values remained within optimal levels, demonstrating balanced stock policies across production scenarios. The cost module effectively identified potential savings by highlighting price differences among suppliers. Overall, the simulator proves valuable for supporting decision-making processes, improving supply-chain responsiveness, cost efficiency, and operational stability in a manufacturing context and was added comparative literature about inputs for this research (See Table 2).

Table 2. Comparative literature about the input on this research.

Author / Application	Practical Application	IoT & Big Data	Predictive ML	Automotive Simulation	Interactive Interface	Cost Analysis
Ivanov et al. (2019)	✔	✔				✔
Turban et al. (2021)		✔				✔
Christopher (2020)	✔					✔
Gutiérrez et al. (2025)	✔	✔	✔	✔	✔	✔

6 Discussion

The automotive simulator successfully integrates production planning, inventory control, and supplier cost management within an interactive analytical environment. Simulation outcomes reveal that adjustments in daily consumption, on-hand stock, and supplier pricing significantly influence DOH performance, procurement savings, and the frequency of pull-in/push-out alerts. Average values remained within optimal levels, demonstrating balanced stock policies across production scenarios. The cost module effectively identified potential savings by highlighting price differences among suppliers. Overall, the simulator proves valuable for supporting decision-making processes, improving supply-chain responsiveness, cost efficiency, and operational stability in a manufacturing context with the main indicators for the organization (See Fig. 2).

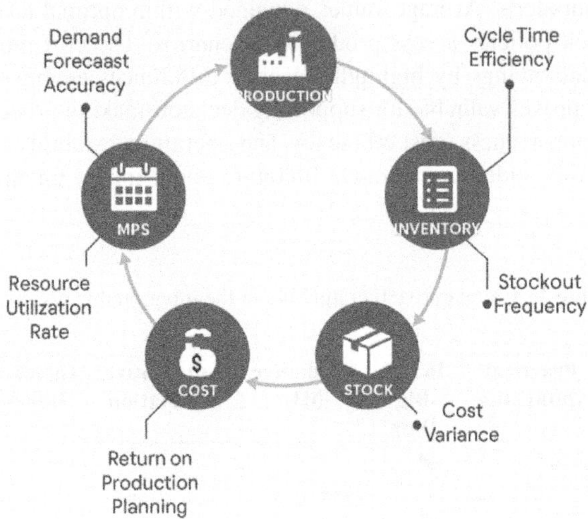

Fig. 2. Circular production cycle with performance indicators.

7 Conclusion

The development of the Interactive Input Optimization Simulator demonstrates how data-driven decision models can significantly enhance production planning, inventory control, and cost management in the automotive supply chain. Through the integration of MPS calculations, projected ending inventory (PEI) tracking, and safety stock estimation, the simulator effectively illustrates the dynamics between production scheduling and demand variability. The weekly scenarios analyzed show that proactive production adjustments maintain optimal inventory levels, prevent shortages, and align operational flow with forecasted demand. The incorporation of DOH metrics into the simulation provides a tangible measure of material coverage and production exposure, allowing planners to visualize supply risks in real time. Similarly, the safety stock model quantifies protection against uncertainty by combining variability in daily usage and lead times. This methodological approach ensures that decision-making is not only reactive to disruptions but also anticipatory, supporting a more stable and efficient supply system. Ultimately, this research validates that integrating quantitative models like MPS, PEI, DOH, and safety stock into a unified digital environment enables companies to achieve higher levels of visibility, responsiveness, and financial efficiency. The proposed framework lays the groundwork for future extensions involving predictive analytics, AI-driven optimization, and digital twin architectures, fostering resilient and sustainable supply.

8 Future Research Lines to Apply

1. Integration of Artificial Intelligence in Production Planning: Applying predictive algorithms and machine learning models to optimize MPS adjustments in real time.
2. Digital Twins for Inventory Management: Developing digital twin architectures to simulate supply and demand variability across production environments.

3. Supplier Evaluation Using Multi-Criteria Decision Models: Implementing AHP, TOPSIS, or fuzzy logic approaches for data-driven supplier ranking and risk mitigation.
4. Sustainability Metrics in Supply Chain Simulations: Integrating carbon footprint, waste reduction, and circular economy indicators into the cost and inventory models.
5. Resilient Supply Chain Optimization under Uncertainty: Extending the simulator with stochastic parameters to analyze disruption scenarios and recovery strategies.
6. Blockchain-Enabled Procurement Tracking: Exploring decentralized ledger systems for transparent monitoring of supplier transactions and performance
7. Human–Machine Collaboration in SCM Decision Systems: Studying how user interfaces and automated recommendations can enhance managerial decision quality and adoption.

References

1. Al-Mahadin, S.N., Gürgün, A.P., Arditi, D.: A digital procurement system for construction projects: a web-based framework for automation and transparency. Autom. Constr. **164**, 105212 (2024). https://doi.org/10.1016/j.autcon.2024.105212
2. Balkan, M., Akyuz, E.: Artificial intelligence and machine learning applications in procurement: a systematic literature review. J. Purch. Supply Manag. **31**(2), 100863 (2025). https://doi.org/10.1016/j.pursup.2025.100863
3. Bittner, E., Nazarian, H., Khan, S.A.: Human-centric and resilient supply chains in the industry 5.0 era. Procedia Manuf. **93**, 211–223 (2024)
4. Demir, K.A., Döven, G., Sezen, B.: Industry 5.0 and human-centric manufacturing: toward collaborative intelligence in production systems. J. Manuf. Syst. **70**, 103–118 (2023)
5. Fares, G., Alshamrani, S., El-Kassar, A.-N.: Supply chain management in the industry 5.0 era: integrating resilience, sustainability, and collaboration through digital transformation. Technol. Forecast. Soc. Change **210**, 123456 (2025). https://doi.org/10.1016/j.techfore.2025.123456
6. Garg, H., Choubey, A.: Hybrid fuzzy-TOPSIS approach for sustainable supplier selection. J. Clean. Prod. **392**, 136285 (2023)
7. Hair, J.F., Hult, G.T.M., Ringle, C.M., Sarstedt, M.: A Primer on Partial Least Squares Structural Equation Modeling (PLS-SEM), 3rd edn. SAGE Publications (2021)
8. Hair, J.F., Hult, G.T.M., Ringle, C.M., Sarstedt, M.: A Primer on Partial Least Squares Structural Equation Modeling (PLS-SEM), 3rd edn. Sage Publications (2022)
9. Ivanov, D., Dolgui, A.: A digital supply chain twin for resilience and sustainability: concept, models, and applications. Int. J. Prod. Res. **61**(7), 2142–2161 (2023)
10. Lamrini, M., Belhadi, A., Benmoussa, R., Rebaï, A.: Distributed-TOPSIS method for large-scale multi-criteria decision-making under big data environment using MapReduce. Expert Syst. Appl. **218**, 119579 (2023). https://doi.org/10.1016/j.eswa.2023.119579
11. Longo, F., Padovano, A., Umbrello, S.: Digital twins and ethical design for sustainable Industry 5.0 systems. Comput. Ind. **149**, 103921 (2023)
12. Ma, J., Li, Z., Zhang, Q.: Digital twin–driven demand-responsive production planning for smart manufacturing systems. Robot. Comput. Integr. Manuf. **86**, 102637 (2024). https://doi.org/10.1016/j.rcim.2024.102637
13. Martini, A.: Human-centered and sustainable artificial intelligence in Industry 5.0 environments. J. Clean. Prod. **438**, 140971 (2024). https://doi.org/10.1016/j.jclepro.2024.140971

14. Nahavandi, S.: Industry 5.0—a human-centric solution. Sustainability **14**(2), 706 (2022)
15. Nazarian, H., Khan, S.A.: Integrating human-centricity, sustainability, and resilience through advanced technologies. Procedia Manuf. **93**, 112–121 (2024)
16. Nicoletti, B., Appolloni, A.: AI foundation models for digital engineering and logistics: toward predictive, integrated supply chains. Comput. Ind. **162**, 104919 (2025). https://doi.org/10.1016/j.compind.2025.104919
17. Prakash, A., Barua, M.K.: Sustainable supplier selection using integrated fuzzy AHP-TOPSIS method. Expert Syst. Appl. **195**, 116547 (2022)
18. Rajabi Asadabadi, M., Tavakkoli-Moghaddam, R., Zavadskas, E.K.: A stratified BWM–TOPSIS model for sustainable supplier selection under uncertainty. J. Clean. Prod. **395**, 136488 (2023). https://doi.org/10.1016/j.jclepro.2023.136488
19. Sarstedt, M., Ringle, C.M., Hair, J.F., Cheah, J.-H.: Advancements in PLS-SEM for predictive modeling in engineering management research. Technol. Forecast. Soc. Change **182**, 121844 (2022)
20. Siciliani, L., Pavanelli, N., Marrone, S.: An AI-based decision support system for public procurement: Leveraging semantic search and natural language processing. Expert Syst. Appl. **228**, 120726 (2023). https://doi.org/10.1016/j.eswa.2023.120726
21. Tarka, P.: Principles for integrating theoretical constructions and measurement models using structural equation modeling (SEM). J. Bus. Res. **146**, 275–286 (2022). https://doi.org/10.1016/j.jbusres.2022.03.045
22. Turban, E., Pollard, C., Wood, G.: Information Technology for Management: Driving Digital Transformation to Increase Local and Global Performance, Growth and Sustainability, 12th edn. Wiley (2021)
23. Venkatesh, R., Kumar, P.: Blockchain-enabled e-procurement for sustainable supply chains: a conceptual framework. Comput. Ind. Eng. **176**, 109029 (2023)
24. Wong, T.C., Cheng, C.H., Zhao, Y.: Gamified supply chain simulation for experiential learning and decision-making in manufacturing education. Comput. Ind. Eng. **190**, 110155 (2024). https://doi.org/10.1016/j.cie.2024.110155
25. Xu, L.D., Wang, J., Kim, S.H.: Artificial intelligence and human collaboration for Industry 5.0 manufacturing. IEEE Trans. Ind. Inform. **19**(4), 5267–5278 (2023)
26. Zhang, Y., Liu, H., Wang, L.: Data preprocessing techniques for intelligent manufacturing systems: a review and future directions. Comput. Ind. Eng. **169**, 108220 (2022)

ECSI 2025

A Multi-objective Decomposition-Based MOPSO with Dynamic Adaptive Penalization for CMOPs

Néstor A. García-Rojas[1], Miguel A. Jiménez-Domínguez[1], Saúl Zapotecas-Martínez[1](✉), Raquel Díaz-Hernández[1], Leopoldo Altamirano-Robles[1], and Bilel Derbel[2]

[1] Instituto Nacional de Astrofísica Óptica y Electrónica, Sta. María Tonantzintla, Puebla 72840, Mexico
{nestor.garcia,miguel.jimenez,szapotecas,raqueld,robles}@inaoep.mx
[2] CNRS, Inria, Centrale Lille, UMR 9189 CRIStAL, Univ. Lille, Lille 59000, France
bilel.derbel@univ-lille.fr

Abstract. This study proposes an algorithm designed to address Constrained Multi-Objective Optimization Problems (CMOPs) within the framework of Multi-Objective Particle Swarm Optimization (MOPSO). The method integrates a decomposition strategy with specialized mechanisms for constraint management. A central component of the approach is an adaptive penalty function, derived from the annealing penalty method, yet reformulated to induce a linear interaction between feasible and infeasible solutions during the search process. As a result of this integration, the capabilities of the dMOPSO algorithm are significantly extended, yielding a novel variant referred to as CdMOPSO-Annealing Penalty (CdMOPSO-AP). The proposed method was rigorously assessed using the CF benchmark suite from the CEC'2009 competition. Comparative analyses, based on convergence and diversity performance indicators, demonstrate that CdMOPSO-AP exhibits competitive efficiency, frequently surpassing four state-of-the-art algorithms considered in the evaluation.

Keywords: Multi-objective constrained optimization · Decomposition-based algorithms · Particle swarm optimization

1 Introduction

In recent years, several enhancements and applications of the Particle Swarm Optimization (PSO) algorithm [14] and its multi-objective version [21] have been developed. This method, which mimics the collective behavior of swarms, enables particles to navigate the search space by adjusting their positions based on individual experience and group knowledge.

Its effectiveness is particularly useful for addressing real-world problems, which often involve constraints and multiple criteria, giving rise to constrained

L. Martínez-Villaseñor et al. (Eds.): MICAI 2025 Workshops, LNAI 16264, pp. 423–435, 2026.
https://doi.org/10.1007/978-3-032-17930-2_30

multi-objective optimization problems (CMOPs). Techniques for handling these constraints, many of which originated for single-objective problems, include rule-based methods, penalty functions, and ε-constraint methods.

An advanced algorithm for highly constrained CMOPs is the feasibility-enhanced PSO (MOFEPSO) [10]. This technique distinguishes between feasible and infeasible particles, guiding the latter through a single "activated constraint" (AC). MOFEPSO ensures compliance with constraints by prohibiting new violations of already satisfied ones and requiring that at least one particle satisfies each constraint.

Cheng *et al.* [4] proposed LOPMOPSO, a hybrid optimizer that combines BOBYQA and PSO to improve convergence and the diversity of non-dominated solutions. It employs a local search and a mutation operator to avoid local optima, handling constraints through an evaluation of the degree of infeasibility.

Long *et al.* [15] proposed a hybrid method that combines PSO with an adaptive constraint-handling technique (ACT) for constrained problems. It employs mutation operators and three adaptive mechanisms that adjust to the population's state to manage the constraints.

Rawhoudine and Bacar [1] proposed a PSO variant that employs local displacements through attractors for multi-objective optimization. It enhances diversity with a square-root distance mechanism in external archives and evaluates its performance on constrained and unconstrained benchmark functions, comparing it with established techniques such as SMPSO, NSGA-II, and SPEA2.

Guo *et al.* [9] proposed a hybrid PSO-DE algorithm for constrained optimization that employs feasibility rules. The PSO updates the top 50% of individuals with the highest constraint violations, while the Differential Evolution (DE) algorithm refines the individual optimal positions.

Nshimirimana *et al.* [20] proposed NF-MOPSO, a multi-objective PSO algorithm that employs constant control parameters, avoiding fine-tuning. It improves convergence to the Pareto front and solution diversity by using fixed coefficients, combined with Gaussian mutation and a penalty function to handle constraints.

Noel [19] presented GPSO, a hybrid algorithm that combines PSO with gradient-based local search to improve convergence speed and accuracy. It uses PSO for global exploration and the gradient method for precise local search, avoiding issues with inertia weights and constriction coefficients.

Zapotecas and Coello [24] introduced dMOPSO, a decomposition-based multi-objective particle swarm optimization algorithm for continuous, unconstrained optimization problems. The algorithm uses a global-best solution set to guide particle position updates and incorporates a memory reinitialization mechanism to preserve and enhance population diversity.

García-Rojas *et al.* [8] introduced CdMOPSO, which is an enhancement of the dMOPSO algorithm designed for CMOPs. This method of multi-objective particle swarm optimization utilizes a decomposition framework and incorporates a dynamically modified penalty function to manage constraints.

In this paper, we propose a modification of the dMOPSO algorithm for CMOPs. The proposed algorithm, called CdMOPSO-AP, employs a dynamic penalty scheme based on the method of Jiménez-Domínguez *et al.* [13], which adjusts the penalties to exhibit linear behavior during the search. The effectiveness of the scheme is evaluated using standardized benchmark functions, showing competitive results compared to other algorithms in the literature.

This document is structured as follows: Sect. 2 presents the fundamental concepts. Section 3 details the proposed methodology integrated into dMOPSO. Section 4 describes the experimental design. Section 5 discusses the obtained results. Finally, Sect. 6 concludes with the findings and future directions.

2 General Background

2.1 Constrained Multi-objective Optimization Problem

In a general context, assuming a minimization framework for all objectives, a constrained multi-objective optimization problem (CMOP) can be rigorously expressed as follows:

$$\begin{aligned} \underset{\mathbf{x} \in \mathbb{R}^n}{\text{minimize:}} \quad & \mathbf{F}(\mathbf{x}) = (f_1(\mathbf{x}), \ldots, f_M(\mathbf{x}))^T \\ \text{subject to} \quad & g_i(\mathbf{x}) \leq 0, \ \forall\, i \in \{1, \ldots, p\} \\ & h_j(\mathbf{x}) = 0, \ \forall\, j \in \{1, \ldots, q\} \end{aligned} \tag{1}$$

In this context, $\mathbf{F}$ represents a vector containing M objective functions, while g_i and $h_j : \mathbb{R}^n \rightarrow \mathbb{R}$ denote the inequality and equality constraints, respectively, which together delineate the feasible search space $\Omega \subset \mathbb{R}^n$. A candidate solution $\mathbf{x} \in \Omega$ is deemed feasible if it adheres to all constraints outlined in Eq. (1); otherwise, it is classified as infeasible. The collection of all feasible solutions forms the feasible region, mathematically represented as:

$$\mathcal{F} = \{\mathbf{x} \in \Omega \subseteq \mathbb{R}^n \mid g_i(\mathbf{x}) \leq 0, h_j(\mathbf{x}) = 0\} \tag{2}$$

for $i = 1, \ldots, p$ and $j = 1, \ldots, q$.

In some cases, it may be advantageous to express all constraints as inequalities by reformulating equality conditions to the form $|h_j(\mathbf{x})| - \varepsilon \leq 0$, $\forall j \in \{1, \ldots, q\}$, where ε is a small positive real number that indicates the tolerance level. To clarify the concept of optimality being addressed, we present the following definitions [17].

Definition 1 (Dominance Relation). *In the context of a multi-objective optimization problem with M objectives, a solution $\mathbf{x} \in \Omega$ is considered to dominate another solution $\mathbf{y} \in \Omega$ (denoted as $\mathbf{x} \prec \mathbf{y}$) if and only if:* 1) *$f_i(\mathbf{x}) \leq f_i(\mathbf{y})$ for every $i = 1, \ldots, M$, and* 2) *$f_j(\mathbf{x}) < f_j(\mathbf{y})$ for at least one index $j \in \{1, \ldots, M\}$.*

Definition 2 (Pareto Optimal Solution). *A solution $\mathbf{x}^\star$ is deemed Pareto optimal if:* 1) *It is part of the search space ($\mathbf{x}^\star \in \Omega$), and* 2) *No other solution $\mathbf{y} \in \Omega$ exists that can dominate $\mathbf{x}^\star$.*

Definition 3 (Pareto Set and Front). *The Pareto Set ($\mathcal{PS}$) encompasses all Pareto optimal solutions within Ω: $\mathcal{PS} = \{\mathbf{x} \in \Omega \mid \text{xisaParetooptimal solution}\}$. The Pareto Front ($\mathcal{PF}$) represents the image of the Pareto Set in the objective space: $\mathcal{PF} = \{\mathbf{F}(\mathbf{x}) \mid \mathbf{x} \in \mathcal{PS}\}$.*

2.2 Decomposing a Multi-objective Optimization Problem

The decomposition approach in multi-objective optimization facilitates the tackling of complex problems by breaking them down into a series of more manageable subproblems. Specifically, scalarization methods allow combining several objective functions into a single-objective framework [7,18], thereby dividing the original problem into subproblems that can be solved independently or in a coordinated fashion. Techniques such as the Weighted Sum and Penalty Boundary Intersection (PBI) have proven effective [25,26]. Among these scalarization techniques, the Chebyshev method [3] stands out due to its widespread application, and it is the method employed in this study. This technique reformulates the objective vector $\mathbf{F}$ into a scalar optimization problem, represented as:

$$\begin{aligned} \text{minimize: } g^{tch}(\mathbf{x}|\mathbf{w},\mathbf{z}) = \max_{1 \le j \le M} \{w_j |f_j(\mathbf{x}) - z_j|\} \\ s.t\ \mathbf{x} \in \Omega \end{aligned} \tag{3}$$

where Ω represents the feasible region, and $\mathbf{z} = (z_1, \ldots, z_k)^T$, with each component defined as $z_j = \min\{f_j(\mathbf{x}) \mid \mathbf{x} \in \Omega\}$ for $j = 1, \ldots, k$. Additionally, $\mathbf{w} = (w_1, \ldots, w_k)^T$ is a weight vector, constrained such that $w_j \ge 0$ for all $j = 1, \ldots, k$ and $\sum_{j=1}^{k} w_j = 1$.

For each Pareto optimal solution $\mathbf{x}$, there exists a corresponding weight vector λ such that $\mathbf{x}$ serves as the optimal solution to Eq. (3), which aligns with a Pareto optimal solution of Eq. (1). Therefore, by solving a set of subproblems through the Chebyshev method using appropriately assigned weight vectors, it is feasible to produce a high-quality approximation of the Pareto front and the Pareto set.

2.3 Constraint Violation Degree

To impose penalties on a candidate solution, it is essential to measure the extent of constraint violations. For a solution $\mathbf{x} \in \Omega$, the total violation can be calculated by summing the individual constraint violations as follows:

$$V(\mathbf{x}) = \sum_{i=1}^{p} \max\{0, g_i(\mathbf{x})\}^{\beta} \tag{4}$$

where β is a positive constant. A solution is deemed feasible if $V(\mathbf{x}) = 0$, and classified as infeasible otherwise. In this study, all constraints are defined in the form $g_i(\mathbf{x}) \le 0$ for $i \in \{1, \ldots, p\}$, with any equality constraints transformed into corresponding inequality forms.

2.4 dMOPSO

In existing research, the Decomposition-based Multi-Objective Particle Swarm Optimizer (dMOPSO) [24] operates within a framework akin to the well-known multi-objective evolutionary algorithm based on decomposition (MOEA/D) [26]. This approach requires a well-distributed collection of weight vectors denoted as $\mathbf{w} = \{\mathbf{w}^1, \ldots, \mathbf{w}^N\}$. For this investigation, the Chebyshev scalarization technique is employed as the chosen decomposition method.

To begin, N candidate solutions, known as particles, are randomly created, forming the set $P = \{\mathbf{x}^1, \ldots, \mathbf{x}^N\}$. Each particle is assigned an initial velocity $\mathbf{v}^i$ and an age a_i, both initialized to zero. The primary objective for each particle is to minimize a specific subproblem associated with its weight vector $\mathbf{w}^i$, focusing on the scalarized single-objective problem represented as $g(\mathbf{x}^i|\mathbf{w}^i, z^\star)$. The personal best position $\mathbf{x}^i_{pb}$ is initially set to the particle's starting location, i.e., $\mathbf{x}^i_{pb} = \mathbf{x}^i$.

During each iteration, the historical trajectories of the particles are examined to pinpoint the best solutions for every subproblem, leading to the formation of the global best set G_{best}. This set is refreshed in each iteration and employs elitism by retaining the top global solutions from both existing and newly generated particle positions.

After establishing G_{best}, the velocity and position of each particle are adjusted accordingly. The algorithm treats all solutions in G_{best} as equally viable and randomly selects one for calculating particle velocity.

To enhance diversity within the swarm, a particle's age increments if it fails to improve its personal best. Should a particle's age surpass a predetermined limit, it undergoes reinitialization, which includes resetting its velocity and personal best. The dMOPSO effectively guides particles toward the global best solutions by using a Gaussian distribution based on the current personal best and the chosen global best particle.

3 Proposed Approach

The proposed CdMOPSO-AP method incorporates a penalty term within the dMOPSO framework [24] to effectively manage problem constraints. This adaptive penalty mechanism can be seamlessly extended to other decomposition-based multi-objective evolutionary algorithms (MOEAs). In the following, we present the fundamental procedures of the method, which are implicitly applied during the evaluation of candidate solutions within the survival selection process. The overall architecture of CdMOPSO-AP is summarized in Algorithm 1.

3.1 Normalized Constraint Violation Degree

To address the issue of varying scales among constraints, all constraints are normalized, allowing for the effective assessment of the extent of violation for a particular solution. The constraint violation of a solution $\mathbf{x}$ is defined as shown in Eq. (4), with all constraints expressed as $g_j(\mathbf{x}) \leq 0$ for $j \in \{1, \ldots, p\}$. The normalized constraint violation for a solution $\mathbf{x} \in \mathbb{R}^n$ is calculated as follows:

$$V_n(\mathbf{x}) = \sum_{j=1}^{p} \phi_j^\beta \tag{5}$$

where β is a positive constant and ϕ_j is defined by:

$$\phi_j = \begin{cases} 0 & \text{if } g_j^{\max} = 0 \\ \max\left\{0, \frac{g_j(\mathbf{x})}{g_j^{\max}}\right\} & \text{otherwise} \end{cases} \tag{6}$$

Here, $g_j^{\max}$ denotes the highest value of the j-th constraint across the current population P, calculated as $g_j^{\max} = \max_{\mathbf{q} \in P}\{0, g_j(\mathbf{q})\}$. It is important to note that if $g_j^{\max} = 0$, then all solutions in P satisfy the j-th constraint.

3.2 Penalty Scheme

In this research, a penalty function inspired by the works of Jiménez-Domínguez *et al.* [13] and Michalewicz and Attia [16] is utilized. For constraints represented as $g_l(\mathbf{x}) \leq 0$ $(l = 1, \ldots, q)$, the j-th objective function is reformulated as follows:

$$f_j^p(\mathbf{x}, t) = f_j(\mathbf{x}) + \varphi(t) V_n(\mathbf{x}) \tag{7}$$

where $V_n(\mathbf{x})$ denotes the normalized constraint violation from Eq. (5). The penalty factor $\varphi(t)$ at generation t is defined as:

$$\varphi(t) = \alpha(1 - \tau(t)) \tag{8}$$

with

$$\tau(t) = 1 - \left(\frac{t}{G_{\max}}\right)^\gamma \tag{9}$$

where α is a scaling parameter, $\tau(t)$ indicates the temperature at generation t, $G_{\max}$ is the total number of generations, and γ regulates the decay rate of the temperature.

Within the dMOPSO framework, the scalarization function is formulated as:

$$\begin{aligned} \text{minimize: } g^{ptch}(\mathbf{x}|\mathbf{w}, \mathbf{z}) &= \max_{1 \leq j \leq M} \{w_j |f_j^p(\mathbf{x}) - z_j|\} \\ \text{s.t. } \mathbf{x} &\in \Omega \end{aligned} \tag{10}$$

where $f_j^p(\mathbf{x})$ represents the objective function adjusted to deal with constraints. This penalty strategy guides the algorithm to systematically explore both the feasible and infeasible regions of the search space.

Algorithm 1: CdMOPSO-AP

Input :
N : Number of decomposition problems;
$\mathbf{w}$: Set of weight vectors $\{w^1, \dots, w^N\}$;
$G_{\max}$: Maximum number of iterations;
Output:
G_{best} : final swarm of particles found by CdMOPSO-AP;

1 Initialize a swarm of N particles $P = \{\mathbf{x}^1, \dots, \mathbf{x}^n\}$;
2 $\mathbf{z} = (+\infty, \dots, +\infty)^T$;
3 $t = 0$;
4 **foreach** $i \in \{1, \dots, N\}$ **do**
5 $\quad F^i = (f_1^p(\mathbf{x}^i, t), f_2^p(\mathbf{x}^i, t), \dots, f_M^p(\mathbf{x}^i, t))^T$;
6 $\quad \mathbf{v}^i = 0$, $\mathbf{x}_{pb}^i = \mathbf{x}^i$, and $a^i = 0$;
7 $\quad$ **if** $f_j^p(\mathbf{x}^i) < z_j$ **then** $z_j = f_j^p(\mathbf{x}^i), \forall j \in \{1, \dots, M\}$;
8 $G_{best} = P$;
9 $t = 1$;
10 **while** $t < G_{max}$ **do**
11 $\quad$ Determine the Normalized Constraint Violation Degree for the complete population P by applying Equation (5);
12 $\quad$ **foreach** $i \in \{1, \dots, N\}$ **do**
13 $\quad\quad$ Select randomly a solution g_{best}^i from G_{best} such that: $\mathbf{x}^i \neq g_{best}^i$;
14 $\quad\quad$ **if** $a^i < T_a$ **then**
15 $\quad\quad\quad \mathbf{v}^i = w\mathbf{v}^i + c_1 r_1(\mathbf{x}_{pb}^i - \mathbf{x}^i) + c_2 r_2(g_{best}^i - \mathbf{x}^i)$;
16 $\quad\quad\quad \mathbf{x}^i = \mathbf{x}^i + \mathbf{v}^i$;
17 $\quad\quad$ **else**
18 $\quad\quad\quad \mathbf{x}_j^i = N((g_{best,j}^i - \mathbf{x}_{pb,j}^i)/2, |g_{best,j}^i - \mathbf{x}_{pb,j}^i|)$;
19 $\quad\quad\quad \mathbf{v}^i = 0$, $\mathbf{x}_{pb}^i = \mathbf{x}^i$, $a^i = 0$;
20 $\quad\quad x_j^i = \begin{cases} x_j^L, & \text{if } x_j^i < x_j^L \\ x_j^U, & \text{if } x_j^i > x_j^U \end{cases}, \; j = 1, \dots, n$;
21 $\quad\quad \mathbf{v}_j^i = -\gamma \mathbf{v}_j^i$, $j = 1, \dots, n$;
22 $\quad\quad F^i = (f_1^p(\mathbf{x}^i, t), f_2^p(\mathbf{x}^i, t), \dots, f_M^p(\mathbf{x}^i, t))^T$;
23 $\quad\quad$ **if** $f_j^p(\mathbf{x}^i) < z_j$ **then** $z_j = f_j^p(\mathbf{x}^i), \forall j \in \{1, \dots, M\}$;
24 $\quad\quad$ **if** $g^{ptch}(\mathbf{x}^i|\mathbf{w}^i, \mathbf{z}) < g^{ptch}(\mathbf{x}_{pb}^i|\mathbf{w}^i, \mathbf{z})$ *or* $a^i = 0$ **then**
25 $\quad\quad\quad \mathbf{x}_{pb}^i = \mathbf{x}^i$, $a^i = 0$;
26 $\quad\quad$ **else**
27 $\quad\quad\quad a^i = a^i + 1$;
28 $\quad T = P \cup G_{best}$;
29 $\quad$ **foreach** $i \in \{1, \dots, N\}$ **do**
30 $\quad\quad \mathbf{g}^i = \left\{\mathbf{x} | \min_{\mathbf{x} \in T} g^{te}(\mathbf{x}|\mathbf{w}^i, \mathbf{z})\right\}$, where $\mathbf{w}^i \in \mathbf{w}$;
31 $\quad\quad T = T \setminus \{\mathbf{x}\}$;
32 $\quad\quad G_{best} = \{\mathbf{g}^1, \dots, \mathbf{g}^N\}$;
33 $\quad t = t + 1$;
34 **return** G_{best};

4 Experimental Study

4.1 Test Problems

The performance of the proposed CdMOPSO-AP is rigorously evaluated against other decomposition-based algorithms that incorporate penalty functions for handling CMOPs. For this purpose, we employ the set of 10 CMOP benchmark problems introduced by Zhang *et al.* [27], which are widely recognized as standard test instances within the Evolutionary Multiobjective Optimization community, specifically from the CEC 2009 Special Session and Competition. Our analysis focuses on problems CF1 through CF10, adhering to the original problem specifications, with all instances defined over ten decision variables. This selection ensures a consistent and challenging testbed, enabling a systematic comparison of algorithmic performance in terms of convergence, diversity, and constraint-handling capability.

4.2 Performance Indicators

To rigorously assess the performance of the multi-objective evolutionary algorithms (MOEAs) included in our comparative study, the following performance indicators were employed:

Inverted Generational Distance Plus. The inverted generational distance plus ($\mathcal{IGD}^{+}$) proposed by Ishibuchi *et al.* [11] serves to evaluate the proximity of a collection of approximate solutions to the actual Pareto front (the set of Pareto optimal solutions). This measure is defined by the following equation:

$$\mathcal{IGD}^{+}(A) = \frac{1}{|Z|}\left(\sum_{i=1}^{|Z|} {d_i^{+}}^{2}\right)^{1/2} \tag{11}$$

where $d_i^{+} = \max\{a_i - z_i, 0\}$ denotes the adjusted distance from z_i to its closest reference point in A, corresponding to the value a_i.

Normalized Hypervolume. The normalized hypervolume metric, first established by Zitzler [28], is highly regarded as a robust measure for assessing the effectiveness of multi-objective optimization algorithms. One of the primary benefits of this metric is its alignment with the principle of Pareto optimality, enabling it to evaluate both how solutions converge to the actual Pareto front and their spread across it. The normalized hypervolume metric for a set of objective vectors S captures the volume of the space dominated by S, constrained by the reference vectors $\mathbf{u}$ and $\mathbf{r}$. It is formally expressed as follows:

$$\mathcal{H}_n(S, \mathbf{u}, \mathbf{r}) = \frac{\mathcal{H}(S, \mathbf{r})}{\prod_{i=1}^{M} |r_i - u_i|} \tag{12}$$

In the above equation, $\mathcal{H}(S, \mathbf{r}) = \mathcal{L}\left(\mathbf{q} \in \mathbb{R}^M | \exists \mathbf{p} \in S : \mathbf{p} \preceq \mathbf{q} \text{ and } \mathbf{q} \preceq \mathbf{r}\right)$, where $\mathcal{L}(\cdot)$ denotes the Lebesgue measure, and M represents the number of objective functions in the associated MOP.

4.3 Experimental Setup

In this research, a systematic evaluation was conducted to compare the effectiveness of GPSOM [19], NSGA-II [5], NSGA-III [6], and CMOEA/D [12] against the newly proposed CdMOPSO-AP algorithm. To achieve a fair and consistent assessment, weight vectors were generated utilizing the simplex lattice design [22], with the population size N adjusted using the parameter H. The weight vectors $\mathbf{w} = w^1, \ldots, w^N$ were formulated such that each component

w_j^i (for $i = 1, \ldots, N$ and $j = 1, \ldots, M$) selected values from the discrete set $0/H, \ldots, H/H$. For problems involving two objectives, H was assigned a value of 99, generating 100 weight vectors, whereas for three-objective problems, H was set to 13, producing 210 weight vectors. Each CMOP was tested over 30 independent runs for each algorithm, maintaining a population size of $N = 100$ for two-objective scenarios and $N = 210$ for three-objective scenarios. A maximum of $G_{\max} = 2,000$ generations was permitted, leading to a total of 200,000 evaluations for bi-objective problems and 420,000 evaluations for three-objective problems. The parameters for the comparative MOEAs were configured based on the guidelines provided by their original authors. For the CdMOPSO-AP algorithm, parameter values were set to $\beta = 2$, $\gamma = 1$, and $\alpha = 1 \times 10^3$, where β influences the handling of constraint violations and γ manages the penalization strategy, constrained to a linear format.

5 Analysis of Results

The performance of the proposed approach and the compared MOEA algorithms was evaluated by applying two performance indicators $\mathcal{H}_n$ and $\mathcal{IGD}^+$ to the obtained reference Pareto fronts. Table 1 shows the average values and their corresponding standard deviations (in parentheses) calculated over 30 runs for each algorithm, with the best average values for each problem highlighted in bold.

To establish statistical differences, the non-parametric Mann-Whitney-Wilcoxon test [23] with a significance level of 0.05 was used, along with the Bonferroni correction [2]. An algorithm that statistically outperformed the other four on a given problem and indicator was considered the best, marked with an underline. The proposed approach (CdMOPSO-AP) was compared with GPSOM, NSGA-II, NSGA-III, and CMOEA/D.

The quantitative evaluation in Table 1, based on the $\mathcal{H}_n$ and $\mathcal{IGD}^+$ indicators, shows a competitive landscape. CdMOPSO-AP outperformed its competitors on CF1, CF4, CF8, CF9, and CF10 in terms of $\mathcal{H}_n$ and $\mathcal{IGD}^+$; NSGA-III performed best on CF2 and CF6, and NSGA-II on CF3, CF5, and CF7.

It is noteworthy that even in problems where it was not the best (CF5, CF7), CdMOPSO-AP performed very close to the leaders, showing solid and competitive results overall, as visually corroborated by Fig. 1.

This analysis suggests that CdMOPSO-AP is an effective method for constrained optimization problems, producing feasible solutions that approximate the true Pareto front. However, future research, detailed in the following section, is required to further explore these findings.

Table 1. Table of results obtained by the proposed CdMOPSO and the adopted MOEAs

	$\mathcal{IGD}^+$					$\mathcal{H}$n				
CF	CdMOPSO-AP	GPSOM	NSGAII	NSGAIII	CMOEA/D	CdMOPSO-AP	GPSOM	NSGAII	NSGAIII	CMOEA/D
1	**1.26E-02** (0.00188)	1.54E-01 (0.03698)	8.33E-02 (0.00637)	8.75E-02 (0.00746)	1.02E-01 (0.01035)	**5.51E-01** (0.00228)	3.68E-01 (0.04297)	4.58E-01 (0.0084)	4.54E-01 (0.00957)	4.35E-01 (0.01257)
2	2.03E-01 (0.00046)	2.83E-01 (0.06097)	7.93E-02 (0.03021)	**6.96E-02** (0.01837)	1.14E-01 (0.04327)	4.71E-01 (0.00108)	3.23E-01 (0.05758)	5.55E-01 (0.03602)	**5.69E-01** (0.02791)	5.17E-01 (0.04574)
3	7.01E-01 (0.15494)	8.49E+00 (2.41067)	**3.79E-01** (0.08363)	4.15E-01 (0.07947)	5.16E-01 (0.09236)	1.26E-02 (0.01538)	0.00E+00 (0)	**7.67E-02** (0.04689)	5.84E-02 (0.03713)	2.15E-02 (0.02882)
4	**1.08E-01** (0.06251)	3.13E-01 (0.06863)	1.29E-01 (0.03268)	1.10E-01 (0.02149)	1.73E-01 (0.06992)	**3.77E-01** (0.05684)	9.25E-02 (0.03057)	3.45E-01 (0.04706)	3.72E-01 (0.02865)	3.06E-01 (0.06175)
5	2.93E-01 (0.05233)	9.50E+00 (2.18411)	**2.77E-01** (0.0787)	3.19E-01 (0.09062)	3.72E-01 (0.10613)	2.21E-01 (0.04629)	0.00E+00 (0)	**2.30E-01** (0.05843)	1.89E-01 (0.07404)	1.41E-01 (0.07537)
6	1.02E-01 (0.01592)	3.74E-01 (0.11981)	9.12E-02 (0.0372)	**8.74E-02** (0.03051)	1.24E-01 (0.04703)	5.84E-01 (0.01491)	1.61E-01 (0.04634)	5.91E-01 (0.0331)	**5.93E-01** (0.02664)	5.49E-01 (0.05076)
7	2.40E-01 (0.03480)	8.16E+00 (1.96907)	**2.18E-01** (0.08328)	2.38E-01 (0.14899)	3.40E-01 (0.10815)	3.57E-01 (0.04222)	0.00E+00 (0)	**4.08E-01** (0.08057)	4.00E-01 (0.12192)	2.98E-01 (0.08407)
8	**1.28E-01** (0.08781)	1.10E+01 (4.12048)	9.06E+00 (16.89043)	7.08E+00 (15.50078)	1.14E+01 (20.52736)	**3.75E-01** (0.07306)	0.00E+00 (0)	9.80E-02 (0.06229)	1.07E-01 (0.05973)	1.16E-01 (0.06873)
9	**8.05E-02** (0.00264)	5.35E-01 (0.2495)	1.65E-01 (0.02134)	1.81E-01 (0.02071)	1.81E-01 (0.05548)	**4.48E-01** (0.00659)	5.94E-02 (0.05303)	3.07E-01 (0.02701)	2.96E-01 (0.02422)	3.05E-01 (0.02674)
10	**5.42E-01** (0.13060)	1.84E+01 (3.8344)	4.61E+01 (17.57067)	4.09E+01 (17.366)	4.56E+01 (16.71656)	**1.97E-02** (0.03031)	0.00E+00 (0)	0.00E+00 (0)	0.00E+00 (0)	2.14E-03 (0.01174)

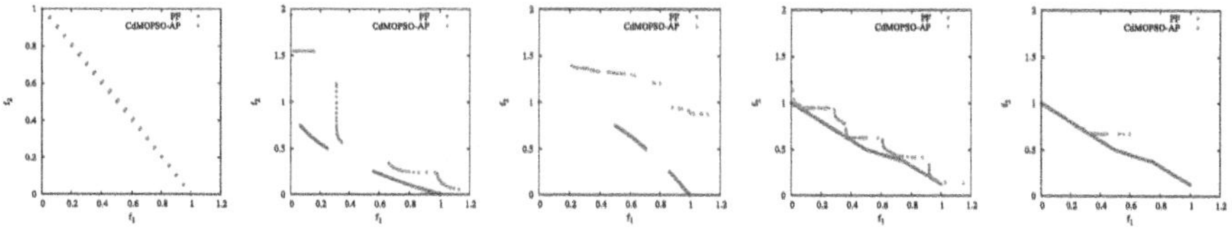

(a) CF1 (b) CF2 (c) CF3 (d) CF4 (e) CF5

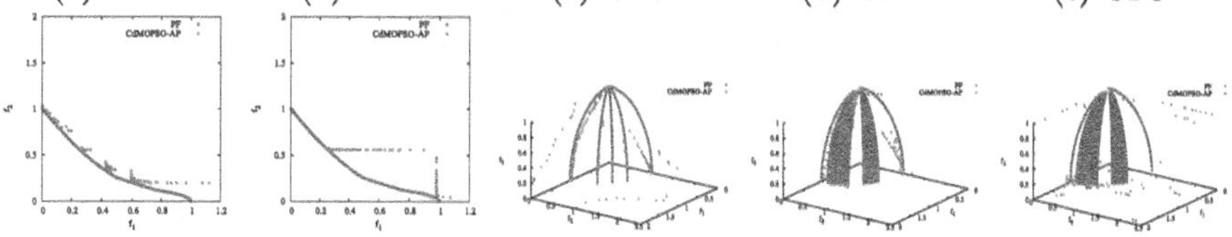

(f) CF6 (g) CF7 (h) CF8 (i) CF9 (j) CF10

Fig. 1. Pareto front approximation obtained by the proposed CdMOPSO-AP in CF1—CF10 test problems.

6 Conclusions

This investigation introduced a new algorithm named CdMOPSO-AP, based on the dMOPSO algorithm and designed to address constrained multi-objective optimization problems. This proposal incorporates an adaptive penalty mechanism, thereby facilitating flexible exploration of the search space through progressive variation in selection pressure on feasible solutions. Although this technique has been implemented within the framework of CdMOPSO-AP, its design allows for easy adaptation to other decomposition-based multi-objective evolutionary algorithms. The experimental results demonstrate that CdMOPSO-AP is highly competitive with other multi-objective evolutionary algorithms (GPSOM, NSGA-II, NSGA-III, and CMOEA/D) on the considered test suites. However, to draw more generalizable conclusions about its performance, it is necessary to evaluate the algorithm on a broader spectrum of optimization problems.

As part of future research, it is planned to deepen the analysis of the proposed penalty function by using indicators that allow for a more detailed characterization of the population's feasibility throughout the search process, such as the evolution of the distance of solutions to the feasible region. A sensitivity analysis will also be conducted to assess the impact of the parameters beta, gamma, and alpha. Likewise, it is projected to evaluate the algorithm's performance on more recent benchmarks and real-world problems, and to compare it with state-of-the-art optimization methods, which constitutes a promising line of research.

Acknowledgments. Néstor A. García-Rojas and Miguel A. Jímenez-Domínguez acknowledge support from SECIHTI and INAOE for their support in pursuing graduate studies for Ph.D. programs in Computational Sciences and Space Science and Technology, respectively. Saúl Zapotecas-Martínez gratefully acknowledges support from the SECIHTI project CBF-2025-I-3114 (Ciencia Básica y de Frontera 2025).

References

1. Bacar, A.H., et al.: A new multiobjective particle swarm optimization using local displacement and local guides. Open J. Optim. **13**(2), 31–49 (2024)
2. Bonferroni, C.E.: Teoria statistica delle classi e calcolo delle probabilita. Pubblicazioni del R Istituto Superiore di Scienze Economiche e Commerciali di Firenze **8**, 3–62 (1936)
3. Bowman, V.J.: On the relationship of the tchebycheff norm and the efficient frontier of multiple-criteria objectives. In: Thiriez, H., Zionts, S. (eds.) Multiple Criteria Decision Making, pp. 76–86. Springer, Berlin Heidelberg, Berlin, Heidelberg (1976). https://doi.org/10.1007/978-3-642-87563-2_5
4. Cheng, S., Zhan, H., Shu, Z.: An innovative hybrid multi-objective particle swarm optimization with or without constraints handling. Appl. Soft Comput. **47**, 370–388 (2016)
5. Deb, K., Pratap, A., Agarwal, S., Meyarivan, T.: A fast and elitist multiobjective genetic algorithm: Nsga-ii. IEEE Trans. Evol. Comput. **6**(2), 182–197 (2002)
6. Deb, K., Jain, H.: An evolutionary many-objective optimization algorithm using reference-point-based nondominated sorting approach, part i: Solving problems with box constraints. IEEE Trans. Evol. Comput. **18**(4), 577–601 (2014)
7. Ehrgott, M.: Multicriteria Optimization. Springer-Verlag, Berlin, Heidelberg (2005)
8. García-Rojas, N.A., Jiménez-Domínguez, M.A., Zapotecas-Martínez, S., Díaz-Hernández, R., Altamirano-Robles, L., Derbel, B.: Constrained multi-objective optimization with dmopso: An adaptive penalty approach. In: 2025 IEEE Conference on Artificial Intelligence (CAI). pp. 1280–1285 (2025)

9. Guo, E., Gao, Y., Hu, C., Zhang, J.: A hybrid pso-de intelligent algorithm for solving constrained optimization problems based on feasibility rules. Mathematics **11**(3) (2023)
10. Hasanoglu, M.S., Dolen, M.: Multi-objective feasibility enhanced particle swarm optimization. Eng. Optim. **50**(12), 2013–2037 (2018)
11. Ishibuchi, H., Masuda, H., Tanigaki, Y., Nojima, Y.: Modified distance calculation in generational distance and inverted generational distance. In: Gaspar-Cunha, A., Henggeler Antunes, C., Coello, C. (eds.) International conference on evolutionary multi-criterion optimization. pp. 110–125. Springer (2015). https://doi.org/10.1007/978-3-319-15892-1_8
12. Jain, H., Deb, K.: An evolutionary many-objective optimization algorithm using reference-point based nondominated sorting approach, part ii: Handling constraints and extending to an adaptive approach. IEEE Trans. Evol. Comput. **18**(4), 602–622 (2014)
13. Jiménez-Domínguez, M.A., García-Rojas, N.A., Zapotecas-Martínez, S., Díaz-Hernández, R., Altamirano-Robles, L., Derbel, B.: Towards a penalty annealing approach in moea/d for constrained multi-objective optimization. In: Proceedings of the Genetic and Evolutionary Computation Conference Companion. p. 1927–1934. GECCO '25 Companion, Association for Computing Machinery, New York, NY, USA (2025)
14. Kennedy, J., Eberhart, R.C.: Swarm intelligence. Morgan Kaufmann Publishers Inc., San Francisco, CA, USA (2001)
15. Long, W., Cai, S., Jiao, J., Zhang, W.: A hybrid constrained optimization approach coupling pso and adaptive constraint-handling technique. WSEAS Trans. Circ. Sys. **15**, 55–63 (2016)
16. Michalewicz, Z., Attia, N.: Evolutionary optimization of constrained problems. In: Proceedings of the 3rd Annual Conference on Evolutionary Programming. pp. 98–108. World Scientific, San Diego, California, USA (1994)
17. Miettinen, K., Neittaanmäki, P., Mäkelä, M.M., Périaux, J. (eds.): Evolutionary algorithms in engineering and computer science. John Wiley & Sons (1999)
18. Miettinen, K.: Nonlinear Multiobjective Optimization, International Series in Operations Research & Management Science, vol. 12. Springer, New York, NY (1998). https://doi.org/10.1007/978-1-4615-5563-6
19. Noel, M.M.: A new gradient based particle swarm optimization algorithm for accurate computation of global minimum. Appl. Soft Comput. **12**(1), 353–359 (2012)
20. Nshimirimana, R., Abraham, A., Nothnagel, G.: A multi-objective particle swarm for constraint and unconstrained problems. Neural Comput. Appl. **33**(17), 11355–11385 (2021). https://doi.org/10.1007/s00521-020-05555-6
21. Reyes-Sierra, M., Coello, C.A.C.: Multi-objective particle swarm optimizers: A survey of the state-of-the-art. Int. J. Comput. Intell. Res. **2**, 287–308 (2006)
22. Scheffé, H.: Experiments with mixtures. J. Royal Statist. Soc.: Series B (Methodol.) **20**(2), 344–360 (1958)
23. Wilcoxon, F.: Individual comparisons by ranking methods. Biom. Bull. **1**(6), 80–83 (1945)
24. Zapotecas Martínez, S., Coello Coello, C.A.: A multi-objective particle swarm optimizer based on decomposition. In: Proceedings of the 13th Annual Conference on Genetic and Evolutionary Computation. p. 69–76. GECCO '11, Association for Computing Machinery, New York, NY, USA (2011)

25. Zapotecas Martínez, S., Coello Coello, C.A.: A multi-objective particle swarm optimizer based on decomposition. In: Proceedings of the 13th Annual Conference on Genetic and Evolutionary Computation. p. 69–76. GECCO '11, Association for Computing Machinery, New York, NY, USA (2011)
26. Zhang, Q., Li, H.: Moea/d: A multiobjective evolutionary algorithm based on decomposition. IEEE Trans. Evol. Comput. **11**(6), 712–731 (2007)
27. Zhang, Q., Zhou, A., Zhao, S., Suganthan, P., Liu, W., Tiwari, S.: Multiobjective optimization test instances for the cec 2009 special session and competition. university of essex, colchester, uk and nanyang technological university. Multiobjective Optimization Test Instances for the CEC 2009 Special Session and Competition pp. 1–30 (2008)
28. Zitzler, E., Thiele, L.: Multiobjective Optimization Using Evolutionary Algorithms—A Comparative Study. In: Eiben, A.E. (ed.) Parallel Problem Solving from Nature V. pp. 292–301. Springer-Verlag (1998). https://doi.org/10.1007/bfb0056872

Enhanced Index Tracking: A Comparison of Multi-objective Evolutionary Approaches

Julián A. Díaz-Ayón[1(✉)], Saúl Zapotecas-Martínez[1], and Julio C. Pérez-Sansalvador[1,2]

[1] Instituto Nacional de Astrofísica, Óptica y Electrónica, 72840 Sta. María Tonantzintla, Puebla, Mexico
{julian.diaz,szapotecas,jcp.sansalvador}@inaoep.mx
[2] Secretaría de Ciencia, Humanidades, Tecnología e Innovación (SECIHTI), Insurgentes Sur 1582, 03940 Ciudad de México, Mexico

Abstract. Portfolio optimization, also known as portfolio selection, is a crucial financial problem that involves allocating a limited budget across a set of assets. In this context, there are two investment strategies: active and passive. One of these passive strategies is known as the enhanced index tracking problem, a multi-objective NP-hard combinatorial optimization problem. Since evolutionary algorithms do not rely on convexity and differentiability assumptions and their population-based nature allows them to obtain many elements of the Pareto front in a single run, their use has gained popularity in the context of portfolio optimization. This study aims to compare the performance of eight state-of-the-art multi-objective evolutionary algorithms in solving the enhanced index tracking problem.

1 Introduction

Investment portfolio optimization is a critical financial problem that involves allocating a limited budget to an optimal selection of assets with their corresponding proportions, intending to maximize expected returns while minimizing risk. There are two types of portfolio optimization strategies, active and passive. In an active strategy, the investor attempts to maximize the expected returns, i.e., to beat the market. The downside of this is that it requires expert knowledge and high-frequency maintenance of the portfolio, incurring high operational and transaction costs; also, it has been shown that active managed funds cannot consistently outperform the *market* over the long term [17]. Passive investment strategies, on the other hand, rely less on expert knowledge and high maintenance and more on a fixed plan, thus reducing operational and transaction costs. One of these strategies is what is known as the Index Tracking Problem (ITP) [17].

The ITP consists of creating a *tracking portfolio* that replicates the returns of a *market index*. Although full replication is possible, where the tracking portfolio

L. Martínez-Villaseñor et al. (Eds.): MICAI 2025 Workshops, LNAI 16264, pp. 436–448, 2026.
https://doi.org/10.1007/978-3-032-17930-2_31

tries to "perfectly replicate" the index, it has some disadvantages such as: 1) frequent changes in the composition of the index and changes in the market require constant rebalancing, which implies high transaction costs, and 2) certain stocks may be held with a tiny proportion, which is a problem if they have minimum quantity limits. The alternative is to use *partial replication*, which consists of selecting only a subset of the stocks in the index [3]. Since partial replication ITP consists of choosing an optimal subset of a set of assets and its corresponding weights, it is a generalization of the knapsack problem, an NP-Hard combinatorial optimization problem [2].

The Enhanced Index Tracking Problem (EITP) extends the ITP by adding a second objective function, making it a multi-objective optimization problem (MOP), where the *tracking error* is minimized and the *excess return* maximized [8]. The addition of the excess return objective enables the investor to seek trade-off solutions between the tracking error and the returns above the underlying market index of the portfolio. Solving an MOP requires finding a set of *Pareto optimal* solutions in the decision space known as *Pareto Set* ($\mathcal{PS}$), whose corresponding image in the objective space is known as *Pareto Front* ($\mathcal{PF}$) [5].

Evolutionary algorithms (EAs) are population-based stochastic optimization/search algorithms that do not rely on convexity and/or differentiability assumptions. The use of EAs in the solution of MOPs is motivated primarily by the population-based nature of EAs to generate many elements of the $\mathcal{PF}$ in a single run; furthermore, the high complexity of some problems may forbid the use of traditional solution methods [5].

The aim of this study is: 1) to solve 24 EITP instances with eight Multi-Objective Evolutionary Algorithms (MOEAs), three based on Pareto dominance, three based on decomposition, and two based on quality indicators; and 2) to compare and analyze the results obtained of each algorithm and type of MOEA approach, to identify which approach should be further investigated in solving other formulations of the EITP.

The remainder of this paper is structured as follows. Section 2 presents a literature review; Sect. 3 introduces the basic concepts and presents the problem formulation; Sect. 4 details the experimental study; Sect. 5 presents the analysis of experimental results; and finally, Sect. 6 concludes this study.

2 Literature Review

Generally, EITPs are formulated as mixed-integer nonlinear programming (MINLP) problems. Still, some EITP formulations can be expressed as mixed-integer linear programming (MILP) and mixed-integer quadratic programming (MIQP) formulations and solved using exact methods. Canakgoz and Beasley [4] expressed the EITP as an MILP and solved it using CPLEX. Guastaroba et al. [12] solved an EITP MILP formulation using CPLEX as well.

Gnägi and Strub [11] proposed MILP and MIQP EITP models and solved them with local branching and iterated greedy heuristics. Guastaroba and Speranza [13] solved an MILP EITP model using a kernel search heuristic. Filippi et al. [10] used and improved the kernel search heuristic in [13] to solve EITP. Beasley et al. [3] solved the MILP formulation of EITP considering transaction cost constraints using the weighted-sum method and their proposed evolutionary population heuristic to solve it. Andriosopoulos et al. [1] used a genetic algorithm (GA) and differential evolution (DE) to solve the single objective EITP using the weighted sum method.

Li and Bao [16] present a four-objective index tracking model that incorporates realistic constraints, and proposed a Pareto-based multi-objective immune algorithm, using real encoding for portfolio weights and incorporating non-dominated sorting, elitist selection, and crowding distance to maintain a diverse and well-converged set of Pareto-optimal solutions; constraint handling is managed through penalty functions and repair strategies.

3 Problem Formulation

This section presents the basic concepts and the enhanced index tracking problem formulation.

Simple Return: Let p_{it} be the price of the asset i at time t. The return of the asset i at time t, r_{it} is the rate of change in the price obtained from holding the asset from time $t-1$ to time t:

$$r_{it} = \frac{p_{it} - p_{i(t-1)}}{p_{i(t-1)}}. \tag{1}$$

Investment Portfolio: A portfolio is a collection of one or more assets, and the value of a portfolio at any given time is the weighted sum of the value of the component assets at that time. Let w_i be the weight of the asset i, and N the total number of assets considered; then, the return of the portfolio at time t is.

$$R_t = \sum_{i=1}^{N} w_i r_{it}. \tag{2}$$

Tracking Error: The tracking error measures how much a portfolio's returns deviate from its benchmark index's returns over time. It is calculated as follows.

$$\mathrm{TE} = \frac{\left[\sum_{t=1}^{T} |R_t - I_t|^{\alpha}\right]^{1/\alpha}}{T}, \tag{3}$$

where I_t is the return of the market index at time t, T is the number of time periods, and α a constant.

Excess Return: The Excess Return measures how much a portfolio return exceeds the one of its underlying index. It is calculated as follows.

$$\mathrm{ER} = \frac{1}{T}\sum_{t=1}^{T}(R_t - I_t)\,. \tag{4}$$

Enhanced Index Tracking Problem. Let K be the maximum desired number of assets in the portfolio, R_t the return of the portfolio, I_t the return of the index. The complete mathematical programming EITP formulation is as follows.

$$\begin{aligned}
\text{Min} \quad & \mathrm{TE} = \frac{1}{T}\left[\sum_{t=1}^{T}|R_t - I_t|^{\alpha}\right]^{1/\alpha} && (5)\\
\text{Max} \quad & \mathrm{ER} = \frac{1}{T}\sum_{t=1}^{T}(R_t - I_t) && (6)\\
\text{Subject to} \quad & \sum_{i=1}^{N} w_i = 1 && (7)\\
& \sum_{i=1}^{N} z_i \leq K && (8)\\
& w_i \in [0,1], \quad \forall i && (9)\\
& z_i \in \{0,1\}, \quad \forall i. && (10)
\end{aligned}$$

Objectives: Equation (5) is the sum of the absolute differences in the portfolio and index returns over all periods. This objective is known as the tracking error. Equation (6) is the excess return of the portfolio over its underlying index.

Constraints: Equation (7) known as *budget constraint* ensures that the whole budget is invested in the portfolio; Eq. (8) known as *cardinality constraint* ensures that the size of the tracking porftolio is no greater than $K < N$; Eq. (9) known as *positivity constraint* states that the weights cannot be negative, i.e., short selling is not allowed; and Eq. 10 states that z_i can only accept binary values.

Decision Variables: The decision variables for the EITP are the vector of weights $\mathbf{w} = (w_1, \ldots, w_N)$ of the portfolio and the vector of binary variables $\mathbf{z} = (z_1, \ldots, z_N)$, where:

$$z_i = \begin{cases} 1 & \text{if} w_i > 0 \\ 0 & \text{if} w_i = 0, \quad \forall i. \end{cases} \tag{11}$$

4 Experimental Study

This section presents the methods of the experimental study.

4.1 Quality Performance Indicators

The algorithms are evaluated based on two quality indicators.

Hypervolume Indicator [22]: The hypervolume indicator (HV)simultaneously captures both convergence toward the Pareto front and diversity among solutions. A higher hypervolume value indicates a better approximation of the Pareto front.

IGD^+ Indicator [14]: The IGD^+ or IGDp indicator is a Pareto-compliant metric that evaluates how well an algorithm's solution set approximates the true Pareto front, considering both convergence and diversity.

4.2 Algorithms for Performance Comparison

Eight algorithms are selected to solve the proposed problems, three based on Pareto dominance, three based on decomposition, and two based on quality indicators, to provide insight into how each approach performs when solving various portfolio models with a different number of objectives.

- **NSGA-II** [7]: NSGA-II is a widely used Pareto-based MOEA for solving MOPs. It ranks solutions using a fast non-dominated sorting procedure and maintains diversity through a crowding distance metric, which estimates the proximity of solutions in the objective space.
- **GDE3** [15]: GDE3 is a Pareto-based multi-objective evolutionary algorithm that extends the classical Differential Evolution (DE) framework to handle multi-objective optimization problems.
- **SPEA2** [21]: SPEA2 is an improved Pareto-based evolutionary algorithm designed to solve multi-objective optimization problems with better convergence and diversity than its predecessor.
- **MOEA/D** [19]: MOEA/D is a decomposition-based evolutionary algorithm that transforms a multi-objective optimization problem into a set of scalar subproblems, each associated with a weight vector representing a particular trade-off among objectives.
- **VaEA** [18]: VaEA is a decomposition-based multi-objective evolutionary algorithm that guides selection by evaluating the vector angles between candidate solutions in the objective space.
- **NSGA-III** [6]: NSGA-III is a decomposition-based algorithm that extends NSGA-II, designed to handle many-objective optimization problems (typically with four or more objectives), where traditional Pareto-based approaches lose selection pressure.
- **SMS-EMOA** [9]: SMS-EMOA is an indicator-based evolutionary algorithm that uses the hypervolume (S-metric) as its primary selection criterion.

- **IBEA** [20]: IBEA is a robust indicator-based multi-objective evolutionary algorithm that guides the selection process using performance indicators rather than Pareto dominance or decomposition.

These algorithms are selected as representatives of their respective classes because they are the precursors of their respective approaches and are also widely popular and available in several frameworks.

4.3 Encoding and Repair Function

The encoding mechanism and repair function are described as follows.

Encoding: Real + Binary encoding is used. Here, each solution i is a vector of the form $\mathbf{x}_i = (r_{i1}, \ldots, r_{iN}, b_{i1}, \ldots, b_{iN})$, where r_{ij} and b_{ij} are the real and binary variables, respectively. The vector of weights of the portfolio is then expressed as $\mathbf{w}_i = (r_{i1}b_{i1}, \ldots, r_{iN}b_{iN})$, with $w_{ij} = r_{ij}b_{ij}$.

Repair Function: The repair function ensures that each $\sum_j b_{ij} \leq K$, by assigning $b_{ij} = 1$, for the K highest $r_{ij}b_{ij}$ values; and $b_{ij} = 0$ for the remainder of the components. Then it normalizes each weight vector so that $\sum_j w_{ij} = 1$.

4.4 Data Sets

The data is taken from the following source: http://people.brunel.ac.uk/~mastjjb/jeb/orlib/indtrackinfo.html. This link provides five datasets containing the historical prices of five major stock market indices and their respective component assets, covering a period of 290 weeks, from March 1992 to September 1997. The indices included are the following. Hang Seng (with 31 assets), DAX 100 (with 85 assets), FTSE 100 (with 89 assets), S&P 100 (with 98 assets) and Nikkei 225 (with 225 assets); and another three unnamed data sets, with 457, 1318 and 2151 assets. A problem is constructed by combining each data set with a value of $K \in \{10, 20, 30\}$. This makes a total of 24 problems.

4.5 Experimental Setup

The experiments are conducted as follows: 1) PlatEMO software is used. For each algorithm, a population size of 100 is set and the maximum number of function evaluations of 10,000 is the stopping criterion. The parameters for the algorithms were set as PlatEMO defaults. Each algorithm is run 30 times on each problem, and the results are stored. 2) Since the $\mathcal{PF}$ of each of the problems is not known, the reference $\mathcal{PF}$ is generated by combining the final population of every run for each algorithm and for each problem and extracting the non-dominated solutions. The reference point for the HV indicator $\mathbf{r} = (r_1, \ldots, r_m)^T$, whith $r_i = 1.1 \cdot f_{i(\text{worst})}$ for $i = 1, \ldots, m$, where $f_{i(\text{worst})}$ is the worst value for the objective i in the reference $\mathcal{PF}$. The reference point set for the IGD+ indicator is the reference $\mathcal{PF}$. 3) For each problem, the HV, IGD$^+$ metrics are calculated for each run. The mean and standard deviation are calculated for each metric. A one-tailed Wilcoxon test, corrected using the Bonferroni method with $\alpha = 0.05$, is used to identify the statistically significant results for each problem.

This experimental design is summarized as follows. A *simple comparative experiment* is used, where *factor* is the combination of a particular *portfolio optimization model* with a particular *data set*, which constitutes a *problem*; and the *two levels* are *two algorithms*; The *response* of this experiment is a *metric* (HV or IGD$^+$) value produced by each algorithm. This simple comparative experiment is conducted seven times, with the best-performing algorithm versus the others. This experimental design is used for each of the 24 problems for each metric. Since the same response data are used to perform 14 Wilcoxon tests per problem (seven for each HV and IGD$^+$ metrics), the Bonferroni correction is used.

5 Analysis of Results

Tables 1 and 2 show the mean values of the 30 runs of each algorithm for each problem of the HV and IGD$^+$ metrics, respectively. The best and worst results are highlighted in orange and blue, respectively; when a value is statistically significant better than the rest, it is underlined. In the bottom row of each table, the average order rank is displayed, where lower values are better.

Hypervolume Discussion: In Table 1, MOEA/D shows the best results in HV consistently, often statistically significant. This indicates its ability to obtain very diverse fronts. GDE3 shows promising results in HV, achieving the best value in several problems, some of which are statistically significant, and ranking second in average, with a consequence fairly close to MOEA/D. IBEA shows consistently above-average results in HV. SPEA2 and NSGA-III exhibit the worst performance in HV, indicating their difficulty in achieving diversity. The rest of the algorithms show below-average performance in HV, obtaining the worst result in some problems.

IGD$^+$Discussion: In Table 2, IBEA has the best performance in IGD$^+$ consistently, achieving the best result in several problems, although none of them are statistically significant. This indicates IBEA's ability to produce fronts with good convergence. MOEA/D exhibits the worst performance in IGD$^+$, yielding the worst results in many problems. This contrasts with the HV results. GDE3 shows poor IGD$^+$ performance, achieving the worst results in some problems. This indicates poor convergence performance. The remaining algorithms exhibit average performance in IGD$^+$, with the best results achieved in some problems.

Figures 1a and 1b display the boxplot (with outliers removed) of the HV and IGD$^+$ values of each algorithm on all problems, respectively. In HV, MOEA/D and GDE3 have the highest mean values, but also the highest variance, with MOEA/D showing the highest of them all; the rest of the algorithms show moderate dispersion of values in comparison. In IGD$^+$, MOEA/D exhibits the highest

Table 1. Mean HV values obtained by each algorithm for each problem are displayed. Best and worst results are highlighted in orange and blue respectively, and best statistically significant result is underlined.

Problem	NSGA-II	GDE3	SPEA2	MOEA/D	VaEA	NSGA-III	IBEA	SMS-EMOA
EITN31K10	0.7272 ± 0.0025	0.7701 ± 0.0082	0.7248 ± 0.0023	0.7816 ± 0.0274	0.7191 ± 0.0032	0.7202 ± 0.0028	0.7304 ± 0.0029	0.7211 ± 0.0032
EITN85K10	0.7392 ± 0.0035	0.8094 ± 0.0136	0.7337 ± 0.0057	0.7807 ± 0.0246	0.7289 ± 0.0052	0.7309 ± 0.0041	0.7402 ± 0.0066	0.7297 ± 0.0106
EITN89K10	0.709 ± 0.0115	0.78 ± 0.0187	0.7045 ± 0.0036	0.7891 ± 0.0252	0.6987 ± 0.0046	0.6977 ± 0.0043	0.7112 ± 0.0047	0.6958 ± 0.0036
EITN98K10	0.7299 ± 0.0098	0.811 ± 0.02	0.7259 ± 0.0037	0.8265 ± 0.0232	0.7244 ± 0.0036	0.7226 ± 0.0052	0.7334 ± 0.0091	0.7265 ± 0.0105
EITN225K10	0.7067 ± 0.0153	0.761 ± 0.0218	0.6984 ± 0.0205	0.751 ± 0.0227	0.6984 ± 0.0083	0.6943 ± 0.0149	0.7174 ± 0.0213	0.6882 ± 0.0208
EITN457K10	0.7108 ± 0.0313	0.78 ± 0.0303	0.6969 ± 0.018	0.7739 ± 0.0632	0.699 ± 0.028	0.7114 ± 0.03	0.7033 ± 0.0254	0.7013 ± 0.0256
EITN1318K10	0.8665 ± 0.125	0.896 ± 0.1171	0.8475 ± 0.1293	0.9809 ± 0.004	0.8882 ± 0.1217	0.8541 ± 0.1308	0.859 ± 0.1278	0.8229 ± 0.1287
EITN2151K10	0.8419 ± 0.1323	0.9411 ± 0.0811	0.8748 ± 0.1288	0.9807 ± 0.0047	0.9025 ± 0.1168	0.8581 ± 0.1323	0.9278 ± 0.0989	0.8871 ± 0.1227
EITN31K20	0.7401 ± 0.0018	0.8429 ± 0.0256	0.7373 ± 0.0021	0.8115 ± 0.0176	0.7349 ± 0.0035	0.7359 ± 0.0018	0.7429 ± 0.0021	0.7375 ± 0.0028
EITN85K20	0.7464 ± 0.0062	0.8404 ± 0.0109	0.7452 ± 0.0026	0.8527 ± 0.0301	0.7427 ± 0.0035	0.7425 ± 0.0024	0.7503 ± 0.0041	0.741 ± 0.0067
EITN89K20	0.7161 ± 0.0043	0.8283 ± 0.01	0.7139 ± 0.0042	0.836 ± 0.0175	0.7136 ± 0.004	0.7117 ± 0.0037	0.7213 ± 0.003	0.7108 ± 0.0037
EITN98K20	0.7261 ± 0.0031	0.8461 ± 0.0165	0.723 ± 0.0105	0.8667 ± 0.0163	0.7281 ± 0.0092	0.7232 ± 0.0029	0.7297 ± 0.011	0.7266 ± 0.0126
EITN225K20	0.7379 ± 0.0135	0.8276 ± 0.0175	0.7365 ± 0.0097	0.8248 ± 0.0182	0.7355 ± 0.0075	0.7366 ± 0.0073	0.758 ± 0.0083	0.7315 ± 0.0087
EITN457K20	0.712 ± 0.02	0.8149 ± 0.0317	0.7096 ± 0.0207	0.8224 ± 0.0605	0.7143 ± 0.0203	0.7108 ± 0.0199	0.7203 ± 0.0252	0.7091 ± 0.0186
EITN1318K20	0.7812 ± 0.1144	0.906 ± 0.1056	0.8144 ± 0.1261	0.9818 ± 0.0065	0.7531 ± 0.0985	0.7776 ± 0.1183	0.8066 ± 0.1253	0.8483 ± 0.126
EITN2151K20	0.868 ± 0.1307	0.9355 ± 0.1016	0.8215 ± 0.1337	0.9831 ± 0.0057	0.9096 ± 0.114	0.8328 ± 0.131	0.8679 ± 0.131	0.8483 ± 0.1325
EITN31K30	0.7216 ± 0.0011	0.8044 ± 0.0254	0.7195 ± 0.0015	0.7956 ± 0.0113	0.7182 ± 0.0042	0.7177 ± 0.0016	0.7245 ± 0.0014	0.7203 ± 0.0018
EITN85K30	0.7528 ± 0.0044	0.8615 ± 0.012	0.7506 ± 0.0025	0.8687 ± 0.0287	0.7517 ± 0.0056	0.7487 ± 0.0043	0.7561 ± 0.0024	0.7498 ± 0.0025
EITN89K30	0.7294 ± 0.0034	0.8598 ± 0.0116	0.7257 ± 0.0032	0.8559 ± 0.0137	0.7309 ± 0.0084	0.7252 ± 0.0042	0.7332 ± 0.0032	0.7258 ± 0.0036
EITN98K30	0.7472 ± 0.0042	0.8756 ± 0.0122	0.7442 ± 0.0025	0.8949 ± 0.0169	0.7516 ± 0.0092	0.746 ± 0.0027	0.7532 ± 0.0098	0.7486 ± 0.0093
EITN225K30	0.7527 ± 0.0114	0.8574 ± 0.0171	0.7481 ± 0.0071	0.8621 ± 0.0099	0.7495 ± 0.0144	0.7485 ± 0.008	0.7639 ± 0.0091	0.7425 ± 0.0081
EITN457K30	0.7106 ± 0.0142	0.8398 ± 0.0279	0.7072 ± 0.0115	0.8239 ± 0.0707	0.7133 ± 0.0165	0.7111 ± 0.017	0.7125 ± 0.0165	0.7124 ± 0.023
EITN1318K30	0.7208 ± 0.0482	0.8782 ± 0.1094	0.769 ± 0.101	0.9842 ± 0.0044	0.7996 ± 0.1227	0.8022 ± 0.1197	0.8367 ± 0.1269	0.8252 ± 0.1265
EITN2151K30	0.8681 ± 0.1292	0.9227 ± 0.1114	0.7795 ± 0.1183	0.9832 ± 0.0053	0.7918 ± 0.1219	0.7998 ± 0.1227	0.8523 ± 0.1311	0.9026 ± 0.1154
Avg. Rank	4.79	1.67	6.38	1.33	5.67	6.58	3.46	6.12

Table 2. Mean IGDp values obtained by each algorithm for each problem are displayed. Best and worst results are highlighted in orange and blue respectively, and best statistically significant result is underlined.

Problem	NSGA-II	GDE3	SPEA2	MOEA/D	VaEA	NSGA-III	IBEA	SMS-EMOA
EITN31K10	1e-04 ± 0	4e-04 ± 2e-04	0 ± 0	0.0013 ± 9e-04	1e-04 ± 0	1e-04 ± 0	0 ± 0	0 ± 0
EITN85K10	1e-04 ± 0	8e-04 ± 2e-04	1e-04 ± 0	0.0014 ± 5e-04	1e-04 ± 0	1e-04 ± 0	1e-04 ± 1e-04	1e-04 ± 1e-04
EITN89K10	1e-04 ± 3e-04	8e-04 ± 4e-04	1e-04 ± 0	0.0024 ± 0.001	1e-04 ± 0	1e-04 ± 0	1e-04 ± 0	1e-04 ± 0
EITN98K10	1e-04 ± 2e-04	0.0013 ± 5e-04	1e-04 ± 0	0.0032 ± 9e-04	1e-04 ± 0	1e-04 ± 0	1e-04 ± 2e-04	1e-04 ± 2e-04
EITN225K10	2e-04 ± 2e-04	6e-04 ± 4e-04	2e-04 ± 2e-04	0.0017 ± 5e-04	1e-04 ± 1e-04	1e-04 ± 1e-04	1e-04 ± 1e-04	2e-04 ± 2e-04
EITN457K10	0.0013 ± 0.0012	0.0052 ± 0.0021	8e-04 ± 7e-04	0.0096 ± 0.0051	0.0012 ± 0.001	0.0014 ± 0.0016	0.001 ± 9e-04	0.0011 ± 0.001
EITN1318K10	0.0233 ± 0.0185	0.0331 ± 0.0181	0.0197 ± 0.0169	0.0529 ± 0.0036	0.0262 ± 0.0159	0.0214 ± 0.0169	0.0216 ± 0.0179	0.0179 ± 0.0187
EITN2151K10	0.0201 ± 0.0186	0.038 ± 0.0127	0.0248 ± 0.0175	0.0516 ± 0.0037	0.0284 ± 0.0164	0.0222 ± 0.0178	0.0321 ± 0.014	0.0257 ± 0.0177
EITN31K20	1e-04 ± 0	0.0036 ± 8e-04	1e-04 ± 0	0.0011 ± 4e-04	1e-04 ± 0	1e-04 ± 0	0 ± 0	0 ± 0
EITN85K20	1e-04 ± 1e-04	0.0013 ± 3e-04	1e-04 ± 0	0.0029 ± 0.001	1e-04 ± 0	1e-04 ± 0	1e-04 ± 0	1e-04 ± 1e-04
EITN89K20	1e-04 ± 0	0.0015 ± 2e-04	1e-04 ± 0	0.0027 ± 6e-04	1e-04 ± 0	1e-04 ± 0	1e-04 ± 0	1e-04 ± 0
EITN98K20	1e-04 ± 0	0.0021 ± 5e-04	2e-04 ± 2e-04	0.0042 ± 8e-04	2e-04 ± 2e-04	1e-04 ± 0	1e-04 ± 2e-04	2e-04 ± 3e-04
EITN225K20	1e-04 ± 1e-04	9e-04 ± 3e-04	1e-04 ± 1e-04	0.0022 ± 4e-04	1e-04 ± 1e-04	1e-04 ± 0	1e-04 ± 1e-04	1e-04 ± 0
EITN457K20	8e-04 ± 9e-04	0.0062 ± 0.002	8e-04 ± 9e-04	0.0115 ± 0.0044	0.001 ± 0.001	8e-04 ± 9e-04	0.001 ± 0.0011	9e-04 ± 9e-04
EITN1318K20	0.0107 ± 0.0154	0.0345 ± 0.0177	0.0155 ± 0.0176	0.0533 ± 0.0051	0.0073 ± 0.0125	0.012 ± 0.0167	0.0136 ± 0.016	0.0197 ± 0.0176
EITN2151K20	0.0224 ± 0.0172	0.0408 ± 0.015	0.0175 ± 0.0177	0.0526 ± 0.0054	0.0287 ± 0.0149	0.0174 ± 0.0171	0.0226 ± 0.0174	0.02 ± 0.0171
EITN31K30	1e-04 ± 0	0.0032 ± 0.001	0 ± 0	0.0011 ± 3e-04	1e-04 ± 0	1e-04 ± 0	0 ± 0	0 ± 0
EITN85K30	1e-04 ± 0	0.002 ± 4e-04	1e-04 ± 0	0.0028 ± 9e-04	1e-04 ± 0	1e-04 ± 0	1e-04 ± 0	1e-04 ± 0
EITN89K30	1e-04 ± 0	0.0021 ± 3e-04	1e-04 ± 0	0.0027 ± 5e-04	1e-04 ± 0	1e-04 ± 0	1e-04 ± 0	1e-04 ± 0
EITN98K30	1e-04 ± 1e-04	0.0025 ± 4e-04	1e-04 ± 0	0.004 ± 8e-04	2e-04 ± 1e-04	1e-04 ± 0	1e-04 ± 2e-04	1e-04 ± 2e-04
EITN225K30	1e-04 ± 1e-04	0.0012 ± 3e-04	1e-04 ± 0	0.0024 ± 4e-04	2e-04 ± 1e-04	1e-04 ± 1e-04	1e-04 ± 1e-04	1e-04 ± 0
EITN457K30	9e-04 ± 0.0011	0.0079 ± 0.0021	6e-04 ± 5e-04	0.0115 ± 0.0041	7e-04 ± 7e-04	8e-04 ± 9e-04	7e-04 ± 7e-04	0.001 ± 0.0014
EITN1318K30	0.0028 ± 0.0062	0.0306 ± 0.0185	0.0077 ± 0.0141	0.0548 ± 0.0043	0.0135 ± 0.0177	0.0127 ± 0.0172	0.0178 ± 0.0185	0.017 ± 0.0184
EITN2151K30	0.0219 ± 0.0169	0.0385 ± 0.0167	0.0107 ± 0.0147	0.0512 ± 0.005	0.0121 ± 0.0165	0.0123 ± 0.0155	0.0205 ± 0.0183	0.0261 ± 0.0152
Avg. Rank	3.67	7.08	2.58	7.92	4.92	3.46	2.46	3.92

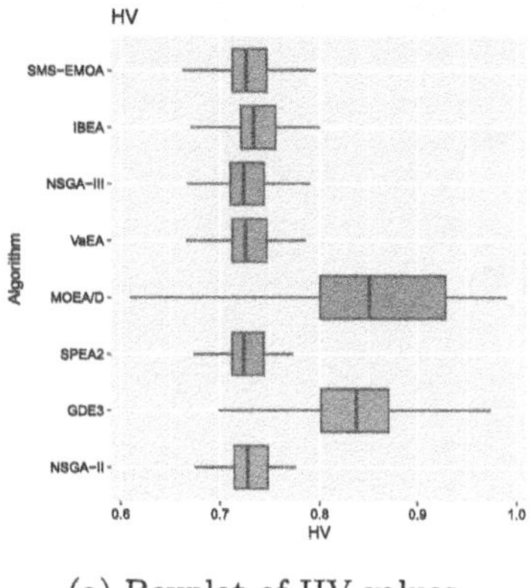

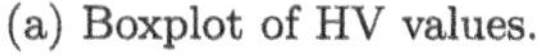
(a) Boxplot of HV values.

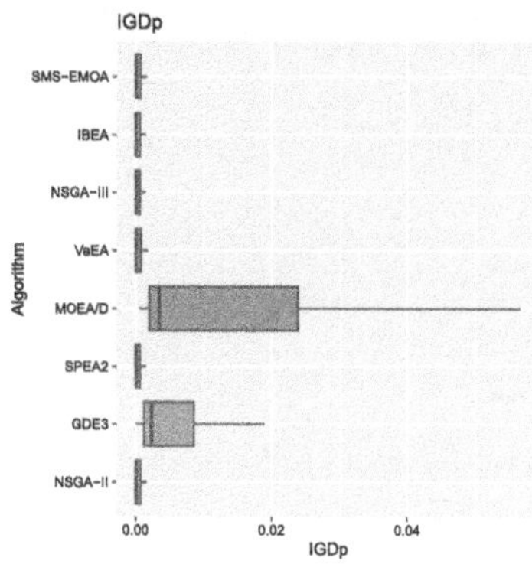

(b) Boxplot of IGD^+ values.

Fig. 1. Boxplot of the HV and IGD^+ values on all problems.

variance, with MOEA/D again showing the worst performance. The remaining algorithms exhibit lower variance in contrast.

Figures 2 show the reference front of the problems EITN31K20, EITN98K20, EITN457K20 and EITN2151 to help visualize the objective space of these problems.

Final Remarks: Based on this analysis, the following key interpretations can be drawn. MOEA/D shows the statistically significant best performance in HV and worst performance in IGD^+, respectively; this indicates that MOEA/D produces fronts with high diversity but poor convergence, and it exhibits the highest variance, indicating inconsistency. IBEA shows the best performance in IGD^+, although not statistically significant, but an average performance in HV, showing a more balanced trade-off between diversity and convergence, and a lower variance in comparison with MOEA/D or GDE3. In general, the best performer is IBEA, which exhibits good convergence, above-average diversity, and moderate variance. Lastly, since the decomposition-based MOEA/D exhibits the highest mean HV, and the indicator-based IBEA shows the most promising results, these approaches should be further studied.

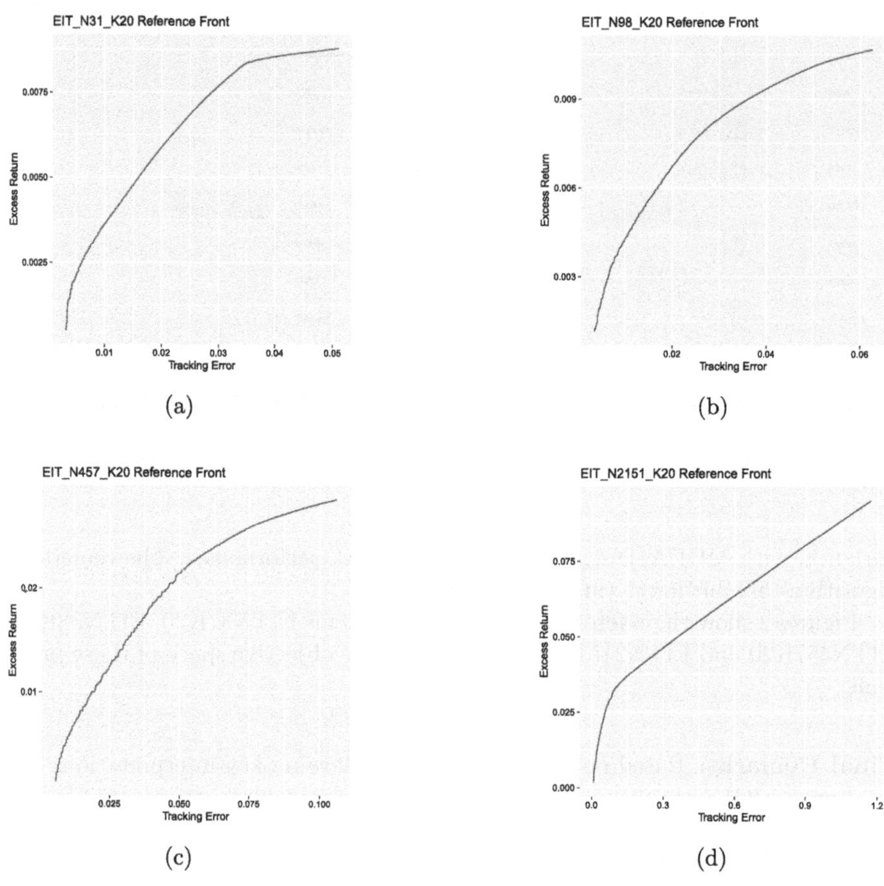

Fig. 2. The reference fronts of four problems: (a) EITN31K20, (b) EITN98K20, (3) EITN457K20 and (4) EITN2151K20.

6 Conclusions

This study compared eight state-of-the-art MOEAs for solving the EITP. IBEA is the best performer in IGD+ and shows average performance in HV. MOEA/D is the best performer in HV, but the worst performer in IGD$^+$. The remaining algorithms exhibit average performance. Therefore, there is no dominant algorithm for these problems. To achieve the best performance in both HV and IGD$^+$ (diversity and convergence), a specialized MOEA tailored for EITP should be developed. Since decomposition-based MOEA/D and indicator-based IBEA show promising results, these approaches should be further studied. In addition, the EITP formulations considered here did not include any additional real-world constraints, which would have made the problem even harder to solve. As future research, we propose: 1) conduct further experiments including real-world constraints; 2) design an MOEA suited for EITP that includes specialized operators to address real-world constraints; 3) conducting experiments with more modern algorithms could provide more valuable insight on how different types of algorithm solve the EITP.

Acknowledgments. Julián Antonio Díaz-Ayón acknowledges support from SECIHTI and INAOE for pursuing graduate studies in the Ph.D. program in Computational Sciences. Saúl Zapotecas-Martínez gratefully acknowledges support from the SECIHTI project CBF-2025-I-3114 (Ciencia Básica y de Frontera 2025).

References

1. Andriosopoulos, K., Doumpos, M., Papapostolou, N.C., Pouliasis, P.K.: Portfolio optimization and index tracking for the shipping stock and freight markets using evolutionary algorithms. Transp. Res. Part E: Logistics Transp. Rev. **52**, 16–34 (2013)
2. Ayón, J.A.D., de Lourdes Sandoval Solis, M., Velázquez, R.G., Ruiz, M.C., Garcés-Báez, A.: Harmony search based metaheuristic for the index tracking problem. In: Figueroa-García, J.C., Hernández, G., Suero Pérez, D.F., García, E.E.G. (eds.) Applied Computer Sciences in Engineering, pp. 15–26, Cham (2025). Springer Nature Switzerland
3. Beasley, J.E., Meade, N., Chang, T.-J.: An evolutionary heuristic for the index tracking problem. Eur. J. Oper. Res. **148**(3), 621–643 (2003)
4. Canakgoz, N.A., Beasley, J.E.: Mixed-integer programming approaches for index tracking and enhanced indexation. Eur. J. Oper. Res. **196**(1), 384–399 (2009)
5. Van Veldhuizen, D.A., Coello Coello, C.A., Lamont, G.B.: Evolutionary Algorithms for Solving Multi-Objective Problems. Genetic and Evolutionary Computation. Springer, 2nd edition (2007)
6. Deb, K., Jain, H.: An evolutionary many-objective optimization algorithm using reference-point-based nondominated sorting approach, part i: solving problems with box constraints. IEEE Trans. Evol. Comput. **18**(4), 577–601 (2013)
7. Deb, K., Pratap, A., Agarwal, S., Meyarivan, T.A.M.T.: A fast and elitist multiobjective genetic algorithm: NSGA-II. IEEE Trans. Evolutionary Comput. **6**(2), 182–197 (2002)
8. Doering, J., Kizys, R., Juan, A.A., Fito, A., Polat, O.: Metaheuristics for rich portfolio optimisation and risk management: Current state and future trends. Oper. Res. Perspect. **6**, 100121 (2019)
9. Emmerich, M., Beume, N., Naujoks, B.: An emo algorithm using the hypervolume measure as selection criterion. In: International Conference on Evolutionary Multi-Criterion Optimization, pp. 62–76. Springer (2005)
10. Filippi, C., Guastaroba, G., Speranza, M.G.: A heuristic framework for the bi-objective enhanced index tracking problem. Omega **65**, 122–137 (2016)
11. Gnägi, M., Strub, O.: Tracking and outperforming large stock-market indices. Omega **90**, 101999 (2020)
12. Guastaroba, G., Mansini, R., Ogryczak, W., Speranza, M.G.: Linear programming models based on omega ratio for the enhanced index tracking problem. Eur. J. Oper. Res. **251**(3), 938–956 (2016)
13. Gianfranco Guastaroba and Maria Grazia Speranza: Kernel search: an application to the index tracking problem. Eur. J. Oper. Res. **217**(1), 54–68 (2012)

14. Ishibuchi, H., Masuda, H., Tanigaki, Y., Nojima, Y.: Modified distance calculation in generational distance and inverted generational distance. In: International Conference on Evolutionary Multi-Criterion Optimization, pp. 110–125. Springer (2015)
15. Kukkonen, S., Lampinen, J.: GDE3: the third evolution step of generalized differential evolution. In: 2005 IEEE Congress on Evolutionary Computation, vol. 1, pp. 443–450. IEEE (2005)
16. Li, Q., Bao, L.: Enhanced index tracking with multiple time-scale analysis. Econ. Model. **39**, 282–292 (2014)
17. Moeini, M.: Solving the index tracking problem: a continuous optimization approach. CEJOR **30**(2), 807–835 (2022)
18. Xiang, Y., Zhou, Y., Li, M., Chen, Z.: A vector angle-based evolutionary algorithm for unconstrained many-objective optimization. IEEE Trans. Evol. Comput. **21**(1), 131–152 (2016)
19. Zhang, Q., Li, H.: MOEA/D: a multiobjective evolutionary algorithm based on decomposition. IEEE Trans. Evol. Comput. **11**(6), 712–731 (2007)
20. Zitzler, E., Künzli, S.: Indicator-based selection in multiobjective search. In: International Conference on Parallel Problem Solving from Nature, pp. 832–842. Springer (2004)
21. Zitzler, E., Laumanns, M., Thiele, L.: SPEA2: improving the strength pareto evolutionary algorithm. TIK Report 103 (2001)
22. Zitzler, E., Thiele, L.: Multiobjective optimization using evolutionary algorithms—a comparative case study. In: International Conference on Parallel Problem Solving from Nature, pp. 292–301. Springer (1998)

Leveraging Adapters for Neural Architecture Search in Large Language Models

Alejandro Rosales-Pérez(✉) and Adrián Pastor López-Monroy

Centro de Investigación en Matemáticas A.C., Avenida Alianza Centro 502, PIIT, Apodaca, Nuevo León, Mexico
{alejandro.rosales,pastor.lopez}@cimat.mx

Abstract. This paper introduces LoRA-NAS, a method that integrates Neural Architecture Search (NAS) with Low-Rank Adaptation (LoRA) to determine optimal adaptation settings for specific tasks. This approach enables the creation of customized Large Language Model (LLM) architectures tailored to individual datasets. LoRA-NAS operates by leveraging an evolutionary algorithm to explore the space of efficient Parameter-Efficient Fine-Tuning (PEFT) configurations. It identifies the optimal layer-wise placement strategy and hyperparameters for LoRA adapters during the PEFT of LLMs. By treating adapter insertion as a search problem, LoRA-NAS aims to customize adapter designing based on task specifics, minimizing redundant parameter updates and accelerating adaptation. A comprehensive evaluation of LoRA-NAS was conducted using the LLaMA-7B model as its base model and benchmarking it against zero-shot classification with LLaMA and the LLaMA fine-tuned with LoRA on a range of natural language understanding tasks. Experimental results demonstrate that LoRA-NAS significantly outperformed reference methods across all evaluated tasks, showing improved accuracy, underscoring the benefits of using architecture search to achieve state-of-the-art results.

Keywords: Neural Architecture Search · Large Language Models · LoRA

1 Introduction

The rise of powerful Large language models (LLMs) like GPT-4 [1], LLaMA-3 [10], among others has revolutionized natural language processing, leading to unprecedented performance in a wide range of applications, from reasoning to text generation. LLMs, however, involve billions or trillions of parameters, rendering traditional fine-tuning methods impractical. Standard fine-tuning usually adjusts most or all of the parameters of a pre-trained model with data specific

This work was supported by project CBF-2023-2024-2797.

L. Martínez-Villaseñor et al. (Eds.): MICAI 2025 Workshops, LNAI 16264, pp. 449–458, 2026.
https://doi.org/10.1007/978-3-032-17930-2_32

to the task [2]. Although effective, this method can be computationally prohibitive, requiring substantial resources and time, particularly for the largest language models, and often suffers from catastrophic forgetting.

To mitigate these challenges, Parameter-Efficient Fine-Tuning (PEFT) has emerged as a critical area of research [3]. PEFT methods efficiently adapt large pre-trained models by fine-tuning only a small portion of their parameters, keeping the original model frozen. This reduces computational and storage overhead. Among PEFT strategies, adapter modules have emerged as a particularly effective and versatile paradigm. Houlsby et al. [5] introduced adapters, which are small, task-specific neural modules inserted into the layers of a pre-trained model. Training is restricted to the parameters of these lightweight adapters, thereby enabling efficient specialization without modifying the base model weights. Further advancements, exemplified by Low-Rank Adaptation (LoRA) [6], have enhanced this concept through low-rank matrix decompositions for parameter updates, resulting in significant efficiency and performance gains.

Despite the success of adapters such as LoRA, the optimal placement of these modules within the intricate architecture of LLMs for performance and efficiency remains a significant, often heuristically addressed, question. Adapters are typically inserted consistently across all applicable layers or according to established configurations [6]. However, recent studies suggest that such uniform placement might be suboptimal and lead to redundant computation, and strategic placement in specific layers can produce significant performance variations depending on the task [14]. Determining the optimal placement configuration manually is challenging and non-scalable, presenting itself as an architectural design problem.

Neural Architecture Search (NAS) automates the design of high-performing neural networks, providing a systematic way to handle complex design decisions [4]. NAS has yielded state-of-the-art architectures over a wide range of vision and language tasks. Our hypothesis is that using NAS can successfully resolve the issue of optimal adapter placement within LLMs. Rather than seeking new layer types or connection structures, NAS can explore the discrete space of potential adapter placements and their hyperparameters.

This paper introduces LoRA-NAS, a method for automatically finding the optimal layer-wise placement strategy and hyperparameters for LoRA adapters during the PEFT of LLMs. Treating adapter insertion as a search problem, we aim to customize adapter deployment based on task specifics, thus minimizing redundant parameter updates and accelerating adaptation. The primary contributions of the paper

The remainder of the paper is organized as follows. Section 2 presents the works related to PEFT and NAS. Section 3 describes the proposed LoRA-NAS, and Sect. 4 details the experimental setup and experimental results. Finally, Sect. 5 presents the main conclusions and details future research paths.

2 Related Work

2.1 Parameter-Efficient Fine-Tunning (PEFT) with Adapters

PEFT aims to adapt large pre-trained models cost-effectively [17]. Adapter-based methods are a cornerstone of PEFT. The original adapter concept introduced small, trainable feed-forward networks inserted sequentially within transformer layers. Pfeiffer et al. [15] explored variations in placement and structure for improved efficiency. These methods isolate task-specific adjustments, enabling modularity. LoRA [6] advanced parameter efficiency further by approximating weight updates with low-rank matrices ($\Delta W \approx BA$), injected typically into attention and feed-forward layers. This approach drastically reduces trainable parameters while maintaining high performance. Extensions like AdaLoRA [18] introduce dynamic rank allocation based on importance scores. While effective, these methods often rely on default placement strategies (e.g., applying LoRA to all query, key, value, and output projections in attention layers, and potentially feed-forward layers), leaving the optimality of this placement largely unexplored. Recent work has started analyzing the impact of placement, confirming that performance varies significantly with adapter location and that optimal placements are task-dependent [14], highlighting the need for systematic placement strategies.

2.2 Neural Architecture Search (NAS)

NAS automates the discovery of optimal neural network architectures, shifting focus from manual design to automated search. Key components include the search space (defining possible architectures), search strategy (e.g., Evolutionary Algorithms (EA) [11]), and performance estimation strategy [4]. Early EA methods were accurate but computationally expensive. Gradient-based methods like DARTS [9] improved efficiency by relaxing the search space but faced stability issues. One-shot methods [16] drastically reduced search cost by training a super-network encompassing all architectures and evaluating candidates via weight sharing. ENAS [16] demonstrated the efficacy of weight sharing combined with an RL controller. NAS has proven successful in various domains but remains computationally intensive, particularly for large models or complex search spaces.

The synergy between PEFT and NAS is an emerging research direction. Initial work focused on using NAS to discover efficient PEFT configurations beyond standard adapters. In [8] a NAS based on pruning was used to find PET architectures for pre-trained LLMs. More recent work has directly incorporated LoRA into NAS frameworks. Approaches like LoNAS [12] and Shears [13], utilize the weight-sharing super-networks NAS principles and NSGA-II to find optimal LoRA ranks for different layers at the time that LLMs are compressed. These methods leverage NAS to optimize the internal configuration of adapters or to use adapters as a tool for broader model compression, demonstrating the potential of combining these techniques for enhanced efficiency.

While existing works [8,12,13] successfully apply NAS to optimize adapter ranks or guide model compression, they do not directly address where to place adapters within the LLM structure for optimal task adaptation. Although in [7,14] establish the importance of placement but often rely on limited search or heuristics, like gradient ranking, for finding good locations. Our proposed LoRA-NAS method specifically tackles this gap. It employs a dedicated NAS algorithm to search the combinatorial space of layer-wise adapter placement decisions (i.e., whether to include a LoRA adapter at each potential site). Unlike LoNAS/Shears which focus on rank search or using adapters for pruning guidance, LoRA-NAS focuses on optimizing the spatial configuration of adapters across the network depth, assuming a fixed (or predefined) adapter structure (e.g., fixed rank LoRA). By automating this critical architectural choice, LoRA-NAS aims to provide a more robust and potentially superior alternative to heuristic or uniform placement strategies commonly used in PEFT, complementing existing methods focused on adapter rank optimization or model compression.

3 LoRA-NAS

In this section, we describe our novel approach, LoRA-NAS, which integrates LoRA into a NAS framework. LoRA-NAS leverages an evolutionary algorithm to explore the space of efficient PEFT configurations, with rapid fitness estimation facilitated by a small subset of the dataset.

Algorithm 1. LoRA-NAS Evolutionary Search

1: **Input:** Population size P, number of generations G, mutation rate r, maximum number of layers M
2: **Output:** Best individual configuration
3: Initialize Population $\mathcal{P} \leftarrow \{ I_1, I_2, \ldots, I_P \}$ where each I is an individual with:
  - A sorted set of randomly chosen layers (from 0 to $M-1$) of size between 1 and 5.
  - Hyperparameters: *rank* and *alpha* sampled from their respective discrete sets.
4: **for** each individual I in $\mathcal{P}$ **do**
5: Evaluate fitness: $I.fitness \leftarrow$ `evaluate_individual`(I)
6: **for** $g \leftarrow 1$ to G **do**
7: **while** $|\mathcal{P}| < 2P$ **do**
8: $(P_1, P_2) \leftarrow$ `tournament_selection`$(\mathcal{P})$
9: $C \leftarrow$ `crossover`(P_1, P_2)
10: `mutate`(C)
11: Add child: $\mathcal{P} \leftarrow \mathcal{P} \cup \{C\}$
12: **for** each individual I in $\mathcal{P}$ with $I.fitness = -1$ **do**
13: Evaluate fitness: $I.fitness \leftarrow$ `evaluate_individual`(I)
14: Sort $\mathcal{P}$ in descending order of fitness.
15: Truncate: $\mathcal{P} \leftarrow$ Top P individuals in $\mathcal{P}$
16: **return** Best individual I^* in $\mathcal{P}$

Algorithm 1 describes LoRA-NAS. It starts with the random initialization of a population of candidate configurations. Each candidate encodes a LoRA-specific architecture by specifying the layers where low-rank modifications will be applied as well as associated hyperparameters (the rank and the scaling factor, α). For each candidate, a PEFT configuration is generated by mapping the selected layers to target modules within the model. The model is then fine-tuned for one training epoch using a fast-evaluation routine. The performance of the candidate, measured via accuracy, determines its fitness. Subsequently, individuals are selected through tournament selection, and evolved via a crossover operator that combines the architectural and hyperparameter choices of parent individuals, and mutation operators. This iterative process is repeated over several generations, with each cycle producing a refined population that progressively converges towards an optimal LoRA configuration.

3.1 Individual Representation and Evolutionary Operators

Individuals in the evolutionary algorithm are represented as a vector with three primary components: a set of chosen layers, and two hyperparameters, *rank* and α. The layers are encoded as a list of layer indices, representing the specific layers in the LLM where LoRA will be applied. The parameters *rank* and α determine the dimensionality of the low-rank approximation and the corresponding scaling factor, respectively. Figure 1 shows an example of how individuals are encoded and the evolutionary operators.

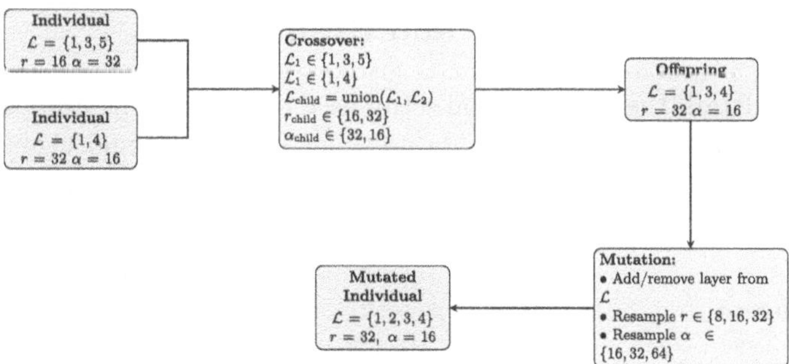

Fig. 1. Individual representation and the evolutionary operators used in the LoRA-NAS method. An individual is represented by a set of chosen layers where LoRA is applied, along with hyperparameters for rank and alpha. The diagram depicts the crossover and mutation operators.

The evolutionary operators are defined as follows. For mutation, each individual undergoes independent probabilistic modifications:

- **Layer Mutation:** With a predetermined probability, the candidate may either eliminate one of its selected layers or incorporate a new layer not currently in the set.

- **Parameter Mutation:** Independently, the values for *rank* and α are subject to change, with new values randomly sampled from discrete predefined sets.

In addition, the crossover operator generates offspring by combining two parent individuals, chosen by tournament selection operator. The crossover works as follows: the offspring's layer set is determined by randomly choosing a subset of layers for each parent, and these layers are inhereted to a new individual. The hyperparameters are inherited by randomly choosing between the corresponding values of the two parents. These evolutionary operators facilitate an effective exploration of the search space while preserving promising architectural traits.

3.2 Fitness Function

The fitness of each individual is determined by its evaluation accuracy as computed on a fine-tuned LoRA model built with the configuration given by an individual. To accelerate the NAS fitness evaluation, only a 1% of the full training data is used to fine-tuning the model, and other 1% of the full training data for evaluating the configuration. This reduced evaluation set significantly speeds-up the training and validation step. The evaluation procedure involves fine-tuning the adapted model for one epoch using a lightweight training configuration, followed by the measurement of accuracy. This efficient fitness estimation ensures that the evolutionary algorithm can operate with high throughput, effectively balancing search speed and predictive performance.

4 Experimental Settings and Results

This section details the experimental setup used to evaluate the proposed LoRA-NAS. We describe the benchmark datasets for fine-tuning and evaluation, the reference methods against which LoRA-NAS is compared, and the metrics for performance assessment.

4.1 Datasets

We used a suite of widely recognized natural language understanding datasets from the GLUE benchmark to assess the effectiveness of LoRA-NAS across diverse tasks. The chosen datasets represent a variety of classification challenges:

- **SST-2**, the Stanford Sentiment Treebank, is a dataset used for binary classification in movie review sentiment analysis. Models classify sentences as either positive or negative in sentiment. We assess the performance on the validation set.
- **MNLI**, Multi-Genre Natural Language Inference, is a massive, crowd-sourced dataset used for natural language inference. Models assess the relationship between a premise and a hypothesis, classifying it as entailment, contradiction, or neutral. We assess performance on matched validation set.

- **QQP**, Quora Question Pairs, is a binary classification dataset that determines whether two Quora questions are semantically similar paraphrases.
- **RTE**, Recognizing Textual Entailment, is a dataset compiling examples from diverse entailment challenges. In this task, models are required to classify text snippets as either containing or not containing a hypothesis.
- **MRPC**, Microsoft Research Paraphrase Corpus, is a news-based dataset used to detect paraphrased text. The models evaluate sentence pairs for semantic equivalence, classifying them as equivalent or not equivalent.

The datasets provide a complete evaluation setting for LoRA-NAS, covering tasks such as sentiment analysis, natural language inference, and paraphrase detection.

4.2 Reference Methods and Evaluation Metrics

The performance of LoRA-NAS is compared against two reference methods based on the LLaMA-7B model:

- **LLaMA-7B Zero-Shot Classification** (LLaMA-ZSC): This baseline reflects the LLaMA 2 model's performance before any fine-tuning for specific downstream tasks. We measure performance by including task instructions or examples in the input prompt.
- **LLaMA-7B Fine-tuned with LoRA** (LLaMA-SFT): This baseline uses a standard LoRA method with a fixed, pre-defined configuration to fine-tune the LLaMA 2 model. We applied LoRA to standard modules like query and value projection layers, using a fixed rank (r) of 8 and alpha (α) of 16 for all layers, and avoiding architectural searches. This directly compares the benefits of using NAS for automated configuration search.

For the proposed LoRA-NAS, we used 10 individuals, which are evolved during 10 generations. The crossover probability is set to 1.0 and mutation probability to 0.20. LoRA-NAS also uses the LLaMA-7B as the base LLM, which has 32 layers. For the LoRA hyperparameters, the rank can take the values of 8, 16, or 32, and the α can take the values of 16, 32, or 64. The comparison between LoRA-NAS and reference methods is carried out using two primary evaluation criteria:

- **Accuracy**: The primary metric to assess the task performance of the resulting models on the corresponding dataset test sets.
- **Running Time**: The computational time required for the fine-tuning process. For LoRA-NAS, this specifically refers to the total time consumed by the evolutionary search process to find the optimal configuration.

All experiments were conducted on workstations equipped with an NVIDIA RTX A4000 graphics processing unit. This hardware configuration provided the computational resources necessary for training and evaluating the models.

4.3 Experimental Results

This section presents the experimental results reported on SST-2, MNLI, QQP, RTE, and MRPC datasets. The performance metric used is accuracy. Table 1 summarizes the performance reported by LLaMA-ZSC, LLaMA-SFT, and LoRA-NAS across the evaluated tasks.

Table 1. Performance Comparison (Accuracy) on Various NLU Tasks

Task	LLaMA-ZSC	LLaMA-SFT	LoRA-NAS
SST-2	0.4713	0.9014	**0.9725**
MNLI	0.3020	0.8699	**0.9140**
QQP	0.4061	0.8802	**0.9069**
RTE	0.5271	0.8520	**0.9134**
MRPC	0.7917	0.8750	**0.8995**

Fine-tuning the LLaMA model significantly improved its performance on the downstream tasks, outperforming zero-shot classification. The performance of LLaMA-ZSC, operating exclusively on its pre-trained parameters without task-specific adaptation, is considerably inferior across all tasks, barely surpassing random chance on certain datasets (including MNLI, SST2-2, and QQP). This underscores the critical need for fine-tuning to attain optimal performance on these particular tasks.

A comparative analysis of the two fine-tuning methods reveals that LoRA-NAS demonstrates superior performance to the standard LLaMA-LoRA approach across all benchmark tasks. LoRA-NAS demonstrates significant improvement, especially on the SST2-2 task, achieving 0.9725 accuracy, a substantial increase over the 0.9014 from LLaMA-SFT. We observed similar improvements on MNLI (0.9140 vs 0.8699), QQP (0.9069 vs 0.8802), RTE (0.9134 vs 0.8520), and MRPC (0.8995 vs 0.8750).

The consistently better results from LoRA-NAS show that its neural architecture search component successfully identifies optimal layer placement and low-rank adaptation configurations for LoRA, surpassing manually configured or default LoRA setups. This results in more precisely tuned models better suited to the specifics of each task. The significant performance improvements show that using NAS to automate LoRA parameter searches is a promising way to search for optimal LLM architectures without requiring a full-training step.

Regarding the running time, LLaMA-ZSC does not require training, making it efficient. LLaMA-SFT required less than two hour for small datasets (61 min for RTE, 87 min for MRPC), and more than two hours for the largest datasets (153 min for SST-2, 447 min for QQP, and 572 min for MNLI). Conversely, LoRA-NAS requires between 12 o 25 h of GPU computation to perform. This can be a shortcoming, however, it has the benefit of designing more accurated and tailored LLM architectures for the given tasks.

5 Conclusions

This paper introduces LoRA-NAS, a method combining NAS and LoRA to automatically find the best adaptation settings for specific tasks, enabling the creation of custom LLM architectures tailored to individual datasets. The LoRA-NAS method used the well-known LLaMA-7b model as its foundation.

A comprehensive evaluation of LoRA-NAS was conducted, benchmarking it against LLaMA-SFT (standard LoRA fine-tuning) and LLaMA-ZSC (zero-shot classification) on a range of natural language understanding tasks including SST-2, MNLI, QQP, RTE, and MRPC, all using the LLaMA model. Experiments revealed that our LoRA-NAS approach outperformed others. Compared to the zero-shot baseline and standard LoRA, LoRA-NAS demonstrated significantly improved accuracy across all evaluated tasks.

The results emphasize the benefits of using architecture search to improve LoRA setups. LoRA-NAS achieves better performance than a generic LoRA approach by customizing its adaptation strategy for each task. This result not only supports our hypothesis but also positions LoRA-NAS as a powerful method for achieving state-of-the-art, parameter-efficient fine-tuning of LLMs.

The success of LoRA-NAS opens up several paths for future research. We might find even better adaptation strategies by exploring different search spaces and algorithms within the NAS framework. Furthermore, to better understand its adaptability, LoRA-NAS should be tested on a broader variety of tasks and model architectures. Finally, reducing the computational cost and time required for NAS is key to making these advanced fine-tuning methods more readily available.

Acknowledgments. This work was supported by the research project *Búsqueda de Arquitecturas Neuronales Eficientes y Efectivas* (CBF-2023-2024-2797) funded by *Secretaría de Ciencia, Humanidades, Tecnología e Innovación*

References

1. Achiam, J., et al.: GPT-4 technical report. arXiv preprint arXiv:2303.08774 (2023)
2. Devlin, J., Chang, M.W., Lee, K., Toutanova, K.: BERT: pre-training of deep bidirectional transformers for language understanding. In: Burstein, J., Doran, C., Solorio, T. (eds.) Proceedings of the 2019 Conference of the North American Chapter of the Association for Computational Linguistics: Human Language Technologies, Volume 1 (Long and Short Papers), pp. 4171–4186. Association for Computational Linguistics, Minneapolis, Minnesota (2019). https://doi.org/10.18653/v1/N19-1423, https://aclanthology.org/N19-1423/
3. Ding, N., et al.: Parameter-efficient fine-tuning of large-scale pre-trained language models. Nature Mach. Intell. **5**(3), 220–235 (2023). https://doi.org/10.1038/s42256-023-00626-4
4. Elsken, T., Metzen, J.H., Hutter, F.: Neural architecture search: a survey. J. Mach. Learn. Res. **20**(55), 1–21 (2019). http://jmlr.org/papers/v20/18-598.html

5. Houlsby, N., et al.: Parameter-efficient transfer learning for NLP. In: Chaudhuri, K., Salakhutdinov, R. (eds.) Proceedings of the 36th International Conference on Machine Learning. Proceedings of Machine Learning Research, vol. 97, pp. 2790–2799. PMLR (2019). https://proceedings.mlr.press/v97/houlsby19a.html
6. Hu, E.J., et al.: LoRA: low-rank adaptation of large language models. ICLR **1**(2), 3 (2022)
7. Hu, Z., et al.: LLM-adapters: an adapter family for parameter-efficient fine-tuning of large language models. arXiv preprint arXiv:2304.01933 (2023)
8. Lawton, N., Kumar, A., Thattai, G., Galstyan, A., Ver Steeg, G.: Neural architecture search for parameter-efficient fine-tuning of large pre-trained language models. In: Findings of the Association for Computational Linguistics: ACL 2023, pp. 8506–8515 (2023)
9. Liu, H., Simonyan, K., Yang, Y.: DARTS: differentiable architecture search. In: International Conference on Learning Representations (2019). https://openreview.net/forum?id=S1eYHoC5FX
10. Llama Team, A.M.: The Llama 3 herd of models (2024). https://arxiv.org/abs/2407.21783
11. Lu, Z., et al.: NSGA-Net: neural architecture search using multi-objective genetic algorithm. In: Proceedings of the Genetic and Evolutionary Computation Conference, pp. 419–427. GECCO '19, Association for Computing Machinery, New York, NY, USA (2019). https://doi.org/10.1145/3321707.3321729
12. Muñoz, J.P., Yuan, J., Jain, N.: Low-rank adapters meet neural architecture search for LLM compression. arXiv e-prints. arXiv–2501 (2025)
13. Munoz, J., Yuan, J., Jain, N.: Shears: unstructured sparsity with neural low-rank adapter search. In: Proceedings of the 2024 Conference of the North American Chapter of the Association for Computational Linguistics: Human Language Technologies (Volume 6: Industry Track), pp. 395–405 (2024)
14. Nowak, A.I., et al.: Towards optimal adapter placement for efficient transfer learning. arXiv preprint arXiv:2410.15858 (2024)
15. Pfeiffer, J., et al.: AdapterHub: a framework for adapting transformers. arXiv preprint arXiv:2007.07779 (2020)
16. Pham, H., Guan, M., Zoph, B., Le, Q., Dean, J.: Efficient neural architecture search via parameters sharing. In: Dy, J., Krause, A. (eds.) Proceedings of the 35th International Conference on Machine Learning. Proceedings of Machine Learning Research, vol. 80, pp. 4095–4104. PMLR (2018). https://proceedings.mlr.press/v80/pham18a.html
17. Zhang, D., et al.: Parameter-efficient fine-tuning for foundation models. arXiv preprint arXiv:2501.13787 (2025)
18. Zhang, Q., et al.: AdaLoRA: adaptive budget allocation for parameter-efficient fine-tuning. arXiv preprint arXiv:2303.10512 (2023)

Optimization of Wave Energy Farms Using Surrogate Models and Metaheuristics

Mario Alberto Martinez Oliveros , Adriana Menchaca-Méndez(✉), and Miguel Raggi

Technologies for Information in Sciences, Escuela Nacional de Estudios Superiores, Unidad Morelia, UNAM, Morelia, México
{amenchaca,mraggi}@enesmorelia.unam.mx

Abstract. Reducing the carbon footprint has motivated the adoption of clean energy generation, with wave energy emerging as a promising alternative. However, the design of wave energy farms poses significant challenges. In this work, we focus on the optimal spatial placement of buoys (WECs) to maximize the power output of a farm. A major limitation in this optimization process is the high computational cost of evaluating objective functions through hydrodynamic simulators. To address this issue, we investigate the use of machine learning models to predict the power output of wave energy farms. We perform a comparative study of four models and use the best-performing one as a surrogate objective function to optimize buoy placement with two well-known metaheuristics: Differential Evolution (DE) and Particle Swarm Optimization (PSO). Experimental results demonstrate that employing support vector machines as surrogate models, combined with DE for optimization, provides an effective alternative for designing wave energy farms.

Keywords: Surrogate modeling · Differential Evolution · Particle Swarm Optimization · Wave energy farms · Renewable energy

1 Introduction

Currently, significant challenges persist in clean energy generation and carbon footprint reduction. Although fossil fuels have traditionally served as the primary energy source, they are finite resources whose exploitation has caused severe environmental impacts, including water and air pollution, ecosystem degradation, and a substantial increase in greenhouse gas emissions. In response, recent years have seen growing interest in clean energy sources capable of generating power without pollutant emissions. Wave energy represents a promising alternative, as it has the potential to supply approximately 10% of the world's electricity demand, equivalent to about 1,400 TWh per year [18]. Nevertheless, several factors have hindered the widespread development of wave energy. Harsh marine conditions, such as storms, can rapidly damage power conversion equipment; current technologies remain costly; and installations may interfere with marine fauna, shipping routes, and fishing activities.

L. Martínez-Villaseñor et al. (Eds.): MICAI 2025 Workshops, LNAI 16264, pp. 459–470, 2026.
https://doi.org/10.1007/978-3-032-17930-2_33

Wave farms consist of arrays of wave energy converters (WECs), whose placement is a critical factor influencing energy capture efficiency, maintenance requirements, environmental compatibility, and economic viability [21]. Designing an optimal wave farm requires optimizing different objectives, such as maximizing energy production, while minimizing costs and environmental impacts. In this work, we focus on maximizing the total energy output of a wave farm by optimizing the spatial configuration of its WEC array, i.e., determining the placement of each WEC to achieve the highest possible power generation. Several studies have shown that environmental characteristics, including wave height, period, and direction, play a decisive role in determining the optimal spatial configuration of WECs [9,14,16,19].

Hydrodynamic simulations and computational models have been employed to predict a wave farm's power output and support its design. Analytical methods have inherent limitations in modeling accuracy, while numerical methods often entail high computational costs, especially for farms with a large number of devices. These challenges have driven the development of more efficient computational models. Currently, specialized tools such as WAMIT and NEMOH provide precise hydrodynamic modeling capabilities [21]. In [14], the authors proposed an alternative model with lower computational cost than its predecessors and released a public dataset through the Machine Learning Repository of the University of California, Irvine [11] to promote the application of machine learning techniques for estimating the power output of wave energy farms.

The main contributions of this work are the following:

1. We present a comparative study of four machine learning techniques (linear regression, CatBoost, support vector machines, and neural networks) for estimating the power output of a wave energy farm based on the spatial placements of its WECs, using the public dataset available through the University of California, Irvine (UCI) Machine Learning Repository under the title "Large-scale Wave Energy Farm".
2. We maximize the power output of a wave energy farm by employing, as the objective function, the approximation model with the highest predictive accuracy identified in our comparative study. To carry out the optimization, we apply two widely used metaheuristics: Differential Evolution and Particle Swarm Optimization.
3. We conduct a comparative analysis of the two optimization methods to evaluate their performance in this context. In addition, we compare our findings with the results reported in [14].

The remainder of this paper is organized as follows. Section 2 reviews the literature on wave energy farm optimization. Section 3 describes the dataset used to approximate the power output of a wave energy farm, along with the data cleaning and preprocessing steps. It also introduces the four machine learning models evaluated and the experimental study conducted to identify the most suitable approach for our problem. Section 4 presents the two optimization methods employed to maximize the power output, together with the experimental evaluation and a comparative analysis of their performance. Finally, Sect. 5 summarizes our findings and outlines directions for future work.

2 Related Work

In [21], the authors investigated the relationship between wave farm layout design and the economic feasibility of ocean wave energy projects. They provided an overview of recent works on wave farm layout optimization, and we can note that numerical models are the most commonly used approach to predict wave farm behavior. Only one study, [2], employed artificial neural networks (ANNs) to estimate dry beach surface differences between a no-wave farm scenario and several wave farm project configurations. They generate the dataset using a suite of numerical models, including a third-generation wave propagation model, a sediment transport formulation, and a shoreline response equation. Using Playa Granada (southern Iberian Peninsula) as a case study, their results indicate that the dry beach surface could increase by up to 5400.18 m^2 per year, demonstrating that ANNs can be a valuable tool for optimizing the design of wave farms for coastal protection. Their study also highlights that various objective functions have been explored in wave farm optimization, such as power smoothing, power output, sea area occupancy, the q-factor (i.e., the ratio of the total output power of a WEC array to the sum of the potential power generated by each device operating in isolation), and production costs. Metaheuristics are widely applied to this problem due to its nonlinear, multi-modal, non-convex, dynamic, and constrained nature, as well as its large search space. Commonly used approaches include genetic algorithms, evolution strategies, particle swarm optimization, and differential evolution.

In the following, we review works that focus on maximizing the power output of a wave farm. In [12], the authors consider fully submerged three-tether converters deployed in arrays and applied heuristic search methods to optimize power generation in a size-constrained environment by configuring both the WEC locations and the power-take-off (PTO) settings of each device. Since the objective function accounts for complex hydrodynamic interactions and is computationally expensive, the search was restricted to a few thousand model evaluations. The authors tested several heuristics in two real wave scenarios, Sydney and Perth, considering farms of two different scales. They conclude that combining the Nelder-Mead algorithm with a back-tracking optimization strategy provides an effective approach to this problem.

In [13], the authors extended their work and proposed a new hybrid approach that combines local search, surrogate power model, and numerical optimization methods. Notably, the surrogate model was not used as the objective function; instead, a numerical model was employed, while the surrogate model was applied within the Smart Local Search + Nelder-Mead (SLS-NM) to guide buoy positions. They prove their proposal in different wave scenarios, including Adelaide, Perth, Tasmania, and Sydney.

Further research by the same group evaluated additional optimization strategies and introduced a new one [15]. Their work was extended to other scenarios, such as Marettimo Island and the Mediterranean Sea, and incorporated a second objective function: levelised energy cost [17]. In [14], the authors proposed a computationally efficient energy model that enabled the design of larger farms with up to 100 WECs. They also released a public dataset that includes 54,000 and 9,600 configurations for farms with 49 and 100 WECs, respectively, including information on individual power, q-factor, and total farm power output [11]. In this work, they further proposed a hybrid multi-strategy evolutionary framework to address this complex optimization problem.

Finally, in [10], the authors used the dataset released in [14] to train a forward-feedback neural network that learns patterns from coordinate locations and predicts energy output. However, they did not search for an optimal configuration of WECs that optimizes the wave energy farm.

3 Approximating Power Output of a Wave Energy Farm via Machine Learning

3.1 Datasets and Preprocessing

The dataset employed in this work is publicly available through the University of California, Irvine (UCI) Machine Learning Repository under the title "Large-scale Wave Energy Farm" [11]. It consists of four subsets derived from simulation studies of wave energy farms in Perth and Sydney, Australia. For each location, two farm sizes were simulated: one with 49 WECs and another with 100 WECs. The dataset includes 54,000 configurations for 49 WECs and 9,600 for 100 WECs. Data manipulation and preprocessing were carried out using the Pandas library, which is available in Python.

Each instance in the dataset includes the following features: the spatial coordinates of each WEC (X_i, Y_i), the individual power generated by each WEC ($Power_i$), the q-factor (qW), and the total farm power output ($Total\_Power$). In this study, we use only the spatial coordinates and the total farm power output, as all WECs in the dataset share the same characteristics, such as the same individual power. The task is formulated as a regression problem, where the goal is to predict the total farm power output based on the spatial distribution of the WECs. The number of features considered in the models is 49×2 or 100×2, corresponding to the X_i and Y_i coordinates of each WEC. Although the datasets contain no missing values, they include a considerable number of duplicate instances, which were removed during preprocessing. The final number of instances in each subset is as follows: 10936 and 2737 instances for Perth (49 and 100 WECs, respectively), and 4816 and 1234 for Sydney (49 and 100 WECs, respectively).

We applied normalization and standardization techniques to ensure that all features contribute equally to the model training process. The spatial coordinates were normalized to the range $[0, 1]$, while the total power was standardized using the Z-score formula, resulting in a mean 0 and a standard deviation of 1. The Python scripts and the processed datasets are publicly available at https://github.com/mariomttz/wec-optimization.

3.2 Comparison of Machine Learning Models

In this study, we evaluated four regression models:

- **Linear regression:** A baseline model that estimates the coefficients β by minimizing the error between the predicted and actual power output, assuming a linear relationship [7].
- **Support vector machines (SVM):** In regression tasks, SVM aims to find a hyperplane that models the relationship between the input variables and the output energy, using kernel functions to capture complex non-linear relationships [3,5].
- **CatBoost:** A gradient boosting algorithm based on decision trees, designed to efficiently handle categorical features and mitigate prediction shift through an ordered boosting scheme [4,20].
- **Deep neural network (DNN):** We implemented a deep neural network with residual connections. In this architecture, a skip connection is applied every two layers, similar to the ResNet model [6]. This technique helps prevent the vanishing gradient problem by allowing the model to learn residual functions, thus enabling the training of deeper and more complex networks without performance degradation.

These four models were selected by the desire to cover a broad spectrum of learning strategies, from a simple linear baseline to complex non-linear approaches. Linear regression is a fundamental benchmark for assessing the degree of linearity in the data [7]. SVM were chosen for their proven effectiveness in high-dimensional spaces and their ability to model complex non-linear relationships through kernel functions [5]. CatBoost represents the state-of-the-art in gradient boosting on tabular data, known for its robustness and high performance [20]. Finally, a DNN with residual connections was included to explore the potential of deep learning models to capture intricate, hierarchical patterns in the data that other models might miss [6].

Linear regression and SVM were developed using *scikit-learn*, CatBoost with its native library, and the neural network with *PyTorch*. The datasets were split for training and testing, allocating 80% of the data for training the models and the remaining 20% for validation. To optimize the hyperparameters of the models, except for linear regression, we employed *Optuna*, an automated optimization framework [1]. Each model underwent 1000 trials where Optuna used adaptive sampling to explore the hyperparameter space efficiently. The key hyperparameters of the best-performing model for each subset are summarized in Table 1.

The best-performing neural network architectures and their training hyperparameters varied significantly: for Perth 49, the model had four hidden layers (254, 166, 63, 182 neurons) and was trained for 215 epochs with a learning rate of 0.0082; for Perth 100, it used two layers (256, 19 neurons), 282 epochs, and a learning rate of 0.0085; the Sydney 49 model had five layers (212, 223, 133, 154, 242 neurons), trained for 300 epochs with a learning rate of 0.0026; and for Sydney 100, the network also had five layers (181, 172, 219, 165, 16 neurons),

Table 1. Optimized hyperparameters for the winning model in each subset.

Subset	Model	Key Hyperparameters
Perth 49	SVM	kernel=rbf, $\gamma = 0.100$, C=8.02
Perth 100	SVM	kernel=rbf, $\gamma = 0.012$, C=83.33
Sydney 49	CatBoost	iterations=951, learning_rate=0.160, depth=4, l2_leaf_reg=4×10^{-6}
Sydney 100	SVM	kernel=rbf, $\gamma = 0.050$, C=6.56

trained for 293 epochs with a learning rate of 0.0005. All neural networks utilized batch normalization.

We evaluated the performance of the models using error-based metrics (mean squared error (MSE), root mean squared error (RMSE), and mean absolute error (MAE)) and correlation-based metrics (the coefficient of determination (R^2), Pearson, Spearman, and Kendall). The results are consolidated in Table 2. The analysis shows that while no single model consistently outperformed the others, the more complex models significantly surpassed the baseline. The SVM model proved to be a strong competitor, achieving the best performance according to error and correlation metrics in three subsets (Perth 49, Perth 100, and Sydney 100). CatBoost achieved the lowest error and strongest correlation on the Sydney 49 subset. The correlation metrics provide further insight into the models' quality. The high R^2 values for the winning models, consistently above 0.92, indicate that they explain a large portion of the variance in the power output. Likewise, the Pearson, Spearman, and Kendall coefficients, all close to 1.0, confirm a robust linear and monotonic relationship between predicted and real values. In contrast, the linear regression model's inadequacy for this non-linear problem is particularly evident in the Sydney 100 case, where its negative R^2 value (-0.5528) indicates a performance worse than a simple mean-based prediction. Although not the top performer, the deep neural network achieved competitive results. This variability underscores the importance of model selection based on dataset characteristics.

Compared with the work of Li et al. [10], who trained feedforward neural networks on the same datasets, our study offers a broader perspective by evaluating four distinct model families. A key finding of our work is the empirical evidence that model choice is a critical and non-trivial factor. While Li et al. focused on a single neural network architecture, our results indicate that models like SVM or CatBoost can outperform neural networks in certain scenarios. This observation suggests that a "one-size-fits-all" approach is inadequate for energy prediction in wave farms and that careful model selection is essential. The model source code, full results, and optimized hyperparameters for each experiment are publicly available in the project's GitHub repository (https://github.com/mariomttz/wec-optimization).

Table 2. Model performance results for all subsets, including correlation metrics. The best performing model for each subset is highlighted in bold.

Location	WECs	Model	MSE	RMSE	MAE	R^2	Pearson	Spearman	Kendall
Perth	49	Linear Regression	0.2617	0.5116	0.3822	0.7353	0.8576	0.8579	0.6785
		SVM	**0.0756**	**0.2750**	**0.1780**	**0.9235**	**0.9610**	**0.9591**	**0.8453**
		CatBoost	0.0775	0.2784	0.1854	0.9216	0.9601	0.9603	0.8430
		Neural Network	0.0802	0.2832	0.1835	0.9203	0.9598	0.9579	0.8421
Perth	100	Linear Regression	0.2442	0.4942	0.3633	0.7396	0.8639	0.8566	0.6798
		SVM	**0.0675**	**0.2599**	**0.1883**	**0.9280**	**0.9636**	**0.9572**	**0.8335**
		CatBoost	0.0833	0.2886	0.2021	0.9112	0.9554	0.9499	0.8202
		Neural Network	0.1213	0.3482	0.2336	0.8829	0.9409	0.9394	0.7994
Sydney	49	Linear Regression	0.2085	0.4566	0.3140	0.7926	0.8919	0.9059	0.7389
		SVM	0.0261	0.1616	0.1041	0.9740	0.9870	0.9866	0.9113
		CatBoost	**0.0167**	**0.1294**	**0.0876**	**0.9833**	**0.9917**	**0.9920**	**0.9283**
		Neural Network	0.0308	0.1754	0.1008	0.9695	0.9848	0.9860	0.9156
Sydney	100	Linear Regression	1.3757	1.1729	0.5454	-0.5528	0.6033	0.8177	0.6568
		SVM	**0.0514**	**0.2268**	**0.1528**	**0.9419**	**0.9712**	**0.9697**	**0.8723**
		CatBoost	0.0739	0.2718	0.1780	0.9166	0.9575	0.9609	0.8479
		Neural Network	0.1321	0.3634	0.2323	0.8502	0.9227	0.9243	0.7952

4 Optimizing Wave Energy Farm via Evolutionary Algorithms

Once the machine learning model with the best performance for each dataset subset was identified, it was employed as the objective function to optimize the spatial configuration of the WECs. The goal is to find the layout that maximizes the total power generated by the farm, as predicted by the surrogate model.

We selected two of the most widely recognized metaheuristics for high-dimensional and nonlinear optimization: Differential Evolution (DE) [22] and Particle Swarm Optimization (PSO) [8]. These algorithms are well-suited to explore complex, multi-modal search spaces. In the case of DE, we tested four variants to analyze different balances between exploration and exploitation of the solution space: *DE/rand/1/bin*, *DE/rand/1/exp*, *DE/best/1/bin*, and *DE/best/1/exp*. PSO and DE implementations were custom-programmed for this work.

To ensure optimal performance, the hyperparameters for each algorithm were tuned using the Optuna framework [1], conducting 100 trials for each algorithm and subset. The best hyperparameters found are shown in Table 3. Finally, each algorithm was executed 100 times with its tuned configuration.

4.1 Results and Discussion

The statistical results from the 100 runs for each algorithm are summarized in Table 4. This table reports the maximum, median, and minimum power (in MW),

Table 3. Best hyperparameters found for each subset.

Algorithm	Differential Evolution				PSO	
Parameter	rand/1/bin	rand/1/exp	best/1/bin	best/1/exp	-	
Perth 49						
F	0.3340	0.2564	0.5539	0.4234	W	0.8241
CR	0.6245	0.9838	0.2946	0.9155	C1	2.0030
Population	123	297	54	170	C2	2.0974
Generations	976	826	981	994	Population	205
-	-	-	-	-	Iterations	273
Perth 100						
F	0.4900	0.3127	0.9990	0.2540	W	0.7140
CR	0.2492	0.9581	0.0191	0.8899	C1	2.0794
Population	263	181	278	193	C2	1.5010
Generations	987	871	900	833	Population	288
-	-	-	-	-	Iterations	336
Sydney 49						
F	0.2003	0.1266	0.7152	0.3987	W	0.5466
CR	0.2026	0.8354	0.2532	0.8536	C1	2.1501
Population	179	58	187	150	C2	2.1882
Generations	757	994	703	713	Population	209
-	-	-	-	-	Iterations	250
Sydney 100						
F	0.5037	0.1193	0.5573	0.2911	W	0.7806
CR	0.2950	0.8688	0.1364	0.8246	C1	1.9373
Population	36	223	220	206	C2	1.6478
Generations	998	724	965	729	Population	149
-	-	-	-	-	Iterations	21

as well as the mean and standard deviation of the obtained power. We applied the Wilcoxon rank-sum test to assess whether the performance differences between DE variants and PSO are statistically significant. The null hypothesis of this test assumes that both samples come from the same distribution. A p-value < 0.05 indicates that the null hypothesis can be rejected, indicating that one algorithm is superior to another with statistical significance.

Across all four subsets, the DE variants consistently demonstrated a superior ability to find higher-quality solutions compared to PSO. Specifically, the *DE/best/1/bin* variant achieved the best maximum solution in all cases. The rank-sum test results confirm this superiority, as DE outperformed PSO with high statistical significance in almost all comparisons. The only notable exception

Table 4. Optimization results for each subset (Power in MW).

Location	Size	Algorithm	Max	Median	Min	Mean	Std. Dev.
Perth	49	DE/rand/1/bin	4.564	4.563	4.100	4.508	0.118
		DE/rand/1/exp	4.562	4.550	4.009	4.467	0.156
		DE/best/1/bin	**4.564**	4.551	3.974	4.489	0.126
		DE/best/1/exp	4.564	4.513	3.925	4.430	0.184
		PSO	4.282	4.203	4.156	4.202	0.023
	Note: All DE variants were statistically superior to PSO ($p \ll 0.05$).						
Perth	100	DE/rand/1/bin	10.100	10.042	7.761	9.726	0.586
		DE/rand/1/exp	10.045	9.678	7.319	9.262	0.833
		DE/best/1/bin	**10.110**	10.056	7.548	9.730	0.657
		DE/best/1/exp	10.052	9.520	7.221	9.223	0.847
		PSO	9.128	8.920	8.476	8.910	0.120
	Note: All DE variants were statistically superior to PSO ($p \ll 0.05$).						
Sydney	49	DE/rand/1/bin	4.465	4.425	4.072	4.383	0.093
		DE/rand/1/exp	4.433	4.386	4.035	4.343	0.097
		DE/best/1/bin	**4.470**	4.418	4.031	4.388	0.087
		DE/best/1/exp	4.423	4.340	3.914	4.295	0.126
		PSO	4.305	4.202	4.120	4.204	0.034
	Note: All DE variants were statistically superior to PSO ($p \ll 0.05$).						
Sydney	100	DE/rand/1/bin	7.896	7.729	7.249	7.723	0.158
		DE/rand/1/exp	7.750	7.620	7.129	7.558	0.158
		DE/best/1/bin	**7.898**	7.837	7.188	7.752	0.175
		DE/best/1/exp	7.721	7.610	7.030	7.531	0.180
		PSO	7.605	7.589	7.570	7.590	0.008
	Note: DE/rand/1/bin and DE/best/1/bin were statistically superior to PSO ($p \ll 0.05$). PSO was superior to DE/rand/1/exp ($p = 0.0068$). No significant difference was found between DE/best/1/exp and PSO ($p = 0.119$).						

Table 5. Best results reported in [14] using a hydrodynamic simulator.

Subset	Best Algorithm	Max Power (MW)
Perth 49	MS-bDE	4.18
Perth 100	MS-bDE	7.35
Sydney 49	MS-bGA	4.15
Sydney 100	DLS(II)	7.36

occurred in the Sydney 100 case, where PSO showed competitive performance, surpassing *DE/rand/1/exp* and resulting in a technical tie with *DE/best/1/exp*.

In the reference work [14], the authors compared 17 different optimization algorithms, using a hydrodynamic simulator as the objective function, and concluded that the variants of their hybrid multi-strategy framework achieve the best performance. Table 5 shows the best results reported in their study. When comparing our results with those of Neshat et al., we observe an improvement in the maximum power obtained. For instance, for Perth 100, our best solution reaches 10.11 MW, exceeding the 7.35 MW they reported. Similarly, for Perth 49, Sydney 100, and Sydney 49, our results of 4.56 MW, 7.90 MW, and 4.47 MW consistently outperformed their 4.18 MW, 7.36 MW, and 4.15 MW, respectively. This improvement can be attributed to the use of a machine learning surrogate model, which, due to its drastically lower computational cost, allows the metaheuristics to perform a much more exhaustive exploration of the solution space. This ability to execute a larger number of objective function evaluations makes it possible to discover more efficient WEC configurations that could not be reached within a reasonable computation time with the direct simulator.

All codes, hyperparameter configurations, and detailed results generated in this study are publicly available in the project's GitHub repository (https://github.com/mariomttz/wec-optimization).

5 Conclusions and Future Work

In this work, our first objective was to approximate the power output of a wave energy farm based on the spatial placements of its WECs. We used four datasets corresponding to farms in Perth and Sydney, Australia, with 49 and 100 WECs, and four machine learning techniques: linear regression, CatBoost, SVM, and neural networks. The SVM model achieved the best performance in three of the four scenarios (Perth with 49 and 100 WECs, and Sydney with 100 WECs), while CatBoost was superior in the case of Sydney with 49 WECs. This highlights the strong dependence between the models and the dataset characteristics.

Our second objective was to maximize the output power of the farm by optimizing the spatial configurations of the WECs. For this task, we employed two well-known metaheuristics: Differential Evolution (DE) and Particle Swarm Optimization (PSO). Among the DE variants tested, *DE/best/1/bin* consistently achieved the best results across all scenarios. However, for Sydney with 100 WECs, PSO was competitive, surpassing *DE/rand/1/exp* and tying with *DE/best/1/exp*. These findings confirm the suitability of DE for this class of problems.

Our results outperform those reported by Neshat et al. [14], who employed 17 optimization methods using a hydrodynamic simulator to compute the objective function. The improvement can be attributed to the use of surrogate models, which allow the computation of a much larger number of objective function evaluations in a reasonable runtime, thus enabling a more exhaustive exploration of the solution space and the discovery of better spatial configurations. This suggests that using surrogate models to approximate complex objective functions associated with real scenarios is a good alternative.

As future work, it would be interesting to expand the datasets by generating additional samples in regions explored by the optimization methods for two main reasons: 1) to validate the power values predicted by the approximation models on instances not included in the UCI datasets, and 2) to improve the accuracy of the surrogate models in areas of interest. Also, we want to incorporate buoy permutations, recognizing that multiple codings can represent the same spatial placements of WECs. If we have 49 buoys, we have 49! equivalent codings of one spatial configuration. Theoretically, the approximation models should predict the same value for all these inputs. However, this dramatically increases the solution space and can add difficulty to the models. Finally, we aim to extend the experimental study with more complex surrogate models, such as deeper neural network architectures, to analyze the trade-off between computational cost and accuracy of the models.

Acknowledgments. The authors gratefully acknowledge the support provided by the PAPIME project PE101325.

References

1. Akiba, T., Sano, S., Yanase, T., Ohta, T., Koyama, M.: Optuna: a next-generation hyperparameter optimization framework. In: Proceedings of the 25th ACM SIGKDD International Conference on Knowledge Discovery and Data Mining, pp. 2623–2631. KDD '19, Association for Computing Machinery, New York, NY, USA (2019). https://doi.org/10.1145/3292500.3330701
2. Bergillos, R.J., Rodriguez-Delgado, C., Iglesias, G.: Optimization of wave farm location and layout for coastal protection. In: Ocean Energy and Coastal Protection. SE, pp. 9–27. Springer, Cham (2020). https://doi.org/10.1007/978-3-030-31318-0_2
3. Burges, C.J.: A tutorial on support vector machines for pattern recognition. Data Mining Knowl. Discov. **2**(2), 121–167 (1998). https://doi.org/10.1023/a:1009715923555
4. Dorogush, A.V., Ershov, V., Gulin, A.: CatBoost: gradient boosting with categorical features support. Workshop on ML Systems at NIPS 2017 (2017). http://learningsys.org/nips17/assets/papers/paper_11.pdf
5. Hastie, T., Tibshirani, R., Friedman, J.: Support vector machines and flexible discriminants, pp. 417–458. Springer New York, New York, NY (2009). https://doi.org/10.1007/978-0-387-84858-7_12
6. He, K., Zhang, X., Ren, S., Sun, J.: Deep residual learning for image recognition (2015). https://arxiv.org/abs/1512.03385
7. James, G., Witten, D., Hastie, T., Tibshirani, R.: Linear regression, pp. 59–128. Springer US, New York, NY (2021). https://doi.org/10.1007/978-1-0716-1418-1_3
8. Kennedy, J., Eberhart, R.: Particle swarm optimization. In: Proceedings of ICNN'95 - International Conference on Neural Networks, vol. 4, pp. 1942–1948 (1995). https://doi.org/10.1109/ICNN.1995.488968

9. Lehmann, M., Karimpour, F., Goudey, C.A., Jacobson, P.T., Alam, M.R.: Ocean wave energy in the united states: Current status and future perspectives. Renew. Sustain. Energy Rev. **74**, 1300–1313 (2017). https://doi.org/10.1016/j.rser.2016.11.101
10. Li, K., Nallaparaju, A., Sha, J.: A novel machine learning approach for the prediction of optimized energy output on large-scale wave energy farms. In: 2024 IEEE MIT Undergraduate Research Technology Conference (URTC), pp. 1–5 (2024). https://doi.org/10.1109/URTC65039.2024.10937646
11. Neshat, M., Alexander, B., Sergiienko, N., Wagner, M.: Large-scale Wave energy farm. UCI Machine Learning Repository (2020). https://doi.org/10.24432/C5GG7Q
12. Neshat, M., Alexander, B., Sergiienko, N.Y., Wagner, M.: A hybrid evolutionary algorithm framework for optimising power take off and placements of wave energy converters. In: Proceedings of the Genetic and Evolutionary Computation Conference, pp. 1293–1301. GECCO '19, Association for Computing Machinery, New York, NY, USA (2019). https://doi.org/10.1145/3321707.3321806
13. Neshat, M., Alexander, B., Sergiienko, N.Y., Wagner, M.: New insights into position optimisation of wave energy converters using hybrid local search. Swarm Evol. Comput. **59**, 100744 (2020). https://doi.org/10.1016/j.swevo.2020.100744
14. Neshat, M., Alexander, B., Sergiienko, N.Y., Wagner, M.: Optimisation of large wave farms using a multi-strategy evolutionary framework. In: Proceedings of the 2020 Genetic and Evolutionary Computation Conference, pp. 1150–1158. GECCO '20, Association for Computing Machinery, New York, NY, USA (2020). https://doi.org/10.1145/3377930.3390235
15. Neshat, M., Alexander, B., Wagner, M.: A hybrid cooperative co-evolution algorithm framework for optimising power take off and placements of wave energy converters. Inf. Sci. **534**, 218–244 (2020). https://doi.org/10.1016/j.ins.2020.03.112
16. Neshat, M., et al.: A new bi-level optimisation framework for optimising a multi-mode wave energy converter design: A case study for the marettimo island, mediterranean sea. Energies **13**(20), 1–23 (2020). https://ideas.repec.org/a/gam/jeners/v13y2020i20p5498-d431953.html
17. Neshat, M., et al.: A new Bi-level optimisation framework for optimising a multi-mode wave energy converter design: a case study for the Marettimo island, Mediterranean sea. Energies **13**(20) (2020). https://doi.org/10.3390/en13205498
18. Noland, J.K., Auxepaules, J., Rousset, A., Perney, B., Falletti, G.: Spatial energy density of large-scale electricity generation from power sources worldwide. Sci. Rep. **12**(1), 21280 (2022). https://doi.org/10.1038/s41598-022-25341-9
19. Pérez-Collazo, C., Greaves, D., Iglesias, G.: A review of combined wave and offshore wind energy. Renew. Sustain. Energy Rev. **42**, 141–153 (2015). https://doi.org/10.1016/j.rser.2014.09.032
20. Prokhorenkova, L., Gusev, G., Vorobev, A., Dorogush, A.V., Gulin, A.: Catboost: unbiased boosting with categorical features (2019). https://arxiv.org/abs/1706.09516
21. Shadmani, A., Nikoo, M.R., Gandomi, A.H.: Layout Design Characteristics and Cost Evaluation, pp. 141–190. Springer Nature Switzerland, Cham (2025)
22. Storn, R., Price, K.: Differential evolution – a simple and efficient heuristic for global optimization over continuous spaces. J. Global Optim. **11**(4), 341–359 (1997). https://doi.org/10.1023/a:1008202821328

Author Index

L. Martínez-Villaseñor et al. (Eds.): MICAI 2025 Workshops, LNAI 16264, pp. 471–472, 2026.
https://doi.org/10.1007/978-3-032-17930-2

The manufacturer's authorised representative in the EU is Springer Nature Customer Service Centre GmbH, Europaplatz 3, 69115 Heidelberg, Germany. If you have any concerns regarding our products, please contact ProductSafety@springernature.com

Printed and bound by CPI Group (UK) Ltd, Croydon, CR0 4YY
13/07/2026
02165297-0003